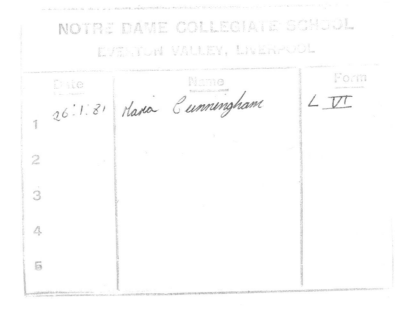

NOTRE DAME COLLEGIATE SCHOOL
EVERTON VALLEY, LIVERPOOL

	Date	Name	Form
1	26.1.81	Maria Cunningham	L VI
2			
3			
4			
5			

PURE
MATHEMATICS
1

S. L. PARSONSON

Senior Mathematics Master
Harrow School

CAMBRIDGE UNIVERSITY PRESS

CAMBRIDGE

LONDON · NEW YORK · MELBOURNE

Published by the Syndics of the Cambridge University Press
The Pitt Building, Trumpington Street, Cambridge CB2 1RP
Bentley House, 200 Euston Road, London NW1 2DB
32 East 57th Street, New York, NY 10022, USA
296 Beaconsfield Parade, Middle Park, Melbourne 3206, Australia

© Cambridge University Press 1970

Library of Congress catalogue card number: 70-100026

ISBN 0 521 07683 8

First published 1970
Reprinted 1972 1974 1975 1977 1978

Printed in Great Britain at the
University Press, Cambridge

Contents

Preface

The present book is the first of a two volume course covering those parts of modern 'A' level pure mathematics syllabuses not normally included in standard calculus texts. The reason for omitting calculus is simply to keep the book within manageable proportions and it is felt that there are a number of excellent modern calculus books available. Although no formal calculus is done here, it is expected that a student will be studying calculus concurrently with this text; thus, for example, it is assumed in Chapter 5 that the reader can differentiate simple algebraic expressions and sketch the graphs of rational functions. In Chapter 16, the exponential function is used.

It is hoped that the order of presentation of topics in this book will offer an effective teaching programme, but variations can be made at the discretion of the teacher. Thus, for example, the chapters on probability can be deferred while the two chapters on trigonometry could be taken in conjunction. Again certain chapters contain work which might be deemed suitable for a second reading; for example, Sections 4 and 5 of Chapter 10. In some ways Chapter 1 offers the most difficult problem of presentation in the whole book: it is necessary later to be able to refer to rational and irrational numbers, and yet to devote too much time in the early stages to such topics may not be desirable. The author hopes that he has found an acceptable compromise but some might yet find parts of Chapter 1 too formal, in which case they are strongly advised to leave the detailed study of Sections 2, 3 and 4 for a second reading.

To learn mathematics, constant practice is necessary, some of it repetitive. The book is therefore liberally supplied with exercises for the student. Most of the questions represent fairly straightforward applications of the bookwork, although in the Miscellaneous Exercises, included at the end of all but two of the chapters, will be found some rather more searching questions. Furthermore, questions marked *Ex.* occur in the text; it is hoped that most, if not all, of these will be attempted by the pupil as he covers the associated bookwork—certainly those marked with an asterisk should be regarded as obligatory.

The syllabuses for M.E.I. 'A' level, the Joint Matriculation Board syllabus in Mathematics (Advanced) and Further Mathematics (Advanced) and the University of London Revised Syllabus in Mathematics (Advanced) have been particularly kept in mind in the writing of this book and the planning of the next. Other boards are in the process of devising new syllabuses and draft copies published by them indicate that this book will probably cover the necessary work. The School Mathematics Project have produced their own text-books but the present book may be used to supplement these if desired.

It is a pleasure to record my thanks to Mr M. J. Rawlinson who read part of the text and made a number of valuable suggestions; to Mr A. J. Moakes who read the entire book and whose detailed criticisms have done much to remove obscurities and improve the presentation; and to my wife, who also read the entire book and who lent invaluable assistance in checking answers. I am grateful for permission to reprint examination questions from the following Boards: Oxford and Cambridge (O & C, M.E.I., S.M.P.), the Joint Matriculation Board (J.M.B.), the Cambridge Local Examination Syndicate (Cambridge), University of London (London), and the Oxford Delegacy of Local Examinations (Oxford); also to the Clarendon Press for permission to use Oxford Scholarship questions (O.S.) and to the Cambridge University Press and University Registry for the use of Cambridge Scholarship (C.S.) and Mathematical Tripos (M.T.) questions.

S.L.P.

1. *Numbers and inequalities*

1. THE INTEGERS AND THEIR REPRESENTATION

The process of counting is deeply rooted in the history of mankind and its development is obscure. Many systems have been evolved but the Arabic (originally Hindu) which we now employ is almost universal.

The entities used for counting are the whole numbers, or *positive integers*, and *zero*. Ten ciphers are used to represent the whole numbers: 0, 1, 2, 3, 4, 5, 6, 7, 8, 9. The introduction of the cipher zero was an advance of considerable significance and it gave to the Arabic system its great flexibility and versatility by making possible a system of place value recording; place value calculation (by the abacus) had already been in use for a long time. A *base* of ten is most frequently used for continued counting; thus, the one hundred and forty second integer is written 142, which stands for

$$1 \times 10^2 + 4 \times 10 + 2 \times 1.$$

The base, 10, of this method of enumeration has no special significance and any other number would do as well. Indeed, were ten not so deeply rooted in us for physical reasons, other bases would no doubt be preferable; for example, eight (2^3) or twelve ($2^2 \times 3$). Had primitive man ignored his thumbs we could well have inherited a more efficient system.

Other bases have been used. A base which has acquired special significance recently is the number two. Counting from 1, with 2 as base, the first eight integers are written: 1, 10, 11, 100, 101, 110, 111, 1000. The value of this, the *binary system*, is clear: it requires only two ciphers, 0 and 1. It is thus eminently suitable for recording numbers in two-state systems as, for example, in electronic digital computers. Conversion from one base to another is easily effected. For example

75 (written in the scale of ten, or the denary scale)

$$= 1 \times 2^6 + 0 \times 2^5 + 0 \times 2^4 + 1 \times 2^3 + 0 \times 2^2 + 1 \times 2^1 + 1$$

$$= 1001011 \text{ (written in the binary scale).}$$

The same result may be arrived at more quickly by continued

division by 2, the remainders recorded being the required digits (in reverse order)

2	75	
2	37	1
2	18	1
2	9	0
2	4	1
2	2	0
2	1	0
	0	1

Ex. 1. Explain why the method of conversion from one scale to another by continued division works.

Ex. 2. Evaluate 11011×1011 in the binary scale. Perform several other multiplications of this type and check your answers by conversion to the denary scale.

Ex. 3. Evaluate $1110011 \div 11011$ in the binary scale. Perform several other divisions of this type and check your answers by conversion to the denary scale.

Exercise 1(a)

1. Solve the following equation for x, working in the binary scale throughout:
   (i) $101x + 11 = 1101$;
   (ii) $11x - 11111 = 1011$;
   (iii) $\dfrac{10x + 11}{101} = 111$;
   (iv) $11(10x - 101) = 10x + 101$.

2. Express the denary number 275 in the scales of 2, 3 and 12. (For the last part, you will need to supplement the digits 0, 1, ..., 9 by $t = $ ten and $e = $ eleven. Why?)

3. With the notation of Question 2, evaluate $4te \times 19t$ in the scale of 12.

4. With the notation of Question 2, evaluate $e89t \div 2ee$ in the scale of 12.

5. Explain the following method of conversion from the binary form 1100110111 to denary form 823

1	100	110	111	Binary
1	4	6	7	Octal

$512 + 256 + 48 + 7 = 823$ Denary

6. Show that 1331 is a perfect cube whatever the base b, provided that b is greater than 3.

7. The number x lies between 100 and 999 (denary scale) and the number y is formed by writing the digits of x in the reverse order. Prove that $x \sim y$ is divisible by 99, where $x \sim y$ means the difference between x and y.

8. Show that the difference between any number with four digits (in the denary scale) and the number with these digits reversed is divisible by 9, and that, if the two middle digits are the same, the difference is also divisible by 37.

2. THE INTEGERS (CONTINUED)

We have already tacitly assumed that the positive integers obey certain laws of combination, which are summarized below. These laws are seen to hold irrespective of the base employed for representing the numbers: the integer seven remains the integer seven, whether it be written 7 or 111 (binary) or 21 (ternary); consistency is all that is demanded.

   (i)   If $a = b$, then $a+c = b+c$ and $ac = bc$.
   (ii) The *commutative laws*: $a+b = b+a$; $ab = ba$.
   (iii) The *associative laws*: $a+(b+c) = (a+b)+c$; $a(bc) = (ab)\,c$.
   (iv) The *distributive law*: $a(b+c) = ab+ac$.
   (v)   The *additive and multiplicative identity laws*:

$$a+0 = a; \quad a1 = a.$$

Considerably later historically, zero and the positive integers were augmented by the *negative integers*; the word 'integer' will in future be taken to mean a positive or negative integer, together with zero. To enable negative integers to be combined, a further rule is required:

   (vi) The *additive inverse law*: $a+(-a) = 0$.

Example 1. *Prove, using only the laws* (i)–(vi) *above, that* $(-a)\,(-b) = ab$.
   First observe that

$$aa+a0 = a(a+0) \quad \text{by (iv)}$$

$$= aa \qquad\quad \text{by (v)}$$

$$= aa+0 \quad\;\; \text{by (v)},$$

$$a0 = 0$$

on adding $-aa$ to both sides and using (ii) and (i). Thus, any integer multiplied by zero gives the answer zero.
   Next, consider

$$ab+[a(-b)+(-a)\,(-b)] = a[b+(-b)]+(-a)\,(-b) \quad \text{by (iii), (iv)}$$

$$= a0+(-a)\,(-b) \qquad\qquad \text{by (vi)};$$

$$= 0+(-a)\,(-b) \qquad\qquad \text{by result} \atop \qquad\qquad\qquad\qquad\qquad\quad \text{proved above};$$

$$= (-a)\,(-b) \qquad\qquad\quad \text{by (v).}$$

3

But
$$ab + [a(-b)+(-a)(-b)] = ab + [a+(-a)](-b) \qquad \text{by (ii) and (iv);}$$
$$= ab + 0(-b) \qquad \text{by (vi);}$$
$$= ab + 0 \qquad \text{by result proved above;}$$
$$= ab \qquad \text{by (v).}$$

Thus
$$ab = (-a)(-b).$$

Laws (i)–(vi) above supply almost all the apparatus required for the manipulation of integers. However, as Example 2 below shows, they need to be supplemented by one more law:

(vii) *The cancellation law*: $ab = ac \Rightarrow b = c$, provided $a \neq 0$. (The sign $\Rightarrow$ is read as 'implies'; $\Leftarrow$ means 'is implied by' and $\Leftrightarrow$ means 'implies and is implied by'.)

In this section we have given only a brief survey of the logical structure of the integers. The reader interested in acquiring a deeper understanding of this topic and, indeed, of the other topics mentioned in this chapter should consult one of the books mentioned in the Bibliography at the end of the book.

Example 2. *Arithmetic modulo* 12 *is defined as follows*: *any two of the integers* 0, 1, 2, ..., 11 *are added or multiplied together and the answer is taken to be the remainder on dividing the sum or product by* 12. *Thus*

$$8+6 \equiv 2 \quad (\bmod\ 12); \quad 4 \times 11 \equiv 8 \quad (\bmod\ 12);$$

and we also write $\qquad 4-6 \equiv 10 \quad (\bmod\ 12).$

Show that arithmetic modulo 12 *satisfies laws* (i)–(vi) *above but that the equation*
$$4x \equiv 4 \quad (\bmod\ 12)$$

does not have a unique solution (*and so law* (vii) *does not hold*).

If $a+b = 12c+r$, then $b+a = 12c+r$ and the commutative rule holds. All the other laws may similarly be verified.

But $x = 1, 4, 7, 10$ all satisfy the equation $4x \equiv 4 \pmod{12}$.

Ex. 4. Prove that $-(a-b) = -a+b$. ($a-b$ means $a+(-b)$.)

Ex. 5. Prove that, if $ax = a$, then $x = 1$, provided $a \neq 0$. (Notice carefully what you have to prove; it is not sufficient merely to verify that $x = 1$ satisfies $ax = a$.)

Ex. 6. Show that arithmetic modulo 11 does not suffer from the same defect as that exhibited by arithmetic modulo 12 in Example 2. Suggest why this is so.

3. RATIONAL NUMBERS

As soon as numbers began to be applied to problems more complex than the mere counting of objects, the value of subdividing the interval between two integers must have become apparent. For example, when a unit of length was defined, lengths must have been met that were not an exact integral number of units. Thus the concept of a *fraction* or, as we shall prefer to call it, a *rational number,* was evolved.

In order to emphasize the fact that we are now dealing with a new type of number, we shall avoid the familiar fractional form for rational numbers at first, and instead we shall *define* a rational number as a pair of integers written in a definite order thus: (p, q), where $q \neq 0$. (We may call this an *ordered pair* of integers: $(2, 3)$ and $(3, 2)$ represent different rational numbers. See Chapter 4.)

(In what follows it may help the reader to see what is happening if he bears in mind that our aim is to demonstrate that the rational number (p, q) is what he would call p/q.)

Two rational numbers (p_1, q_1) and (p_2, q_2) are said to be *equal* if $p_1 q_2 - p_2 q_1 = 0$; if $p_1 q_2 - p_2 q_1 \neq 0$, they are said to be *unequal*.

Ex. 7. Is it true that $(a, b) \neq (b, a)$?

Ex. 8. Prove that $(1, 2)$, $(2, 4)$, $(13, 26)$ are all equal. Prove more generally that $(p, q) = (kp, kq)$, provided $k \neq 0$.

Since rational numbers are newly defined objects, rules for adding, subtracting, multiplying and dividing them must be given, for these operations have so far only been applied to integers. The rules are

$$(p_1, q_1) + (p_2, q_2) = (p_1 q_2 + p_2 q_1, q_1 q_2); \quad (p_1, q_1) - (p_2, q_2) = (p_1 q_2 - p_2 q_1, q_1 q_2);$$

$$(p_1, q_1) \times (p_2, q_2) = (p_1 p_2, q_1 q_2); \quad (p_1, q_1) \div (p_2, q_2) = (p_1 q_2, p_2 q_1),$$

provided $p_2 \neq 0$, otherwise the left-hand side is undefined.

Example 3. *Verify that the distributive law holds for rational numbers.*
We have to show that

$$(p_1, q_1) \times [(p_2, q_2) + (p_3, q_3)] = (p_1, q_1) \times (p_2, q_2) + (p_1, q_1) \times (p_3 q_3),$$

$$\text{L.H.S.} = (p_1, q_1) \times (p_2 q_3 + p_3 q_2, q_2 q_3)$$

$$= (p_1 p_2 q_3 + p_1 p_3 q_2, q_1 q_2 q_3),$$

5

$$\text{R.H.S.} = (p_1, q_1) \times (p_2, q_2) + (p_1, q_1) \times (p_3, q_3)$$
$$= (p_1 p_2, q_1 q_2) + (p_1 p_3, q_1 q_3)$$
$$= (p_1 p_2 q_1 q_3 + p_1 p_3 q_1 q_2, q_1^2 q_2 q_3)$$
$$= (p_1 p_2 q_3 + p_1 p_3 q_2, q_1 q_2 q_3), \quad \text{by Ex. 8, since}$$
$$q_1 \neq 0.$$

In a similar way, all the rules for combining integers may be verified to hold also for rational numbers.

Ex. 9. Verify the laws (i)–(vii) for rational numbers.

Ex. 10. Verify that, if the rule for division is ignored, rational numbers of the form $(p, 1)$ have properties identical to those possessed by the integers.

Ex. 11. Verify that, if $(a, 1) \times (x, 1) = (b, 1)$, then $(x, 1) = (b, a)$, provided $a \neq 0$.

Ex. 10 shows us that we may identify the integers with rational numbers of the form $(p, 1)$; Ex. 11 then shows us that the rational number (b, a), when multiplied by the integer $(a, 1)$ gives the integer $(b, 1)$. In more familiar language (b, a) has just the properties we associate with the 'number' b/a. We may thus regard a rational number as 'the quotient of two integers'.

It thus follows that the statement 'x is a rational number' is equivalent to the statement 'integers p and q may be found such that $x = p/q$'.

The reader will be familiar with the process of expressing a rational number as a decimal. For example,

$$\frac{18}{625} = 0 \cdot 024 = 0 \times \frac{1}{10} + 2 + \frac{1}{10^2} + 4 \times \frac{1}{10^3}.$$

Conversely, a *terminating decimal* can always be expressed as a rational number in the form p/q; for example

$$0 \cdot 175 = \tfrac{175}{1000} = \tfrac{7}{40}.$$

However, the terms 'rational number' and 'terminating decimal' are not synonymous. Thus, $\tfrac{8}{7}$ is certainly a rational number, but

$$\tfrac{8}{7} = 1 \cdot 142857142857142857\ldots$$

and the process of division cannot be brought to an exact conclusion. However, this expression does *recur*; the reader will probably be familiar with the notation.
$$\tfrac{8}{7} = 1 \cdot \dot{1}4285\dot{7}.$$

In fact, any rational number may be expressed either as a terminating or a recurring decimal, and conversely, *any terminating or recurring decimal represents a rational number*. The proof of the italicized part of this state-

6

ment depends upon the notion of a limit (see Chapter 8; geometric sequences) but good grounds for believing it are given in the following particular example.

Example 4. *Express* $2 \cdot 3 \dot{7} \dot{8}$ *as a rational number in standard form.*
    Let $x = 2 \cdot 3 \dot{7} \dot{8}$; then

$$1000x = 2378 \cdot \dot{3} \dot{7} \dot{8}$$
$$x = 2 \cdot \dot{3} \dot{7} \dot{8}$$

$$\overline{999x = 2376} \quad \text{by subtraction}$$
$$x = \tfrac{2376}{999}$$
$$= \tfrac{88}{37}.$$

Ex. 12. Express the following recurring decimals as fractions:

$$\text{(i)} \ 0 \cdot \dot{7}, \quad \text{(ii)} \ 0 \cdot 40 \dot{2}, \quad \text{(iii)} \ 6 \cdot 2 \dot{8}.$$

Ex. 13. Using only the digits 0 and 1 we may express any rational number as a bicimal. For example

$$11 \cdot 01101 = 1 \times 2 + 1 + 0 \times \frac{1}{2} + 1 \times \frac{1}{2^2} + 1 \times \frac{1}{2^3} + 0 \times \frac{1}{2^4} + 1 \times \frac{1}{2^5}.$$

Express as bicimals the decimals 3·75, 0·703125, 4·6, 0·82.
    [*Hint*: see Ex. 1 and substitute repeated multiplication for repeated division.]

Ex. 14. Compare $0 \cdot \dot{9}$ (decimal) with $0 \cdot \dot{1}$ (bicimal).

Ex. 15. Express $0 \cdot 0 \dot{1}$ and $1 \cdot \dot{1} 0 \dot{1}$ (both bicimals) as decimals.

4. IRRATIONAL NUMBERS

It is useful to depict the integers and rational numbers as points on a straight line. In Figure 1.1, an origin O is taken, representing the number zero, and equal intervals are measured to the right, the end-points representing 1, 2, 3, ... and to the left representing $-1, -2, -3, \dots$. The position of a point representing a rational number may be defined quite simply;

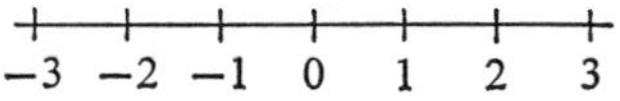

Fig. 1.1

for example, the point representing 3·28 is obtained by sub-dividing the interval between 3 and 4 equally into 100 divisions and marking the end-point of the twenty-eighth division. We may thus associate with the rational numbers a definite ordering: x is greater than y (written $x > y$) if the point representing x lies to the *right* of that representing y.

7

All rational numbers may thus be represented by points on the line and, furthermore, however close together two points representing rational numbers may be there will always be another point representing a rational number lying between them. For example, between the points representing 3·286 and 3·287 lies the point representing 3·2865.

Ex. 16. Show that $\frac{1}{2}(x+y)$ always lies between x and y.

Our last remark shows that, however close together we choose two rational numbers, we can always fit another rational number in between them; surprisingly, however, we can never succeed in 'filling the line up' with points representing rational numbers. In Figure 1.2 an isosceles right-angled triangle OPQ has been drawn in which $OQ = QP = 1$. The theorem of Pythagoras tells us that, if OP represents the number x, then $x^2 = 2$; our next example shows that P does not represent a rational number.

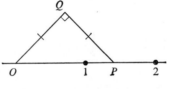

Fig. 1.2

Example 5. *Prove that* $\sqrt{2}$ *is not a rational number.*

We have to prove that $\sqrt{2}$ cannot be expressed in the form p/q where p, q are integers. Our method of proof will consist in assuming that $\sqrt{2}$ can be expressed in the form p/q and showing that this leads to a contradiction.

Suppose that $\sqrt{2} = p/q$, where p, q have no common factors.

Then $p^2 = 2q^2$; but, if the square of an integer is even, the integer itself must be even, and so $p = 2r$ where r is an integer

$$\therefore \quad 4r^2 = 2q^2 \quad \text{and so} \quad 2r^2 = q^2.$$

By the same token q must be even.

Thus, p, q must both be even, contradicting our initial assumption.

Numbers such as $\sqrt{2}$ which are not rational are called *irrational*. Since rational numbers are represented by terminating or recurring decimals, *the decimal representation (if it exists) of an irrational number is non-terminating and non-recurring.*

Irrational numbers obey the same laws of combination as rational numbers. The proof of this lies beyond the scope of this book, as it requires a systematic definition of irrational numbers in terms of the rationals;

we shall be content to assume this result, which is intuitively fairly obvious if we consider rational (terminating decimal) approximations to irrational numbers.

Exercise 1(b)

1. Where does the proof of Example 5 break down if you try to prove $\sqrt{4}$ is irrational?

2. By assuming that $\sqrt[3]{2} = p/q$, where p, q are integers cancelled down into their lowest form, show that $\sqrt[3]{2}$ is irrational.

3. Prove that $\sqrt{3}$ is irrational.

4. Express as (i) a decimal, (ii) a bicimal, the fraction $\frac{1}{3}$ (denary notation). If a decimal recurs, does it bicimal representation necessarily recur?

5. Prove that, if a rational number of the form p/q (cancelled down into its lowest form) is expanded as a recurring decimal, the length of the block of digits that recurs is less than q.

6. Which of the following statements are always true and which are not? If a statement is true, prove it; if it may be false, give a counter-example (that is, an example that illustrates its falsity):
    (i) rational+rational = rational;
    (ii) rational+irrational = irrational;
    (iii) irrational+irrational = irrational;
    (iv) rational×rational = rational;
    (v) rational×irrational = irrational;
    (vi) irrational×irrational = irrational.

7. If a and b are integers and $\sqrt{b}$ is irrational, prove that $(a+\sqrt{b})^3$ is irrational. (The results of Question 6 may be used in this question.)

8. Prove that it is always possible to find an irrational number that lies between two given rational numbers a and b.

9. If p_1, p_2, p_3 are three unequal prime numbers, prove that

$$\frac{1}{p_1}+\frac{1}{p_2}+\frac{1}{p_3}$$

is a rational number, but not an integer.
    Can you generalize this result?

10. You are given a ruler with only integral units of length marked on it. Show how to construct, geometrically, the following lengths:

$$\text{(i) } \sqrt{3}; \quad \text{(ii) } \sqrt{7}; \quad \text{(iii) } \sqrt{(2+\sqrt{2})}.$$

11. Prove that, if k is an integer and $\sqrt{k}$ is rational, then $\sqrt{k}$ is an integer. Show further that, for $k > 1$, $\sqrt{(k^2-1)}$ is irrational and deduce that, for $k \geqslant 1$, $\sqrt{(k-1)}+\sqrt{(k+1)}$ is irrational.

5. SURDS

Although the existence of irrational numbers is mathematically significant, from the point of view of practical arithmetic all numbers may be regarded as rational, since any irrational number may be approximated to by a terminating decimal. Indeed, wherever measurements are concerned, the answers obtained must necessarily be in the form of rational numbers, since every measuring device must eventually reach the limits of its possible accuracy. However, just as $\frac{1}{3}$ is simpler to handle than its decimal approximation 0·3333, so $\sqrt{2}$ is often easier to deal with than its approximation 1·414.

An expression involving only rational numbers and their roots (not necessarily square roots) is called a *surd*; thus surds form a class of irrational numbers, though there are irrational numbers, such as π, which cannot be expressed as surds.

Examples of surds are:

$$\sqrt{2}; \quad \sqrt[3]{\frac{3}{5}}; \quad \left(\sqrt{2}+\frac{1}{\sqrt{2}-1}\right)^2; \quad \sqrt[3]{3}+\sqrt{2}.$$

Note: if x is positive, $\sqrt[m]{x} = x^{1/m}$ means the positive m^{th} root of x; by convention, the 2 is omitted for square roots, e.g. $\sqrt{9} = 3$. Again, $\sqrt[2m]{(-x)}$ has no meaning, while

$$\sqrt[2m+1]{(-x)} = (-x)^{1/(2m+1)} = -(x)^{1/(2m+1)}.$$

A great number of complicated surds may be simplified using the three results:

$$\text{(i) } \sqrt{(ab)} = \sqrt{a}\sqrt{b}; \quad \text{(ii) } \sqrt{\frac{a}{b}} = \frac{\sqrt{(ab)}}{b};$$

$$\text{(iii) } (\sqrt{a}+\sqrt{b})(\sqrt{a}-\sqrt{b}) = a-b.$$

Example 6. Simplify the expression $\sqrt{128}-\sqrt{32}-\sqrt{8}+\sqrt{2}$.

$$\sqrt{128}-\sqrt{32}-\sqrt{8}+\sqrt{2} = \sqrt{(2^6.2)}-\sqrt{(2^4.2)}-\sqrt{(2^2.2)}+\sqrt{2}$$
$$= 2^3\sqrt{2}-2^2\sqrt{2}-2\sqrt{2}+\sqrt{2}$$
$$= 8\sqrt{2}-4\sqrt{2}-2\sqrt{2}+\sqrt{2}$$
$$= 3\sqrt{2}.$$

The process of removing surds from the denominator of surd expressions is known as *rationalizing the denominator*.

Conventionally, a surd is usually expressed with its denominator rationalized.

Example 7. *Rationalize the denominators of the following surds*:

(i) $\sqrt{\dfrac{3}{5}}$;   (ii) $\dfrac{1}{\sqrt{5}-\sqrt{2}}$;   (iii) $\dfrac{\sqrt{2}+1}{\sqrt{3}+\sqrt{2}}$.

(i) $\sqrt{\dfrac{3}{5}} = \dfrac{\sqrt{3}}{\sqrt{5}} = \dfrac{\sqrt{3}\sqrt{5}}{\sqrt{5}\sqrt{5}} = \dfrac{\sqrt{15}}{5}$;

(ii) $\dfrac{1}{\sqrt{5}-\sqrt{2}} = \dfrac{1}{\sqrt{5}-\sqrt{2}}\left(\dfrac{\sqrt{5}+\sqrt{2}}{\sqrt{5}+\sqrt{2}}\right) = \dfrac{\sqrt{5}+\sqrt{2}}{3}$;

(iii) $\dfrac{\sqrt{2}+1}{\sqrt{3}+\sqrt{2}} = \left(\dfrac{\sqrt{2}+1}{\sqrt{3}+\sqrt{2}}\right)\left(\dfrac{\sqrt{3}-\sqrt{2}}{\sqrt{3}-\sqrt{2}}\right) = \dfrac{(\sqrt{2}+1)\,(\sqrt{3}-\sqrt{2})}{3-2}$

$$= \sqrt{6}+\sqrt{3}-\sqrt{2}-2.$$

Ex. 17. $\sqrt{45} = 3\sqrt{5}$. Simplify in a similar fashion the surds: (i) $\sqrt{8}$; (ii) $\sqrt{18}$; (iii) $\sqrt{54}$; (iv) $\sqrt{250}$; (v) $\sqrt{5292}$.

Ex. 18. Simplify the following surd expressions.
(i) $(\sqrt{3}+2\sqrt{2})^2$;   (ii) $\sqrt{216}-\sqrt{150}+\sqrt{24}$;   (iii) $\sqrt{75}+\sqrt{147}-\sqrt{300}$;
(iv) $(\sqrt{32}+\sqrt{50}-\sqrt{98})^2$.

Ex. 19. Rationalize the denominators of the following expressions:

(i) $\dfrac{1}{\sqrt{3}}$;   (ii) $\dfrac{\sqrt{2}+1}{\sqrt{2}}$;   (iii) $\dfrac{1}{2-\sqrt{2}}$;   (iv) $\dfrac{\sqrt{3}}{\sqrt{3}-\sqrt{2}}$;   (v) $\dfrac{2-\sqrt{3}}{2+\sqrt{3}}$.

We conclude this section with some further examples of manipulation of surd quantities and the use of the $\sqrt{}$ sign.

Example 8. *Simplify*:

(i) $\dfrac{1}{1+\sqrt{3}-\sqrt{2}}$;   (ii) $\sqrt{(14-4\sqrt{6})}$.

(i) $\dfrac{1}{1+\sqrt{3}-\sqrt{2}} = \dfrac{1-(\sqrt{3}-\sqrt{2})}{1-(\sqrt{3}-\sqrt{2})^2}$

$$= \dfrac{1-\sqrt{3}+\sqrt{2}}{1-(5-2\sqrt{6})}$$

$$= \dfrac{1+\sqrt{2}-\sqrt{3}}{2(\sqrt{6}-2)}$$

$$= \dfrac{(1+\sqrt{2}-\sqrt{3})\,(\sqrt{6}+2)}{2(6-4)}$$

$$= \dfrac{\sqrt{6}+2+\sqrt{12}+2\sqrt{2}-\sqrt{18}-2\sqrt{3}}{4}$$

$$= \dfrac{2+\sqrt{6}-\sqrt{2}}{4}.$$

(ii) Suppose $14-4\sqrt{6} = (\sqrt{a}-2\sqrt{b})^2$.

Then $14-4\sqrt{6} = (a+4b)-4\sqrt{(ab)}$.

11

These two expressions will be equal if

$$a+4b = 14,$$

$$ab = 6.$$

By inspection (or by solution of the simultaneous quadratic equations) $a = 2, b = 3$.

Thus

$$\sqrt{(14-4\sqrt{6})} = 2\sqrt{3}-\sqrt{2}.$$

(Notice that we must choose the positive square root.)

Example 9. Solve the equation

$$\sqrt{(3x+4)}-\sqrt{(x+2)} = 2.$$

(i) Squaring both sides,

$$(3x+4)+(x+2)-2\sqrt{(3x^2+10x+8)} = 4.$$

(ii) Collecting terms and dividing both sides by 2,

$$2x+1 = \sqrt{(3x^2+10x+8)}.$$

(iii) Squaring both sides and collecting terms,

$$x^2-6x-7 = 0.$$

This gives $x = 7$ or $x = -1$. However, we must check both of these solutions in the original equation since, after step (iii), we could equally well have been solving the equation

$$\sqrt{(3x+4)}+\sqrt{(x+2)} = 2. \quad \text{(Why?)}$$

Inspection shows us that only $x = 7$ is a valid root of the original equation.

Exercise 1(c)

1. Express in the form $a\sqrt{b}$, where b has no perfect squares as factors
   (i) $\sqrt{50}$;   (ii) $\sqrt{363}$;   (iii) $\sqrt{2400}$;   (iv) $\sqrt{192}$;   (v) $\sqrt{1452}$.

2. Simplify the following surds:
   (i) $(\sqrt{5}-1)^2$;   (ii) $(2\sqrt{3}-\sqrt{2})^2$;   (iii) $(\sqrt{3}+1)^3$;   (iv) $(\sqrt{3}-\sqrt{2})^3$;
   (v) $(\sqrt{3}-1)^4$.

3. Simplify the following expressions:
   (i) $\sqrt{18}-\sqrt{2}$;   (ii) $\sqrt{80}-\sqrt{5}$;   (iii) $\sqrt{108}-\sqrt{75}+\sqrt{48}$;
   (iv) $\dfrac{\sqrt{117}}{3}$;   (v) $\dfrac{\sqrt{147}-\sqrt{3}}{4}$.

4. Rationalize the denominators of the following expressions:

(i) $\dfrac{1}{\sqrt{5}}$; (ii) $\sqrt{\left(\dfrac{7}{3}\right)}$; (iii) $\dfrac{2}{\sqrt{7}-2}$; (iv) $\dfrac{2\sqrt{3}+1}{2\sqrt{3}-1}$; (v) $\dfrac{1+\sqrt{2}}{\sqrt{3}+\sqrt{2}}$.

5. Simplify:

(i) $\sqrt{(6-2\sqrt{5})}$; (ii) $\sqrt{(10-\sqrt{96})}$; (iii) $\sqrt{(30+12\sqrt{6})}$; (iv) $\sqrt{(47-6\sqrt{60})}$;
(v) $3/\sqrt{(7-\sqrt{40})}$.

6. Solve for x the following equations:

(i) $3\sqrt{x}-\sqrt{(x+5)} = 3$,
(ii) $\sqrt{(2x+5)}-\sqrt{(x+2)} = 1$,
(iii) $\sqrt{(x+6)}+\sqrt{(4-x)} = \sqrt{(1-3x)}$.

7. Rationalize the denominators of the expressions:

(i) $\dfrac{1}{\sqrt{3}+\sqrt{2}+1}$; (ii) $\dfrac{1}{2\sqrt{2}+\sqrt{5}-1}$.

8. The equation
$$\sqrt{(x+4\cdot7)}+\sqrt{(x+4\cdot9)} = \sqrt{33}$$

was solved to give an answer $x = 3\cdot1$ (to one decimal point). Without using tables, state why this is clearly wrong.

9. Given that $\sqrt{5} \approx 2\cdot23607$, $\sqrt{2} \approx 1\cdot41421$, evaluate:

(i) $\dfrac{1}{\sqrt{5}}$; (ii) $\dfrac{1}{\sqrt{5}+\sqrt{2}}$,

giving your answers to the greatest accuracy that you can guarantee.

10. Given that, to six significant figures, $\sqrt{6} = 2\cdot44949$, $\sqrt{3} = 1\cdot73205$, evaluate as accurately as possible $1/(2\sqrt{3}-\sqrt{6})$, justifying the accuracy you give.

11. Rationalize the denominator of the expression $\sqrt[3]{3}/(\sqrt[3]{3}+1)$, by using the factorization $a^3+b^3 = (a+b)(a^2-ab+b^2)$.

12. Rationalize the denominators, and simplify as far as possible the following expressions:

(i) $\dfrac{1}{\sqrt{(x+1)}-\sqrt{(x-1)}}$; (ii) $\sqrt{(x+1)}+\dfrac{1}{\sqrt{(x+1)}}$;

(iii) $\dfrac{1}{\sqrt{(2x+a)}}-\dfrac{1}{\sqrt{(2x-a)}}$; (iv) $\dfrac{1}{\sqrt{(x-1)}+1}-\dfrac{1}{\sqrt{(x+1)}-1}$.

6. SETS OF NUMBERS

Suppose we have a collection of numbers, the whole collection being denoted by the letter $\mathfrak{U}$. Suppose, too, we ask a question which may be answered unambiguously 'Yes' or 'No' for each number (or element) of $\mathfrak{U}$. Then the collection of those elements of $\mathfrak{U}$ for which the answer is 'Yes' is said to form a *set S*, which is a *subset* of the *universal set* $\mathfrak{U}$,

13

written $S \subseteq \mathfrak{U}$. The collection of those elements of $\mathfrak{U}$ for which the answer is 'No' is called the *complement of S*, written S'.

It may happen that the answer to the question is 'No' for each element of $\mathfrak{U}$; in this case we say S is *empty* and write this as $S = \varnothing$. ($\varnothing$ is usually referred to as the *null set*, or *empty set*.)

As an example, suppose that $\mathfrak{U}$ is the set of integers from 1 to 10. We may write this as
$$\mathfrak{U} = \{1, 2, 3, ..., 10\}.$$

The question may be posed: 'Is the element x of $\mathfrak{U}$ divisible by 3?' Those elements for which the answer is 'Yes' form a set A where

$$A = \{3, 6, 9\}.$$

The complement of A is given by

$$A' = \{1, 2, 4, 5, 7, 8, 10\}.$$

Again, the alternative question 'Is the element x of $\mathfrak{U}$ irrational?' may be asked and unambiguously answered for each element of $\mathfrak{U}$. The answer is 'No' in every case; the set defined is thus $\varnothing$ and its complement is $\mathfrak{U}$.

In this example, the universal set $\mathfrak{U}$ contains only a finite number of elements. It may well happen, however, that $\mathfrak{U}$ contains an infinite number of elements; for example, $\mathfrak{U}$ might be the set of all positive integers. The *proper subset E* defined by the question 'Is the element x of $\mathfrak{U}$ even?' also contains an infinite number of elements. (P is a *proper subset of Q* if P is contained in Q but is not the whole of Q, written $P \subset Q$. $P \subseteq Q$ means that P is a subset of Q, but may be the whole of Q.)

It is convenient to develop a shorthand notation for the somewhat cumbersome method we have used so far in defining our sets. The method adopted is to use braces $\{:\}$ with a colon (:) or vertical line (|) (read as 'such that') separating the two necessary pieces of information:

(i) within the bracket and to the left of the colon is stated the universal set from which the elements are drawn;

(ii) within the bracket and to the right of the colon is the statement defining which particular elements of the universal set are to be chosen.

For instance, for the sets $\mathfrak{U}$ and A mentioned above we may write

$$A = \{x \in \mathfrak{U} : x \text{ is divisible by 3}\}.$$

The sign $\in$ means 'is a member of' or 'is an element of'.

Ex. 20. If $\mathfrak{U}$ is the set of positive integers $\{1, 2, 3, ..., 9\}$ write down the elements of the following sets:
  (i) $\{x \in \mathfrak{U} : x+4 \in \mathfrak{U}\}$;   (ii) $\{x \in \mathfrak{U} : \sqrt{x} \text{ is rational}\}$.

14

Ex. 21. If $\mathfrak{U}$ is the set of all positive integers $\{1, 2, 3, ...\}$ describe in words the following sets:

   (i) $\{x \in \mathfrak{U}: \frac{1}{2}(x+1) \in \mathfrak{U}\}$;   (ii) $\{x \in \mathfrak{U}: x-1 \in \mathfrak{U}\}$;

   (iii) $\{x \in \mathfrak{U}: \frac{1}{10}x \in \mathfrak{U}\}$;   (iv) $\{x \in \mathfrak{U}: x^2-5x-6 = 0\}$;

   (v) $\{x \in \mathfrak{U}: x^2-5x-7 = 0\}$.

Ex. 22. Two sets A and B which are both subsets of the same universal set $\mathfrak{U}$ are said to be *equal* $(A = B)$ if they contain precisely the same elements.

   Show that $A = B \Leftrightarrow A \subseteq B$ and $B \subseteq A$.

We may combine two subsets $A \subseteq \mathfrak{U}$ and $B \subseteq \mathfrak{U}$ according to the two rules of *union* ($\cup$) and *intersection* ($\cap$) defined as follows:

$A \cup B$ is the set of all elements of $\mathfrak{U}$ that are members of *either A or B or both.*

$A \cap B$ is the set of all elements of $\mathfrak{U}$ that are members of *both A and B.*

From these definitions it follows at once that the operations of union and intersection are commutative; that is,

$$A \cup B = B \cup A \quad \text{and} \quad A \cap B = B \cap A.$$

The operations of union, intersection and complementation may be exhibited pictorially using a *Venn diagram*. In a Venn diagram, the universal set $\mathfrak{U}$ is represented by a rectangle; any subset $A \subseteq \mathfrak{U}$ is depicted by a closed region lying within the rectangle; see Figure 1.3.

In Figures 1.4, 1.5, 1.6, $A \cup B$, $A \cap B$ and A' are shown shaded:

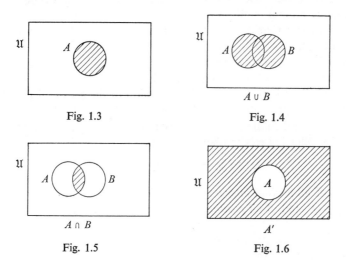

Fig. 1.3 $A \cup B$

                               Fig. 1.4

$A \cap B$ A'

Fig. 1.5   Fig. 1.6

Ex. 23. Verify, using Venn diagrams, that the operations of union and intersection are associative; that is

$$A \cup (B \cup C) = (A \cup B) \cup C; \quad A \cap (B \cap C) = (A \cap B) \cap C.$$

15

Ex. 24. Verify, using Venn diagrams, that the operation of union is distributive over intersection, and that intersection is distributive over union; that is

$$A \cup (B \cap C) = (A \cup B) \cap (A \cup C); \quad A \cap (B \cup C) = (A \cap B) \cup (A \cap C).$$

Ex. 25. Verify *de Morgan's Laws*, using a Venn diagram:

$$\text{(i) } (A \cup B)' = A' \cap B'; \quad \text{(ii) } (A \cap B)' = A' \cup B'.$$

(The reader may be able to identify these laws with the logic of AND ($\cap$), OR ($\cup$) and NOT (').)

Ex. 26. If $\mathfrak{U}$ is the set of all positive integers and

$$A = \{x \in \mathfrak{U} : \tfrac{1}{2}x \in \mathfrak{U}\}, \quad B = \{x \in \mathfrak{U} : \tfrac{1}{3}x \in \mathfrak{U}\}$$

describe $A \cap B$, using the $\{:\}$ notation.

Ex. 27. If $\mathfrak{U} = \{a, b, c, d, e\}$ and $A = \{a, c, e\}$ write down the subsets:
(i) $A \cup A'$; (ii) $A \cap A'$; (iii) $A \cup \mathfrak{U}$; (iv) $A \cap \mathfrak{U}$; (v) $A \cup \varnothing$; (vi) $A \cap \varnothing$; (vii) $\mathfrak{U}'$; (viii) $\varnothing'$.

Ex. 28. If, with the notation of Ex. 27, $B = \{a, b, e\}$, write down the subsets

$$\text{(i) } A \cap B; \quad \text{(ii) } A' \cup B; \quad \text{(iii) } A \cap B'.$$

Verify de Morgan's Laws (see Ex. 25) in this particular case.

Three particular sets, the set of all integers, the set of all rational numbers and the set of all real numbers occur throughout mathematics with such unfailing regularity that it is convenient to introduce a notation by which to refer to them.

The set of all *integers* is denoted by Z.

The set of all *rational numbers* is denoted by Q.

The set of all *real numbers* (that is, the union of the set of all rational numbers and the set of all irrational numbers) is denoted by R.

With a suitable definition of each of the terms integer, rational and real we have the following relation between them

$$Z \subset Q \subset R.$$

The sets of all *positive integers* is denoted by Z^+, of all *positive rational numbers* by Q^+ and of all *positive real numbers* by R^+.

Ex. 29. Enumerate the elements of the following sets:
(i) $\{x \in Z : (x-2)(2x+1)(x^2-2) = 0\}$;
(ii) $\{x \in Q^+ : (x-2)(2x+1)(x^2-2) = 0\}$;
(iii) $\{x \in Q : (x-2)(2x+1)(x^2-2) = 0\}$;
(iv) $\{x \in R^+ : (x-2)(2x+1)(x^2-2) = 0\}$;
(v) $\{x \in R : (x-2)(2x+1)(x^2-2) = 0\}$.

7. INEQUALITIES

We have already asserted that the integers and the rational numbers may be ordered; that is, given two integers (or rational numbers) x and y, we may answer the question 'Is x greater than y?' The same is true for the set of all irrational numbers, or, indeed, for the union of the sets of rational and irrational numbers (the set of real numbers).

If x, y are two real numbers, $x > y$ (read 'x is greater than y') means that the point representing the number x lies to the right of the point representing the number y. Similarly for $x < y$ ('x is less than y'). When comparing two positive or negative numbers x and y in this way, we see that

$$x > y \Leftrightarrow x-y > 0 \quad (i.e.\ x-y\ is\ positive),$$
$$x < y \Leftrightarrow x-y < 0 \quad (i.e.\ x-y\ is\ negative),$$
$$x = y \Leftrightarrow x-y = 0 \quad (i.e.\ x-y\ is\ zero).$$

The number zero separates the positive and negative numbers; it is itself neither positive nor negative.

By continued use of these results we see that we may add or subtract any number from both sides of an inequality without altering the validity of the inequality sign.

Inequalities are of value in defining sets. Thus, for example, to take a rather trivial case,
$$\{x \in Z: 0 < x < 3\} = \{1, 2\}.$$

A more substantial example would be
$$\{x \in R: x^2 < 4\}.$$

Solving an inequality means redefining the set of elements which satisfy the given inequality in as simple a manner as possible.

Ex. 30. What does 'solving an equation' mean?

Example 10. *If x is a real number, solve the inequality $3-x > 2$.*
The question asks us to redefine the set
$$\{x \in R: 3-x > 2\}$$
as simply as possible.
Since
$$3-x > 2$$
$$\Rightarrow 3 > 2+x \quad \text{(by adding x to both sides)}$$
$$\Rightarrow 1 > x \quad \text{(by subtracting 2 from both sides)}$$
the solution set may be rewritten
$$\{x \in R: x < 1\}.$$

17

The rule for redefining a set by multiplying or dividing both sides of an inequality by a number is slightly more complicated. If $x-y$ and z are both positive, then $(x-y)z$ is positive, thus

$$x > y \quad \text{and} \quad z > 0 \Rightarrow xz > yz.$$

If, on the other hand, $x-y$ is positive but z is negative, then $(x-y)z$ is negative and thus
$$x > y \quad \text{and} \quad z < 0 \Rightarrow xz < yz.$$

Thus, if a set is defined by an inequality $x > y$, the same set is defined by

$$xz > yz \quad \text{if } z \text{ is } positive,$$

or by $\qquad\qquad\qquad xz < yz \quad$ if z is *negative*.

A similar result holds for division.

We now append an alternative solution to Example 10:

$$3-x > 2$$
$$\Rightarrow -3+x < -2, \quad \text{multiplying both sides by } -1,$$
$$\Rightarrow \qquad x < 1, \qquad \text{adding 3 to both sides,}$$

and we have, as before, the solution set

$$\{x \in R : x < 1\}.$$

Ex. 31. Solve the inequalities
  (i) $3+x < 1$; (ii) $2-3x > -1$; (iii) $3-4x > 1$.

The reader should have observed that in, for example, the result

$$x > y \quad \text{and} \quad z > 0 \Rightarrow xz > yz$$

the two-way implication was not used: it is not valid to deduce from $xz > yz$ that $x > y$ and $z > 0$. However, inequalities involving products may be solved by observing that, if the product is positive, then the factors are either both positive or both negative. Another useful observation is that a squared number is always positive or zero.

Example 11. *Solve the inequality* $(x+2)(x-1) > 0$ *(x real)*.
  If $(x+2)(x-1) > 0$ then

either $\qquad\qquad$ (i) $(x+2) > 0 \quad$ and $\quad (x-1) > 0$,
or $\qquad\qquad$ (ii) $(x+2) < 0 \quad$ and $\quad (x-1) < 0$.

The first pair of inequalities has as solution set

$$\{x \in R : x > -2\} \cap \{x \in R : x > 1\} = \{x \in R : x < 1\}.$$

18

The second pair of inequalities has as solution set

$$\{x \in R: x < -2\} \cap \{x \in R: x < 1\} = \{x \in R: x < -2\}.$$

The complete solution is thus the union of these two sets

$$\{x \in R: \text{ either } x < -2 \text{ or } x > 1\}.$$

Alternatively, the argument may be presented very clearly in the following tabular form. The critical values of x for which $(x+2)(x-1)$ changes sign are $x = -2$ and $x = 1$. We divide the possible values of x into the three ranges $x < -2$, $-2 < x < 1$ and $x > 1$ and consider the signs of $(x+2)$, $(x-1)$ and hence of $(x+2)(x-1)$ in each interval.

	$x < -2$	$-2 < x < 1$	$x > 1$
$x+2$	$-$	$+$	$+$
$x-1$	$-$	$-$	$+$
$(x+2)(x-1)$	$+$	$-$	$+$

Example 12. *Prove that the expression* $y = x^2 + x + 1$ *is positive for all real values of* x, *and find its minimum value.*

It will be useful in the solution of this example to employ the notation $\geqslant$: $x \geqslant y$ means 'x is greater than, or equal to, y'.

Now

$$y = x^2 + x + 1$$
$$= (x + \tfrac{1}{2})^2 + \tfrac{3}{4},$$
$$\therefore \quad y - \tfrac{3}{4} = (x + \tfrac{1}{2})^2,$$
$$\therefore \quad y - \tfrac{3}{4} \geqslant 0 \quad \text{or} \quad y \geqslant \tfrac{3}{4}.$$

Thus y is always positive and has a minimum value of $\tfrac{3}{4}$ (when $x = -\tfrac{1}{2}$).

Given two positive numbers x and y we define
(i) the *arithmetic mean* (A.M.) as $A = \tfrac{1}{2}(x+y)$;
(ii) the *geometric mean* (G.M.) as $G = \sqrt{(xy)}$.

We conclude this chapter by proving a famous theorem (which may be extended, see Miscellaneous Exercise 1, Question 13).

Theorem 1.1. *The* A.M. *of two positive numbers is at least as great as their* G.M.

Proof. Since the two numbers are positive, we may write them as u^2 and v^2.

Let $A = (u^2 + v^2)/2$, $G = uv$; we have to prove that

$$A - G \geqslant 0,$$

19

that is
$$\frac{u^2+v^2}{2} - uv \geqslant 0,$$

$$\text{L.H.S.} = \tfrac{1}{2}(u^2+v^2-2uv)$$
$$= \tfrac{1}{2}(u-v)^2$$
$$> 0, \quad \text{unless} \quad u = v.$$

We have thus proved that $A > G$ unless $u^2 = v^2$ in which case $A = G$.

Example 13. 200 *m of wattle fencing are to be bent to form three sides of a rectangular enclosure, the fourth side being a straight hedge. Find the length of the rectangle if the area to be enclosed is to be a maximum.*

Let x m be the length, y m the breadth, A m² the area of the enclosure. Then we have

(i) $x+2y = 200$,   (ii) $xy = A$.

Both x and $2y$ are positive; thus, by the theorem just proved, their A.M. is at least as great as their G.M. That is

$$\tfrac{1}{2}(x+2y) \geqslant \sqrt{(2xy)}.$$

Using (i) and (ii), this gives
$$100 \geqslant \sqrt{(2A)},$$

i.e.
$$A \leqslant 5000.$$

Equality occurs only if $x = 2y$, i.e. $x = 100$, $y = 50$. Thus the maximum area occurs when the length is 100 m.

Exercise 1(d)

1. Verify, using a Venn diagram, the results:
  (i) $A \cup (A' \cup B)' = A \cap (B' \cup A)$,
  (ii) $(A \cup B) \cap (A' \cap C)' = A \cup (B \cap C')$,
  (iii) $[A' \cup (B' \cap C')]' = (A \cap B) \cup (A \cap C)$.

2. If R is the set of real numbers and
$$A = \{x \in R \colon x > 3\}, \quad B = \{x \in R; \, x < 4\}$$
describe, using the $\{:\}$ notation
  (i) $A \cup B$;   (ii) $A \cap B$;   (iii) $A' \cup B$.

3. Taking the universal set, $\mathfrak{U}$ as the set of all integers, describe using the $\{:\}$ notation
  (i) the set of all negative integers;
  (ii) the set of all positive integers divisible by 6;
  (iii) the set of all integers, excluding 0, ± 1, ± 2.

4. $A = \{x \in R \colon -1 \leqslant x < 3\}$, $B = \{x \in R \colon 2 \leqslant x < 4\}$, $C = \{x \in R \colon x > 3\}$.
Find expressions for the following sets, using the $\{:\}$ notation:
  (i) $A \cap B$; (ii) $A' \cap C$; (iii) $(A \cup B) \cap C'$; (iv) $A \cup (B \cap C')$; (v) $(A' \cup B') \cap C$; (vi) $A' \cup (B' \cap C)$; (vii) $A' \cap B \cap C$.

5. $A = \{x \in R: x > 0\}, \quad B = \{x \in R: x \leqslant 1\}, \quad C = \{x \in R: -1 < x < 2\},$
$D = \{x \in R: -2 \leqslant x < 1\}.$

Find expressions for the following sets, using the {:} notation:
(i) $A \cap B \cap C \cap D$;   (ii) $A' \cap B \cap C \cap D'$;
(iii) $(A \cup B') \cap (C \cap D')$;   (iv) $(A' \cap B') \cup (C' \cap D)$.

6. Solve the following inequalities:
(i) $x+2 < -3$;   (ii) $3x-1 > 5$;   (iii) $4x-3 < 3x+4$;   (iv) $2x > x$;
(v) $x^2 > x$.

7. Solve the following inequalities:
(i) $(x+3)(x-1) > 0$;   (ii) $(2x-1)(3x+1) > 0$;   (iii) $(x-3)(2x+3) < 0$;
(iv) $x^2-6x+9 < 0$; (v) $x^2-4x-5 < 0$.

8. Solve the inequality
$$(2x+1)(x-2)(x+3) > 0.$$

9. Prove that the following expressions are positive, for all real values of x, and find their minimum values:
(i) x^2+2x+2;   (ii) $x^2-6x+12$;   (iii) $2x^2-2x+1$.

10. Find the signs, for all values of x, of:
(i) $2x-x^2-2$;   (ii) $2x^2-x+1$.

11. For what values of x is the expression
$$(x-1)(x+2)(x-3)(x+4)$$
positive?

12. If $xy = 25$, find the least possible value for $x+y$, if both x and y are positive.

13. If $xy = 18$, find the least possible value for $2x+y$, if both x and y are positive.

14. If $x+y = 2$, find the maximum value of xy.

15. If $2x+3y = 120$, find the maximum value of xy.

16. Some netting is required to make three sides of a rectangular chicken-run, the fourth side being an existing wall. Find the least length of netting needed for an area of 50 m².

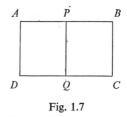

17. Figure 1.7 shows part of the framework of a kite. $ABCD$ is a rectangle; P and Q are the mid-points of AB, CD respectively. Find the maximum area of $ABCD$ that can be made if 4 m of wood are available.

Fig. 1.7

What are the dimensions of the kite necessary to attain this area?

Miscellaneous Exercise 1

1. Express 120 as a binary number.
Find the least number of stamps required so that any value from ½p to 60p (in steps of ½p) may be selected, and give their values. (You may assume stamps of any value are available if required.)

2. Show that it is impossible to choose values of a and b so that the number written as ab in the scale of ten is equal to the number written as ba in the scale of twelve.

Show, however, that ab (scale of ten) $= ba$ (scale of seven) is possible, and give an example.

3. Prove the well known result that the remainder on dividing a number by 9 is the same as the remainder on dividing the sum of its digits by 9.

Show that this result may be generalized as follows: if a number is divided by s then the remainder is the same as the remainder on dividing by s the sum of its digits, when it is expressed to the base $s+1$.

4. Prove that, if a number is divided by 11, the remainder is either the same as the remainder on dividing the difference between the sums of the digits in the even and odd places, or else the sum of the two remainders is 11.

Generalize this result along the lines of Question 3.

5. Prove that, if the digits of an integer (expressed to the base ten) are re-arranged in any way to form another integer, the difference between the two integers is divisible by 9.

6. If $abc + abc = cba$ in the scale of five (when abc here means $5^2a + 5b + c$) find values for a, b, c.

Show that this question is always soluble provided a base of $3n-1$ is used, where n is a positive integer.

7. Prove that $\sqrt{3} - \sqrt{2}$ is irrational.

8. Solve the equation
$$\sqrt{(4x-2)} + \sqrt{(x+1)} - \sqrt{(7-5x)} = 0. \qquad \text{(O \& C)}$$

9. Verify that the expression
$$a^2 + b^2 + c^2 - 2bc - 2ca - 2ab$$
is equal to $(a+b-c)^2 - 4ab$. Hence, or otherwise, prove that the expression is equal to
$$(\alpha + \beta + \gamma)(\alpha - \beta - \gamma)(\alpha - \beta + \gamma)(\alpha + \beta - \gamma),$$
where
$$\alpha = \sqrt{a}, \quad \beta = \sqrt{b}, \quad \gamma = \sqrt{c}.$$

Hence, or otherwise, find one solution of each of the equations
(i) $\sqrt{(x-6)} + \sqrt{(x-1)} = \sqrt{(3x-5)}$;
(ii) $\sqrt{(6-x)} - \sqrt{(1-x)} = \sqrt{(5-3x)}$. \qquad (O \& C)

10. If $a > b$ and $c > d$, prove that $ac + bd > bc + da$.
What happens to the third inequality if $a < b$, $c < d$?

11. If the universal set is taken as the set R of all real numbers, the three sets A, B and C are defined as follows:

$$A = \{x \in R: x > 2\}; \quad B = \{x \in R: 1 < x < 4\}; \quad C = \{x \in R: x < 3\}.$$

Express, in terms of any or all of A, B, C (and using the notation of union, intersection and complement) the following sets:
(i) $\{x \in R: 2 < x < 3\}$;   (ii) $\{x \in R: x \leqslant 1\}$;
(iii) $\{x \in R: 3 \leqslant x < 4\}$;   (iv) $\{x \in R: 1 < x \leqslant 2 \text{ or } 3 \leqslant x < 4\}$.

12. Show that the expression $x^2+8xy-5y^2-k(x^2+y^2)$ can be put in the form $a(x+by)^2$ when k has either one or other of two values. Find these values and the values of a and b corresponding to each value of k.

Prove that when the variables x and y are restricted by the relation

$$x^2+y^2 = 1,$$

but are otherwise free, then

$$-7 \leqslant x^2+8xy-5y^2 \leqslant 3. \qquad \text{(O \& C)}$$

13. a, b, c, d are four unequal positive numbers. By using Theorem 1.1 and considering first the pair of numbers $\frac{1}{2}(a+b)$ and $\frac{1}{2}(c+d)$, and then, separately, the pairs a, b and c, d, prove that

$$\tfrac{1}{4}(a+b+c+d) > (abcd)^{\frac{1}{4}}.$$

Deduce, by considering the four unequal numbers a, b, c and $\frac{1}{3}(a+b+c)$, that

$$\tfrac{1}{3}(a+b+c) > (abc)^{\frac{1}{3}}.$$

What happens to the last inequality (i) if $a = b = c$; (ii) $a = b \neq c$?
Suggest a generalization of the results proved above.

14. If $x+2y+3z = 1$, where x, y, z are positive numbers, find the maximum value of xyz.

If $u+v = 1$, where u, v are positive numbers, find the maximum value of u^2v.

15. A cylindrical vessel, with one end open, is made from a given piece of material. Show that its volume is greatest if the height and radius are equal.

16. a, b, c are non-zero rational numbers. Show that, if

$$a^{\frac{1}{3}}+b^{\frac{1}{3}}+c^{\frac{1}{3}} = 0,$$

and if none of $a^{\frac{1}{3}}$, $b^{\frac{1}{3}}$, $c^{\frac{1}{3}}$ is rational, then $a^{\frac{1}{3}}$, $b^{\frac{1}{3}}$, $c^{\frac{1}{3}}$ are each rational multiples of the same irrational number.

17. Show that, if p/q is a good approximation to $\sqrt{2}$, then $(p^2+2q^2)/(2pq)$ is a better one. Starting with $p = q = 1$, show that $\sqrt{2} \approx 577/408$, and estimate the accuracy of this approximation.

2. *Vectors and vector geometry*

1. SCALAR AND VECTOR QUANTITIES

Many physical quantities are completely specified by their magnitude alone. For example, if the mass of the box is m kg and we are told that $m = 8$, we know the mass of the box precisely. Not all physical quantities are so easily described as this; for example, if the position of the point P relative to the fixed point O is denoted by $\mathbf{r}$, then the statement '$\mathbf{r} = 8$ m' is not sufficient for us to locate P: it may be anywhere on a sphere, centre O and radius 8 m. In order to determine the position of P we need to be given its direction, specified in any suitable way.

The position of P relative to O is an example of a *displacement*; that is, a line segment whose length, direction and sense are given. Experimental evidence reveals that many physical quantities obey the same mathematical laws as do displacements; such quantities are called *vector quantities*. We shall give a precise definition of a vector quantity in the next section, observing here merely that vector quantities require a direction and sense, as well as a magnitude, for their specification. Physical quantities which require only a magnitude (that is, a pure number) to describe them are called *scalar quantities*. Here are a few examples of each type:

Vector quantities: displacement, velocity, acceleration, force, momentum, electric intensity.

Scalar quantities: mass, time, temperature, energy, electric charge, electrostatic potential.

2. VECTORS AND THE TRIANGLE RULE

Since all vector quantities obey the same mathematical laws as displacements we shall concern ourselves exclusively with displacements in building up the relevant mathematics. It should be borne in mind, however, that the theory being developed is applicable to a wide range of physical quantities.

Before embarking upon a study of operations involving displacements we must define what we mean by the *equality* of two such quantities. A displacement is typified by its magnitude, sense and direction and so it seems reasonable to regard two displacements of the same magnitude which are parallel in the same sense to be equal. Thus, in Figure 2.1, we have

AB = **CD** = **EF** = **GH** = ... We shall use a single symbol to represent any member of the class of such equal displacements

$$\mathbf{a} = \mathbf{AB} = \mathbf{CD} = \mathbf{EF} = ...$$

Such a representative of a whole class of displacements is called a *vector*. In other words, a vector is a mathematical entity, to which a whole class of geometrical objects correspond. Vectors are usually printed in bold face type: **a**, **b**, **c**, ... In manuscript they should be indicated by a wavy line beneath the letters, a͜, b͜, c͜.

The equality of two vectors **a** = **b**, *means that* **a** *and* **b** *are both representative of the same class of parallel and equal displacements.*

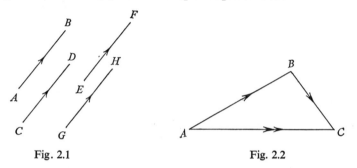

Fig. 2.1   Fig. 2.2

The *magnitude of a vector*, **a**, written |**a**|, is the magnitude of any one of the displacements of which it is representative. It is most important to remember that |**a**| = |**b**| does NOT imply that **a** = **b**; put another way, two unequal vectors may have the same magnitude.

Two displacements **AB** and **BC** may be combined together, or *added*, according to the *triangle rule*, **AB**+**BC** = **AC** (see Figure 2.2).

Two vectors may similarly be added: to find **a**+**b** we draw any displacement **AB** represented by **a**; we then select the unique displacement **BC**, represented by **b** which has as its initial point the point B and the vector **a**+**b** will be representative of that class of displacements of which **AC** is a typical member.

We have said that vector quantities are physical quantities that may be completely represented by a displacement. Since displacements obey the triangle rule of combination, so must vector quantities generally. Indeed, we are now in the position to make a formal definition:

A physical quantity is a vector quantity if
(i) *it has magnitude, direction and sense;*
(ii) *it obeys the triangle law of addition.*†

† The reader should observe that certain vector quantities must have their position specified too. For example, to describe a force we need to know not only its magnitude and direction, but also its line of application.

25

The observation that any particular physical quantity is indeed a vector quantity is the result of experimental evidence, which must include a verification of the triangle rule.

Ex. 1. Can you suggest any addition to the list of vector and scalar quantities given in Section 1?

Ex. 2. Can three displacements be added together? Does it matter in what order it is done?

Ex. 3. A rotation may be given a magnitude (size of angle turned through), direction (axis of rotation) and sense (positive being direction for which rotation is anticlockwise). Show that rotations are NOT vector quantities. (This example shows that physical quantities exist that are neither scalar nor vector quantities.)

3. OPERATIONS WITH VECTORS

Since all parallel and equal line segments represent the same vector **a** we may, when verifying the various rules of vector algebra geometrically, choose as representative those line segments which are most convenient.

Rule 1. *Vector addition is commutative.* $\mathbf{a} + \mathbf{b} = \mathbf{b} + \mathbf{a}$.

If $\mathbf{AB} = \mathbf{DC} = \mathbf{a}$ and $\mathbf{BC} = \mathbf{AD} = \mathbf{b}$, $ABCD$ is a parallelogram and

$$\mathbf{a} + \mathbf{b} = \mathbf{AC} = \mathbf{b} + \mathbf{a}.$$

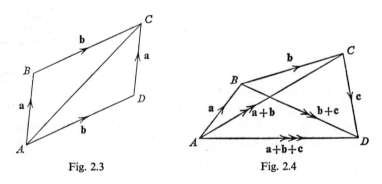

Fig. 2.3 Fig. 2.4

Rule 2. *Vector addition is associative.* $(\mathbf{a} + \mathbf{b}) + \mathbf{c} = \mathbf{a} + (\mathbf{b} + \mathbf{c})$.

If $\qquad \mathbf{AB} = \mathbf{a}, \quad \mathbf{BC} = \mathbf{b}, \quad \mathbf{CD} = \mathbf{c},$

then $\qquad (\mathbf{a} + \mathbf{b}) + \mathbf{c} = \mathbf{AC} + \mathbf{CD} = \mathbf{AD},$

and $\qquad \mathbf{a} + (\mathbf{b} + \mathbf{c}) = \mathbf{AB} + \mathbf{BD} = \mathbf{AD}.$

We may thus drop the brackets when adding three vectors together, and write $\mathbf{a} + \mathbf{b} + \mathbf{c}$ without ambiguity.

If **AB** represents the vector **a** then **BA** will be said to represent the vector

26

$-\mathbf{a}$. We shall write $\mathbf{a}+(-\mathbf{a}) = \mathbf{0}$ for all $\mathbf{a}$ and call $\mathbf{0}$ the *zero vector*. (Note that the zero vector, unlike all others, has no direction.)

If $\mathbf{AB} = \mathbf{a}$ and $\mathbf{AC} = \mathbf{b}$ then, since $\mathbf{CA}+\mathbf{AB} = \mathbf{CB}$, the line segment $\mathbf{CB}$ represents $\mathbf{a}-\mathbf{b}$ (see Figure 2.5). (Notice that we have used the commutativity of vector addition here.)

To develop the algebra of vectors further, we need a new definition, the *multiplication of a vector by a number (scalar)*.

If k is any positive number, $k\mathbf{a}$ is the vector of magnitude $k|\mathbf{a}|$ in the same direction as $\mathbf{a}$ and with the same sense.

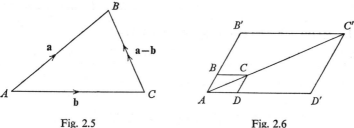

Fig. 2.5   Fig. 2.6

If k is any negative number, $k\mathbf{a}$ is the vector of magnitude $-k|\mathbf{a}|$ in the same direction as $\mathbf{a}$ and with the opposite sense.

Thus, multiplying a vector by a number simply stretches or contracts the vector along its length. Notice that $-\mathbf{a} = -1\mathbf{a}$.

Rule 3. Multiplication by numbers is associative.

$$k(l\mathbf{a}) = (kl)\,\mathbf{a}.$$

This is immediately apparent, since $\mathbf{a}$, $l\mathbf{a}$ and $(kl)\mathbf{a}$ all have the same direction, and the magnitude and senses of $k(l\mathbf{a})$ and $(kl)\mathbf{a}$ are both $(kl)\,|\mathbf{a}|$.

Rule 4. Multiplication by numbers is distributive over vector addition.

$$k(\mathbf{a}+\mathbf{b}) = k\mathbf{a}+k\mathbf{b}.$$

Representing $\mathbf{a}$ by $\mathbf{AB}$ and $\mathbf{b}$ by $\mathbf{BC}$, $k\mathbf{a}$ by $\mathbf{AB'}$ and $k\mathbf{b}$ by $\mathbf{B'C'}$, ACC' is a straight line by similar triangles and the result follows, since the corresponding sides are in proportion (Figure 2.6).

Rule 5. Multiplication by numbers is also distributive in the following sense.

$$(k+l)\,\mathbf{a} = k\mathbf{a}+l\mathbf{a}.$$

The vectors on either side of the above identity have the same magnitude, sense and direction, as can be seen immediately from a diagram.

*Ex. 4. Prove that $0.\mathbf{a} = \mathbf{0}$. What does this tell us about the magnitude of the zero vector?

Ex. 5. If **a** is a vector of magnitude 4 units due north and **b** is a vector of magnitude 1 unit due east, describe the vectors:

(i) 2**a**;   (ii) −3**b**;   (iii) **a**−4**b**;   (iv) 2(**a**+**b**);   (v) 2**a**−6**b**.

Ex. 6. If **a** = 3**x**+**y**, **b** = **x**−2**y**, find **x**, **y** in terms of **a**, **b**, justifying your argument in terms of Rules 1–5.

Ex. 7. If **a** is a vector of magnitude 1 unit due north and **b** is a vector of magnitude 1 unit in the direction N 60° E, describe the following vectors (using a scale drawing or trigonometry, if necessary):

(i) 2**a**+**b**;   (ii) −(2**a**−**b**);   (iii) **b**−**a**;   (iv) −**a**−2**b**.

Ex. 8. If **a** is a vector of 2 units due north in a horizontal plane, **b** is a vector of 3 units due east in a horizontal plane and **c** is a vector of 1 unit vertically up out of the plane, describe the vectors:

(i) **a**−2**c**; (ii) −**b**−3**c**; (iii) 3**a**+2**b**+6**c**; (iv) 3**a**−2**b**−6**c**.

Ex. 9. *ABCD* is a parallelogram with *AB* 2 units and *BC* 1 unit. If **a** is a vector of 1 unit in the direction *AB* and **b** is a vector of 1 unit in the direction of *BC*, and if *E* is the mid-point of *CD*, find, in terms of **a** and **b**, the vectors **AC**, **DB**, **AE**, **EB**.

4. COMPONENTS OF A VECTOR

It is often useful to express a given vector **r** as the sum of a number of vectors in specified directions

$$\mathbf{r} = \mathbf{a}_1 + \mathbf{a}_2 + \ldots + \mathbf{a}_n.$$

If this is done, $\mathbf{a}_1$, $\mathbf{a}_2$, ..., $\mathbf{a}_n$ are called *components* of **r**.

Given a vector **r** and specified directions two questions immediately arise:

(i) Can **r** be split into components in these directions?

(ii) If the answer to (i) is 'Yes', in how many alternative ways can this be done?

We shall answer these questions for a vector **r** and three non-parallel, non-coplanar directions in three dimensions by proving two theorems of types that constantly recur in mathematics. The first theorem is an example of an *Existence Theorem*: it will answer question (i) above, telling us that a solution does exist; the second theorem is a *Uniqueness Theorem*: it will answer question (ii) above, telling us that the solution which we know exists is the only possible one, that is, that it is unique. The significance of these two theorems will become apparent as we proceed.

Theorem 2.1 (*The Existence Theorem*). *Given a non-zero vector* **r** *and* *three non-coplanar†, non-parallel vectors* **a**, **b**, **c**, *there exist numbers* λ, μ, ν, *such that*
$$\mathbf{r} = \lambda\mathbf{a} + \mu\mathbf{b} + \nu\mathbf{c}.$$

† That is, displacements represented by **a**, **b**, **c**, cannot all be chosen to lie in one plane.

28

Proof. Represent the vectors **a**, **b**, **c**, **r**, by line segments **OA**, **OB**, **OC**, **OP** respectively. Through P draw a plane parallel to the plane OBC to cut the line OA at A' (this may always be done, by the data). Let P' be the point in the plane OBC such that **OP′** = **A′P**. Through P' draw a line parallel to CO to cut OB at B' (this again may be done using the data). The constructions are illustrated in Figure 2.7.

$$\mathbf{r} = \mathbf{OA'} + \mathbf{A'P}$$
$$= \lambda\mathbf{a} + \mathbf{OP'}$$
$$= \lambda\mathbf{a} + \mathbf{OB'} + \mathbf{B'P'}$$
$$= \lambda\mathbf{a} + \mu\mathbf{b} + \nu\mathbf{c}.$$

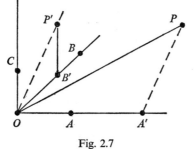

Fig. 2.7

We have thus proved our Existence Theorem by showing that, with the given data, a set of components may be constructed. To demonstrate the truth of the Uniqueness Theorem we employ a common device in mathematical arguments: we assume that it is false and show that this leads to a contradiction (see Chapter 9).

Theorem 2.2 (*The Uniqueness Theorem*). *The solution shown to exist in Theorem* 2.1 *is unique.*

Proof. By Theorem 2.1 a solution exists, say

$$\mathbf{r} = \lambda_1\mathbf{a} + \mu_1\mathbf{b} + \nu_1\mathbf{c}.$$

Assume that a different solution also exists

$$\mathbf{r} = \lambda_2\mathbf{a} + \mu_2\mathbf{b} + \nu_2\mathbf{c}$$

where, say, $\lambda_1 \neq \lambda_2$. Then

$$\lambda_1\mathbf{a} + \mu_1\mathbf{b} + \nu_1\mathbf{c} = \lambda_2\mathbf{a} + \mu_2\mathbf{b} + \nu_2\mathbf{c}.$$

and so $$(\lambda_2 - \lambda_1)\,\mathbf{a} = (\mu_1 - \mu_2)\,\mathbf{b} + (\nu_1 - \nu_2)\,\mathbf{c}.$$

But $(\mu_1 - \mu_2)\,\mathbf{b} + (\nu_1 - \nu_2)\,\mathbf{c}$ is a vector in the plane determined by **b** and **c** and any non-zero multiple of **a** cannot lie in this plane, by the data. Thus $\lambda_1 = \lambda_2$, which contradicts our initial assumption.

Theorems 2.1 and 2.2 have been proved for three dimensions; they hold equally well in two dimensions, for a vector **r** lying in the plane determined by **a** and **b**, where $\mathbf{a} \neq k\mathbf{b}$.

An expression such as $\lambda\mathbf{a} + \mu\mathbf{b} + \nu\mathbf{c}$ is called a *linear combination* of the vectors **a**, **b**, **c**. The theorems we have just proved may be restated in the form 'Given three non-parallel, non-coplanar vectors **a**, **b**, **c** any non-zero vector **r** may be expressed uniquely as a linear combination of **a**, **b**, **c**'.

If numbers λ, μ, ν (not all zero) exist such that

$$\lambda\mathbf{a} + \mu\mathbf{b} + \nu\mathbf{c} = 0$$

the vectors **a**, **b**, **c** are said to be *linearly dependent*; if no such numbers exist, **a**, **b**, **c** are said to be *linearly independent*.

Ex. 10. Prove that, if O, A, B, C are coplanar, then the position vectors **a**, **b**, **c** are linearly dependent and, conversely, if **a**, **b**, **c** are linearly dependent, then O, A, B, C are coplanar.

Ex. 11. Prove the Existence and Uniqueness Theorems for components in two dimensions.

Ex. 12. $ABCD$ is a parallelogram, and E is the mid-point of CD. $\mathbf{AB} = \mathbf{a}$, $\mathbf{AD} = \mathbf{b}$, $\mathbf{AE} = \mathbf{x}$, $\mathbf{BE} = \mathbf{y}$. Express **x** and **y** in terms of components in the directions **a** and **b** and also express **a** and **b** in terms of components in the directions **x** and **y**.

Ex. 13. Do either the Existence or the Uniqueness Theorems hold in three dimensions if four directions **a**, **b**, **c**, **d** are given?

Exercise 2a

1. If $\mathbf{v} = \mathbf{a} + 2\mathbf{b}$, $\mathbf{w} = 2\mathbf{a} - \mathbf{b}$, express the following vectors in the form

$$\lambda\mathbf{a} + \mu\mathbf{b}.$$

(i) $\mathbf{v} + \mathbf{w}$; (ii) $2\mathbf{v} + 3\mathbf{w}$; (iii) $\mathbf{v} - 3\mathbf{w}$; (iv) $2(\mathbf{v} - \mathbf{w})$.

2. If $\mathbf{u} = \mathbf{a} + 3\mathbf{b}$, $\mathbf{v} = 2\mathbf{a} - \mathbf{b}$, express **a** and **b** in terms of **u** and **v**.

3. If $\mathbf{u} = \mathbf{a} + \mathbf{b} + \mathbf{c}$, $\mathbf{v} = \mathbf{a} + 2\mathbf{b} + \mathbf{c}$, $\mathbf{w} = \mathbf{a} - \mathbf{b} - 2\mathbf{c}$, find, in terms of **a**, **b**, **c**:
(i) $\mathbf{u} + \mathbf{v} + \mathbf{w}$; (ii) $\mathbf{u} - \mathbf{v} - \mathbf{w}$; (iii) $2\mathbf{u} + \mathbf{v} - \mathbf{w}$; (iv) $\mathbf{u} + 2\mathbf{v} + 3\mathbf{w}$.

4. If $\mathbf{u} = \mathbf{a} + \mathbf{b} - \mathbf{c}$, $\mathbf{v} = 2\mathbf{a} - \mathbf{b} + \mathbf{c}$, $\mathbf{w} = 3\mathbf{a} + 2\mathbf{b} + \mathbf{c}$, find **a**, **b**, **c** in terms of **u**, **v**, **w**.

5. If **i** and **j** are perpendicular vectors of unit magnitude, **i** pointing due east and **j** due north, find the magnitudes and directions of the following vectors:
(i) $2\mathbf{i}$; (ii) $-3\mathbf{j}$; (iii) $3\mathbf{i} + 4\mathbf{j}$; (iv) $\mathbf{i} - \mathbf{j}$; (v) $-3\mathbf{i} + 4\mathbf{j}$.

6. If **p** is a vector of magnitude 2 pointing due east and **q** is a vector of magnitude 5 pointing due south, find the magnitudes and directions of the following vectors:
(i) 6**p**+**q**; (ii) 6**p**−**q**; (iii) −**p**−**q**.

7. If **p** is a vector of magnitude 1 pointing due east and **q** is a vector of magnitude 2 pointing north-west find (by accurate drawing, if you wish) the vectors
(i) 2**p**+**q**; (ii) **p**−**q**; (iii) −**p**−**q**; (iv) −4**p**+2**q**.

8. **x** is a vector of magnitude 1 pointing due east; **y** is a vector of magnitude 2 pointing south-west; **z** is a vector of magnitude 20 pointing due north. Express **z** in the form λ**x**+μ**y**, giving the explicit numerical values of λ and μ.

9. If **a** is a vector of magnitude 1 pointing due north, **b** is a vector of magnitude 1 pointing N 20° E and **c** is a vector of magnitude 2 pointing N 70° W, express **c** in the form **c** = λ**a**+μ**b**.
   If **d** is a vector of magnitude 2 pointing N 10° E, find approximate values for λ', μ' where **d** = λ'**a**+μ'**b**.

10. If **i**, **j**, **k** are vectors of unit magnitude pointing respectively due east, due north and vertically upwards out of the plane containing **i**, **j**, find the magnitude of the vector **u** = 4**i**+**j**+8**k**.
   If **v** = 4**i**−**j**+8**k** and **w** = 4**i**−**j**−8**k**, find the angles between the vectors (i) **u**, **v**; (ii) **v**, **w**.

11. Figure 2.8 represents a lattice of congruent parallelograms; **OA** = **a**, **OB** = **b**, **AB** = **c**. Express **OP** in terms of
(i) **a**, **b**; (ii) **a**, **c**; (iii) **b**, **c**;

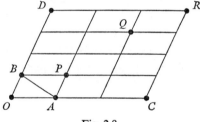

Fig. 2.8

and do the same for the vectors **OQ** and **OR**. Express **PQ** in terms of **a**, **b**, and **RQ** in terms of **b**, **c**. Find two different expressions of the form α**a**+β**b**+γ**c** for the vector **OQ**, with none of α, β, γ zero. Show that, if one of these expressions is subtracted from the other, the known relation **b** = **c**+**a** is obtained.

12. In Figure 2.8 **OC** = **u**, **OD** = **v**, **QP** = **w**. Obtain expressions for **OP**, **OQ**, **OR** in terms of **u**, **v** and hence obtain **w** in terms of **u** and **v**.
   Why is it not possible to express **CD** in terms of the two vectors **PQ**, **AR**?

13. *ABCDEF* is a regular hexagon, and **AB** = **a**, **BC** = **b**. Find **CD**, **DE**, **EF**, **FA** in terms of **a** and **b**.

14. *ABCDA'B'C'D'* is a cuboid whose base *ABCD* is a square of side 2 units. The sides *AA'*, etc., are vertical and of magnitude 4 units. *E* is the mid-point

31

of AB, G is the mid-point of $B'C'$ and F is the mid-point of CC'. **a**, **b**, **c** are three vectors, each of magnitude 1 unit in the directions AB, AD, AA' respectively. Find, in terms of **a**, **b**, **c** the vectors DE, AF, EF, GF, GE.

15. With the data of Question 14, express **ED′**, **EG** and **EF** in terms of components in the directions **a**, **b** and **c** and also express **a**, **b**, **c** in terms of components in the directions **ED′**, **EG** and **EF**.

16. $OABCO'A'B'C'$ is a rectangular box with square ends $OABC$ and $O'A'B'C'$. OO', AA', BB', CC' are parallel edges. If $AO = OC = 1$ unit, $OO' = 2$ units, and if **i**, **j**, **k** are unit vectors (that is, vectors of unit magnitude) along OA, OC, OO' respectively, find, in terms of **i**, **j**, **k**:
   (i) **OC′**;   (ii) **OB′**;   (iii) **C′A**;   (iv) **OD**,
where D is the point on $C'B'$ produced such that $C'B' = B'D$;
   (v) **OM**, where M is the mid-point of AA';   (vi) **MD**.

17. $OABC$ is a regular tetrahedron of side a; **p**, **q**, **r** are unit vectors (see Question 16) along OA, OB, OC respectively. Find in terms of **p**, **q**, **r**:
   (i) **AB**;   (ii) **OD**, where $ABCD$ is a rhombus.

18. $ABCD$ is a square and P, Q are the mid-points of BC, CD respectively. Find, in terms of $\mathbf{u} = \mathbf{AP}$ and $\mathbf{v} = \mathbf{AQ}$,
   (i) **AB**;   (ii) **AD**;   (iii) **BD**.

19. With the notation of Question 16, $\mathbf{OB'} = \mathbf{u}$, $\mathbf{AC'} = \mathbf{v}$, $\mathbf{O'B} = \mathbf{w}$; find, in terms of **u**, **v**, **w**:
   (i) **OA′**;   (ii) **BC′**;   (iii) **O′B′**;   (iv) **BC**.

20. With the notation of Question 19, if $\mathbf{CA'} = \mathbf{x}$, find two distinct expressions for **CB′** in terms of **u**, **v**, **w**, **x**.

21. $ABCDA'B'C'D'$ is a cube, with faces $ABCD$, $A'B'C'D'$ and edges AA', etc. Find, in terms of **AD′**, **AC′**, **AC**, the vectors **D′B** and **A′C**.

22. $ABCDEFGH$ is a regular octagon. If $\mathbf{AB} = \mathbf{a}$, $\mathbf{BC} = \mathbf{b}$, find, in terms of **a**, **b**, the displacements CD, DE, EF, FG, GH, HA.

5. APPLICATIONS TO GEOMETRY

So far we have developed the algebra of vectors using geometrical arguments; we now reverse the process and show that the algebra of vectors may usefully be employed to deduce geometrical results. The vector treatment of geometrical problems has the great advantage that it is equally applicable to two or three dimensions.

To describe a geometrical configuration consisting of a number of points A, B, C, ... we must be able to locate each point. This may be done by taking a fixed point O (called the *origin*) and referring to a point A by the line segment **OA**. If **a** is the vector representative of all the line segments equal and parallel to **OA**, then **a** is called *the position vector of the point A with respect to the origin O*. Thus, given an origin O, we may refer to all points in the plane by their position vectors relative to this origin O.

First, we establish a result known as the *Section Formula*. This theorem enables us to write down the position vector of any point on a given line and so is of importance in setting up a vectorial description of a geometrical configuration.

Theorem 2.3 (The Section Formula). If APB is a straight line, with

$$AP/PB = \lambda/\mu,$$

and if the position vectors of A, P, B, relative to any origin O, are **a, p, b** *respectively, then*

$$\mathbf{p} = \frac{\lambda \mathbf{b} + \mu \mathbf{a}}{\lambda + \mu}.$$

Proof. We have (Figure 2.9)

$$\mathbf{AB} = \mathbf{b} - \mathbf{a}$$

and

$$\mathbf{AP} = \mathbf{p} - \mathbf{a}.$$

But

$$\mathbf{AP} = \frac{\lambda}{\lambda + \mu} \mathbf{AB}$$

and so

$$(\lambda + \mu)(\mathbf{p} - \mathbf{a}) = \lambda(\mathbf{b} - \mathbf{a}),$$

or

$$(\lambda + \mu)\mathbf{p} = \lambda \mathbf{b} + \mu \mathbf{a}$$

and the result follows.

Notice that the proof holds equally well for positive or negative values of the ratio λ/μ.

Notice also the important special case in which $\lambda = \mu$: the mid-point of AB has position vector $\frac{1}{2}(\mathbf{a} + \mathbf{b})$.

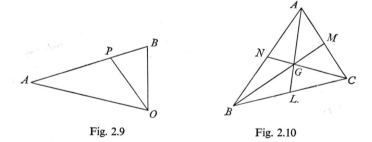

Fig. 2.9   Fig. 2.10

Example 1. Show that the medians of a triangle ABC are concurrent and find the position vector of the centroid (meet of the medians) in terms of the position vectors **a, b, c,** *referred to some origin O.*

Let the mid-points of BC, CA, AB be L, M, N respectively and call their position vectors **l, m, n** (Figure 2.10).

33

Then, by the Section Formula

$$\mathbf{l} = \tfrac{1}{2}(\mathbf{b}+\mathbf{c}), \quad \mathbf{m} = \tfrac{1}{2}(\mathbf{c}+\mathbf{a}); \quad \mathbf{n} = \tfrac{1}{2}(\mathbf{a}+\mathbf{b}).$$

Any point on AL has a position vector

$$\frac{\lambda\mathbf{l}+\mu\mathbf{a}}{\lambda+\mu},$$

i.e.
$$\frac{\tfrac{1}{2}\lambda(\mathbf{b}+\mathbf{c})+\mu\mathbf{a}}{\lambda+\mu}.$$

For varying values of λ and μ we obtain different points of the line AL; in particular, if we choose $\lambda = 2$, $\mu = 1$, we obtain a point whose position vector is symmetrical in $\mathbf{a}$, $\mathbf{b}$, $\mathbf{c}$ and so lies equally well on BM or CN.

Thus, the medians of a triangle are concurrent at the centroid, G, whose position vector is given by
$$\mathbf{g} = \frac{\mathbf{a}+\mathbf{b}+\mathbf{c}}{3}.$$

Notice, incidentally, that we have shown that $AG/GL = 2$, etc.

Example 2. Show that the mid-points of the sides of a skew quadrilateral form the vertices of a parallelogram.

Let $ABCD$ be the skew quadrilateral and the mid-points of AB, BC, CD, DA be P, Q, R, S respectively.

Take any point O as origin, let $\mathbf{a}$ denote the position vector of A with respect to O and similarly for the other points.

Then we have, on using the Section Formula,

$$\mathbf{p} = \tfrac{1}{2}(\mathbf{a}+\mathbf{b}), \quad \mathbf{q} = \tfrac{1}{2}(\mathbf{b}+\mathbf{c}), \quad \mathbf{r} = \tfrac{1}{2}(\mathbf{c}+\mathbf{d}), \quad \mathbf{s} = \tfrac{1}{2}(\mathbf{d}+\mathbf{a})$$

and so
$$\mathbf{p}-\mathbf{q} = \tfrac{1}{2}(\mathbf{a}-\mathbf{c})$$

and
$$\mathbf{s}-\mathbf{r} = \tfrac{1}{2}(\mathbf{a}-\mathbf{c}).$$

Thus $\mathbf{QP} = \mathbf{RS}$ and so $PQRS$ is a parallelogram (one pair of sides equal and parallel).

Ex. 14. Show that the joins of mid-points of opposite edges of the tetrahedron $ABCD$ are concurrent at a point G.

Ex. 15. Show that, in a tetrahedron $ABCD$, the joins of vertices to the centroids of opposite faces are concurrent at the same point G as that obtained in Ex. 14.

*Ex. 16. What condition must the numbers α, β possess for the points with position vectors $\mathbf{a}$, $\mathbf{b}$ and $\alpha\mathbf{a}+\beta\mathbf{b}$ to be collinear?

34

The Section Formula may be restated in a form that gives a test for the collinearity of three points whose position vectors are known.

Theorem 2.4 (*condition for three distinct points to lie in a line*).

*Three points A, B, C have position vectors **a**, **b**, **c**. Then* (i) *if A, B, C lie on a straight line, there exist numbers α, β, γ, not all zero, such that*

$$\alpha\mathbf{a}+\beta\mathbf{b}+\gamma\mathbf{c} = \mathbf{0}$$

and
$$\alpha+\beta+\gamma = 0.$$

Conversely, (ii) *if there exist numbers α, β, γ not all zero such that*

$$\alpha\mathbf{a}+\beta\mathbf{b}+\gamma\mathbf{c} = \mathbf{0}$$

and
$$\alpha+\beta+\gamma = 0$$
then A, B, C are collinear.

Proof. (i) Given that A, B, C are collinear, suppose $AB/BC = \lambda/\mu$. Then by the Section Formula
$$\mathbf{b} = \frac{\mu\mathbf{a}+\lambda\mathbf{c}}{\mu+\lambda},$$

i.e.
$$\mu\mathbf{a}-(\mu+\lambda)\,\mathbf{b}+\lambda\mathbf{c} = \mathbf{0}.$$

Take $\alpha = \mu$, $\beta = -(\mu+\lambda)$, $\gamma = \lambda$ and the result follows.

(ii) Given that numbers α, β, γ exist such that

$$\alpha\mathbf{a}+\beta\mathbf{b}+\gamma\mathbf{c} = \mathbf{0}$$

and
$$\alpha+\beta+\gamma = 0$$

we have $\alpha\mathbf{a}+\beta\mathbf{b} = (\alpha+\beta)\,\mathbf{c}$,   by substitution.

Now we know that α, β, γ are not all zero and we may assume, without any loss of generality, that $\gamma \neq 0$. It follows that $\alpha+\beta \neq 0$ and so

$$\mathbf{c} = \frac{\alpha\mathbf{a}+\beta\mathbf{b}}{\alpha+\beta},$$

i.e. **c** is the position vector of the point dividing AB in the ratio $\beta:\alpha$, from which it follows, that A, B, C are collinear.

Example 3 (*Desargues's Theorem*). *Two triangles ABC, A'B'C' (not necessarily in the same plane) are so positioned that AA', BB', CC' all pass through a point V. BC, B'C' meet at L; CA, C'A' at M; AB, A'B' at N. Prove that L, M, N are collinear.*

35

Denoting the position vectors of the various points in the usual way, we have, using Theorem 2.4:

$$\begin{cases} \mathbf{v}+\alpha\mathbf{a}+\alpha'\mathbf{a}' = \mathbf{0}, \\ 1+\alpha+\alpha' = 0; \end{cases}$$

$$\begin{cases} \mathbf{v}+\beta\mathbf{b}+\beta'\mathbf{b}' = \mathbf{0}, \\ 1+\beta+\beta' = 0; \end{cases}$$

$$\begin{cases} \mathbf{v}+\gamma\mathbf{c}+\gamma'\mathbf{c}' = \mathbf{0}, \\ 1+\gamma+\gamma' = 0. \end{cases}$$

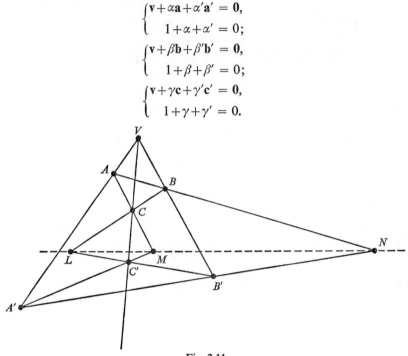

Fig. 2.11

From the second and third pairs of equations

$$\frac{\beta\mathbf{b}-\gamma\mathbf{c}}{\beta-\gamma} = \frac{\beta'\mathbf{b}'-\gamma'\mathbf{c}'}{\beta'-\gamma'}$$

and, by the Section Formula, these must both represent $\mathbf{l}$. Thus

$$(\beta-\gamma)\,\mathbf{l} = \beta\mathbf{b}-\gamma\mathbf{c}.$$

Similarly, $(\gamma-\alpha)\,\mathbf{m} = \gamma\mathbf{c}-\alpha\mathbf{a}$ and $(\alpha-\beta)\,\mathbf{n} = \alpha\mathbf{a}-\beta\mathbf{b}.$

Thus $$\begin{cases} (\beta-\gamma)\,\mathbf{l}+(\gamma-\alpha)\,\mathbf{m}+(\alpha-\beta)\,\mathbf{n} = \mathbf{0}, \\ (\beta-\gamma)+(\gamma-\alpha)+(\alpha-\beta) = 0 \end{cases}$$

and so L, M, N are collinear.

Ex. 17. If *ABC, A'B'C'* are two triangles not in the same plane and such that *AA', BB', CC'* all pass through a point *V*, prove Desargues's Theorem by showing that the meets of corresponding sides of the two triangles must all lie on the line of intersection of the planes *ABC, A'B'C'*.

Ex. 18. Prove the Converse of Desargues's Theorem.

36

6. THE VECTOR EQUATIONS OF LINES AND PLANES

Throughout the present section we shall adhere to the generally accepted custom that P denotes a variable point whose position vector is $\mathbf{r}$.

A *locus* is a set of points (in a plane or in space) subject to some condition; examples are a straight line, a plane, a sphere, the interior of a sphere, etc. In this section we shall confine our attention to lines and planes.

The *equation of a line* is the algebraic condition that is satisfied by the positions vector $\mathbf{r}$ of a general point P lying on the line. Similarly for the *equation of a plane*. Later we shall meet loci that are defined by inequalities; the interior of a sphere would be such a locus.

A straight line is completely specified if two points A, B of the line are given. Suppose that an origin O is taken and that the position vectors of A and B relative to O are $\mathbf{a}$ and $\mathbf{b}$ respectively. The equation of the line AB is the condition satisfied by the position vector $\mathbf{r}$ of a general point on AB. (Of course, if a different origin O' were chosen, a different equation would be obtained: the equation of any locus depends upon the choice of origin.) Now, since P lies on AB, or AB produced (Fig. 2.12), $\mathbf{AP} = \lambda\mathbf{AB}$, where λ is a number. For different points on the line, different values of λ are taken. This equation may be rewritten in terms of position vectors as

$$\mathbf{r} - \mathbf{a} = \lambda(\mathbf{b} - \mathbf{a})$$

which represents the equation of the line AB.

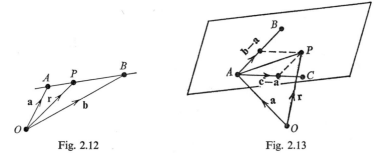

Fig. 2.12   Fig. 2.13

A plane is completely specified by three (non-collinear) points A, B, C (see Chapter 3, Section 5). For a general point P of the plane, $\mathbf{AP}$ is a vector lying in the plane of $\mathbf{AB}$ and $\mathbf{AC}$ and so we may split $\mathbf{AP}$ into components in these two directions (remember that A, B, C were non-collinear and so two directions are defined). Thus $\mathbf{AP} = \lambda\mathbf{AB} + \mu\mathbf{AC}$ (Fig. 2.13) and so, in terms of position vectors relative to some origin O,

$$\mathbf{r} - \mathbf{a} = \lambda(\mathbf{b} - \mathbf{a}) + \mu(\mathbf{c} - \mathbf{a})$$

37

which may be rewritten as

$$\mathbf{r} = -(\lambda+\mu-1)\,\mathbf{a}+\lambda\mathbf{b}+\mu\mathbf{c}.$$

Our final theorem of this chapter is essentially a re-phrasing of the result above. It is structurally very similar to Theorem 2.4 and the reader is advised to refer back to that theorem before continuing.

Theorem 2.5 (condition for four points to lie on a plane). Four points A, B, C, D have position vectors **a, b, c, d.**

Then

(i) *If A, B, C, D lie on a plane, there exist numbers* α, β, γ, δ, *not all zero, such that*

$$\alpha\mathbf{a}+\beta\mathbf{b}+\gamma\mathbf{c}+\delta\mathbf{d} = 0,$$

$$\alpha+\beta+\gamma+\delta = 0.$$

Conversely,

(ii) *If there exist numbers* α, β, γ, δ, *not all zero, such that*

$$\alpha\mathbf{a}+\beta\mathbf{b}+\gamma\mathbf{c}+\delta\mathbf{d} = \mathbf{0},$$

$$\alpha+\beta+\gamma+\delta = 0$$

then A, B, C, D are coplanar.

Proof. (i) Given that *A, B, C, D* are coplanar, **d** satisfies an equation of the form

$$\mathbf{r} = -(\lambda+\mu-1)\,\mathbf{a}+\lambda\mathbf{b}+\mu\mathbf{c},$$

i.e. $$-(\lambda+\mu-1)\,\mathbf{a}+\lambda\mathbf{b}+\mu\mathbf{c}-\mathbf{d} = \mathbf{0}$$

and the first result follows if we set

$$\alpha = -(\lambda+\mu-1), \quad \beta = \lambda, \quad \gamma = \mu, \quad \delta = -1.$$

(ii) Given that numbers α, β, γ, δ exist such that

$$\alpha\mathbf{a}+\beta\mathbf{b}+\gamma\mathbf{c}+\delta\mathbf{d} = \mathbf{0},$$

$$\alpha+\beta+\gamma+\delta = 0.$$

We have $$-(\beta+\gamma+\delta)\,\mathbf{a}+\beta\mathbf{b}+\gamma\mathbf{c}+\delta\mathbf{d} = 0,$$

i.e. $$\beta(\mathbf{b}-\mathbf{a})+\gamma(\mathbf{c}-\mathbf{a}) = \delta(\mathbf{a}-\mathbf{d}),$$

or $$\beta\mathbf{AB}+\gamma\mathbf{AC} = \delta\mathbf{DA}.$$

But **AB, AC** both lie in the plane *ABC* and so therefore does δ**DA**. It follows that *D* lies in the plane *ABC* and the proof is complete.

*Ex. 19. Show that the equation of the line through *A* parallel to the direction defined by the vector **u** is $\mathbf{r} = \mathbf{a}+\lambda\mathbf{u}$.

Ex. 20. Show that the equation of the plane through A parallel to the directions defined by the two vectors **m**, **n** is $\mathbf{r} = \mathbf{a} + \lambda\mathbf{m} + \mu\mathbf{n}$.

Ex. 21. Show that the mid-points of two pairs of opposite edges of a tetrahedron $ABCD$ are coplanar.

Example 4. *ABCD is the base of a cube whose vertical edges are AA′, BB′, CC′, DD′. X is the point of trisection of BB′ nearer B, Y is the point of trisection of CC′ nearer C′ and M is the mid-point of BC.*

    If D′M cuts the plane AXY at Z, find the ratio in which Z divides D′M.

    Take side of cube as 6 units and call vectors of unit magnitude in the directions *AB, AD, AA′* respectively **i, j, k**.

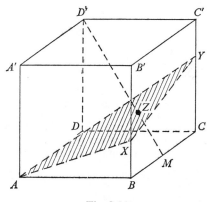

Fig. 2.14

    Working with A as origin, and denoting the position vector of X by **x**, etc., we have

$$\mathbf{x} = 6\mathbf{i} + 2\mathbf{k},$$

$$\mathbf{y} = 6\mathbf{i} + 6\mathbf{j} + 4\mathbf{k}$$

and so the position vector of any point on the plane AXY is given by

$$\mathbf{r} = \lambda\mathbf{x} + \mu\mathbf{y}$$

$$= 6(\lambda + \mu)\,\mathbf{i} + 6\mu\mathbf{j} + 2(\lambda + 2\mu)\,\mathbf{k}.$$

Again, $\mathbf{m} = 6\mathbf{i} + 3\mathbf{j}$,

$$\mathbf{d}' = 6\mathbf{j} + 6\mathbf{k}$$

and so $\mathbf{D}'\mathbf{M} = 6\mathbf{i} - 3\mathbf{j} - 6\mathbf{k}$.

The position vector of any point on $D'M$ is given by

$$\mathbf{r} = \mathbf{AD'} + \mathbf{D'P}$$
$$= \mathbf{d'} + \nu\mathbf{D'M}$$
$$= 6\mathbf{j} + 6\mathbf{k} + \nu(6\mathbf{i} - 3\mathbf{j} - 6\mathbf{k})$$
$$= 6\nu\mathbf{i} + (6 - 3\nu)\,\mathbf{j} + (6 - 6\nu)\,\mathbf{k}.$$

Thus, the point of intersection is given by

$$6\nu\mathbf{i} + (6 - 3\nu)\,\mathbf{j} + (6 - 6\nu)\,\mathbf{k} = 6(\lambda + \mu)\,\mathbf{i} + 6\mu\mathbf{j} + 2(\lambda + 2\mu)\,\mathbf{k}.$$

But $\mathbf{i}$, $\mathbf{j}$, $\mathbf{k}$ are non-coplanar vectors so, by the Uniqueness Theorem,

$$\begin{cases} \nu = \lambda + \mu, \\ 1 - \tfrac{1}{2}\nu = \mu, \\ 3 - 3\nu = \lambda + 2\mu \end{cases}$$

and thus $$\nu = \tfrac{4}{7}.$$

Thus $D'Z:ZM = 4:3$.

Exercise 2(*b*)

1. ABC is a triangle. U lies on AB produced so that $AB = \tfrac{1}{4}AU$, V lies on AC so that $AV = 2VC$. Find, in terms of the position vectors $\mathbf{a}$, $\mathbf{b}$, $\mathbf{c}$ of A, B, C, the position vectors of U, V and the mid-point of UV.

2. Draw a diagram showing the relative positions of the points whose position vectors are $\mathbf{a}$, $\mathbf{b}$ and $3\mathbf{a} - 2\mathbf{b}$.

Prove that these three points are collinear.

3. If G is the centroid of the triangle ABC, prove that

$$\mathbf{GA} + \mathbf{GB} + \mathbf{GC} = \mathbf{0}.$$

Suggest a generalization of this result.

4. ABC is an equilateral triangle of side 3 cm. P, Q lie on BC, CA respectively and are such that $AQ = CP = 2$ cm. R lies on AB produced so that $BR = 1$ cm. Prove that PQR is a straight line.

5. $OABC$ is a parallelogram and the position vectors of A, B, C relative to O are respectively $\mathbf{a}$, $\mathbf{b}$, $\mathbf{c}$. M is the mid-point of BC. Write down, in terms of $\mathbf{b}$ and $\mathbf{c}$, and hence in terms of $\mathbf{a}$ and $\mathbf{c}$, the position vector of a general point X on the line OM. Deduce that, if X lies on AC, then X is the point of trisection of AC nearer C and also the point of trisection of OM nearer M.

6. OAB is a triangle; M is the mid-point of AB and T is the point of trisection of OB nearer B. TM produced meets OA at X. If $\mathbf{OA} = \mathbf{a}$ and $\mathbf{OB} = \mathbf{b}$, write down the position vectors of T and M, and hence of a general point P of TM. Deduce the position vector of X and find a relation between the points O, A and X.

7. The position vectors of the vertices A, B, C of a triangle are respectively **a**, **b**, **c**. M is the point of trisection of AC nearer A, N is the point of trisection of AB nearer B. Write down the position vectors of M and N and hence of general points of BM, CN. Deduce the position vector of X, the intersection of BM and CN.

8. $ABCDA'B'C'D'$ is a parallelepiped, with parallel edges AA', BB', CC', DD'. U is the point of trisection of AA' nearer A, V is the point of trisection of $C'D'$ nearer C' and W is the mid-point of $B'C'$. With A as origin, the position vectors of B, D, A' are respectively **b**, **d**, **a**'. Write down the position vectors of U, V, W and a general point of DD'. Locate the point at which the plane UVW cuts DD'.

9. $OUVW$ is a tetrahedron, the position vectors of U, V, W being **u**, **v**, **w**. A is a vertex of the parallelogram $OUAV$, B is the mid-point of VW, C is the reflection in the origin of the point of trisection of UV nearer U. Find, in terms of **u**, **v**, **w**, the position vectors of A, B, C and hence find where the plane ABC cuts OW.

10. $ABCD$ is a tetrahedron, P is the mid-point of AB, Q is the mid-point of AD and R is the point of trisection of AC nearer C. Taking A as the origin, write down the position vector of the general point X of the plane PQR in terms of the position vectors of B, C and D. Write down also, in terms of the same frame of reference, the position vector of the general point Y of the line DM, where M is the mid-point of BC.

The plane PQR cuts the line DM at Z; find the ratio ZM/MD.

11. Four points P, Q, R, S in a plane through the origin O have position vectors **OP**, **OQ**, **OR**, **OS** given by

$$2\mathbf{i}+3\mathbf{j}, \quad 3\mathbf{i}+2\mathbf{j}, \quad 4\mathbf{i}+6\mathbf{j}, \quad 9\mathbf{i}+6\mathbf{j}$$

respectively, where **i** and **j** are given non-parallel vectors. Express the vectors **PR** and **QS** in terms of **i** and **j**.

Show that the position vectors **OA** and **OB** of the points A and B on PQ and RS respectively, and such that $PA/PQ = a$ and $RB/RS = b$, are

$$(2+a)\,\mathbf{i}+(3-a)\,\mathbf{j} \quad \text{and} \quad (4+5b)\,\mathbf{i}+6\mathbf{j},$$

respectively. Hence determine the position vector with respect to O of the point of intersection of the lines PQ and RS. (J.M.B.)

12. Two vectors are represented by **OP**, **OQ** and R divides PQ in the ratio $n:m$. Show that

$$m\mathbf{OP}+n\mathbf{OQ} = (m+n)\,\mathbf{OR}.$$

The points D, E, F divide the sides BC, CA, AB of a triangle in the ratios $1:4$, $3:2$, $3:7$ respectively. Show that the sum of the vectors **AD**, **BE**, **CF** is parallel to CX, where X divides AB in the ratio $1:3$. (J.M.B.)

13. $ABCD$ is a skew quadrilateral and a plane cuts AB, BC, CD, DA at W, X, Y, Z respectively. Prove that

$$\frac{AW}{WB} \cdot \frac{BX}{XC} \cdot \frac{CY}{YD} \cdot \frac{DZ}{ZA} = 1.$$

Suggest a generalization of this result.

14. $ABCD$ is a parallelogram and O is a point in the same plane. OD cuts AB at P and BC at Q; OB cuts CD at R and DA at S. Prove that PS and QR are parallel.

15. $OABC$ is a square of side $2a$. $\mathbf{i}$, $\mathbf{j}$ are unit vectors along OA, OC. The mid-point of AB is L; the mid-point of BC is M; OL, AM meet at P; BP meets OA at N. Show that the segment $\mathbf{OP}$ can be measured by the vector $\lambda(2a\mathbf{i}+a\mathbf{j})$ and also by the vector $2a\mathbf{i}+\mu(2a\mathbf{j}-a\mathbf{i})$. Hence determine λ and μ. Prove that $ON = \frac{2}{3}OA$.

(O & C)

Miscellaneous Exercise 2

1. $ABCDE$ is a regular pentagon. $\mathbf{AB} = \mathbf{a}$ and $\mathbf{AE} = \mathbf{b}$. Show that
$$\mathbf{CD} = (\mathbf{b}-\mathbf{a})/(1+2\cos 72°)$$
and express $\mathbf{BC}$ and $\mathbf{ED}$ in terms of $\mathbf{a}$ and $\mathbf{b}$.

2. ABC is a triangle. L divides BC in the ratio $1:2$, M divides CA in the ratio $1:2$ and N divides AB in the ratio $1:2$. Prove that the triangles ABC and LMN have the same centroid.

Suggest a generalization of this result and prove your assertion.

3. Referred to some origin O, the position vectors of A, B, C, D are $\mathbf{a}$, $\mathbf{b}$, $\mathbf{c}$, $\mathbf{d}$ respectively. Express in terms of $\mathbf{a}$, $\mathbf{b}$, $\mathbf{c}$, $\mathbf{d}$ the displacements $\mathbf{BD}$, $\mathbf{AC}$. What can be said about the quadrilateral $ABCD$:
  (i) If $\mathbf{a}+\mathbf{c} = \mathbf{b}+\mathbf{d}$;
  (ii) if $|\mathbf{a}-\mathbf{c}| = |\mathbf{b}-\mathbf{d}|$;
  (iii) if both (i) and (ii) hold?

4. The triangles ABC, $A'B'C'$ have centroids respectively at G and G'. Prove that
$$\mathbf{AA'}+\mathbf{BB'}+\mathbf{CC'} = 3\mathbf{GG'}.$$

5. P, Q are the mid-points of the sides BC and CD respectively of the parallelogram $ABCD$. Prove that:
$$\mathbf{AB}+\mathbf{AC}+\mathbf{AD} = \tfrac{4}{3}\,(\mathbf{AP}+\mathbf{AQ}).$$

6. $ABCD$ is a tetrahedron and B', C', D' lie on AB, AC, AD produced. The centroids of the triangles $BC'D'$, $B'CD'$, $B'C'D$ are G_1, G_2, G_3 respectively and the centroids of the triangles $B'CD$, $BC'D$, BCD' are H_1, H_2, H_3 respectively. If the centroids of the triangles BCD, $G_1G_2G_3$, $H_1H_2H_3$ are F, G, H respectively, prove that FGH is a straight line.

7. $ABCD$ is a parallelogram and points X, Y are taken on the diagonal BD such that $\mathbf{BX} = \mathbf{YD}$. Prove vectorially that $AXCY$ is a parallelogram.

8. ABC is a triangle and Y, Z are points on AC, AB respectively such that ZY is parallel to BC. BY and CZ meet at P. Prove vectorially that AP produced bisects BC.

9. ABC, $A'B'C'$ are two skew lines (that is, no plane contains both lines). If $AB:BC = A'B':B'C'$ prove that the mid-points of the lines AA', BB', CC' are collinear. Is the converse true?

10. Prove that, if ABC is a plane through the origin O from which position vectors are measured, and if A, B, C have position vectors $\mathbf{a}$, $\mathbf{b}$, $\mathbf{c}$, then there necessarily exits a relation of the form

$$p\mathbf{a}+q\mathbf{b}+r\mathbf{c} = 0 \quad (p, q, r \neq 0)$$

where 0 is the zero vector.

The lines AO, BO, CO meet BC, CA, AB in L, M, N respectively. Prove that the position vector of L is

$$\frac{q}{q+r}\mathbf{b}+\frac{r}{q+r}\mathbf{c}.$$

Deduce that
$$\frac{BL.CM.AN}{LC.MA.NB} = +1,$$

where the magnitude and sense of each line segment is taken into account. (M.E.I.)

(The result proved in Question 10 is known as *Ceva's Theorem*: it and its converse are very useful for proving concurrency theorems.)

11. If a transversal cuts the sides BC, CA, AB of a triangle ABC at L, M, N respectively, prove that
$$\frac{BL.CM.AN}{LC.MA.NB} = -1,$$

magnitudes and senses of each line segment being taken into account.

(This result is known as *Menelaus's Theorem*: with its converse it is useful for proving collinearity properties.)

12. $ABCD$ is a plane quadrilateral. AB and DC meet at P; BC and AD meet at Q. Prove that the mid-points of AC, BD and PQ are collinear.

13. P, Q are variable points on two skew lines. Find the locus of the mid-point of PQ. Can you generalize this result?

14. $ABCDA'B'C'D'$ is a parallelepiped, with $ABCD$, $A'B'C'D'$ congruent parallelograms and AA', etc., edges. The tetrahedron $ACB'D'$ is inscribed in the parallelepiped. Prove that AC' passes through the centroid X of $B'CD'$ and deduce that the joins of the vertices of the tetrahedron to the centroids of opposite faces are concurrent at a point G. Determine the ratios $AG:GX:XC'$.

15. Two vectors $\mathbf{a}$ and $\mathbf{b}$, such that $\mathbf{b}$ is not a multiple of $\mathbf{a}$, are given in a plane. Two other vectors $\mathbf{c}$ and $\mathbf{d}$ are defined by the equations

$$\mathbf{c} = \gamma_1\mathbf{a}+\gamma_2\mathbf{b},$$

$$\mathbf{d} = \delta_1\mathbf{a}+\delta_2\mathbf{b}.$$

Prove that any vector $\alpha\mathbf{a}+\beta\mathbf{b}$ can be expressed in terms of $\mathbf{c}$ and $\mathbf{d}$ provided $\gamma_1\delta_2-\gamma_2\delta_1 \neq 0$. Find the coefficients of $\mathbf{c}$ and $\mathbf{d}$.
Explain the geometrical significance of the condition $\gamma_1\delta_2-\gamma_2\delta_1 \neq 0$. (O & C)

16. Let O, A, B, C be four distinct points in three-dimensional space, no three of which are collinear. The position vectors of A, B, C with respect to O are **a, b, c** respectively and X is the point given by $\mathbf{x} = \lambda\mathbf{a} + \mu\mathbf{b} + \nu\mathbf{c}$. Prove that:

   (i) If X is a point of the line AB, then $\lambda + \mu = 1$, $\nu = 0$.

   (ii) If X is a point of the plane ABC, then $\lambda + \mu + \nu = 1$.

   (iii) X is in the interior of triangle ABC if and only if $\lambda + \mu + \nu = 1$ and $\lambda > 0$, $\mu > 0$, $\nu > 0$ and indicate on a sketch the regions in the plane ABC in which X lies for other combinations of the signs λ, μ, ν. Obtain an expression for the position vector **x** of a general point X in the interior of the tetrahedron $OABC$ and find the values of λ, μ, ν corresponding to the centroid.   (M.E.I.)

3. *Coordinates*

1. UNIT VECTORS

A unit vector is a vector of unit magnitude. Thus, a unit vector is a sort of 'signpost' giving a direction and sense; any vector may be split into the product of a number (its magnitude) and a unit vector with the required sense and direction. Thus we may write

$$\mathbf{r} = r\hat{\mathbf{r}},$$

where $r = |\mathbf{r}|$ and $\hat{\mathbf{r}}$ is a unit vector in the direction of $\mathbf{r}$. (The notation employed here is useful and should be adopted by the reader: given any vector $\mathbf{x}$, its magnitude may be written simply as x while a unit vector with the same sense and direction as $\mathbf{x}$ is written $\hat{\mathbf{x}}$.) Unit vectors are useful in that they enable us to deal separately with the magnitude and direction of a given vector.

Now suppose we choose two directions in a plane and specify them by unit vectors $\mathbf{i}$ and $\mathbf{j}$. By the Existence and Uniqueness Theorem for a plane (see Chapter 2) any displacement AB in the plane, represented by $\mathbf{d}$ may be split into components in the $\mathbf{i}$ and $\mathbf{j}$ directions

$$\mathbf{d} = p\mathbf{i} + q\mathbf{j}$$

where p and q are uniquely determined. The vector $\mathbf{d}$, which is representative of a whole class of displacements, of which $\mathbf{AB}$ is a typical member, may be written in the alternative form

$$\mathbf{d} = \begin{pmatrix} p \\ q \end{pmatrix}.$$

Thus, $\begin{pmatrix} 2 \\ -1 \end{pmatrix}$ represents the vector $2\mathbf{i} - \mathbf{j}$, $\begin{pmatrix} 1 \\ 0 \end{pmatrix}$ the vector $\mathbf{i}$ and $\begin{pmatrix} 0 \\ -1 \end{pmatrix}$ the vector $-\mathbf{j}$. Of course, the representation of a vector in this new notation depends upon our original choice of base vectors $\mathbf{i}$ and $\mathbf{j}$. Again, there is no necessity for the base vectors to be unit vectors, though they will almost invariably be so. To illustrate these last two remarks, consider two unit vectors $\mathbf{i}$ and $\mathbf{j}$ and the vector $\mathbf{a}$ where

$$\mathbf{a} = 3\mathbf{i} - \mathbf{j}.$$

Now
$$\mathbf{a} = (\mathbf{i} + \mathbf{j}) + 2(\mathbf{i} - \mathbf{j})$$
and so we have
$$\mathbf{a} = \begin{pmatrix} 3 \\ -1 \end{pmatrix} \quad \text{with} \quad \mathbf{i}, \mathbf{j} \quad \text{as base vectors,}$$

while $\quad\quad \mathbf{a} = \begin{pmatrix} 1 \\ 2 \end{pmatrix}\quad$ with $\quad(\mathbf{i}+\mathbf{j}), (\mathbf{i}-\mathbf{j})\quad$ as base vectors.

Notice that $(\mathbf{i}+\mathbf{j})$ and $(\mathbf{i}-\mathbf{j})$ are not unit vectors. (For example, if $\mathbf{i}$ and $\mathbf{j}$ are perpendicular, neither $(\mathbf{i}+\mathbf{j})$ nor $(\mathbf{i}-\mathbf{j})$ is a unit vector.)

Similarly, in three dimensions, if non-coplanar base vectors $\mathbf{i}, \mathbf{j}, \mathbf{k}$ are chosen, any vector $\mathbf{d}$ may be split into three components in the $\mathbf{i}, \mathbf{j}, \mathbf{k}$ directions

$$\mathbf{d} = p\mathbf{i}+q\mathbf{j}+r\mathbf{k}$$

and $\mathbf{d}$ may be represented in the alternative notation as

$$\mathbf{d} = \begin{pmatrix} p \\ q \\ r \end{pmatrix}$$

relative to the base vectors $\mathbf{i}, \mathbf{j}, \mathbf{k}$.

We shall now adopt the convention that $\mathbf{i}, \mathbf{j}, \mathbf{k}$ represent unit vectors each one of which is perpendicular to the other two. Furthermore, positive senses are determined by the following rule: if the thumb, first and second fingers of the right hand are splayed out at right angles to one another, the thumb points in the positive $\mathbf{i}$ direction, the first finger in the positive $\mathbf{j}$ direction and the second finger in the positive $\mathbf{k}$ direction. $\mathbf{i}, \mathbf{j}, \mathbf{k}$ are then said to form a *right-handed orthogonal triple* of unit vectors. (Orthogonal means 'at right-angles to one another'.) Similarly, but more simply, one may define a right-handed orthogonal pair of unit vectors $\mathbf{i}, \mathbf{j}$ for a plane.

Example 1. *If* $\mathbf{a} = \mathbf{i}+2\mathbf{j}+3\mathbf{k}$, *express* $\mathbf{a}$ *as a column vector*

(i) *with* $\mathbf{i}, \mathbf{j}, \mathbf{k}$ *as base vectors*;

(ii) *with* $\mathbf{i}+\mathbf{j}, \mathbf{i}-\mathbf{k}, \mathbf{k}-2\mathbf{j}$ *as base vectors*.

(i) With $\mathbf{i}, \mathbf{j}, \mathbf{k}$ as base vectors,

$$\mathbf{a} = \begin{pmatrix} 1 \\ 2 \\ 3 \end{pmatrix}.$$

(ii) Write $\mathbf{u} = \mathbf{i}+\mathbf{j}, \mathbf{v} = \mathbf{i}-\mathbf{k}, \mathbf{w} = \mathbf{k}-2\mathbf{j}$.
Solving for $\mathbf{i}, \mathbf{j}, \mathbf{k}$ we have

$$\mathbf{i} = \tfrac{1}{3}(2\mathbf{u}+\mathbf{v}+\mathbf{w}); \quad \mathbf{j} = \tfrac{1}{3}(\mathbf{u}-\mathbf{v}-\mathbf{w}); \quad \mathbf{k} = \tfrac{1}{3}(2\mathbf{u}-2\mathbf{v}+\mathbf{w}).$$

Thus, $\quad\quad \mathbf{a} = \mathbf{i}+2\mathbf{j}+3\mathbf{k}$

$$= (\tfrac{2}{3}\mathbf{u}+\tfrac{1}{3}\mathbf{v}+\tfrac{1}{3}\mathbf{w})+(\tfrac{2}{3}\mathbf{u}-\tfrac{2}{3}\mathbf{v}-\tfrac{2}{3}\mathbf{w})+(2\mathbf{u}-2\mathbf{v}+\mathbf{w})$$

$$= \tfrac{10}{3}\mathbf{u}-\tfrac{7}{3}\mathbf{v}+\tfrac{2}{3}\mathbf{w}$$

and we have, with **u**, **v**, **w** as base vectors,

$$\mathbf{a} = \begin{pmatrix} \frac{10}{3} \\ -\frac{7}{3} \\ \frac{2}{3} \end{pmatrix}.$$

Ex. 1. Rewrite $3\mathbf{i}+4\mathbf{j}-\mathbf{k}$ and $(\mathbf{i}+\mathbf{j})-2(\mathbf{j}-2\mathbf{k})$ in the column vector notation, with **i**, **j**, **k** as base vectors.

Ex. 2. Express $3\mathbf{i}-\mathbf{j}-\mathbf{k}$ as a column vector with $(\mathbf{j}+\mathbf{k})$, $(\mathbf{k}+\mathbf{i})$, $(\mathbf{i}+\mathbf{j})$ as base vectors. Where do you use the Uniqueness Theorem in your solution?

Ex. 3. Evaluate $\mathbf{a}+\mathbf{b}$, $2\mathbf{a}-3\mathbf{b}$ and $3(\mathbf{a}-2\mathbf{b})$ where

$$\mathbf{a} = \begin{pmatrix} 1 \\ 0 \\ -1 \end{pmatrix}, \quad \mathbf{b} = \begin{pmatrix} 2 \\ 1 \\ -1 \end{pmatrix}.$$

Ex. 4. If

$$2\begin{pmatrix} x \\ 3 \\ -1 \end{pmatrix} = \begin{pmatrix} -4 \\ y \\ -2 \end{pmatrix}$$

what are the values of x and y? Explain how you make your deductions.

2. COORDINATES

Suppose we now have some geometrical configuration in a plane which we want to describe algebraically. Let us choose any point O of the plane as origin; then all the points of the plane may be specified by their position vectors with respect to O. To give more detailed information, these position vectors may be split into their components in the direction defined by the right-handed pair of orthogonal unit vectors **i**, **j**.

Thus, if

$$\mathbf{r} = \mathbf{OP}$$

we may write

$$\mathbf{r} = x\mathbf{i}+y\mathbf{j}.$$

x and y are called, respectively, *the x and y coordinates of the point P* and are usually written as (x, y). The lines through O in the **i** and **j** directions are called the x and y *axes* respectively, and may be denoted by Ox and Oy.

In Figure 3.1 the following points have been plotted:

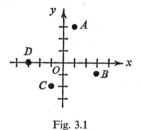

Fig. 3.1

$A(1, 3)$; $B(3, -1)$; $C(-1, -2)$; $D(-3, 0)$.

Note that the x coordinate is always written first.

47

The reader should note the distinction between (1, 3) and $\binom{1}{3}$: the first gives the x and y coordinates of the unique point A, while the second denotes the vector (referred to $\mathbf{i}, \mathbf{j}$ as base) representative of the class of displacements of which $\mathbf{OA}$ is a typical member.

Coordinates may similarly be defined in three dimensions, though now we require a right-handed triplet of orthogonal unit vectors $\mathbf{i}, \mathbf{j}, \mathbf{k}$ to define the directions of the coordinate axes OX, OY, OZ through the origin O. Thus, if P is the point $(2, -1, -3)$, the position vector of P is $2\mathbf{i}-\mathbf{j}-3\mathbf{k}$. Note again that the coordinates are given in the order x, y, z.

Ex. 5. Draw a sketch to denote the approximate positions of the points:

$$A(1, 0), \quad B(-2, -1), \quad C(1, -3), \quad D(-2, 0), \quad E(-1, -2).$$

Ex. 6. Write down the position vectors of the points

$$A(1, -2), \quad B(3, 4).$$

Deduce the coordinates of the mid-point of AB. Can you state a general rule for finding the coordinates of the mid-point of a line?

Ex. 7. Write down the position vectors of the points

$$A(1, -1), \quad B(5, -5).$$

Use the Section Formula to deduce the coordinates of the two points of trisection of AB.

Ex. 8. What are the coordinates of the mid-point of the line joining

$$A(0, -1, 2) \quad \text{and} \quad B(2, 3, 2)?$$

Ex. 9. If $ABCD$ is a parallelogram, what relation must hold between the position vectors $\mathbf{a}, \mathbf{b}, \mathbf{c}, \mathbf{d}$? Find the coordinates of the vertex D of the parallelogram $ABCD$ whose other vertices are given by

$$A(1, 2), \quad B(4, 3), \quad C(3, 5).$$

Ex. 10. The coordinates of the points A, B, C are as follows:

$$A(-1, 1, 2), \quad B(1, 0, -3), \quad C(0, 2, 4).$$

Find the coordinates of the fourth vertex D of the parallelogram $ABCD$ and of the fourth vertex E of the parallelogram $ACBE$.

Ex. 11. Find the coordinates of the centroid of the triangle ABC of Ex. 9.

Ex. 12. A rectangular box $ABCD\ A'B'C'D'$ has base $ABCD$ and the edges AA', BB', CC', DD' are all vertical. M, N, P are the mid-points of BC, CC' and $A'B'$ respectively. AB has magnitude 3 units, BC 2 units and CC' 1 unit. If A is taken as origin and unit vectors $\mathbf{i}, \mathbf{j}, \mathbf{k}$ are taken along AB, AD, AA' respectively, find the position vector of the centroid of triangle MNP and deduce its coordinates.

48

3. DISTANCES IN TERMS OF COORDINATES

Before proceeding with our study of coordinates we shall develop an economic notation whose value should be readily apparent to the reader. It would be convenient to refer to all points by using, say, the letter P, to all x coordinates by x, to all y coordinates by y and to all z coordinates by z but to do so without further clarification would clearly lead to appalling confusion. We may, however, differentiate between the various points and their coordinates by the use of *suffixes* : thus we may call two points P_1 and P_2 and take as their coordinates (x_1, y_1, z_1) and (x_2, y_2, z_2) respectively. One advantage of such a notation is obvious: without further explanation we know that P_n stands for a point, that x_n is its x coordinate and so on. (The reader must guard against confusion between suffixes and indices: x_2 simply means the x coordinate of the point P_2, whereas x^2 represents the result of multiplying the number x by itself.) The choice of a good notation is often more than half the battle in the solution of a mathematical problem; as he gains experience in its use, the reader will come to appreciate the deeper significance of the suffix notation. One evident further advantage may, however, be noted here: the use of suffixes effects a considerable economy in notation if we have to deal with a large (or indeterminate) number of points. (It should be noted that not all sets may be enumerated, that is, counted in the form 1, 2, 3, ... In such cases, the suffix notation as we have presented it breaks down. Consider, for example, the problem of naming all the points on the line segment joining $A(0, 0)$ and $B(1, 0)$.)

Now consider a plane and two points P_1 and P_2 lying in it whose coordinates relative to perpendicular axes through some origin O are (x_1, y_1) and (x_2, y_2).

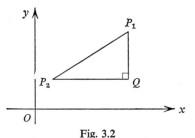

Fig. 3.2

From Figure 3.2 we have

$$\mathbf{P_2P_1} = \mathbf{P_2Q} + \mathbf{QP_1}$$
$$= (x_1 - x_2)\,\mathbf{i} + (y_1 - y_2)\,\mathbf{j}.$$

Thus, applying Pythagoras's Theorem to the right-angled triangle P_2P_1Q,

$$P_1P_2 = \sqrt{[(x_1 - x_2)^2 + (y_1 - y_2)^2]}.$$

49

For three-dimensional coordinates the same argument applies but Pythagoras's Theorem must be applied twice. In Figure 3.3, the feet of the perpendicular from P_1, P_2 to the plane Oxy are Q_1, Q_2, and RQ_1, Q_2R are respectively parallel to Oy and Ox. Thus we have

$$\mathbf{P_2P_1} = \mathbf{P_2Q} + \mathbf{QP_1}$$
$$= \mathbf{Q_2R} + \mathbf{RQ_1} + \mathbf{QP_1}$$
$$= (x_1 - x_2)\,\mathbf{i} + (y_1 - y_2)\,\mathbf{j} + (z_1 - z_2)\,\mathbf{k}$$

and so $\quad P_1P_2 = \sqrt{[(x_1 - x_2)^2 + (y_1 - y_2)^2 + (z_1 - z_2)^2]}$

on applying Pythagoras's Theorem to triangles P_1P_2Q and Q_1Q_2R.

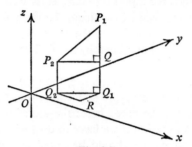

Fig. 3.3

Example 2. (i) The distance between $A(3, -1)$ and $B(-1, 2)$ is
$$\sqrt{[(3 - -1)^2 + (-1 - 2)^2]} = 5.$$

(ii) The distance between $A(1, 0, -2)$ and $B(-1, 2, -3)$ is
$$\sqrt{[(1 - -1)^2 + (0 - 2)^2 + (-2 - -3)^2]} = 3.$$

Ex. 13. A, B, C, D, E, F have coordinates as follows:
$$A(-1, -2), B(-3, 2); \quad C(-1, -2, 4), D(0, -4, 3);$$
$$E(a, -a, 0), F(-k, -k, k).$$
Find the lengths of AB, CD and EF.

Ex. 14. Show that $ABCD$ is a rectangle, A, B, C, D having coordinates:
$$A(1, 2), \quad B(5, -1), \quad C(8, 3), \quad D(4, 6).$$

Ex. 15. What is the fourth vertex of the parallelogram $ABCD$ where
$$A \text{ is } (1, 1, 2), \quad B(2, 0, -1), \quad C(3, 3, 0)?$$

Ex. 16. Find the circumcentre of the triangle
$$A(0, -1, 1), \quad B(1, 0, -1), \quad C(-1, 1, 0).$$

What is the circumradius? (The *circumcentre* of a triangle is the centre of the circle which passes through the three vertices.)

50

Exercise 3(a)

1. Evaluate as single column vectors:

(i) $\begin{pmatrix} 1 \\ 3 \\ -1 \end{pmatrix} - \begin{pmatrix} 1 \\ 1 \\ -3 \end{pmatrix}$;

(ii) $2 \begin{pmatrix} 1 \\ 2 \\ -1 \end{pmatrix} + 3 \begin{pmatrix} 1 \\ 0 \\ -2 \end{pmatrix}$;

(iii) $\begin{pmatrix} 0 \\ 1 \\ -1 \end{pmatrix} + 4 \begin{pmatrix} 1 \\ -1 \\ 0 \end{pmatrix}$;

(iv) $\begin{pmatrix} 2 \\ 1 \\ 3 \end{pmatrix} + 3 \begin{pmatrix} 1 \\ -1 \\ -2 \end{pmatrix} + 2 \begin{pmatrix} 0 \\ 1 \\ 1 \end{pmatrix}$;

(v) $2 \begin{pmatrix} 1 \\ 2 \\ -1 \end{pmatrix} - 3 \begin{pmatrix} 2 \\ 1 \\ -2 \end{pmatrix} + 4 \begin{pmatrix} 1 \\ -1 \\ 1 \end{pmatrix}$.

2. If

$$a = \begin{pmatrix} -1 \\ 1 \\ -3 \end{pmatrix}, \quad b = \begin{pmatrix} 1 \\ 3 \\ -2 \end{pmatrix}, \quad c = \begin{pmatrix} 1 \\ -3 \\ 3 \end{pmatrix},$$

find, in column vector form, the vectors:
(i) $2a - b$; (ii) $a + b - 3c$; (iii) $(3a + b) - 2(b + 3c)$.

3. If a, b, c are defined as in Question 2, solve for x the equations:
(i) $2x = a - b$; (ii) $3(x + a) = b - 2c$
giving your answers in column vector form.

4. Again using the notation of Question 2, solve for x, y, z the following systems of linear equations, giving your answers in column vector form:

(i) $\begin{cases} 3x - y = a + 2b, \\ x + 2y = b - c; \end{cases}$

(ii) $\begin{cases} x + y - z = 2a + 2b, \\ 2x + y + z = a + 3b + 2c, \\ x - y - 3z = 4a - 4c. \end{cases}$

5. Two vectors p, q (where $p \neq kq$) are given in a plane. Referred to p, q as base, the vectors a, b, c, d are given by:

$$a = \begin{pmatrix} 2 \\ 0 \end{pmatrix}, \quad b = 4 \begin{pmatrix} 0 \\ -1 \end{pmatrix}, \quad c = 2 \begin{pmatrix} 1 \\ -4 \end{pmatrix}, \quad d = \begin{pmatrix} 4 \\ -4 \end{pmatrix}.$$

Express a, b, c, d as column vectors, taking $p - 2q, p + 2q$ as base.

6. Three non-coplanar vectors u, v, w are given. Referred to these vectors as base vectors, the vectors, e, f, g, h are given by:

$$e = \begin{pmatrix} 1 \\ 0 \\ 0 \end{pmatrix}, \quad f = \begin{pmatrix} 1 \\ 1 \\ 1 \end{pmatrix}, \quad g = \begin{pmatrix} 2 \\ 3 \\ 3 \end{pmatrix}, \quad h = 4 \begin{pmatrix} -1 \\ 1 \\ 0 \end{pmatrix}.$$

Express e, f, g, h as column vectors taking $v + w, w + u, u + v$ as base vectors.

7. Write down the coordinates of the mid-points of the lines joining the following pairs of points:
(i) $(2, 4), (4, 6)$;   (ii) $(-2, 4), (4, 2)$;   (iii) $(-1, -3), (2, -4)$;
(iv) $(3, 1, -5), (2, -4, 0)$;   (v) $(a + b, a, a - b), (a - b, -a, -a - b)$.

8. Write down the coordinates of the two points of trisection of the lines joining each of the following pairs of points:

(i) (1, 4), (4, 10);　(ii) $(-2, 1)$, (1, 8);　(iii) $(a+2b, b-2a)$, $(a-b, a+b)$;
(iv) $(1, 2, -1)$, $(2, 1, -5)$;　(v) $(a, 2a, b)$, $(a-b, b-2a, a+b)$.

9. Find the lengths of each of the line segments of Question 7. (Leave your answers in the form $\sqrt{m}$.)

10. $A(3, 0)$, $B(4, -1)$, $C(6, 2)$ are vertices of a parallelogram $ABCD$. Find the coordinates of D. Find also the coordinates of E if $ACBE$ is a parallelogram.

11. Prove that the triangle whose vertices are $A(-1, 2)$, $B(3, 5)$, $C(-4, 6)$ is isosceles. What is its area?

12. $A(3, 1, -1)$, $B(1, 2, -2)$, $C(0, 0, 2)$ are vertices of a parallelogram $ABCD$. Find the coordinates of D. What are the coordinates of the meet of the diagonals?

13. Find the area of the triangle whose vertices are $A(1, -3)$, $B(2, 5)$, $C(-4, -3)$.

14. Show that the line joining $A(-1, 4, -3)$ and $B(5, -8, 6)$ meets the x axis. If the point of intersection is C, find the ratio AC/CB.

4. COORDINATE GEOMETRY IN A PLANE; STRAIGHT LINES AND THEIR GRADIENTS

Throughout this section we shall confine our attention to a plane, so that only two coordinates are required to specify a point.

The reader will recall that the vector equation of a straight line is the algebraic condition that must be satisfied by the position vector $\mathbf{r}$ of a point P if P is to lie on the line. In the same way, the *Cartesian equation* of a straight line is the algebraic condition that must be satisfied by the coordinates x, y, of a point $P(x, y)$ of the line (and, conversely, no point P not on the line has coordinates satisfying the equation).

The equations of lines parallel to the coordinate axes may readily be obtained. For example, the reader should have no difficulty in seeing that the line through $(-3, 1)$ parallel to the x axis is $y = 1$; similarly, the line through this point parallel to the y axis is $x+3 = 0$. In particular, the equations of the x and y axes are respectively $y = 0$ and $x = 0$.

A straight line is determined completely by two points on it. Suppose now that we wish to find the Cartesian equation of the straight line through $P_1(x_1, y_1)$ and $P_2(x_2, y_2)$, where $x_1 \neq x_2$ and $y_1 \neq y_2$ and so the line is not parallel to the axes. Let the position vectors of P_1 and P_2 be $\mathbf{r}_1$ and $\mathbf{r}_2$ respectively. Then (see page 37) the vector equation of the line P_1P_2 is

$$\mathbf{r} = \mathbf{r}_1 + \lambda(\mathbf{r}_2 - \mathbf{r}_1)$$

where $\mathbf{r}_1 = x_1\mathbf{i} + y_1\mathbf{j}$ and $\mathbf{r}_2 = x_2\mathbf{i} + y_2\mathbf{j}$.

52

This may be rewritten in column vector notation (with **i, j** as base)

$$\begin{pmatrix} x \\ y \end{pmatrix} = \begin{pmatrix} x_1 \\ y_1 \end{pmatrix} + \lambda \begin{pmatrix} x_2 - x_1 \\ y_2 - y_1 \end{pmatrix}.$$

By the Uniqueness Theorem in two dimensions this gives the equations

$$\begin{cases} x - x_1 = \lambda(x_2 - x_1), \\ y - y_1 = \lambda(y_2 - y_1). \end{cases}$$

Eliminating λ between these two equations we obtain the following result. *The Cartesian equation of the line joining the points $P_1(x_1, y_1)$ $P_2(x_2, y_2)$ is*

$$\frac{x - x_1}{x_2 - x_1} = \frac{y - y_1}{y_2 - y_1}. \tag{1}$$

(The reader must note carefully the distinction in this equation between x, y on the one hand and x_1, y_1, x_2, y_2 on the other: x, y are the coordinates of a general point P on the line; x_1, y_1, x_2, y_2 are the coordinates of two specified fixed points of the line. If we take $\mathfrak{U}$ as the set of all points (x, y) in the plane, the equation (1) is the defining condition for the set of points comprising the line; that is, the set

$$\left\{ (x, y) \in \mathfrak{U} : \frac{x - x_1}{y - y_1} = \frac{x_2 - x_1}{y_2 - y_1} \right\}.$$

The same remarks hold for the vector equation $\mathbf{r} = \mathbf{r}_1 + \lambda(\mathbf{r}_2 - \mathbf{r}_1)$, in which $\mathbf{r}_1$, $\mathbf{r}_2$ are the position vectors of two given points.)

Equation (1) may be rewritten in the form

$$\left. \begin{aligned} y - y_1 &= \frac{y_2 - y_1}{x_2 - x_1}(x - x_1), \\ y - y_1 &= m(x - x_1), \\ m &= \frac{y_2 - y_1}{x_2 - x_1}. \end{aligned} \right\} \tag{2}$$

or

where

The number m is called *the gradient of the line*. The sign of the gradient tells us which way the line is sloping (see Figures 3.4 and 3.5). In case (i), $x_1 - x_2$ and $y_1 - y_2$ have the same sign and $m > 0$; in case (ii) $x_1 - x_2$ and $y_1 - y_2$ have opposite signs and $m < 0$. In both cases, the positive value of m is equal to $\tan \alpha$, where α is the acute angle made by the line with the x axis. Equation (2) gives the form for the straight line when a point on the line and its gradient are known.†

† The reader who has already met trigonometric ratios of obtuse angles will realize that if the straight line AB meets the x axis at P, then the gradient of AB is $\tan \angle xPA$ in all cases, where $\angle xPA$ is measured in the positive (anticlockwise) sense from the x axis (see Chapter 6).

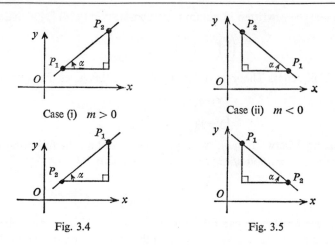

Fig. 3.4   Fig. 3.5

Equation (2) may be rewritten as

$$y = mx + c. \tag{3}$$

Here the constant c represents the intercept cut off on the y axis, as may easily be seen by setting $x = 0$.

Having derived these various forms for the equation of a straight line, we may easily deduce the result that any equation of degree 1 in the two variables x, y represent a straight line (hence the word *linear* usually applied to such equations).

Consider the general linear equation in the two variables x, y:

$$ax + by + c = 0.$$

If $a = 0$ or $b = 0$ this represents a line parallel to one of the axes. If $b \neq 0$, the equation may be rewritten in the form

$$y = -\frac{a}{b}x - \frac{c}{b}$$

and comparison with (3) shows that this is the equation of a line with gradient $-a/b$ and making an intercept $-c/b$ on the y axis.

Example 3. Find the equation of the line L_1 through $(2, -1)$ with gradient $-\frac{1}{2}$ and the equation of the line L_2 joining the points $(0, 7)$ and $(-1, 4)$. What are the coordinates of the intersection of L_1 and L_2?

Draw a sketch showing the relative positions of L_1 and L_2 and the coordinate axes.

L_1 has equation $y + 1 = -\frac{1}{2}(x - 2),$

i.e. $x + 2y = 0,$

54

L_2 has equation
$$\frac{x-0}{-1-0} = \frac{y-7}{4-7},$$

i.e.
$$3x - y + 7 = 0.$$

Since all points lying on L_1 satisfy the $x + 2y = 0$ and all points lying on L_2 satisfy $3x - y + 7 = 0$, the point of intersection of the two lines must satisfy both equations simultaneously.

Solving
$$\begin{cases} x + 2y = 0, \\ 3x - y = -7 \end{cases}$$

we have
$$x = -2, \quad y = 1$$

and so the point of intersection of L_1 and L_2 is $(-2, 1)$.

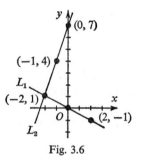

(In this case the sketching of the lines L_1 and L_2 is straightforward: we know two points on L_2, and L_1 clearly passes through the origin. In general, to sketch the position of a straight line whose equation is given, first find the coordinates of the points where it cuts through the coordinate axes.)

Fig. 3.6

Ex. 17. Draw a sketch to show the positions of the straight lines:
(i) $3x - 2y - 6 = 0$;   (ii) $2x + y + 3 = 0$;   (iii) $2x - 5y = 0$.

Ex. 18. Find the equations of the lines through $(2, -3)$ with gradients:
(i) 2;   (ii) $-\frac{2}{3}$.

Ex. 19. Find the equations of the lines joining the pairs of points:
(i) $(2, -3)$, $(3, 2)$;   (ii) $(0, 1)$, $(2, -1)$;
(iii) $(-3, -1)$, $(-1, 2)$;   (iv) $(1, 2)$, $(-3, 2)$.

Ex. 20. What are the gradients of the following lines:
(i) $2x - y - 3 = 0$;   (ii) $x + y + 1 = 0$;   (iii) $3x + 4y + 2 = 0$?

Suppose now we have two lines, L_1 and L_2, the gradients of which are respectively m_1 and m_2.

(i) If L_1 and L_2 are parallel, the angles that they make with the x axis are equal and
$$m_1 = m_2.$$

(ii) If L_1 and L_2 are perpendicular then either they are parallel to the coordinate axes or they have gradients of opposite sign: in the second case,

55

if $m_1 = \mp \tan \alpha_1$ and $m_2 = \pm \tan \alpha_2$ then $m_1 m_2 = -\tan \alpha_1 \tan \alpha_2 = -1$, i.e.

$$m_1 m_2 = -1.$$

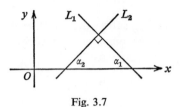

Fig. 3.7

*Ex 21. With the notation above, prove that, if $m_1 = m_2$, L_1 and L_2 are parallel.

*Ex. 22. Again with the notation above, prove that, if $m_1 m_2 = -1$, L_1 and L_2 are perpendicular.

Example 4. Find the equations of the lines L_1, through $(1, -1)$ parallel to $3x - y + 7 = 0$ and L_2, through $(2, -3)$ perpendicular to $2x + 5y + 1 = 0$. Find also the equation of the line L_3 joining the origin to the intersection of L_1 and L_2.

The gradient of $3x - y + 7 = 0$ is $+3$ and so L_1 has equations

$$y + 1 = 3(x - 1),$$

i.e. $\qquad\qquad 3x - y - 4 = 0.$

The gradient of $2x + 5y + 1 = 0$ is $-\frac{2}{5}$ and so the gradient of a perpendicular line is $+\frac{5}{2}$. Thus, the equation of L_2 is

$$y + 3 = \tfrac{5}{2}(x - 2),$$

i.e. $\qquad\qquad 5x - 2y - 16 = 0.$

(With practice, the reader will soon be able to derive such equations more rapidly than is done here. For example, in the second case, any line perpendicular to $2x + 5y + 1 = 0$ is clearly of the form $5x - 2y = k$ and, since the required line passes through $(2, -3)$, $k = 5(2) - 2(-3) = 16$.)

Now consider the equation

$$(3x - y - 4) + \lambda(5x - 2y - 16) = 0,$$

where λ is any number. This is a linear equation and so represents a straight line; furthermore, the point common to L_1 and L_2 clearly satisfies this equation. Thus

$$(3x - y - 4) + \lambda(5x - 2y - 16) = 0$$

56

represents a straight line through the intersection of L_1 and L_2. If it passes through the origin, $(0, 0)$,

$$-4 + \lambda(-16) = 0,$$
$$\lambda = -\tfrac{1}{4}$$

and the equation simplifies down to

$$7x - 2y = 0$$

which is the required equation of L_3.

Ex. 23. Find the equations of the lines L_1, through $(4, -10)$ parallel to $3x - y = 0$ and L_2, through $(1, 2)$ perpendicular to $2x - y - 1 = 0$. What are the coordinates of the intersection of L_1 and L_2?

Ex. 24. Find the line joining the point $(-1, 2)$ to the meet of the two lines $x + 3y - 1 = 0, x - 4y + 2 = 0$.

Ex. 25. Find the equation of the line through the meet of the two lines

$$3x - y + 1 = 0, \quad 4x - 3y + 2 = 0$$

perpendicular to the line $3x - y - 1 = 0$.

Ex. 26. Find the intercept cut off on the transversal $5x - 2y + 3 = 0$ by the two parallel lines $3x - y + 1 = 0$ and $3x - y + 4 = 0$.

Exercise 3(b)

1. Find the equations of the lines through the stated points with the given gradients:
    (i) $(0, -2), 2$;   (ii) $(-1, -1), -2$;   (iii) $(3, -1), -\tfrac{1}{2}$;   (iv) $(a, b), -a/b$.

2. Find the equations of the lines joining the following pairs of points:
    (i) $(1, -2), (2, 1)$;   (ii) $(-2, -3), (-1, 4)$;   (iii) $(2, -1), (-1, -1)$; (iv) $(a, b), (2a, -\tfrac{1}{2}b)$.

3. Write down the gradients of the following lines:
    (i) $2x - 3y + 1 = 0$;   (ii) $3x + 6y + 2 = 0$;   (iii) $5x - y + 1 = 0$; (iv) $(a + b)x + (a - b)y + ab = 0$.

4. Find the equations of the lines through $(3, -1)$ (*a*) parallel and (*b*) perpendicular to:
    (i) $2x - y + 3 = 0$;   (ii) $5x + 4y + 3 = 0$;   (iii) $x + 7 = 0$.
In case (i), what is the distance between the two parallel lines?

5. Find the points of intersection of the following pairs of lines:

(i) $\begin{cases} 4x + 3y - 6 = 0, \\ x - y - 5 = 0; \end{cases}$ (ii) $\begin{cases} ax + by + a^2 = 0, \\ bx - ay + b^2 = 0. \end{cases}$

6. The two lines $3x - 5y - 7 = 0, 4x + 4y + 5 = 0$ meet at the point A. Find the equations of the line through A
    (i) which passes through the origin;
    (ii) is parallel to $7x - y + 2 = 0$;
    (iii) is perpendicular to $3x + 5y - 1 = 0$.

7. Find the orthocentre of the triangle whose vertices are $(0, 1), (1, 2), (4, 3)$. (The orthocentre is the meet of the altitudes of a triangle.)

8. The mid-points L, M, N of the sides, BC, CA, AB of a triangle ABC have coordinates $(2, 1), (3, -3), (4, -5)$. Find the coordinates of A, B, C.

9. The coordinates of the vertices of a triangle are $(6, 0), (-1, 1)$ and $(5, -7)$. Find the coordinates of the centre of the circumcircle.

10. The coordinates of the vertices of a triangle are $(1, -4), (3, -2)$ and $(-11, 12)$. Find the coordinates of the centre of the circumcircle and determine the coordinates of the points where this circle cuts the axes.

11. Show that, for all values of λ, the line whose equation is $\lambda x + y = 1 - 2\lambda$ always passes through the point $(-2, 1)$. What is the equation (in terms of λ) of the perpendicular line through $(1, 2)$? Show that, whatever the value of λ, the intersection of these two lines always satisfies the equation

$$x^2 + y^2 + x - 3y = 0.$$

What locus does this last equation represent?

12. $OABC$ is a rectangle in which $OA = 3OC$. M is the mid-point of OC and L is the point of trisection of CB nearer C. OL, AM meet at X. By setting up axes along OA and OC and assigning suitable coordinates to the various points, determine the ratio in which X divides OL.

13. Prove that, for all values of λ, the line

$$(1 - \lambda) x + \lambda y = 3 - 7\lambda$$

passes through a fixed point. What are the coordinates of the point?

14. Find the coordinates of the centre of the circumcircle of the triangle ABC, where A, B, C have coordinates $(-1, -3), (-2, -2), (5, 5)$ respectively. Prove that the point $P(6, 4)$ lies on the circumcircle and prove further that the feet of the perpendiculars from P on to BC, CA, AB are collinear.

15. Find the equation of the line joining $A(a, 0)$ and $B(0, b)$. A', B' are the feet of the perpendiculars from A, B to a variable line through the origin. If $A'P, B'P$ are respectively parallel to the y and x axes, what can be said about the position of P?

16. What are the equations of the reflections of the line $2x - 3y + 6 = 0$ in
   (i) the x axis;   (ii) the y axis;
   (iii) the line $2x - 3y = 0$;   (iv) the line $2x - 3y = 3$?

5. COORDINATE GEOMETRY IN SPACE: THE PLANE AND STRAIGHT LINE

The effective use of Cartesian coordinates in three dimensions requires rather more vector technique than we have at present at our disposal and so a more detailed study will be deferred until a later chapter (Chapter 11).

We shall content ourselves for the moment with demonstrating the general form of the Cartesian equations of lines and planes in space.

We may define a plane as a set of points in space which

(i) contains at least three non-collinear points;

(ii) has the property that, given any two points R_1 and R_2 of the set, all points of the line $R_1 R_2$ belong to the set.

From this definition, three non-collinear points

$$P_1 (x_1, y_1, z_1), \quad P_2 (x_2, y_2, z_2), \quad P_3 (x_3, y_3, z_3)$$

clearly define a plane. If $\mathbf{r}_1, \mathbf{r}_2, \mathbf{r}_3$ are respectively the position vectors of P_1, P_2, P_3, we have seen that the plane $P_1 P_2 P_3$ is (see Chapter 2.6)

$$\mathbf{r} = \mathbf{r}_1 + \lambda(\mathbf{r}_2 - \mathbf{r}_1) + \mu(\mathbf{r}_3 - \mathbf{r}_1).$$

In column vector form this may be written

$$\begin{pmatrix} x \\ y \\ z \end{pmatrix} = \begin{pmatrix} x_1 \\ y_1 \\ z_1 \end{pmatrix} + \lambda \begin{pmatrix} x_2 - x_1 \\ y_2 - y_1 \\ z_2 - z_1 \end{pmatrix} + \mu \begin{pmatrix} x_3 - x_1 \\ y_3 - y_1 \\ z_3 - z_1 \end{pmatrix}$$

which, by the Uniqueness Theorem, yields three equations:

$$x = x_1 + \lambda(x_2 - x_1) + \mu(x_3 - x_1),$$

$$y = y_1 + \lambda(y_2 - y_1) + \mu(y_3 - y_1),$$

$$z = z_1 + \lambda(z_2 - z_1) + \mu(z_3 - z_1).$$

Solving the first two equations simultaneously we obtain λ and μ as linear expressions in x and y. Hence, substituting these values of λ and μ in the third equation, we see that the Cartesian equation of a plane is linear in x, y, z.

Now let us prove the converse result: a linear equation in x, y, z represents the equation of a plane.

Consider the equation $ax + by + cz + d = 0$ where we shall suppose, for simplicity, that $a \neq 0, b \neq 0, c \neq 0, d \neq 0$. (The fact that one or several of them may be zero requires a modification of the proof given below; see Ex. 30.) The three points $(-d/a, 0, 0)$, $(0, -d/b, 0)$, $(0, 0, -d/c)$ certainly all satisfy the equation and are non-collinear (since the first two have zero z coordinate, for example). Thus condition (i) for a plane is satisfied.

To demonstrate condition (ii), suppose P_1 and P_2 satisfy the given equation. Then

$$\begin{cases} ax_1 + by_1 + cz_1 + d = 0, \\ ax_2 + by_2 + cz_2 + d = 0 \end{cases}$$

3   P P M

and thus, for any values of k and l

$$a\left(\frac{lx_1+kx_2}{k+l}\right)+b\left(\frac{ly_1+ky_2}{k+l}\right)+c\left(\frac{lz_1+kz_2}{k+l}\right)=0.$$

But, by the Section Formula,

$$\mathbf{r}=\frac{l\mathbf{r}_1+k\mathbf{r}_2}{k+l}=\left(\frac{lx_1+kx_2}{k+l}\right)\mathbf{i}+\left(\frac{ly_1+ky_2}{k+l}\right)\mathbf{j}+\left(\frac{lz_1+kz_2}{k+l}\right)\mathbf{k}$$

is the position vector of a point on the line joining P_1 and P_2. Thus, the coordinates of any point on the line joining $P_1 P_2$ satisfies the given equation.

In three dimensions two intersecting (that is, non-parallel) planes define a straight line and we should therefore expect a line to be represented by two linear equations in x, y, z.

The vector equation of the line through P, parallel to the vector

$$\mathbf{u}=l\mathbf{i}+m\mathbf{j}+n\mathbf{k}$$

is (see Chapter 2) $\qquad \mathbf{r}=\mathbf{r}_1+\lambda\mathbf{u}.$

In column vector form this reads

$$\begin{pmatrix}x\\y\\z\end{pmatrix}=\begin{pmatrix}x_1\\y_1\\z_1\end{pmatrix}+\lambda\begin{pmatrix}l\\m\\n\end{pmatrix}$$

and so, by the Uniqueness Theorem, we have three equations:

$$x=x_1+\lambda l,\quad y=y_1+\lambda m,\quad z=z_1+\lambda n$$

giving the equation of the line in the form

$$\frac{x-x_1}{l}=\frac{y-y_1}{m}=\frac{z-z_1}{n}=\lambda. \tag{4}$$

We use this form even if one or more of l, m, n are zero. For example, the line through the point $(1, -1, 2)$ in the direction of the vector $2\mathbf{i}-3\mathbf{k}$ may be written as

$$\frac{x-1}{2}=\frac{y+1}{0}=\frac{z-2}{-3}=\lambda$$

or $\qquad \dfrac{x-1}{2}=\dfrac{z-2}{-3},\quad y+1=0.$

Notice that the Cartesian coordinates of a second general point of the line (4) may be expressed in terms of one variable as

$$(x_1+\lambda l, y_1+\lambda m, z_1+\lambda n).$$

λ is called a *parameter* for points of the line.

60

The vector **u** defines the direction of the line and may be termed a *direction vector*. Since $\mathbf{u} = l\mathbf{i}+m\mathbf{j}+n\mathbf{k}$, l, m, n are proportional to the cosines of the angles that **u** makes with the directions **i**, **j**, **k**, that is, with the directions of the coordinate axes. l, m, n are usually called *direction ratios* for the line; if **u** is a unit vector, the constant of proportionality is one and l, m, n are called *direction cosines* (see Figure 3.8, where $l = \cos\theta_1$, $m = \cos\theta_2$, $n = \cos\theta_3$).

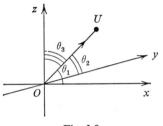

Fig. 3.8

Example 5. Find the equation of the plane through $A\,(1, 1, 1)$, $B\,(0, 1, -2)$, $C\,(0, 0, -1)$ and the point of intersection of this plane with the line

$$\frac{x-3}{1} = \frac{y-2}{-2} = \frac{z-2}{3}.$$

Let the equation of the required plane be

$$ax+by+cz+d = 0.$$

Since the coordinates of A, B, C all satisfy this equation,

$$\begin{cases} a+b+c = -d, \\ \quad b-2c = -d, \\ \qquad -c = -d \end{cases}$$

which gives $a = -3d$, $b = d$, $c = d$.

The equation of the plane ABC is thus

$$3x-y-z-1 = 0.$$

Any point of the given line has coordinates

$$(3+\lambda, 2-2\lambda, 2+3\lambda).$$

This lies on the plane if

$$3(3+\lambda)-(2-2\lambda)-(2+3\lambda)-1 = 0$$

giving

$$\lambda = -2$$

and so the point of intersection has coordinates

$$(1, 6, -4).$$

Example 6. *Two straight lines are given parametrically by*

$$L_1: x = 1-4\lambda, \quad y = 1+\lambda, \quad z = 1+\lambda$$

and $\qquad L_2: x = 2\mu, \qquad y = 1-\mu, \quad z = 2+\mu.$

Prove that L_1 *and* L_2 *intersect, and find the equation of the plane containing the two lines.*

If we can choose λ, μ such that the three equations

$$1-4\lambda = 2\mu,$$
$$1+\lambda = 1-\mu,$$
$$1+\lambda = 2+\mu$$

are simultaneously satisfied, then L_1 and L_2 intersect. By inspection, $\lambda = \frac{1}{2}, \mu = -\frac{1}{2}$ fulfils the required condition (giving the point of intersection $(-1, \frac{3}{2}, \frac{3}{2})$).

Eliminating λ (*a*) between the x and y coordinates of a general point of L_1, and (*b*) between the y and z coordinates, we see that the two planes

$$x+4y = 5, \quad y-z = 0$$

both contain L_1. It follows that, for all values of k, the equation

$$(x+4y-5)+k(y-z) = 0 \qquad (1)$$

represents a plane containing L_1.

By setting $\mu = 0$, we see that the point $(0, 1, 2)$ lies on L_2 (but not on L_1). This lies on the plane (1) if

$$(0+4-5)+k(1-2) = 0,$$

i.e. $\qquad\qquad\qquad k = -1.$

The equation of the plane containing L_1 and L_2 is thus seen to be

$$x+4y-5-1(y-z) = 0,$$

i.e. $\qquad\qquad\qquad x+3y+z-5 = 0.$

Ex. 27. What is the equation of the plane
(i) containing Ox and Oy;
(ii) through $(1, -1, 2)$ perpendicular to Oz?

Ex. 28. Describe the position of the plane $ax+by = 0$.

Ex. 29. Why was condition (i) included in the definition of a plane?

*Ex. 30. Show that three non-collinear points may be found on

$$ax+by+cz+d = 0$$

in the following cases:

(i) $d = 0, a \neq 0, b \neq 0, c \neq 0$;   (ii) $d \neq 0, a = b = 0, c \neq 0$;

(iii) $d = a = 0, b \neq 0, c \neq 0$;   (iv) $a = 0, b \neq 0, c \neq 0, d \neq 0$.

Ex. 31. Find the equation of the plane through the line of intersection of the planes $x-y+2z+1 = 0$, $2x+y-z+2 = 0$ which contains the origin.

Ex. 32. What are the coordinates of a general point of the line

$$\frac{x-3}{2} = \frac{y+2}{-1} = \frac{z+5}{-3}?$$

Where does this line cut the plane $x+y+z+2 = 0$?

Ex. 33. What are the equations of the line joining $(-3, 1, 1)$ and $(2, 2, -1)$?

Ex. 34. Find the equation of the plane containing the origin and the line

$$\frac{x-2}{2} = \frac{y-3}{3} = \frac{z+4}{-1}.$$

Exercise 3 (c)

1. Find (*a*) direction ratios, (*b*) the direction cosines, for the lines joining the following pairs of points:

(i) $(1, 2, 3), (2, 3, 4)$;   (ii) $(2, -1, 3), (1, 1, 2)$;

(iii) $(3, 1, 2), (5, -1, 1)$;   (iv) $(1, 3, 5), (5, 3, 1)$;

(v) $(2, -3, -4), (-3, 2, 1)$;

(vi) $(a+\lambda, 2a+2\lambda, 3a+3\lambda), (a-\mu, 2a-2\mu, 3a-3\mu)$;

(vii) $(a^2, ab, b^2), (a^2, ac, c^2)$;   (viii) $(1, a, a^2), (a^2, a, 1)$.

2. Find the equations of the planes through the following sets of points:

(i) $(1, 0, 0), (0, 1, 0), (0, 0, 1)$;

(ii) $(3, 2, 0), (0, 3, -1), (1, 0, -2)$;

(iii) $(2, 0, 0), (1, 1, -1), (6, -5, 3)$;

(iv) $(2, 2, 0), (-1, 1, -4), (1, 1, -1)$;

(v) $(-1, 3, 1), (1, -3, -3), (3, -1, 5)$;

(vi) $(1, 2, 3), (2, -2, 8), (-1, 2, -7)$.

3. Find the equations of the lines joining the following pairs of points:

(i) $(0, 0, 0), (2, 1, -3)$;   (ii) $(1, 2, -1), (2, 3, -3)$;

(iii) $(1, 1, -1), (-1, 4, 2)$;   (iv) $(-2, 1, 3), (2, 1, -3)$;

(v) $(1, 4, 2), (1, -1, 2)$;   (vi) $(a, 2a, 3a), (-a, a, 2a)$.

4. Find the equation of the plane through the line of intersection of the planes $x+y-3z = 2$, $2x-y-z = 1$

(i) containing the origin;

(ii) containing the point $(1, 1, -1)$;

(iii) parallel to the *x* axis.

5. Find the equation of the plane through the line of intersection of the planes

$$2x+2y+3z-1 = 0, \quad 3x-y-z+2 = 0$$

(i) containing the origin;

(ii) containing the point $(1, 1, 1)$;

(iii) parallel to the *z* axis.

6. Write down the equation of the plane parallel to the x axis which contains the line

$$\frac{x-1}{-1} = \frac{y-3}{2} = \frac{z+1}{-3}.$$

Find the equation of the plane containing this line and the origin.

7. Find the equation of the plane through the point $(1, 1, -5)$ containing the line

$$\frac{x+1}{3} = \frac{y+5}{4} = \frac{z}{-5}.$$

8. Write down, in terms of a parameter λ, the coordinates of a general point of the line

$$\frac{x-8}{3} = \frac{y-1}{1} = \frac{z-1}{0}.$$

Where does this line cut the plane $x-2y-3z-2 = 0$?

9. Find the coordinates of the point where the line joining $(2, 3, 1)$ and $(4, 7, 3)$ cuts the plane $2x+y-z-3 = 0$.

10. Find the equations of the line joining $(2, 1, 1)$ and $(1, -1, 2)$. Where does this line meet the plane $x-y+az = 0$?

Is your result true for all a? Explain.

11. Determine the direction cosines of the line of intersection of the planes

$$2x-y+z-9 = 0, \quad 4x+y+2z-6 = 0.$$

Where does this line meet the plane $x+y+z = 0$?

12. Prove that the two lines

$$\frac{x-1}{1} = \frac{y+1}{2} = \frac{z+2}{3},$$

$$\frac{x+1}{1} = \frac{y}{1} = \frac{z-1}{1},$$

are skew.

13. Prove that the two lines

$$\frac{x-2}{3} = \frac{y+4}{1} = \frac{z-1}{-1}$$

and

$$\frac{x+1}{2} = \frac{y+4}{1} = \frac{z+2}{-2}$$

meet. What are the coordinates of their point of intersection? Find the equation of the plane containing them.

14. Prove that the two lines

$$\frac{x-3}{2} = \frac{y-2}{1} = \frac{z-4}{1}$$

and

$$\frac{x+1}{2} = \frac{y-1}{0} = \frac{z}{3}$$

meet. What are the coordinates of their point of intersection? Find the equation of the plane containing them.

64

15. Find the coordinates of the point common to the three planes:

$$x-3y+z-6 = 0,$$
$$2x-y+2z-2 = 0,$$
$$3x+2y+z+2 = 0.$$

16. Find the coordinates of the point common to the three planes:

$$x-2y+z-7 = 0,$$
$$2x+3y-4z+26 = 0,$$
$$3x+y+3z+7 = 0.$$

17. Find the coordinates of the point where the line determined by the two planes

$$x-3y-z+8 = 0,$$
$$x-y+z-2 = 0$$

cuts the plane containing the x and y axes.

Miscellaneous Exercise 3

1. Find the area of the trapezium whose vertices are:

$$(x_2, y_2), \quad (x_3, y_3), \quad (x_2, 0), \quad (x_3, 0).$$

Deduce that the area of the triangle $P_1(x_1, y_1)$, $P_2(x_2, y_2)$, $P_3(x_3, y_3)$ is

$$\tfrac{1}{2}(x_2y_3 - x_3y_2 + x_3y_1 - x_1y_3 + x_1y_2 - x_2y_1).$$

What is the condition that the three points $P_1P_2P_3$ should be collinear?

2. $ABCD$ is a rectangle with $AB = 2AD$. E is the mid-point of AB and F is the mid-point of BC. CE, AF meet at X. By setting up a suitable coordinate system, prove that DXB is a straight line and determine the ratio DX/XB.

What is the area of the quadrilateral $AXCD$?

3. $ABCD$ is a rectangle and points P, Q are taken on AB, AD respectively. The rectangle $APRQ$ is completed. If the lines BQ, DP meet at X, prove that X, R, C lie on a straight line.

4. Find, in terms of a parameter m, representing the gradient, the equation of a variable straight line through the fixed point (a, b).

If this line cuts the x and y axes at A and B respectively, and the parallelogram $OABP$ is completed, prove that, whatever the value of m, the point P lies on the curve

$$xy = xb - ay.$$

Sketch this curve for the case $a = b = 1$ for values of $x > -1$.

5. Show that, by a suitable choice of coordinate system, the equations of two coplanar non-parallel lines may be taken in the form

$$y = ax, \quad y = -ax.$$

Two fixed lines OA, OB are drawn and a variable line, passing through the fixed point C, cuts OA, OB at P and Q respectively. If the feet of the perpendiculars from P, Q to OB, OA are U, V, prove that UV passes through a fixed point.

6. Two fixed straight lines, L_1 and L_2, meet at O. Through a fixed point A two lines AP_1P_2 and AQ_1Q_2 are drawn to cut L_1 at P_1 and Q_1, and L_2 at P_2 and Q_2. Prove that whatever the position of the two lines drawn through A, the point of intersection of P_1Q_2 and P_2Q_1 lies on a fixed straight line through O.

7. Points P_1, P_2, P_3 are taken on the x axis, and Q_1, Q_2, Q_3 on the y axis. L_1 is the point of intersection of P_2Q_3 and P_3Q_2, I_2 of P_3Q_1 and P_1Q_3, L_3 of P_1Q_2 and P_2Q_1. Prove that L_1, L_2, L_3 lie on a straight line.

(This is a particular case of Pappus's Theorem, which holds more generally for two sets of three collinear points on any two straight lines.)

8. Prove that the lines
$$\frac{x+1}{-2} = \frac{y-1}{2} = \frac{z-3}{1}$$
and
$$\frac{x-1}{3} = \frac{y-3}{1} = \frac{z-2}{6}$$
are skew.

By considering the family of planes through one of the lines, prove that there is just one common transversal to the two lines which passes through the origin and find its equation.

9. Prove that no three of the points $(1, 1, 2), (-2, -6, 3), (-1, 1, 5), (2, 4, 2)$ are collinear but that all four points lie on a plane.

10. Explain why the three planes
$$x-z+1 = 0,$$
$$x-y-z+5 = 0,$$
$$x+2y-z+2 = 0$$
have no common point.

What can you say about the intersections of the planes:
$$x-z+1 = 0,$$
$$x-y-z+5 = 0,$$
$$x+2y-z-7 = 0?$$

11. $ABCDA'B'C'D'$ is a cube, with square faces $ABCD$, $A'B'C'D'$ and vertical edges AA' etc. M is the mid-point of $C'D'$. The plane $AB'M$ cuts BD' at X and CC' produced at Y. Find the ratios $BX:XD'$ and $CC':C'Y$.

12. Prove that the three lines
$$L_1: \frac{x}{1} = \frac{y}{2} = \frac{z}{3},$$
$$L_2: \frac{x-1}{2} = \frac{y}{3} = \frac{z}{1},$$
$$L_3: \frac{x+1}{3} = \frac{y}{1} = \frac{z}{2}$$
are skew.

66

If general points of L_1 and L_2 have parameters λ and μ respectively, find the condition that the line joining the point on L_1 with parameter λ to the point on L_2 with parameter μ should intersect L_3.

Deduce that a unique common transversal to the three lines may be drawn through a given point on L_1.

13. In the tetrahedron $ABCD$, each of the faces ABC, ABD, ACD has a right angle at A, and $AB = AC = AD$. X is the point on AD such that $AX = 2XD$ and Y is the point on BC such that $CY = 2YB$. The mid-point of AY is Z. Prove that the mid-point of DZ lies on the plane BCX.

14. A is the fixed point $(a, 0, 0)$ and variable points $Q\,(0, \lambda, 0)$, $R\,(0, 0, \mu)$ (λ, μ positive) are taken on the y and z axes such that the plane AQR passes through the fixed point $B\,(\alpha, \beta, \gamma)$. Prove that

$$(\alpha - a)\,\lambda\mu + \alpha\beta\mu + \alpha\gamma\lambda = 0.$$

Find the value of λ that makes the triangle OQR isosceles.

15. Explain why the equation

$$x^2 + y^2 + z^2 = 1$$

represents the surface of a sphere, centre the origin.

Find the equations of the planes through the point $(2, 0, 0)$ which are tangential to the sphere and parallel to the y axis.

4. *Polynomials*

1. POLYNOMIALS

Expression of the form
$$x^3 - 3x^2 + 4x + 2$$

and
$$x^5 - x + 1$$

are called *polynomials*. More generally, a *polynomial of degree n* is an expression of the form

$$a_0 x^n + a_1 x^{n-1} + a_2 x^{n-2} + \ldots + a_{n-1} x + a_n \quad (a_0 \neq 0)$$

involving only multiples of positive integral powers of x and a *constant term*, a_n. A polynomial of degree n is completely determined if its $(n+1)$ coefficients (including the constant term or coefficient of x^0) are given and two polynomials of degree n are said to be *identically equal* if the coefficient of x^r in each polynomial is the same for all values of r, and conversely. For example, writing $\equiv$ to mean 'identically equal to'

$$ax^3 - x - 2 \equiv 2x^3 - bx^2 - x + c$$
$$\Leftrightarrow \quad a = 2, \quad b = 0, \quad c = -2.$$

Ex. 1. If $ax^2 + bx + c \equiv 3x^2 + 2ax + b$, find a, b and c.

A convenient shorthand is to write a polynomial as $P(x)$; for example, if we are considering the polynomial $x^3 - 3x - 2$ we could write 'Let

$$P(x) \equiv x^3 - 3x - 2'$$

and subsequently refer to this polynomial simply as $P(x)$. By $P(1)$ we mean the value of the polynomial when $x = 1$; that is, the numerical value attained by the polynomial when 1 is substituted for x. In the case just quoted, $P(1) = 1 - 3 - 2 = -4$ and $P(-2) = -8 + 6 - 2 = -4$.

Ex. 2. If $P(x) \equiv x^4 - 3x^3 + 4x^2 - x - 1$, show that $P(1) = 0$ and find $P(-1)$, $P(0)$ and $P(2)$.

Ex. 3. Show that, if $P(x) \equiv Q(x)$, then $P(k) = Q(k)$ for all values of k. The converse of this proposition is also true: if $P(k) = Q(k)$ for all values of k, then the coefficients of x^r in $P(x)$ and $Q(x)$ are the same for all r (see Ex. 7). Either statement may be taken as the definition of 'identically equal to'.

68

A non-zero number may be regarded as a polynomial of degree zero, or a constant polynomial. The number zero may be regarded as the *zero polynomial*.†

No ambiguity will arise if we write the zero polynomial as 0. A polynomial is identically equal to the zero polynomial if all its coefficients are zero, and conversely.

Ex. 4. If $(a-1) x^2+(a+b) x+(a+b+c) \equiv 0$, find the values of a, b, c.

Example 1. *If* $P(x) \equiv ax^2+bx+c$, *distinguish between the identity* $P(x) \equiv 0$ *and the equation* $P(x) = 0$.

$P(x) \equiv 0$ means that $P(x)$ is identically equal to the zero polynomial and so we deduce that $a = b = c = 0$. Thus, whatever value x may have, say $x = k$, then $P(k) = 0$.

$P(x) = 0$ is a *statement* which holds only for certain values of x. In fact, provided $b^2 > 4ac$ and $a \neq 0$,

$$P\left[\frac{-b+\sqrt{(b^2-4ac)}}{2a}\right] = P\left[\frac{-b-\sqrt{(b^2-4ac)}}{2a}\right] = 0$$

and $P(x) \neq 0$ for any other value of x.

Exercise 4(a)

1. If $P(x) \equiv x^3+5x^2+3x+1$; find $P(1)$, $P(-1)$, $P(\frac{1}{2})$, $P(3)$.

2. If $(x-2) (x-3) (x-4) \equiv ax^3+bx^2+cx+d$, find a, b, c, d.

3. Prove that $(x-a)^3 \equiv x^3-3ax^2+3a^2x-a^3$. For what real values of x does $(x-a)^3 = -a^3$?

4. If $a(x-2)^2+b(x-2)+c \equiv 3x^2-8x-1$, find a, b, c.

5. Express $7x^3-x^2+3x-4$ in the form $a(x-1)^3+b(x-1)^2+c(x-1)+d$.

6. Express $4x^3+12x^2+6x$ in the form $a(x+1)^3+b(x+1)^2+c(x+1)+d$.

7. Express $3x^3+2x^2-11x-10$ in the form $a(x+1)^3+b(x+1)^2+c(x+1)+d$ and also in the form $\alpha(x-2)^3+\beta(x-2)^2+\gamma(x-2)+\delta$.
Find the three roots of the cubic equation $3x^3+2x^2-11x-10 = 0$.

8. Express $x^3+4kx^2+3k^2x-k^3$ in the form $a(x+k)^3+b(x+k)^2+c(x+k)+d$.

9. If $(ax^2+bx+c) (x+1) \equiv 0$, prove that $ax^2+bx+c \equiv 0$.

† We shall not associate a degree with the zero polynomial. The reader will appreciate that, by elementary algebra, the product of a polynomial of degree m by a polynomial of degree n is a polynomial of degree $m+n$. This result holds good even if one or both of the polynomials is a constant polynomial, but fails if one of the polynomials is the zero polynomial if a finite degree is associated with this polynomial.

10. If $(ax+b)(cx+d) \equiv (ax+c)(bx+d)$ prove that:
(i) if $a \neq 0$, then $b = c$; (ii) if $b \neq c$, then $a = d = 0$.

11. If $(x-c)^3 \equiv x^3+ax^2+bx-27$, find a, b, c.

12. If $(x-a)(x-b)(x-c) \equiv (x+\alpha)(x+\beta)(x+\gamma)$, prove that

$$\{a, b, c\} = \{-\alpha, -\beta, -\gamma\}.$$

2. THE FACTOR AND REMAINDER THEOREMS

If $P(x) \equiv (x-a)Q(x)$, where $P(x)$ is a polynomial of degree n and $Q(x)$ is a polynomial of degree $n-1$, $P(x)$ is said to have *a linear factor*. Conversely, if $P(x)$ has a linear factor, then $P(x)$ may be expressed in the form

$$P(x) \equiv (x-a)Q(x).$$

For example, $2x^3+5x^2-3x-10 \equiv (x+2)(2x^2+x-5)$

and so the cubic polynomial $2x^3+5x^2-3x-10$ has a linear factor $(x+2)$. (It also has a quadratic factor $(2x^2+x-5)$.)

It is important to realise at the outset that possession of a factor is not an absolute property of a polynomial but depends on the restrictions we place upon the coefficients. For example, if we restrict our polynomials to have only rational numbers as coefficients, the polynomial x^2-2 has no linear factors; on the other hand, if we allow our coefficients to be real numbers, $x^2-2 = (x-\sqrt{2})(x+\sqrt{2})$. (This is often expressed by the statement: 'x^2-2 is irreducible over the rational field but reducible over the real field'. The word 'field' has a technical meaning and will be defined in Volume 2; all that is necessary at the moment is to realize that 'over the rational field' means that all polynomials under discussion must have rational numbers as coefficients.)

The theorems we are about to prove do not depend upon whether we choose the rational field or the real field for our coefficients provided, of course, that we are consistent. We shall not, therefore, allude to the field from which the coefficients are drawn, but the reader may, if he wishes interpret all the coefficients as, say, rational numbers.

It is easy to see that, if $P(x)$ has a factor $(x-\alpha)$, then $P(\alpha) = 0$. For $P(x)$ has a factor $(x-\alpha)$

$$\Leftrightarrow \quad P(x) \equiv (x-\alpha)Q(x)$$

$$\Rightarrow \quad P(\alpha) = 0 \cdot Q(\alpha)$$

$$\Rightarrow \quad P(\alpha) = 0.$$

A converse of this result is known as the *Factor Theorem*.

70

Theorem 4.1 (*The Factor Theorem*). *If* $P(x)$ *is a polynomial and if* $P(\alpha) = 0$, *then* $P(x)$ *has a linear factor* $x-\alpha$.

Proof. First observe that

$$x^r - \alpha^r \equiv (x-\alpha)(x^{r-1} + \alpha x^{r-2} + \alpha^2 x^{r-3} + \ldots + \alpha^{r-1}).$$

Suppose $\quad P(x) \equiv b_0 x^n + b_1 x^{n-1} + b_2 x^{n-2} + \ldots + b_{n-1} x + b_n,$

Then $\quad P(\alpha) = b_0 \alpha^n + b_1 \alpha^{n-1} + b_2 \alpha^{n-2} + \ldots + b_{n-1} \alpha + b_n$

and so

$$P(x) - P(\alpha) \equiv b_0(x^n - \alpha^n) + b_1(x^{n-1} - \alpha^{n-1}) + \ldots + b_{n-1}(x-\alpha)$$

$$\equiv (x-\alpha)[b_0(x^{n-1} + \ldots + \alpha^{n-1}) + b_1(x^{n-2} + \ldots + \alpha^{n-2}) + \ldots + b_{n-1}].$$

But $P(\alpha) = 0$ thus we have

$$P(x) \equiv (x-\alpha) Q(x)$$

and therefore $P(x)$ has a linear factor $(x-\alpha)$.

Consider now the following division process:

$$
\begin{array}{r}
x^2 - 2x - 3 \\
x-2 \overline{)\, x^3 - 4x^2 + x + 2} \\
\underline{x^3 - 2x^2} \\
-2x^2 + x \\
\underline{-2x^2 + 4x} \\
-3x + 2 \\
\underline{-3x + 6} \\
-4
\end{array}
$$

In elementary algebra the result of this process would be described by saying that, if $x^3 - 4x^2 + x + 2$ is divided by $x-2$, the *quotient* is $x^2 - 2x - 3$ and the *remainder* is -4. There are advantages, however, in restating the process as follows: $x^3 - 4x^2 + x + 2$ is identically equal to the product of $(x-2)$ by the quotient $(x^2 - 2x - 3)$, plus the remainder -4. In symbols

$$x^3 - 4x^2 + x + 2 \equiv (x-2)(x^2 - 2x - 3) - 4. \tag{1}$$

This identity holds for all values of x, whereas the division process given above is true for all values of x other than $x = 2$.

Ex. 5. Check that $x = 2$ does indeed satisfy (1).

We now prove our second result, *the Remainder Theorem*, which generalizes the ideas outlined above.

Theorem 4.2 (*The Remainder Theorem*). *If $P(x)$ is any polynomial of degree $n \geqslant 1$, and $x-\alpha$ is any linear polynomial, then $P(x)$ may be expressed in the form*

$$P(x) \equiv (x-\alpha)\, Q(x) + R$$

where $Q(x)$ is a polynomial of degree $n-1$ and $R = P(\alpha)$.

Proof. As in Theorem 1, we have

$$P(x) - P(\alpha) \equiv (x-\alpha)\, Q(x)$$

and the result follows immediately.

Note (i). The Remainder Theorem is often stated in the following form: if a polynomial $P(x)$ is divided by $x-\alpha$, then the remainder is $P(\alpha)$.

(ii) Strictly speaking, we should prove that the expression given above for $P(x)$ is unique in the sense that, if $P(x) \equiv (x-\alpha)\, Q_1(x) + R_1$, then $Q_1(x) \equiv Q(x)$ and $R_1 = R$. The proof of this result should be supplied by the reader.

Example 2. *Find the remainder when $x^3 - 5x^2 - x + 2$ is divided* by (i) $x-1$; (ii) $x+2$; (iii) $2x+1$.

Write
$$P(x) \equiv x^3 - 5x^2 - x + 2.$$

(i) $P(x) \equiv (x-1)\, Q_1(x) + R_1$;

put $x = 1$: $R_1 = P(1) = 1 - 5 - 1 + 2 \equiv -3$;

(ii) $P(x) \equiv (x+2)\, Q_2(x) + R_2$;

put $x = -2$: $R_2 = P(-2) = -8 - 20 + 2 + 2 \equiv -24$;

(iii) $P(x) \equiv (2x+1)\, Q_3(x) + R_3$;

put $x = -\frac{1}{2}$: $R_3 = P(-\frac{1}{2}) = -\frac{1}{8} - \frac{5}{4} + \frac{1}{2} + 2 = \frac{9}{8}$.

Exercise 4(b)

1. Find the remainder when:
(i) $x^3 - x + 2$ is divided by $x-4$;
(ii) $3x^3 - 5x^2 + x + 2$ is divided by $x-2$;
(iii) $4x^4 - 2x^2 + x - 3$ is divided by $x+1$;
(iv) $x^5 - x - 1$ is divided by $x+3$;
(v) $4x^3 - 5x^2 + 2$ is divided by $2x-1$;
(vi) $4x^3 - 8x + 1$ is divided by $2x+1$.

2. Show that $x-2$ is a factor of the polynomial $x^3 - 4x^2 + x + 6$ and hence factorize the expression completely.

3. Factorize the following polynomials over the rational field as far as possible:

(i) $2x^3 + 7x^2 - 5x - 4$; (ii) $12x^3 + 5x^2 - 19x - 12$;

(iii) $2x^3 + 7x^2 - 17x - 10$; (iv) $x^3 + 3x^2 - 2x - 6$;

(v) $x^3 - x^2 - x - 2$; (vi) $x^3 - 7x^2 + 7x + 15$;

(vii) $x^3 + 2x^2 - 7x - 2$; (viii) $8x^3 + 12x^2 - 2x - 3$.

4. Factorize the polynomials given in Question 3 over the real field as far as possible.

5. If $x^3 - 5x^2 + 7x - a$ has a factor $x - 2$, find a.

6. If $2x^3 + ax^2 - 5x - 1$ is divisible by $2x + 1$, find a.

7. If $x^3 + 3x^2 + ax - 1$ leaves a remainder of 3 on division by $(2x + 1)$, find a.

8. If $3x^3 + ax^2 + bx - 2$ is divisible by both $x + 2$ and $3x + 1$, find a and b.

9. If $ax^3 + 3x^2 + bx - 3$ is divisible by both $x - 1$ and $2x + 3$, find a and b.

10. By expressing $x^4 + 1$ in the form $x^4 + 2x^2 + 1 - 2x^2$, show that $x^4 + 1$ is reducible over the real field.

11. Factorize $x^4 + 3x^3 - 15x^2 + 9x + 2$: (i) over the rational field; (ii) over the real field.

12. $ax^4 + 2x^3 - 4x^2 - 2x + b$ has factors $(x - 1)$ and $(x - 2)$, find a and b and factorize the expression completely.

3. THE FACTOR THEOREM (CONTINUED)

We now show how the Factor Theorem may be extended for cubic polynomials and, in particular, how this extended result may be used to derive certain algebraic identities. The results we prove are valid for the general polynomial (substituting n for 3 in their enunciation) but proofs for this require the use of mathematical induction (see Chapter 9).

Theorem 4.3. *If $P(x)$ is a cubic polynomial with leading term $a_0 x^3$, and if $P(\alpha) = P(\beta) = P(\gamma) = 0$ for 3 unequal numbers α, β, γ, then*

$$P(x) = a_0(x - \alpha)(x - \beta)(x - \gamma).$$

Proof. Since $P(\alpha) = 0$, $P(x) \equiv (x - \alpha) Q_1(x)$, where $Q_1(x)$ is a polynomial of degree 2.

Thus, since $P(\beta) = 0$, $0 = (\beta - \alpha) Q_1(\beta)$. But $\beta - \alpha \neq 0$ and so $Q_1(\beta) = 0$. $Q_1(x)$ therefore has a factor $(x - \beta)$.

$Q_1(x) \equiv (x - \beta) Q_2(x)$, where $Q_2(x)$ is a polynomial of degree 1.

By the same argument,

$Q_2(x) \equiv (x - \gamma) Q_3(x)$, where $Q_3(x)$ is a polynomial of degree 0, that is, $Q_3(x) = k$, where k is some number. Substituting,

$$P(x) \equiv k(x - \alpha)(x - \beta)(x - \gamma).$$

Since these two polynomials are identically equal, the coefficient of x^3 must be the same in each, and so $k = a_0$ and the proof is complete.

Corollary (The Identity Theorem). If $P(x)$ is a cubic polynomial and if 4 unequal numbers α, β, γ, δ can be found such that

$$P(\alpha) = P(\beta) = P(\gamma) = P(\delta) = 0, \quad then \quad P(x) \equiv 0.$$

Proof. By Theorem 4.3,

$$P(x) \equiv a_0(x-\alpha)(x-\beta)(x-\gamma).$$

But $P(\delta) = 0$ and so

$$0 = a_0(\delta-\alpha)(\delta-\beta)(\delta-\gamma).$$

Now $\delta \neq \alpha$, $\delta \neq \beta$, $\delta \neq \gamma$ and it follows that $a_0 = 0$. $P(x)$ thus reduces to a quadratic polynomial $a_1 x^2 + a_2 x + a_3$ which vanishes for 4 distinct values of x. Successive repetitions of the argument show that $a_1 = a_2 = a_3 = 0$ and the corollary is proved.

Ex. 6. Prove that, if $P(x)$ is a quadratic polynomial and if 3 unequal numbers α, β, γ can be found such that $P(\alpha) = P(\beta) = P(\gamma) = 0$, then $P(x) \equiv 0$.

Ex. 7. If $P(x)$ and $Q(x)$ are cubic polynomials, and if unequal numbers α, β, γ, δ can be found such that $P(\alpha) = Q(\alpha)$, ..., $P(\delta) = Q(\delta)$, prove that $P(x) \equiv Q(x)$.

Example 3. Establish the identity

$$\frac{x^2-a^2}{(a-b)(a-c)} + \frac{x^2-b^2}{(b-c)(b-a)} + \frac{x^2-c^2}{(c-a)(c-b)} + 1 \equiv 0 \quad (a \neq b \neq c).$$

Write

$$P(x) \equiv \frac{x^2-a^2}{(a-b)(a-c)} + \frac{x^2-b^2}{(b-c)(b-a)} + \frac{x^2-c^2}{(c-a)(c-b)} + 1,$$

then

$$P(a) = 0 + \frac{a+b}{c-b} + \frac{a+c}{b-c} + 1$$

$$= \frac{-b+c}{b-c} + 1$$

$$= 0.$$

Similarly

$$P(b) = P(c) = 0.$$

But $P(x)$ is a quadratic polynomial and so must vanish identically.

Exercise 4(c)

1. Prove that

$$\frac{(x-b)(x-c)}{(a-b)(a-c)} + \frac{(x-c)(x-a)}{(b-c)(b-a)} + \frac{(x-a)(x-b)}{(c-a)(c-b)} - 1 \equiv 0.$$

2. Prove that

$$\frac{(x-b)\,(x-c)\,(x-d)}{(a-b)\,(a-c)\,(a-d)} + \frac{(x-c)\,(x-d)\,(x-a)}{(b-c)\,(b-d)\,(b-a)} + \frac{(x-d)\,(x-a)\,(x-b)}{(c-d)\,(c-a)\,(c-b)}$$

$$+ \frac{(x-a)\,(x-b)\,(x-c)}{(d-a)\,(d-b)\,(d-c)} - 1 \equiv 0.$$

3. Prove that

$$\frac{a(x-b)\,(x-c)}{(a-b)\,(a-c)} + \frac{b(x-c)\,(x-a)}{(b-c)\,(b-a)} + \frac{c(x-a)\,(x-b)}{(c-a)\,(c-b)} - x \equiv 0.$$

4. Prove that

$$\frac{x(x-a)}{bc(c-a)\,(a-b)} + \frac{x(x-b)}{ca(a-b)\,(b-c)} + \frac{x(x-c)}{ab(b-c)\,(c-a)} - \frac{x}{abc} \equiv 0.$$

5. By considering the quadratic polynomial $ax^2 + bx + c$, show that, if $n \neq 0$, $n \neq 1$ and

$$a+b+c = 0,$$
$$an^2 + bn + c = 0,$$
$$a + bn + cn^2 = 0,$$

then $a = b = c = 0$.

6. Prove that the cubic polynomial $P(x)$ defined by

$$P(x) \equiv \frac{a(x-\beta)\,(x-\gamma)\,(x-\delta)}{(\alpha-\beta)\,(\alpha-\gamma)\,(\alpha-\delta)} + \frac{b(x-\alpha)\,(x-\gamma)\,(x-\delta)}{(\beta-\alpha)\,(\beta-\gamma)\,(\beta-\delta)} + \frac{c(x-\alpha)\,(x-\beta)\,(x-\delta)}{(\gamma-\alpha)\,(\gamma-\beta)\,(\gamma-\delta)}$$

$$+ \frac{d(x-\alpha)\,(x-\beta)\,(x-\gamma)}{(\delta-\alpha)\,(\delta-\beta)\,(\delta-\gamma)}$$

is the *unique* cubic polynomial such that $P(\alpha) = a$, $P(\beta) = b$, $P(\gamma) = c$, $P(\delta) = d$. Find the cubic polynomial $P(x)$ such that

$$P(-1) = -3, \quad P(0) = 2, \quad P(1) = 5, \quad P(2) = 12.$$

7. Find the cubic polynomial $P(x)$ such that

$$P(0) = 1, \quad P(1) = -1, \quad P(2) = -1, \quad P(3) = 13.$$

8. Find the cubic polynomial $P(x)$ which takes the value -5 when x has the values -1, 0, 1 and is such that $P(2) = 1$.

9. State and prove the identity theorem for quartic polynomials.

Miscellaneous Exercise 4

1. We shall say that a polynomial $P(x)$ 'has the property R' if the remainder on division of $P(x)$ by the fixed factor $x-a$ is R. Prove that
   (i) if $P_1(x)$ and $P_2(x)$ both have the property R, so also has the polynomial $P(x)$ where $P(x) = P_1(x) + P_2(x)$;
   (ii) if $P_3(x)$ has the property R and $P_4(x)$ has the property S, show that the polynomial $Q(x) \equiv P_3(x)\,P_4(x)$ has the property RS.
   What can be said about the polynomial $P(x)$ if it has the property 0?

2. Prove that, if $P(x)$ is any polynomial of degree $n \geqslant 2$, then $P(x)$ may be expressed in the form

$$P(x) \equiv (x-a)\,(x-b)\,Q(x) + Rx + S,$$

where R, S are numbers and $Q(x)$ is a polynomial of degree $n-2$ (all numbers and coefficients taken from the same field—say the rationals).

Express $5x^3 + 9x^2 - 8x - 11$ in the form

$$(x-1)\,(x+2)\,Q(x) + Rx + S$$

and show you can check your values for R and S by putting $x = 1$ and $x = -2$.

3. Find the remainder on dividing the following polynomials by $x^2 - x - 6$:
(i) $7x^3 - x^2 - 30x - 30$; (ii) $x^8 - 1$.

4. The remainder when the polynomial $P(x)$ is divided by $(x-a)\,(x-b)$, where $a \neq b$, is expressed in the form $A(x-a) + B(x-b)$. Find explicit values for A and B.

Prove that, if identically equal remainders are obtained on division by

$$(x-a)\,(x-b) \quad \text{and} \quad (x-a)\,(x-c),$$

then $$(b-c)\,P(a) + (c-a)\,P(b) + (a-b)\,P(c) = 0.$$

What can you deduce about the remainder when $P(x)$ is divided by

$$(x-b)\,(x-c)?$$

5. By using the Remainder Theorem or otherwise, find the factors of

$$a^2(b+c) + b^2(c+a) + c^2(a+b) + 2abc.$$

Hence or otherwise show that, if $a+b+c = 0$, then

$$a^3 + b^3 + c^3 = 3abc.$$

Find (i) the factors of

$$(p+2q-3r)^3 + (-3p+q+2r)^3 + (2p-3q+r)^3,$$

(ii) the prime factors of
$$73^3 - 47^3 - 26^3.$$
(Cambridge)

6. If $ax^2 + 2bx + c$ can be written in the form

$$A(x-\alpha)^2 + B(x-\beta)^2,$$

prove that $$a\alpha\beta + b(\alpha+\beta) + c = 0.$$

Is it true that, if numbers α, β can be found such that

$$a\alpha\beta + b(\alpha+\beta) + c = 0$$

then $ax^2 + 2bx + c$ can be written in the form $A(x-\alpha)^2 + B(x-\beta)^2$?

7. Prove that, if $lx^2 + mx + n$ is equal to zero for three distinct values of x, then $l = m = n = 0$.

Hence, or otherwise, prove the identity

$$\frac{a^2(x-b)\,(x-c)}{(a-b)\,(a-c)} + \frac{b^2(x-c)\,(x-a)}{(b-c)\,(b-a)} + \frac{c^2(x-a)\,(x-b)}{(c-a)\,(c-b)} \equiv x^2.$$

Prove also that

$$\frac{(x+a)^3}{(a-b)\,(a-c)}+\frac{(x+b)^3}{(b-c)\,(b-a)}+\frac{(x+c)^3}{(c-a)\,(c-b)} \equiv 3x+a+b+c.$$

(O & C)

8. Factorize:
   (i) $bc(b-c)+ca(c-a)+ab(a-b)$;
   (ii) $a(b-c)^2+b(c-a)^2+c(a-b)^2+8abc$;
   (iii) $a(b-c)^3+b(c-a)^3+c(a-b)^3$.

9. Given that p, q, r are distinct values of x which satisfy the equation

$$\frac{a}{x-\alpha}+\frac{b}{x-\beta}+\frac{c}{x-\gamma} = 1,$$

prove that, for all values of x other than $x = \alpha$, $x = \beta$, $x = \gamma$

$$\frac{a}{x-\alpha}+\frac{b}{x-\beta}+\frac{c}{x-\gamma} \equiv 1-\frac{(x-p)\,(x-q)\,(x-r)}{(x-\alpha)\,(x-\beta)\,(x-\gamma)}.$$

By considering the value of $P(x) \equiv (x-p)\,(x-q)\,(x-r)$ for different values of x, prove that, if a, b, c are all positive and $\alpha < \beta < \gamma$, then p, q, r lie one in each of the sets
$$\{x \in R: \alpha < x < \beta\}, \quad \{x \in R; \beta < x < \gamma\}, \quad \{x \in R: x > \gamma\}.$$

Prove also that
$$a = \frac{(p-\alpha)\,(q-\alpha)\,(r-\alpha)}{(\alpha-\beta)\,(\alpha-\gamma)}$$

and that
$$\frac{a}{(p-\alpha)^2}+\frac{b}{(p-\beta)^2}+\frac{c}{(p-\gamma)^2} = \frac{(p-q)\,(p-r)}{(p-\alpha)\,(p-\beta)\,(p-\gamma)}.$$

(O & C adapted)

10. When divided by (x^2+x+1), a cubic polynomial $F(x)$ leaves a remainder $(2x+3)$. When $F(x)$ is divided by $x(x+3)$, the remainder is $5(x+1)$. Find $F(x)$.
(Cambridge)

11. $f(x)$, $g(x)$ and $G(x)$ are cubic polynomials in x. The polynomials $h(x)$ and $H(x)$ are respectively the remainders left when $f(x)$ is divided by $g(x)$ and by $G(x)$. Prove that, if ax^3 and Ax^3 are respectively the terms of highest degree in $g(x)$ and $G(x)$, then

$$[aG(x)-Ag(x)]f(x) \equiv aG(x)\,h(x) - Ag(x)\,H(x). \quad \text{(Cambridge)}$$

5. *Functions and inequalities*

1. FUNCTIONS

The concept of an association between the elements of two sets is of prime importance in mathematics. For example, the table of sines in a book of mathematical tables exhibits an association between the set A of angles between $0°$ and $90°$ and the set B of real numbers between 0 and 1. We could exhibit the fact that $\sin 30° = 0.5$ by writing the *ordered pair* $(30°, 0.5)$. The word '*ordered*' used here reminds us that the order in which we write the elements down within each pair must be taken into account; that is, the ordered pair (a, b) is not the same as the ordered pair (b, a).

We can put this concept of an association between the elements of two sets in a more precise way if we introduce the idea of the *Cartesian product of two sets A and B*. The Cartesian product of A and B, written $A \times B$ is the set of all ordered pairs (a, b) where $a \in A$ and $b \in B$. For example, if

$$A = \{1, 2, 3\}, \quad B = \{3, 4, 5\},$$

then

$$A \times B = \{(1, 3), (1, 4), (1, 5), (2, 3), (2, 4), (2, 5), (3, 3), (3, 4), (3, 5)\}.$$

Ex. 1. If the set A has m elements and the set B has n elements, how many elements has the set $A \times B$?

A *relation* between two sets A and B is a proper subset of $A \times B$. Thus, a relation is a set of ordered pairs (a, b) containing at least one pair, but not all the pairs, of $A \times B$. Of course, relation is a very wide term as defined here. For example, both $\{(1, 3)\}$ and $\{(1, 3), (1, 4), (1, 5), (2, 3), (2, 4), (2, 5), (3, 3), (3, 4)\}$ define perfectly respectable relations between A and B. Of particular significance are the (1-1) *relations* (read as 'one-to-one' relations) which associate with each element of A just one element of B in such a way that no element of B arises from more than one element of A; in our example above, such a relation could be $\{(1, 3), (2, 4), (3, 5)\}$.

In this chapter we shall be concerned with perhaps the most important of all types of relation, the *function*. A *function f from A to B*, written $f : A \to B$, is a subset of $A \times B$ with the property that each element of A appears just once. Another word for function is *mapping*: *A is mapped by f into B*. A function may be looked upon as something which associates

78

with *each* element of A a *unique* element of B. In Figure 5.1 a function is pictured diagrammatically; notice that the arrows, indicating the paths by which elements of A are to find their assigned destination in B, start from each point of A. Notice too that there is no restriction on the number of elements of A for which $b \in B$ is the image. (The *image* of the element $a \in A$ is the element which a is mapped into by f.)

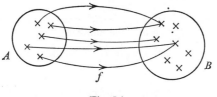

Fig. 5.1

If we have a function $f: A \to B$ the set A is called the *domain* of f and the set of image points (a subset of B in general, but possibly the whole of B) is called the *range* of f. The set B is called the *codomain* of f. The image of the element $a \in A$ is written $f(a)$, thus, $f(a)$ is an element of B or, in other words, $(a, f(a))$ is an element of $A \times B$.

Example 1. *The function* $f: R^+ \to R^+$ *is defined by*

$$f(x) = \frac{1}{1+x} \quad (x \in R^+).$$

Find:
  (i)   *the range of* f;
  (ii) $f(2)$ *and* $f(\sqrt{2})$;
  (iii) *the value of* x *which maps into* $\frac{1}{4}$.
  (i) For $0 < x_1 < x_2$,
$$1 > \frac{1}{1+x_1} > \frac{1}{1+x_2} > 0.$$

Thus, since $1/(1+x)$ can take any positive value less than 1 by a suitable choice of positive x, the range of f is the set $\{y \in R^+ : 0 < y < 1\}$.
  (ii) $f(2) = 1/(1+2) = \frac{1}{3}; f(\sqrt{2}) = 1/(1+\sqrt{2}) = \sqrt{2}-1$. (Notice that both 2 and $\sqrt{2}$ belong to R^+ and so $f(2), f(\sqrt{2})$ are defined.)
  (iii) If $1/(1+x) = \frac{1}{4}$, $x = 3$.

If there is no doubt as to the domain, a particular function is often defined by phrases such as 'the function $f(x) = x^2 - 3x - 2$' or 'y is a function of x such that $y = x^2 - 3x - 2$' or even 'the function $x^2 - 3x - 2$'. From the context we are presumed to appreciate that x is, say, a real number. Even so, the phraseology is loose: the notation $f(x)$ (or y) stands for the image of x under f, not for the function itself.

*Ex. 2. Comment upon the statement

$$
\text{`} \quad \frac{1}{1+\sqrt{x}} \quad \text{and} \quad \frac{1-\sqrt{x}}{1-x}
$$

represent the same function'.

Ex. 3. $f: R \to R$ is defined by $f(x) = x^3 - 3x^2 - 5x + 2$. Evaluate $f(0)$, $f(-1)$, $f(2)$, $f(3)$. Which elements of R map into the number 2?

Ex. 4. Answer the same question as in Ex. 3 for the function $g: Q \to R$ defined by $g(x) = x^3 - 3x^2 - 5x + 2$.

A useful pictorial representation of certain functions $f: R \to R$ (or subsets of these sets) may be obtained by taking the x axis to represent the domain and the y axis to contain the range. If y is the image of the number x under f, that is, if $y = f(x)$, we represent the element (x, y) of f as the point with Cartesian coordinates (x, y). The set of all such points is called the *graph* of the function. For example, suppose $f: R \to R$ is defined by the equation $f(x) = x^2 - 5x + 4$. The graph of this function for the part of the domain $-1 \leqslant x \leqslant 6$ is shown in Figure 5.2. This graph may alternatively be referred to as 'the *curve* $y = x^2 - 5x + 4$'.

Certain relations which are not functions may also be represented graphically; for example, consider the subset of $R \times R$ consisting of all ordered pairs of the form (x, y) where $x \in R$, $y \in R$ such that $y^2 = x$. That part of the graph for $x < 6$ is shown in Figure 5.3.

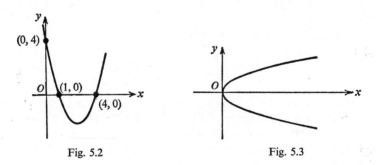

Fig. 5.2   Fig. 5.3

Ex. 5. Explain why the relation depicted in Figure 5.3 is not a function.

Suppose now we have a function $f: A \to B$; under what circumstances will the set of all ordered pairs $(f(a), a)$, $a \in R$, constitute a function $F: B \to A$?

80

Viewed pictorially, the question may be rephrased: if all the arrows in a diagram such as Figure 5.4 were reversed, under what circumstances would we still have a diagram depicting a function?

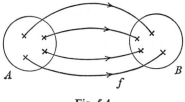

Fig. 5.4

The question is easily answered if we recall what is demanded of such a function F: it must associate *each* point of B with a *unique* point of A. Thus, the range of f must be the *whole* of B (since each point of B has an image under F) and f must be (1-1) (since each point of B has a unique image under F). If f satisfies both of these conditions F is defined as a function: it is called the *inverse function of* f: $A \rightarrow B$ and is written

$$f^{-1}: B \rightarrow A.$$

Ex. 6. Show that no inverse function exists for the function $f: R \rightarrow R$ where $f(x) = x^2$, but that an inverse function does exist for the function $g: R^+ \rightarrow R^+$, where $g(x) = x^2$.

Exercise 5(a)

1. The function $f: R \rightarrow R$ is defined by $f(x) = x^3 - x - 1$. Find $f(0)$, $f(1)$, $f(2)$, $f(3), f(-1)$.

2. The function $g: R^+ \rightarrow R$ is defined by

$$g(x) = \frac{x^2 + x + 1}{x + 1}.$$

Find $g(1)$, $g(2)$, $g(3)$.

3. The function $f: R \rightarrow R$ is defined by

$$f(x) = \begin{cases} -x & \text{if } x < 0, \\ 0 & \text{if } x = 0, \\ x & \text{if } x > 0. \end{cases}$$

(This is normally written $f(x) = |x|$; read '$f(x)$ equals the *modulus* of x'.) What is the range of f? Sketch the graph of f.

A second function $g: R \rightarrow R$ is defined by $g(x) = x - |x|$. What is the range of g? Sketch the graph of g.

4. The function $f: R \to R$ is defined by

$$f(x) = \begin{cases} \dfrac{x}{|x|}, & x \neq 0, \\ 0, & x = 0. \end{cases}$$

Write down the values of $f(-1)$ and $f(1)$. Sketch the graph of f.

5. $A \subseteq R$ and $B \subseteq R$. The set f of all ordered pairs (x, y) is formed, where $x \in A$, $y \in B$ and $y = \sqrt[4]{x}$. Show that f is *not* a function if
  (i) $A = R^+$, $B = Q$; (ii) $A = Q$, $B = R$.
Suggest sets A and B for which f is a function.

6. $A = \{x \in R: 1 \leqslant x \leqslant 2\}$ and $f: A \to R$ is defined by $f(x) = 2/x$. The function $g: A \to R$ is defined by $g(y) = 1+y^2$. A new function $h: A \to R$ is defined by $h(x) = g[f(x)]$ (this is usually written $h = g \circ f$). Find
  (i) $h(\tfrac{3}{2})$; (ii) the range of h.

7. Sketch the graph of the function $f: R \to R$ where $f(x) = |x+1|$.

8. Sketch the graph of the function $g: R \to R$ where
$$g(x) = |x+1| + |x+2| + |x+3|.$$

9. $A = \{x \in R: 0 < x < 3\}$ and $f: A \to R$ is defined by $f(x) = x^2 - 3x + 2$. Find
  (i) $f(1), f(2)$;
  (ii) the range of f;
  (iii) the subset of A whose elements have the image 1 under f;
  (iv) the subset of A whose elements have the image 2 under f.

10. $A = \{x \in R: -\sqrt{6} \leqslant x \leqslant \sqrt{6}\}$ and $f: A \to R$ is defined by $f(x) = x^3 - 6x$. Find the range and sketch the graph of f.

11. If $f: R \to R$ is defined by $f(x) = (x-1)^3$, show that $f^{-1}: R \to R$ exists and determine its form explicitly.

12. Determine the numbers which are invariant† under the mapping $f: R \to R$ where f is defined by

$$f(x) = \begin{cases} (x^2+x+1)(x+3)^{-1} & (x \neq -3), \\ 0 & (x = -3). \end{cases}$$

Show how to illustrate invariance graphically for a general function $g: R \to R$.

13. $f: R \to R$ is a given function, $A \subset R$ and the set of images of all the elements in A is denoted by B. If C is the set of numbers whose images belong to B, prove that $A \subset C$ and that the inclusion may not be strict.

14. $f: R \to R$ is a given function, $X \subset R$ and the set of images of all the elements in X is denoted by $f(X)$. If $A \subset R$, $B \subset R$ is it necessarily true that
  (i) $f(A \cap B) = f(A) \cap f(B)$; (ii) $f(A \cup B) = f(A) \cup f(B)$?

15. Sketch the graph of the function $f: R^+ \to R$ defined by $f(x) = x^2$. Show that the function $g: R^+ \to R$, where $g(x) = x^{\frac{1}{2}}$, is the inverse of f. Sketch the graph of g.
  What connection exists between the graphs of f and g?

† An element a is *invariant* under the mapping f if $f(a) = a$.

16. If x is a real number, $[x]$ denotes the greatest integer less than or equal to x. (For example, $[-2\frac{1}{2}] = -3$, $[4\frac{1}{4}] = 4$, $[-1] = -1$.) The function $f: R \rightarrow Z$ is defined by $f(x) = [x]$; sketch its graph.

A function f is called *periodic* if there exists a number k such that $f(x+k) = f(x)$, for all x in the domain; k is then called the *period* of f. Show that the function defined by $f(x) = x - [x]$ is periodic and find its period.

What feature does the graph of any periodic function possess?

2. INEQUALITIES

The function, f, defined by
$$f(x) = \frac{1}{3-2x}$$

has for its domain the set R with the single point $x = \frac{3}{2}$ deleted; if we call this set D, we may write $D = R - \{\frac{3}{2}\}$. The inequality

$$\frac{1}{3-2x} < 1 \tag{1}$$

defines a set $A \subset D$, where
$$A = \left\{x \in D: \frac{1}{3-2x} < 1\right\};$$

that is, A is the subset of elements of D which map into elements less than 1. By 'the *solution*' of the inequality (1) is meant the determination of the simplest expression for the set A.

It is always good practice, in solving an inequality, to express one side of the inequality as zero. Thus

$$A = \left\{x \in D: \frac{1}{3-2x} - 1 < 0\right\} = \left\{x \in D: \frac{2(x-1)}{3-2x} < 0\right\}.$$

To determine the values of x satisfying the inequality

$$\frac{2(x-1)}{3-2x} < 0$$

it is best to express the working in tabular form (see Chapter 1.7). The critical values of $x \in R$ are $x = 1$ and $x = \frac{3}{2}$.

D	$x < 1$	$x = 1$	$1 < x < \frac{3}{2}$	$x > \frac{3}{2}$
$x-1$	$-$	0	$+$	$+$
$3-2x$	$+$	$+$	$+$	$-$
$\frac{x-1}{3-2x}$	$-$	0	$+$	$-$

Thus $$A = \{x \in D : x < 1\} \cup \{x \in D : x > \tfrac{3}{2}\}.$$

Figure 5.5 shows a graph of the function f defined above; the domain of f is denoted by the whole of the x axis with the point $x = \tfrac{3}{2}$ deleted, the range of f is represented by the y axis, with $y = 0$ deleted. The subset A of D is denoted by that part of the x axis drawn in a thick line. (Note carefully that $1 \notin A, \tfrac{3}{2} \notin A$; indeed, $\tfrac{3}{2} \notin D$.)

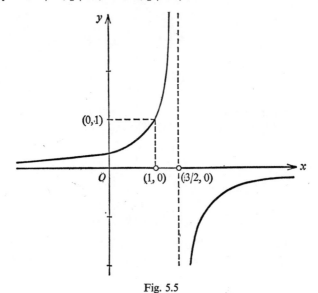

Fig. 5.5

Example 2. Solve the inequality

$$\frac{x}{(x-3)\,(x+1)} \leqslant -\tfrac{2}{5}$$

and illustrate your answer by means of a sketch of the curve

$$y = \frac{x}{(x-3)\,(x+1)}.$$

The function f defined by

$$f(x) = \frac{x}{(x-3)\,(x+1)}$$

has as its domain the set D where

$$D = R - \{-1, 3\};$$

that is, the set of real numbers, less the two numbers -1 and 3. (D may be written alternatively as the complement of the set

$$\{x \in R : x = -1 \quad \text{or} \quad x = 3\}.)$$

Now
$$\frac{x}{(x-3)(x+1)}+\frac{2}{5}=\frac{5x+2x^2-4x-6}{5(x-3)(x+1)}$$
$$=\frac{2x^2+x-6}{5(x-3)(x+1)}$$
$$=\frac{(2x-3)(x+2)}{5(x-3)(x+1)}.$$

We thus seek a simpler description of the set A, where

$$A=\left\{x\in D:\frac{(2x-3)(x+2)}{5(x-3)(x+1)}\leqslant 0\right\}.$$

The critical values of $x\in R$ are $x=-2$, $x=-1$, $x=\frac{3}{2}$, $x=3$.
As above, we set out the work in tabular form.

D	$x<-2$	$x=-2$	$-2<x<-1$	$-1<x<\frac{3}{2}$	$x=\frac{3}{2}$	$\frac{3}{2}<x<3$	$x>3$
$x+2$	$-$	0	$+$	$+$	$+$	$+$	$+$
$2x-3$	$-$	$-$	$-$	$-$	0	$+$	$+$
$x-3$	$-$	$-$	$-$	$-$	$-$	$-$	$+$
$x+1$	$-$	$-$	$-$	$+$	$+$	$+$	$+$
$\frac{(x+2)(2x-3)}{5(x-3)(x+1)}$	$+$	0	$-$	$+$	0	$-$	$+$

Thus $A=\{x\in D:-2\leqslant x<-1\}\cup\{x\in D:\frac{3}{2}\leqslant x<3\}$.

Figure 5.6 shows the graph of f, the set A is represented by that part of the x axis drawn in thick lines.

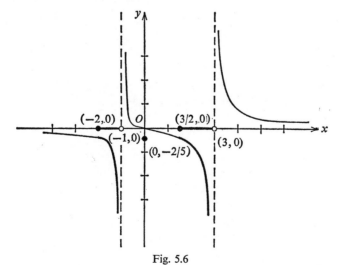

Fig. 5.6

Ex. 7. Verify the solution of Example 2 by evaluating $f(-3)$, $f(-1\frac{1}{2})$, $f(0)$, $f(2)$, $f(4)$. Explain why these are appropriate values to use for checking.

*Ex. 8. Show that the two expressions

$$\frac{(2x-3)\,(x+2)}{(x-3)\,(x+1)} \quad \text{and} \quad (x-3)\,(x-\tfrac{3}{2})\,(x+1)\,(x+2)$$

have the same sign for all values of $x \neq -1$ or 3. Hence solve the inequality of Example 2.

Exercise 5(b)

Solve the following inequalities, illustrating your solutions by means of a sketch.

1. $\dfrac{1}{x} < 2;$ 2. $\dfrac{3-x}{x} < 2;$ 3. $\dfrac{1}{1-x} < 1;$

4. $\dfrac{x}{1+x} < 2;$ 5. $\dfrac{2}{3-x} \geqslant 1;$ 6. $\dfrac{x}{2-3x} > -1;$

7. $\dfrac{2}{x-1} \geqslant x;$ 8. $\dfrac{x-4}{x-3} \leqslant x;$ 9. $\dfrac{x}{x+1} < \dfrac{1}{3};$

10. $\dfrac{2}{x^2-5x+6} < 1;$ 11. $\dfrac{x-4}{x^2-1} < -2;$ 12. $\dfrac{5x+7}{x^2+5x+6} > 1;$

13. $\dfrac{x-4}{x^2-4} < 1;$ 14. $\dfrac{6(3x+1)}{(x-1)\,(x-2)\,(x+3)} < 1;$

15. $\dfrac{x-3}{x^2+x-3} < 1;$ 16. $\dfrac{1}{x^2-3} < -1;$

17. $-1 \leqslant \dfrac{1}{2-x} < 2;$ 18. $0 < \dfrac{1}{2x-5} < 3;$

19. $\left|\dfrac{3}{2-3x}\right| < 1;$ 20. $\left|\dfrac{1}{x^2-1}\right| < 1;$

21. $\left|\dfrac{x^2-3x+3}{x^2-4x+3}\right| \leqslant 1;$ 22. $\left|\dfrac{x^2-21}{x^2-7x+6}\right| < 1.$

6. *The trigonometric functions*

1. RADIANS

We shall assume in this chapter that the reader is familiar with the usual measurement of angles in degrees and also with the definitions of the sines, tangents, etc., of acute angles in terms of the sides of a right-angled triangle. We shall also assume that arc-lengths in circles may be satisfactorily defined and measured and, in particular, that the circumference and area of a circle of radius r are respectively $2\pi r$ and πr^2.

An alternative measure of angle may be defined as follows. Figure 6.1 shows a circle of radius r, centre O. The magnitude of the angle $\angle AOP$ may be defined as the ratio of the arc-length, s, of AP to the radius, r. In the particular case in which $s = r$, the angle $\angle AOP$ is called a *radian*. Thus, an arc-length of $2r$ subtends an angle of 2 radians at the centre of the circle. (We may write this '$\angle AOP = 2\,\text{rad}$', or, since a ratio of two lengths is a pure number, simply '$\angle AOP = 2$' provided no confusion is likely to arise.)

Fig. 6.1

*$Ex.$ 1. Show that a right-angle is $\frac{1}{2}\pi$ rad. Convert 180° to radians and use your result to express in radians the following angles: 30°, 60°, 45°, 75°, 135°, 225°, 330°.

*$Ex.$ 2. Express in degrees the following angles: $\frac{1}{4}\pi$ rad, $\frac{5}{6}\pi$ rad, $\frac{2}{3}\pi$ rad, $\frac{5}{9}\pi$ rad, $\frac{7}{12}\pi$ rad, $\frac{1}{5}\pi$ rad, $\frac{4}{15}\pi$ rad.

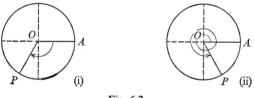

Fig. 6.2

We shall adopt the usual convention that angles are measured as *positive in the anticlockwise sense*, the sense being denoted, when necessary, by an arrow. Figure 6.2(i) shows an angle of $-\frac{2}{3}\pi$, Figure 6.2(ii) an angle of $\frac{11}{3}\pi$, both measured from OA.

One advantage of measuring angles in radians is that the expressions for arc-lengths and the area of a sector take on a particularly simple form. Indeed, if in Figure 6.1 $\angle AOP = \theta$ rad, we have

$$s = r\theta;$$

also, assuming that the area of a sector is proportional to the angle subtended at the centre,

$$\text{area of sector } AOP = \pi r^2(\theta/2\pi)$$
$$= \tfrac{1}{2}r^2\theta.$$

(A further advantage of using radians will become apparent later when the reader learns to differentiate the trigonometric functions: if the angles are measured in radians, the derivatives of these functions take on a particularly simple form.)

Exercise 6(a)

1. Express in radians the following angles: 20°, 45°, 105°, 150°, 210°, 270°, 315°, 330°, 450°, 570°.

2. Express in degrees the following angles: $\tfrac{1}{6}\pi$ rad, $\tfrac{1}{3}\pi$ rad, $\tfrac{3}{4}\pi$ rad, $\tfrac{5}{12}\pi$ rad, $\tfrac{7}{6}\pi$ rad, $\tfrac{9}{2}\pi$ rad, $\tfrac{3}{10}\pi$ rad, 5π rad, $\tfrac{5}{18}\pi$ rad, $\tfrac{7}{20}\pi$ rad.

3. Express in radians, to 3 D.P.: 25° 30′, 71° 15′, 146° 12′.

4. Express in degrees, to 1 D.P.: 0·48 rad, 0·65 rad, 2·18 rad.

5. Taking $\pi = 3\cdot141593$, show that 1 rad $\approx$ 57·296°. (Use a calculating machine if you have one available.)

6. If the earth is taken to be a sphere of radius 3960 miles, find the length in feet of arc which subtends an angle of 1 minute at the centre of the earth.

7. A circle has radius 10 cm. Calculate the length of the smaller arc cut off by a chord of length 16 cm.

8. The chord PQ subtends an angle $\tfrac{1}{3}\pi$ at the centre, O, of a circle of radius 10 cm. Find:
  (i) the length of arc PQ;
  (ii) the area of the triangle OPQ;
  (iii) the area of the minor segment cut off by PQ.

9. A chord of a circle of radius r cm subtends an angle of 2θ *degrees* at its centre. Obtain expressions for the length of the chord and the length of the minor arc which it cuts off.
  If the arc has length 3 cm and the chord 2·7 cm, prove that

$$\pi\theta = 200 \sin \theta. \qquad \text{(O \& C 'O')}$$

10. The section of a tunnel consists of the major segment of a circle standing on a chord of length 2 m. If the greatest height of the tunnel is 3 m, calculate the radius of the circle.
  Prove that the angle subtended by the chord at the centre is approximately 1·287 rad, and hence find the area of the cross-section of the tunnel, correct to the nearest square metre. (O & C 'O' adapted)

11. Two circles of radii 6 cm and 8 cm respectively have their centres 10 cm apart. Calculate the length of their common chord, and the area common to the two circles.   (O & C 'O')

12. The vertex of a hollow cone is A and BC is a diameter of the base; $BC = 6$ cm and $AB = AC = 5$ cm. The cone is unrolled into a sector of a circle. Find :
   (i)   the angle of the sector;
   (ii)   the area of the curved surface of the cone;
   (iii)   the shortest distance on the surface of the cone from C to the mid-point of AB.   (O & C 'O')

2. THE TRIGONOMETRIC FUNCTIONS

Figure 6.3 shows a circle of unit radius; $\mathbf{OA} = \mathbf{i}$, $\mathbf{OB} = \mathbf{j}$ (where as usual, $\mathbf{i}$ and $\mathbf{j}$ are perpendicular). The angle θ, measured in radians from OA as initial line, defines a unique unit vector $\mathbf{OP}$. Now $\mathbf{OP}$ may be expressed uniquely in terms of the unit vectors $\mathbf{i}$, $\mathbf{j}$ (see Chapter 2)

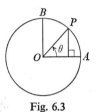

$$\mathbf{OP} = x\mathbf{i} + y\mathbf{j}.$$

Fig. 6.3

Thus, given any $\theta \in R$, we determine uniquely two numbers $x \in R$, $y \in R$, which may be taken as the images of two functions $R \to R$, called respectively the *cosine* and *sine* functions. We write $x = \cos \theta$, and $y = \sin \theta$; the reader will have no difficulty in appreciating that our definitions lead to the familiar sine and cosine of acute angles if $0 \leqslant \theta \leqslant \frac{1}{2}\pi$. We have to be a little careful if we measure θ in degrees: strictly speaking, the sine and cosine functions would then be different functions $R \to R$. Of course, given an angle, the image of the appropriate sine function in either case would be the same number: for example with angles measured in radians, $\sin \frac{1}{6}\pi = 0\cdot 5$; with angles measured in degrees, $\sin 30° = 0\cdot 5$. We adopt the same name for the two functions, as not to do so would lead to confusion; if extra clarity is required, we may always write '$\sin \theta$ rad' or '$\sin \theta°$'. (In this chapter, '$\sin \theta$' will mean '$\sin \theta$ rad' and similarly for the other trigonometric functions; if we wish to measure θ in degrees, we write '$\sin \theta°$'.)

Since $-1 \leqslant x \leqslant 1$ and $-1 \leqslant y \leqslant 1$, the range of both the sine and cosine functions is the set $\{x \in R: -1 \leqslant x \leqslant 1\}$.

The reader will no doubt suspect that a tangent function will now be defined by $\tan \theta = y/x$. However, we must be careful here, for y/x is not defined if $x = 0$; this occurs whenever θ is an odd number of right-angles, or, to be more precise, when $\theta = (2k+1)\frac{1}{2}\pi$, where k is any integer. We must therefore restrict our domain to $R \cap A'$, where

$$A = \{\theta \in R, k \in Z: \theta = (2k+1)\tfrac{1}{2}\pi\}.$$

89

With this restriction, the *tangent* function $R \cap A' \to R$ is defined by $\tan \theta = y/x$.

Similarly, if $B = \{\theta \in R, k \in Z : \theta = k\pi\}$, the *cotangent* function

$$R \cap B' \to R \quad \text{is defined by} \quad \cot \theta = x/y.$$

If the reader finds the notation of the previous two paragraphs difficult to digest, he may simply remember that

(i) $\tan \theta = y/x$ provided $x \neq 0$; $\tan \theta$ is undefined if $x = 0$.

(ii) $\cot \theta = x/y$, provided $y \neq 0$; $\cot \theta$ is undefined if $y = 0$.

In similar fashion, the *secant* and *cosecant* functions are defined by

(iii) $\sec \theta = 1/x$, provided $x \neq 0$; $\sec \theta$ is undefined if $x = 0$.

(iv) $\operatorname{cosec} \theta = 1/y$, provided $y \neq 0$; $\operatorname{cosec} \theta$ is undefined if $y = 0$.

In terms of the sets A and B defined above, the domain of the secant function is $R \cap A'$; the domain of the cosecant function is $R \cap B'$.

Ex. 3. Prove that the range of both the tangent and cotangent function is the set R.

Ex. 4. Prove that the range of the secant and cosecant function is the complement of the set $\{x \in R : -1 < x < 1\}$.

The following table of the images of the sine, cosine and tangent functions for some commonly occurring angles is worth memorizing:

	0	$\pi/6$	$\pi/4$	$\pi/3$	$\pi/2$
sin	0	1/2	$1/\sqrt{2}$	$\sqrt{3}/2$	1
cos	1	$\sqrt{3}/2$	$1/\sqrt{2}$	1/2	0
tan	0	$1/\sqrt{3}$	1	$\sqrt{3}$	Undefined

The corresponding images of the secant, cosecant and cotangent functions may be obtained from the following important identities, which are valid for all angles θ at which the functions are defined:

$$\cot \theta \equiv \frac{\cos \theta}{\sin \theta} \equiv \frac{1}{\tan \theta}; \quad \sec \theta \equiv \frac{1}{\cos \theta}; \quad \operatorname{cosec} \theta \equiv \frac{1}{\sin \theta}.$$

(Proofs follow immediately from the definitions. The sign $\equiv$ emphasizes that these are *identities*, true for *all* values of θ for which the functions are defined.)

Example 1. Find the value of:

(i) $\sin \frac{5}{6}\pi$; (ii) $\cos \frac{2}{3}\pi$; (iii) $\tan \frac{1}{4}\pi$; (iv) $\operatorname{cosec} \frac{9}{4}\pi$; (v) $\sec(-\frac{3}{4}\pi)$; (vi) $\cot(-\frac{7}{6}\pi)$.

In each case we find:

(a) the correct sign to attach (by considering signs of x and y),

(b) the acute angle which defines the same numerical values of x and y.

(i) For $\theta = \frac{5}{6}\pi$, $y > 0$ and so $\sin \frac{5}{6}\pi > 0$.

Also the acute angle which defines the same numerical values of x and y is $\frac{1}{6}\pi$ (see Figure 6.4(i)).

Thus, $\sin \frac{5}{6}\pi = +\sin \frac{1}{6}\pi = +\frac{1}{2}$.

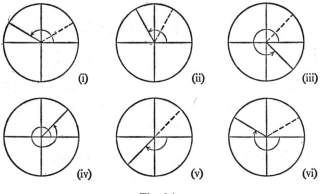

(i)   (ii)   (iii)

(iv)   (v)   (vi)

Fig. 6.4

(ii) $\theta = \frac{2}{3}\pi$, $x < 0$ and the corresponding acute angle is $\frac{1}{3}\pi$ (Figure 6.4 (ii)).

Thus, $\cos \frac{2}{3}\pi = -\cos \frac{1}{3}\pi = -\frac{1}{2}$.

(iii) For $\theta = \frac{7}{4}\pi$, $x > 0$, $y < 0$ and the corresponding acute angle is $\frac{1}{4}\pi$ (Figure 6.4 (iii)).

Thus, $\tan \frac{7}{4}\pi = -\tan \frac{1}{4}\pi = -1$.

(iv) For $\theta = \frac{9}{4}\pi$, $y > 0$ and the corresponding acute angle is $\frac{1}{4}\pi$ (Figure 6.4(iv)).

Thus, $\operatorname{cosec} \frac{9}{4}\pi = +\operatorname{cosec} \frac{1}{4}\pi = +\sqrt{2}$.

(v) For $\theta = -\frac{3}{4}\pi$, $x < 0$ and the corresponding acute angle is $\frac{1}{4}\pi$ (Figure 6.4(v)).

Thus, $\sec(-\frac{3}{4}\pi) = -\sec \frac{1}{4}\pi = -\sqrt{2}$.

(vi) For $\theta = -\frac{7}{6}\pi$, $x < 0$, $y > 0$ and the corresponding acute angle is $\frac{1}{6}\pi$ (Figure 6.4(vi)).

Thus, $\cot(-\frac{7}{6}\pi) = -\cot \frac{1}{6}\pi = -\sqrt{3}$.

Figure 6.5 gives a useful method for seeing which sign to attach according to the quadrant in which the angle falls. A stands for all, S for sine, T for tangent and C for cosine. In the A quadrant, all trigonometric ratios are positive; in the S quadrant, only

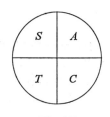

Fig. 6.5

sines (and cosecants) are positive; in the T quadrant, only tangents (and cotangents) are positive; in the C quadrant, only cosines (and secants) are positive. Notice, as an aid to remembering the diagram, that the letters (read anticlockwise) spell the word 'CAST'.

Example 2. Solve for θ the equation

$$2 \sin^2 \theta + \sin \theta - 1 = 0$$

giving all solutions in the interval $0 \leqslant \theta \leqslant 2\pi$.

The left-hand-side factorizes: $(2 \sin \theta - 1)(\sin \theta + 1) = 0$ and so is satisfied by values of θ such that either

(i) $\sin \theta = +\frac{1}{2}$, or (ii) $\sin \theta = -1$.

The relevant solutions of (i) are $\theta = \frac{1}{6}\pi$, $\theta = \frac{5}{6}\pi$; and of (ii) $\theta = \frac{3}{2}\pi$. Thus, the required set of solutions of the given equation is

$$\{\tfrac{1}{6}\pi, \ \tfrac{5}{6}\pi, \ \tfrac{3}{2}\pi\}.$$

Since **OP** is a unit vector, $x^2 + y^2 = 1$ for all θ. Thus,

$$\sin^2 \theta + \cos^2 \theta \equiv 1, \quad \text{for all } \theta.$$

Division by $\cos^2 \theta$ gives

$$1 + \tan^2 \theta \equiv \sec^2 \theta, \quad \text{for all } \theta \neq (2k+1)\,\pi/2.$$

Division by $\sin^2 \theta$ gives

$$1 + \cot^2 \theta \equiv \operatorname{cosec}^2 \theta, \quad \text{for all } \theta \neq k\pi.$$

These three identities are true for all values of θ, provided the functions mentioned are defined.

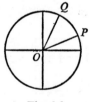

Fig. 6.6

Suppose **OP** is the unit vector defined by the angle θ and **OQ** the unit vector defined by the angle $\frac{1}{2}\pi - \theta$ (see Figure 6.6). If **OP** $= x\mathbf{i} + y\mathbf{j}$, then **OQ** $= y\mathbf{i} + x\mathbf{j}$. It follows that

$$\sin(\tfrac{1}{2}\pi - \theta) \equiv \cos \theta, \quad \cos(\tfrac{1}{2}\pi - \theta) \equiv \sin \theta, \quad \tan(\tfrac{1}{2}\pi - \theta) \equiv \cot \theta,$$

$$\operatorname{cosec}(\tfrac{1}{2}\pi - \theta) \equiv \sec \theta, \quad \sec(\tfrac{1}{2}\pi - \theta) \equiv \operatorname{cosec} \theta, \quad \cot(\tfrac{1}{2}\pi - \theta) \equiv \tan \theta$$

(provided, of course, that θ lies in domains for which both sides are defined).

*Ex. 5. Find similar simplifications for the values of the trigonometric functions for the angles
  (i) $\frac{1}{2}\pi+\theta$; (ii) $\pi-\theta$; (iii) $\pi+\theta$.
N.B. Be careful about the signs!

Example 3. Solve the equation $\sin\theta+\cos 2\theta = 0$, *giving all values of* θ *between* 0 *and* 2π.
  Since $\cos(\frac{1}{2}\pi+\theta) = -\sin\theta$, the equation may be rewritten

$$\cos 2\theta = \cos(\tfrac{1}{2}\pi+\theta).$$

Now
  $\cos\theta = \cos\phi$ if $\theta = \pm\phi$ or $\theta = 2\pi\pm\phi$ or $\theta = 4\pi\pm\phi$ ....

Thus the original equation is satisfied for values of θ given by

$$2\theta = \pm(\tfrac{1}{2}\pi+\theta); \qquad 2\theta = 2\pi\pm(\tfrac{1}{2}\pi+\theta);$$
$$2\theta = 4\pi\pm(\tfrac{1}{2}\pi+\theta); \quad 2\theta = 6\pi\pm(\tfrac{1}{2}\pi+\theta); \;\dots$$

Trial of these solutions shows that the values of θ lying in the given range are
$$\{\tfrac{1}{2}\pi,\ \tfrac{7}{6}\pi,\ \tfrac{11}{6}\pi\}.$$

Example 4. Prove that the identity

$$\frac{1}{\sin\theta+\cos\theta} \equiv \frac{\tan\theta+\cot\theta}{\sec\theta+\operatorname{cosec}\theta}$$

holds, provided $\theta \neq \frac{1}{2}k\pi$, $\theta \neq n\pi-\frac{1}{4}\pi$.
  The restrictions on θ ensure
  (i) $(\theta \neq \frac{1}{2}k\pi)$ that $\tan\theta$, $\cot\theta$, $\sec\theta$, $\operatorname{cosec}\theta$ are defined;
  (ii) $(\theta \neq n\pi-\frac{1}{4}\pi)$ that $\sin\theta+\cos\theta \neq 0$ and $\sec\theta+\operatorname{cosec}\theta \neq 0$.
With these restrictions

$$\text{R.H.S.} = \left(\frac{\sin\theta}{\cos\theta}+\frac{\cos\theta}{\sin\theta}\right)\Big/\left(\frac{1}{\cos\theta}+\frac{1}{\sin\theta}\right)$$

$$\equiv (\sin^2\theta+\cos^2\theta)/(\sin\theta+\cos\theta)$$

$$\equiv 1/(\sin\theta+\cos\theta)$$

$$= \text{L.H.S.}$$

Example 5. Eliminate θ *between the equation*

$$x = a\cos\theta, \tag{1}$$

$$y = b\sec\theta+c\tan\theta, \tag{2}$$

$$x = a \cos \theta \quad \text{and} \quad y = b \sec \theta + c \tan \theta$$

$$\Rightarrow \quad xy = a \cos \theta \,(b \sec \theta + c \tan \theta),$$

$$\Rightarrow \quad xy = ab + ac \sin \theta$$

$$\Leftrightarrow \quad ac \sin \theta = xy - ab.$$

But $\qquad\qquad\qquad ac \cos \theta = cx.$

Squaring and adding $\qquad a^2 c^2 = c^2 x^2 + (xy - ab)^2.$

Exercise 6(b)

1. Write down the values of $\cos \frac{4}{3}\pi$, $\tan \frac{3}{4}\pi$, $\operatorname{cosec} \frac{5}{6}\pi$, $\cot \frac{2}{3}\pi$, $\sin \frac{7}{4}\pi$, $\sec \frac{5}{3}\pi$, $\cos \frac{3}{2}\pi$, $\tan \frac{7}{6}\pi$, $\operatorname{cosec} (-\frac{3}{4}\pi)$, $\sec (-\frac{5}{6}\pi)$.

2. Write down the values of $\cos 315°$, $\tan 135°$, $\operatorname{cosec} 330°$, $\sin (-135°)$, $\cot (-120°)$, $\sec 240°$, $\sin 480°$, $\sec (-210°)$, $\cot (-60°)$, $\sin 1020°$.

3. Use your tables to find the values of $\sin 215°$, $\cos 128°$, $\tan (-40°)$, $\operatorname{cosec} 161°$, $\sin (-200°)$.

4. Solve the following equations for θ, giving all values lying in the interval $0 \leqslant \theta \leqslant 2\pi$:
(i) $\sin \theta = -\frac{1}{2}$;   (ii) $\tan \theta + 1 = 0$;   (iii) $\sec \theta + 2 = 0$;
(iv) $\cot \theta = \sqrt{3}$;   (v) $4 \sin^2 \theta = 3$;   (vi) $2 \cos (\theta - \frac{1}{4}\pi) + \sqrt{3} = 0$;
(vii) $\sin \theta + \cos \theta = 0$;   (viii) $2 \sin 3\theta = 1$;   (ix) $\sec (\theta + \frac{1}{3}\pi) = 1$;
(x) $3 \sec^2 (\theta + \frac{1}{6}\pi) = 4$; (xi) $\operatorname{cosec}^2 (\theta + \frac{1}{3}\pi) = 1$; (xii) $\tan^2 2\theta = 3$.

5. Solve the following equations for θ, giving all values lying in the interval $-\pi \leqslant \theta \leqslant \pi$:
(i) $2 \sin^2 \theta + \sin \theta = 0$;   (ii) $2 \cos^2 \theta + 3 \sin \theta = 0$;
(iii) $\cos 2\theta = \sin \theta$;   (iv) $2 \tan \theta + \sin \theta = 0$;
(v) $\sin (\frac{1}{4}\pi - \theta) + \cos \theta = 0$;   (vi) $\cos \theta = 2 \cot \theta$;
(vii) $\tan \theta + \cot (\frac{1}{3}\pi - \theta) = 0$;   (viii) $\tan \theta + \cot \theta + \sec \theta = 0$;
(ix) $\cot^2 \theta + \operatorname{cosec} \theta + 1 = 0$;   (x) $\sec 3\theta + \operatorname{cosec} \theta = 0$.

6. Find the maximum and minimum values of:
(i) $3/(2 + \sin \theta)$;   (ii) $(1 + \cos 2\theta)^2$;   (iii) $\sin^2 \theta + 2 \sin \theta + 2$.

7. No tables to be used in this question.
(i) If $\frac{1}{2}\pi < x < \pi$ and $\sin x = \frac{1}{3}$, find $\cos x$ and $\tan x$.
(ii) If $\frac{1}{2}\pi < x < \pi$ and $\tan x = -\frac{1}{2}$, find $\sin x$ and $\cos x$.
(iii) If $\pi < x < \frac{3}{2}\pi$ and $\sec x = -3$, find $\cos x$ and $\tan x$.
(iv) If $\frac{1}{2}\pi < x < \pi$ and $\sin x = \frac{1}{4}$, find $\tan x$ and $\sec x$;
(v) If $\frac{3}{2}\pi < x < 2\pi$ and $\sec x = 4$, find $\operatorname{cosec} x$ and $\cot x$.

8. Prove that, provided $\sin \theta \neq 0$.

$$\frac{1 - \cos \theta}{\sin \theta} \equiv \frac{1}{\operatorname{cosec} \theta + \cot \theta}.$$

94

9. Prove that, provided $\sin \theta \neq 0$, $\cos \theta \neq 0$,

$$\tan \theta + \cot \theta \equiv \sec \theta \operatorname{cosec} \theta.$$

10. Prove that, provided all the values of the functions are defined,

$$\operatorname{cosec}^2 \theta \equiv 1 + \cos \theta \cot \theta \operatorname{cosec} \theta.$$

11. If $\sin \theta = \frac{4}{5}$ find, without using tables, the possible values of $\sec \theta + \operatorname{cosec} \theta$.

12. If $\tan = \frac{1}{3}$ find, without using tables, the possible values of $2 \cos \theta + \cot \theta$.

13. Use your tables to find all values of θ, lying in the interval $0° \leqslant \theta° \leqslant 360°$, which satisfy the following equations:

(i) $2 \sec^2 \theta° = 5 - \tan \theta°$;   (ii) $3 \cos^2 \theta° = 7 \cos \theta° - 2$;

(iii) $2 \sin^2 \theta° - \sin \theta° \cos \theta° - \cos^2 \theta° = 0$;

(iv) $\cot^2 \theta° = \operatorname{cosec} \theta°$;   (v) $16 \tan^2 \theta° = 9$;

(vi) $3 \sec^2 \theta° = 2 \operatorname{cosec} \theta°$;   (vii) $\tan \theta° = 2(\sec \theta° + \cos \theta°)$;

(viii) $\sec^2 \theta° = 1 + 2 \tan \theta°$.

14. Eliminate θ between the following pairs of equations:

(i) $x = 2 \cos \theta$, $y = 3(1 + \sin \theta)$;

(ii) $x = \cos \theta - \sin \theta$, $y = \cos \theta + \sin \theta$;

(iii) $x = 2 \cos \theta - \sin \theta$, $y = \cos \theta + \sin \theta$;

(iv) $x = 3 \tan \theta$, $y = 4 \sin \theta$;

(v) $x = \operatorname{cosec} \theta - 1$, $y = \cos \theta + 1$.

15. A particle oscillates along the x axis in such a manner that its coordinates at time t seconds after the start of the motion are $(\sin (\omega t + \epsilon), 0)$.

(i)   Where is the particle at the start of the motion?

(ii) Between what two points does the particle oscillate?

(iii) How long does the particle take to move from one extreme point to the other?

16. If a particle is projected with a velocity $V \cos \alpha \mathbf{i} + V \sin \alpha \mathbf{j}$ under gravity then its position vector at time t is given by

$$\mathbf{r} = (Vt \cos \alpha) \, \mathbf{i} + (Vt \sin \alpha - \tfrac{1}{2} gt^2) \mathbf{j}.$$

If $\mathbf{r}$ is written in the form $\mathbf{r} = x\mathbf{i} + y\mathbf{j},$

prove that $y = x \tan \alpha - \dfrac{1}{2} \left(\dfrac{gx^2}{V^2} \right) \sec^2 \alpha.$

Deduce that, if x, y, g, V are known, there are in general two values of α in the interval $0 \leqslant \alpha \leqslant \frac{1}{2}\pi$ which satisfy this equation. Under what circumstances is there only one such angle?

17. Prove that the equation $x^2 + y^2 + z^2 = a^2$

represents the surface of a sphere.

Show that the point P whose position vector is

$$\mathbf{r} = a \cos \theta \cos \phi \mathbf{i} + a \sin \theta \cos \phi \mathbf{j} + a \sin \phi \mathbf{k}$$

lies on the sphere, for all values of θ and ϕ.

Is the following converse result true? Values of θ and ϕ can be found such that any point on the surface has a position vector of the form

$$\mathbf{r} = a\cos\theta\cos\phi\mathbf{i} + a\sin\theta\cos\phi\mathbf{j} + a\sin\phi\mathbf{k}.$$

18. Discuss the possibility of solving the following equations for θ:
  (i) $\sin\theta = a + 1/a$;   (ii) $2ab\cos\theta = a^2 + b^2$;
  (iii) $\cos^2\theta + 4 = \sin\theta + 4\cos\theta$.

19. What are the maximum and minimum values of the expression $4/(2+\sin x)$? Without attempting to solve the equations exactly, state how many values of x in the range $0 < x < 2\pi$ satisfy
  (i) the equation $\cos x(2+\sin x) = 4$;
  (ii) the equation $\tan x(2+\sin x) = 4$.

3. THE GRAPHS OF THE TRIGONOMETRIC FUNCTIONS

Since revolutions through angles 2π, 4π, ... about O brings the unit vector **OP** into coincidence with its original position, it follows that, for any integer k and any of the six trigonometric functions $f: R \to R$

$$f(2k\pi + x) = f(x).$$

Thus, a trigonometric function is a periodic function, period 2π (see Exercise $5(a)$, Question 16).

Figure 6.7 shows the graphs of the sine function (continuous line) and cosine function (dotted line), for values of the domain $-2\pi \leqslant x \leqslant 2\pi$.

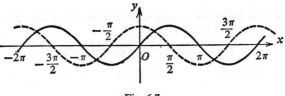

Fig. 6.7

Ex. 6. How do the graphs of $\sin x$ and $\cos x$ illustrate the identities

$$\sin(\tfrac{1}{2}\pi - x) \equiv \cos x, \quad \sin(\tfrac{1}{2}\pi + x) \equiv \cos x,$$
$$\sin(\tfrac{3}{2}\pi - x) \equiv -\cos x, \quad \sin(\tfrac{3}{2}\pi + x) \equiv -\cos x?$$

Ex. 7. Sketch roughly the graphs of $2\sin x$, $\sin 2x$, $|\sin x|$.

Figure 6.8 shows the graph of the tangent function (continuous line) and cotangent function (dotted line) for values of the domain $-2\pi < x < 2\pi$. Recall that the tangent function is undefined at values of x which are odd multiples of $\tfrac{1}{2}\pi$ but, by taking x sufficiently close to such

96

values, we make $|\tan x|$ arbitrarily large. A similar remark holds for the cotangent function at values of x which are even multiples of $\frac{1}{2}\pi$. (A line such as $x = \frac{1}{2}\pi$ is called an asymptote for the curve $y = \tan x$.)

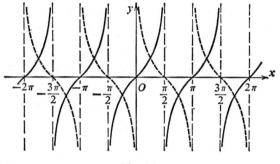

Fig. 6.8

Ex. 8. How does Figure 6.8 illustrate the identities $\tan\left(\frac{1}{2}\pi - x\right) \equiv \cot x$, $\tan\left(\frac{1}{2}\pi + x\right) \equiv -\cot x$, $\tan\left(\frac{3}{2}\pi - x\right) = \cot x$, $\tan\left(\frac{3}{2}\pi + x\right) \equiv -\cot x$?

Ex. 9. Sketch roughly the graphs of $\tan 3x$ and $|\tan x|$.

Figure 6.9 shows the secant function (continuous line) and cosecant function (dotted line).

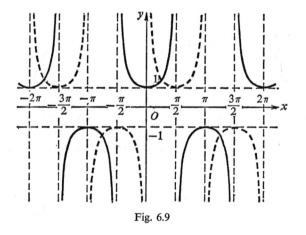

Fig. 6.9

Ex. 10. How does Figure 6.9 illustrate the identities

$$\sec\left(\tfrac{1}{2}\pi - x\right) \equiv \operatorname{cosec} x, \quad \sec\left(\tfrac{1}{2}\pi + x\right) \equiv -\operatorname{cosec} x,$$
$$\sec\left(\tfrac{3}{2}\pi - x\right) \equiv -\operatorname{cosec} x, \quad \sec\left(\tfrac{3}{2}\pi + x\right) \equiv \operatorname{cosec} x?$$

Ex. 11. Sketch roughly the graphs of $\sec 2x$ and $|\operatorname{cosec} x|$.

4. INVERSE TRIGONOMETRIC FUNCTIONS

The sine function has no inverse, because if we take any number z in the range $-1 \leqslant z \leqslant 1$, we can find any number of values x such that $\sin x = z$. However, if we *restrict the domain of the sine function to*

$$-\tfrac{1}{2}\pi \leqslant x \leqslant \tfrac{1}{2}\pi \quad \text{(the range remaining } -1 \leqslant y \leqslant 1\text{)}$$

then the inverse function does exist, for the mapping becomes one to one. The inverse function so defined is called the *arcsine* function. Thus, arc-sine is a function from

$$\{x \in R: -1 \leqslant x \leqslant 1\} \quad \text{to} \quad \{y \in R: -\tfrac{1}{2}\pi \leqslant y \leqslant \tfrac{1}{2}\pi\}$$

with the property that $\arcsin x = y$ if $\sin y = x$, and conversely. (Notice that we retain x as an element of the domain.) Another notation for $\arcsin x$ is $\sin^{-1} x$; the slight drawback to this notation is that it suggests that the unrestricted sine function has an inverse, which is, of course, false.

The graph of the arcsine function may be obtained directly from the graph of the sine function for the restricted domain $-\tfrac{1}{2}\pi \leqslant x \leqslant \tfrac{1}{2}\pi$ by interchanging the x and y axes. If we retain x as an element of the domain, so that $y = \arcsin x$, the graph is as shown in Figure 6.10.

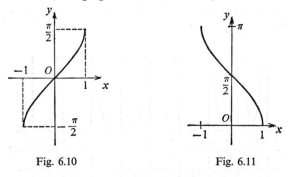

Fig. 6.10   Fig. 6.11

The *arccosine* function may be similarly defined, with domain

$$\{x \in R: -1 \leqslant x \leqslant 1\} \quad \text{and range} \quad \{0 \leqslant y \leqslant \pi\}.$$

If $y = \arccos x$, then $\cos y = x$. The graph is shown in Figure 6.11.

Again, the *arctangent* may be defined, with domain R and range $\{-\tfrac{1}{2}\pi < y < \tfrac{1}{2}\pi\}$ (notice the strict inequality). If $y = \arctan x$, then $\tan y = x$. The graph is shown in Figure 6.12.

Ex. 12. Suggest appropriate domains and ranges for arccotangent, arcsecant and arccosecant.

Ex. 13. Write down the values of $\arcsin \tfrac{1}{2}$, $\arccos 1/\sqrt{2}$ and $\arctan(-1)$.

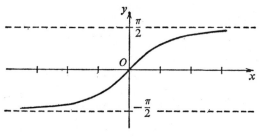

Fig. 6.12

Example 6. Simplify cos (arcsin x).

Let arcsin $x = y$; then $-\frac{1}{2}\pi \leqslant y \leqslant \frac{1}{2}\pi$ and sin $y = x$

$$\cos^2 y = 1 - \sin^2 y = 1 - x^2.$$

Thus cos $y = \pm \sqrt{(1-x^2)}$; but $-\frac{1}{2}\pi \leqslant y \leqslant \frac{1}{2}\pi$ and so cos $y > 0$; it follows that cos (arcsin x) $= \sqrt{(1-x^2)}$.

Exercise 6(c)

1. Show that the function f defined by

$$f(x) = \cos x + \sin x$$

is periodic and sketch its graph.

2. Draw the graph of the function f defined by

$$f(x) = \sin x + \sin 2x$$

for values of x in the interval $0 \leqslant x \leqslant 2\pi$. Solve the equation

$$\sin x + \sin 2x = 0,$$

giving values of x for which $0 \leqslant x \leqslant 2\pi$.

3. Draw the graph of $y = \tan x°$, from $x = -20$ to $x = 70$, plotting points at intervals of $10°$.

Using the same axes and intervals, draw also the graph of

$$y = \cos (x+10)° \quad \text{from} \quad x = 20 \quad \text{to} \quad x = 50.$$

Read from your graph the value of x when tan $x° = \cos (x+10)°$.

(O & C 'O')

4. It is required to find an angle x such that

$$\sin x = \tfrac{4}{5}x$$

where x is measured in radians.

Draw on the same diagram the graphs of $y = \sin x$ and $y = \frac{4}{5}x$ for values of x from 0 to $\frac{1}{2}\pi$, taking 1 in. (or 2 cm) to represent $\frac{1}{12}\pi$ on the scale for x, and 0·2 on the scale for y.

99

Estimate from your graphs the required angle, giving your answer in degrees to the nearest degree. (O & C 'O')

5. Solve graphically the equation $\tan 2x° = 2 \cot x°$, giving all solutions x such that $0° < x° < 180°$.

6. Draw the graph of $y = 1 - 2 \sin 60x°$ for values of x from 0 to 6, using 2 cm as unit on both axes. By drawing a suitable straight line on the same diagram, read the solutions, within the given range of values of x, of the equation

$$2(1 - 2 \sin 60x°) = x. \qquad \text{(O & C 'O')}$$

7. Solve graphically the equation

$$\sin x = \cos 2x + 1$$

for values of x for which $0 < x < \pi$.

8. Using the same axes sketch the graphs of: (i) $\sin x$, (ii) $2 \sin x$, (iii) $1 + 2 \sin x$.

9. Using the same axes, sketch the graphs of (i) $\sin x$, (ii) $-\sin x$, (iii) $2 - \sin x$.

10. Sketch the graph of $2(1 - \cos x)$.

11. Sketch the graph of $1 - \tan x$.

12. Sketch the graph of $1 + |\sin x|$.

13. Sketch the graph of $\sin (x + \frac{1}{4}\pi)$.

14. Sketch the graph of $1 + 2 \cos (x - \frac{1}{4}\pi)$.

15. Find the values of:
(i) $\sin (\arccos \frac{1}{2})$;
(ii) $\cos (\arcsin -\frac{1}{2})$;
(iii) $\tan (\text{arccot } \sqrt{3})$;
(iv) $\sin (\arctan -1)$;
(v) $\cos (\text{arccot } -1/\sqrt{3})$;
(vi) $\sec (\arccos \frac{1}{3})$;
(vii) $\text{cosec} (\arcsin \frac{1}{4})$;
(viii) $\cot (\arcsin -\frac{1}{2}\sqrt{3})$.

16. Simplify the expressions (i) $\tan (\arcsin x)$; (ii) $\sin (\arctan x)$.

17. Sove for x the equation $\tan (\text{arccot } x) = 2 \sin (\arccos x)$.

18. Simplify the expression $\sec \{\arccos [\tan (\text{arccot } x)]\}$.
What restriction must be placed upon the value of x?

19. If $\arcsin x = \pi - \arccos y$, find a relation between x and y.

20. Prove that:
(i) $\arcsin x + \arccos x = \frac{1}{2}\pi$;
(ii) $\arcsin [\cos (\arcsin x)] + \arccos [\sin (\arccos x)] = \frac{1}{2}\pi$.

(O & C modified)

Miscellaneous Exercise 6

1. A chord PQ of a circle of radius r subtends an angle 2θ rad at the centre of the circle and $2\theta < \pi$. Find an expression for the area of the smaller of the two portions into which PQ divides the circle.

If this area is a fraction $1/2\pi$ of the area of the circle, prove that $\sin 2\theta = 2\theta - 1$. Obtain graphically an approximate solution in radians of this equation.

(O & C 'O')

2. If a circle of radius a is drawn with its centre on the circumference of another circle of radius a, find the area common to both circles.

3. Find the maximum and minimum values of the expression

$$\sin^2 \theta + 6 \sin \theta + 4.$$

4. Solve the equation

$$12 \cos^2 \theta = 6 + \sin \theta$$

giving all values of θ, in radians, lying between 0 and 2π.

5. A globe representing the earth consists of a sphere of radius 10 cm. Find the length of the circumference of the small circle representing the 30° parallel of latitude.

Two points A, B on the 30° parallel of latitude differ in longitude by 90°. Calculate:
(i) the length of the straight line joining A and B;
(ii) the angle subtended by AB at the centre of the globe;
(iii) the great circle distance between A and B, in cm, correct to 3 s.f.

(O & C 'O')

6. Show, by sketching the appropriate graphs, that the equation

$$x + \cos x = 1$$

has only one root. What is this root?

7. Prove that the identity

$$\sin^2 x \cos^2 y - \cos^2 x \sin^2 y \equiv \sin^2 x - \sin^2 y$$

is true for all values of x, y. Is the identity

$$\frac{\sin^2 x \cos^2 y - \cos^2 x \sin^2 y}{\sin^2 x - \sin^2 y} \equiv 1$$

also true for all values of x and y? Give reasons for your answer.

8. Solve the simultaneous equations

$$\sin (x+y) = \tfrac{1}{2}\sqrt{3},$$
$$\cos (2x-y) = -\tfrac{1}{2}\sqrt{2},$$

giving all pairs of values of x, y, lying between 0 and π.

9. Eliminate θ between the two equations

$$x = \tan \theta - \sin \theta,$$
$$y = \tan \theta + \sin \theta.$$

10. Sketch the graphs of $y = x$ and $y = \cos x$ and hence sketch the graph of $y = x + \cos x$.
Sketch the graphs of:
(i) $y = |x + \cos x|$; (ii) $y = |x| + \cos x$; (iii) $y = x + |\cos x|$.

11. Draw an accurate graph of the function $y = \frac{1}{2}\pi \sin x$ between $x = 0$ and $x = \pi$. Draw in the same diagram the lines $y = mx$ for $m = \frac{1}{5}, \frac{2}{5}, \frac{3}{5}, \frac{4}{5}, 1$.

Determine the values of x where these lines cut the graph of $y = \frac{1}{2}\pi \sin x$ giving your answers in the form $k\pi$, where k is correct to two decimal places.

Use the values obtained to draw a separate graph of

$$y = \frac{1}{2}\pi \frac{\sin x}{x} \quad \text{between} \quad x = \frac{1}{2}\pi \quad \text{and} \quad x = \pi.$$

12. Show by means of a rough graph that the equation $\cos x = x/2n\pi$ has $2n+1$ positive roots when n is a positive integer. Show also that, if r is a positive integer less than n, the root nearest to $2r\pi$ is $2r\pi + \alpha$ where α is the smallest positive root of the equation

$$\cos x = \frac{r}{n} + \frac{x}{2n\pi}.$$

Draw a careful graph of $y = \cos x$ for $-\frac{1}{2}\pi < x < \frac{1}{2}\pi$ and from it find the five positive roots of the equation

$$4\pi \cos x = x.$$

Give your answers in the form $k\pi$, where k is correct to two decimal places.

(O & C)

13. Show that $\theta = 2n\pi + \alpha$ and $\theta = (2n+1)\pi - \alpha$, where n is an integer, both satisfy the equation $\sin\theta = \sin\alpha$. Prove, furthermore, that any solution of the equation must have one or other of these forms.

$\theta = 2n\pi + \alpha$ or $\theta = (2n+1)\pi - \alpha$ is called the *general solution* of the equation $\sin\theta = \sin\alpha$. Find forms for the general solution of

$$\cos\theta = \cos\alpha \quad \text{and} \quad \tan\theta = \tan\alpha.$$

14. Find the general solutions of the equations

(i) $\tan x = \cot(x + \frac{1}{6}\pi)$; (ii) $2\cos^2 x - \cos x - 1 = 0$.

15. AB is a chord of a given circle, centre O and radius a, subtending an angle θ at 0 $(0 < \pi)$. Prove (i) that the area of the triangle OAB is $\frac{1}{2}a^2 \sin\theta$, and (ii) that the area of the minor segment of the circle of which AB is the chord is $\frac{1}{2}a^2(\theta - \sin\theta)$.

Prove also that the area of the part of the circumcircle of the triangle AOB lying outside the given circle is

$$\frac{1}{2}a^2 \left(\frac{\sin\theta - \theta\cos\theta}{1 + \cos\theta} \right).$$

(O & C)

16. In a circle centre O, two radii OP, OQ contain an angle θ radians $(\theta < \pi)$. If the area of the sector OPQ is A and the length of the chord PQ is $2c$ show that $1 - \cos\theta = c^2\theta/A$. Draw on the same diagram on squared paper the graphs of the functions $y = 1 - \cos\theta$ and $y = c^2\theta/A$ in the particular case where

$$A = \pi \text{ cm}^2, \quad c = 1\cdot3 \text{ cm}$$

for values of θ between 0 and π. (Take 1 cm to represent $\frac{1}{10}\pi$ on the x axis and 4 cm to represent one unit on the y axis.) Read off from your graphs the value of θ between 0 and π which satisfies the equation $1 - \cos\theta = c^2\theta/A$ in this particular case. Use your value of θ to find the radius of the circle in this case.

(Cambridge)

17. The function $f: R^+ \to R$ is defined by $f(x) = x \sin 1/x$. Sketch the graph of the function.

7. *Probability in finite outcome spaces*

1. ARRANGEMENTS AND SELECTIONS: COUNTING LARGE NUMBERS

Before discussing the question of probability, we shall introduce a few techniques whereby the procedure for counting up large numbers may be made more efficient. Our reason for doing so is that, in probability, we are frequently faced with the problem of deciding in how many ways an event can occur; since the numbers involved might be large, it is desirable to arrive at them by the simplest method available.

Consider first the following problem: *in how many ways may the four aces from a pack of cards be arranged in a row on a table?* By direct counting, it is not difficult to arrive at the correct answer, which is twenty-four. However, it is simpler to argue thus: consider four spaces on the table; the first space may be filled in any one of four ways: for each of these four ways, the next space may be filled in three ways and so on. The total number of ways is thus $4 \times 3 \times 2 \times 1 = 24$.

The result of multiplying together all the integers from 1 to n is written $n!$ (read '*factorial n*'). Thus, the number of ways of arranging the four aces may be written $4!$.

Ex. 1. Verify that $2! = 2$, $3! = 6$, $4! = 24$. Write down the values of $5!$, $6!$, $7!$.

The result above may be generalized in an obvious way: the number of ways of arranging n unlike objects in a row is $n!$.

Now suppose we alter our question: *how many different rows of four cards may be made, given a standard pack of fifty-two cards?* Direct counting is now out of the question—it would take far too long. But an identical argument to that employed above shows us that the number of ways is $52 \times 51 \times 50 \times 49 = 6497400$. We may write this in the alternative form $\dfrac{52!}{48!}$.

Again, our argument may be generalized in an obvious way: the number of ways of arranging r objects chosen from n unlike objects is

$$n \times (n-1) \times (n-2) \times \ldots \times (n-r+1) = \frac{n!}{(n-r)!}.$$

This is often referred to as the number of *permutations of n unlike objects r at a time* and is written $_nP_r$. Thus

$$_nP_r = \frac{n!}{(n-r)!}.$$

(Note that 0! is defined to have the value 1 and so this formula remains true when $r = n$.)

Ex. 2. Evaluate $_4P_2$, $_3P_3$, $_6P_6$.

Ex. 3. How many different 'words' can be made using the five letters of the word 'AFTER'? How many of these begin with A and end with R?

We may modify our question again and ask: '*how many different hands of four cards may be dealt from a standard pack?*' The difference here is that we are not concerned with the order in which the cards are dealt: we only want to know the number of *selections* (sometimes called *combinations*) of four cards that can be made from fifty-two cards. Suppose for the moment that this number is N. Then each of these N different hands may be rearranged in 4! = 24 ways. There are then $24N$ different arrangements of four cards. But we already know that the number of different arrangements is $52 \times 51 \times 50 \times 49$. Thus

$$N = \frac{52 \times 51 \times 50 \times 49}{24} = 270725.$$

Once more, our argument may be generalized: since there are $_nP_r$ possible arrangements of n objects taken r at a time, the number of selections, or combinations, of n unlike objects, taken r at a time, is

$$\frac{_nP_r}{r!} = \frac{n!}{r!(n-r)!}.$$

The number of combinations of n unlike objects, taken r at a time, is written either as $_nC_r$ or $\binom{n}{r}$. The latter notation is used almost universally now, although the former has its merits: we can read $_nC_r$ as 'n choose r', reminding us that we are choosing, or selecting, rather than arranging. We shall retain $_nC_r$ in this chapter, but revert to $\binom{n}{r}$ in later chapters, when the need arises.

$$\binom{n}{r} = {_nC_r} = \frac{n!}{r!(n-r)!}.$$

(Notice that again, since 0! has been defined as 1, $_nC_n = 1$ by the formula, which accords with the commonsense result that there is just one way of selecting n objects from n.)

104

Ex. 4. Evaluate $_5C_2$, $_6C_3$.

*Ex. 5. Evaluate $_nC_0$ by the formula, and interpret your result.

*Ex. 6. Evaluate $_nC_r$ and $_nC_{n-r}$ by the formula and interpret your result.

Ex. 7. In how many ways may a cricket team of eleven boys be chosen from four-teen boys available? If three particular boys are certain to be chosen, how many ways are there of completing the team?

Example 1. *A committee of three is to be chosen from four men and three women. If at least one man is to be included, how many possible selections are there?*

First solution. There are three possibilities:

(i) Two women included: number of ways of selecting the women $= _3C_2 = 3$; for each of these choices there are $_4C_1 = 4$ ways of selecting the remaining committee member, who must be a man.

Total (i): $3 \times 4 = 12$.

(ii) One woman included: number of ways of selecting the woman $= _3C_1 = 3$; for each of these choices there are

$$_4C_2 = \frac{4 \times 3}{1 \times 2} = 6$$

ways of selecting the remaining committee members.

Total (ii): $3 \times 6 = 18$.

(iii) No woman included: the committee is selected entirely from men, $_4C_3 = 4$ ways.

Total (iii): 4.

The total of possible committttees is thus

$$12 + 18 + 4 = 34.$$

Second solution. There are

$$_7C_3 = \frac{7 \times 6 \times 5}{1 \times 2 \times 3} = 35$$

possible committees in all. Just one of the committees consists entirely of women, and so $35 - 1 = 34$ contain at least one man.

It is often necessary in probability questions to know in how many ways it is possible to arrange n objects in a row, given that r are alike of one kind, s are alike of a second kind and so on. We start by distinguishing between the like objects by attaching suffixes to them: for example, if we have r letters a, s letters b, ... then we write our n letters as

$$a_1, a_2, a_3, ..., a_r, b_1, b_2, b_3, ..., b_s, ...$$

There are $n!$ ways of arranging these n letters. But, in any one of these arrangements, the letter $a_1, a_2, a_3, ..., a_r$ may be rearranged amongst themselves in $r!$ ways; similarly the letter $b_1, b_2, b_3, ..., b_s$ may be arranged in $s!$ ways and so on. Thus, if we drop the suffixes, the number of distinguishable arrangements becomes

$$\frac{n!}{r!\,s!\,...}.$$

Hence we have the following important rule.

Given n objects, r alike of one kind, s alike of another kind and so on, the number of arrangements of the n objects in a row is

$$\frac{n!}{r!\,s!\,...}.$$

For example, the number of different arrangements of the letters of the word SELECTIONS is

$$\frac{10!}{2!\,2!} = 907\,200.$$

Ex. 8. In how many ways may four letters P and six letters Q be arranged in a row?

We complete this section by mentioning one further technique for counting which is frequently useful in probability: to find the number of ways of arranging n objects, r at a time, if repetitions are allowed. We shall illustrate the method adopted in Example 2.

Example 2. In a simplified football coupon there are ten matches whose results (home win, 1; away win, 2; draw, ×) are to be forecast. In how many ways may the coupon be completed?

The first result may be forecast in three different ways (1, 2, ×); for each of these choices there are three different choices for the second match (1, 2, ×) and so on. The total number of ways of completing the coupon is thus $3^{10} = 59\,049$.

Ex. 9. A multiple choice paper consists of ten questions, to each of which is attached five possible answers, labelled A, B, C, D, E. A candidate selects one of these answers for each question; in how many ways may he complete the paper?

Exercise 7(a)

1. Five boats are entered for a race. Assuming that they all finish and that there are no dead heats, in how many possible orders can they pass the finishing line?

2. In a form of thirty boys, a first and a second prize are to be awarded; in how many ways can this be done?

3. You have a form on which you have to give your first six choices for university, in order of preference. If you have a list of twelve universities offering the course you want, in how many ways can you complete the form?

4. A fruit machine has three windows, in each of which appears independently one of six pictures. How many different arrangements (taking the order into account) are possible?

5. How many five-digit numbers can be formed from the digits 1, 2, 3, 4, 5, using each digit once? How many of them are even? How many are even and greater than 30000?

6. A committee of four is to be selected from six Labour and six Conservative M.P.s. How many possible committees are there? In how many will the members of the Labour Party have a majority?

7. In how many ways may a tennis team of six members be selected from fifteen available players? In how many ways may a first and second team be chosen?

8. Twelve people are to divide up into three sets of four players for a whist drive. In how many ways can this be done?

9. Of ten electric light bulbs, three are faulty but it is not known which. In how many ways may three bulbs be selected? How many of these selections will include at least one faulty bulb?

10. How many different bridge hands (thirteen cards) are there which contain (i) all four aces, (ii) three aces and one king? (Leave your answer in factorial form.)

11. Criticize the following attempted solution of Example 1:
'A man must sit on the committee, and he can be chosen in four ways. The remaining two members may now be chosen arbitrarily from among the six remaining people: this may be done in $^6C_2 = 15$ ways. Thus, the total number of possible committees is $4 \times 15 = 60$.'

12. Prove that the numbers of distinguishable arrangements of n objects in a row, if two are alike and the rest different, is $\frac{1}{2}n!$.
What is the number of distinguishable arrangements if three are alike and the rest different?
How many different telephone numbers can be made using all the digits of the number 4225267?

13. How many different arrangements are there of the letters of the word QUEUE? In how many of these arrangements do the letters QU appear together, in that order?

14. Find in how many ways a batting order (eleven men) may be made if Smith is to bat before Brown.

15. A diagonal of an n-sided polygon is a line joining two non-adjacent vertices. How many diagonals does an n-sided polygon possess?

16. In how many ways can two 1s, two 2s and two 3s be thrown with six dice?

107

17. Given n unlike objects, find the number of ways of dividing them into three unequal groups of sizes p, q, r where $p+q+r = n$.

In how many ways can they be divided into two groups of size p and one of size $n-2p$, if no attention is paid to the order of the groups?

18. A pair of integers is selected from the set of positive integers 1, 2, 3, ..., n. In how many ways may this be done? [In each pair the order of the integers is immaterial, e.g. (2, 3) and (3, 2) count as one pair only.]

If the integers in each pair are multiplied together show that, in the case when n is odd, the number of products which will be odd integers is $\frac{1}{8}(n^2-1)$. If n is large show that this number is approximately one-quarter of the total number of products.   (Cambridge)

2. RANDOM EXPERIMENTS AND OUTCOME SPACES

The subject of probability deals with 'experiments' which may have a number of possible outcomes; more specifically, it seeks to assign a numerical measure to the likelihood of obtaining various possible results if such an experiment is conducted, and thereby enable us to analyse the situation mathematically. Experiments of this nature, in which the results obtained depend upon chance, may be called *random experiments*.

We may take, as three typical examples of random experiments:

(i) A coin is tossed and the result (head or tail) noted.

(ii) From the very large output of a machine producing electrical components, a sample of twenty components is drawn and each component in the sample is tested in turn to decide whether or not it is faulty.

(iii) A person is tested for blood group (A, B, AB or O).

Each of the above experiments has the property that its outcome may be one of a (finite) number of possibilities. *A set whose elements represent all the various distinct possible outcomes of a random experiment is called an outcome space for that experiment and its elements are called elementary events.* Notice particularly the words 'all' and 'distinct' in this definition: all the possible outcomes must be represented in the set and no elementary event can correspond to more than one possible outcome of the experiment. (The word 'space' is used because the outcomes of an experiment are frequently represented as points in geometrical space; 'outcome set' would perhaps be a preferable term but we shall follow the customary usage. Alternative terms in use are 'sample space' and 'possibility space'.)

For example, denoting by r the numbers of defectives found in a sample in experiment (ii) above, a possible outcome space would be

$$S_1 = \{r \in Z : 0 \leqslant r \leqslant 20\}.$$

It should be noticed that we have talked of *an* outcome space rather than

108

the outcome space: any other set whose elements represent distinct possible outcomes and which exhausts all the possibilities will do, e.g.

$$S_2 = \{G, F, P\},$$

where *G* denotes a good result (no defectives);

    F denotes a fair result (one or two defectives);

    P denotes a poor result (more than two defectives).

Generally speaking, it is best to choose as an outcome space one that gives as much detail as possible about the result obtained, but there are exceptions to this and other criteria may be adopted.

Ex. 10. Two coins are tossed and the result (in terms of heads and tails) noted. Suggest three possible outcome spaces.

Ex. 11. A card is drawn from a pack and its value and suit noted. Criticize the following outcome space:

    S = {card is an ace, card is a heart, card is neither a heart nor an ace}.

Ex. 12. Suggest an outcome space for Ex. 11 if the experiment is concerned only with the drawing of a heart or an ace from a pack of cards.

Ex. 13. A count is made of the numbers of girls and boys in a family. Under what circumstances would the set

    S = {there are more girls than boys, there are more boys than girls}

constitute an outcome space?

3. PROBABILITY DISTRIBUTIONS

We now assign to each elementary event s_i of our outcome space S a positive fraction p_i (i.e. $0 \leqslant p_i \leqslant 1$) called the *probability* that the outcome of our experiment will be s_i. Furthermore, for consistency, we shall make the sum of all the probabilities p_i over the entire outcome space 1. Thus, the probabilities associated with an outcome space $S = \{s_1, s_2, ..., s_n\}$ are real numbers such that

$$0 \leqslant p_i \leqslant 1, \tag{1}$$

$$p_1 + p_2 + p_3 + ... + p_n = 1. \tag{2}$$

Such a set of probabilities is said to constitute a *probability distribution* for the given outcome space.

It will be observed that so far we have attached no meaning to the numbers p_i—we have only placed certain restrictions upon their possible values. Provided we observe these restrictions we have a mathematically meaningful system. However, it is desirable that a mathematical system should have some relevance to the physical world. If a mathematical system describes some physical situation, we are said to have created a

109

mathematical model of that situation. In using a probability distribution as a mathematical model of a situation we shall demand that the probability p_i shall be, in some sense, a numerical measure of our degree of belief that the experiment will result in the outcome s_i.

It should be carefully noted that the assigning of a probability distribution to an outcome space S constitutes an assumption about the experiment under consideration. Certain 'natural' ways of assigning probabilities are discussed below. In many cases, a 'natural' way of assigning probabilities will appear so obvious that the tacit assumptions made may be overlooked. It is a sound point of self-discipline to pause to consider the assumptions made when embarking upon any question in probability.

We now give two examples of ways in which probabilities may be assigned to the elementary events of typical outcome spaces. The final justification for such probability distributions is that calculations based upon them are supported by empirical evidence.

(i) Symmetry among the possible outcomes may make it reasonable to assume that all the elementary events have equal probability. For example, in the case of a die, it may reasonably be assumed that no one face is more or less likely to appear uppermost if the die is thrown than any other. Then since $p_1+p_2+\ldots+p_6 = 1$,

$$p_1 = p_2 = p_3 = p_4 = p_5 = p_6 = \tfrac{1}{6}.$$

If the same probability is assigned to each elementary event of an outcome space S, the resulting probability distribution is said to be *uniform* and the elementary events are said to be *equiprobable*.

(ii) Previous repetitions of an experiment (conducted under constant conditions) show that outcome A occurs a per cent of the time, B occurs b per cent of the time, etc., where $A, B, \ldots$ are quite distinct. Then our accumulated experience suggests that the probability of securing outcome A is $a/100$, that of securing B is $b/100$, etc. As an example, suppose that a large number of samples of size 20 are taken from the output of a machine manufacturing electrical components and that, on average, 0·94 per sample turn out to be defective. Then we may reasonably take the probability of any components being defective as $0·94/20 = 0·047$. Notice that such an assignment of probabilities satisfies the requirements (1) and (2) on p. 109.

Ex. 14. Of the outcome spaces you suggested for Ex. 10 which do you think may reasonably be supposed to be uniform?

Ex. 15. Two dice are thrown and the total score is noted. Criticize the assigning of a uniform distribution to the outcome space

$$S = \{2, 3, 4, \ldots, 12\}.$$

3] PROBABILITY DISTRIBUTIONS

Ex. 16. Suggest an outcome space for the experiment of throwing two dice that may be given a uniform distribution.

Ex. 17. From the weather records of a certain town taken over the past thirty years, on the average five days in November have been recorded as foggy. Is it justifiable to assume that the probability of a November day in that town being foggy is $\frac{1}{6}$?

Ex. 18. The number of boys and girls in a family of five children are noted. Justify the assumption that the outcome space

$$S = \{\text{there are more girls than boys, there are more boys than girls}\}$$

has a uniform distribution (i.e. $\rho = \frac{1}{2}$ for each of the two elementary events).

4. PROBABILITIES OF EVENTS

Any subset E of the outcome space S of an experiment is called an *event*. (Notice that the use of the word in 'elementary events' is consistent with this definition, since $\{s\} \subset S$.) If we have assigned a probability distribution to our outcome space it becomes meaningful to consider the probability of the event E (by which we would mean, in a practical example, a measure of our degree of belief that the experiment will result in one of the elementary events belonging to E). A moment's consideration should show that the following definition is plausible, at least in simple cases.

Given a sample space S with associated probability distribution, and an event $E \subseteq S$, then *the probability of the event E*, written Pr $(E|S)$ (read: 'the probability of event E given S'—more explicitly, 'the probability of E given the probability distribution of the outcome space S') is defined as the sum of the probabilities of all the elementary events belonging to E.

More formally, if $S = \{s_1, s_2, ..., s_n\}$ and p_i is the probability associated with s_i, and if $E = \{s_{r_1}, s_{r_2}, ..., s_{r_m}\}$ then

$$\text{Pr } (E|S) = p_{r_1} + p_{r_2} + p_{r_3} + ... + p_{r_m}.$$

Example 3. *If a card is drawn from a well-shuffled pack, what is the probability that it will be an ace?*

A suitable outcome space, S, is the set of 52 elementary outcomes corresponding to the fifty-two different cards in the pack.

To continue, we must make an assumption about the probability distribution. Since the pack is well shuffled, we shall consider this as a case of fifty-two equiprobable events and so associate with each element of S the probability $\frac{1}{52}$. The event E is the subset of S consisting of the drawing of the ace of spades, hearts, diamonds or clubs.

Then $$\text{Pr } (E|S) = \tfrac{1}{52} + \tfrac{1}{52} + \tfrac{1}{52} + \tfrac{1}{52} = \tfrac{1}{13}.$$

Example 4. *What is the probability of securing a hand of thirteen cards all of one suit in a game of bridge?*

We take as our outcome space the set consisting of all possible distinct bridge hands, i.e. a set with $_{52}C_{13}$ elements.

If the cards have been well shuffled we may assume that these hands are equiprobable and so the probability of getting a specified hand is $13! \, 39!/52!$.

Of these hands, four consist of one suit only. The required probability is thus $13! \, 39! \, 4/52!$, which works out to be roughly 1.6×10^{-11}.

*Ex. 19. How would you interpret the probabilities obtained in Examples 3 and 4?

Ex. 20. What is the probability of obtaining one head and two tails if three coins are tossed?

Ex. 21. What is the probability of obtaining a total of more than 10 from the throw of two dice?

Ex. 22. There are one thousand tickets issued in a lottery and prizes are awarded for twenty of them. What is the probability of any specified ticket securing a prize?

Ex. 23. What is the probability that a bridge hand contains (i) just one heart (a singleton heart); (ii) a singleton in just one suit? (Leave your answers in factorial form.)

Probability is occasionally formulated in terms of *odds* rather than as a fraction. If the probability that a horse will win a race is estimated as $\frac{1}{4}$, then the probability that it will not win is $\frac{3}{4}$ and the *odds against its winning* are 3 to 1 (sometimes written as '3 to 1 against'). Again, if the probability that another horse will win a race is $\frac{2}{3}$, then the *odds in favour of its winning* are 2 to 1 (or '2 to 1 on').

Ex. 24. The odds on horse A to win a race are 3 to 1 on and on horse B 4 to 1 against. Write down the probabilities
   (i) that A wins;
   (ii) that B wins;
   (iii) that A does not win.

Exercise 7(b)

1. Consider families consisting of six children, all of different ages. The 'type' of family is defined by an ordered set of the form $\{B, B, G, B, G, B\}$ the elements of which represent the sex of each child, starting with the eldest. How many different types are there? In how many different types are there three boys and three girls? What is the probability that a family of six children will consist of three boys and three girls?

2. In question 1 an outcome space

$$S = \{0, 1, 2, ..., 6\}$$

is given, where the elements represent each of the possible number of boys in a family. Assign a probability distribution to this space.

3. A number is chosen at random from among the integers 1, 2, 3, ..., 20. What is the probability that
   (i) it is a multiple of 3 or 7?
   (ii) it is a multiple of 3 or 5?

4. If a committee of four is chosen at random from ten women and ten men, what is the probability that there will be two women and two men serving?

5. If, in Question 4, the male chairman is certain to be re-elected, what is now the probability of equal numbers of men and women?

6. Two numbers are selected at random from the integers 1 to 10. (You may assume that all numbers are equally likely to be selected and that the same number may be selected twice.)
   The elements 0, 1, 2, ..., 9 of the outcome space represent the magnitude of the difference between the two numbers. Assign a probability distribution to this space which you feel represents a suitable mathematical model for the experiment.

7. If two numbers are selected at random from the numbers 1 to 10, what is the probability that the larger number will be greater than 8?

8. If two cards are drawn from a pack of fifty-two cards, what is the probability that
   (i) they will both be spades,
   (ii) they will be of the same suit?

9. Two people are asked independently to write down an integer between 1 and 10 (inclusive). The sum, s, of the two numbers is then calculated. Write out an outcome space for the possible values of s and assign a probability distribution, on the assumption that each person is equally likely to select any one of the ten numbers.
   What is the probability that s will be prime?

10. In a mixed bag of screws there are twice as many large as small. 10 % of the large screws are defective and so are 5 % of the small screws. Assuming that every screw has an equal probability of being selected, what is the chance of picking a defective screw?
   Comment upon the assumption made.

5. THE ADDITION LAWS

We are now in a position to prove some simple theorems concerning the probabilities of compound events. Throughout we shall suppose that the outcome space S and the probability distribution are given.

113

Theorem 7.1. If E_1, E_2 are two events, then

$$\Pr(E_1 \cup E_2 | S) = \Pr(E_1 | S) + \Pr(E_2 | S) - \Pr(E_1 \cap E_2 | S).$$

Proof. The sum of the probabilities of the elementary events in $E_1 \cup E_2$ is equal to the sum of the probabilities in E_1 and E_2, less the sum of the probabilities in $E_1 \cap E_2$, since this has been included twice. The result now follows from the definition of the probability of an event.

Theorem 7.2. If the events E_1, E_2 are mutually exclusive (i.e. if $E_1 \cap E_2 = \varnothing$), then

$$\Pr(E_1 \cup E_2 | S) = \Pr(E_1 | S) + \Pr(E_2 | S).$$

Proof: $\Pr(E_1 \cap E_2 | S) = \Pr(\varnothing | S) = 0$, by the definition of the probability of an event. The result now follows immediately from Theorem 7.1.

Theorem 7.3. If E is any event

$$\Pr(E' | S) = 1 - \Pr(E | S).$$

Proof. Since $E \cup E' = S$ and $E \cap E' = \varnothing$, this is a special case of Theorem 2.

Theorem 7.4. If E_1, E_2, ..., E_n are mutually exclusive events

$$(E_i \cap E_j = \varnothing, \quad i \neq j)$$

then $\quad \Pr\left(\bigcup_{i=1}^{n} E_i \Big| S\right) = \Pr(E_1 | S) + \Pr(E_2 | S) + ... + \Pr(E_n | S).$†

A formal proof of this theorem may be had by employing mathematical induction (see Chapter 9). However, its truth is intuitively fairly obvious if we consider a Venn diagram and note that, since no two of the E_i intersect, the sum of the probabilities in UE_i is obtained by adding up the probabilities for E_1 then for E_2 and so on.

Example 5. Two dice are thrown. What is the probability of scoring either a double, or a sum greater than 9?

We take as our outcome space the set of 36 pairs (i, j), where i, j run independently from 1 to 6. We make the assumption that the events are equiprobable and so attach a probability to each elementary event of $\frac{1}{36}$.

Write
$$E_1 = \{(1, 1), (2, 2)\ (3, 3)\ (4, 4)\ (5, 5)\ (6, 6)\},$$
$$E_2 = \{(4, 6)\ (5, 5)\ (6, 4)\ (5, 6)\ (6, 5)\ (6, 6)\},$$

† The notation $\bigcup_{i=1}^{n}$ means the union of the n sets E_1, E_2, ..., E_n; that is
$$E_1 \cup E_2 \cup ... \cup E_n.$$

and so $$E_1 \cap E_2 = \{(5, 5), (6, 6)\}.$$

We thus have

$$\Pr(E_1|S) = \Pr(E_2|S) = \tfrac{6}{36}; \quad \Pr(E_1 \cap E_2|S) = \tfrac{2}{36}$$

and so $\Pr(E_1 \cup E_2|S) = \tfrac{1}{6} + \tfrac{1}{6} - \tfrac{1}{18}$, by Theorem 7.1,

$$= \tfrac{5}{18}.$$

Example 6. Two dice are thrown. What is the probability of not getting a double?

Making the same assumptions as in Example 5 and using the same notation,
$$\Pr(E_1'|S) = 1 - \Pr(E_1|S), \quad \text{by Theorem 7.3,}$$

$$= 1 - \tfrac{1}{6}$$

$$= \tfrac{5}{6}.$$

Ex. 25. In a class of boys, one-third have black hair and one-quarter have brown eyes. What deductions can you make?

Ex. 26. If a card is drawn from a well-shuffled pack what is the probability that it is either an ace or a king?

Ex. 27. If a card is drawn from a well-shuffled pack, what is the probability that it is an ace or a heart?

Ex. 28. If a number is selected at random from the integers 1, 2, ..., 30 what is the probability that it is
  (i) divisible by 2;
  (ii) divisible by 3;
  (iii) divisible by 6;
  (iv) not a multiple of 2 or 3?

Ex. 29. If one thousand tickets are issued in a lottery in which there are two first prizes, eight second prizes and ten third prizes, what is the probability of not securing a prize with one ticket?

6. THE MULTIPLICATION LAWS

We shall now consider how we must modify our estimate of the probability of an event E if we are given information in addition to our outcome space and its allied probability distribution. Suppose that E and F are two events (with $\Pr(F|S) \neq 0$) and we require to estimate the probability of E knowing that F occurs. Essentially, we have a new outcome space F and we have to determine $\Pr(E|F)$. (We *define* $\Pr(E|F)$ to mean

$$\Pr(E \cap F|F).)$$

Now since F is the new outcome space, the new probability distribution for F must have the property that the probabilities of the elementary events contained in F sum to 1. Making the plausible assumption that the relative proportion of the weights attached to the elementary events of F remain unaltered, this is equivalent to scaling up the probabilities in F by a factor $1/\mathrm{Pr}\,(F|S)$. The probability that E will occur is thus $\mathrm{Pr}\,(E \cap F|S)$, scaled up by this factor $1/p(F|S)$. We are thus led to make the following definition:

$$\mathrm{Pr}\,(E|F) = \frac{\mathrm{Pr}\,(E \cap F|S)}{\mathrm{Pr}\,(F|S)}.$$

Example 7. A bag contains twenty balls, ten of which are red, eight white and two blue. The balls are indistinguishable apart from the colour. Two balls are drawn in succession, without replacement. What is the probability that they will both be red?

We take as our outcome space S the set of $20 \times 19 = 380$ possible selections of two balls. Since the balls are indistinguishable apart from colour, we may impose a uniform probability distribution upon S.

Now define R_1 as the event 'the first ball picked is red', R_2 as the event 'the second ball picked is red' and similarly W_1, W_2, B_1, B_2.

We require to find $\mathrm{Pr}\,(R_1 \cap R_2|S)$.

Now $\mathrm{Pr}\,(R_1|S) = \frac{10}{20}$ and $\mathrm{Pr}\,(R_2|R_1)$—the probability that a red ball is selected from a bag now containing nine red, eight white and two blue balls is $\frac{9}{19}$.

Thus,
$$\mathrm{Pr}\,(R_1 \cap R_2|S) = \mathrm{Pr}\,(R_2|R_1).\mathrm{Pr}\,(R_1|S)$$
$$= \tfrac{9}{19}.\tfrac{10}{20}$$
$$= \tfrac{9}{38}.$$

Example 8. With the data of Example 7, what is the probability that we obtain a blue and a white ball (in either order)?

Adopting the notation of Example 7, we are required to calculate the probability of obtaining one or other of the two mutually exclusive events $B_1 \cap W_2$ and $W_1 \cap B_2$; that is $\mathrm{Pr}\,\{(B_1 \cap W_2) \cup (W_1 \cap B_2)|S\}$.

Now
$$\mathrm{Pr}\,\{(B_1 \cap W_2) \cup (W_1 \cap B_2)|S\} = \mathrm{Pr}\,(B_1 \cap W_2|S) + \mathrm{Pr}\,(W_1 \cap B_2|S),$$

since the events are mutually exclusive using Theorem 2;

$$= \mathrm{Pr}\,(W_2|B_1).\mathrm{Pr}\,(B_1|S) + \mathrm{Pr}\,(B_2|W_1).\mathrm{Pr}\,(W_1|S)$$
$$= \tfrac{8}{19}.\tfrac{2}{20} + \tfrac{2}{19}.\tfrac{8}{20}$$
$$= \tfrac{8}{95}.$$

The arguments employed for the solution of the preceding examples may be represented diagrammatically by a *probability tree* (see Figure 7.1).

Starting at O on the extreme left, the end-points of the first three branches represent all the possible (mutually exclusive) results of the first draw. The end-points of the next three sets of branches represent all the possible

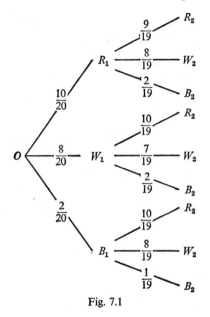

Fig. 7.1

outcomes of the second draw, the various sets corresponding to the different draws on the first round. The various probabilities are then attached to the branches as shown and the probability of any desired path from O to some end-point on the right may be found by multiplying the successive branch probabilities together.

For example

$$\text{Pr}\,(W_1 \cap R_2|S) = \tfrac{8}{20} \times \tfrac{10}{19} = \tfrac{4}{19},$$

$$\text{Pr}\,(B_2|S) = \text{Pr}\,(R_1 \cap B_2|S) + \text{Pr}\,(W_1 \cap B_2|S) + \text{Pr}\,(B_1 \cap B_2|S)$$
$$\text{(events mutually exclusive)}$$
$$= \text{Pr}\,(R_1|S).\text{Pr}\,(B_2|R_1) + \text{Pr}\,(W_1|S).\text{Pr}\,(B_2|W_1)$$
$$+ \text{Pr}\,(B_1|S).\text{Pr}\,(B_2|B_1)$$
$$= \tfrac{10}{20}.\tfrac{2}{19} + \tfrac{8}{20}.\tfrac{2}{19} + \tfrac{2}{20}.\tfrac{1}{19}$$
$$= \tfrac{1}{10}.$$

(Can you see a simpler method of arriving at this last probability?)

117

Probability trees are particularly helpful if a number of probabilities have to be read off. If only one probability is required, a simplified tree may often help. For example, in Example 7 we are essentially concerned with two alternatives: red and not red. Figure 2 shows a suitable tree for this example.

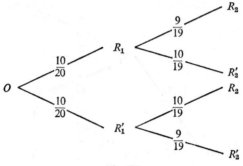

Fig. 7.2

$$Pr\,(R_1 \cap R_2|S) = Pr\,(R_1|S).Pr\,(R_2|R_1)$$

$$= \tfrac{10}{20}.\tfrac{9}{19}$$

$$= \tfrac{9}{38}.$$

A particularly important case of the multiplication law arises in the case of independent events. Intuitively, two events are independent if neither has an effect upon the other. To make this notion mathematically precise we define two events A and B to be *independent* if

$$Pr\,(A \cap B|S) = Pr\,(A|S).Pr\,(B|S).$$

Comparison of this definition with that given above for conditional probabilities shows that the assumption of independence is equivalent to the assumption that

$$Pr\,(A|S) = Pr\,(A|B).$$

In words, the occurrence of B does not lead us to review our estimate of the probability of A.

Ex. 30. Prove that, if $Pr\,(A \cap B|S) = Pr\,(A|S)\,Pr\,(B|S)$, then $Pr\,(A|S) = Pr\,(A|B)$.

Example 9. A coin is tossed and a die thrown. What is the probability of securing a head and a six?
    On the assumption that the two events are independent, the required probability is clearly $\tfrac{1}{2} \times \tfrac{1}{6} = \tfrac{1}{12}$.

Ex. 31. A bag contains two white balls and six red balls; a second bag contains four white balls and four red balls. The balls are indistinguishable apart from colour. What is the probability of obtaining two white balls if
  (i) one ball is drawn from each bag;
  (ii) two balls are drawn from the first bag;
  (iii) two balls are drawn from the second bag?

Ex. 32. Criticize the following argument:
  'A ring of anti-ballistic missiles is estimated to give a probability of 0·2 of destroying any incoming missile. A set of five such rings will therefore render a city immune to missile attack.'

Ex. 33. 'In a form of twenty-four boys, six failed their English examination and four failed their Mathematics. The probability that a boy, selected at random from the form, failed in both English and Mathematics is thus $\frac{6}{24} \times \frac{4}{24} = \frac{1}{24}$.' Do you think this argument is essentially correct?

Ex. 34. A coin is spun twice and a die is thrown twice. Find the probability of obtaining at least one head or at least one six (or possibly both).

Exercise 7(c)

1. What is the probability of not throwing a six with four throws of an un-biased die? What is the probability of throwing at least one six?

2. On average, 2 % of the electric light bulbs of a certain type prove to be faulty: what is the probability that a batch of twelve such bulbs will be free of defectives?

3. If four people are chosen at random, find the probability that no two of them were born on the same day of the week.   (M.E.I. 'O')

4. A bag contains a dozen apples, of which three are bad. If two apples are withdrawn at random, find the probability that
  (i) both are good ;
  (ii) both are bad;
  (iii) one is good and one bad.   (M.E.I. 'O')

5. Show that there is a better chance of throwing at least one 6 with four throws of a single die than there is of throwing at least one double 6 with twenty-five throws of a pair of dice. (This is a modification of a famous problem in the history of probability, first proposed by a gambler, the Chevalier de Méré and transmitted by him to the French mathematician Fermat, who managed to solve it.)

6. A bag contains two red, three white and four blue balls. If two balls are drawn in succession without replacement, what is the probability of drawing a red and a blue ball, in either order? What is the corresponding probability if the first ball is replaced before the second is drawn?

7. A bridge hand consisting of thirteen playing cards contains two aces. If five cards are drawn at random from the hand, find the probability that the five will contain neither of the aces.   (M.E.I. 'O')

119

8. A teacher has twelve pupils in his form, eight boys and four girls. On a school outing he can provide transport in his car for three pupils and decides to draw lots for the seats. Construct a tree to show on its branches the probabilities as to the sex of the winning pupils in the different stages of the draw. Hence, or otherwise, find the probability that those winning will contain

    (i) two boys and one girl,

    (ii) at least two girls. (M.E.I. 'O')

9. Given five different letters and their respective envelopes, in how many ways can one letter be placed in each envelope if this is done at random?

    Find in how many cases only two of the letters will be in their correct envelopes.

    What is the probability that at least three of the letters are in their correct envelopes? (M.E.I. 'O')

10. What is the probability that, after a pack of cards has been well shuffled, two aces will lie at the top?

11. A bag contains three red, four white and five blue balls, indistinguishable apart from their colour. If two balls are drawn successively, without replacement, estimate the probability of obtaining two balls of different colours.

12. A machine has N components, each of which has a probability of $2/3$ of breaking down. The machine will function provided at least one of its components is functioning. What value should be chosen for N if the machine is to be 99 % efficient?

13. A pack of fifty-two ordinary playing cards is shuffled and a card is withdrawn. D denotes the event that the card is a diamond, K that it is a king, R that it is red. Prove by calculating the appropriate probabilities that D and K are independent, that K and R are independent, but that D and R are not independent.

    What is the value of $\Pr [(D' \cap K) \cup (D \cap K')]$? (M.E.I.)

14. Three cards are drawn from a pack of fifty-two cards and, when they have been replaced and the pack shuffled, a second set of three cards is drawn. Find the chance that the six cards drawn should include at least one ace. (M.E.I.)

15. A bag contains five white and three red balls. Balls are drawn in succession and are not replaced. Show that the chance that the first red ball will appear at the fifth draw is $3/56$. (M.E.I.)

16. Three bags, A, B, C, contain respectively three white and two red balls, four white and four red balls, five white and two red balls. A ball is drawn unseen from A and placed in B; then a ball is drawn from B and placed in C. Find the chance that if a ball is now drawn from C it will be red. (M.E.I.)

17. How many times should an unbiased die be thrown if the probability that a six should appear at least once is to be greater than $9/10$? (M.E.I.)

18. A batch of fifty articles contains three which are defective. The particles are drawn in succession (without replacement) from the batch and tested. Show that the chance that the first defective met will be the rth article drawn is

$$(50-r)(49-r)/39\,200. \qquad \text{(M.E.I.)}$$

19. Two men A and B play a game in which A should win eight games to every seven won by B. If they play three games, show that the probability that A will win at least two games is approximately 0·55. (Cambridge)

20. The chance of any one engine of a four-engined aeroplane failing on a long journey is 5 %. If only one engine fails the chance of the aeroplane completing the journey is 80 %; if two engines on opposite wings fail, its chance of completing the journey is 50 %. It cannot fly with two engines out of action on the same wing. Find the chance that the aeroplane will complete the journey. (O & C)

21. (i) From a bag containing five red, four white and three green balls, three are drawn together at random. Find the chance of their being

    (*a*) all of different colours,

    (*b*) all of the same colour.

    (ii) Two six-faced dice whose faces bear the numbers 1 to 6 respectively are thrown together. Find the chance of

    (*a*) the total score being exactly 8,

    (*b*) the total score being greater than 8. (O & C)

7. EXTENDED USE OF THE MULTIPLICATION LAWS

Note. To gain precision we have so far always specified the conditioning set, even if it is the entire sample space (whose associated probability distribution is known). In this latter case, however, little harm is done by dropping the reference to S; thus, if the outcome space is S and an event E is considered as a subset of S, it is customary to refer to $\Pr(E|S)$ simply as $\Pr(E)$. Provided no ambiguity arises we shall adopt this simplified notation.

For example, if A, B are independent, we shall write

$$\Pr(A \cap B) = \Pr(A) . \Pr(B).$$

More generally, if A, B are any two events in an outcome space S

$$\Pr(A \cap B) = \Pr(A|B) . \Pr(B).$$

In pursuing applications of the multiplication law, we first notice that, since the operation of intersection is commutative, that is, since

$$A \cap B = B \cap A$$

we have, for any two events A, B

$$\Pr(A|B) . \Pr(B) = \Pr(A \cap B) = \Pr(B \cap A) = \Pr(B|A) . \Pr(A).$$

This form of the multiplication law is often useful, for example, when it is desired to calculate $\Pr(A|B)$ and the three probabilities $\Pr(A)$, $\Pr(B)$, $\Pr(B|A)$ are known or easily found.

121

Example 10. *Two bags contain coloured balls as shown in the table below.*

	Red	White	Blue
Bag I	3	2	1
Bag II	0	4	2

*A die is thrown; if a 1 or 6 appears, then bag I is chosen, otherwise bag II.
A ball is then drawn from the selected bag. If the result of the throw of the die
is unknown, but merely that a white ball is drawn, what is the probability that
it came from bag I?*

We begin by making the assumption that the balls are indistinguishable
apart from colour and that we have an equiprobable outcome space.

Let I denote the event 'bag I is selected',

II denote the event 'bag II is selected',

W denote the event 'a white ball is selected'.

Then $\Pr(\text{I}) = \frac{1}{3}$; $\Pr(\text{II}) = \frac{2}{3}$.

W may occur in either of two mutually exclusive ways: bag I is selected
and a white ball is drawn; bag II is selected and a white ball is drawn.
Thus we have

$$\Pr(W) = \Pr(W \cap \text{I}) + \Pr(W \cap \text{II})$$
$$= \Pr(W|\text{I}).\Pr(\text{I}) + \Pr(W|\text{II}).\Pr(\text{II})$$
$$= \tfrac{2}{6}.\tfrac{1}{3} + \tfrac{4}{6}.\tfrac{2}{3}$$
$$= \tfrac{1}{9} + \tfrac{4}{9}$$
$$= \tfrac{5}{9}.$$

Thus
$$\Pr(\text{I}|W) = \frac{\Pr(\text{I} \cap W)}{\Pr(W)}$$
$$= \frac{\Pr(W \cap \text{I})}{\Pr(W)}$$
$$= \frac{\Pr(W|\text{I}).\Pr(\text{I})}{\Pr(W)}$$
$$= \tfrac{1}{9}/\tfrac{5}{9}$$
$$= \tfrac{1}{5},$$

which is the required probability.

The technique mentioned above may be generalized to yield a result
commonly known as Bayes's Theorem. (The Reverend Thomas Bayes
(1702–61) was one of the earlier writers on the subject of probability. The
theorem which bears his name was published posthumously in 1764.)

Before considering the general theorem we shall solve an example for a special case ($n = 3$).

Example 11. *Three machines produce the same type of electrical component, 20 % of the total output coming from machine A, 50 % from machine B and 30 % from machine C. Tests conducted in the past show that 5 % of the components from A and 1 % from each of B and C prove faulty. A component selected at random from the total output is proved to be faulty. What is the probability that it came from machine A?*

Call A the event 'component comes from machine A',
  B the event 'component comes from machine B',
  C the event 'component comes from machine C',
  F the event 'component found faulty'.
We have to determine $\Pr(A|F)$.
Now, from the data, we may assign the following probabilities:

$$\Pr(F|A) = \tfrac{5}{100}; \quad \Pr(F|B) = \tfrac{1}{100}; \quad \Pr(F|C) = \tfrac{1}{100};$$

$$\Pr(A) = \tfrac{20}{100}; \quad \Pr(B) = \tfrac{50}{100}; \quad \Pr(C) = \tfrac{30}{100}.$$

Now $\Pr(A|F) = \Pr(A \cap F)/\Pr(F)$ and so the problem reduces to determining $\Pr(A \cap F)$ and $\Pr(F)$, given the numerical values above. But

$$\Pr(A \cap F) = \Pr(F \cap A)$$
$$= \Pr(F|A).\Pr(A)$$
$$= \tfrac{1}{100}.$$

Again $F = (F \cap A) \cup (F \cap B) \cup (F \cap C)$ and these three events are mutually exclusive (no component can come from more than one machine).
Thus
$$\Pr(F) = \Pr(F \cap A) + \Pr(F \cap B) + \Pr(F \cap C)$$
$$= \Pr(F|A).\Pr(A) + \Pr(F|B).\Pr(B) + \Pr(F|C).\Pr(C)$$
$$= \tfrac{1}{100} + \tfrac{1}{200} + \tfrac{3}{1000}$$
$$= \tfrac{9}{500}.$$

Thus
$$\Pr(A|F) = \frac{\Pr(A \cap F)}{\Pr(F)}$$
$$= \tfrac{5}{9}.$$

Ex. 35. Of two pennies, one is double-headed, the other normal. If one of the pennies is selected at random and tossed twice, what is the probability of obtaining two heads? If one of the coins is selected at random, tossed twice and gives two heads, what is the probability that it is double-headed?

Ex. 36. Find the probabilities that the faulty article of Example 11 came from (i) machine B, (ii) machine C.

Ex. 37. With the data of Example 11, find the probability that a component selected at random and shown to be not faulty comes from machine *A*.

Ex. 38. Two articles come from one of the machines of Example 11, but it is not known which one. On testing, both are found to be faulty. Find the respective probabilities that they come from machines *A*, *B* and *C*.

Notice that in Example 11 we had an outcome space partitioned into three mutually exclusive and exhaustive events *A*, *B*, *C*, and were required to find the probability of *A* conditional upon the occurrence of some event *F*. More generally, we define a *partition* of a set *S* as a set of subsets

$$\{H_1, H_2, H_3, ..., H_n\}$$

such that the intersection of any two of the *H*'s is empty and the union of the *H*'s is *S*, that is

Given a set S, the set $\{H_1, H_2, ..., H_n\}$ of subsets forms a partition of S if

(i) $H_i \cap H_j = \varnothing, 1 \leqslant i < j \leqslant n$;

(ii) $\bigcup_{i=1}^{n} H_i = S$.

Theorem 7.5 (*Bayes's Theorem*). *Given a partition $H_1, H_2, ..., H_n$ of an outcome space S and an event $E \subseteq S$,*

$$\Pr(H_j|E) = \frac{\Pr(E|H_j)\Pr(H_j)}{\Pr(E|H_1).\Pr(H_1)+\Pr(E|H_2).\Pr(H_2)+...+\Pr(E|H_n).\Pr(H_n)}.$$

Proof. Since the H_i are exhaustive,

$$E = (E \cap H_1) \cup (E \cap H_2) \cup ... \cup (E \cap H_n).$$

But the H_i are mutually exclusive and it follows that the $E \cap H_i$ are also mutually exclusive. Thus, by Theorem 7.4

$$\Pr(E) = \Pr(E \cap H_1)+\Pr(E \cap H_2)+...+\Pr(E \cap H_n)$$

$$= \Pr(E|H_1).\Pr(H_1)+\Pr(E|H_2).\Pr(H_2)+...+\Pr(E|H_n).\Pr(H_n),$$

but

$$\Pr(H_j|E) = \frac{\Pr(H_j \cap E)}{\Pr(E)}$$

$$= \frac{\Pr(E \cap H_j)}{\Pr(E)}$$

$$= \frac{\Pr(E|H_j).\Pr(H_j)}{\Pr(E)}$$

$$= \frac{\Pr(E|H_j).\Pr(H_j)}{\Pr(E|H_1).\Pr(H_1)+\Pr(E|H_2).\Pr(H_2)+...+\Pr(E|H_n).\Pr(H_n)}.$$

The value of this theorem lies largely in its application to inferential problems in statistics. A number of hypotheses H_i are made (hence the conventional use of the letter H in the theorem) and the probability of one hypothesis H_j given the occurrence of some event E is determined in terms of the probabilities of the H_i without the prior knowledge of the event E. (This is sometimes referred to as the determination of the *a posteriori* probability of the event H_j given the *a priori* probabilities of the events H_i, $1 \leqslant i \leqslant n$.) The major practical difficulty in its application lies in the estimation of the *a priori* probabilities $\Pr(H_i)$.

In solving problems involving Bayes's Theorem it is advisable always to work from first principles as in Example 11, and not to quote the theorem in its general form.

Exercise 7(d)

1. One of four dice is known to be biased, showing a 6, on average, three times as often as each of the other scores. A die is chosen at random and thrown three times and three 6s appear. What is the probability that it is one of the unbiased dice?

2. A factory manufactures three different qualities of light bulb, A, B and C in the ratio 1:2:3. The bulbs are indistinguishable in external appearance but extensive tests indicate that, on the average, 1 % of type A, 4 % of type B and 5 % of type C are below the advertised standard. A batch of six, all of the same type is sent in error without a distinguishing label. If none of these turns out to be defective, estimate the probability that they were of type A.

3. Of a large sample of items, 40 % were produced by machine A and 30 % by each of machines B and C. The machinery was very unreliable, machine A producing 10 % defective items, machine B 20 % defective items and machine C 30 %. If an item, selected at random from the sample, proves to be defective, what is the probability that it came from machine A?

4. A card is missing from a pack of 52 cards. If this is the only information you have, what is the probability that the missing card is a spade? The pack is well shuffled and the first card is removed and proves to be a spade. What would your assessment of the probability that the missing card is a spade be now? The card removed is now replaced and the pack shuffled. The top card again proves to be a spade. What is your assessment of the probability now?

5. Four bags, I, II, III, IV, contain white and black balls as shown in the following table.

Bag	I	II	III	IV
Number of white balls	1	2	3	4
Number of black balls	9	8	7	6

A die is thrown; if a one appears, bag I is chosen, if a two or three, bag II, if a four or five, bag III and if a six, bag IV. A ball is then drawn at random from the bag selected.

If you are told that a black ball has been drawn, what should your assessment be of the probability that it came from bag I?

6. A certain rare disease from which one in ten thousand of the population suffers is diagnosed by a test which reveals the presence of the disease in 95 % of the cases of those tested who actually have the disease. However, it also incorrectly yields a positive reaction in 1 % of the cases of those who are not suffering from the disease. If a person selected at random from the population shows a positive reaction, what is the probability that he is actually suffering from the disease?

7. One of four pennies is known to be double-headed, the other three being normal. One of the pennies is selected at random and tossed three times. If the result is three heads, what is the probability that the coin tossed is the double-headed penny?

8. An engineer is responsible for servicing three small computer installations A, B, C. The probability that A, B, C will break down on any day are $\frac{1}{40}$, $\frac{1}{50}$, $\frac{1}{100}$ respectively. The probabilities that the three computers will not be in operation after 7 p.m. are $\frac{5}{9}$, $\frac{2}{3}$, $\frac{3}{4}$ respectively. On one day the engineer receives a message that one of the computer installations has broken down at 8 p.m. but the message does not specify which computer. Calculate the probabilities that the breakdown is at A, B, C and so decide the first installation which should be checked by the engineer. (M.E.I. adapted)

9. The probability that a radio message sent from a ship is not picked up by a land-station is p. The land-station replies to all messages received and its transmission back has probability q of not being picked up by the ship. Find the probability that the land-station failed to receive the message if the ship gets no reply.

Miscellaneous Exercise 7

1. A number is drawn at random from the set of thirty-seven numbers

$$0, 1, 2, ..., 36,$$

and is then replaced.

(i) What is the chance that the number drawn will be odd?

(ii) What is the chance that in two consecutive draws the numbers drawn will be the same?

(iii) What is the chance that in one hundred consecutive draws the number 0 will not be drawn?

(iv) What is the chance that in five consecutive draws none of the numbers will be odd?

Give the answers to (i) and (ii) as vulgar fractions, and evaluate the answers to (iii) and (iv) approximately as decimals. (Cambridge)

2. An encyclopaedia consisting of n ($\geqslant 4$) similar volumes is kept on a shelf with the volumes in correct numerical order; that is, with volume one on the left, volume two next and so on. The volumes are taken down for cleaning and replaced on the shelf in random order. What are the probabilities of finding exactly n, $(n-1)$, $(n-2)$, $(n-3)$ volumes in their correct order on the shelf? (Cambridge)

3. You have available two pairs of dice. The dice of one pair are both true but, in the other pair, one is true and the other is known to be biased in some way. Which pair would you choose if you were playing a game in which to win you had to throw (*a*) a score of 7; (*b*) a double?

4. Two persons X and Y play a game in which X deals from a standard pack of fifty-two cards. Each player receives three cards and the game is won by X if he holds more red cards than there are black cards held by Y.

By considering the number of black cards in play or otherwise, calculate the probability that the dealer wins a game. What odds should be fixed by the dealer in order that he may expect just to show a profit?   (M.E.I. 'A')

5. Four cards, the aces of hearts, diamonds, spades and clubs are well shuffled and then dealt two to player A, the other two to player B. A is then asked whether at least one of his two cards is red. He replies in the affirmative. In the light of this information we wish to calculate the probability that he holds both the red aces. Consider the argument:

'We know that he has one red ace; without loss of generality we may suppose that it is the heart ace. Among the other three cards there is no reason why one more than another should be the diamond ace: one only out of three equally likely possibilities gives A both the red cards: the required chance is thus $\frac{1}{3}$.'

Criticize this argument and produce a correct argument and answer.   (C.S.)

6. A bag contains twelve coloured balls: 4 yellow, 3 white, 2 black, 2 red and 1 green. A prize is offered for obtaining 2 red balls in two draws, there being an option of either replacing or not replacing the first ball. Which would you choose?

Generalize your result to the case of a bag containing N balls of s different colours where there are m_i balls of colour i, and prove your conjecture.

7. Raffles of two types, A and B, are held. In raffles of type A there are $2N$ tickets, of which $2n$ carry prizes; in those of type B there are N tickets of which n carry prizes. Which would you prefer: two tickets in a raffle of type A, or two tickets in separate raffles of type B?

8. A six-digit telephone number (i.e. any number between 100000 and 999999) is dialled at random. Show that the probability that one or more digits are dialled in succession (as in 322916 or 322216 or 322911 but not as in 329216) is about 41%.   (Cambridge)

9. An experiment consists in drawing balls one at a time from a bag containing eight white and two black balls initially. Balls drawn from the bag are not replaced. A note is kept of the number r ($1 \leqslant r \leqslant 9$) of the draw which first yields a black ball. If the experiment is repeated many times what is (i) the most probable value of r; (ii) the probability that r exceeds 5?   (Cambridge)

10. Articles are distributed among three boxes in such a way that each article has the same chance of being placed in any one of the boxes. Find the probability that at least one of the boxes remains empty when r articles have been distributed.

Deduce that, if r articles are similarly distributed among five boxes, the probability that exactly two boxes remain empty is $6(3^{r-1} - 2^r + 1)/5^{r-1}$.   (Oxford)

11. A bag contains m oranges and n lemons: sampling is at random without replacement. Obtain the probabilities of the following events:
  (i) the first draw is an orange;
  (ii) the first two draws are oranges;
  (iii) the second draw is a lemon, given that the first was an orange;
  (iv) the third fruit is an orange. (Cambridge)

12. In a game of bridge each of four players is dealt thirteen cards after the pack has been shuffled. One of the players has four diamond cards and he can see four more diamonds in the exposed dummy hand, which has been put down on the table by one of the players. What is the chance that the five remaining diamond cards are split three in one hand and two in the other?

If, in the first three rounds of play, each player has used exactly one diamond and two other cards, what is the chance that one of the players has no diamond cards remaining in his hand? (M.E.I.)

13. Half the population of the city of Ekron are Philistines and the other half are Canaanites. A Philistine never tells the truth but a Canaanite speaks truthfully with probability $\frac{2}{5}$ and falsely with a probability $\frac{3}{5}$. What is the probability that a citizen encountered at random will give a correct answer to a question?

Tabulate (as fractions, decimals or percentages) the probabilities that 0, 1, 2, 3 men out of a sample of three citizens taken at random from Ekron will affirm a proposition (i) when it is true, (ii) when it is false.

The proposition has a prior probability of $\frac{3}{4}$ of being true. What is the (posterior) probability of its being true conditional on its being affirmed by only one out of three? (Cambridge)

14. A farmer keeps two breeds (A, B) of chicken; 70% of the egg production is from birds of breed A. Of the eggs laid by the A hens, 30% are large, 50% standard and the remainder small; for the B hens the corresponding proportions are 40%, 30% and 30%. Egg colour (brown or white) is manifested independently of size in each breed: 30% of A eggs and 40% of B eggs are brown. Find
  (i) the probability that an egg laid by an A hen is large and brown;
  (ii) the probability that an egg is large and brown;
  (iii) the probability that a brown egg is large;
  (iv) which size grade contains the largest proportion of brown eggs;
  (v) whether colour and size are manifested independently in the total egg production. (Cambridge)

15. A and B are two events and B' is the complementary event to B. Show that Pr (A) is between Pr $(A|B)$ and Pr $(A|B')$. (M.E.I.)

16. Prove that, if A and B are independent events, so also are A and B'. If A_1, A_2, A_3 are three mutually independent events such that

$$\text{Pr} (A_i \cap A_j' \cap A_k') = p_i \quad (i \neq j \neq k),$$

then $$\text{Pr} (A_i) = p_i/(p_i+\lambda),$$

where λ is a root of a certain cubic equation, which should be found.

17. A motorist driving along the main street of a town encounters two sets of traffic lights 660 feet apart. Both sets of lights change every 30 seconds and the second set are timed to change to 'Go' 10 seconds after the first set. The motorist drives at 30 m.p.h. but if forced to stop at the lights, he accelerates uniformly from rest at 4 ft/s² until he attains that speed. Estimate the probabilities of his finding

(i) both sets of lights in his favour;

(ii) both sets of lights against him;

(iii) only one set of lights against him.

Suggest two ways in which the relative timing of the two sets of lights could be adjusted to ensure that the probabilities would be the same if travelling in either direction and calculate the probabilities.

(Assume throughout that his progress is not interfered with by other vehicles, and also, that he drives at 30 m.p.h. right up to the lights and then stops instantaneously if they are red at that instant.)   (SMP)

18. Three players, X, Y, Z, play a game and at each round of the game they have an equal probability of winning that round. The player who wins each round scores one point and the game is won by the first person to score a total of 3 points. X wins the first round; calculate the probability that Y wins the game.

(M.E.I.)

19. The basic premium under a certain motor insurance policy is £λ p.a. The scale of No Claims Bonus provides 25% discount after the first year without claim, $33\frac{1}{3}$% after two consecutive years free of claim and 50% after three or more consecutive years free of claim. In addition a preferred policy holder's discount of 20% is given on the basic premium (which may already be discounted by the No Claims Bonus) for four consecutive years without claim. If a preferred policy holder's discount has been granted it is not lost by reason of a claim. Suppose that for a given driver there is a constant probability q of no claim in a given year. Evaluate the probabilities for the possible premiums in the sixth year of the policy, in terms of q.   (M.E.I.)

20. n^2 balls, of which n are black and the rest white, are distributed at random into n bags, so that each bag contains n balls. Determine the probability that at least one bag contains no black ball.

8. *Finite series and the Binomial Theorem*

1. SEQUENCES, SERIES AND THE Σ NOTATION

In Chapter 4, we saw that a function maps each element of the domain into an element of the range. A function whose domain is the set of positive integers, $Z^+ = \{1, 2, 3, 4, ...\}$, is called a *sequence* and the elements of the range are called *terms* of the sequence.†

For example, we could have as the terms of a sequence the numbers

$$1, 3, 5, 7, 9, ...,$$

where 1 (the first term) is the image of the integer 1; 3 (the second term) is the image of the integer 2; 5 (the third term) is the image of the integer 3 and so on (see Figure 8.1).

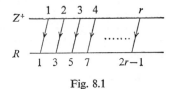

Fig. 8.1

It is common usage to refer to the range of a sequence simply as 'a sequence'; thus we should say that the numbers 1, 3, 5, 7, 9, ... 'form a sequence'. Other examples of sequences are

$$1, 2, 4, 8, 16, ...,$$
$$1, 4, 9, 16, 25, ...,$$
$$1, 1\tfrac{1}{2}, 2, 2\tfrac{1}{2}, 3, ...,$$
$$1, \sqrt{2}, 2, 2\sqrt{2}, 4, ...$$

If we call the first term of a sequence u_1, the second term u_2 and so on, the rth term (general term) of the sequence will be denoted by u_r. A sequence itself is often written $\{u_r\}$ (provided this notation causes no confusion with the set consisting of the single element u_r). For example, the first few terms

† It is possible to extend the definition of a sequence to include Z as the domain, but we shall restrict ourselves to Z^+ in this book, or, occasionaly to $Z^+ \cup \{0\}$, that is, the set of natural numbers with zero.

130

of the sequence $\{r^3-1\}$ are 0, 7, 26, 80, 124, ... Again, the sequence 1, 3, 5, 7, 9, ... could be written $\{2r-1\}$—but see Ex. 5, which illustrates the danger of assuming that the form of the rth term is determined by the first few terms of a sequence.

Sequences are sometimes defined by giving, say, the first term and a relation between the $(r-1)$th and rth terms. For example, the sequence defined by the relation

$$u_r = ru_{r-1}+1 \qquad\qquad (1)$$

and the first term $\qquad\qquad u_1 = 1$

has, for its second term $2.1+1 = 3$, for its third term $3.3+1 = 10$, for its fourth term $4.10+1 = 41$ and so on.

*Ex. 1. What are the first four terms of the sequence given by

$$u_r = ru_{r-1}+1,$$

(i) if $u_1 = 0$;   (ii) if $u_1 = 2$?

A relation such as (1), connecting general terms of a sequence, is called a *recurrence relation*. As another example of a recurrence relation we might have

$$u_r = u_{r-1}+u_{r-2}. \qquad\qquad (2)$$

To define this sequence $\{u_r\}$ we need two initial terms (why?). Thus, if

$$u_1 = 1, \quad u_2 = 1$$

then (2) defines the sequence

$$1, 1, 2, 3, 5, 8, 13, ...$$

Ex. 2. Write down the first four terms of the sequences defined by the following recurrence relations and initial terms:

(i) $u_r = 2u_{r-1}, u_1 = 1$;   (ii) $u_r = u_{r-1}+1, u_1 = 1$;
(iii) $u_r = ru_{r-1}+r^2, u_1 = 0$;   (iv) $u_r-u_{r-1} = r(u_{r-1}-u_{r-2})$,
$\qquad\qquad\qquad\qquad\qquad\qquad\qquad\qquad\qquad u_1 = 1, u_2 = 2$;

(v) $u_r = \dfrac{1}{2}\left(u_{r-1}+\dfrac{2}{u_{r-1}}\right)$, $u_1 = 1{\cdot}5$.

Ex. 3. Write down the first six terms of the following sequences:

(i) $\{3r\}$;   (ii) $\{3r-5\}$;   (iii) $\{2^{r-1}\}$;   (iv) $\{r(r^2-1)\}$;
(v) $\{1+(-1)^r\}$;   (vi) $\{1/[r(r+1)]\}$;   (vii) $\{r^{r-3}\}$;
(viii) $\{r+(-1)^r (r+1)\}$.

Ex. 4. Suggest possible fifth and sixth terms for the following sequences, whose first four terms are given, indicating how you arrived at them:

(i) $\{1, 4, 7, 10, ...\}$;   (ii) $\{1, -\frac{1}{2}, \frac{1}{4}, -\frac{1}{8}, ...\}$;
(iii) $\{1, 2, 4, 7, ...\}$;   (iv) $\{0, 3, 8, 15, ...\}$;
(v) $\{1, 3, 6, 11, ...\}$.

*Ex. 5. Why was the word 'suggest' used in Exercise 4?

Work out the first four terms of the sequence $\{r^4 - 10r^3 + 35r^2 - 50r + 25\}$.

Work out the fifth term of this sequence.

Can you see an easy way of constructing the general term of a sequence which has the property that its first five terms are zero, but its sixth term is non-zero?

Given a sequence it is often necessary to obtain the *sum* of its first n terms. If the first n terms of a sequence are written down and connected by + signs, we are said to have a *series*. For example

$$1+3+5+7+\ldots+(2n-1),$$

$$1+\tfrac{1}{2}+\tfrac{1}{3}+\tfrac{1}{4}+\ldots+1/n$$

are the series obtained respectively from the sequences $\{2r-1\}$ and $\{1/r\}$.

If n is known, such sums may be found simply by obtaining the necessary terms and adding them one by one, but the process is naturally laborious. In this chapter we shall explore more sophisticated methods for summing certain simple series, but, before doing so, it is desirable to introduce a shorthand notation for sums, the Σ *notation* (read 'sigma notation').

We write $u_1 + u_2 + u_3 + \ldots + u_n$ as $\sum_{r=1}^{n} u_r$. Thus, for example,

$$\sum_{r=1}^{4} r = 1+2+3+4 = 10;$$

$$\sum_{r=1}^{5} (3r-1) = 2+5+8+11+14 = 40.$$

It is possible to assume that u_r is defined by values of $r \notin Z^+$:

$$\sum_{r=0}^{3} (r^2+1) = 1+2+5+10 = 18;$$

$$\sum_{r=-1}^{2} (r^2+r+1) = 1+1+3+7 = 12.$$

The general rule for finding $\sum_{r=m}^{n} u_r$ is to determine the value of u_r for $r = m$ and all subsequent r, in steps of 1, until we arrive at u_n and then to sum all the terms so obtained.

Ex. 6. Write out in full:

(i) $\sum_{r=1}^{3} r^2$;

(ii) $\sum_{r=1}^{4} (r^2 - r)$;

(iii) $\sum_{r=1}^{4} r(2^r - 1)$;

(iv) $\sum_{r=1}^{5} (-1)^r r$;

(v) $\sum_{r=0}^{3} (r^3 + 2)$;

(vi) $\sum_{r=-2}^{3} (r^2 - 1)$;

(vii) $\sum_{r=0}^{4} \dfrac{r}{r+2}$.

132

Ex. 7. Evaluate:

(i) $\sum_{r=1}^{4} (r+2)$;   (ii) $\sum_{r=1}^{3} r^2$;   (iii) $\sum_{r=1}^{4} r^3$;

(iv) $\sum_{r=0}^{3} (r-1)^2$;   (v) $\sum_{r=0}^{2} \frac{1}{r+2}$;   (vi) $\sum_{r=1}^{5} (-1)^r r^2$;

(vii) $\sum_{r=0}^{4} 2^r$;   (viii) $\sum_{r=2}^{4} \left(\frac{1}{r} - \frac{1}{r+1}\right)$.

Ex. 8. Write in Σ notation:

(i) $1+2+3+4$;   (ii) $1-2+3-4$;
(iii) $2+4+6+8$;   (iv) $1+2+4+8+16$;
(v) $1+\frac{1}{2}+\frac{1}{3}+\frac{1}{4}+\frac{1}{5}+\frac{1}{6}$;   (vi) $1.2+2.3+3.4+4.5+5.6+6.7$;
(vii) $1-1+1-1+1-1+1-1$;   (viii) $1+2+3+4+...+n$.

Ex. 9. Prove that, if $\{u_r\}$ and $\{v_r\}$ are two sequences, then

$$\sum_{r=m}^{n} (u_r+v_r) = \sum_{r=m}^{n} u_r + \sum_{r=m}^{n} v_r.$$

Ex. 10. Prove that, if $\{u_r\}$ is any sequence and a a fixed number, then

$$\sum_{r=m}^{n} a u_r = a \sum_{r=m}^{n} u_r.$$

Ex. 11. Interpret and evaluate $\sum_{r=1}^{n} c$, where c is fixed. (That is, find the sum of the first n terms of the constant sequence defined by $u_r = c$, all r.)

2. ARITHMETIC SEQUENCES

Sequences such as $\{1, 3, 5, 7, ...\}$, $\{1\frac{1}{4}, 2\frac{1}{2}, 3\frac{3}{4}, 5, ...\}$, $\{4, 1, -2, -5, ...\}$ are called *arithmetic sequences*, their distinguishing feature being that the difference between any pair of successive terms is constant. If we call this *common difference* d, and the *first term* a, then the arithmetic sequence takes the form $\{a+(r-1)d\}$.

Ex. 12. Write down the rth terms of each of the following arithmetic sequences:

$$\{1, 4, 7, ...\}, \quad \{1, 2\frac{1}{2}, 4, ...\}, \quad \{2, 0, -2, ...\}.$$

Ex. 13. Find to which integer r the following terms correspond in the given arithmetic sequences:

(i) 91 in $\{1, 3, 5, ...\}$;   (ii) 139 in $\{3, 7, 11, ...\}$;
(iii) -253 in $\{2, -1, -4, ...\}$;   (iv) $61\cdot7$ in $\{3\cdot2, 4\cdot7, 6\cdot2, ...\}$;
(v) -67 in $\{7\frac{1}{4}, 6\frac{1}{2}, 5\frac{3}{4}, ...\}$.

Ex. 14. Taking what you consider to be the simplest continuation in each case, write down, in Σ form, the sum of the first n terms of each of the following series:

(i) $1.4.7+4.7.10+7.10.13+10.13.16+...;$

(ii) $2.3.5+4.6.9+6.9.13+8.12.17+...;$

(iii) $2^1+4^4+6^7+8^{10}+...;$

(iv) $\dfrac{1.3}{2}+\dfrac{3.7}{5}+\dfrac{5.11}{8}+\dfrac{7.15}{11}+...;$

(v) $\dfrac{1}{1.2.3}-\dfrac{2}{3.5.10}+\dfrac{3}{5.8.17}-\dfrac{4}{7.11.24}.$

The sum to n terms of the *arithmetic series* (sometimes called the *arithmetic progression* and abbreviated A.P.) is easily obtained by the following argument.

Consider first the sum of the first n positive integers, that is $\sum\limits_{r=1}^{n} r$. Writing this sum as S we have

$$S = 1+2+3+...+n$$

and $$S = n+(n-1)+(n-2)+...+1.$$

Adding: $$2S = (n+1)+(n+1)+(n+1)+...+(n+1)$$
$$= n(n+1).$$

Thus $$S = \tfrac{1}{2}n(n+1).$$

Now, for the general arithmetic series,

$$\sum_{r=1}^{n} [a+(r-1)\,d] = \sum_{r=1}^{n} a+d\sum_{r=1}^{n} r- \sum_{r=1}^{n} d \quad \text{(see Ex. 9 and Ex. 10)}$$

$$= na+\tfrac{1}{2}dn(n+1)-nd$$

$$= \tfrac{1}{2}n[2a+(n-1)\,d].$$

This method is easily applicable to any arithmetic series and depends only upon memorizing the single important result

$$\sum_{r=1}^{n} r = \tfrac{1}{2}n(n+1).$$

Example 1. *The tenth term of a certain arithmetic series is* -29 *and the twentieth term is* -69. *Find the sum of the first twenty terms.*

Let the first term be a and the common difference d. Then

$$a+9d = -29, \qquad a+19d = -69,$$

giving $a = 7$, $d = -4$. The rth term of the arithmetic series is thus

134

$7+(r-1)(-4) = 11-4r$ and the sum of twenty terms is given by

$$\sum_{r=1}^{20} (11-4r) = 220 - 2.20.21$$
$$= -620.$$

Exercise 8(a)

1. Evaluate:

(i) $\sum_{r=1}^{6} (r^2+r)$;   (ii) $\sum_{r=1}^{4} \frac{1}{r}$;   (iii) $\sum_{r=-2}^{2} (1+r+r^2)$.

2. Write in Σ notation:
   (i) $1.3+4.6+7.9+...$ (to n terms);
   (ii) $1.2.3-2.3.4+3.4.5-4.5.6+...$ (to n terms);
   (iii) $1^2-3^2+5^2-7^2+...$ (to n terms).

3. Find the first four terms of each of the sequences defined by the following recurrence relations and initial terms:
   (i) $u_r = 3u_{r-1}+1$, $u_1 = 1$;
   (ii) $u_r+2u_{r-1}-3u_{r-2} = 0$, $u_1 = 1$, $u_2 = 1$;
   (iii) $u_r = u_{r-1}^2$, $u_1 = 2$;
   (iv) $2u_r u_{r-1}-u_{r-1}^2 = 3$, $u_1 = 1$.

4. If $\{u_r\}$ is an arithmetic sequence with common difference d and first term a, show that u_r satisfies the recurrence relation

$$u_r = u_{r-1}+d.$$

If $s_n = \sum_{r=1}^{n} u_r$, determine a recurrence relation involving only s_n, s_{n-1}, s_{n-2} and d. What is s_1?

5. Find the rth term of the following arithmetic sequences:
   (i) $\{3, 12, 21, ...\}$;   (ii) $\{\frac{1}{4}, \frac{3}{4}, \frac{5}{4}, ...\}$;   (iii) $\{12, 4, -4, ...\}$.

6. Find the number of terms in the following arithmetic series:
   (i) $1+3+5+...+101$;   (ii) $2+9+16+...+485$;
   (iii) $5+2+(-1)+...+(-82)$.

7. Sum each of the series in Question 6.

8. The fourth term of an arithmetic series is -14 and the tenth term is -44. Find an expression for the rth term and hence obtain the sum of the first twenty terms.

9. The first term of an arithmetic series is 9 and the sum of the first ten terms is 450. Find an expression for the rth term and deduce an expression for the sum to n terms. Check your final result by setting (i) $n = 1$; (ii) $n = 10$.

10. The ninth term of an arithmetic series is 24 and the sum of the first nine terms is 126. Find an expression for the rth term and deduce an expression for the sum to n terms.

11. How many terms of the series $1+8+15+...$ are required to give a sum of 5500?

12. How many terms of the series $12+6+0+...$ are required to give a sum of -3348?

13. Show that
$$\sum_{r=1}^{n}(r+1)^2 = \sum_{r=1}^{n}r^2+2\sum_{r=1}^{n}r+n$$
and deduce that
$$\sum_{r=1}^{n}r = \tfrac{1}{2}n(n+1).$$

14. If $\sum_{r=1}^{n}s_r = n^2+n$, prove that $\{s_r\}$ is an arithmetic sequence, and find the first three terms.

15. Prove that the sum of n terms of any arithmetic series may be written in the form an^2+bn+c. Prove the converse of this result: that if
$$\sum_{r=1}^{n}s_r = an^2+bn+c,$$
then $\{s_r\}$ is an arithmetic sequence.

16. If a^2, b^2, c^2 are the first three terms of an arithmetic sequence, prove that $(b+c)^{-1}, (c+a)^{-1}, (a+b)^{-1}$ are the first three terms of another arithmetic sequence (provided $b+c \neq 0, c+a \neq 0, a+b \neq 0$).

17. If $3+x+y+29$ is an arithmetic series, find x and y.
If $a+x_1+x_2+...+x_n+b$ are the $(n+2)$ terms of an arithmetic series, find x_r in terms of a, b, r and n.

18. An arithmetic sequence whose first term is 8 has a common difference of $\tfrac{1}{4}$. Find N, given that the sum of the first $2N$ terms is equal to the sum of the next N terms.

3. GEOMETRIC SEQUENCES

Sequences such as $\{1, 2, 4, 8, ...\}, \{3, -6, 12, -24, ...\}, \{1\cdot5, 0\cdot75, 0\cdot375...\}$, in which each term is a fixed multiple of the preceding term are called *geometric sequences*. If we call the *first term* of the sequence a, and the fixed multiple, or *common ratio*, ρ then the geometric sequence takes the form $\{a\rho^{r-1}\}$.

Ex. 15. Which of the following sets of numbers could be the first three terms of geometric sequences?
  (i) $\{1, -5, 25, ...\}$; (ii) $\{2, 2\tfrac{1}{4}, 2\tfrac{17}{32}, ...\}$ (iii) $\{1, 4, 9, ...\}$;
  (iv) $\{1, -1\cdot1, 1\cdot21, ...\}$; (v) $\{7, -1, -\tfrac{1}{7}, ...\}$; (vi) $\{1, -1, 1, ...\}$.

Ex. 16. Find to which value of r the following terms correspond in the given geometric sequences:
  (i) 256 in $\{2, 4, 8, ...\}$; (ii) 1458 in $\{2, 6, 18, ...\}$;
  (iii) 10^{-30} in $\{10, 1, 0\cdot1, ...\}$.

A *geometric series* (*geometric progression*, G.P.) is a series obtained from a geometric sequence. The sum of the first n terms of such a series may be obtained as follows:

Let
$$S = \sum_{r=1}^{n} a\rho^{r-1}.$$

If $\rho = 1$, then $S = na$.
If $\rho \neq 1$, then
$$S = a + a\rho + a\rho^2 + \ldots + a\rho^{n-1}$$
$$\rho S = \quad\; a\rho + a\rho^2 + \ldots + a\rho^{n-1} + a\rho^n$$
$$\therefore \;\; (1-\rho)S = a \qquad\qquad\qquad\qquad -a\rho^n.$$

Since $1-\rho \neq 0$ we may divide by $(1-\rho)$ to obtain the following important result:
$$\sum_{\rho=1}^{n} a\rho^{r-1} = \frac{a(1-\rho^n)}{1-\rho} \quad (\rho \neq 1).$$

Since, for $|\rho| < 1$, $\lim_{n\to\infty} \rho^n = 0$ (consult a calculus text-book for the definition of limits and the proof of this result), we may take
$$\sum_{r=1}^{n} a\rho^{r-1} - a/(1-\rho)$$

less than any positive number, however small, by taking a sufficiently large n, provided $|\rho| < 1$. Thus, if we write
$$\lim_{n\to\infty} \sum_{r=1}^{n} a\rho^{r-1} \quad \text{as} \quad \sum_{r=1}^{\infty} a\rho^{r-1}$$

we have
$$\sum_{r=1}^{\infty} a\rho^{r-1} = \frac{a}{1-\rho}, \quad \text{provided} \quad |\rho| < 1.$$

(The *sum to infinity* of a geometric series.)

Example 2. Find the sum of money that must be invested to yield an income of £50 at the end of that year, and at the end of each of the subsequent nine years, reckoning on a return of 5 % compound interest on money remaining invested. (Assume that interest is payable once a year.)

For every £1 invested, its value at the end of one year is £1·05, its value at the end of two years is £1·05² and so on. Thus, to obtain £50 at the end of the first year, we must invest £P_1, where
$$P_1 \times 1{\cdot}05 = 50.$$

Again, to obtain £50 at the end of the second year, we must invest £P_2, where
$$P_2 \times 1{\cdot}05^2 = 50$$
and so on.

The total sum to be invested is given by

$$P_1+P_2+\ldots+P_{10} = 50[1\cdot05^{-1}+1\cdot05^{-2}+\ldots+1\cdot05^{-10}]$$

$$= \frac{50[1-1\cdot05^{-10}]}{1-1\cdot05^{-1}}1\cdot05^{-1}$$

$$= 1000[1-1/1\cdot05^{10}]$$

$$= 1000[1-1/1\cdot6289]$$

$$= 386\cdot2.$$

Ex. 17. Comment upon the number of decimal points used in the calculations in Example 2 and on the accuracy achieved.

Exercise 8(b)

1. Find the sum of the following geometric series, simplifying your answers as far as possible, but without evaluating terms of the form ρ^n:

(i) $1+4+16+\ldots$ (12 terms); (ii) $1-2+4-8+\ldots$ (20 terms);
(iii) $\sqrt{2}+2+2\sqrt{2}+\ldots$ (16 terms); (iv) $1+\frac{1}{3}+\frac{1}{9}+\ldots$ (50 terms)

2. The third term of a geometric sequence is 5 and the eighth is 160. Find the first term and the common ratio.

3. Find two possible geometric sequences whose fourth term is 9 and whose eighth term is 144.

4. Which is the first term of the geometric sequence 1, $\frac{1}{3}$, $\frac{1}{9}$, ... which is less than 10^{-8}?

5. How many terms of the geometric series $1+\frac{1}{2}+\frac{1}{4}+\ldots$ must be taken to give a sum greater than $2-10^{-6}$?

6. How many terms of the geometric series $1+\frac{3}{4}+\frac{9}{16}+\ldots$ must be taken to give a sum greater than $4-10^{-3}$?

7. If $x-4$, x, $x+6$ are the first three terms of a geometric sequence, find x and the fourth term.

8. How many terms of the series $1+5+25+\ldots$ must be taken to give a sum greater than 10^{10}?

9. A piece of paper is $0\cdot1$ mm thick (so that when it is folded over, the resulting thickness is $0\cdot2$ mm). If a very large sheet of paper could be folded fifty times, what would be the resulting thickness? (This is a variant of a famous problem; another form it can take is to find how much corn is required if one grain is to be placed on the first square of a chess board, two on the second, four on the third and so on. The answers, when first met, are surprising.)

10. The sum of the first n terms of the sequence $\{s_r\}$ is $\frac{1}{6}(3^n-1)$. Prove that the sequence is geometric, and write down the first three terms.

138

11. If £250 is invested at 4 % compound interest, reckoned annually, what will be its value after six years?

12. What sum of money must be invested to give an annuity, starting ten years after investment, of £100 p.a. for five years, reckoning on 4 % compound interest (calculated annually) on money remaining invested?

13. Sum to infinity the following geometric series:

(i) $1+\frac{1}{10}+\frac{1}{100}+...$;   (ii) $3+1\frac{1}{2}+\frac{3}{4}+...$;

(iii) $1-\frac{1}{2}+\frac{1}{4}-....$

14. A recurring decimal may be regarded as the sum of an infinite geometric series; for example

$$0\cdot\dot{2}\dot{1} = \frac{21}{100}+\frac{21}{10000}+\frac{21}{1\,000\,000}+....$$

Use this approach to express $0\cdot3\dot{1}\dot{5}$ as a fraction p/q.

15. If the population of a country increases by 3 % each year, how many years will it take for the population to double?

16. If
$$s_n = \sum_{r=1}^{n} a\rho^{r-1}, \quad \text{evaluate} \sum_{r=1}^{n} s_r.$$

17. If $\{u_r\}$ is a geometric sequence with common ratio ρ, find a recurrence relation involving u_r and u_{r-1}. If $s_n = \sum_{r=1}^{n} u_r$, show that s_r satisfies the recurrence relation

$$s_n - \rho s_{n-1} = a.$$

What is s_1?

18. If $a_1, a_2, a_3, a_4, ...$ are terms of a geometric sequence with common ratio r, find the sum of n terms of the series

$$(a_1 - a_2)^2 + (a_2 - a_3)^2 + (a_3 - a_4)^2 + ...$$

4. FURTHER SUMMATION; THE USE OF DIFFERENCES

By factorizing the algebraic expression $r(r+1)(r+2)-(r-1)r(r+1)$ we see that
$$r(r+1) \equiv \tfrac{1}{3}[r(r+1)(r+2)-(r-1)r(r+1)].$$

Now suppose we let r take successively the values 1, 2, 3, ..., n in this identity. Writing the resulting equalities one below the other we have

$$1.2 = \tfrac{1}{3}[1.2.3-0.1.2],$$
$$2.3 = \tfrac{1}{3}[2.3.4-1.2.3],$$
$$3.4 = \tfrac{1}{3}[3.4.5.-2.3.4],$$
$$\vdots$$
$$(n-1).n = \tfrac{1}{3}[(n-1)n(n+1)-(n-2)(n-1)n],$$
$$n.(n+1) = \tfrac{1}{3}[n(n+1)(n+2)-(n-1)n(n+1)].$$

139

...

If all the terms on the left-hand side are added together we have precisely $\sum_{r=1}^{n} r(r+1)$; if all the terms on the right-hand side are added together, we are left with $-\frac{1}{3}0.1.2$ at the beginning and $\frac{1}{3}n(n+1)(n+2)$ at the end, all the others having cancelled out in pairs. Thus

$$\sum_{r=1}^{n} r(r+1) = \tfrac{1}{3}n(n+1)(n+2).$$

Ex. 18. Show that
$$\frac{1}{r(r+1)} = \frac{1}{r} - \frac{1}{r+1}$$

and deduce the result
$$\sum_{r=1}^{n} \frac{1}{r(r+1)} = 1 - \frac{1}{n+1}.$$

More generally, if the rth term of the sequence $\{s_r\}$ can be expressed as the difference between the $(r+1)$th term and the rth term of a new sequence $\{u_r\}$, that is, if we can find a new sequence $\{u_r\}$ with the property that, for all r,
$$s_r = u_{r+1} - u_r,$$

then
$$\sum_{r=1}^{n} s_r = \sum_{r=1}^{n}(u_{r+1} - u_r) = u_{n+1} - u_1.$$

In the example given above, $s_r = r(r+1)$ and $u_r = \tfrac{1}{3}(r-1)r(r+1)$; in Ex. 18,
$$s_r = \frac{1}{r(r+1)} \quad \text{and} \quad u_r = -1/r.$$

This technique for summing series is called the *method of differences*; its use depends, of course, upon our ability to discover the new sequence $\{u_r\}$.

Ex. 19. Show that
$$r(r+1)(r+2) = \tfrac{1}{4}[r(r+1)(r+2)(r+3) - (r-1)r(r+1)(r+2)]$$

and deduce that
$$\sum_{r=1}^{n} r(r+1)(r+2) = \tfrac{1}{4}n(n+1)(n+2)(n+3).$$

Ex. 20. Show that
$$\frac{1}{r(r+1)(r+2)} = \frac{1}{2}\left[\frac{1}{r(r+1)} - \frac{1}{(r+1)(r+2)}\right]$$

and deduce that
$$\sum_{r=1}^{n} \frac{1}{r(r+1)(r+2)} = \frac{1}{4} - \frac{1}{2(n+1)(n+2)}.$$

Ex. 21. Prove that
$$\sum_{r=1}^{n} r(r+1)(r+2)(r+3) = \tfrac{1}{5}n(n+1)(n+2)(n+3)(n+4)$$

and evaluate
$$\sum_{r=1}^{n} r(r+1)(r+2)(r+3)(r+4).$$

140

Ex. 22. Prove that

$$\sum_{r=1}^{n} \frac{1}{r(r+1)(r+2)(r+3)} = \frac{1}{18} - \frac{1}{3(n+1)(n+2)(n+3)}$$

and evaluate

$$\sum_{r=1}^{n} \frac{1}{r(r+1)(r+2)(r+3)(r+4)}.$$

It is sometimes worthwhile to manipulate s_r into a slightly different form before applying the method of differences.

Example 3. *Evaluate*

$$\sum_{r=1}^{n} \frac{1}{r(r+2)},$$

$$\frac{1}{r(r+2)} = \frac{r+1}{r(r+1)(r+2)} = \frac{1}{(r+1)(r+2)} + \frac{1}{r(r+1)(r+2)}.$$

Then

$$\sum_{r=1}^{n} \frac{1}{r(r+2)} = \sum_{r=1}^{n} \frac{1}{(r+1)(r+2)} + \sum_{r=1}^{n} \frac{1}{r(r+1)(r+2)}$$

$$= \sum_{r=1}^{n} \left[\frac{1}{r+1} - \frac{1}{r+2} \right] + \frac{1}{2} \sum_{r=1}^{n} \left[\frac{1}{r(r+1)} - \frac{1}{(r+1)(r+2)} \right]$$

$$= \left[\frac{1}{2} - \frac{1}{n+2} \right] + \frac{1}{2} \left[\frac{1}{2} - \frac{1}{(n+1)(n+2)} \right]$$

$$= \frac{3}{4} - \frac{2n+3}{2(n+1)(n+2)}.$$

(Note the check by putting $n = 1$.)

The method of difference is thus seen to constitute a powerful technique for summing series. The reader should commit the method to memory, especially the particular approach used for the series given at the beginning of this section and in Ex. 19 and Ex. 20. We shall complete this section by using the results already proved to deduce two more important sums:

(i) $\sum_{r=1}^{n} r^2 = \frac{1}{6}n(n+1)(2n+1);$ (ii) $\sum_{r=1}^{n} r^3 = \frac{1}{4}n^2(n+1)^2.$

Proof of (i): Since

$$r^2 = r(r+1) - r,$$

$$\sum_{r=1}^{n} r^2 = \sum_{r=1}^{n} r(r+1) - \sum_{r=1}^{n} r$$

$$= \frac{1}{3}n(n+1)(n+2) - \frac{1}{2}n(n+1)$$

$$= \frac{1}{6}n(n+1)(2n+1).$$

141

Proof of (ii):

$$r(r+1)(r+2) = r^3+3r^2+2r$$

and so
$$r^3 = r(r+1)(r+2)-(3r^2+2r)$$
$$= r(r+1)(r+2)-3r(r+1)+r.$$

Thus
$$\sum_{r=1}^{n} r^3 = \sum_{r=1}^{n} r(r+1)(r+2)-3\sum_{r=1}^{n} r(r+1)+\sum_{r=1}^{n} r$$
$$= \tfrac{1}{4}n(n+1)(n+2)(n+3) - n(n+1)(n+2)+\tfrac{1}{2}n(n+1)$$
$$= \tfrac{1}{4}n^2(n+1)^2, \quad \text{on simplification.}$$

$$\left(\text{Observe that } \sum_{r=1}^{n} r^3 = \left(\sum_{r=1}^{n} r\right)^2.\right)$$

Example 4. Evaluate
$$\sum_{r=1}^{n}(r+1)(n+r).$$

$$\sum_{r=1}^{n}(r+1)(n+r) = \sum_{r=1}^{n}(r^2+r(n+1)+n)$$
$$= \sum_{r=1}^{n} r^2+(n+1)\sum_{r=1}^{n} r+n^2, \text{ by Exs. 9, 10, 11}$$
$$= \tfrac{1}{6}n(n+1)(2n+1)+\tfrac{1}{2}n(n+1)^2+n^2$$
$$= \tfrac{1}{6}n(5n^2+15n+4).$$

Exercise 8(c)

1. Sum the following series:
   (i) $1^2+2^2+3^2+\ldots+12^2$; (ii) $1^3+2^3+3^3+\ldots+12^3$;
   (iii) $3^2+4^2+5^2+\ldots+20^2$; (iv) $1^2+3^2+5^2+7^2+\ldots+(2n-1)^2$.

2. By expressing $r(r+1)(r+3)$ in the form $r(r+1)(r+2)+r(r+1)$, sum the series
$$\sum_{r=1}^{n} r(r+1)(r+3).$$

   Find the value of
$$\sum_{r=1}^{n} r(r+1)(r+4).$$

3. Find
$$\sum_{r=1}^{n} r^2(r+1).$$

4. Find
$$\sum_{r=1}^{n}(r^3+r+2).$$

5. Find
$$\sum_{r=1}^{n} r(n-r)^2.$$

142

6. Find $\displaystyle\sum_{r=1}^{n} (r^2 + 2r)$

(i) by expressing it as $\displaystyle\sum_{r=1}^{n} r^2 + \sum_{r=1}^{n} 2r$;

(ii) by expressing it as $\displaystyle\sum_{r=1}^{n} (r+1)^2 - \sum_{r=1}^{n} 1$.

7. Show that, for $r \geqslant 0$,

$$\frac{r}{(r+1)(r+2)(r+3)} = \frac{1}{(r+2)(r+3)} - \frac{1}{(r+1)(r+2)(r+3)}.$$

Hence evaluate $\displaystyle\sum_{r=1}^{n} \frac{r}{(r+1)(r+2)(r+3)}.$

8. Evaluate $\displaystyle\sum_{r=1}^{n} \frac{r-1}{r(r+1)(r+2)(r+3)}.$

9. Evaluate $\displaystyle\sum_{r=1}^{n} \frac{1}{r(r+1)(r+2)(r+4)}.$

10. Find the sums to n terms of the following series:
(i) $1.4 + 4.7 + 7.10 + 10.13 + \dots$;
(ii) $1^2.2 + 2^2.3 + 3^2.4 + 4^2.5 + \dots$;
(iii) $1.2.3 + 4.5.6 + 7.8.9 + 10.11.12 + \dots$;
(iv) $1^2.2.3 + 2^2.3.4 + 3^2.4.5 + 4^2.5.6 + \dots$.

11. Show that

$$x(x+1)(2x+1) \equiv Ax(x+1)(x+2)(x+3) + B(x-2)(x-1)x(x+1)$$

for certain constant values of A and B, and find these values. Hence find the sum of the first n terms of the series

$$1.2.3 + 2.3.5 + 3.4.7 + 4.5.9 + \dots. \qquad \text{(O \& C)}$$

12. Prove that

$$\frac{(2n+1)(2n+3)}{(n+1)(n+2)} - \frac{(2n-1)(2n+1)}{n(n+1)} \equiv \frac{2(2n+1)}{n(n+1)(n+2)}.$$

Find the sum of the first n terms of the series

$$\frac{3}{1.2.3} + \frac{5}{2.3.4} + \frac{7}{3.4.5} + \dots \qquad \text{(O \& C)}$$

13. Deduce $\displaystyle\sum_{r=1}^{n} r^2$ from the identity $(2r+1)^3 - (2r-1)^3 \equiv 24r^2 + 2.$

14. Evaluate $\displaystyle\sum_{r=2}^{n} \frac{1}{r(r^2-1)}.$

15. Prove that the sum of the squares of the first n even numbers exceeds the sum of the squares of the first n odd numbers by $n(2n+1)$. Hence, or otherwise, find the sum of the squares of the first n odd numbers. (O \& C)

5. THE BINOMIAL THEOREM

By ordinary multiplication of algebraic expressions

$$(x+a)^1 = x+a$$
$$(x+a)^2 = x^2+2xa+a^2$$
$$(x+a)^3 = x^3+3x^2a+3xa^2+a^3$$
$$(x+a)^4 = x^4+4x^3a+6x^2a^2+4xa^3+a^4$$
$$(x+a)^5 = x^5+5x^4a+10x^3a^2+10x^2a^3+5xa^4+a^5$$

Notice the following features possessed by these expressions:
(i) the number of terms in the expansion of $(x+a)^n$ is $n+1$;
(ii) the degree of each term in the expansion of $(x+a)^n$ is n;
(iii) The coefficients of the terms in the expansion of $(x+a)^n$ are given by the nth line of *Pascal's triangle* (Blaise Pascal, 1623–62); see Figure 8.2.

```
      1   1
    1   2   1
  1   3   3   1
1   4   6   4   1
1   5   10   10   5   1
```

Fig. 8.2

Each line of Pascal's triangle starts and finishes with a 1; terms in between are obtained by adding together the two terms on either side of it in the row above.

Ex. 23. Supply the sixth, seventh and eighth lines of Pascal's triangle.

Ex. 24. Check that the expansion of $(x+a)^6$ satisfies conditions (i), (ii) and (iii) above.

Ex. 25. Show that, if we add the 'zeroth' line, 1, to Pascal's triangle, the expansion of $(x+a)^0$ satisfies conditions (i), (ii) and (iii).

By direct verification as above, we may show that conditions (i), (ii) and (iii) hold for all suitably small values of n; the *Binomial Theorem* can be used to show that they are true for all positive integers n. However, before proceeding to the general theorem, we shall solve an example by means of Pascal's triangle.

144

Example 5. Obtain the expansion of $(2x-3y)^5$. *Hence obtain an approximate value for* $199 \cdot 7^5$, *and comment upon the accuracy of the result.*

From the fifth line of Pascal's triangle

$$(2x-3y)^5 = (2x)^5 + 5(2x)^4(-3y) + 10(2x)^3(-3y)^2 + 10(2x)^2(-3y)^3$$
$$+ 5(2x)(-3y)^4 + (-3y)^5$$
$$= 32x^5 - 240x^4y + 720x^3y^2 - 1080x^2y^3 + 810xy^4 - 243y^5.$$

If we put $x = 10^2$, $y = 10^{-1}$, then $(2x-3y)^5 = 199 \cdot 7^5$. Hence,

$$199 \cdot 7^5 = 3 \cdot 2 \times 10^{11} - 2 \cdot 4 \times 10^9 + 7 \cdot 2 \times 10^6 \ldots$$

and the last three terms will not affect the first six significant figures. Direct calculation of the line above shows us that

$$199 \cdot 7^5 = 3 \cdot 17607 \times 10^{11}, \quad \text{correct to six significant figures.}$$

Ex. 26. Write down the expansions of
(i) $(3x-y)^4$;   (ii) $(2x+y)^6$;   (iii) $(2x-1)^7$;   (iv) $(3x+2y)^5$.

The Binomial Theorem states that, for any positive integer n,

$$(x+a)^n = x^n + \binom{n}{1}x^{n-1}a + \binom{n}{2}x^{n-2}a^2 + \ldots + \binom{n}{r}x^{n-r}a^r + \ldots + a^n$$
$$= \sum_{r=0}^{n}\binom{n}{r}x^{n-r}a^r. \quad \left(\text{Recall that } \binom{n}{0} = 1.\right)$$

Proof. $(x+a)^n = (x+a)(x+a)(x+a)\ldots(x+a)$. [$n$ brackets in all.]

Since, in forming the product on the right-hand side, one term is chosen from each bracket, each term in the expansion must be of the form $x^{n-r}a^r$ (choose $(n-r)$ terms x, and r terms a). Now the term $x^{n-r}a^r$ may be obtained by selecting any r brackets and choosing the a term and then choosing an x from each of the remaining $(n-r)$ brackets. But there are $\binom{n}{r}$ different ways of doing this and so the coefficient of $x^{n-r}a^r$ is $\binom{n}{r}$. The proof of the Binomial Theorem is now complete.†

We make the following observations:
(i) Since r runs through all integral values from 0 to n, there are $(n+1)$ terms in the expansion.
(ii) The degree of each term is $(n-r)+r = n$.

† An alternative proof of the Binomial Theorem is given in Chapter 9.3.

(iii) Since

$$\binom{n-1}{r-1} + \binom{n-1}{r} = \frac{(n-1)!}{(r-1)!\,(n-r)!} + \frac{(n-1)!}{r!\,(n-r-1)!}$$

$$= \frac{(n-1)!}{(r-1)!\,(n-r-1)!} \left[\frac{1}{n-r} + \frac{1}{r} \right]$$

$$= \frac{n!}{r!\,(n-r)!}$$

$$= \binom{n}{r},$$

the coefficients in the expansion of $(x+a)^n$ are connected to those of the expansion of $(x+a)^{n-1}$ in precisely the same way as was previously observed for Pascal's triangle.

The result

$$\binom{n-1}{r-1} + \binom{n-1}{r} = \binom{n}{r}$$

is of some importance and will be used later; it is generally known as *Vandermonde's Theorem*.

Example 6. Obtain the first three terms in the expansion of $(1-2x)^{20}$ in ascending powers of x.

$$(1-2x)^{20} = (1)^{20} + \binom{20}{1}(1)^{19}(-2x)^1 + \binom{20}{2}(1)^{18}(-2x)^2$$

$$= 1 + 20(-2x) + \frac{20.19}{1.2}(4x^2) \ldots$$

$$= 1 - 40x + 760x^2 \ldots.$$

Exercise 8(d)

1. Write down the expansions of
  (i) $(x-y)^6$;
  (iii) $(1+2x)^7$;
  (ii) $(2x+\frac{1}{2}y)^5$;
  (iv) $(2x+6y)^6$.

2. Find the coefficient of x^2 in the expansions of each of the following expressions:
  (i) $(3x+1)^4$;   (ii) $(2-x)^7$;   (iii) $(1+2x)^{12}$;   (iv) $(3-4x)^6$.

3. Write down the first three terms in the expansions of each of the following expressions in ascending powers of x:
  (i) $(1+2x)^8$;   (ii) $(1+\frac{1}{2}x)^{15}$;   (iii) $(2-x)^{10}$;   (iv) $(3x-y)^7$.

4. Write down the general term in the expansion of

$$\left(2x - \frac{1}{x}\right)^8.$$

146

Hence determine the constant term in this expansion (that is, the term not involving x).

5. Determine the constant term in the expansion of

$$\left(x^2 - \frac{1}{3x}\right)^6.$$

6. Find correct to five significant figures, the values of
(i) $(1 \cdot 01)^6$;　　　(ii) $(0 \cdot 998)^8$;　　　(iii) $(9 \cdot 99)^5$;　　　(iv) $(2 \cdot 98)^5$.
In each case, justify the accuracy of your result.

7. Find, without using tables, the value of

$$(2 + \sqrt{5})^4 + (2 - \sqrt{5})^4.$$

8. Write down the coefficient of a^3x^7 in the expansion of $(a+x)^{10}$. Find the co-efficient of $a^3b^4c^3$ in the expansion of $(a+b+c)^{10}$.

9. Expand in ascending powers of x, as far as terms in x^2, each of the following expressions:
(i) $(1+x+x^2)^4$;　　(ii) $(1-x+x^2)^6$;　　(iii) $(1+2x-x^2)^5$;　　(iv) $(2-x-2x^2)^6$.

10. If a device measures linear dimensions with an error of less than $\frac{1}{2}\%$, find the possible percentage margin of error if it is used to measure the volume of a cube.

11. Find the sum of the coefficients of the powers of x (including x^0) in the expansion of $(1+x)^n$.
If $(1+x+x^2)^4 = a_0 + a_1x + a_2x^2 + \ldots + a_8x^8$, evaluate

(i) $\sum_{r=0}^{8} a_r$;　　(ii) $\sum_{r=0}^{8} (-1)^r a_r$.

12. Prove Vandermonde's Theorem by considering the identity

$$(1+x)^{n+1} \equiv (1+x)(1+x)^n.$$

Prove that
$$\binom{n+2}{r} = \binom{n}{r-2} + 2\binom{n}{r-1} + \binom{n}{r},$$

and suggest a generalization of this result.

Miscellaneous Exercise 8

1. Find (i) the sum, (ii) the product, of the first n terms of the geometric sequence $\{1, 3, 9, \ldots\}$.

2. The first term of a geometric series is 18 and the sum to infinity is 20. Find the common ratio and the sum of the first six terms. Find also in its simplest form the ratio of the nth term to the sum of all the subsequent terms of the infinite series.　　　　　　　　　　　　　　　　　　　　　　(J.M.B.)

147

3. In the expansion in powers of x of the function

$$(1+x)(a-bx)^{12}$$

the coefficient of x^8 is zero. Find in its simplest form the value of the ratio a/b.

(J.M.B.)

4. Write down the sum of the geometric series

$$1+x+x^2+x^3+\ldots+x^n.$$

Deduce the sum of the series

$$1+2x+3x^2+\ldots+nx^{n-1}$$

by differentiating, with respect to x, the expression for the sum of the original series.

Find the sum of the series

$$1^2+2^2x+3^2x^2+\ldots+n^2x^{n-1}.$$

5. Use Vandermonde's Theorem to evaluate

$$\sum_{r=p}^{n}\binom{r}{p}.$$

6. Numbers $C_1, C_2, C_3, \ldots$ are defined as follows:

$$C_1 = 2, \quad C_{n+1} = 2(C_1+C_2+\ldots+C_n)$$

for $n = 1, 2, \ldots$. Find C_2, C_3 and C_4 and prove that the numbers $C_2, C_3, C_4, \ldots$ form a geometric progression.

Find the sum of n terms of the series

$$C_1+C_2+C_3+\ldots. \qquad\qquad \text{(O \& C)}$$

7. The numbers $a_0, a_1, \ldots, a_n$; $c_0, c_1, \ldots, c_{n-1}$ are the coefficients in the two expansions

$$(1+x)^n = a_0+a_1x+a_2x^2+\ldots+a_nx^n,$$

$$(1+x)^{n-1} = c_0+c_1x+c_2x^2+\ldots+c_{n-1}x^{n-1}.$$

Prove that:

(a) $a_0 = c_0$ and $a_n = c_{n-1}$;
(b) $c_{r-1}+c_r = a_r$ for $1 \leqslant r \leqslant n-1$;
(c) $ra_r = nc_{r-1}$ for $1 \leqslant r \leqslant n$.

Use these results to show that

$$a_r-a_{r-1}+\ldots\pm a_0 = \frac{r+1}{n}a_{r+1}$$

for $0 \leqslant r \leqslant n-1$. (O \& C)

8. Integers a, b, d are connected by the relation $a = b+d$. By using the binomial expansion of $(b+d)^n$, where n is a positive integer, show that $a^n-b^{n-1}(b+nd)$ is exactly divisible by d^2.

Replace b by $a-d$ in this result, and hence show that if a is the first term, d the common difference and l the nth term of an arithmetic progression, then $a^n-(a-d)^{n-1}l$ is exactly divisible by d^2.

Show that $5^{10}-2^{14}$ is exactly divisible by 9. (Cambridge)

148

9. Prove that
$$1+2+3+\ldots+n = \tfrac{1}{2}n(n+1).$$
Prove also that
$$1^2-2^2+3^2-4^2+\ldots+(2n+1)^2 = (n+1)(2n+1).$$

Show that, when m is any positive integer, odd or even, the sum of the first m terms of the series
$$1^2-2^2+3^2-4^2+\ldots$$
is $(-1)^{m-1}\tfrac{1}{2}m(m+1).$ (O & C)

10. Prove that $(\sqrt{2}+1)^{2n} = A\sqrt{2}+B$, where A and B are integers. Prove further that $B^2-2A^2 = 1.$

11. Show that
$$\binom{n}{r} = \binom{n}{n-r}.$$

By considering the identity
$$(1+x)^{2m}(1-x)^{2m} \equiv (1-x^2)^{2m},$$
prove that
$$\binom{2m}{0}^2 - \binom{2m}{1}^2 + \binom{2m}{2}^2 - \ldots + \binom{2m}{2m}^2 = (-1)^m \frac{(2m)!}{(m!)^2}.$$

12. Prove that, when n is a positive integer and $a \neq 1$,
$$1+(1+a)+(1+a+a^2)+\ldots+(1+a+a^2+\ldots+a^{n-1}) = \frac{a(a^n-1)}{(a-1)^2} - \frac{n}{a-1}.$$

Show that the sum may also be written
$$n+(n-1)a+(n-2)a^2+\ldots+a^{n-1}$$
and deduce from this the sum to n terms of the series
$$1+2b+3b^2+\ldots+(n-1)b^{n-2}+nb^{n-1}.$$ (O & C)

13. Find, in binary form, the square of the number whose expression in binary notation consists of the r digits 1.

14. Evaluate
$$\sum_{r=1}^{n}\left(\sum_{s=1}^{m} rs\right).$$

By putting $m = n$, deduce that the sum of the product in pairs of the first n integers is
$$\tfrac{1}{24}n(n^2-1)(3n+2).$$

15. Verify that
$$r^2(r+1)^2-(r-1)^2 r^2 = 4r^3$$
and deduce that
$$1^3+2^3+\ldots+n^3 = \tfrac{1}{4}n^2(n+1)^2.$$
Prove that
$$1^3+3^3+5^3+\ldots+(2n-1)^3 = n^2(2n^2-1)$$
and find the sum of the cubes of all odd numbers less than 50 that are not multiples of 5.

149

16. Prove that $1^2 + 2^2 + 3^2 + \ldots + n^2 = \frac{1}{6}n(n+1)(2n+1)$.

A non-degenerate triangle is to be made from three rods chosen from $2n$ straight rods whose lengths are 1, 2, 3, ..., $2n$ units respectively. If the length of the longest side is $2r$ units, show that $(r-1)^2$ such triangles can be made.

Deduce that the total number of possible triangles whose longest side is an even number of units is
$$\tfrac{1}{6}n(n-1)(2n-1).$$
(J.M.B.)

17. The salary scale for certain employees begins at £630 a year and rises to a maximum of £855 by fifteen annual increments of £15 each. After the maximum has been reached the annual salary remains constant. Find expressions for the total amount received by an employee in n years (i) when $n \leqslant 16$; (ii) when $n > 16$.

Find the value of the second expression when $n = 24$.

It is proposed to revise the salary scale so that it begins at £720 a year and rises to a maximum by 10 equal annual increments. If each annual increment is £d find an expression for the total amount to be received in salary by an employee in n years when $n > 11$.

Find the integral value of d which would make the total amount to be received in twenty years on the new scale as nearly as possible equal to the total amount received in twenty-four years on the old scale.   (Cambridge)

18. The series of natural numbers is grouped as follows:

$$(1), \quad (2, 3, 4), \quad (5, 6, 7, 8, 9), \quad \ldots$$

(i.e. each bracket contains two integers more than the preceding bracket).

(i)   Find the total number of integers in the first $(n-1)$ brackets.

(ii) Show that the first number in the nth bracket is $n^2 - 2n + 2$.

(iii) Show that the sum of the numbers in the nth bracket is $n^3 + (n-1)^3$.

(iv) If the first number in the nth bracket is denoted by a and the first number in the $(n+1)$th bracket is denoted by b show that the sum of the numbers in the nth bracket is exactly divisible by $(b-a)$ and that the quotient is an odd number.
(Cambridge)

Revision exercise A

1. If the expressions

$$x^3 - (a+2)\,x + 2b \quad \text{and} \quad 2x^3 + ax^2 - 4x - b$$

have a common factor $x+3$, find the values of a and b, and find a second common factor. $\hfill$ (O & C 'O')

2. Find the mid-point of the line joining the points $(-4, 2)$ and $(2, -6)$, and show that the equation of the perpendicular bisector of this line is $3x - 4y = 5$.

Prove that the point $(3, 1)$ is one vertex of a square of which the points $(-4, 2)$ and $(2, -6)$ are opposite vertices, and find the coordinates of the fourth vertex. $\hfill$ (O & C 'O')

3. You are given that the equation

$$3x^5 - 9x + 5 = 0$$

has a root approximately equal to 1. By substituting $x = 1+h$, and neglecting h^2 and higher powers show that $x = 1\frac{1}{6}$ is a closer approximation to this root.

4. (i) The fourth term of an arithmetic series is 55, and the tenth term is 45. Calculate the sum of all the positive terms.

(ii) Find, correct to one decimal point, the sum of the first fifteen terms of the geometric series
$$1 + (1\cdot02) + (1\cdot02)^2 + (1\cdot02)^3 + \dots. \hfill \text{(O \& C 'O')}$$

5. In how many distinct ways may the letters of the word SYZYGY be arranged? In how many of these do the three Ys appear together?

(What does the word syzygy mean?)

6. Without using tables, prove that $\tan 60° = \sqrt{3}$.

A rectangle $ABCD$ lies in a horizontal plane and DE is a line of length h drawn vertically upwards from D; EA, EB, EC are joined. If the lines AE, CE make angles of $60°$, $45°$ respectively with the horizontal, express AD and CD in terms of h, and hence calculate the angle which BE makes with the horizontal. $\hfill$ (O & C 'O')

7. Find the equation of the line of gradient -1 which passes through the point of intersection of the lines $x + 3y - 5 = 0$ and $2x - y - 7 = 0$.

8. If $x^2 + 2x + 2$ is a factor of $x^4 + ax^2 + b$, find a and b. Express $x^4 + 16$ as the product of two quadratic factors whose coefficients are real numbers.

9. ABC is a triangle: points Q, R are taken on AC, AB respectively so that

$$AQ = 2QC, \quad 2AR = RB.$$

Express **AB**, **AC** in terms of **RQ**, **BC**.

10. If $\frac{1}{2}\pi < x < \pi$ and $\sin x = \frac{2}{3}$, find (i) $\cos x$, (ii) $\tan x$, (iii) $\operatorname{cosec} x$.

11. Write down the expansion of $(1+x)^5$ in ascending powers of x. If
$$(1+x+x^2)^5 = 1+ax+bx^2+\ldots,$$
find a and b.

12. Given that $(2x+1)$ is a factor of the expression
$$6x^3+ax^2+6x+1$$
find a, and hence find the other two linear factors.

13. Three integers (not necessarily distinct) are chosen at random from the set of integers $\{1, 2, 3, \ldots, 10\}$. What is the probability that their sum is 10? What is the probability that their sum is 10 or less?

14. By considering a suitable rhombus of side 1 unit, show that, if $\sin\theta = a$, then $\sin 2\theta = 2a\sqrt{(1-a^2)}$.
Deduce that
$$\sin 15° = \frac{\sqrt{3}-1}{2\sqrt{2}}.$$

15. Show that
$$4r^3 \equiv [r(r+1)]^2 - [r(r-1)]^2.$$
Hence evaluate $\sum_{r=1}^{n} r^3$.

16. How many terms are there in the expansion of $(a+b+c)^6$?
Can you generalize your result for $(a+b+c)^n$?

17. Show that it is not possible to find a number which is written abc in the scale of 4 and bca in the scale of 5.

18. Two points, P and Q, on the circumference of a circle of radius 10 cm are such that PQ subtends an angle of 1 radian ($57° 18'$) at its centre. State the length of the minor arc PQ of this circle, and calculate the length of the chord PQ.
   If the above circle is drawn on the surface of a sphere of radius 15 cm, find the angle which the chord PQ subtends at the centre of the sphere, and hence find the length of the minor arc PQ of the great circle of the sphere which passes through P and Q. (O & C 'O')

19. I take my wife out to buy her a new hat. There is a probability of $\frac{9}{10}$ that I shall approve of the first hat that we are shown, but if I approve, there is only a probability of $\frac{1}{20}$ that my wife will agree with my choice. If we both like the hat, I purchase it. If I dislike the first hat that we are shown, there is a probability of $\frac{3}{5}$ that my wife will like it. If she does like it she naturally overrules my choice but, when I hear the price, there is a $\frac{4}{5}$ probability that I shall veto the purchase. What is the probability that I buy her the first hat we are shown? If I do buy her the hat, what is the probability that we both like it?

20. Prove that, if n is an integer, none of the numbers $7n+3$, $7n+5$, $7n+6$ can be a perfect square.

21. Find the equation of the plane through the point $(1, 1, 1)$ containing the line
$$\frac{x-3}{5} = \frac{y-1}{2} = \frac{z}{-4}.$$
   Find also the direction cosines of the line of intersection of this plane with the plane Oxy.

152

22. The set S consists of all points in a plane whose coordinates relative to a given pair of perpendicular axes are both integers (in the units used). If A, B, C are members of S, prove that the area of the triangle ABC is a rational number of square units.

23. Eliminate θ between the pair of equations

$$a \sec \theta + b \operatorname{cosec} \theta = c,$$

$$a' \sec \theta - b' \operatorname{cosec} \theta = c'.$$

24. Solve the inequality

$$\frac{x-1}{x^2 - 3x - 4} < -2$$

and illustrate your answer by sketching the graph of

$$y = \frac{x-1}{x^2 - 3x - 4}.$$

25. Evaluate

$$\sum_{r=1}^{n} r(r+1)(2r+3).$$

26. $A = \{x \in R : -3 < x \leqslant 2\}$, $B = \{x \in R : -2 \leqslant x < 3\}$,
$C = \{x \in R : 1 < x\}$.
Express, in the form $\{:\}$, the sets

$$A \cap B, \quad A \cap C', \quad A' \cap B, \quad A \cap B \cap C, \quad A \cup (B \cap C').$$

27. Show, by drawing a rough sketch, that the equation

$$x = 2 \cos x$$

has just one positive solution.

By drawing an accurate graph, estimate this value of x as accurately as you can.

28. A five digit number (that is, a number lying between 10000 and 99999 inclusive) is selected at random. What is the probability that it contains either the digit 8 or the digit 9 (or both)?

29. Show that the plane containing the points with position vectors

$$\mathbf{i} - 2\mathbf{j}, \quad \mathbf{i} + \mathbf{j} + \mathbf{k}, \quad 2\mathbf{i} - \mathbf{j} + 2\mathbf{k}$$

has vector equation

$$\mathbf{r} = \mathbf{i} - 2\mathbf{j} + \lambda(3\mathbf{j} + \mathbf{k}) + \mu(\mathbf{i} + \mathbf{j} + 2\mathbf{k}).$$

Find the position vector of the point of intersection of this plane with the line

$$\mathbf{r} = 3\mathbf{i} + 5\mathbf{j} - 5\mathbf{k} + \nu(2\mathbf{i} + 3\mathbf{j} - \mathbf{k}).$$

30. a, b are rational approximations to the irrational numbers $\sqrt{A}$, $\sqrt{B}$. An approximation to $\sqrt{(AB)}$ is calculated by using the formulae:
   (i) $\sqrt{(AB)} \approx ab$;   (ii) $\sqrt{(AB)} \approx \frac{1}{2}[(a+b)^2 - (A+B)]$;
   (iii) $\sqrt{(AB)} \approx \frac{1}{2}[(A+B) - (a-b)^2]$.
The errors in the three cases are respectively E_1, E_2, E_3. Find a relation connecting E_1, E_2, E_3.

153

31. A bag contains three white and four red balls, another bag contains four white and three red balls. One of the bags is selected at random and two balls are drawn from it. If both balls are red, what is the probability that, of the five balls remaining in the selected bag, two are red?

32. A and B are two points with position vectors $\mathbf{a}$, $\mathbf{b}$ relative to a given origin O. Prove that the equation of the internal bisector of the angle AOB is

$$\mathbf{r} = \lambda(\hat{\mathbf{a}} + \hat{\mathbf{b}}).$$

(Recall that $\hat{\mathbf{a}}$ is a unit vector in the direction of $\mathbf{a}$.)

What is the equation of the external angle bisector?

Find the position vector of the incentre of the triangle ABO in terms of $a = |\mathbf{a}|$, $b = |\mathbf{b}|$, $c = |\mathbf{AB}|$ and the unit vectors $\hat{\mathbf{a}}$, $\hat{\mathbf{b}}$. (The *incentre* of a triangle is the point of intersection of the bisectors of the angles of the triangle.)

33. Evaluate the expressions

(i) $\sqrt{[1 + \sqrt{\{1 + \sqrt{(1 + ...)}\}}]}$; (ii) $\sqrt{[2 + \sqrt{\{2 + \sqrt{(2 + ...)}\}}]}$.

If n is an integer, when is an expression of the form

$$\sqrt{[n + \sqrt{\{n + \sqrt{(n + ...)}\}}]}$$

a rational number?

34. Two cards are missing from a pack. If three cards are drawn at random from the remaining fifty (without replacement) and all are found to be aces, what is the probability that, if a fourth card is drawn, it will also be an ace?

9. *Mathematical induction*

1. A NOTE ON MATHEMATICAL PROOFS

In a mathematical proof we proceed from one step to the next by processes of deductive logic; that is, each step is logically implied by the previous step or steps of the proof. In other words, a mathematical argument has a *direction*. The first step must depend upon certain premises or known theorems which may or may not be stated explicitly. For example, in the traditional form of proof for a geometrical problem, the premises (data) are usually stated before the proof commences and the argument leads from this statement to the final deduction, using previously proved results of elementary geometry. If, however, we are asked to prove that the probability of a double with a throw of two unbiased dice is $\frac{1}{6}$, we must commence by asserting that the set consisting of the thirty-six pairs of numbers $(1, 1), (1, 2), ..., (1, 6), (2, 1), (2, 2), ..., (6, 6)$ constitutes a possible outcome space and that we assume that each of these elementary events has a probability of $\frac{1}{36}$. ('The dice are unbiased.') We are then able to deduce the required probability.

Since a mathematical argument has a direction, we shall frequently meet the situation in which a sequence of statements p, q, r are strung together in the form 'statement p *implies* the statement q which, in turn, implies the statement r and so on'. The notation

$$p \Rightarrow q \quad \text{(read '}p \text{ implies } q\text{')}$$

has already been used; its use in mathematical proofs can lead to conciseness of expression.

Example 1. *Prove that* $x^2+y^2+z^2-yz-zx-xy \geqslant 0$ *for real x, y, z.*

$$E = x^2+y^2+z^2-yz-zx-xy$$

$$\Rightarrow 2E = (y-z)^2+(z-x)^2+(x-y)^2$$

$$\Rightarrow 2E \geqslant 0, \quad \text{for real} \quad x, y, z,$$

$$\Rightarrow E \geqslant 0, \quad \text{for real} \quad x, y, z.$$

The reader must always be on his guard, when writing $p \Rightarrow q$, that this is indeed what he means: a genuine deduction from the immediately preceding statement is implied. One of the principle sources of error among beginners attempting to prove mathematical results is to confuse the implication $p \Rightarrow q$ with the implication $q \Rightarrow p$. $p \Rightarrow q$ means that, whenever p is true, q is true; it does not tell us anything about the truth of the statement p if q is true. (We shall not discuss the meaning of the statement $p \Rightarrow q$ in the case when p is false; the bibliography refers to books in which problems concerning the use of implication are discussed at length.)

Ex. 1. 'If $-1 > 0$, then $(-1)^2 > 0$, which is true, and so $-1 > 0$.' Comment.

Ex. 2. A class is asked to prove that, if $a/b = c/d$, then

$$(a+b)/(a-b) = (c+d)/(c-d) \quad (a, b, c, d \text{ unequal and non-zero}).$$

Criticize the following proof:

$$\text{'}\frac{a+b}{a-b} = \frac{c+d}{c-d} \Rightarrow (a+b)(c-d) = (a-b)(c+d)$$

$$\Rightarrow ac+bc-ad-bd = ac+ad-bc-bd$$

$$\Rightarrow 2bc = 2ad$$

$$\Rightarrow a/b = c/d$$

which is true and so the original proposition is true.'

Ex. 3. Criticize the proof of the identity $\operatorname{cosec}^2 A \tan^2 A - 1 \equiv \tan^2 A$ given below:
'If $\operatorname{cosec}^2 A \tan^2 A - 1 \equiv \tan^2 A$, then

$$\frac{1}{\sin^2 A} \frac{\sin^2 A}{\cos^2 A} \equiv 1 + \tan^2 A \equiv \sec^2 A$$

which is manifestly true, since

$$\frac{1}{\cos A} = \sec A.\text{'}$$

If the implication $p \Rightarrow q$ is reversible, that is, if $p \Rightarrow q$ and $q \Rightarrow p$ both hold, then we may write

$$p \Leftrightarrow q \quad \text{(read '}p \text{ implies and is implied by } q\text{').}$$

Example 2. *Solve the equation* $\sqrt{(2x+1)} + \sqrt{x} = 5$.

$$\sqrt{(2x+1)} + \sqrt{x} = 5$$

$$\Rightarrow 2x+1+x+2\sqrt{[x(2x+1)]} = 25$$

$$\Leftrightarrow \qquad 2\sqrt{[x(2x+1)]} = -(3x-24)$$

$$\Rightarrow \qquad 4(2x^2+x) = 9x^2-144x+576$$

$$\Leftrightarrow \qquad x^2-148x+576 = 0$$

$$\Leftrightarrow \qquad (x-4)(x-144) = 0.$$

Thus $\sqrt{(2x+1)}+\sqrt{x} = 5 \Rightarrow (x-144)(x-4) = 0$, but two of the steps of the argument are not reversible, and so it is not possible to infer that $(x-144)(x-4) = 0 \Rightarrow \sqrt{(2x+1)}+\sqrt{x} = 5$. To express it another way, if $x = a$ is a root of $\sqrt{(2x+1)}+\sqrt{x} = 5$, then it is certainly a root of

$$(x-144)(x-4) = 0,$$

but, if $x = a$ is a root of $(x-144)(x-4) = 0$ it may not be a root of $\sqrt{(2x+1)}+\sqrt{x} = 5$. To complete the solution of the given equation we must substitute back the two possible solutions $x = 4$ and $x = 144$. It is then seen that $x = 4$ is a root of the original equation, but that $x = 144$ is not.

Ex. 4. In Example 2, how do you know that $x = 4$ is the *only* root of the equation $\sqrt{(2x+1)}+\sqrt{x} = 5$?

Ex. 5. Solve Question 6, Exercise 1 *c*, using the implication signs, and explaining carefully which steps are not reversible.

If a result is stated in the form $p \Rightarrow q$, the *converse* result (if it holds) is $q \Rightarrow p$. For example, if p and q are defined as follows:

p is the statement 'the triangle ABC has $AB = AC$',

q is the statement 'the triangle ABC has $\angle B = \angle C$',

then a well-known theorem of elementary geometry asserts that $p \Rightarrow q$. The converse theorem, $q \Rightarrow p$, is also true and the two theorems may be combined together in the single two-way implication $p \Leftrightarrow q$.

It is by no means always the case that, if a theorem is true, then its converse is also true. Indeed, if a theorem takes the form

$$p \text{ and } q \Rightarrow r$$

a converse is not clearly defined. In the case in which a theorem $p \Rightarrow q$ and its converse $q \Rightarrow p$ both hold, we may use the two-way implication $\Leftrightarrow$ in its formulation; alternatively, we may use the phrase '*if and only if*' —sometimes abbreviated to 'iff'.

In proving the truth of a two-way implication it is vital to remember that two separate proofs are needed. For example, referring again to the proposition about the triangle ABC mentioned above, we

(i) assume $AB = AC$ and deduce that

$$\angle B = \angle C \quad (AB = AC \Rightarrow \angle B = \angle C$$

or alternatively, $AB = AC$ *only if* $\angle B = \angle C$);† and

† From the purely linguistic points of view, the words 'only if' are somewhat ambiguous; mathematically, however, no ambiguity can arise if we define 'p only if q' to mean '$p \Rightarrow q$'.

(ii) assume $\angle B = \angle C$ and deduce that

$$AB = AC \quad (\angle B = \angle C \Rightarrow AB = AC$$

or, alternatively, $AB = AC$ if $\angle B = \angle C$).†

Ex. 6. The triangle ABC is right-angled at A if and only if $BC^2 = CA^2 + AB^2$. What would you assume if asked to prove the 'only if' part of this proposition?

Ex. 7. Correct the following statement: 'The integer N (expressed in the denary scale) is divisible by 5 if and only if the units digit of N is 5.'

Ex. 8. Correct the following statement: 'Two vectors **a** and **b** are equal if and only if $|\mathbf{a}| = |\mathbf{b}|$.'

Ex. 9. Is it true to say that, if $x > 0$ then $ax > x^2$ only if $a > x$?

It is often necessary to disprove an implication; that is, to show that the truth of statement p does not imply the truth of statement q. In this situation we write $p \not\Rightarrow q$ (read 'p does not imply q'). Since $p \Rightarrow q$ means that, in all cases in which p holds, q holds too, to show that $p \not\Rightarrow q$ we have merely to exhibit one case in which p holds and q does not hold (a *counter example*). For example, if we have

p is the statement 'x is of the form $(6n \pm 1)\,\pi/3$, n integral',

q is the statement '$\sin x = \sin 2x$'

it is a fairly straightforward matter to prove that, if p is true, then q is true; that is, $p \Rightarrow q$. To disprove the converse, $q \Rightarrow p$, we have simply to find a counter example, e.g. $x = 0$, which certainly satisfies q, but is not of the form $(6n \pm 1)\,\pi/3$.

Ex. 10. Prove that $x = (6n \pm 1)\,\pi/3 \Rightarrow \sin x = \sin 2x$.

Ex. 11. If p is the statement 'n is an odd number' and q is the statement 'an integer k can be found so that $n = 4k + 1$' prove that $q \Rightarrow p$ and disprove the converse result $p \Rightarrow q$.

To complete this section we mention one final method of proving that the implication $p \Rightarrow q$ holds. If a statement p is modified by the addition of the word '*not*', a new statement '*not p*', written p' (sometimes $\sim p$) is obtained. For example, if p is the statement 'the integer n is divisible by 3' p' is the statement 'the integer n is not divisible by 3'. p' is called the *negation* of p.

† Another way of expressing implications is by using the phrases '*necessary condition*' and '*sufficient condition*'. *A necessary condition for p is q* means that $p \Rightarrow q$; a *sufficient condition for p is q* means that $q \Rightarrow p$. A *necessary and sufficient condition for p is q* means that $p \Leftrightarrow q$.

The implication $p \Rightarrow q$ is equivalent to saying that we cannot have p true without q being true or, using negatives, if q' is true, then p' is true; in terms of implication, $q' \Rightarrow p'$. The argument also works in reverse and thus the two implications $p \Rightarrow q$ and $q' \Rightarrow p'$ are equivalent. Expressed more succinctly

$$(p \Rightarrow q) \Leftrightarrow (q' \Rightarrow p').$$

The mathematical value of this equivalence is that it is often easier to prove the implication $q' \Rightarrow p'$ rather than the implication $p \Rightarrow q$.

Ex. 12. In Ex. 11, prove that $p' \Rightarrow q'$.

Example 3. *To prove that there is an unlimited number of primes.*

Let q be the statement '1 has no prime factor' and r be the statement 'there is an unlimited number of primes'. The statement q is true, since the smallest prime number is 2; we shall show that $q \Rightarrow r$, and so r is true.

Now the negation of r is the statement r': 'there is a finite number of primes'.

$r' \Rightarrow$ there is a greatest prime number, p say;

$\Rightarrow (k+1)$ is not prime, where k is the product of all the primes, $k = 2.3.5\ldots p$;

$\Rightarrow (k+1)$ has some member of the set $\{2, 3, 5, \ldots, p\}$ as a factor;

$\Rightarrow$ both k and $(k+1)$ have some member of the set $\{2, 3, 5, \ldots, p\}$ as a common factor;

$\Rightarrow 1$ has some number of the set $\{2, 3, 5, \ldots\}$ as a factor;

$\Rightarrow q'$.

Thus $r' \Rightarrow q'$ and so $q \Rightarrow r$.

A number of important points have been glossed over in the discussion of implication in this section. The reader should consult one of the books mentioned in the bibliography for a more thorough and rigorous treatment of the subject.

Exercise 9(a)

1. Disprove the converse of the result 'if a quadrilateral is a rectangle then its diagonals are equal'.

2. All angles θ of the form $\theta = k\pi$ (k an integer) have the property that $\sin \theta = \tan \theta$. Is the converse result true?

3. If $a, b \in Z^+$ and if the operation o is defined by

$$a \circ b = \frac{ab - a - b}{a + 1},$$

prove that $a \circ b = b \circ a \Leftrightarrow a = b$.

159

4. Solve the equation $\sqrt{(x-4)}+2 = \sqrt{(x+12)}$, stating which steps in your solution are reversible and which are not.

5. Solve the equation $\sqrt{(2x+1)}-\sqrt{x} = 1$, stating which steps in your solution are reversible and which are not.

6. Solve the equation $\sqrt{(2x-1)}+\sqrt{(x+3)} = 9$, stating which steps in your solution are reversible and which are not.

7. Explain the fallacy in the following argument:
   'n^2+1 has no real factors. Put $n = 3$: thus 10 is a prime number.'

8. Prove that the difference of the squares of two odd numbers is divisible by 8. State and prove a converse theorem.

9. Prove that $(x+h)$ is a factor of ax^2+bx+c if and only if $ah^2-bh+c = 0$.

10. Prove that, if $a \neq -1$, then the simultaneous equations in x, y:
$$\begin{cases} ax+y = b, \\ x+ay = b \end{cases}$$
can be solved for x and y.
   What happens if $a = 1$?
   Is it true that the equations cannot be solved if $a = -1$?

11. Two well-known theorems of number theory are:
   (i) any odd prime of the form $4n+1$ is expressible as the sum of the squares of two integers;
   (ii) any odd prime of the form $4n+3$ is not expressible as the sum of the squares of two integers.
   Combine these two theorems into a single theorem by using the phrase 'if and only if'.

12. a, b, c, d are four unequal, positive numbers. Prove that
$$\frac{a-c}{b-d} = \sqrt{\left(\frac{a^2+c^2}{b^2+d^2}\right)} \quad \text{if and only if} \quad \frac{a}{b} = \frac{c}{d}.$$

13. If $P(x)$ is a polynomial with a repeated linear factor, that is, if
$$P(x) = (x-h)^2\, Q(x),$$
where $Q(x)$ is a polynomial, prove that $(x-h)$ is also a factor of $P'(x)$. ($P'(x)$ is the derivative of $P(x)$.)

14. Prove that, if $0 < x < 1$,
   then
$$(1-x)^{\frac{1}{2}} < \frac{4-3x}{4-x}.$$

15. ABC is any triangle and M is the mid-point of BC. Prove that
$$AB^2+AC^2 = 2AM^2+BM^2+CM^2 \quad \text{(Apollonius's Theorem)}.$$
Is it true that, if M is a point on BC such that
$$AB^2+AC^2 = 2AM^2+BM^2+CM^2$$
then M is the mid-point of BC?

160

16. If p is a prime number greater than 3, prove that either $p+1$ or $p-1$ is divisible by 6.

Show that the statement 'if x is a number such that $x+1$ or $x-1$ is divisible by 6, then x is a prime' is false.

Show further that the statement 'if x is divisible by 6, then at least one of $x+1$ or $x-1$ is a prime number' is also false.

17. Prove that a sufficient condition for the integer x to be divisible by 17 is that there exists an integer n such that

$$x = 35^n - 18^n.$$

Prove further that this is not a necessary condition for x to be divisible by 17.

2. MATHEMATICAL INDUCTION;
AN INTRODUCTORY EXAMPLE

Consider the series

$$\frac{1}{1.2} + \frac{1}{2.3} + \frac{1}{3.4} + \ldots.$$

Suppose we define the sequence $\{s_n\}$ in such a way that s_n represents the sum of the first n terms of this series. Then by direct computation,

$$s_1 = \tfrac{1}{2}, \quad s_2 = \tfrac{2}{3}, \quad s_3 = \tfrac{3}{4}, \quad s_4 = \tfrac{4}{5}.$$

The form taken by the first few values of s_n suggests that

$$s_n = \frac{n}{n+1} \quad (n \in Z^+).$$

Let us define a new sequence $\{f_n\}$ in such a way that

$$f_n = \frac{n}{n+1}.$$

Then we wish to prove that the two sequences $\{s_n\}$ and $\{f_n\}$ are the same, in the sense that $s_n = f_n$ for all $n \in Z^+$.

As a first step, we observe that

$$f_{n+1} = \frac{n+1}{n+2}, \quad \text{by the definition of } f_n$$

$$= \frac{n}{n+1} + \frac{1}{(n+1)(n+2)}$$

$$= f_n + \frac{1}{(n+1)(n+2)}. \tag{1}$$

Also,

$$s_{n+1} = s_n + \frac{1}{(n+1)(n+2)}, \quad \text{by the definition of } s_n. \tag{2}$$

(1) and (2) define recurrence relations (see chapter 8.1); with the initial terms they enable us to determine *uniquely* any term of either of the sequences $\{s_n\}$, $\{f_n\}$. But we further observe, in this case, that
  (i) the two recurrence relations are the same;
  (ii) $s_1 = \frac{1}{2} = f_1$.
Since the recurrence relations (1) and (2) develop successive terms of the sequences $\{s_n\}$ and $\{f_n\}$ in the same way, and since the two sequences have the same starting point, we deduce that $s_n = f_n$ for all n.

The observation that (1) and (2) represent the same recurrence relation enables us to deduce that if $s_n = f_n$, then $s_{n+1} = f_{n+1}$, or, expressed alternatively,

$$s_n = f_n \Rightarrow s_{n+1} = f_{n+1}.$$

The fact that $s_1 = f_1$ then enables us to infer the equality of s_n and f_n for all $n \in Z^+$; for

$$s_1 = f_1 \Rightarrow s_2 = f_2 \Rightarrow s_3 = f_3 \dots .$$

Ex. 13. Define sequences s_n and f_n as follows

$$s_n = 1.2 + 2.3 + 3.4 + \dots + n(n+1),$$
$$f_n = \tfrac{1}{3}n(n+1)(n+2).$$

Show that (i) $s_1 = f_1$, (ii) s_n and f_n satisfy the same recurrence relation. Deduce that $s_n = f_n$.

3. THE METHOD OF MATHEMATICAL INDUCTION

Suppose that p_n is some statement about the positive integer n. For example (see example 5 below), we might have

p_n: 'the expression $13^n - 6^{n-2}$ is divisible by 7'.

Then, if we can show
  (i) that p_m is true for some specific integer m (in our example, $m = 2$ would do); and
  (ii) that $p_k \Rightarrow p_{k+1}$ for all $k \geqslant m$ (in our example, p_{k+1} is the statement '$13^{k+1} - 6^{k-1}$') we have

$$p_m \Rightarrow p_{m+1} \Rightarrow p_{m+2} \Rightarrow \dots$$

and the truth of the statement p_n may be asserted for all $n \geqslant m$. Such a process is called *proof by mathematical induction*.

The method of mathematical induction is used to prove a conjecture about the positive integer n. The conjecture itself is usually arrived at by inductive argument from a few simple cases—hence the use of the word 'induction', though the method of proof is deductive.

162

To summarize: given the statement p_n about the positive integer n, to prove the truth of p_n we

(i) verify that the induction starts; that is, we find an integer m for which p_m is true;

(ii) prove the implication $p_k \Rightarrow p_{k+1}$ for a general positive integer $k \geqslant m$.

*Ex. 14. Show that n^2+n+41 is a prime number if $n = 1, 2, 3$. Prove that the statement 'n^2+n+41 is a prime number for all positive integers n' is false. (n^2+n+41 is, in fact, prime for $n = 1, 2, 3, ..., 39$ but it is false when $n = 40$ and whenever n is a multiple of 41: $p_k \not\Rightarrow p_{k+1}$.)

*Ex. 15. If p_n is the statement '$5n^2-5n+2$ is divisible by 10', prove that $p_k \Rightarrow p_{k+1}$. Prove also that p_n is false for all positive integers n. (The induction has no starting point.) *Hint.* To prove the falsity of p_n, observe that $p_k \Leftrightarrow p_{k+1}$ and thus $p'_k \Rightarrow p'_{k+1}$.

Example 4. Prove that

$$1.1!+2.2!+3.3!+...+n.n! = (n+1)!-1.$$

Write $\qquad s_n = 1.1!+2.2!+3.3!+...+n.n!.$

We have to prove that $s_n = (n+1)!-1$; let p_n be the statement

$$'s_n = (n+1)!-1'.$$

(i) p_1 is true, for $s_1 = 1.1! = 1$ and $(1+1)!-1 = 1$: the induction starts.

(ii) To prove $p_k \Rightarrow p_{k+1}$:

$$s_{k+1} = s_k+(k+1)(k+1)!, \quad \text{by the definition of } s_k;$$

$$\Rightarrow s_{k+1} = (k+1)!-1+(k+1)(k+1)!, \quad \text{by } p_k;$$

$$\Rightarrow s_{k+1} = (k+1)![1+k+1]-1$$

$$\Rightarrow s_{k+1} = (k+2)!-1$$

and thus $p_k \Rightarrow p_{k+1}$ and the result is true for all $n \geqslant 1$, by mathematical induction.

Example 5. Prove that 13^n-6^{n-2} is divisible by 7 for all positive integers greater than m, where m is a certain integer, to be specified.

Write $u_n = 13^n-6^{n-2}$; we have to prove that u_n is divisible by 7 for all $n \geqslant m$, where m is some integer, to be found.

(i) u_1 is a fraction, and the concept of divisibility does not apply. $u_2 = 13^2-6^0 = 168 = 7.24$ and u_2 is therefore divisible by 7: the induction starts.

Let p_n be the statement 'u_n is divisible by 7'.

163

(ii) To prove $p_k \Rightarrow p_{k+1}$:

$$u_{k+1} = 13^{k+1} - 6^{k-1} \quad \text{and} \quad u_k = 13^k - 6^{k-2}$$

$$\Rightarrow u_{k+1} - 6u_k = (13 \cdot 13^k - 6 \cdot 6^{k-2}) - (6 \cdot 13^k - 6 \cdot 6^{k-2})$$

$$\Rightarrow u_{k+1} - 6u_k = 7 \cdot 13^k$$

$$\Rightarrow \qquad u_{k+1} = 7 \cdot 13^k + 6u_k$$

$\Rightarrow u_{k+1}$ is divisible by 7, by p_k, since the sum of two integers divisible by 7 is itself divisible by 7.

Thus, $13^n - 6^{n-2}$ is divisible by 7 for all $n \geqslant 2$.

Example 6 (the Binomial Theorem). Prove that

$$(x+a)^n = \binom{n}{0} x^n + \binom{n}{1} x^{n-1} a + \binom{n}{2} x^{n-2} a^2 + \ldots + \binom{n}{r} x^{n-r} a^r + \ldots + \binom{n}{n} a^n$$

for positive integral n.

(i) $(x+a)^1 = x+a = \binom{1}{0} x^1 a^0 + \binom{1}{1} x^0 a^1$ and the induction starts.

(ii) Consider the product

$$(x+a) \left[x^n + \binom{n}{1} x^{n-1} a + \binom{n}{2} x^{n-2} a^2 + \ldots + \binom{n}{r} x^{n-r} a^r + \ldots + a^n \right].$$

Each term in the product is of degree $(n+1)$, the first is x^{n+1}, the last is a^{n+1} and the term containing $x^{n+1-r} a^r$ is

$$x \binom{n}{r} x^{n-r} a^r + a \binom{n}{r-1} x^{n+1-r} a^{r-1}$$

$$= \left[\binom{n}{r} + \binom{n}{r-1} \right] x^{n+1-r} a^r$$

$$= \binom{n+1}{r} x^{n+1-r} a^r, \qquad \text{by Vandermondes} \\ \text{Theorem (see Chapter 8).}$$

Thus

$$(x+a) \left[x^n + \binom{n}{1} x^{n-1} a + \binom{n}{2} x^{n-2} a^2 + \ldots + \binom{n}{r} x^{n-r} a^r + \ldots + a^n \right]$$

$$= x^{n+1} + \binom{n+1}{1} x^n a + \binom{n+1}{2} x^{n-1} a^2 + \ldots + \binom{n+1}{r} x^{n+1-r} a^r + \ldots + a^{n+1}$$

and hence

$$(x+a)^n = x^n + \binom{n}{1} x^{n-1} a + \binom{n}{2} x^{n-2} a^2 + \ldots + \binom{n}{r} x^{n-r} a^r + \ldots + a^n$$

$$\Rightarrow (x+a)^{n+1} = x^{n+1} + \binom{n+1}{1} x^n a + \binom{n+1}{2} x^{n-1} a^2 + \ldots$$

$$+ \binom{n+1}{r} x^{n+1-r} a^r + \ldots + a^{n+1}$$

and the proof is complete, by mathematical induction.

164

It should be noted in passing that the proof of the Binomial Theorem given in Chapter 8.5 strictly speaking requires induction, to justify the process of selection from each bracket. The student is recommended to supply the necessary details.

In our next example, we make an assumption (sometimes called *inductive hypothesis*) of a slightly different form to those of the preceding examples. The reader should observe that, to start the induction, we have to verify that the result holds for *two* successive values of n.

Example 7. If a sequence u_n is defined by the recurrence relation

$$u_{n+1} = 3u_n - 2u_{n-1} \quad (n \geqslant 2)$$

and the initial values $u_1 = 0$, $u_2 = 2$, prove that

$$u_n = 2^n - 2.$$

(i) Since $2^1 - 2 = 0$ and $2^2 - 2 = 2$, the result holds for $n = 1$ and $n = 2$.

(ii) Suppose

$$u_k = 2^k - 2 \quad \text{and} \quad u_{k-1} = 2^{k-1} - 2 \quad (k \geqslant 2).$$

Then,

$$u_{k+1} = 3u_k - 2u_{k-1}, \quad \text{by the given recurrence relation;}$$

$$= 3(2^k - 2) - 2(2^{k-1} - 2), \quad \text{by the assumption made above;}$$

$$= 6.2^{k-1} - 6 - 2.2^{k-1} + 4$$

$$= 4.2^{k-1} - 2$$

$$= 2^{k+1} - 2.$$

Thus $\quad u_k = 2^k - 2 \quad \text{and} \quad u_{k-1} = 2^{k-1} - 2 \Rightarrow u_{k+1} = 2^{k+1} - 2.$

But the result is true for $n = 1$ and $n = 2$, hence it is true for $n = 3$ and so on.

*Ex. 16. If $\{u_n\}$ is a sequence defined by the relation $u_n = \sum_{r=1}^{n-1} u_r$, $n \geqslant 2$ and the initial value $u_1 = 4$, prove that $u_n = 2^n$ $(n \geqslant 2)$. (Make the assumption that, for $k \geqslant 2$, $u_s = 2^s$ for *all* s in the interval $2 \leqslant s \leqslant k$.)

Example 8. Prove Theorem 7.4, using mathematical induction.

Theorem 7.4 states that, if $E_1, E_2, \ldots, E_n$ are mutually exclusive events, $(E_i \cap E_j = \phi, i \neq j)$, then

$$\Pr\left(\bigcup_{i=1}^{n} E_i \mid S\right) = \sum_{i=1}^{n} \Pr(E_i \mid S).$$

(i) The result is certainly true if $n = 2$, by Theorem 7.2, and the induction starts.

(ii) Write $F = \overset{k-1}{\underset{i=1}{\cup}} E_i$ and suppose that $\Pr(F|S) = \overset{k-1}{\underset{i=1}{\sum}} \Pr(E_i|S)$.

Now $F \cap E_k = \phi$, since the events are mutually exclusive. Thus

$$\Pr(F \cup E_k|S) = \Pr(F|S) + \Pr(E_k|S), \quad \text{by Theorem 7.2}$$

$$= \overset{k-1}{\underset{i=1}{\sum}} \Pr(E_i|S) + \Pr(E_k|S), \quad \text{by the assumption made above}$$

$$= \overset{k}{\underset{i=1}{\sum}} \Pr(E_i|S)$$

and the theorem is proved, by mathematical induction.

Exercise 9(b)

Throughout this exercise, n represents a positive integer. Prove the results 1–14. using the principle of mathematical induction.

1. $1+2+3+4+\ldots+n = \frac{1}{2}n(n+1)$.

2. $1+3+5+\ldots+(2n-1) = n^2$.

3. $1^2+2^2+3^2+4^2+\ldots+n^2 = \frac{1}{6}n(n+1)(2n+1)$.

4. $1^3+2^3+3^3+\ldots+n^3 = \frac{1}{4}n^2(n+1)^2$.

5. $1.1+3.2+5.4+\ldots+(2n-1).2^{n-1} = 3+2^n(2n-3)$.

6. $3.1!+7.2!+13.3!+\ldots+(n^2+n+1)\,n! = (n+1)^2\,n!-1$.

7. $\dfrac{1}{1.2.3}+\dfrac{1}{2.3.4}+\dfrac{1}{3.4.5}+\ldots+\dfrac{1}{n(n+1)(n+2)} = \dfrac{1}{4}-\dfrac{1}{2(n+1)(n+2)}$.

8. $\dfrac{1}{1.3}+\dfrac{1}{2.4}+\dfrac{1}{3.5}+\ldots+\dfrac{1}{n(n+2)} = \dfrac{3}{4}-\dfrac{2n+3}{2(n+1)(n+2)}$.

9. n^5-n is divisible by 30.

10. $12^n+2.5^{n-1}$ is divisible by 7.

11. $2^{6n}+3^{2n-2}$ is divisible by 5.

12. $5^{2n}+2^{2n-2}.3^{n-1}$ is divisible by 13.

13. $3.7^{3n}+3^{2n-1}.15^{n-1}$ is divisible by 8.

14. $(1+x)^n > 1+nx$, provided $x > -1, n > 1$.

15. The terms of the sequence $\{u_r\}$ are all positive and $s_n = \overset{n}{\underset{r=1}{\sum}} u_r$. Prove that

$$(1+u_1)(1+u_2)(1+u_3)\ldots(1+u_n) > 1+s_n \quad \text{for} \quad n \geqslant 2.$$

16. Prove that $5^n < n!$ for all sufficiently large n. Add such precision as you can to the phrase 'sufficiently large n'.

17. Prove by mathematical induction that the sum of the angles of a convex n-sided polygon is $(2n-4)$ right-angles.

18. Prove that an n-sided convex polygon has $\frac{1}{2}n(n-3)$ diagonals.

19. A straight line separates a plane into 2 regions; two straight lines separate the plane into 4 regions and so on. If n straight lines (no three concurrent, no two parallel) separate the plane into u_n regions, prove that

$$u_n = \tfrac{1}{2}(n^2+n+2).$$

20. If n is a positive integer, prove that

$$5^{2n+2}-24n-25$$

is divisible by 576. (Cambridge)

21. If
$$f(n) = 1+\frac{1}{2^2}+\frac{1}{3^2}+\dots+\frac{1}{n^2}$$

prove that $\displaystyle\sum_{r=1}^{n}[(3r^2+3r+1)f(r)] = (n+1)^3 f(n)-\tfrac{1}{2}n(n+1).$ (Cambridge)

22. Prove that
$$\sum_{r=1}^{n} r(r+1)(r+2)\dots(r+k-1) = \frac{n(n+1)\dots(n+k)}{k+1}.$$

23. If $a_1, a_2, a_3, \dots, a_n$ are all positive, prove that

$$(a_1+a_2+\dots+a_n)\left(\frac{1}{a_1}+\frac{1}{a_2}+\dots+\frac{1}{a_n}\right) \geqslant n^2.$$

24. Prove that, for any positive integer n,

$$\frac{2n}{2n-1}+\frac{2n(2n-2)}{(2n-1)(2n-3)}+\frac{2n(2n-2)(2n-4)}{(2n-1)(2n-3)(2n-5)}+\dots \quad \text{(to n terms)} = 2n.$$

(O & C)

25. A motorist estimates that, by travelling along a main road at a certain steady speed, the probability that the next set of traffic lights will be green if the last set was green is $\frac{3}{4}$ and that the probability that the next set of lights will be green if the last set was red is $\frac{1}{2}$. He sets out one day to test his theory. Prove that, if the first lights he meets are green and if

$$p_n = \text{Pr (the nth set of lights is green when he reaches them)}$$

then
$$p_n = \tfrac{2}{3}+\tfrac{1}{3}(\tfrac{1}{4})^{n-1} \quad (n \geqslant 1).$$

26. A man repeatedly tosses an unbiased coin, scoring 1 for each head and 2 for each tail. If p_n is the probability that his score will ever be n, prove that

$$p_n = \tfrac{2}{3}+\tfrac{1}{3}(-\tfrac{1}{2})^n.$$

27. n bags, numbered 1 to n, each contain one white and one black ball. A ball is taken at random from bag one and placed in bag two; a ball is then taken from bag two and placed in bag three and so on, until finally a ball is taken from bag n. Prove that the probability that this ball is white is

$$\frac{1}{2}\left(1+\frac{1}{3^{n-1}}\right)$$

given that the first ball drawn was white.

28. The sequence $\{u_n\}$ is defined by the recurrence relation

$$u_n - 5u_{n-1} + 6u_{n-2} = 0 \quad (n \geqslant 3)$$

and the initial values $u_1 = 7$, $u_2 = 17$. Prove that

$$u_n = 2^{n+1} + 3^n.$$

29. The sequence $\{u_n\}$ is defined by the recurrence relation

$$u_{n+2} + u_{n+1} - 2u_n = 0 \quad (n \geqslant 1)$$

and the initial values $u_1 = 4$, $u_2 = -2$. Prove that

$$u_n = 2 - (-2)^n.$$

30. The sequence $\{u_n\}$ is defined by the recurrence relation

$$u_{n+3} + 2u_{n+2} - u_{n+1} - 2u_n = 0 \quad (n \geqslant 1)$$

and the initial values $u_1 = -1$, $u_2 = 7$, $u_3 = -7$. Prove that

$$u_n = 2 + (-1)^n (1 + 2^n).$$

31. (The Fibonacci Series.) The sequence $\{u_n\}$ is defined by the equations

$$u_1 = u_2 = 1, \quad u_{n+1} = u_n + u_{n-1} \quad (n \geqslant 2);$$

prove that

$$u_n = \frac{1}{\sqrt{5}}(\alpha^n - \beta^n) \quad \text{where} \quad \alpha = \frac{1+\sqrt{5}}{2} \quad \text{and} \quad \beta = \frac{1-\sqrt{5}}{2}$$

are the roots of the quadratic equation $x^2 = x + 1$.

32. Prove that, for positive integral n, $3^{2n} - 5^n$ is divisible by 7 if and only if n is even.

10. *Expectation*

1. RANDOM VARIABLES

In Chapter 7 we considered random experiments described by outcome spaces. With each elementary event we associated a number, its probability, which denoted our degree of belief that the experiment would result in that particular events occurring. The elementary events themselves may be described in various ways: in some cases, it is natural to denote them by a number, e.g. for the fall of a die we could denote our elementary events by the numbers 1, 2, 3, ..., 6; but sometimes no such natural numerical description exists. For example, for a single toss of a coin, the two element set {heads, tails} is the natural choice of outcome space, the elements being labelled by the descriptions 'heads' and 'tails'. In order to make a mathematical analysis of random experiments it is helpful to describe the possible outcomes numerically even in those cases where no such 'natural' description exists. Thus, in the case of coin spinning, the event 'tails' could be denoted by the number 0, the event 'heads' by the number 1. Such values are called *values of a random variable*.

Let us pause here to recapitulate. Suppose we have a random experiment whose possible outcomes are the n elementary events $s_1, s_2, ..., s_n$. Then we may take as our outcome space the set

$$S = \{s_1, s_2, ..., s_n\}.$$

We now attach two numerical 'labels' to each element s_i of S:

(i) the probability, p_i, of that event occurring;

(ii) the corresponding value x_i of the random variable (see Figure 10.1).

To help fix ideas, consider the following examples:

1. An unbiased die is thrown and the score noted. The outcome space with the associated probabilities and values of a possible choice of random variable are shown in Figure 10.2. If the experiment is repeated a number of times, then the sum of the values of the random variable obtained gives us our aggregate score.

2. Two unbiased dice are thrown in an attempt to score a double. Since we are interested in just two possible outcomes, we may take our outcome space, S, as shown in Figure 10.3. Associated probabilities together with a possible choice for values of a random variable are as indicated. In this case, if the experiment is repeated, the sum of the values of the random variables obtained gives us the number of doubles thrown.

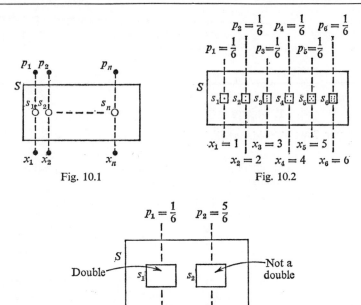

Fig. 10.1   Fig. 10.2

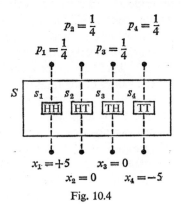

Fig. 10.3

3. A simple coin-tossing game is played as follows: *A* pays 5 pence for the privilege of tossing two unbiased coins. If he gets two heads, *B* pays him 5 pence and his stake money is returned; if he gets a head and a tail (in either order), his stake money is returned; if he gets two tails, *B* keeps the stake. A possible choice of outcome space, with associated probabilities attached, is shown in Figure 10.4. In this experiment we are primarily con-

$$p_1 = \frac{1}{4} \qquad p_2 = \frac{1}{4} \qquad p_3 = \frac{1}{4} \qquad p_4 = \frac{1}{4}$$

S | s_1 | s_2 | s_3 | s_4
HH | HT | TH | TT

$$x_1 = +5 \qquad x_3 = 0$$
$$x_2 = 0 \qquad x_4 = -5$$

Fig. 10.4

cerned with the financial outcome and our choice of random variable reflects this concern. If the experiment is repeated a number of times, the sum of the values of the random variable obtained denotes A's net gain in pence.

With these examples behind us we now make the following definition: a variable whose value is a number determined by the outcome of a random experiment is called a *random variable*.

The discerning reader will have observed that a random variable is a function from a given sample space into a set of numbers, the values of the random variable being the images under this function. The words 'random variable', however, are often loosely used to denote the image—a vice to which we ourselves shall succumb from time to time for the sake of brevity.

In the same way that a function is denoted by f and the image of z under f by $f(z)$, so a random variable may be denoted by X and its associated value for the ith element of the outcome space by x_i.

Ex. 1. A man pays 10 pence to throw two dice. For any double he receives his stake momey back, together with a prize: one pound for a double six and 20 pence for any other double. Suggest a suitable outcome space, probability distribution and random variable for this experiment.

Ex. 2. A man insures his life for £1000, paying a premium of £X. Suggest a suitable choice of random variable to describe the situation.

2. EXPECTATION

A mass of numerical data often has an indigestible appearance and conveys very little, unless subjected to considerable analysis. A device commonly used to give an overall impression of the data is to determine their *average value*. For example, if the heights of a hundred boys are measured, the complete set of results may usefully be characterized by giving their average height.

We shall now investigate what meaning can be attached to the phrase 'the average value of the random variable X associated with a given probability distribution'. If an experiment is repeated N times, where N is a large number, our interpretation of the probability p, as a measure of our confidence in securing the outcome s_1 leads us to expect roughly $p_1 N$ occurrences of s_1, with similar results for s_2, s_3, etc. Thus we should anticipate a score of x_1 on $p_1 N$ occasions, x_2 on $p_2 N$ occasions and so on, giving an approximate average value of our random variable X for all N

repetitions as

$$\frac{p_1 N x_1 + p_2 N x_2 + \ldots + p_n N x_n}{N} = p_1 x_1 + p_2 x_2 + \ldots + p_n x_n$$

$$= \sum_{i=1}^{n} p_i x_i.$$

The larger the value of N, the more confidence we should place in the value of $\sum_{i=1}^{n} p_i x_i$ as an estimate of the average. We are thus led to formulate the following definition:

The *expectation* $\mathscr{E}(X)$ of the random variable X is defined by the equation

$$\mathscr{E}(X) = \sum_{i=1}^{n} p_i x_i.$$

Example 1. *An unbiased die is thrown; what is the expected score?*

Here $p_i = \frac{1}{6}$ for each elementary event, and the associated values of the random variable X are the integers 1, 2, 3, 4, 5, 6. Thus

$$\mathscr{E}(X) = \sum_{i=1}^{6} \frac{r}{6}$$

$$= \frac{21}{6}$$

$$= 3 \cdot 5.$$

It is perhaps surperfluous to remark that no one sufficiently familiar with an unbiased die would expect a score of 3·5 on any one throw. 3·5 simply represents the best estimate available, prior to the actual experiment, that we can make of the final average score if the die is thrown a number of times; the larger the number of throws, the better we expect our estimate to be. (The reader is strongly recommended to test the accuracy of this forecast if ever he finds time lying heavily on his hands by throwing a die, say a hundred times, and computing his average score.)

Example 2. *Two players, A and B, play the following game with three coins: A pays a stake of* 10 *pence and tosses the three coins in turn. If he obtains three heads, his stake is returned, together with a prize of* 30 *pence; for two consecutive heads, his stake money is returned, together with a prize of* 10 *pence. In all other cases, B wins the stake money. Is the game fair?*

We must first consider what is meant by the question 'is the game fair?' Intuitively it seems reasonable to label a game as 'fair' if, in the long-run neither side anticipates any considerable financial gain. Mathematically, a game between two players is *fair* if the expectation of gain for either player is zero.

172

To continue with the solution of the problem, we choose as our outcome space the four-element set

$$S = \{(HHH), (HHT), (THH), (anything\ else)\}.$$

On the assumption that the coins are unbiased and that the results of the tosses are independent, Pr (HHH) $= (\frac{1}{2})^3 = \frac{1}{8}$; similarly,

$$Pr\ (HHT) = Pr\ (THH) = \frac{1}{8} \quad and \quad Pr\ (anything\ else) = 1 - \frac{3}{8} = \frac{5}{8}.$$

As our random variable we take the net gain, in pence, for A on each particular elementary event: $x_1 = +30$, $x_2 = +10$, $x_3 = +10$, $x_4 = -10$.
Summarizing in tabular form, we have:

S	HHH	HHT	THH	Anything else
P	$\frac{1}{8}$	$\frac{1}{8}$	$\frac{1}{8}$	$\frac{5}{8}$
X	30	10	10	-10

$$\begin{aligned}\mathscr{E}(X) &= \tfrac{1}{8}.30 + \tfrac{1}{8}.10 + \tfrac{1}{8}.10 + \tfrac{5}{8}(-10) \\ &= 0.\end{aligned}$$

The game is therefore, according to our definition proposed above, fair.

Ex. 3. An experiment with three possible outcomes s_1, s_2, s_3, has probability distribution $\{\frac{1}{7}, \frac{2}{7}, \frac{4}{7}\}$ and associated random variables 3, 2, 1. Determine the expectation.

Ex. 4. A man pays 1 penny to throw three unbiased dice. If at least one six appears he receives back his stake money together with a prize consisting of the number of pennies equal to the number of sixes thrown. Does he expect to win or lose?

Ex. 5. An experiment can result in three possible outcomes, whose probabilities are $\frac{1}{4}, \frac{1}{2}, \frac{1}{4}$. A random variable is assigned whose values are respectively x^2, $-x$, 1. Show that, if the experiment is repeated a number of times, the player may possibly finish with a negative score but can anticipate an aggregate score which is positive. Can his expectation be zero?

Exercise 10(a)

1. The values of a random variable, together with their associated probabilities for four different experiments, are given in the tables below. Calculate $\mathscr{E}(X)$ in the four cases.

(i)

x_i	0	1	2	3	4	5
p_i	$\frac{1}{15}$	$\frac{2}{15}$	$\frac{1}{3}$	$\frac{1}{5}$	$\frac{2}{15}$	$\frac{2}{15}$

(ii)

x_i	-2	-1	0	1	2
p_i	$\frac{1}{10}$	$\frac{2}{5}$	$\frac{3}{10}$	$\frac{1}{10}$	$\frac{1}{10}$

(iii)

x_i	1	2	3	4	5	6
p_i	$\frac{1}{20}$	$\frac{3}{20}$	$\frac{1}{5}$	$\frac{2}{5}$	$\frac{1}{10}$	$\frac{1}{10}$

(iv)

x_i	1	2	3	4	5	6	7	8	9	10
p_i	0	$\frac{1}{8}$	0	$\frac{3}{8}$	0	$\frac{1}{4}$	0	$\frac{1}{8}$	0	$\frac{1}{8}$

2. In Question 1, a new random variable Y is constructed so that $Y = 2X-1$. If the probability distributions remain the same, calculate $\mathscr{E}(Y)$ in the four cases. Can you generalize your result in any way?

3. A player pays a certain sum of money to spin two coins. For two heads he receives back 10p, for two tails he receives 2p, for a head and a tail he receives nothing. In all four cases he forfeits his stake money. What should the stake money be for the game to be fair?

4. Two dice are thrown; find the expectation of the higher score showing (or the score of one of them, if they fall alike).

5. If the probability that a man aged sixty will survive another year is 0·9, what premium should he be charged for a life insurance policy of £1000? (If he survives the year, he receives no money back.)

6. X_1 and X_2 are two random variables, each with values 0, 1, 2, 3, ..., 9, and each possessing a uniform probability distribution. Evaluate
   (i) $\mathscr{E}(X_1 - X_2)$;   (ii) $\mathscr{E}(|X_1 - X_2|)$.

7. Two bags each contain ten coloured discs as shown.

	Red	Green	Blue
Bag I	4	3	3
Bag II	5	3	2

A player stakes a certain sum of money for the privilege of drawing two discs, one from each bag. For two discs of the same colour his stake is returned and, in addition, he is awarded a prize of 10p for two reds, 20p for two greens and 25p for two blues. For two discs of different colours he loses his stake.

Show that, if the stake money is 8p, he can anticipate gaining in the long run, but that with the stake at 9p he should expect to lose.

8. The game of Question 7 is repeated, but the player now tosses a coin to decide which bag he must choose from: if he tosses a head, he chooses bag I, if a tail, bag II; he then draws a disc at random from the chosen bag, notes its colour and replaces the disc. He repeats the process again and is paid prizes as in the previous question. Determine the minimum stake (to the nearest penny) required to ensure that the player will show a loss in the long run.

9. The game of Question 8 is repeated but the discs are not replaced between draws. Determine the minimum stake (to the nearest penny) required to ensure that the player will show a loss in the long run.

10. The game of Question 7 is repeated, but the player is now required to place his stake after the result of the first draw from bag I is known. If he draws a red disc first time he pays 2p, if a green, 9p, if a blue, 12p. Show that, in the long run, the player expects to win.

Show further that the above stakes are the fairest available that still give an advantage to the player, in the sense that, if any one of the stakes were increased by 1p, the bank would then expect to win.

11. A man pays a stake to throw two dice. If he scores a total of 3 or 11, he receives 40p. For a total of 5 or 9 he receives 20p, and for a total of 7, 10p (in each case the stake money being returned too). He loses his stake money for any even score. Show that he expects to win if the stake money is 21p, but that, if the prizes for scoring 5 or 9 and 7 are reversed, he would then expect to lose.

12. Two identical bags contain respectively (i) four fivepenny pieces and twelve tenpenny pieces, (ii) nine fivepenny and seven tenpenny pieces. You are allowed to select a bag and draw a coin at random from it. If the coin you draw is a fivepenny piece, what would be a fair price for you to offer for the bag you did not select?

13. The path in Figure 10.5 represents a simple maze along which a rat is made to run. It starts at S and has to finish at F. If it makes a mistake at A by turning along AA' it will return to A and be forced by the construction of the maze, to turn towards F, and similarly at each of the other junctions. The probability of taking either of the two paths available at each junction is $\frac{1}{2}$. Find the expected number of mistakes the rat will make in running from S to F.

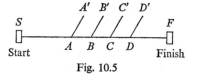

Fig. 10.5

14. What is the expected number of moves that can be made by (i) a bishop, (ii) a knight, placed at random on an empty chess board?

15. Two dice are thrown in 'one turn', each turn costing 5p. If a prize of 40p is given for a double six and a prize of 20p for any other double (together, in both cases, with the stake money), determine the loss to a person playing the game one hundred times.

16. A man puts three coins into a bag, deciding at random for each coin separately whether it is to be a fivepenny or a tenpenny piece. Calculate the expected total value of the coins he puts in his pocket.

17. A man puts three £5 notes into one envelope and three £1 notes into a similar envelope. Each year at Christmas, he chooses one envelope at random and gives his nephew a note from it. As soon as either envelope is emptied by his taking the last note from it, the process ends.
   (i) State the different totals which the nephew may have received when the process ends;
   (ii) for each of these totals calculate the chance of its occurrence;
   (iii) deduce that the nephew's expectation of gain is £12·375.

(Cambridge adapted)

3. STANDARD DEVIATION; EXPECTATION OF FUNCTIONS OF RANDOM VARIABLES

The expectation $\mathscr{E}(X)$ of the random variable X is often called the *mean* of X and is frequently denoted by the letter μ (or, occasionally, when it is necessary to avoid ambiguity by referring to the random variable under consideration, μ_x). μ gives us a forecast of the average value obtained for the random variable if the experiment is repeated a great number of times; it does not, however, give us any indication of how the individual results will be spread out.

By way of illustration, consider two unbiased dice, one of which has its faces printed in the usual way, but the other has three faces showing one dot and three faces showing six dots. It is readily verified that the expected score for the second die is 3·5, just as it is for the first but clearly, if each die is thrown one hundred times, the separate scores in the two cases will present a very different appearance: the *spreads* of the distributions are quite different. To measure the spreads of these distributions it might seem plausible to consider a new random variable Y whose value for a particular face equals the difference between the score showing and the mean (commonly called the *deviation from the mean*) and to calculate the expectation of Y. However, a calculation in the above example shows that such a quantity is quite unsuitable.

For the first die, Y takes the values $\{-2·5, -1·5, -0·5, 0·5, 1·5, 2·5\}$ with corresponding probabilities $\{\frac{1}{6}, \frac{1}{6}, \frac{1}{6}, \frac{1}{6}, \frac{1}{6}, \frac{1}{6}\}$. For the second die, the values of Y are $\{-2·5, 2·5\}$ with corresponding probabilities $\{\frac{1}{2}, \frac{1}{2}\}$.

176

For die I, $\mathscr{E}(Y) = \frac{1}{6}(-2\cdot5-1\cdot5-0\cdot5+0\cdot5+1\cdot5+2\cdot5) = 0.$

For die II, $\mathscr{E}(Y) = \frac{1}{2}(-2\cdot5+2\cdot5) = 0.$

A moment's consideration should show that our obtaining the answer zero in both cases is no coincidence. Indeed, for any distribution, the expectation of the deviation from the mean is zero. Why?

To avoid the cancelling out of the positive and negative scores a plausible precaution would be to choose as our new random variable not Y, the deviation from the mean, but Z, the *squared* deviation from the mean and this does, indeed, prove a very satisfactory measure of spread.

Let us see how such a new choice of random variable works in our example of the two dice. For die I, Z takes the values $\{6\cdot25, 2\cdot25, 0\cdot25\}$ each with associated probability $\frac{1}{3}$, while for die II, Z takes the value $\{6\cdot25\}$, with associated probability 1.

For die I, $\mathscr{E}(Z) = \frac{1}{3}(6\cdot25+2\cdot25+0\cdot25) = 2\cdot92.$

For die II, $\mathscr{E}(Z) = 6\cdot25.$

The precise meaning of these two numbers in probabilistic terms will be more fully explained in the next section (see Chebyshev's Theorem); for the moment it suffices to point out that the larger answer obtained for the second die corresponds to the fact that the scores obtained from this die are, on the average, farther from the mean than they are for the normal die.

Summarizing the results, we make the following definition: given a random variable X, with mean μ, the *variance*, σ_x^2, of X is the expectation of the squared deviations from the mean. That is, if a new choice of random variable, Z, is made, where $z_i = (x_i - \mu_x)^2$, then

$$\sigma_x^2 = \mathscr{E}(Z)$$
$$= \sum_{i=1}^{n} p_i(x_i - \mu_x)^2.$$

The positive square root of the variance, σ_x, is called the *standard deviation of X*; it has the advantage of being measured in the same units as X. The standard deviation (or, equivalently, the variance) has been shown, in an intuitive sense, to give a measure of spread; its deeper significance will be appreciated by the reader only as he gains a fuller grasp of the subject, when it will be seen that standard deviation plays a central part in the development of probability theory.

There is no difficulty in extending the concept of expectation to other functions of a random variable. Indeed, given a function f that maps the random variable X into another random variable Y, where $y_i = f(x_i)$, we may define the expectation of $f(X)$, $\mathscr{E}[f(X)]$, by

$$\mathscr{E}[f(X)] = \sum_{i=1}^{n} p_i f(x_i);$$

with this notation $\qquad \sigma_x^2 = \mathscr{E}[(X-\mu_x)^2].$

Ex. 6. Find the mean and variance of the random variable X whose probability distribution is shown in the table below:

X	0	1	2	3	4
p	$\frac{1}{8}$	$\frac{1}{4}$	$\frac{1}{4}$	$\frac{1}{4}$	$\frac{1}{8}$

Ex. 7. Find the variance for the number of heads showing if three unbiased coins are tossed.

*Ex. 8. A random variable has mean μ and variance σ^2. If a constant c is added to each value of the random variable, describe (without embarking upon any detailed working) what difference this will make to (i) the mean, (ii) the variance.

4. SOME THEOREMS CONCERNING THE MEAN AND STANDARD DEVIATION OF A RANDOM VARIABLE

Throughout this section we shall assume that, for some random experiment, an outcome space S with known probability distribution is given and a random variable, X, assigned, where $\mathscr{E}(X) = \mu$ and $\mathscr{E}[(X-\mu)^2] = \sigma^2$.

Our first theorem enables us to determine μ and σ in terms of the expectation of $X-a$ and $(X-a)^2$. Its value lies in the fact that these latter quantities are frequently a great deal less troublesome to calculate than are μ and σ^2 directly from the definition.

Theorem 10.1. *If a is any number, then*

(i) $\mathscr{E}[(X-a)] = \mu-a;$ $\qquad$ (ii) $\mathscr{E}[(X-a)^2] = \sigma^2+(\mu-a)^2.$

Proof. (i) $\mathscr{E}[(X-a)] = \sum_{i=1}^{n} p_i(x_i-a)$

$$= \sum_{i=1}^{n} p_i x_i - \sum_{i=1}^{n} p_i a$$

$$= \mu-a \sum_{i=1}^{n} p_i$$

$$= \mu-a, \quad \text{since} \quad \sum_{i=1}^{n} p_i = 1.$$

178

(ii) $\mathscr{E}[(X-a)^2] = \sum_{i=1}^{n} p_i(x_i-a)^2$

$$= \sum_{i=1}^{n} p_i[(x_i-\mu)+(\mu-a)]^2$$

$$= \sum_{i=1}^{n} p_i(x_i-\mu)^2+2(\mu-a)\sum_{i=1}^{n} p_i(x_i-\mu)$$

$$+(\mu-a)^2 \sum_{i=1}^{n} p_i,$$

since $2(\mu-a)$ and $(\mu-a)^2$ are common factors and thus may be taken outside the summation; thus

$$\mathscr{E}[(X-a)^2] = \sigma^2+(\mu-a)^2, \quad \text{since } \sum_{i=1}^{n} p_i = 1$$

and $\sum_{i=1}^{n} p_i(x_i-\mu) = 0$ (from Theorem 10.1 (i) putting $a = \mu$).

Example 3. Find the mean and variance of the numbers 1, 2, ..., 20, *assuming that they are uniformly distributed.*

We use Theorem 10.1, with $a = 10$,

$$\mathscr{E}[(X-10)] = \tfrac{1}{20}[-(9+8+...+1)+(1+2+...+9)+10]$$

$$= 0.5,$$

$$\mu = 10.5;$$

$$\mathscr{E}[(X-10)^2] = \tfrac{1}{20}[2(1^2+2^2+...+9^2)+10^2]$$

$$= \tfrac{1}{20}[\tfrac{1}{3}.9.10.19+100]$$

$$= 33.5,$$

$$\sigma^2 = 33.5-(0.5)^2$$

$$= 33.25.$$

The next theorem determines the mean and standard deviation of a linear function of the random variable. Intuitively, the results are easy to understand: multiplication of every value of X by λ clearly results in a proportionate increase in the measures of the average (mean) and spread (standard deviation), while a shift of origin shifts the average by the same amount but has no effect upon the spread.

Theorem 10.2. If λ, a are any numbers:
  (i) *the mean of the random variable $Y = \lambda X+a$ is $\lambda\mu+a$,*
  (ii) *the standard deviation of the random variable $Y = \lambda X+a$ is $\lambda\sigma$.*

Proof. (i) $\mathscr{E}[\lambda X+a)] = \sum_{i=1}^{n} p_i(\lambda x_i+a)$

$$= \lambda \sum_{i=1}^{n} p_i x_i+a \sum_{i=1}^{n} p_i$$

$$= \lambda\mu+a.$$

179

(ii) The mean of Y is $\lambda\mu + a$, by (i) and the variance of Y is given by

$$\mathscr{E}\{[Y - (\lambda\mu + a)]^2\} = \mathscr{E}\{[(\lambda X + a) - (\lambda\mu + a)]^2\}$$

$$= \sum_{i=1}^{n} p_i[\lambda x_i - \lambda\mu]^2$$

$$= \lambda^2 \sum_{i=1}^{n} p_i(x_i - \mu)^2$$

$$= \lambda^2 \sigma^2.$$

Our final theorem of this section is a result due to the great Russian mathematician P. L. Chebyshev (1821–94). Its importance lies in the fact that it gives us an interpretation for standard deviation in terms of probabilities; that is, it gives us, in terms of λ, an upper limit for the probability that a value of the random variable lies further away from the mean than λ standard deviations, whatever the associated probability distribution. (Of course, if we are given some information about the probability distribution we can usefully refine the inequality, but this does not detract from Chebyshev's result viewed as a general theorem.)

Theorem 10.3 (*Chebyshev's Theorem*). *If λ is any positive number,*

$$\Pr\left(|x_i - \mu| > \lambda\sigma\right) < 1/\lambda^2.$$

Proof. Define the subset A of the outcome space S by

$$A = \{x_i : |x_i - \mu| > \lambda\sigma\} = \{x_i : (x_i - \mu)^2 > \lambda^2\sigma^2\}.$$

Now $S = A \cup A'$ and $A \cap A' = \varnothing$. Denoting by $\sum_A$ summations over those values of i for which $x_i \in A$, and similarly $\sum_{A'}$ and $\sum_S$, we have,

$$\sigma^2 = \sum_S p_i(x_i - \mu)^2$$

$$= \sum_A p_i(x_i - \mu)^2 + \sum_{A'} p_i(x_i - \mu)^2$$

$$\geqslant \sum_A p_i(x_i - \mu)^2, \quad \text{since} \quad \sum_{A'} p_i(x_i - \mu)^2 \geqslant 0,$$

$$> \sum_A p_i\lambda^2\sigma^2, \quad \text{by the definition of } A,$$

$$= \lambda^2\sigma^2 \sum_A p_i.$$

Since $\lambda^2\sigma^2 > 0$ we may divide both sides of the inequality by $\lambda^2\sigma^2$:

$$\frac{1}{\lambda^2} > \sum_A p_i = \Pr\left(x_i : |x_i - \mu| > \lambda\sigma\right).$$

Ex. 9. A probability distribution has mean 3 and variance $\sigma^2 = 1\cdot2$. Give an approximate limit for the probability

$$\Pr\left(|x-3| > 2\sigma\right).$$

The probability distribution for the random variable X ($X = 1, 2, ..., 5$) is given in the following table:

X	1	2	3	4	5
p	$\frac{1}{10}$	$\frac{1}{5}$	$\frac{2}{5}$	$\frac{1}{5}$	$\frac{1}{10}$

Find the mean and standard deviation. What is $\Pr\left(|x-3| > 2\sigma\right)$? Comment upon the results obtained and any discrepancy you observe.

Ex. 10. Find an expression for $\mathscr{E}[(X-\mu)^3]$ in terms of $\mathscr{E}(X^3)$, μ and σ.

5. PROBABILITY GENERATING FUNCTIONS

We now introduce a technique of considerable value in dealing with probability distributions of an integral variable. Given a random experiment the outcome space for which has associated integral random variable X, the expectation of the function t^X is called the *probability generating function* (*p.g.f.*), $G(t)$, for the distribution. Thus

$$G(t) = \mathscr{E}[t^x] = \sum_{i=1}^{n} p_i t^{x_i}.$$

For example, suppose a card is drawn at random from a well-shuffled pack and that we score the face value of the card drawn (an ace scoring 1 and a picture card 10). The probabilities of scoring 1, 2, 3, ..., 9 are each $\frac{1}{13}$, while the probability of scoring 10 is $4/13$. Thus

$$G(t) = \tfrac{1}{13}(t^1+t^2+t^3+...+t^9)+\tfrac{4}{13}t^{10}.$$

The quantity t has no particular significance: it is simply used as a 'carrier' for the values x_i of the random variable. Since the coefficient of t^{x_i} is p_i, the probability of each value of the random variable may be read off if we know the form of the p.g.f. Thus, if we are able to deduce the form of the p.g.f. we have a concise summary of the probability distribution. Theorem 10.4 gives a method of building up the p.g.f. for a complicated distribution but, before we embark upon its enunciation and proof, we must make the following definition:

Two random variables X and Y defined on the same sample space are said to be *independently distributed* if

$$\Pr\left(X = x_i \quad \text{and} \quad Y = y_j\right) = \Pr\left(X = x_i\right)\Pr\left(Y = y_j\right).$$

Our next theorem shows that, if X and Y are independently distributed, then the new random variable $Z = X+Y$ has as its generating function

181

the product of the generating functions of X and Y. For simplicity, we shall consider the particular case in which X can take the $n+1$ values $0, 1, 2, \ldots, n$ with $\Pr(X = i) = p_i$ and that Y can take the $(n+1)$ values $0, 1, 2, \ldots, n$, with $\Pr(Y = j) = q_j$. Then Z can take the $2n+1$ values $0, 1, 2, \ldots, 2n$, with $\Pr(Z = k) = r_k$, say.

Theorem 10.4. *If X and Y are independently distributed random variables taking the values $0, 1, 2, \ldots, n$ and if the p.g.f.s of X and Y are $G_x(t)$, $G_y(t)$ respectively, then the random variable $Z = X + Y$ has p.g.f. $G_z(t)$ where*

$$G_z(t) = G_x(t)\, G_y(t).$$

Proof. $r_k = \Pr(Z = k)$

$\qquad = \Pr(X = 0 \text{ and } Y = k) + \Pr(X = 1 \text{ and } Y = k-1) + \ldots$

$\qquad\qquad\qquad\qquad\qquad\qquad + \Pr(X = k \text{ and } Y = 0)$

$\qquad = p_0 q_k + p_1 q_{k-1} + p_2 q_{k-2} + \ldots + p_k q_0,$

but $\quad G_x(t)\, G_y(t) = (p_0 + p_1 t + p_2 t^2 + \ldots + p_n t^n)(q_0 + q_1 t + q_2 t^2 + \ldots + q_n t^n)$

$\qquad\qquad = p_0 q_0 + (p_0 q_1 + p_1 q_0) t + (p_0 q_2 + p_1 q_1 + p_2 q_0) t^2 + \ldots$

$\qquad\qquad = G_z(t).$

Before giving an example of the application of this theorem, we prove one further result to illustrate the value of developing the theory of p.g.f.s: we show that they may be used to calculate the mean and standard deviation of a distribution.

Theorem 10.5. *If the random variable X, whose p.g.f. is $G(t)$, has mean μ and standard deviation σ, then,*

(i) $G(1) = 1;$

(ii) $G'(1) = \mu;$

(iii) $G''(1) = \sigma^2 + \mu^2 - \mu.$

Proof. (i) $\quad G(t) = \sum_{r=1}^{n} p_r t^r$

$\qquad \therefore \quad G(1) = \sum_{r=1}^{n} p_r$

$\qquad\qquad\quad = 1;$

(ii) $\quad G'(t) = \sum_{r=1}^{n} r p_r t^{r-1}$

$\qquad \therefore \quad G'(1) = \sum_{r=1}^{n} r p_r$

$\qquad\qquad\quad = \mathscr{E}(X)$

$\qquad\qquad\quad = \mu;$

(iii) $G''(t) = \sum_{r=1}^{n} r(r-1) p_r t^{r-2}$

$\therefore \quad G''(1) = \sum_{r=1}^{n} r(r-1) p_r$

$$= \sum_{r=1}^{n} r^2 p_r - \sum_{r=1}^{n} r p_r$$

$$= \mathscr{E}(X^2) - \mathscr{E}(X)$$

$$= (\sigma^2 + \mu^2) - \mu, \quad \text{by Theorem 10.1, with } a = 0.$$

Example 4. Two unbiased dice are thrown. Find the expectation of the total score, and its variance.

Let the random variable X denote the score from the first die; the random variable Y the score from the second die. Then we have to calculate the expectations and variance of the random variable $Z = X + Y$. Now

$$G_X(t) = \tfrac{1}{6}(t^1 + t^2 + \dots + t^6),$$

$$G_Y(t) = \tfrac{1}{6}(t^1 + t^2 + \dots + t^6),$$

$$\therefore \quad G_Z(t) = \tfrac{1}{36}(t^1 + t^2 + \dots + t^6)^2,$$

assuming that the dice fall independently. Thus

$$G_Z'(t) = \tfrac{1}{18}(t^1 + t^2 + \dots + t^6)(1 + 2t + 3t^2 + 4t^3 + 5t^4 + 6t^5),$$

$$G_Z''(t) = \tfrac{1}{18}(t^1 + t^2 + \dots + t^6)(2 + 6t + 12t^2 + 20t^3 + 30t^4)$$
$$+ \tfrac{1}{18}(1 + 2t + 3t^2 + 4t^3 + 5t^4 + 6t^5)^2,$$

$$\therefore \quad G_Z'(1) = 7,$$

$$G_Z''(1) = 47\tfrac{5}{6}.$$

By Theorem 10.5, $\mu = 7$

$$\mu^2 + \sigma^2 - \mu = 47\tfrac{5}{6},$$

$$\mu = 7, \quad \sigma^2 = 5\tfrac{5}{6}.$$

Ex. 11. Three coins are tossed and the number of heads noted. Find the p.g.f. for the resulting distribution and determine μ and σ^2.

6. EXPERIMENTS WITH INFINITE OUTCOME SPACES

Experiments with an infinite number of possible discrete outcomes are easy to visualize. For example, suppose a coin is spun until a head appears. Take as random variable X, the number of tails obtained before the first head is tossed; then X has possible values 0, 1, 2, 3, ... and

$$\Pr(X = r) = \frac{1}{2^{r+1}}.$$

Notice that

$$\sum_{r=0}^{\infty} \Pr(X = r) = \frac{\frac{1}{2}}{1-\frac{1}{2}} = 1,$$

which is as it should be. Indeed, all the results of Chapter 7 hold for such outcome spaces; detailed proofs will be omitted, because they depend upon the manipulation of convergent series. However, assuming the obvious generalizations of the definitions and theorems, the calculations involved are not difficult. For instance, in the example above

$$\mathscr{E}(X) = \sum_{r=1}^{\infty} r \cdot \frac{1}{2^{r+1}}.$$

But

$$\sum_{r=0}^{\infty} x^r = (1-x)^{-1} \quad (|x| < 1)$$

and so

$$\sum_{r=0}^{\infty} r x^{r-1} = (1-x)^{-2},$$

assuming that the infinite series may be differentiated term by term (a result always true, in fact, for convergent power series). Thus

$$\sum_{r=0}^{\infty} r x^{r+1} = x^2 (1-x)^{-2}$$

and, putting $x = \frac{1}{2}$, $\qquad \mathscr{E}(X) = 1.$

Example 5. A and B alternately throw a die, the game terminating in a win for A if he throws a 1 or a 6, or in a win for B if he throws a 2, 3, 4, 5. Find the probability that A wins and, if he wins, find the average number of throws he takes, given that A commences the play.

$\Pr(A$ *throws 1 or 6 on a particular toss*$) = \frac{1}{3}$,

$\Pr(B$ *throws 2, 3, 4 or 5 on a particular toss*$) = \frac{2}{3}$,

$\Pr(A$ *wins on* $(2r+1)$*th. play*$)$
$\qquad = \Pr(A$ *and B fail alternately on first $2r$ plays*$)$
$\qquad\qquad\qquad\qquad \times \Pr(A$ *throws 1 or 6 on* $(2r+1)$*th. play*$)$
$\qquad = (\frac{2}{3})^r (\frac{1}{3})^r (\frac{1}{3})$,

$\qquad \therefore \quad \Pr(A$ *wins*$) = \sum_{r=0}^{\infty} (\frac{2}{9})^r (\frac{1}{3}) = \frac{\frac{1}{3}}{1-\frac{2}{9}} = \frac{3}{7}.$

We now have to find the expected number of throws taken by A, given that A wins. We take as our random variable X where

$$X = r \quad \text{if} \quad A \text{ wins on his } r\text{th turn.}$$

Since the game can go on indefinitely, X may take any positive integral value 1, 2, 3, ...

$$\Pr\,(X = r\,|\,A \text{ wins}) = \frac{(\frac{2}{3}.\frac{1}{3})^{r-1}\frac{1}{3}}{\frac{3}{7}}$$

$$= \tfrac{7}{9}(\tfrac{2}{9})^{r-1}$$

and

$$\mathscr{E}(X) = \sum_{r=1}^{\infty} \tfrac{7}{9}.r(\tfrac{2}{9})^{r-1}$$

$$= \tfrac{7}{9}.\frac{1}{(1-\tfrac{2}{9})^2}$$

$$= \tfrac{9}{7}$$

(on using the result proved above: $\sum_{r=0}^{\infty} rx^{r-1} = (1-x)^{-2}$).

Ex. 12. A man tosses a coin until a head appears and is paid a number of pence equal to the number of tosses he makes. What is his expectation?

Exercise 10(b)

1. X is a random variable with mean μ and standard deviation σ. Write down the means and standard deviations of the following random variables:

(i) $-X$;   (ii) $X+1$;   (iii) $3X-1$;   (iv) $(X-\mu)/\sigma$.

2. Calculate the mean and variance for each of the following distributions:

(i)

X	0	1	2	3	4	5
p	$\frac{1}{4}$	$\frac{1}{8}$	$\frac{1}{16}$	$\frac{1}{16}$	$\frac{1}{8}$	$\frac{3}{8}$

(ii)

X	1	2	3	4	5	6
p	$\frac{1}{10}$	$\frac{1}{10}$	$\frac{2}{10}$	$\frac{3}{10}$	$\frac{2}{10}$	$\frac{1}{10}$

(iii)

X	-3	-2	-1	$0.$	1	2	3	4
p	$\frac{1}{20}$	$\frac{3}{20}$	$\frac{1}{4}$	$\frac{3}{20}$	$\frac{3}{20}$	$\frac{1}{10}$	$\frac{1}{10}$	$\frac{1}{20}$

(iv)

X	50	100	150	200	250
p	$\frac{1}{10}$	$\frac{1}{5}$	$\frac{2}{5}$	$\frac{1}{5}$	$\frac{1}{10}$

3. Calculate the means and variances for X^2 in each part of Question 2.

4. A cubical die is so weighted that the probability of obtaining any face is proportional to the score showing on that face. Find the mean and variance of the score obtained.

5. If the random variable X can take the values 1, 2, 3, ..., n, all values being equally likely, calculate the mean and variance for X.

185

6. *A, B* and *C* repeatedly throw a die, *A* starting, then *B*, then *C*, then *A* again and so on. The winner is the first to throw a six. What are their respective chances of success?

7. *A* throws a pair of unbiased dice, *B* a pair of dice of which one is unbiased and the other is such that the probability of a six is *p*. If they throw in turn and the winner is the first to throw a double six, find *p*, given that, when *A* has the first throw, the game is fair.

8. An unbiased coin is tossed *n* times. If a head appears, $+1$ is scored, if a tail, -1 is scored. Prove that the p.g.f. for the random variable *X*, where x_i = total score after *i* turns, is given by

$$G(t) = (2t)^{-n}(t^2+1)^n.$$

9. A die is thrown *n* times. An odd face makes the score showing, an even face scores zero. Determine the p.g.f. and hence the mean score for *n* throws.

10. Two dice are thrown together and the scores added. What is the chance that the total score exceeds 8?

Find the mean and standard deviation of the total score. What is the standard deviation of the score for a single die? (Cambridge)

11. A card is drawn at random from a standard pack and scores the face value of the card (with ace one and picture cards 10 each). Find the mean and variance of the score.

If the card is replaced, the pack well shuffled and a second card drawn, find the probability that the total score for both draws is 12.

12. Two unbiased dice are given, one of which has the faces numbered in the usual way 1, 2, ..., 6, but the other has two faces numbered 1, two numbered 3 and two numbered 5. Both dice are thrown and the total score, *X*, is recorded. Find the mean μ and standard deviation, σ, of *X*.

Find also

(i) $\Pr(|X-\mu| > \sigma)$; (ii) $\Pr(|X-\mu| > 2\sigma)$.

Miscellaneous Exercise 10

1. Two bags contain red and white discs as shown in the table below:

	Red	White
Bag I	5	15
Bag II	10	10

One of the bags is selected at random and a disc drawn from it proves to be red. If the red discs are now valued at £1 each and the white discs are valueless, what would be a fair price to pay for the remaining discs in the selected bag?

2. (The St Petersburg Paradox.) A coin is spun. If a head is obtained first time you are paid 1p; if you get a tail followed by a head you receive 2p; for two tails followed by a head 4p, the next prize being 8p and so on. Show that, however much you are prepared to pay to play the game, your expected profit will be positive.

Criticise any assumptions you have made and indicate what further know-ledge you would require before offering a more realistic 'fair price' for the game. If the banker against whom you are playing starts with a capital of 100p, what would be a fair price for you to offer him before playing the game?

3. A and B alternately throw an unbiased die, A having the first throw. The game terminates when a six is thrown. B agrees to pay A £1 if A throws a six on his first throw, £3 for a six on his second throw, £5 for a six on his third throw, and so on. What would be a fair price for A to offer to play the game?

4. Two men play a game with two dice. A has a true die, whereas B has a die which is biased so that each of the even faces is twice as likely to occur as each of the odd faces. The two players throw their own die and A wins from B the sum of the numbers thrown when the sum is even and the numbers are unequal. B wins the sum from A when it is odd; and the game is drawn when the two numbers are equal.
Calculate the expectation of the game to A.

5. X and Y are two random variables defined over the same probability distribution. A new random variable Z is constructed, where $Z = X + Y$. Prove that the mean of Z is the sum of the means of X and Y.
Is it also true that the variance of Z is the sum of the variances of X and Y?

6. If X is a random variable with mean μ and standard deviation σ prove that the standard deviation of the random variable $(X - \mu)^2$ is

$$\{\mathscr{E}[(x - \mu)^4] - \sigma^4\}^{\frac{1}{2}}.$$

7. n points are marked on a line at 1 cm intervals. If two of the points are chosen at random, find the probability that they will be r cm apart. Deduce that the expected distance apart of the two points is $\frac{1}{3}(n + 1)$.

8. A and B play a game in which A's chance of winning is p, while B's is q, where $p + q = 1$. They have a contest, the winner being the first to score two consecutive successes. Prove that the expected number of games is

$$(2 + pq)(1 - pq)^{-1}.$$

9. X is a random variable such that $\Pr(X < 0) = 0$ and the mean and standard deviation of X are respectively μ and σ. Prove that, for any $k \geqslant 1$,

$$\Pr(X < k\mu) \geqslant \frac{k - 1}{k}.$$

Deduce Chebyshev's result, that

$$\Pr(\mu - \lambda\sigma < X < \mu + \lambda\sigma) \geqslant 1 - \frac{1}{\lambda^2}.$$

10. The random variable Y has a distribution such that $\Pr(Y = r)$ is given by the coefficient of θ^{r-t} in $p^t(1 - \theta q)^{-t}$ for $r \geqslant t$ and zero otherwise, where $0 < p < 1$, $q = 1 - p$. Find the expectation of Y.   (M.E.I.)

11. X is a random variable that can take all positive integral values 0, 1, 2, 3, ... If

$$p_r = \Pr(X = r) \quad \text{and} \quad q_r = \sum_{s=r+1}^{\infty} p_s$$

and if the p.g.f. for X is $G(t)$ and

$$H(t) = \sum_{r=0}^{\infty} q_r t^r,$$

prove that $$H(t) = \frac{\{1-G(t)\}}{1-t}.$$

Prove, furthermore, that $H(1) = \mu$ where μ is the mean of X, and determine the value of $H'(1)$.

12. A die is thrown n times. If S denotes the total sum obtained, prove that $\mathscr{E}(S^2) = 7n(21n+5)/12$.

13. n identical cards are numbered 1, 2, 3, ..., n, and a random sample (with re-placement) of size k is drawn. If the number on the highest card is taken as the value of the random variable X, prove that

$$\Pr(X = r) = [r^k - (r-1)^k]/n^k$$

and deduce that, for large n, the mean value of X is approximately

$$\frac{nk}{k+1}.$$

14. A and B play a game of golf. At each hole A's chance of winning is a and B's is b. Find the chance, h, that the hole is halved, in terms of a and b.

Show that the chance of A being r up after n holes is the coefficient of x to the power $(n+r)$ in the expansion of $(ax^2 + hx + b)^n$.

If $a = b = h$, find the chance that A wins 5 and 4, i.e. that he was either 5 up with 5 to play and then halved the fourteenth hole, or was 4 up with 5 to play and won it.

Leave your answer in terms of powers of 3 and binomial coefficients.

(M.E.I.)

15. A man consistently stakes a fixed proportion of his available capital on a fair bet, that is, a bet with zero expectation of gain. If he wins, his existing capital is increased by $a\%$, but, if he loses, he decreases it by $b\%$. Show that he must expect to lose in the long run, whatever values a and b might take.

16. Two numbers X and Y between 1 and 100 (inclusive) are selected at random, all possible pairs (X, Y) having equal probabilities. Let Z denote the maximum of X and Y. What is the probability that $Z \leqslant 50$? By use of the formulae

$$\sum_{r=1}^{n} r = \tfrac{1}{2}n(n+1)$$

and $$\sum_{r=1}^{n} r^2 = \tfrac{1}{6}n(n+1)(2n+1)$$

or otherwise, show that the mean of Z is just over 67. Find a median of Z. (A *median* of Z is any number ζ such that $\Pr(Z \leqslant \zeta) \geqslant \tfrac{1}{2}$ and $\Pr(Z \geqslant \zeta) \geqslant \tfrac{1}{2}$.)

(C.S.)

17. Is it possible to devise a coin tossing experiment with a single unbiased coin to give a probability of $\tfrac{1}{3}$ for some event?

If you are given a coin which is biased in some unknown way, show how to devise an experiment in which the probability of success, to be defined, is $\tfrac{1}{2}$.

188

11. *Further vectors*

1. THE DOT (SCALAR, INNER) PRODUCT OF TWO VECTORS

We have defined the combination of two vectors by the triangle rule, an operation which we called *addition* and for which we used the sign $+$. The choice of the word 'addition' was not entirely arbitrary, for it transpired that the addition of vectors bore resemblances to the addition of numbers, in the sense that certain algebraic properties of addition in the two cases were strikingly similar.

We shall now define a new way of combining two vectors, which we shall call *dot multiplication* (otherwise variously called *scalar multiplication*, or the formation of the *inner product*) and denoted by . . The use of a familiar name and notation is again dictated by the fact that dot multiplication and the ordinary multiplication of two numbers display a strong resemblance to one another. However, the reader should again be on his guard and realize that the two operations are quite different as they operate on different types of quantities. Having issued this caveat, we now make our definition of the dot product of two vectors **a** and **b**:

$$\mathbf{a}.\mathbf{b} = |\mathbf{a}||\mathbf{b}| \cos \theta,$$

where θ is the angle between the vectors **a** and **b**. Note that the multiplication on the right-hand side of this equation is the ordinary multiplication of three real numbers, $|\mathbf{a}|, |\mathbf{b}|$, and $\cos \theta$, of which the first two are positive (or zero).

Before proceeding we must clarify one apparent ambiguity in the definition given above: the angle θ between two vectors is chosen as that angle

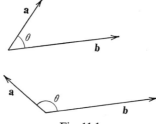

Fig. 11.1

(between 0° and 180°) through which one of the vectors must be rotated to bring it into coincidence in the same sense as the other vector (see Figure 11.1). It follows that the sign of the dot product is positive if the angle thus defined between the two vectors is acute and negative if the angle is obtuse.

We have said that the word 'multiplication' is used in this context because of the similarity shown between dot products and ordinary products. This similarity we now endeavour to display, but to give added force to our warning against pressing the analogy too far, we start by observing two laws of multiplication of ordinary numbers that do NOT hold for dot products.

Dot multiplication does NOT give closure; that is, **a.b** is not a vector.

Dot multiplication is NOT associative; indeed, **(a.b).c** is not even defined, for **(a.b)** is a number, not a vector. (On the other hand, we can talk about **(a.b) c**, which represents a vector in the direction of **c** and whose magnitude is $|\mathbf{a}|\,|\mathbf{b}|\cos\theta$ times that of **c**.)

However, there is a sort of associative rule that holds: if **a**, **b** are two vectors and k is a number,

$$k(\mathbf{a.b}) = (k\mathbf{a}).\mathbf{b} = \mathbf{a}.(k\mathbf{b}).$$

The proof of this follows immediately from the definitions and may be left as an exercise for the diligent reader.

Another reassuring note may be struck by observing that the commutative law holds for dot products

$$\mathbf{a.b} = \mathbf{b.a}.$$

Again, the proof of this is immediate from the definition and may, with even more confidence, be left as an exercise for the reader.

The final rule for dot products, that of distributivity over vector addition, i.e.

$$\mathbf{a.(b+c)} = \mathbf{a.b} + \mathbf{a.c}$$

is more subtle and the proof is not immediately obvious. However, the effort expended in demonstrating this result is amply rewarded, for with it we shall have set up all the apparatus necessary for an effective algebra of vectors.

We begin by defining the *projection* of a vector **a** in a direction specified by a unit vector **u**. Suppose the displacement **OA** represents **a**; draw the plane π through O perpendicular to **u**. Then, if D is the foot of the perpendicular from A to π,

$$\mathbf{a} = \mathbf{OD} + \mathbf{DA}$$

$$= \mathbf{OD} + p\mathbf{u}$$

(see Figure 11.2). Further, the expression of **a** as the sum of two vec-

190

tors, one in the plane π and one in the direction $\mathbf{u}$ is unique. For suppose that

$$\mathbf{a} = \mathbf{OD} + p\mathbf{u}$$

$$= \mathbf{OD'} + p'\mathbf{u},$$

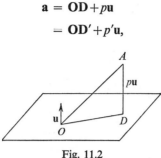

Fig. 11.2

where D, D' both lie in π. Then, by subtraction

$$0 = \mathbf{OD} - \mathbf{OD'} + p\mathbf{u} - p'\mathbf{u}$$

$$= \mathbf{D'D} + (p - p')\,\mathbf{u}$$

and so $$\mathbf{DD'} = (p - p')\,\mathbf{u}.$$

But this is impossible unless D and D' coincide and $p = p'$, for $\mathbf{DD'}$ and $(p - p')\,\mathbf{u}$ lie in different planes and so cannot possibly be equal, unless each is the zero vector.

The number p that arises in this construction is called the *projection* of $\mathbf{a}$ in the direction $\mathbf{u}$. We now prove the fundamental result for projections: if the projection of $\mathbf{a}_1$ in the direction $\mathbf{u}$ is p_1 and the projection of $\mathbf{a}_2$ in the direction of $\mathbf{u}$ is p_2, then the projection of $\mathbf{a}_1 + \mathbf{a}_2$ in the direction $\mathbf{u}$ is $p_1 + p_2$.

Suppose, with the obvious notation, that

$$\mathbf{a}_1 = \mathbf{OD}_1 + p_1\mathbf{u},$$

$$\mathbf{a}_2 = \mathbf{OD}_2 + p_2\mathbf{u};$$

then $$\mathbf{a}_1 + \mathbf{a}_2 = (\mathbf{OD}_1 + \mathbf{OD}_2) + (p_1 + p_2)\,\mathbf{u}.$$

But $\mathbf{OD}_1 + \mathbf{OD}_2$ is certainly a vector in the plane π, and so, by the uniqueness of the expression for $\mathbf{a}_1 + \mathbf{a}_2$ as the sum of two vectors, one in π and the other in the direction of $\mathbf{u}$, the projection of $\mathbf{a}_1 + \mathbf{a}_2$ in the direction of $\mathbf{u}$ is $p_1 + p_2$.

Having defined the projection of a vector in a given direction we may obtain a simple geometrical interpretation for the dot product of two vectors $\mathbf{a}$ and $\mathbf{b}$. Represent $\mathbf{a}$, $\mathbf{b}$ by the displacements $\mathbf{OA}$, $\mathbf{OB}$; let C be the foot of the perpendicular from A to OB, and D the foot of the perpendicular from B to OA. Then OC is the projection of $\mathbf{a}$ in the direction of $\mathbf{b}$, and OD is the projection of $\mathbf{b}$ in the direction of $\mathbf{a}$ (see Figure 11.3).

191

Now $\qquad$ $\mathbf{a.b} = OA(OB \cos \theta)$

$\qquad\qquad\quad = OA.OD$

and $\qquad$ $\mathbf{a.b} = OB(OA \cos \theta)$

$\qquad\qquad\quad = OB.OC,$

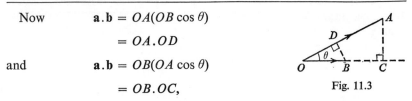

Fig. 11.3

and thus the value of $\mathbf{a.b}$ is the product of the magnitude of either of the vectors with the projection of the other in its direction.

Our proof of distributivity for dot multiplication over vector addition has been long delayed but our result, which we shall state as a theorem, now follows very readily and the results we have proved concerning projections have an interest and importance in their own right and were doubly worth pursuing.

Theorem 11.1. *For any vectors* $\mathbf{a}$, $\mathbf{b}$, $\mathbf{c}$,

$$\mathbf{a.(b+c)} = \mathbf{a.b} + \mathbf{a.c}.$$

Proof. Let the projection of $\mathbf{b}$ and $\mathbf{c}$ in the direction $\mathbf{a}$ be p_1 and p_2 respectively. Then

$$\mathbf{a.(b+c)} = |\mathbf{a}| \, (p_1 + p_2) = |\mathbf{a}| \, p_1 + |\mathbf{a}| \, p_2$$

$$= \mathbf{a.b} + \mathbf{a.c}$$

(by distributive law for ordinary numbers).

Ex. 1. A, B have position vectors $\mathbf{a}$, $\mathbf{b}$ referred to some origin O. If OA is perpendicular to OB, show that $\mathbf{a.b} = 0$. Is the converse result true?

Ex. 2. If $\mathbf{a}$ is the position vector of the point A, interpret the scalar product $\mathbf{a.a}$.

Ex. 3. Show that $\qquad (\mathbf{a-b}) \,.(\mathbf{a-b}) = \mathbf{a.a} + \mathbf{b.b} - 2\mathbf{a.b}.$
If $\mathbf{a}$, $\mathbf{b}$ are the position vectors of the points A, B, interpret this equation (i) when OA and OB are perpendicular; (ii) when OA, OB are not perpendicular.

Example 1. *Prove that, if the sum of the squares of two opposite edges of a tetrahedron is equal to the sum of the squares of another pair of opposite edges, then the remaining pair of opposite edges are perpendicular.*

We are given that

$$AB^2 + CD^2 = BC^2 + DA^2$$

and have to prove that

$$AC \perp DB.$$

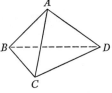

Fig. 11.4

Take any origin O and let the position vectors of A, B, C, D be $\mathbf{a}$, $\mathbf{b}$, $\mathbf{c}$, $\mathbf{d}$. Then, in terms of these position vectors, we are given that

$$(\mathbf{b-a}).(\mathbf{b-a}) + (\mathbf{d-c}).(\mathbf{d-c}) = (\mathbf{c-b}).(\mathbf{c-b}) + (\mathbf{d-a}).(\mathbf{d-a}).$$

Now

$$(\mathbf{b}-\mathbf{a}).(\mathbf{b}-\mathbf{a})+(\mathbf{d}-\mathbf{c}).(\mathbf{d}-\mathbf{c}) = (\mathbf{c}-\mathbf{b}).(\mathbf{c}-\mathbf{b})+(\mathbf{d}-\mathbf{a}).(\mathbf{d}-\mathbf{a})$$

$$\Leftrightarrow \mathbf{b}.\mathbf{b}-2\mathbf{a}.\mathbf{b}+\mathbf{a}.\mathbf{a}+\mathbf{d}.\mathbf{d}-2\mathbf{c}.\mathbf{d}+\mathbf{c}.\mathbf{c}=\mathbf{c}.\mathbf{c}-2\mathbf{b}.\mathbf{c}+\mathbf{b}.\mathbf{b}+\mathbf{d}.\mathbf{d}-2\mathbf{d}.\mathbf{a}+\mathbf{a}.\mathbf{a}$$

$$\Leftrightarrow \mathbf{b}.\mathbf{c}+\mathbf{d}.\mathbf{a} = \mathbf{a}.\mathbf{b}+\mathbf{c}.\mathbf{d}$$

$$\Leftrightarrow (\mathbf{c}-\mathbf{a}).(\mathbf{b}-\mathbf{d}) = 0.$$

But $\mathbf{c}-\mathbf{a} \neq 0$, $\mathbf{b}-\mathbf{d} \neq 0$,

$$\therefore \quad AC \perp BD.$$

Exercise 11(a)

1. Show that $\mathbf{a}.\mathbf{a}-\mathbf{b}.\mathbf{b} = (\mathbf{a}-\mathbf{b}).(\mathbf{a}+\mathbf{b})$.
Interpret this equation geometrically and discuss the particular case $|\mathbf{a}| = |\mathbf{b}|$.

2. If $\mathbf{a}$, $\mathbf{b}$ are non-zero vectors such that $|\mathbf{a}+\mathbf{b}| = |\mathbf{a}-\mathbf{b}|$, show that $\mathbf{a}$ and $\mathbf{b}$ are perpendicular.

3. A is a fixed point with position vector $\mathbf{a}$ and $\mathbf{c}$ is a constant vector. If the variable point P has position vector $\mathbf{r}$ where $\mathbf{r}$ satisfies the equation

$$(\mathbf{r}-\mathbf{a}).(\mathbf{r}-\mathbf{a}) = \mathbf{c}.\mathbf{c}$$

what can be said about the position of P?

4. Prove that $\quad \mathbf{b}+\mathbf{c} = 0 \quad$ and $\quad |\mathbf{a}| = |\mathbf{b}| \Leftrightarrow (\mathbf{a}-\mathbf{b}).(\mathbf{a}-\mathbf{c}) = 0$.

Interpret this result as a geometrical theorem.

5. $OXYZ$ is a rhombus of side a; P is any point of OY (or OY produced). Prove that $OP.YP = XP^2-a^2$.

6. $ACBD$ is a straight line and O is a point not on the line. $\angle AOB$, $\angle COD$ are both right-angles. If $\mathbf{OA} = \mathbf{a}$, $\mathbf{OB} = \mathbf{b}$, $AC = x$, $CB = y$, $BD = z$, find the position vectors (relative to O) of C and D.
Deduce that

$$\frac{CB.BD}{AC.AD} = \frac{OB^2}{OA^2}.$$

7. $ABCD$ is a tetrahedron in which $AB \perp CD$ and $AC \perp BD$. Prove that $AD \perp BC$ and that

$$AB^2+CD^2 = AC^2+BD^2 = AD^2+BC^2.$$

8. If each edge of a tetrahedron is equal to the opposite edge, prove that the line joining the mid-points of any two opposite edges is at right-angles to each of these edges.

9. Prove that, if two of the joins of mid-points of opposite edges of a tetrahedron are at right-angles, the remaining edges are equal.

10. $ABCD$ is a skew quadrilateral (that is, the vertices A, B, C, D do not all lie in the same plane). The mid-points of AC, BD are P, Q respectively. Prove that

$$AB^2+BC^2+CD^2+DA^2 = AC^2+BD^2+4PQ^2.$$

193

11. $ABCD$ is a tetrahedron; X, Y, Z are the mid-points of AB, AC, AD and P, Q, R are the mid-points of CD, BD, BC. Prove that

$$AB^2 + DC^2 + 2PX^2 = AC^2 + BD^2 + 2QY^2 = AD^2 + BC^2 + 2RZ^2.$$

12. $ABCD$ is a tetrahedron and G is the centroid of the base BCD. Prove that

$$AB^2 + AC^2 + AD^2 = GB^2 + GC^2 + GD^2 + 3GA^2.$$

2. THE DOT PRODUCT (CONTINUED); COMPONENT FORM

If $\mathbf{i}, \mathbf{j}, \mathbf{k}$ form a right-handed set of orthogonal unit vectors, the following equalities immediately follow from the definition of the dot product:

$$\mathbf{i}.\mathbf{i} = \mathbf{j}.\mathbf{j} = \mathbf{k}.\mathbf{k} = 1, \tag{1}$$

$$\mathbf{j}.\mathbf{k} = \mathbf{k}.\mathbf{i} = \mathbf{i}.\mathbf{j} = 0. \tag{2}$$

Theorem 11.2. *If* $\mathbf{a} = a_1\mathbf{i} + a_2\mathbf{j} + a_3\mathbf{k}$ *and* $\mathbf{b} = b_1\mathbf{i} + b_2\mathbf{j} + b_3\mathbf{k}$,

then $\qquad\qquad \mathbf{a}.\mathbf{b} = a_1 b_1 + a_2 b_2 + a_3 b_3.$

Proof: $\mathbf{a}.\mathbf{b} = (a_1\mathbf{i} + a_2\mathbf{j} + a_3\mathbf{k}).(b_1\mathbf{i} + b_2\mathbf{j} + b_3\mathbf{k})$

$$= a_1 b_1 \mathbf{i}.\mathbf{i} + a_2 b_2 \mathbf{j}.\mathbf{j} + a_3 b_3 \mathbf{k}.\mathbf{k} + a_1 b_2 \mathbf{i}.\mathbf{j} + a_1 b_3 \mathbf{i}.\mathbf{k}$$

$$+ a_2 b_1 \mathbf{j}.\mathbf{i} + a_2 b_3 \mathbf{j}.\mathbf{k} + a_3 b_1 \mathbf{k}.\mathbf{i} + a_3 b_2 \mathbf{k}.\mathbf{j}$$

$$= a_1 b_1 + a_2 b_2 + a_3 b_3 \quad \text{by virtue of equations (1) and (2).}$$

From Theorem 11.2 it follows that

$$|\mathbf{a}|^2 = \mathbf{a}.\mathbf{a} = a_1^2 + a_2^2 + a_3^2$$

and that $\qquad \cos\theta = \dfrac{\mathbf{a}.\mathbf{b}}{|\mathbf{a}||\mathbf{b}|} = \dfrac{a_1 b_1 + a_2 b_2 + a_3 b_3}{\sqrt{(a_1^2 + a_2^2 + a_3^2)}\sqrt{(b_1^2 + b_2^2 + b_3^2)}}.$

Example 2. A, B, C have Cartesian coordinates $(2, 3, 4)$, $(-2, 1, 0)$, $(4, 0, 2)$ *respectively. Find:*
   (i) $\cos \angle BAC$;
   (ii) *the unit vector perpendicular to the plane ABC.*

$$\mathbf{x} = \mathbf{AB} = -4\mathbf{i} - 2\mathbf{j} - 4\mathbf{k},$$

$$\mathbf{y} = \mathbf{AC} = 2\mathbf{i} - 3\mathbf{j} - 2\mathbf{k}$$

giving $\qquad\qquad \mathbf{x}.\mathbf{y} = -8 + 6 + 8 = 6.$

But $\qquad\qquad \mathbf{x}.\mathbf{y} = |\mathbf{x}||\mathbf{y}| \cos \angle BAC$

$$= \sqrt{36}\sqrt{17} \cos \angle BAC.$$

Thus $$6 = 6\sqrt{17}\cos \angle BAC,$$

$$\therefore \quad \cos \angle BAC = 1/\sqrt{17}.$$

Now suppose $\mathbf{u} = l\mathbf{i}+m\mathbf{j}+n\mathbf{k}$ is a unit vector perpendicular to the plane ABC. Then

$$\begin{cases} \mathbf{u}.\mathbf{x} = 0, \\ \mathbf{u}.\mathbf{y} = 0, \end{cases}$$

$$\therefore \quad \begin{cases} -4l-2m-4n = 0, \\ 2l-3m-2n = 0, \end{cases}$$

$$\therefore \quad -4m-4n = 0$$

and so $l:m:n = 1:2:-2$, on solving for the ratios $l:m:n$. Thus

$$\mathbf{u} = \lambda\mathbf{i}+2\lambda\mathbf{j}-2\lambda\mathbf{k}$$

where λ must be so chosen that $|\mathbf{u}| = 1$,

i.e. $$\lambda^2+4\lambda^2+4\lambda^2 = 1,$$

i.e. $$\lambda = \tfrac{1}{3}$$

and so $$\mathbf{u} = \tfrac{1}{3}\mathbf{i}+\tfrac{2}{3}\mathbf{j}-\tfrac{2}{3}\mathbf{k}.$$

Ex. 4. If $\mathbf{a} = \mathbf{i}-3\mathbf{j}+\mathbf{k}$, $\mathbf{b} = 2\mathbf{i}+2\mathbf{j}-\mathbf{k}$, find $\mathbf{a}.\mathbf{b}$.

Ex. 5. Show that the two skew lines

$$\begin{cases} \dfrac{x-1}{2} = \dfrac{y+1}{3} = \dfrac{z+1}{2}, \\[2mm] \dfrac{x+1}{1} = \dfrac{y-2}{2} = \dfrac{z}{-4} \end{cases}$$

are perpendicular.

Ex. 6. Find the unit vector perpendicular to the plane A (3, 1, 1), B (2, 5, 0), $C(-1, -1, 15)$.

Ex. 7. Deduce the two distance formulae of Chapter 3 using dot products.

Ex. 8. Prove vectorially that the angle between two diagonals of a cube is $\arccos \tfrac{1}{3}$.

3. FURTHER COORDINATE GEOMETRY OF TWO DIMENSIONS

Throughout this section we shall suppose a right-handed set of axes Ox, Oy is given, their directions being defined by unit vectors $\mathbf{i}$, $\mathbf{j}$. $P_1(x_1, y_1)$, $P_2(x_2, y_2)$ ... are given points with position vectors $\mathbf{r}_1, \mathbf{r}_2 ...$; $P(x, y)$ is a general point with position vector $\mathbf{r}$.

A line is specified given a point P_1 lying upon it and its direction; let us suppose its direction is defined by the unit vector $\mathbf{u} = l\mathbf{i} + m\mathbf{j}$. Here $l = \cos\theta_1$ and $m = \cos\theta_2$, where θ_1 and θ_2 are the angles made by the vector $\mathbf{u}$ with the axes Ox and Oy respectively (senses being taken into account) (see Figure 11.5).

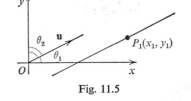

Fig. 11.5

The line through $P_1(x_1, y_1)$ in the direction $\mathbf{u}$ thus has the equation

$$\frac{x-x_1}{l} = \frac{y-y_1}{m} = \lambda$$

(see Figure 11.5, where $\theta_1 \neq \tfrac{1}{2}\pi$). Since $\cos\theta_2 = \sin\theta_1$, this equation may be rearranged in the form

$$y - y_1 = \frac{\sin\theta_1}{\cos\theta_1}(x - x_1)$$

or $$y - y_1 = \tan\theta_1(x - x_1)$$

agreeing with the form given in Chapter 3. (Notice, however, that the letter m was used differently on that occasion.)

Given two lines, one through P_1 in the direction $\mathbf{u}_1 = l_1\mathbf{i} + m_1\mathbf{j}$, the other in the direction $\mathbf{u}_2 = l_2\mathbf{i} + m_2\mathbf{j}$, the angle ϕ between the two lines may be found by computing the dot product $\mathbf{u}_1 . \mathbf{u}_2$

$$\mathbf{u}_1 . \mathbf{u}_2 = |\mathbf{u}_1||\mathbf{u}_2|\cos\phi$$

$$= \cos\phi \quad \text{(since } \mathbf{u}_1, \mathbf{u}_2 \text{ are unit vectors)}$$

and thus $$\cos\phi = l_1 l_2 + m_1 m_2. \tag{3}$$

For example, the lines $2x - y + 1 = 0$, $3x + 2y - 3 = 0$ may be put in the form

$$\frac{x}{1} = \frac{y-1}{2}; \quad \frac{x-1}{-2} = \frac{y}{3}$$

or, equivalently, by making the denominators components of unit vectors $(l^2 + m^2 = 1)$

$$\frac{x}{1/\sqrt{5}} = \frac{y-1}{2/\sqrt{5}}; \quad \frac{x-1}{-2/\sqrt{13}} = \frac{y}{3/\sqrt{13}}.$$

196

The angle between the lines is thus given by

$$\cos \phi = -\frac{1}{\sqrt{5}} \cdot \frac{2}{\sqrt{13}} + \frac{2}{\sqrt{5}} \cdot \frac{3}{\sqrt{13}}$$

$$= \frac{4}{\sqrt{65}}.$$

Notice in particular that, from equation (3) the two lines are perpendicular

$$\Leftrightarrow l_1 l_2 + m_1 m_2 = 0.$$

Provided $m_1 \neq 0$, $m_2 \neq 0$ this second condition may be written

$$\frac{l_1}{m_1} \frac{l_2}{m_2} = -1.$$

But, as was noted above, l_1/m_1 and l_2/m_2 are the gradients of the two lines; we have thus regained, by an alternative method, the result of Chapter 3.4.

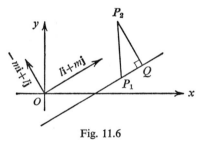

Fig. 11.6

It is frequently required to find the perpendicular distance from a point to a line. Suppose we are given a line through $P_1(x_1, y_1)$ in the direction $\mathbf{u} = l\mathbf{i} + m\mathbf{j}$ and a point $P_2(x_2, y_2)$. Let Q be the foot of the perpendicular from P_2 to the given line. Then the unit vector in the direction of QP_2 is $-m\mathbf{i} + l\mathbf{j}$ (consider the dot product with $\mathbf{u}$). Thus

$$P_2Q = \mathbf{P_1P_2}.(-m\mathbf{i} + l\mathbf{j})$$

$$= ([x_2 - x_1]\mathbf{i} + [y_2 - y_1]\mathbf{j}).(-m\mathbf{i} + l\mathbf{j})$$

$$= -m(x_2 - x_1) + l(y_2 - y_1).$$

Although this gives the required perpendicular distance, it may not be a very convenient form to handle: the equation of a line is generally given in the form $ax + by + c = 0$ and we shall now deduce, as a theorem, the perpendicular distance from the point $P_2(x_2, y_2)$ to this line.

197

Theorem 11.3. *The perpendicular distance from the point* $P_2(x_2, y_2)$ *to the line* $ax+by+c = 0$ *is*

$$\frac{ax_2+by_2+c}{\sqrt{(a^2+b^2)}} \cdot$$

Proof. The given line may be rewritten in the form

$$\frac{x+c/a}{b} = \frac{y}{-a}$$

or, making the denominators components of a unit vector, in the equivalent form

$$\frac{x+c/a}{b/\sqrt{(a^2+b^2)}} = \frac{y}{-a/\sqrt{(a^2+b^2)}} \cdot$$

Thus the unit vector defining the direction of the line is

$$\mathbf{u} = \frac{b}{\sqrt{(a^2+b^2)}}\,\mathbf{i} - \frac{a}{\sqrt{(a^2+b^2)}}\,\mathbf{j},$$

and a perpendicular unit vector is

$$\mathbf{u}' = \frac{a}{\sqrt{(a^2+b^2)}}\,\mathbf{i} + \frac{b}{\sqrt{(a^2+b^2)}}\,\mathbf{j}.$$

If $P_1(x_1, y_1)$ is some (arbitrary) point of the given line, the perpendicular distance, d, from P_2 is given by

$$d = \mathbf{P_1P_2} \cdot \mathbf{u}'$$
$$= \frac{a(x_1-x_2)}{\sqrt{(a^2+b^2)}} + \frac{b(y_1-y_2)}{\sqrt{(a^2+b^2)}} \cdot$$

But $ax_1+by_1 = -c$, since P_1 lies on the line and hence

$$d = \frac{ax_2+by_2+c}{\sqrt{(a^2+b^2)}} \cdot$$

For example, the perpendicular distance from the point (1, 2) to the line $2x-5y+1 = 0$ is

$$\frac{2-10+1}{\sqrt{29}} = -\frac{7}{\sqrt{29}} \cdot$$

(The significance of the negative sign is explained below; the magnitude of the perpendicular distance is $7/\sqrt{29}$.)

Suppose now that the line joining OP_2 cuts the line

$$ax+by+c = 0$$

at P_1 (see Figure 11.7). Then, if $OP_1:P_1P_2 = 1:\lambda$, the coordinates of P_1 are

$$\left(\frac{x_2}{1+\lambda}, \frac{y_2}{1+\lambda}\right).$$

198

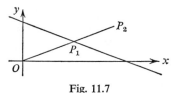

Fig. 11.7

But P_1 lies on the line $ax+by+c = 0$ and thus

$$\frac{ax_2}{1+\lambda}+\frac{by_2}{1+\lambda}+c = 0$$

or $$ax_2+by_2+c = -\lambda c.$$

From this equation it follows at once that, if ax_2+by_2+c and c have the same sign, λ is negative and, if they have opposite signs, λ is positive. Since c may be written as $a.0+b.0+c$, we may summarize the result as follows.

If, in the expression $ax+by+c$, the substitution of the quantities (i) $x = 0, y = 0$; (ii) $x = x_2, y = y_2$ gives two values of the same sign, then P_2 and O lie on the same side of the line (for, in this case, P_1 divides OP_2 externally and so $\lambda < 0$); if on the other hand, it yields values of opposite signs, P_2 and O lie on opposite sides of the line.

Ex. 9. Find the perpendicular distances of the point $(2, -1)$ from the lines $3x+4y+3 = 0$ and $4x-3y-6 = 0$. What can you deduce about the position of $(2, -1)$ relative to the two given lines?

Ex. 10. Sketch the two lines $3x+y-3 = 0, 3x+y-6 = 0$ and shade in the region determined by the four inequalities $x > 0, y > 0, 3x+y-3 > 0, 3x+y-6 < 0$.

Ex. 11. Find the equation of the bisector of the acute angle between the lines $x = 0$ and $5x+12y-60 = 0$. Find the incentre of the triangle formed by the lines $x = 0, y = 0, 5x+12y-60 = 0$.

Ex. 12. a, b, c are constants. Show that, as θ varies, the straight line

$$x \cos \theta + y \sin \theta + a \cos \theta + b \sin \theta + c = 0$$

touches a certain circle. Find the centre and radius of the circle.

Ex. 13. Find the equations of the lines parallel to $8x+6y+3 = 0$, and distant 1 unit from it.

Exercise 11 (b)

1. Determine the projection upon (*a*) the x axis, (*b*) the line $3x-4y+1 = 0$ of the line segments joining the following pairs of points:

   (i) $(2, 3), (4, 4)$;   (ii) $(-1, 2), (1, 5)$;

   (iii) $(-1, 2), (2, -3)$;   (iv) $(a, b), (a+b, a-b)$.

2. Find the cosines of the acute angles between the following pairs of lines:

(i) $x-y+1 = 0, 3x-y+2 = 0$;   (ii) $3x+2y+1 = 0, x-2y-3 = 0$;

(iii) $4x-y+1 = 0, 3x+4y = 0$;   (iv) $ax+by = 0, ax-by = 0$.

3. Determine the perpendicular distances between the following points and lines. (Leave your answers in surd form.)

(i) $(0, 0), x+4y-1 = 0$;   (ii) $(-1, 2), 2x-3y-4 = 0$;

(iii) $(-2, -3), x-3y+5 = 0$;   (iv) $(h, -k), hx-ky+2hk = 0$.

4. Find the distances between the following pairs of parallel lines:

(i) $x-2y+1 = 0, x-2y+3 = 0$;   (ii) $2x+y-3 = 0, 4x+2y+3 = 0$;

(iii) $5x-y-1 = 0, 5x-y+3 = 0$;   (iv) $ax+by+a = 0, ax+by-b = 0$.

5. Find the equations of the pairs of lines, parallel to the following lines, and distant three units from them:

(i) $3x-4y+1 = 0$;   (ii) $8x+6y+5 = 0$;

(iii) $5x+12y+2 = 0$;   (iv) $3x+2y+1 = 0$.

6. Draw rough sketches and shade in the areas determined by the following inequalities:

(i) $x > 0, y > 0, y < 2, 2x+3y-8 < 0$;

(ii) $x > 0, y > 0, x-y-1 < 0, 3x+y-7 < 0$;

(iii) $2x-y > 0, x-2y < 0, 2x-y+2 > 0, x-2y+4 > 0$;

(iv) $|x+y| < 1; |x-y| < 1$;

(v) $|x+y-1| < 1; |2x-3y-1| < 1$.

7. Find the equations of the bisectors of the *acute* angles between the following pairs of lines:

(i) $x = 0, 3x-4y = 0$;   (ii) $3x-4y-1 = 0, 4x-3y-2 = 0$;

(iii) $5x+12y+3 = 0, 6x-8y+3 = 0$.

8. Find the equation of the image by reflection of the line $x-y = 4$ in the line $2x+y = 1$.   (London)

9. ABC is a triangle; A is the point $(0, 3)$ and B is the point $(-5, -2)$. The orthocentre (meet of the altitudes) of the triangle is the point $(-1, 1)$. Find

(i) the coordinates of C;   (ii) the area of the triangle;

(iii) the tangent of the angle ACB.

10. Show that the reflection of the point (α, β) in the line $y = mx$ is the point

$$\left(\frac{(1-m^2)\,\alpha+2m\beta}{1+m^2}, \frac{2m\alpha-(1-m^2)\,\beta}{1+m^2}\right).$$

A is the point (p, q), B is the reflection of A in the line $y = x$ and C is the reflection of B in the line $y = -x$. Find the coordinates of C.

Show that C is the reflection of A in the line $px+qy = 0$.   (London)

200

11. A triangle ABC lies wholly within the first quadrant and has an area of $4\frac{1}{2}$ sq. units. The equation of one side is $2x-5y+23 = 0$ and the vertices A and B are (1, 5) and (3, 4) respectively. Find the equations of the other two sides, the angle ABC, and the coordinates of the orthocentre of the triangle.   (London)

12. If $f(x, y) \equiv ax+by+c$, discuss the changes in value and sign of $f(X, Y)$, when the point P with coordinates (X, Y) moves in the x, y plane, in relation to the line whose equation is $f(x, y) = 0$.

Determine the smallest value attained by the expression

$$22x+11y-21,$$

when x and y vary subject to the simultaneous restrictions

$$3x+4y \geqslant 12,$$

$$2x-y \geqslant 2.   \text{(Cambridge)}$$

4. FURTHER COORDINATE GEOMETRY
OF THREE DIMENSIONS

As a straight line in two dimensions may be completely defined by a point and a gradient, so a plane may be defined, given a point lying on it and the direction of its normal. Suppose that a plane passes through the point A (position vector **a**) and is perpendicular to the directions defined by the unit normal **n**. Then, if P (position vector **r**) is any point of the plane,

$$\mathbf{AP} = \mathbf{r} - \mathbf{a}$$

(Figure 11.8). But

$$\mathbf{AP}.\mathbf{n} = 0,$$

$$\therefore \quad (\mathbf{r}-\mathbf{a}).\mathbf{n} = 0,$$

i.e. $$\mathbf{r}.\mathbf{n} = \mathbf{a}.\mathbf{n}. \tag{4}$$

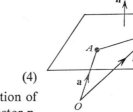

Fig. 11.8

Equation (4) represents the vector equation of the plane through A with unit normal vector **n**. If Cartesian axes are taken in the directions **i, j, k** and $\mathbf{n} = l_1\mathbf{i}+l_2\mathbf{j}+l_3\mathbf{k}$, $\mathbf{a} = a_1\mathbf{i}+a_2\mathbf{j}+a_3\mathbf{k}$, $\mathbf{r} = x\mathbf{i}+y\mathbf{j}+z\mathbf{k}$, then (4) takes the Cartesian form $$l_1x+l_2y+l_3z = l_1a_1+l_2a_2+l_3a_3. \tag{5}$$

Thus, equation (5) represents the Cartesian equation of the plane through $A(a_1, a_2, a_3)$ with normal whose direction cosines are l_1, l_2, l_3.

Conversely, $$\mathbf{r}.\mathbf{n} = p \quad (p \text{ constant}) \tag{6}$$

represents a plane with unit normal vector **n**. For **r.n** is the length of the projection of OP in the direction **n**, and, if this is constant for all P, P clearly lies on a plane perpendicular to **n**. Thus, (using components),

$$ax+by+cz = d$$

201

is the equation of a plane. The unit normal vector is

$$\left(\frac{a}{\sqrt{(a^2+b^2+c^2)}}\right)\mathbf{i}+\left(\frac{b}{\sqrt{(a^2+b^2+c^2)}}\right)\mathbf{j}+\left(\frac{c}{\sqrt{(a^2+b^2+c^2)}}\right)\mathbf{k}$$

and it follows from equation (6), that the perpendicular distance from the origin to this plane is the numerical value of

$$\frac{d}{\sqrt{(a^2+b^2+c^2)}}.$$

Ex. 14. Write down the unit vectors perpendicular to

(i) $x-2y+2z = 0$; (ii) $3x-y+z = 6$; (iii) $3x+2y+z = 2$.

Ex. 15. Write down the equation of the planes through the given points and perpendicular to the given vectors:

(i) $(1, 2, 0), \mathbf{i}-3\mathbf{j}+\mathbf{k}$; (ii) $(2, -1, -1), \mathbf{i}-\mathbf{j}+\mathbf{k}$;

(iii) $(3, -4, 2), 2\mathbf{i}+3\mathbf{j}-5\mathbf{k}$.

Theorem 11.4. *The perpendicular distance from the point* $P_1(x_1, y_1, z_1)$ *to the plane* $ax+by+cz+d = 0$ *is*

$$\frac{ax_1+by_1+cz_1+d}{\sqrt{(a^2+b^2+c^2)}}.$$

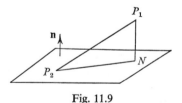

Fig. 11.9

Proof. Let $P_2(x_2, y_2, z_2)$ be any point of the plane $ax+by+cz+d = 0$ and let N be the foot of the perpendicular from P_1 to the plane (Figure 11.9). If $\mathbf{n}$ is the unit vector perpendicular to the plane, then

$$P_1N = \mathbf{P_2P_1.n}$$

$$= [(x_1-x_2)\mathbf{i}+ (y_1-y_2)\mathbf{j}+ (z_1-z_2)\mathbf{k}]$$

$$\cdot\left[\frac{a}{\sqrt{(a^2+b^2+c^2)}}\mathbf{i}+ \frac{b}{\sqrt{(a^2+b^2+c^2)}}\mathbf{j}+\frac{c}{\sqrt{(a^2+b^2+c^2)}}\mathbf{k}\right]$$

$$= \frac{a(x_1-x_2)+b(y_1-y_2)+c(z_1-z_2)}{\sqrt{(a^2+b^2+c^2)}}.$$

202

But $ax_2+by_2+cz_2 = -d$, since P_2 lies on the plane. Thus

$$P_1N = \frac{ax_1+by_1+cz_1+d}{\sqrt{(a^2+b^2+c^2)}}.$$

Again, $ax_1+by_1+cz_1+d$ may be positive or negative, depending upon which side of the plane P_1 lies. The result is completely analogous to that for the straight line.

We conclude this chapter by giving some worked examples of coordinate geometry in two and three dimensions.

Example 3. *Find the complete locus of a point which moves so that its perpendicular distance from* $8x-y+18 = 0$ *is twice its perpendicular distance from* $7x+4y+6 = 0$. (O & C)

Let $P(x, y)$ be any point of the plane. If d_1, d_2 represent the perpendicular distances from P to the two lines

$$d_1 = \pm\frac{8x-y+18}{\sqrt{65}}; \quad d_2 = \pm\frac{7x+4y+6}{\sqrt{65}}.$$

The required locus is the totality of points P which satisfy $d_1 = 2d_2$; that is

$$\left\{(x, y) : \pm\frac{8x-y+18}{\sqrt{65}} = \pm\frac{14x+8y+12}{\sqrt{65}}\right\}.$$

This is equivalent to

$$\left\{(x, y) : \frac{8x-y+18}{\sqrt{65}} = \frac{14x+8y+12}{\sqrt{65}}\right\}$$

$$\cup \left\{(x, y): \frac{8x-y+18}{\sqrt{65}} = -\frac{14x+8y+12}{\sqrt{65}}\right\}$$

$$= \{(x, y): 2x+3y-2 = 0\} \cup \{(x, y) : 22x+7y+30 = 0\}.$$

The locus is thus the pair of straight lines

$$2x+3y-2 = 0, \quad 22x+7y+30 = 0.$$

Example 4. *Prove that the lines*

$$\frac{x-3}{1} = \frac{y-2}{1} = \frac{z-4}{3}$$

and

$$\frac{x}{1} = \frac{y+1}{0} = \frac{z-1}{1}$$

are skew, and find the perpendicular distance between them.

The given lines may be written

$$\frac{x-3}{1} = \frac{y-2}{1} = \frac{z-4}{3} = \lambda,$$

$$\frac{x}{1} = \frac{y+1}{0} = \frac{z-1}{1} = \mu$$

and so a general point P of the first line has coordinates $(\lambda+3, \lambda+2, 3\lambda+4)$ and a general point Q of the second line has coordinates $(\mu, -1, \mu+1)$.

The two lines are clearly not parallel, since their direction cosines are different. Thus they are either skew or else they meet in a point. If they meet in a point, we must have

$$\begin{cases} \lambda+3 = \mu, \\ \lambda+2 = -1, \\ 3\lambda+4 = \mu+1, \end{cases}$$

for some λ, μ. But solution of the first two equations gives $\lambda = -3$, $\mu = 0$ and these values clearly do not satisfy the third equation. The lines are therefore skew. Now

$$\mathbf{OP} = (\lambda+3)\,\mathbf{i}+(\lambda+2)\,\mathbf{j}+(3\lambda+4)\,\mathbf{k},$$

$$\mathbf{OQ} = \mu\mathbf{i}-\mathbf{j}+(\mu+1)\,\mathbf{k},$$

$$\therefore \quad \mathbf{QP} = (\lambda-\mu+3)\,\mathbf{i}+(\lambda+3)\,\mathbf{j}+(3\lambda-\mu+3)\,\mathbf{k}.$$

But the directions of the two given lines are given by the vectors

$$\mathbf{i}+\mathbf{j}+3\mathbf{k}$$

and $$\mathbf{i}+\mathbf{k}.\dagger$$

Thus QP is perpendicular to both lines

$$\Leftrightarrow (\lambda-\mu+3)+(\lambda+3)+3(3\lambda-\mu+3) = 0$$

and $$(\lambda-\mu+3) \qquad + (3\lambda-\mu+3) = 0.$$

Solving these two equations gives $\lambda = -1$, $\mu = 1$ and so the coordinates of the end-points of the common perpendicular to the two lines are $(2, 1, 1)$ and $(1, -1, 2)$ and the length of the common perpendicular

$$= \sqrt{[(2-1)^2+(1+1)^2+(1-2)^2]}$$

$$= \sqrt{6}.$$

† Since we are going to use the condition for perpendicularity, in which the right-hand side of the dot product is zero, there is no need to make these vectors unit vectors since this would only introduce a factor that would divide out.

Note: A more elegant method for finding the direction of the common perpendicular to two skew lines will be described when the vector product is introduced.

Example 5. Find the image by reflection of the point $(11, -13, 8)$ *in the plane* $2x - 3y + z + 1 = 0$.

The vector $2\mathbf{i} - 3\mathbf{j} + \mathbf{k}$ is perpendicular to the given plane and so the line through $(11, -13, 8)$ perpendicular to the plane has equations

$$\frac{x-11}{2} = \frac{y+13}{-3} = \frac{z-8}{1} = \lambda.$$

The coordinates of a general point P of this line are

$$(2\lambda + 11, -3\lambda - 13, \lambda + 8)$$

and $\quad\quad\quad\quad$ *P lies in the plane*

$$\Leftrightarrow 2(2\lambda + 11) - 3(-3\lambda - 13) + (\lambda + 8) + 1 = 0$$

$$\Leftrightarrow \quad\quad\quad\quad\quad\quad\quad\quad 14\lambda + 70 = 0$$

$$\Leftrightarrow \quad\quad\quad\quad\quad\quad\quad\quad\quad \lambda = -5.$$

Thus, the reflection of $(11, -13, 8)$ in the plane is given by $\lambda = -10$, i.e.

$$(-9, 17, -2).$$

Exercise 11(c)

1. Prove that the vectors:

$$\mathbf{a} = \mathbf{i} + 2\mathbf{j} + 4\mathbf{k}, \quad \mathbf{b} = 2\mathbf{i} - 3\mathbf{j} + \mathbf{k}$$

are perpendicular.

Find the angle between the vectors

$$\mathbf{c} = 3\mathbf{i} + \mathbf{j} + 2\mathbf{k}, \quad \mathbf{d} = \mathbf{i} - 2\mathbf{j} - 3\mathbf{k}.$$

2. Find the equations of the planes through the given points which are normal to the given vectors:

(i) $(0, 0, 0)$, $\mathbf{i} - \mathbf{j} + \mathbf{k}$; $\quad\quad\quad\quad$ (ii) $(1, 2, -3)$, $2\mathbf{i} + \mathbf{j} - 3\mathbf{k}$;

(iii) $(-1, 2, -4)$, $3\mathbf{i} - \mathbf{k}$; $\quad\quad\quad$ (iv) $(2, 4, -1)$, $6\mathbf{i} - 3\mathbf{j} - 2\mathbf{k}$;

(v) $(2, 3, 4)$, $4\mathbf{i} + \mathbf{j} - 3\mathbf{k}$; $\quad\quad\quad$ (vi) (a, b, c), $a\mathbf{i} + b\mathbf{j} + c\mathbf{k}$.

3. Find the cosines of the angles between the following pairs of lines. (Leave your answers in surd form.)

(i) $\dfrac{x}{2} = \dfrac{y-1}{-3} = \dfrac{z+1}{-1}$, $\dfrac{x-1}{1} = \dfrac{y+2}{0} = \dfrac{z-1}{-2}$;

(ii) $\dfrac{x-2}{1} = \dfrac{y-3}{-1} = \dfrac{z-3}{4}$, $\dfrac{x+1}{-3} = \dfrac{y}{2} = \dfrac{z-4}{1}$;

(iii) $\dfrac{x+1}{-2} = \dfrac{y+2}{3} = \dfrac{z-1}{4}$, $\dfrac{x-1}{5} = \dfrac{y}{0} = \dfrac{z+1}{2}$;

(iv) $\dfrac{x}{1} = \dfrac{y}{0} = \dfrac{z-a}{-1}$, $\dfrac{x-a}{1} = \dfrac{y-a}{-1} = \dfrac{z}{0}$.

4. Find the cosines of the angles between the following pairs of planes. (Leave your answers in surd form.)

(i) $3x-y+z = 0$, $x = 0$;   (ii) $2x-y = 0$, $x+y+z = 0$;

(iii) $2x-y-z+3 = 0$, $3x-y+z-1 = 0$;

(iv) $x+y-4z+1 = 0$, $2x-3y+4z+5 = 0$;

(v) $ax+by = 0$, $ay-bz = 0$;

(vi) $ax+by-cz = 0$, $bx-cy+ax = 0$.

5. Find the cosines of the acute angles between the following lines and planes. (Leave your answers in surd form.)

(i) $\dfrac{x-1}{1} = \dfrac{y-2}{2} = \dfrac{z-3}{3}$, $x+y+z = 0$;

(ii) $\dfrac{x-3}{-1} = \dfrac{y+2}{0} = \dfrac{z+1}{2}$, $2x-y-z = 0$;

(iii) $\dfrac{x-2}{2} = \dfrac{y-1}{2} = \dfrac{z}{-1}$, $3x-2y+2z+4 = 0$;

(iv) $\dfrac{x-3}{4} = \dfrac{y-4}{-3} = \dfrac{z+3}{4}$, $4x-3y-4z = 0$;

(v) $\dfrac{x-1}{1} = \dfrac{y+1}{0} = \dfrac{z-2}{-1}$, $y-z = 0$;

(vi) $\dfrac{x-a}{l} = \dfrac{y-b}{m} = \dfrac{z-c}{n}$, $px+qy+rz = 0$.

6. Find the unit vectors normal to the planes through the following sets of points, and deduce the equations of the planes:

(i) $(1, 1, -1), (2, 3, 1), (5, -1, -13)$;

(ii) $(2, 6, 1), (0, 3, 1), (4, 0, -2)$;

(iii) $(1, 4, 1), (2, 7, 2), (-3, 0, -1)$;

(iv) $(1, 0, -1), (0, -4, -1), (3, 2, 2)$;

(v) $(1, 1, 2), (2, 2, 3), (-2, 1, 11)$;

(vi) $(0, c/b, b/c), (c/a, 0, -a/c), (b/a, a/b, 0)$.

206

7. Find the coordinates of points where the line

$$\frac{x-2}{1} = \frac{y-3}{2} = \frac{z+1}{-2}$$

meets the planes

(i) $x - y - z = 0$;   (ii) $2x - y - z - 6 = 0$;

(iii) $3x + 4y + 2z - 9 = 0$;   (iv) $2x + 3y + z = 0$.

8. Find the reflections of the following points in the given planes:

(i) $(-1, 7, 5)$, $5x - y - z - 10 = 0$;

(ii) $(5, -9, -6)$, $2x - y + 3z - 8 = 0$;

(iii) $(6, 13, -3)$, $4x - y - 3z + 19 = 0$;

(iv) $(3, 5, 8)$, $3x - y - z + 26 = 0$;

(v) $(-5, 11, 6)$, $5x - 6y - 2z - 27 = 0$;

(vi) $(0, 0, 0)$, $ax + by + cz + d = 0$.

9. Find the feet of the perpendiculars from the origin to the lines

(i) $\dfrac{x+1}{2} = \dfrac{y}{1} = \dfrac{z-4}{-1}$;   (ii) $\dfrac{x-3}{1} = \dfrac{y-1}{-2} = \dfrac{z-5}{1}$;

(iii) $\dfrac{x-7}{-1} = \dfrac{y+1}{3} = \dfrac{z-4}{0}$;   (iv) $\dfrac{x-3}{3} = \dfrac{y-8}{-4} = \dfrac{z-3}{-2}$.

10. Find the foot of the perpendicular from $(7, -1, 2)$ to the line

$$\frac{x-9}{1} = \frac{y-5}{3} = \frac{z-5}{5}.$$

11. Where does the line

$$\frac{x-2}{1} = \frac{y-7}{3} = \frac{z-2}{-1}$$

cut the plane $x - y + z = 0$?

Find the image by reflection of the line in the given plane.

12. Find the image by reflection of the line

$$\frac{x-10}{9} = \frac{y-4}{-1} = \frac{z-2}{0}$$

in the plane $3x - y + 2z - 2 = 0$.

13. Find the image by reflection of the line

$$\frac{x}{1} = \frac{y-3}{-1} = \frac{z+6}{5}$$

in the line

$$\frac{x}{2} = \frac{y-3}{1} = \frac{z+6}{1}$$

14. Prove that the following pairs of lines are skew:

$$\frac{x}{1} = \frac{y-3}{1} = \frac{z}{-1},$$

$$\frac{x-5}{3} = \frac{y-8}{7} = \frac{z-2}{-1}.$$

Find the direction ratios of the common perpendicular and determine the shortest distance between the two lines.

15. $ABCD$ is a rectangle and O is a point on the normal at C to the plane of this rectangle. $AB = a$, $AD = b$, and $CO = h$. P is a point on AO and the line through P in the plane AOB which is perpendicular to AO meets AB at M.
   If $AP = x$, show that

$$PM = x\sqrt{(b^2+h^2)}/a; \quad AM = x\sqrt{(a^2+b^2+h^2)}/a.$$

Prove that the cosine of the acute angle between the planes OAB and OAD is

$$ab/\sqrt{[(a^2+h^2)(b^2+h^2)]}. \qquad \text{(London)}$$

16. Define the scalar product of two three-dimensional Euclidean vectors $\mathbf{u}$, $\mathbf{v}$. Deduce an expression for the angle between the vectors

$$\mathbf{u} = u_1\mathbf{i}+u_2\mathbf{j}+u_3\mathbf{k},$$

$$\mathbf{v} = v_1\mathbf{i}+v_2\mathbf{j}+v_3\mathbf{k},$$

in terms of $u_1, u_2, u_3, v_1, v_2, v_3$.
   A regular tetrahedron has vertices O, A, B, C, where O is the origin, and A, B, C have position vectors with respect to O given by

$$\mathbf{OA} = -\mathbf{i}+\mathbf{j},$$

$$\mathbf{OB} = a\mathbf{i}+b\mathbf{j},$$

$$\mathbf{OC} = p\mathbf{i}+q\mathbf{j}+r\mathbf{k}.$$

Find the numerical values of a, b, p, q, r given that $a > 0$ and $r > 0$.   (SMP)

17. Show that the line L given by

$$\frac{x+1}{5} = \frac{y-1}{3} = \frac{z+1}{2}$$

is the intersection of the planes

$$3x-5y+8 = 0 \quad \text{and} \quad 2y-3z-5 = 0.$$

Show that every plane containing the line L can be expressed in the form

$$\lambda(3x-5y+8)+\mu(2y-3z-5) = 0.$$

How should λ, μ be chosen in order to ensure that the plane is perpendicular to the plane

$$5x-y+2z = -2?$$

208

Hence or otherwise obtain the equation of the orthogonal projection of the line L on the plane

$$5x - y + 2z = -2,$$

expressing your answer in vector form, $\mathbf{x} = t\mathbf{a} + \mathbf{b}$. (M.E.I.)

18. Prove that the equation of the plane which cuts off intercepts a, b, c on the axes of x, y, z respectively is

$$\frac{x}{a} + \frac{y}{b} + \frac{z}{c} = 1.$$

The foot of the perpendicular from the origin to a plane is $P(2, -1, 2)$. Find the equation of the plane. If the plane meets the axes of x, y, z at A, B, C respectively, prove that AP is perpendicular to BC, and find the angle between AP and CP. (J.M.B.)

19. Two planes, π_1 and π_2, have equations

$$2x + y + z = 1 \quad \text{and} \quad 3x + y - z = 2,$$

respectively. Prove that the plane π_3, which is perpendicular to π_1, and contains the line of intersection of π_1 and π_2 has the equation

$$x - 2z = 1.$$

Points P and Q lie on the planes π_1 and π_3 respectively and the line PQ is perpendicular to π_2. If the coordinates of P are $(-2, 4, 1)$, find the coordinates of Q. Determine the angle between the line PQ and the perpendicular from P to the line of intersection of the three planes. (J.M.B.)

20. The straight line whose equations are

$$\frac{x-2}{-2} = \frac{y}{1} = \frac{z+1}{2}$$

meets the plane $x + 2y - 2z = 8$ at B, and A is the point $(2, 0, -1)$ on the line. The foot of the perpendicular from A to the plane is C. Find
(i) the coordinates of B and C;
(ii) the length of AC.
Show that the sine of the acute angle between BA and BC is $\frac{4}{9}$.
The line AC is produced to D so that $AC = 2CD$. Find the coordinates of D. (J.M.B.)

Miscellaneous Exercise 11

1. The perpendicular distance from the origin to a straight line l is of length p and makes an angle α with the positive x axis. Prove that the equation of the line may be taken in the form

$$x \cos \alpha + y \sin \alpha = p.$$

What is the equation of the parallel line through the point $P_1(x_1, y_1)$? Deduce the perpendicular distance from P_1 to the given line.

2. Find the equations of the straight lines which bisect the angles between the straight lines

$$3x - 4y - 11 = 0, \quad 12x + 5y - 2 = 0. \quad \text{(O \& C)}$$

3. Find the equation of the bisector of the acute angle between the lines

$$4x+3y-12 = 0, \quad 12x+5y-60 = 0. \qquad \text{(O \& C)}$$

4. Sketch the triangle formed by the lines

$$3x-4y-4 = 0, \quad 12x-5y+6 = 0, \quad 7x+24y-56 = 0,$$

and verify by calculation and reference to your sketch that the point (1, 1) is the centre of the inscribed circle. (O & C)

5. A straight line is drawn through $A(h, k)$ and $P(x, y)$ so that AP makes an angle θ with the positive direction of the x axis, and $AP = r$. Prove that

$$\frac{x-h}{\cos \theta} = \frac{y-k}{\sin \theta} = r.$$

Three vertices of a square are $E(2, 2)$, $F(-2, 2)$ and $G(-2, -2)$; a straight line of gradient $\frac{3}{4}$ is drawn from $A(-3, -1)$ to meet FG at P and EF at Q. Use the formulae in the first part of the equation to find the length of PQ.

Find also the radius of the circle with centre at the origin to which APQ is a tangent. (O & C)

6. Points A and B lie on the same side of a line l, C is the optical image of A in l, and BC meets l at P. Prove that l is a bisector of $\angle APB$. Given that l has the equation $x+3y = 5$, and that the coordinates of A and B are $(1, -2)$ and $(-11, 2)$ respectively, verify that these points lie on the same side of l. Prove that the coordinates of C are $(3, 4)$, and find the coordinates of P. (O & C)

7. Prove that the equation of the circle, centre (12, 13), radius 7, is

$$x^2+y^2-24x-26y+264 = 0.$$

Two sides of a triangle are

$$5x-12y+5 = 0, \quad 12x-5y+12 = 0$$

and the incentre is the point (12, 13). Prove that the third side touches the circle

$$x^2+y^2-24x-26y+264 = 0. \qquad \text{(O \& C)}$$

8. Prove that the perpendicular bisectors of the sides of a triangle are concurrent (at the *circumcentre*) and that the altitudes of a triangle are concurrent (at the *orthocentre*).

9. Prove that the circumcentre S, the centroid G and the orthocentre H of a triangle ABC have position vectors (referred to any origin O) which satisfy the relation

$$\mathbf{h}+2\mathbf{s}-3\mathbf{g} = 0.$$

Deduce that SGH is a straight line and determine the ratio $SG:GH$.

Prove further that the mid-point, N, of the line SH is the centre of the circle through the mid-points of the triangle ABC. What is the radius of this circle?

10. $OABC$ is a tetrahredron in which OA is perpendicular to BC and OB is perpendicular to AC. PQR is a triangle such that A is the mid-point of QR, B is the mid-point of RP and C is the mid-point of PQ.

210

Taking O as the origin, express the position vectors of P, Q, R in terms of those of A, B, C. Hence prove that $OP = OQ = OR$.

If D is the foot of the perpendicular from O to the plane ABC, prove that D is the circumcentre of the triangle PQR.

11. $ABCDA'B'C'D'$ is a cube with edges AA', BB', CC', DD' and diagonal AC'. Show that $B'C$ is perpendicular to the plane ABC'. Find a line in the figure perpendicular to the plane ACC'. What is the angle between the planes ABC' and ACC'?

12. In a tetrahedron $PQRS$, the edges PQ, RS are perpendicular to the faces PRS, PQS respectively; L is the mid-point of PS and M is the mid-point of QR. Prove that
$$PQ^2 + RS^2 = QR^2 - PS^2,$$
$$PM = SM = \tfrac{1}{2}QR,$$
$$4LM^2 = PQ^2 + RS^2. \qquad \text{(O \& C)}$$

13. Prove that there is one and only one line which joins two given skew lines and is perpendicular to each of them.

Two fixed skew lines AL, BM have a common perpendicular AB, and the angle between them is θ. Prove that
$$LM^2 = AL^2 + BM^2 - 2AL \cdot BM \cos \theta.$$

Prove that, if $\theta = \tfrac{1}{2}\pi$ and the points L and M vary on the fixed skew lines so that LM is constant, the locus of the mid-point of LM is a circle. (O \& C)

14. The common perpendicular of two skew lines l and l' meets them at A and A' respectively. Points P and P' are taken on l and l' respectively so that $AP + A'P'$ is constant, where the sense of AP and $A'P'$ is taken into account.

Show that the locus of the mid-point M of PP' is a straight line m, and describe its relation to l and l'.

If $AP - A'P'$ is constant, show that the locus of M is another straight line m', and describe the relation of m and m'. (O \& C)

15. Find the reflection of the line
$$\frac{x-7}{3} = \frac{y+2}{1} = \frac{z-2}{-1}$$
in the plane $x - y - z + 2 = 0$.

16. Prove that, given two skew lines and a point O not lying on either of them, that just one transversal may be drawn through O to cut each of the lines. Prove that the lines
$$\frac{x+5}{1} = \frac{y-7}{-1} = \frac{z}{2}$$
and
$$\frac{x-4}{2} = \frac{y+3}{0} = \frac{z+2}{-1}$$
are skew and find the equation of the common transversal that passes through the origin.

17. Obtain the equation of a plane in the vector form
$$\mathbf{n.r} = p \quad \text{(n a unit vector)},$$
explaining precisely what you mean by each of the three symbols $\mathbf{n}$, $\mathbf{r}$, p.

Prove that the length of the perpendicular to the plane from the point S with position vector s is $|n.s-p|$; and find the position vector t of the mirror image T of S in the plane—that is, of the point T such that TS is perpendicular to the plane and bisected by it. (M.E.I.)

18. Referred to a given system of rectangular coordinates in space of three-dimensions, the points A, B have coordinates $(1, 0, 0)$, $(-1, 0, 0)$ respectively.

A variable point P has coordinates (x, y, z). Write down the direction-cosines of PA, PB and prove that, if θ is the angle between them, then

$$\cos^2\theta = \frac{(x^2+y^2+z^2-1)^2}{[(x^2+y^2+z^2+1)-2x].[(x^2+y^2+z^2+1)+2x]}.$$

Deduce that, if P is restricted to lie in the plane $z = 0$, then

$$(x^2+y^2-1)^2 = [(x^2+y^2-1)^2+4y^2]\cos^2\theta$$

and find the equations of the two circles on which P must lie if the angle θ is kept constant. (M.E.I.)

19. Two planes
$$x-3y+2z = 2,$$
$$2x-y-z = 9,$$

meet in the line l. Find the equations of

(i) the plane through the origin which contains l,
(ii) the plane through the origin which is perpendicular to l.

Find also the coordinates of the reflection of the origin in l. (C.S.)

20. Find the value of k such that the line joining the points $(-2, k, -9)$, $(2, 1, 7)$ intersects the line joining $(-2, -4, 4)$, $(7, 2, 1)$.

What are the coordinates of the point of intersection?

21. A regular tetrahedron $ABCD$ has the face ABC in the xy plane, the origin is the centre of that face, the vertex A is at the point $(1, 0, 0)$ and the vertex D is on the positive half of the z axis. Find the coordinates of B, C, D and of the centre of the tetrahedron, and the direction ratios of the normals to the four faces.

Hence or otherwise show that, if any line makes angles α, β, γ, δ with the faces of a regular tetrahedron, then

$$\sin^2\alpha+\sin^2\beta+\sin^2\gamma+\sin^2\delta = \tfrac{4}{3}.$$

22. Prove that the equation of the straight line through the given point A, position vector a, and in the direction of the unit vector b is

$$r = a+tb,$$

where t is the distance from A of the variable point P of the line whose position vector is r.

Prove also that the equation of the plane through the point C (position vector c) whose normal is in the direction given by the unit vector d can be expressed in the form
$$r.d = c.d.$$

The plane through the point $C(1, 2, 4)$ has normal in the direction
$$\mathbf{d} = \tfrac{3}{13}\mathbf{i} + \tfrac{4}{13}\mathbf{j} + \tfrac{12}{13}\mathbf{k}.$$
Find the length of the shortest distance from the point $A(3, 4, 5)$ to the plane.
(M.E.I.)

23. To find the position of an underground rock layer a number of vertical borings are made at points on horizontal ground which form a coordinate grid. Results are as follows, the unit of distance both horizontally and vertically being 300 m:

Grid-point	$(0, 0)$	$(2, 0)$	$(0, 2)$	$(2, 2)$
Depth	0·270	0·225	0·162	0·117

Show that these results are consistent with this part of the rock layer being a plane. Find the (x, y) equation of the line in which this plane when produced would meet the ground, and show that the plane would be inclined at about $3\tfrac{1}{2}°$ to the ground.

What would you conclude if a boring at $(1, 1)$ gave a depth of about 0·18?
(M.E.I.)

24. Calculate the shortest distance between the line of intersection of the planes
$$x - 8y + 2z + 9 = 0, \quad x - 2y - z + 6 = 0$$
and the line of intersection of the planes
$$2x + y + 8z - 12 = 0, \quad x - y + z - 6 = 0;$$
and show that the line which cuts both these lines at right-angles passes through the point $(-4, 12, 8)$.

25. Find the coordinates of the mirror image of the point (p, q, r) in the plane
$$ax + by + cz + d = 0.$$

A ray from the origin is reflected successively in the planes
$$x + y - z + 1 = 0$$
and
$$x - y + 2z - 1 = 0,$$
and then passes again through the origin. Find the points at which it meets the two planes.

26. Prove that the lines
$$\frac{x+1}{2} = \frac{y+1}{3} = \frac{z+2}{1}, \quad \frac{x-1}{3} = \frac{y+3}{1} = \frac{z}{-2}$$
do not intersect.

Find the equation of the plane through the origin which contains the first line, and find also the direction cosines of the line through the origin which meets both lines.
(Oxford Mod.)

27. The line $x/l = y/m = z/n$ is reflected in the plane $ax + by + cz + d = 0$. Show that the equation of the resulting line is
$$\frac{(a^2 + b^2 + c^2)\,x + 2ad}{(a^2 + b + c^2)\,l - 2a(al + bm + cn)} = \frac{(a^2 + b^2 + c^2)\,y + 2bd}{(a^2 + b^2 + c^2)\,m - 2b(al + bm + cn)}$$
$$= \frac{(a^2 + b^2 + c^2)\,z + 2cd}{(a^2 + b^2 + c^2)\,n - 2c(al + bm + cn)}.$$

Hence, or otherwise, find the equation of the plane such that the angle between it and the plane $lx+my+nz = 0$ is bisected by the plane $ax+by+cz = 0$.

(Oxford Mod.)

28. Write down the equations of the axes Ox, Oy, Oz. What is the equation of the plane containing Ox and the point (a, b, c)?

The roof of a rectangular house consists of four inclined planes, each sloping upwards at an angle of $45°$ to the horizontal. What is the angle between two adjacent faces of the roof?

29. $ABCDA'B'C'D'$ is a cubical box, with faces $ABCD$, $A'B'C'D'$ and edges AA', BB', CC', DD'. E is the point on BB' such that $BE = \frac{1}{2}EB'$; F is the mid-point of CC'. Find the angles between

(i) the line $A'B$ and the plane AEF;

(ii) the plane $A'BC$ and the plane AEF.

30. Two lines through the origin have unit direction vectors $l_1\mathbf{i}+m_1\mathbf{j}+n_1\mathbf{k}$ and $l_2\mathbf{i}+m_2\mathbf{j}+n_2\mathbf{k}$. Prove that the locus of points equidistant from the two lines is a pair of planes and deduce the equations of the straight lines which bisect the angles between the given lines.

31. Two straight paths on a plane hillside are at right-angles, and make angles θ and ϕ respectively with the horizontal. If the hillside itself makes an angle α with the horizontal, prove that
$$\sin^2\theta + \sin^2\phi = \sin^2\alpha.$$

Prove also that the acute angle between the projections of the paths on a horizontal plane is
$$\arccos(\tan\theta\tan\phi).$$

32. A line of slope, in an easterly direction, of a plane hillside is inclined at an angle α to the horizontal. A line of slope of the hillside in a southerly direction is inclined at an angle β to the horizontal. Prove that the actual inclination, θ, of the hillside to the horizontal is
$$\theta = \arctan(\tan^2\alpha+\tan^2\beta)^{\frac{1}{2}}.$$

A vertical pole of height h is placed on top of the hill. Show that the angle ϕ subtended by it at a point distant a down the line of greatest slope through the foot of the pole is given by
$$\tan\phi = \frac{h}{a\sec\theta+h\tan\theta}.$$

Find ϕ, if $h = 16$, $a = 36$, $\alpha = 30°$ and $\beta = 45°$.   (London)

33. Let G be the centroid of the acute-angled triangle ABC of circumradius R. Show that
$$AG^2+BG^2+CG^2 \geqslant 2R^2.$$

34. If O is the point on AB such that $AO = 2OB$, and if P is any point, prove that
$$AP^2+2BP^2-3OP^2$$
is independent of the position of P.

What is the locus of a point which moves so that the sum of the squares of its distances from the vertices of an equilateral triangle is constant?

214

12. *Further trigonometry*

1. FORMULAE FOR COMPOUND AND MULTIPLE ANGLES

In many applications of trigonometry it is essential to be able to deal with expressions such as $\sin(A+B)$ or $\sin 2A$ in terms of the trigonometric functions of the simpler angles A and B. Angles such as $A+B$ are called *compound* angles; in particular, those like $2A$ are called *multiple* angles.

Ex. 1. By taking $A = B = 30°$, show that $\sin(A+B) \neq \sin A + \sin B$ in general. Is it possible to find values of A and B such that $\sin A + \sin B$ cannot be expressed as the sine of a single angle?

We shall now establish the fundamental compound angle formulae for $\sin(\theta+\phi)$, $\cos(\theta+\phi)$. The proof depends upon the fact that we may express a unit vector **OP** in the form

$$\cos\theta\mathbf{i} + \sin\theta\mathbf{j},$$

where $\mathbf{i}$, $\mathbf{j}$ are two perpendicular unit vectors and θ is the angle between $\mathbf{i}$ and **OP** measured anticlockwise from $\mathbf{i}$; see Figure 12.1 which represents a circle of unit radius, with

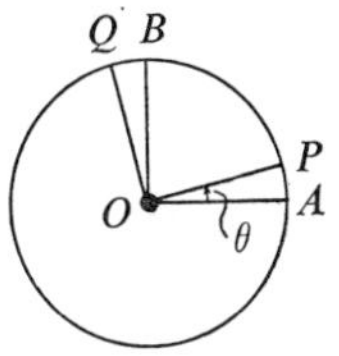

Fig. 12.1

$$\mathbf{OA} = \mathbf{i}, \quad \mathbf{OB} = \mathbf{j}, \quad \mathbf{OP} = \mathbf{p}, \quad \text{where} \quad \mathbf{p} = \cos\theta\mathbf{i} + \sin\theta\mathbf{j}.$$

Similarly, if **OQ** makes an angle $90°+\theta$ with $\mathbf{i}$ (that is, if $\angle POQ = 90°$, measured anticlockwise), then

$$\mathbf{OQ} = \mathbf{q} = \cos(90°+\theta)\mathbf{i} + \sin(90°+\theta)\mathbf{j}$$
$$= -\sin\theta\mathbf{i} + \cos\theta\mathbf{j}.$$

These expressions for $\mathbf{p}$, $\mathbf{q}$ hold for angles of any size and either sense.

Theorem 12.1. *For any two angles*:

   (i) $\cos(\theta+\phi) \equiv \cos\theta\cos\phi - \sin\theta\sin\phi$;

   (ii) $\sin(\theta+\phi) \equiv \sin\theta\cos\phi + \cos\theta\sin\phi$;

   (iii) $\cos(\theta-\phi) \equiv \cos\theta\cos\phi + \sin\theta\sin\phi$;

   (iv) $\sin(\theta-\phi) \equiv \sin\theta\cos\phi - \cos\theta\sin\phi$.

Proof. Take points $APRBQ$ as a unit circle, centre O. $\mathbf{OA} = \mathbf{i}$, $\mathbf{OB} = \mathbf{j}$; $\mathbf{OP} = \mathbf{p}$, $\mathbf{OQ} = \mathbf{q}$; $\mathbf{OR} = \mathbf{r}$. $\angle AOP = \theta$, $\angle POR = \phi$ (see Figure 12.2).

215

The proof of (i) and (ii) is effected by expressing the unit vector $\mathbf{r}$ (a) in terms of $\mathbf{i}$ and $\mathbf{j}$ directly and (b) in terms of $\mathbf{p}$ and $\mathbf{q}$ and hence in terms of $\mathbf{i}$ and $\mathbf{j}$.

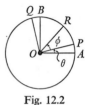

Thus $\qquad$ (a) $\mathbf{r} = \cos(\theta+\phi)\,\mathbf{i} + \sin(\theta+\phi)\,\mathbf{j}$

and $\qquad$ (b) $\mathbf{r} = \cos\phi\,\mathbf{p} + \sin\phi\,\mathbf{q}$.

But $\qquad$ $\mathbf{p} = \cos\theta\,\mathbf{i} + \sin\theta\,\mathbf{j}$

and $\qquad$ $\mathbf{q} = -\sin\theta\,\mathbf{i} + \cos\theta\,\mathbf{j}$

Fig. 12.2

(see remarks preceding this theorem).

Substituting for $\mathbf{p}$ and $\mathbf{q}$ in (b) this gives

(c) $\mathbf{r} = \cos\phi(\cos\theta\,\mathbf{i} + \sin\theta\,\mathbf{j}) + \sin\phi(-\sin\theta\,\mathbf{i} + \cos\theta\,\mathbf{j})$

$\qquad = (\cos\theta\cos\phi - \sin\theta\sin\phi)\,\mathbf{i} + (\sin\theta\cos\phi + \cos\theta\sin\phi)\,\mathbf{j}$.

But, in a plane, the expressions for the components of a vector $\mathbf{r}$ in the two directions $\mathbf{i}$ and $\mathbf{j}$ are unique (see Chapter 2) and so, comparing (a) and (c),

(i) $\cos(\theta+\phi) \equiv \cos\theta\cos\phi - \sin\theta\sin\phi$;

(ii) $\sin(\theta+\phi) \equiv \sin\theta\cos\phi + \cos\theta\sin\phi$.

Formulae (iii) and (iv) now follow immediately, on writing $-\phi$ for ϕ and recalling that $\sin(-\phi) \equiv -\sin\phi$, $\cos(-\phi) \equiv \cos\phi$,

(iii) $\cos(\theta-\phi) \equiv \cos\theta\cos\phi + \sin\theta\sin\phi$;

(iv) $\sin(\theta-\phi) \equiv \sin\theta\cos\phi - \cos\theta\sin\phi$.

Ex. 2. Express sin 15° and cos 15° in surd form by writing 15° = 45° − 30°.

Ex. 3. Express cos 165° and sin 105° in surd form.

Ex. 4. If $\sin x = \frac{5}{13}$ and $\sin y = \frac{4}{5}$ find $\sin(x+y)$ and $\cos(x+y)$
(i) when x and y are both acute angles;
(ii) when x is acute and y is obtuse;
(iii) when x and y are both obtuse angles.

Ex. 5. Express $\cos(A+B) - \cos(A-B)$ in terms of $\sin A$ and $\sin B$.

The results of Theorem 12.1 are important and should be committed to memory. They give rise immediately to the following results which we shall also state in the form of a theorem:

Theorem 12.2. For any angles θ, ϕ for which all of the expressions appearing are defined

(v) $\tan(\theta+\phi) \equiv \dfrac{\tan\theta+\tan\phi}{1-\tan\theta\tan\phi}$;

(vi) $\tan(\theta-\phi) \equiv \dfrac{\tan\theta-\tan\phi}{1+\tan\theta\tan\phi}$;

(vii) $\sin 2\theta \equiv 2 \sin \theta \cos \theta$;

(viii) $\cos 2\theta \equiv \cos^2 \theta - \sin^2 \theta \equiv 2 \cos^2 \theta - 1 \equiv 1 - 2 \sin^2 \theta$;

(ix) $\tan 2\theta \equiv \dfrac{2 \tan \theta}{1 - \tan^2 \theta}$.

Proof. (v) The right-hand side is not defined if θ or $\phi = (2k+1)\frac{1}{2}\pi$; neither side is defined if $\theta + \phi = (2k+1)\frac{1}{2}\pi$. For any other values of θ and ϕ

$$\tan (\theta + \phi) \equiv \frac{\sin \theta \cos \phi + \cos \theta \sin \phi}{\cos \theta \cos \phi - \sin \theta \sin \phi} \quad \text{by formulae (i) and (ii)};$$

divide top and bottom of the fraction on the right-hand side by $\cos \theta \cos \phi$ (a non-zero expression, by the restrictions on θ and ϕ).

(vi) As for (v) by using (iii) and (iv);

(vii) set $\theta = \phi$ in (ii);

(viii) set $\theta = \phi$ in (i), and recall that $\sin^2 \theta + \cos^2 \theta \equiv 1$;

(ix) set $\theta = \phi$ in (v).

Ex. 6. What values of θ and ϕ must be excluded in (*a*) formula (vi); and (*b*) formula (ix)?

Example 1. *Find an expression for* cos 75° *in surd form.*

   Method (i). $\cos 75° = \cos (30° + 45°)$

$$= \cos 30° \cos 45° - \sin 30° \sin 45°$$

$$= \frac{\sqrt{3}}{2} \cdot \frac{1}{\sqrt{2}} - \frac{1}{2} \cdot \frac{1}{\sqrt{2}}$$

$$= \frac{\sqrt{3} - 1}{2\sqrt{2}}.$$

   Method (ii). $\cos 150° = 2 \cos^2 75° - 1$,

$$\therefore \quad -\tfrac{1}{2}\sqrt{3} = 2 \cos^2 75° - 1,$$

or $\dfrac{4 - 2\sqrt{3}}{8} = \cos^2 75°.$

Thus $\cos 75° = \dfrac{\sqrt{3} - 1}{2\sqrt{2}}.$

(We reject the negative square root since cos 75° > 0.)

Example 2. *Prove the identity*

$$\frac{\cos \theta - \sin \theta}{\cos \theta + \sin \theta} \equiv \sec 2\theta - \tan 2\theta \quad (\theta \neq (2n+1)\tfrac{1}{4}\pi).$$

217

The R.H.S. is defined, by the restriction on θ.

$$\text{R.H.S.} = \frac{1}{\cos 2\theta} - \frac{\sin 2\theta}{\cos 2\theta}$$

$$= \frac{1 - \sin 2\theta}{\cos 2\theta},$$

$$\text{L.H.S.} = \frac{(\cos \theta - \sin \theta)^2}{\cos^2 \theta - \sin^2 \theta}, \qquad (\sin^2 \theta \neq \cos^2 \theta, \text{ since } \theta \neq (2n+1)\tfrac{1}{4}\pi)$$

$$= \frac{\cos^2 \theta + \sin^2 \theta - 2 \sin \theta \cos \theta}{\cos 2\theta}$$

$$= \frac{1 - \sin 2\theta}{\cos 2\theta}.$$

The formulae we have proved are also useful in dealing with combinations of inverse trigonometric functions, as is shown in the next example.

Example 3. Find the value of arctan $2+$ arctan 3.
Write $x = \arctan 2$; $y = \arctan 3$, then

$$\tfrac{1}{4}\pi < x < \tfrac{1}{2}\pi, \quad \tfrac{1}{4}\pi < y < \tfrac{1}{2}\pi \quad \text{and so} \quad \tfrac{1}{2}\pi < x+y < \pi,$$

$$\tan(x+y) = \frac{\tan x + \tan y}{1 - \tan x \tan y}$$

$$= \frac{2+3}{1-6}$$

$$= -1.$$

Since $\tfrac{1}{2}\pi < x+y < \pi$, this gives

$$x+y = \pi + \arctan(-1)$$

$$= \pi - \tfrac{1}{4}\pi.$$

Thus $\qquad\qquad\qquad \arctan 2 + \arctan 3 = \tfrac{3}{4}\pi.$

Example 4. Find angles θ between $0°$ and $360°$ satisfying the equation

$$5 \cos \theta - 6 \sin \theta = 3.$$

Observe that 5 and 6 are two sides of a right-angled triangle whose hypotenuse is $\sqrt{61}$. Thus, dividing both sides of the equation by $\sqrt{61}$,

$$\cos \alpha \cos \theta - \sin \alpha \sin \theta = \frac{3}{\sqrt{61}},$$

where $\tan \alpha = \tfrac{6}{5}$, i.e. $\alpha = 50° \ 12'$. Also, using tables,

$$\frac{3}{\sqrt{61}} = \cos 67° \ 25'.$$

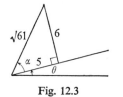

Fig. 12.3

No.	Log.
3	0·4771
61	1·7853
$\sqrt{61}$	0·8926
$\cos 67° 25'$	$\overline{1}$·5845

Thus, $\cos 50° 12' \cos \theta - \sin 50° 12' \sin \theta = \cos 67° 25'$,

i.e. $\cos (50° 12' + \theta) = \cos 67° 25'$,

$\therefore$ $50° 12' + \theta = 67° 25'$ or $292° 35'$

and $\theta = 17° 13'$ or $242° 23'$.

Example 5. Find maximum and minimum values for the expression
$$y = \sin 2\theta + 4 \cos 2\theta.$$

This may be solved by a process similar to that employed in Example 4. Thus

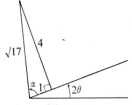

$$y = \sqrt{17} \left(\frac{1}{\sqrt{17}} \sin 2\theta + \frac{4}{\sqrt{17}} \cos 2\theta \right)$$

$$= \sqrt{17} \sin (2\theta + \alpha),$$

Fig. 12.4

where $\tan \alpha = 4$. But $-1 \leqslant \sin \phi \leqslant 1$,

$$\therefore \quad -\sqrt{17} \leqslant y \leqslant \sqrt{17}.$$

Observe that, since $\tan 76° \approx 4$, y attains its maximum when
$$2\theta + 76° \approx 90°,$$
i.e. $\theta \approx 7°$, and its minimum when $2\theta + 76° \approx 270°$, i.e. $\theta \approx 97°$.

Ex. 7. Find the maximum and minimum values of the following expressions:

(i) $\sin x - 3 \cos x$;   (ii) $2 \cos x + \sin x$;   (iii) $5 + 3 \sin x + 4 \cos x$;

(iv) $1 - \sin x - \cos x$;   (v) $1/(2 - \sin x + \cos x)$.

Ex. 8. Solve the following equations, giving all solutions lying between 0° and 360° inclusive:

(i) $\cos x - \sin x = 1$;   (ii) $3 \cos x + 4 \sin x = 5$;

(iii) $\sin x + 2 \cos x = 1$;   (iv) $12 \sin x - 5 \cos x = -4$.

Ex. 9. If $\tan A = \frac{1}{2}$, and $\tan B = \frac{1}{3}$, find $\tan (A + B)$ and $\cot (A - B)$.

Ex. 10. If $x + y = \frac{1}{4}\pi$ and $\tan x = \frac{1}{4}$, find $\tan y$.

Ex. 11. If $\cos x = \frac{1}{3}$, find $\cos 2x$. If, furthermore, $0 < x < \pi$, find $\sin 2x$.

Ex. 12. Find the maximum and minimum values of $1 + \sin x \cos x$.

Ex. 13. Find the values of x in the interval $0 \leqslant x \leqslant 2\pi$ which satisfy the equation $\cos 2x = 3 \sin x - 1$.

Ex. 14. Find the value of $\tan \frac{1}{8}\pi$ without using your tables.

Ex. 15. Find $\sin (2 \arcsin x)$ and $\cos (2 \arccos y)$.

Ex. 16. By writing $x = \arctan \frac{1}{2}$ and $y = \arctan \frac{1}{3}$ and considering $\tan (x+y)$, show that $\arctan \frac{1}{2} + \arctan \frac{1}{3} = \arctan \frac{7}{9}$.

Ex. 17. Express $\arcsin \frac{3}{5} + \arcsin \frac{5}{13}$ in the form $\arcsin x$.

The multiple angle formulae can be used to derive three very useful expressions, for $\sin \theta$, $\cos \theta$ and $\tan \theta$, in terms of $\tan \frac{1}{2}\theta$. Their value derives from the fact that, with their help, a trigonometric expression may be written as a rational function† of a single variable $t = \tan \frac{1}{2}\theta$. The reader will find that they have applications to problems in calculus as well as ordinary trigonometry.

Theorem 12.3. If $\tan \frac{1}{2}\theta = t$, *then*

(i) $\sin \theta \equiv \dfrac{2t}{1+t^2}$;

(ii) $\cos \theta \equiv \dfrac{1-t^2}{1+t^2}$;

(iii) $\tan \theta \equiv \dfrac{2t}{1-t^2}$ $(|t| \neq 1)$.

Proof. (i) $\sin \theta = 2 \sin \frac{1}{2}\theta \cos \frac{1}{2}\theta$

$= \dfrac{2 \tan \frac{1}{2}\theta}{\sec^2 \frac{1}{2}\theta}$

$= \dfrac{2t}{1+t^2}$;

(ii) $\cos \theta = \cos^2 \frac{1}{2}\theta - \sin^2 \frac{1}{2}\theta$

$= \dfrac{1-\tan^2 \frac{1}{2}\theta}{\sec^2 \frac{1}{2}\theta}$

$= \dfrac{1-t^2}{1+t^2}$;

(iii) $\tan \theta = \dfrac{2t^2}{1-t^2}$, by dividing (i) by (ii).

† A *rational function* is defined as the ratio of two polynomials.

220

Example 6. Prove the identity

$$\frac{1+\sin\theta}{\cos\theta} \equiv \tan\left(\tfrac{1}{4}\pi+\tfrac{1}{2}\theta\right) \quad (\theta \neq (2n+1)\,\tfrac{1}{2}\pi),$$

$$\text{L.H.S.} = \frac{1+\dfrac{2t}{1+t^2}}{\dfrac{1-t^2}{1+t^2}} \quad \text{by (i), (ii),}$$

$$= \frac{(1+t)^2}{1-t^2}, \quad \text{on multiplying numerator and denominator by } (1+t^2),$$

$$= \frac{1+t}{1-t}, \quad 1+t \neq 0 \quad (\tfrac{1}{2}\theta \neq (2n+1)\,\tfrac{1}{4}\pi),$$

$$\text{R.H.S.} = \frac{\tan\tfrac{1}{4}\pi + \tan\tfrac{1}{2}\theta}{1 - \tan\tfrac{1}{4}\pi\,\tan\tfrac{1}{2}\theta}$$

$$= \frac{1+t}{1-t}, \quad \text{since } \tan\tfrac{1}{4}\pi \neq 1.$$

Example 7. Solve the equation of Example 4, using the substitution

$$\tan\tfrac{1}{2}\theta = t.$$

$$5\cos\theta - 6\sin\theta = 3,$$

$$\therefore \quad \frac{5(1-t^2)}{1+t^2} - \frac{12t}{1+t^2} = 3,$$

$$5 - 5t^2 - 12t = 3 + 3t^2,$$

$$4t^2 + 6t - 1 = 0,$$

$$t = \frac{-6 \pm \sqrt{(36+16)}}{8}$$

$$= \tfrac{1}{4}(-3 \pm \sqrt{13})$$

$$= 0.151 \quad \text{or} \quad -1.651,$$

$$\therefore \quad \tfrac{1}{2}\theta = 8°\,35' \quad \text{or} \quad 121°\,12',$$

$$\theta = 17°\,10' \quad \text{or} \quad 242°\,24'.$$

Note. Some discrepancy arises between the results obtained here and in Example 4. Rounding-off explains the error in the larger answer; the smaller answer is seriously affected in Example 7, since the subtraction $-3 + \sqrt{13}$ loses a significant figure.

Ex. 18. Express $\sin x + \cos x$ in terms of t, where $t = \tan\tfrac{1}{2}x$.

8-2

2. SUM AND PRODUCT FORMULAE

The expansions derived for $\cos (A \pm B)$ and $\sin (A \pm B)$ lead to a further series of identities between trigonometric functions which prove of great value in the manipulation of trigonometric expressions. The identities which we are about to deduce may be divided into two groups:

1. The expression of products of trigonometric functions as sums.

2. Conversely, the expression of sums of trigonometric functions as products.

We shall state and prove these two sets of identities as two theorems.

Theorem 12.4.

(i) $\sin A \sin B \equiv \frac{1}{2}[\cos (A-B) - \cos (A+B)]$;

(ii) $\cos A \cos B \equiv \frac{1}{2}[\cos (A+B) + \cos (A-B)]$;

(iii) $\sin A \cos B \equiv \frac{1}{2}[\sin (A+B) + \sin (A-B)]$;

(iv) $\cos A \sin B \equiv \frac{1}{2}[\sin (A+B) - \sin (A-B)]$.

Proof. (i) R.H.S. $= \frac{1}{2}[(\cos A \cos B + \sin A \sin B)$
$\qquad\qquad\quad - (\cos A \cos B - \sin A \sin B)]$

$\qquad = \frac{1}{2} . 2 \sin A \sin B$

$\qquad = $ L.H.S.;

(ii), (iii), (iv) are all proved in a similar fashion.

Theorem 12.5.

(i) $\sin A + \sin B \equiv 2 \sin \dfrac{A+B}{2} \cos \dfrac{A-B}{2}$;

(ii) $\sin A - \sin B \equiv 2 \cos \dfrac{A+B}{2} \sin \dfrac{A-B}{2}$;

(iii) $\cos A + \cos B \equiv 2 \cos \dfrac{A+B}{2} \cos \dfrac{A-B}{2}$;

(iv) $\cos A - \cos B \equiv 2 \sin \dfrac{A+B}{2} \sin \dfrac{B-A}{2}$.

Proof.

(i) R.H.S. $= \sin \left[\dfrac{A+B}{2} + \dfrac{A-B}{2}\right] + \sin \left[\dfrac{A+B}{2} - \dfrac{A-B}{2}\right]$,

$\qquad\qquad\qquad\qquad\qquad\qquad$ by Theorem 12.4(iii)

$\qquad = \sin A + \sin B$

$\qquad = $ L.H.S.

(ii), (iii), (iv) are all proved in similar fashion.

222

Example 8. If $A+B+C = 180°$, prove that

$$\cos A+\cos B+\cos C = 1+4 \sin \frac{A}{2} \sin \frac{B}{2} \sin \frac{C}{2}.$$

L.H.S. $= \cos A+[\cos B+\cos C]$

$$= 1-2 \sin^2\frac{A}{2}+2 \cos \frac{B+C}{2} \cos \frac{B-C}{2}$$

$$= 1-2 \sin^2\frac{A}{2}+2 \sin \frac{A}{2} \cos \frac{B-C}{2}, \quad \text{since} \quad \frac{B+C}{2} = 90°-\frac{A}{2}$$

$$= 1-2 \sin \frac{A}{2} \left[\sin \frac{A}{2}-\cos \frac{B-C}{2} \right]$$

$$= 1-2 \sin \frac{A}{2} \left[\cos \frac{B+C}{2}-\cos \frac{B-C}{2} \right]$$

$$= 1-4 \sin \frac{A}{2} \sin \frac{B}{2} \sin \frac{C}{2}$$

$= $ R.H.S.

Example 9. Solve the equation

$$\sin 3x+\sin x = \cos x$$

giving all roots in the range $0° \leqslant x \leqslant 360°$.

$$\sin 3x+\sin x = \cos x$$

$$\Leftrightarrow 2 \sin 2x \cos x = \cos x$$

$$\Leftrightarrow \cos x(2 \sin 2x-1) = 0$$

$$\Rightarrow \text{either} \quad \cos x = 0 \quad \text{or} \quad \sin 2x = \tfrac{1}{2}.$$

(1) $\cos x = 0$ gives $x = 90°$ or $270°$.

(2) $\sin 2x = \tfrac{1}{2}$ gives $2x = 30°$ or $150°$ or $390°$ or $510°$

and $\qquad\qquad x = 15°$ or $75°$ or $195°$ or $255°$.

Thus $x = 15°$ or $75°$ or $90°$ or $195°$ or $225°$ or $270°$.

Note. A very common error made in equations of the type in Example 8 is to forget the solution $\cos x = 0$.

Ex. 19. Express in factor form:

(i) $\sin x+\sin 3x$;

(ii) $\cos 4x+\cos 2x$;

(iii) $\cos 3x-\cos x$;

(iv) $\sin x+\cos x$;

(v) $\cos (\tfrac{1}{4}\pi - x)-\cos (\tfrac{1}{4}\pi + x)$.

Ex. 20. Prove the identity $\sin x + \sin 2x + \sin 3x \equiv \sin 2x(2\cos x + 1)$. Hence find all values of x in the interval $0 \leqslant x \leqslant 2\pi$ satisfying the equation

$$\sin x + \sin 2x + \sin 3x = 0.$$

*Ex. 21. Solve the equation $\sin x + \sin 2x = 0$ by expressing the left-hand side in factor form, giving all solutions in the interval $0 \leqslant x \leqslant 2\pi$. Solve the equation again in the following alternative ways:

   (i) by rewriting it as $\sin 2x = \sin(-x)$, etc.;

   (ii) by rewriting it as $\sin x + 2\sin x \cos x = 0$.

Exercise 12(a)

1. Evaluate in surd form:

   (i) $\sin 75°$;   (ii) $\cos 105°$;   (iii) $\tan 105°$;   (iv) $\cot 75°$.

2. Prove that $\sin 3A = 3\sin A - 4\sin^3 A$ and that $\cos 3A = 4\cos^3 A - 3\cos A$. By considering the equation $\sin 2A = \cos 3A$, express in surd form:

   (i) $\sin 18°$;   (ii) $\cos 18°$;   (iii) $\sin 54°$;   (iv) $\tan 108°$.

3. Prove that the following identities hold for all angles A, B for which the expressions appearing are defined:

   (i) $\sin(A+B)\sin(A-B) \equiv \cos^2 B - \cos^2 A$;

   (ii) $\cos(A-B) - \sin(A+B) \equiv (\cos A - \sin A)(\cos B - \sin B)$;

   (iii) $\dfrac{\cos(A+B) + \cos(A-B)}{\sin(A+B) - \sin(A-B)} \equiv \cot B$;

   (iv) $\sin(A+B)\sin B \equiv \cos A - \cos(A+B)\cos B$;

   (v) $\sec(A+B) \equiv \dfrac{\sec A \sec B \operatorname{cosec} A \operatorname{cosec} B}{\operatorname{cosec} A \operatorname{cosec} B - \sec A \sec B}$;

   (vi) $\tan 2A(\cot A - \tan A) \equiv 2$;

   (vii) $\cos 4A \equiv 4(\cos^4 A + \sin^4 A) - 3$;

   (viii) $\cot A - \cot 2A \equiv \operatorname{cosec} 2A$;

   (ix) $\dfrac{\sin A + \sin B}{\cos A + \cos B} \equiv \tan \tfrac{1}{2}(A+B)$;

   (x) $\dfrac{\sin A + \sin 2A + \sin 3A}{\cos A + \cos 2A + \cos 3A} \equiv \tan 2A$.

4. If A, B, C are the angles of a triangle, prove the following identities:

   (i) $\sin A + \sin B + \sin C \equiv 4\cos\dfrac{A}{2}\cos\dfrac{B}{2}\cos\dfrac{C}{2}$;

   (ii) $\cos 2A + \cos 2B + \cos 2C + 4\cos A \cos B \cos C + 1 \equiv 0$;

224

(iii) $\cos^2 A + \cos^2 B + \cos^2 C \equiv 1 - 2\cos A \cos B \cos C$;

(iv) $\tan A + \tan B + \tan C \equiv \tan A \tan B \tan C$ (provided that the triangle is not right-angled).

5. Solve the following equations for x, giving values between $0°$ and $360°$ inclusive:

(i) $2\sin x = \sin(x+45°)$;　　　　(ii) $2\cos x = \cos(x+60°)$;

(iii) $\sin(30°+x) = \cos(15°-x)$;

(iv) $\cos(x-30°)+\sin(x-20°) = \cos x$.

6. Solve the following equations for x, giving values of x between $0°$ and $360°$ inclusive:

(i) $\cos x + \sin x + \sqrt{2} = 0$;　　(ii) $\sin x + \sqrt{3}\cos x - 1 = 0$;

(iii) $3\sin x - 4\cos x + 2 = 0$;　　(iv) $3\sin x + 2\cos x - 3 = 0$.

7. Solve the following equations, giving all solutions between $0°$ and $360°$:

(i) $\sin 2x + \sin^2 x = 0$;

(ii) $\cos 2x - 3\cos x = 4$;

(iii) $\cos x + \cos 2x + \cos 3x = 0$;

(iv) $\cos x - \sin x = \cos 2x$.

8. (i) Prove that, when $\cos\phi = -\frac{1}{2}$, the value of the expression

$$\sin\theta + \sin(\theta+\phi) + \sin(\theta+2\phi)$$

is zero, whatever the value of θ.

(ii) Prove that if

$$5\tan x = \tan(x+\alpha),$$

then

$$\sin(2x+\alpha) = \tfrac{3}{2}\sin\alpha,$$

stating what restrictions you impose on the value of $\sin\alpha$ for a solution to be possible. Hence find the values of x between $0°$ and $360°$ which satisfy the equation

$$5\tan x = \tan(x+30°). \qquad\qquad (\text{O \& C})$$

9. Prove the identities:

(i) $\dfrac{\sec^2\theta + 2\tan\theta}{(\cos\theta+\sin\theta)^2} \equiv \sec^2\theta$;

(ii) $4\cos\theta\cos(\theta+120°)\cos(\theta-120°) \equiv \cos 3\theta$. $\qquad (\text{O \& C})$

10. Prove that $\cos[(n+2)\theta] \equiv 2\cos\theta\cos[(n+1)\theta] - \cos n\theta$.

Hence express $\cos 3\theta$ and $\cos 4\theta$ in terms of $\cos\theta$, and prove that

$$\cos 5\theta \equiv 16\cos^5\theta - 20\cos^3\theta + 5\cos\theta. \qquad (\text{O \& C})$$

11. Prove that　　$\dfrac{\sin 5\theta + 2\sin 3\theta + \sin\theta}{\cos\theta - \cos 5\theta} \equiv \cot\theta$

and hence, using the formula $\sin 3\theta \equiv 3\sin\theta - 4\sin^3\theta$, show that $\cos 36°$ is a root of the equation

$$8x^4 - 8x^2 + x + 1 = 0.$$ (O & C)

12. (i) Prove that
$$\cos 2\theta \equiv \frac{1 - \tan^2\theta}{1 + \tan^2\theta}$$

and, without using tables, deduce that
$$\tan 22\tfrac{1}{2}° = \sqrt{2} - 1$$

(ii) Prove that $\cos 3\theta \equiv 4\cos^3\theta - 3\cos\theta$ and deduce that

$$\cos^3\theta + \cos^3(\theta + 60°) + \cos^3(\theta + 120°) \equiv \tfrac{3}{2}\cos(\theta + 60°) + \tfrac{1}{4}\cos 3\theta.$$ (O & C)

13. (i) If $a = \sin\theta + \cos\phi$ and $b = \cos\theta + \sin\phi$, prove that
$$\cos(\theta - \phi) = 2ab/(a^2 + b^2)$$

and hence, or otherwise, find $\tan(\theta - \phi)$ in terms of a and b.

(ii) Express $11\sin^2 x + 12\sin x\cos x + 6\cos^2 x$ in the form $a + b\sin(2x - \theta)$ where a, b and θ are constants to be determined.
Hence prove that

$$2 \leqslant 11\sin^2 x + 12\sin x\cos x + 6\cos^2 x \leqslant 15.$$ (Cambridge)

14. Prove that
$$\sec x + \tan x = \tan(\tfrac{1}{4}\pi + \tfrac{1}{2}x)$$

and express in a similar way (i.e. as the tangent of an angle)

(i) $\sec x - \tan x$; (ii) $\operatorname{cosec} x - \cot x$. (Cambridge)

15. Prove
$$2\sin\theta(\cos 2\theta + \cos 4\theta + \cos 6\theta) \equiv \sin 7\theta - \sin\theta.$$

Deduce that $\cos\tfrac{2}{7}\pi + \cos\tfrac{4}{7}\pi + \cos\tfrac{6}{7}\pi = -\tfrac{1}{2}.$

Show also that $\cos\tfrac{1}{7}\pi + \cos\tfrac{3}{7}\pi + \cos\tfrac{5}{7}\pi = +\tfrac{1}{2}.$ (Cambridge)

16. Express the function $\cos x + 2\sin x$ in the form $R\sin(x + \alpha)$ where R is positive and $0° < \alpha < 360°$. State the values of R and α. Hence, or otherwise, find the values of x in the range $0°$ to $360°$ inclusive which satisfy the equations

(i) $2\cos x + 4\sin x = 1$; (ii) $\cos x(\cos x + 2\sin x) = 1$. (Cambridge)

17. If $u = \cos\theta + \sin\theta$, $v = \cos\theta - \sin\theta$, prove that
$$\cos 2\theta = uv, \quad \sin 2\theta = u^2 - 1, \quad u^2 + v^2 = 2.$$

Prove that, if θ is a root lying between $-180°$ and $180°$ of the equation
$$\cos 2\theta + a\sin 2\theta = \cos\theta - \sin\theta,$$

then it is either $0°$ or $90°$ or it is a root of the equation
$$(a+1)\cos\theta + (a-1)\sin\theta + a = 0.$$

Solve the equation
$$\cos 2\theta + 7\sin 2\theta = \cos\theta - \sin\theta$$

for values of θ between $-180°$ and $180°$. (O & C)

226

18. Find all the pairs of values (θ, ϕ) lying between 0 and 2π that satisfy the equations

$$\cos\theta + \cos\phi = \cos\tfrac{1}{4}\pi,$$
$$\sin\theta + \sin\phi = \sin\tfrac{1}{4}\pi. \qquad\qquad \text{(O & C)}$$

19. Prove, by induction or otherwise, that

$$\cos\alpha + \cos(\alpha+\beta) + \cos(\alpha+2\beta) + \ldots + \cos[\alpha+(n-1)\beta]$$
$$\equiv \cos[\alpha+\tfrac{1}{2}(n-1)\beta]\sin\tfrac{1}{2}n\beta\operatorname{cosec}\tfrac{1}{2}\beta,$$

provided that β is not a multiple of 2π.

A regular polygon has n sides of length a; the vertices of the polygon are $V_1, V_2, \ldots, V_n$. Show that

$$(V_1 V_2)^2 + (V_1 V_3)^2 + \ldots + (V_1 V_n)^2 = \tfrac{1}{2}na^2\operatorname{cosec}^2(\pi/n). \qquad \text{(Cambridge)}$$

3. THE SOLUTION OF TRIANGLES

One of the most important applications of elementary trigonometry is to the solution of triangles; that is, the determination of the remaining sides and angles of a triangle some of whose sides and/or angles are given. For consistency, we employ the following notation: ABC is a triangle with sides $BC = a$, $CA = b$, $AB = c$ and the radius of the circumcircle of $\triangle ABC$ is R.

A triangle may be solved uniquely in the following three cases:

(i) given the three sides;

(ii) given two sides and the included angle;

(iii) given two angles and a side.

A triangle may also be solved (but not necessarily uniquely) in the following case:

(iv) given two sides and a non-included angle.

The *Cosine* and *Sine Rules* of elementary trigonometry are employed in the solution, the Cosine Rule in cases (i) and (ii), the Sine Rule in cases (iii) and (iv). Before illustrating their use, we give the proofs for the benefit of the reader unfamiliar with them.

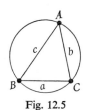

Fig. 12.5

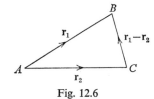

Fig. 12.6

The Cosine Rule.

In the $\triangle ABC$,
$$a^2 = b^2 + c^2 - 2bc\cos A,$$
$$b^2 = c^2 + a^2 - 2ca\cos B,$$
$$c^2 = a^2 + b^2 - 2ab\cos C.$$

227

Proof. Take A as origin and let the position vectors of B, C be $\mathbf{r}_1, \mathbf{r}_2$ respectively. (Thus $|\mathbf{r}_1| = c$, $|\mathbf{r}_2| = b$ and $|\mathbf{r}_1 - \mathbf{r}_2| = a$.) We have

$$|\mathbf{r}_1 - \mathbf{r}_2|^2 = (\mathbf{r}_1 - \mathbf{r}_2).(\mathbf{r}_1 - \mathbf{r}_2)$$

$$= \mathbf{r}_2.\mathbf{r}_2 + \mathbf{r}_1.\mathbf{r}_1 - 2\mathbf{r}_1.\mathbf{r}_2$$

$$= b^2 + c^2 - 2bc \cos A.$$

The other two forms are proved similarly, using a new origin.

Ex. 22. Prove the vector identity

$$2\mathbf{r}_1.(\mathbf{r}_2 - \mathbf{r}_1) = \mathbf{r}_2.\mathbf{r}_2 - \mathbf{r}_1.\mathbf{r}_1 - (\mathbf{r}_2 - \mathbf{r}_1).(\mathbf{r}_2 - \mathbf{r}_1)$$

and show that, with the notation used above, this reduces to the second form of the Cosine Rule.

The Sine Rule.

In the $\triangle ABC$ $$\frac{a}{\sin A} = \frac{b}{\sin B} = \frac{c}{\sin C} = 2R.$$

Proof. Draw the diameter BD.
If $\angle A$ is acute (Figure 12.7(i)), $\angle BDC = \angle A$.
If $\angle A$ is obtuse (Figure 12.7(ii)), $\angle BDC = 180° - \angle A$.
In both cases

$$\frac{a}{\sin A} = 2R$$

and the result follows by symmetry.

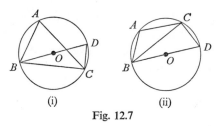

(i)   (ii)

Fig. 12.7

Ex. 23. Show that the area, $\triangle$, of the $\triangle ABC$ is given by the formula

$$\triangle = \tfrac{1}{2}bc \sin A.$$

Write down the two similar expressions for $\triangle$ and deduce the Sine Rule in the form

$$\frac{a}{\sin A} = \frac{b}{\sin B} = \frac{c}{\sin C}.$$

Example 10. *In* $\triangle ABC$, $BC = 6$ cm, $CA = 4$ cm, $AB = 5$ cm. *Find the angles of the triangle.*

228

Clearly we must use the Cosine Rule to begin with. We select the angle B, since this is the smallest angle, and the tables of cosines are marginally more accurate for smaller than larger angles.

$$16 = 25 + 36 - 60 \cos \angle B,$$

$$\cos \angle B = 0 \cdot 75,$$

$$\angle B = 41° \, 24'.$$

By the Sine Rule $\qquad \dfrac{\sin A}{6} = \dfrac{\sin 46° \, 24'}{2},$

$$\sin \angle A = 0 \cdot 9919(5),$$

$$\angle A = 82° \, 42'.$$

By the angle sum property of a triangle

$$\angle C = 55° \, 54'.$$

Example 11. *Discuss the solution of a triangle in which A, a, c are given.* (This is often called the *ambiguous case*, since it is sometimes possible to draw two triangles.)

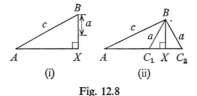

Fig. 12.8

Construct the point X such that $\angle AXB = 90°$, $\angle BAX = \angle A$.
If

$$c \sin A > a, \quad \sin C = \frac{c \sin A}{a} > 1,$$

and no triangle can be drawn (Figure 12.8(i)).

If $c \sin A = a$, $\angle C = 90°$ a unique right-angled triangle can be drawn.

If $c \sin A < a < c$, $\sin C = c \sin A / a < 1$ and two angles C may be found, one acute and one obtuse (see Figure 12.8(ii)); two triangles can be drawn.

Finally, if $a > c$, then $A > C$ and the obtuse value for C must be rejected (see Figure 12.8(ii) again).

Ex. 24. Interpret the four congruency conditions for triangles in terms of the solution of triangles by trigonometry.

4. SOLUTION OF PROBLEMS, PARTICULARLY IN THREE DIMENSIONS

We recall that the angle between two planes is equal to the angle between the normals to the two planes and that the angle between a line and a plane is equal to the angle between the line and its projection in the plane. It is important to remember, too, that *bearings are always given in a horizontal plane.*

Many problems are best done by setting up coordinate systems and applying the methods of Chapters 2 and 11. The reader must learn to develop a flexible attitude towards problem solving and be prepared to try several techniques in a search for the simplest approach.

Example 12. *A hillside faces due north and is inclined at* 20° *to the horizontal. A path up the hill has a bearing of* 120°. *Find the angle the path makes with the horizontal.*

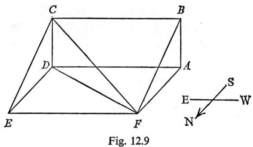

Fig. 12.9

ABCD is a vertical rectangle; *ADEF* a horizontal rectangle. The hillside is represented by *BCEF*; *AF* points due north, *FE* due east. *FC* represents the path.

We have $\angle AFB = 20°$, $\angle AFD = 60°$, and we have to calculate $\angle DFC$. Let $\angle DFC = \theta$, $AB = h$ units.

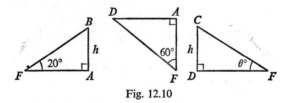

Fig. 12.10

In $\triangle AFB$, $\qquad AF = h \cot 20°$.

In $\triangle AFD$, $\qquad FD = AF \sec 60° = h \cot 20° \sec 60°$.

230

In $\triangle DFC$, $\tan \theta = h/DF = \tan 20° \cos 60°$

$$= 0{\cdot}1820,$$

$$\theta = 10° \; 19'.$$

Example 13. *Prove the theorem of Apollonius that, in any triangle ABC with median AM,* $AB^2 + AC^2 = 2AM^2 + 2BM^2.$

An aircraft flying on a constant course and at constant height with speed V is observed from a station on the ground at times 0, *t*, 2*t* *to have elevations* α, β, γ *respectively. Prove that*

$$V = h\sqrt{(\cot^2 \alpha - 2 \cot^2 \beta + \cot^2 \gamma)}/t\sqrt{2}.$$

If the bearings of the aircraft from the station at times 0 *and* 2*t are* θ_1 *and* θ_2 *respectively, determine the course of the aircraft.*

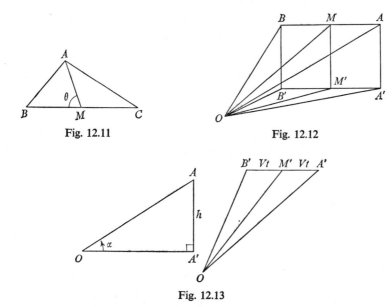

Fig. 12.11   Fig. 12.12

Fig. 12.13

Let $\angle AMB = \theta$ (Figure 12.11).

In $\triangle AMB$, $AB^2 = AM^2 + BM^2 - 2AM.BM \cos \theta.$

In $\triangle AMC$, $AC^2 = AM^2 + MC^2 - 2AM.MC \cos (180° - \theta).$

But $BM = MC$ and $\cos \theta = -\cos (180° - \theta)$ whence the theorem of Apollonius, by addition.

AB represents the course of the aircraft, A, M, B being its position at times 0, t, 2t. The projections of A, M, B on the ground are A', M', B', and O is the observation point. We are given that $AM = MB = Vt$ and that $\angle AOA' = \alpha$, $\angle MOM' = \beta$, $\angle BOB' = \gamma$.

In $\triangle OA'A$, $\qquad\qquad\qquad OA' = h\cot\alpha.$

Similarly $\qquad\qquad OB' = h\cot\gamma; \quad OM' = h\cot\beta.$

In $\triangle AO'B'$, $\qquad h^2\cot^2\alpha + h^2\cot^2\gamma = 2h^2\cot^2\beta + 2V^2t^2$

by Apollonius's Theorem, whence

$$V = h\sqrt{(\cot^2\alpha - 2\cot^2\beta + \cot^2\gamma)}/t\sqrt{2}.$$

Furthermore, if ϕ is the bearing of the course of the aircraft

$$\angle A'OB' = \theta_1 - \theta_2; \quad \angle B'A'O = \phi - \theta_1$$

and we have, by applying the Sine Rule in $\triangle OA'B'$

$$\frac{2Vt}{\sin(\theta_1 - \theta_2)} = \frac{h\cot\gamma}{\sin(\phi - \theta)},$$

i.e. $\qquad \sin(\phi - \theta_1) = \dfrac{h\cot\gamma\sin(\theta_1 - \theta_2)}{h\sqrt{2}\sqrt{(\cot^2\alpha - 2\cot^2\beta + \cot^2\gamma)}},$

i.e. $\qquad \phi = \theta_1 + \arcsin\left[\dfrac{\cot\gamma\sin(\theta_1 - \theta_2)}{\sqrt{(2\cot^2\alpha - 4\cot^2\beta + 2\cot^2\gamma)}}\right].$

Exercise 12(b)

1. Two points B and C on the bank of a straight river are 120 metres apart. It is observed that a point A on the opposite bank is such that the angle ABC is 72° 15′ and the angle ACB is 38° 30′. Find the width of the river, correct to the nearest metre. $\qquad\qquad$ (O & C 'O')

2. In $\triangle ABC$, $s = \frac{1}{2}(a+b+c)$; deduce from the Cosine Rule that

$$\cos\frac{A}{2} = \sqrt{\left[\frac{s(s-a)}{bc}\right]}.$$

If the area of the triangle is $\triangle$, use this result to prove

(i) $\sin\dfrac{A}{2} = \sqrt{\left[\dfrac{(s-b)(s-c)}{bc}\right]};$ $\qquad$ (ii) $\triangle = \sqrt{[s(s-a)(s-b)(s-c)]}.$

3. In the $\triangle ABC$, $a = 14$, $b = 15$, $c = 13$. Calculate
   (i) the area of the triangle;
   (ii) $\sin A$;
   (iii) the radius of the circumcircle. $\qquad\qquad$ (O & C 'O')

4. Prove that, in any triangle ABC,

(i) $\dfrac{a-b}{a+b} = \dfrac{\sin A - \sin B}{\sin A + \sin B};$

(ii) $\tan\dfrac{A-B}{2} = \dfrac{a-b}{a+b}\cot\dfrac{C}{2}.$

In a triangle ABC, $a = 13\cdot41$ cm, $b = 9\cdot63$ cm and $\angle C = 34°$. Find the size of the angles $\angle A$ and $\angle B$.

If in a triangle $a = 5$, $b = 4$ and $\cos(A-B) = \frac{31}{32}$, prove that $\cos C = \frac{1}{8}$ and that $c = 6$.   (O & C)

5. A straight river is 80 m wide. A man on one bank observed that the angle of elevation of the top of a tree directly opposite him is $18°\ 20'$. He walks 60 m along the bank. Find the angle of elevation of the top of the tree from his new position.   (O & C 'O')

6. In a triangle ABC, $a = 20$ m, $b = 28$ m, $c = 32$ m. Prove that $\angle B = 60°$. From the points A, B, C which are on level ground, the top of a flagstaff has the same angle of elevation, $30°$. Calculate the height of the flagstaff.

(O & C 'O')

7. A snow-slope is a plane inclined to the horizontal at an angle of α. A man on skis traverses this slope in a straight line which makes an angle β with the horizontal. Show that the angle θ which his path makes with the line of greatest slope of the plane is given by the equation

$$\cos \theta = \sin \beta \, \operatorname{cosec} \alpha.$$

If $\alpha = 25°$ and $\beta = 20°$, calculate the size of the angle θ.   (O & C 'O')

8. Two adjacent sides of a roof, whose horizontal bases meet at right-angles, slope at $30°$ and $45°$ to the horizontal. At what angle do the roofs intersect?

9. A right pyramid, vertex O, stands on a square horizontal base $ABCD$; $AB = 2a$ and the height of the pyramid is h. Express the sines of the following angles in terms of h and a:
  (i)   the inclination of OB to the horizontal;
  (ii) the inclination of a slant face to the horizontal;
  (iii) the angle between the faces OAB, ODC;
  (iv) one-half of the angle between the faces OAB, OBC.   (O & C)

10. $ABCD$ is a regular tetrahedron and M is the mid-point of the edge CD. Find the angle between the plane ABC and

  (i) the plane ABM;   (ii) the line AM.

11. From the top of a cliff the angle of depression of a ship, steaming on a constant course at 12 km per hour, is $15°$ and its true bearing is $75°$ north of west. Two minutes later, the angle of depression is $12°$ and the true bearing is due west. Find
  (i) the height of the cliff (to the nearest metre);
  (ii) the ship's course (to the nearest half-degree).

12. A and B are two points on one bank of a straight stretch of a river, P is a chimney exactly opposite A and 20 m from the other bank. The angles of elevation of the top of the chimney from A and B are α and β respectively. Calculate the width of the river to the nearest metre, given that

$$\alpha = 45°, \quad \beta = 30° \quad \text{and} \quad AB = 200 \text{ m}.$$

233

Prove that, if the angle of elevation of the top of the chimney from a point C, midway between A and B, is γ, then

$$4 \cot^2 \gamma = 3 \cot^2 \alpha + \cot^2 \beta$$

whatever the height of the chimney, the width of the river, and the distance AB may be.　　　　　　　　　　　　　　　　　　　(O & C)

13. In the quadrilateral $ABCD$, $AB = 13$ cm, $BC = 20$ cm, $CD = 48$ cm, $\angle BCD$ is $90°$ and $\angle BAC = \angle DBC$. Without using tables
   (i) prove that $\cos \angle BAC = \frac{5}{13}$;
   (ii) prove that $\cos \angle ACB = \frac{4}{5}$;
   (iii) find the area of the quadrilateral by adding the areas of the triangles ABC and ACD.　　　　　　　　　　　　　　　(Cambridge)

14. A right pyramid has vertex V and rectangular base $ABCD$. $AB = 4$ cm, $BC = 6$ cm and the height of the pyramid is 8 cm. Find
   (i) the angle a sloping edge makes with the base;
   (ii) the angle the face VAB makes with the base;
   (iii) the angle between two adjacent sloping faces.

15. From a point P in a horizontal plane a man observes the summit S of a mountain to be due north at an elevation θ. When the man has walked a distance $2a$ on a bearing α east of north to a point Q in the horizontal plane, he observes that the elevation of S from Q is again θ. If h is the height of S above the horizontal plane containing P and Q, show that $h = a \tan \theta \sec \alpha$. When the man has walked a further distance a in the same plane and in the same direction to a point R he observes that the elevations of S from R is ϕ. Show that

$$\cot^2 \phi = (3 \cos^2 \alpha + 1) \cot^2 \theta$$

and that the distance RS is

$$a(\sec^2 \alpha \sec^2 \theta + 3)^{\frac{1}{2}}.　　　　　　　　　　　\text{(Cambridge)}$$

16. An observer situated at a point O in a horizontal plane observes two other points P and Q. The point P is in the horizontal plane containing O on a bearing α west of north from O. The point Q is situated due north of O at an angle of elevation β as observed from O. If $OP = OQ = r$, show that the length l of the straight line PQ is given by

$$l^2 = 2r^2(1 - \cos \alpha \cos \beta).$$

   Hence, or otherwise, show that $\cos \angle POQ = \cos \alpha \cos \beta$.
   If $\alpha = 60°$, $\beta = 30°$ find the length of the arc PQ of the circle which passes through P and Q and has its centre at O. Give the answer in terms of r correct to two decimal places.　　　　　　　　　　　　　　(Cambridge)

17. ABC is an equilateral triangle of side 1 m marked out on level ground. Three vertical posts are driven in at the vertices; AP is of height a m; BQ is of height b m; CR is of height c m $(a > b; c > b)$. The line PQ meets the ground at U; the line RQ meets the ground at V. Prove that

$$BU = \frac{lb}{a-b}; \quad BV = \frac{lb}{c-b}.$$

If $l = 2$, $a = 6$, $b = 3$, $c = 4$, calculate the length of the perpendicular from B to the line UV and hence find the inclination of the plane PQR to the horizontal.

(O & C)

18. A tower stands on a level plane. The inclinations of its top from three points A, B, C in the plane are α, β, γ. The points A, B, C are in a line which does not go through the foot of the tower and $AB = p$, $BC = q$. Prove that the height h of the tower is given by

$$h^2[p(\cot^2 \alpha - \cot^2 \beta) + q(\cot^2 \alpha - \cot^2 \beta)] = pq(p+q).$$ (O & C)

19. In the tetrahedron $OABC$, $BC = a$, $CA = b$ and $AB = c$;

$$\angle BOC = \angle COA = \angle AOB = 90°.$$

Find the angle between the planes OAB and ABC.

Miscellaneous Exercise 12

1. Prove that $\arctan \frac{2}{3} + \arctan \frac{1}{5} = \frac{1}{4}\pi$ and that

$$\arctan \tfrac{1}{3} + \arctan \tfrac{1}{4} + \arctan \tfrac{2}{9} = \tfrac{1}{4}\pi.$$

2. Solve the equations:
   (i) $\arctan \frac{1}{2} + \arctan x = \arctan \frac{2}{3}$;
   (ii) $2 \arcsin (x-y) = 3 \arccos (x+y) = \pi$.

3. Two circles with centres O and C meet in P and Q. The radii of the circles are a and b and the angle CPO is α. Prove that the angle between the common tangents of the circles is θ, where

$$(a-b)^2 \cot^2 \tfrac{1}{2}\theta = 4ab \sin^2 \tfrac{1}{2}\alpha.$$ (O & C)

4. Find the set of values of x which satisfy the inequality

$$2 \sin x + \sin 2x > 0.$$ (SMP)

5. Under what circumstances is it true that

$$\arctan x + \arctan y = \arctan \frac{x+y}{1-xy} \,?$$

Find values of x, y for which the relationship above is (i) true, (ii) untrue.

6. Prove that, in any triangle ABC,

$$\frac{a}{\sin A} = \frac{b}{\sin B} = \frac{c}{\sin C}.$$

In the triangle ABC the angle B is a right-angle and O is a point inside the triangle at which all the sides subtend the angle 120°. If θ is the angle CBO, prove that

$$\tan \theta = \frac{c + a\sqrt{3}}{a + c\sqrt{3}}.$$

If the angle $C = 30°$, show that $CO = 2AO$.   (O & C)

7. Show that $4 \arctan \frac{1}{5} - \arctan \frac{1}{239} = \frac{1}{4}\pi$ (a result commonly known as *Machin's Formula*).

8. Find all pairs of angles x, y such that $0 < x < \pi$, $0 < y < \pi$ which satisfy the simultaneous equations

$$\sin x \sin y = \tfrac{1}{4}(\sqrt{3}-1); \quad \cos x \cos y = \tfrac{1}{4}(\sqrt{3}+1).$$

9. A man stands facing the rectangular front of a building and is in the same plane as one of the ends of the building. The elevation of the nearer top corner A is α and of the further top corner B is β. The man walks towards the vertical edge through B until the elevation of B is also α, and he finds that he has walked a distance a. Show that the height of the face of the building is

$$a \sin \alpha \sin \beta / \sin (\alpha - \beta).$$

Show also that its length is $a[\sin (\alpha + \beta)/\sin (\alpha - \beta)]^{\frac{1}{2}}$.   (O & C)

10. Find the maximum and minimum values of the expression $a \sin \theta + b \cos \theta$.

By making the substitution $t = \tan \tfrac{1}{2}\theta$, deduce the condition for the existence of real roots of the quadratic equation

$$(b+c) t^2 - 2at + (c-b) = 0.$$

11. An aircraft is observed flying on a constant course γ east of north at a constant height. When its true bearing is θ west of north, the angle of elevation is α, and when its true bearing is ϕ east of north, the angle of elevation is β. Prove that γ is given by

$$\tan \gamma = \frac{\sin \phi \tan \alpha + \sin \theta \tan \beta}{\cos \phi \tan \alpha - \cos \theta \tan \beta}.$$

Prove that, if $\theta = \phi$, the angle of elevation δ, when the true bearing is north, is given by

$$\tan \delta = \tfrac{1}{2}(\tan \alpha + \tan \beta) \sec \theta.\qquad\qquad \text{(O \& C)}$$

12. Prove that
$$\tan 3x \equiv \frac{3 \tan x - \tan^3 x}{1 - 3 \tan^2 x}$$

provided both sides of the identity are defined.

Deduce that the three roots of the cubic equation

$$t^3 - 3t^2 - 3t + 1 = 0$$

are $\tan \tfrac{1}{12}\pi$, $\tan \tfrac{5}{12}\pi$, $\tan \tfrac{3}{4}\pi$.

13. Sketch the graph of the function defined by

$$f(x) = |\sin x + \cos x|.$$

For what values of x in the interval $0 \leqslant x \leqslant \pi$ does $|\sin x + \cos x| = 1$?

14. Find the maximum and minimum values of the expression

$$\sin x(\sin x + \cos x).$$

15. Eliminate x and y between the equations

$$\sin x + \sin y = a,$$

$$\cos x + \cos y = b,$$

$$x + y = \alpha.$$

16. The wave-train well away from a ship is modelled by the equation

$$z = a \sin \left[(x+y-ct)/p\right]$$

where z is the height of the sea's surface above the mean horizontal plane in which (x, y) are Cartesian coordinates, a is the maximum height of the waves, c is the fixed speed, and p a fixed length. Sketch a diagram showing an airman's view of the waves, indicating the lines of the crests and troughs and the direction in which the waves are travelling; and prove that the wave velocity and distance between successive waves are $c/\sqrt{2}$ and $\pi p\sqrt{2}$ respectively.

The wave train of another ship, given by

$$z = a \sin \left[(x-y-ct)/p\right]$$

is superimposed on the other one. Prove that on the lines $y = (N+\frac{1}{2})\,\pi p$, where N is an integer, the sea is undisturbed.   (SMP)

17. Find the range or ranges of values of c such that the simultaneous equations

$$\cos\theta + \sin\phi = 1,$$

$$\sec\theta + \operatorname{cosec}\phi = c$$

are satisfied by real values of θ and ϕ.

Obtain the general solutions of these equations when $c = 6\frac{1}{4}$.

13. *Matrices I*

1. INTRODUCTION

Any pair of simultaneous equations in two unknowns, x and y,

$$\begin{cases} ax+by = c, \\ dx+ey = f \end{cases}$$

is completely specified if we know

(i) the coefficients on the left-hand side, which we may write as the rectangular array

$$\begin{pmatrix} a & b \\ d & e \end{pmatrix}$$

and (ii) the two numbers on the right-hand side, which we may write as the rectangular array

$$\begin{pmatrix} c \\ f \end{pmatrix}.$$

Ex. 1. Solve the simultaneous equations whose coefficients are given by the rectangular array

$$\begin{pmatrix} 2 & -1 \\ 1 & 2 \end{pmatrix}$$

and whose right-hand sides are given by the rectangular array

$$\begin{pmatrix} 11 \\ -2 \end{pmatrix}.$$

The answer is the pair of values 4 (for x) and -3 (for y), which can be expressed as an array

$$\begin{pmatrix} 4 \\ -3 \end{pmatrix},$$

as we saw in Chapter 2.

Such rectangular arrays of numbers are called *matrices*; in the example above they exhibit the known quantities in a pair of simultaneous equations but they may be used in other contexts too, to display information.

Suppose 23 boys take examinations in Mathematics (M), English (E) and French (F). In each examination there are five grades A, B, C, D, E. Then the fate of the boys may be summarized in the following 3×5 matrix (read 'three by five matrix'; that is, a matrix with three *rows* and five *columns*):

$$
\begin{array}{c}
\\
M \\
E \\
F
\end{array}
\begin{array}{ccccc}
A & B & C & D & E \\
\left(\begin{array}{ccccc}
2 & 5 & 7 & 6 & 3 \\
1 & 6 & 8 & 6 & 2 \\
3 & 5 & 8 & 7 & 0
\end{array}\right).
\end{array}
$$

Ex. 2. In the example just quoted, describe what information is represented by each of the following :
   (i) the 3×1 matrix (or *column-vector*)

$$
\begin{pmatrix} 7 \\ 8 \\ 8 \end{pmatrix};
$$

  (ii) the 3×2 matrix
$$
\begin{pmatrix} 2 & 5 \\ 1 & 6 \\ 3 & 5 \end{pmatrix};
$$

 (iii) the 1×5 matrix (or *row-vector*)

$$(3 \ 5 \ 8 \ 7 \ 0).$$

More generally, any rectangular array of m rows and n columns of elements is called an $m \times n$ *matrix*:

$$
\begin{pmatrix}
a_{11} & a_{12} & a_{13} & \cdots & a_{1n} \\
a_{21} & a_{22} & a_{23} & \cdots & a_{2n} \\
\multicolumn{5}{c}{\dotfill} \\
a_{m1} & a_{m2} & a_{m3} & \cdots & a_{mn}
\end{pmatrix}.
$$

We may, if we so wish, denote the whole matrix by a single capital letter **A** (printed in bold-face type; in script, write a capital A and underline). The element a_{ij} in the ith row and jth column, is called the i, jth *element* or *entry* of the matrix. A *real matrix* is a matrix all of whose elements are real numbers.

2. LINEAR TRANSFORMATIONS

If we are given a pair of axes in a plane, any point P may be located by its coordinates (x, y), so that $\mathbf{OP} = x\mathbf{i} + y\mathbf{j}$. Suppose we now associate with each point $P(x, y)$ a unique point $P'(x', y')$ such that

$$x' = x + 2y,$$

$$y' = x - y.$$

For example, the point $P(1, 2)$ gives rise to $P'(5, -1)$; the point $Q(-2, 3)$ gives rise to $Q'(4, -5)$. Such an association of points is a mapping, or function, of the set of points in the plane into itself and is often referred to as a *transformation of the plane into itself*. We may specify our mapping by the 2×2 matrix

$$\begin{pmatrix} 1 & 2 \\ 1 & -1 \end{pmatrix}$$

which we call the matrix of the given transformation. For the present, such a matrix is to be regarded simply as an inert array of coefficients defining a transformation. In Section 3 we shall consider combinations of transformations and the resulting matrices; in Section 4, rules for combining matrices will be developed and the inert arrays which we have at present will come to life. Finally, in Section 5 matrices, with their new-found vitality, will be used to illuminate the concept of a geometrical transformation.

We may also regard the transformation as mapping the vector **OP** into the vector **OP'** and the vector **OQ** into the vector **OQ'**. If we call the transformation T, then we write

$$T(\mathbf{OP}) = \mathbf{OP'}$$

and $$T(\mathbf{OQ}) = \mathbf{OQ'}.$$

Notice carefully that $T(\mathbf{OP})$ *is a vector*: *the position vector of P'*. $T(\mathbf{OP})$ is called the *image* of **OP**; P' is the *image* of P and may be written $T(P)$.

The transformation defined above has an important property: it maps the vector **OP**+**OQ** into the vector sum of $T(\mathbf{OP})$ and $T(\mathbf{OQ})$. Let us demonstrate this property first with the points P and Q above:

$$\mathbf{OP} = \mathbf{i}+2\mathbf{j}, \quad \mathbf{OQ} = -2\mathbf{i}+3\mathbf{j}.$$

Let $$\mathbf{OR} = \mathbf{OP}+\mathbf{OQ}$$

so that R is the point $(-1, 5)$ and $\mathbf{OR} = -\mathbf{i}+5\mathbf{j}$. By the definition of T, R' has coordinates $(-1+2.5, -1-5)$, i.e. $(9, -6)$ and so

$$\mathbf{OR'} = 9\mathbf{i}-6\mathbf{j}.$$

But $$\mathbf{OP'}+\mathbf{OQ'} = (5\mathbf{i}-\mathbf{j})+(4\mathbf{i}-5\mathbf{j})$$

$$= (9\mathbf{i}-6\mathbf{j})$$

$$= \mathbf{OR'}.$$

Now let P be any point (h_1, k_1), Q any point (h_2, k_2) and let $R(h_3, k_3)$ be the point such that $$\mathbf{OR} = \mathbf{OP}+\mathbf{OQ},$$

or $$h_3\mathbf{i}+k_3\mathbf{j} = (h_1+h_2)\,\mathbf{i}+(k_1+k_2)\,\mathbf{j},$$

240

then $\quad T(\mathbf{OR}) = T(h_3\mathbf{i}+k_3\mathbf{j})$

$$= (h_3+2k_3)\,\mathbf{i}+(h_3-k_3)\,\mathbf{j}, \quad \text{by the definition of } T,$$

$$= (h_1+h_2+2k_1+2k_2)\,\mathbf{i}+(h_1+h_2-k_1-k_2)\,\mathbf{j}$$

$$= [(h_1+2k_1)\,\mathbf{i}+(h_1-k_1)\,\mathbf{j}] + [(h_2+2k_2)\mathbf{i}+(h_2-k_2)\mathbf{j}]$$

$$= T(\mathbf{OP})+T(\mathbf{OQ}), \quad \text{again using the definition of } T.$$

The result we have just proved for the transformation T can be generalized. If $S(h_4, k_4)$ is the point whose position vector is given by

$$\mathbf{OS} = \lambda\mathbf{OP}+\mu\mathbf{OQ},$$

where λ, μ are any numbers, so that $h_4 = \lambda h_1+\mu h_2$, $k_4 = \lambda k_1+\mu k_2$, then

$$T(\mathbf{OS}) = T(h_4\mathbf{i}+k_4\mathbf{j})$$

$$= (h_4+2k_4)\,\mathbf{i}+(h_4-k_4)\,\mathbf{j}, \quad \text{by the definition of } T,$$

$$= (\lambda h_1+\mu h_2+2\lambda k_1+2\mu k_2)\,\mathbf{i}+(\lambda h_1+\mu h_2-\lambda k_1-\mu k_2)\,\mathbf{j}$$

$$= \lambda[(h_1+2k_1)\,\mathbf{i}+(h_1-k_1)\,\mathbf{j}]+\mu[(h_2+2k_2)\,\mathbf{i}+(h_2-k_2)\,\mathbf{j}]$$

$$= \lambda T(\mathbf{OP})+\mu T(\mathbf{OQ}).$$

The property which we have just demonstrated for the transformation holds for a wide class of transformations, called *linear transformations*. A *linear transformation* T is a transformation such that the image of the vector $\lambda\mathbf{x}+\mu\mathbf{y}$ is the vector sum of λ times the image of $\mathbf{x}$ and μ times the image of $\mathbf{y}$. In symbols, T is a linear transformation if, for any vectors $\mathbf{x}$, $\mathbf{y}$ and any numbers λ, μ

$$T(\lambda\mathbf{x}+\mu\mathbf{y}) = \lambda T(\mathbf{x})+\mu T(\mathbf{y}).$$

Ex. 3. By writing $\mathbf{x}$ in the form $\mathbf{x}+\mathbf{0}$, show that, for any linear transformation T, $T(\mathbf{O}) = \mathbf{0}$.

An example of a mapping, T, that is particularly easy to visualize geometrically is that in which the image P' of P is obtained by a half-turn about the origin (see Figure 13.1). The coordinates of $P'(x',y')$ in terms of $P(x,y)$ are given by

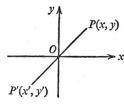

Fig. 13.1

$$x' = -x,$$

$$y' = -y$$

and thus the matrix of this transformation is

$$\begin{pmatrix} -1 & 0 \\ 0 & -1 \end{pmatrix}.$$

To see that T is a *linear* transformation, consider the points $P(h_1, k_1)$ and $Q(h_2, k_2)$ and suppose that

$$\mathbf{OR} = \lambda \mathbf{OP} + \mu \mathbf{OQ},$$

where

$$\mathbf{OR} = h_3\mathbf{i} + k_3\mathbf{j} = (\lambda h_1 + \mu h_2)\,\mathbf{i} + (\lambda k_1 + \mu k_2)\,\mathbf{j},$$

then

$$
\begin{aligned}
T(\mathbf{OR}) &= T(h_3\mathbf{i} + k_3\mathbf{j}) \\
&= -h_3\mathbf{i} - k_3\mathbf{j}, \quad \text{by the definition of } T, \\
&= -(\lambda h_1 + \mu h_2)\,\mathbf{i} - (\lambda k_1 + \mu k_2)\,\mathbf{j} \\
&= \lambda(-h_1\mathbf{i} - k_1\mathbf{j}) + \mu(-h_2\mathbf{i} - k_2\mathbf{j}) \\
&= \lambda T(\mathbf{OP}) + \mu T(\mathbf{OQ}).
\end{aligned}
$$

Thus, T is a linear transformation.

Ex. 4. Write down the matrix for the transformation

$$x' = kx,$$

$$y' = ky.$$

This transformation is called the *enlargement transformation*, or *dilatation transformation*. Draw a diagram and consider the effect on the points (2, 3), $(-1, 2)$ when k is (i) 2, (ii) $\frac{1}{2}$. Can you suggest a reason for the name?

Ex. 5. Prove that the enlargement transformation is linear.

Ex. 6. The function $f: R \to R$ defined by $f(x) = ax + b$ is a linear function (that is, its graph is a straight line). Show that, regarded as a mapping of points of the x axis into points of the x axis, it is not a linear transformation.

Ex. 7. The function $f: R \to R$ defined by $f(x) = x^2$ maps the x axis into itself. Prove that f is neither a linear function nor a linear transformation.

Example 1. *The transformation T maps the vector $\mathbf{OP}$ into the vector $\mathbf{OP}'$ where*

$$|\mathbf{OP}| = |\mathbf{OP}'| \quad \text{and} \quad \angle POP' = \alpha,$$

a fixed angle measured in the anticlockwise sense. Find the matrix for T and verify that T is a linear transformation.

Suppose $\mathbf{OP}$ makes an angle β with the x axis (see Figure 13.2). Writing $|\mathbf{OP}| = |\mathbf{OP}'| = r$ we have

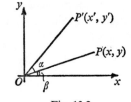

$$x' = r\cos(\alpha + \beta) = (r\cos\beta)\cos\alpha - (r\sin\beta)\sin\alpha,$$

$$y' = r\sin(\alpha + \beta) = (r\cos\beta)\sin\alpha + (r\sin\beta)\cos\alpha$$

and the transformation is given by

Fig. 13.2

$$x' = x\cos\alpha - y\sin\alpha,$$

$$y' = x\sin\alpha + y\cos\alpha.$$

The matrix of the transformation is therefore

$$\begin{pmatrix} \cos\alpha & -\sin\alpha \\ \sin\alpha & \cos\alpha \end{pmatrix}.$$

To prove that T is linear, consider $P(h_1, k_1)$, $Q(h_2, k_2)$, $R(h_3, k_3)$ where

$$\mathbf{OR} = \lambda\mathbf{OP} + \mu\mathbf{OQ},$$

$$T(\mathbf{OR}) = T(h_3\mathbf{i} + k_3\mathbf{j})$$

$$= (h_3\cos\alpha - k_3\sin\alpha)\,\mathbf{i} + (h_3\sin\alpha + k_3\cos\alpha)\,\mathbf{j}, \text{ by the equations for } T \text{ defined above,}$$

$$= [(\lambda h_1 + \mu h_2)\cos\alpha - (\lambda k_1 + \mu k_2)\sin\alpha]\,\mathbf{i}$$
$$+ [(\lambda h_1 + \mu h_2)\sin\alpha + (\lambda k_1 + \mu k_2)\cos\alpha]\,\mathbf{j}$$

$$= \lambda[(h_1\cos\alpha - k_1\sin\alpha)\,\mathbf{i} + (h_1\sin\alpha + k_1\cos\alpha)\,\mathbf{j}]$$
$$+ \mu[(h_2\cos\alpha - k_2\sin\alpha)\,\mathbf{i} + (h_2\sin\alpha + k_2\cos\alpha)\,\mathbf{j}]$$

$$= \lambda T(\mathbf{OP}) + \mu T(\mathbf{OQ})$$

and the result is complete.

3. LINEAR TRANSFORMATIONS AND THEIR MATRICES

Suppose we have a linear transformation T whose matrix A is given by

$$\mathbf{A} = \begin{pmatrix} a & b \\ c & d \end{pmatrix}.$$

Since $\mathbf{i}$ is the position vector of the point $I(1, 0)$ and $\mathbf{j}$ is the position vector of the point $J(0, 1)$, we have

$$T(\mathbf{i}) = a\mathbf{i} + c\mathbf{j}, \quad T(\mathbf{j}) = b\mathbf{i} + d\mathbf{j}.$$

Recalling that vectors may be written in column form, this result shows us that the first column of $\mathbf{A}$, regarded as a vector, is the position vector of the image of I and the second column of $\mathbf{A}$, regarded as a vector, is the position vector of J.

Ex. 8. Prove the converse of the result above that, if

$$T(\mathbf{i}) = a\mathbf{i} + c\mathbf{j} \quad \text{and} \quad T(\mathbf{j}) = b\mathbf{i} + d\mathbf{j},$$

then the matrix of T is A where

$$\mathbf{A} = \begin{pmatrix} a & b \\ c & d \end{pmatrix}.$$

(The results above show us that we are entitled to talk of **A** as *the matrix of a given linear transformation T only if we take* **i, j** *as our base vectors*: to put it another way, *if we change our coordinate system, we change the equations which define the linear transformation.* We shall continue in this chapter, unless specifically stated otherwise, to assume that our base vectors are **i** and **j**.)

Since any vector **x** may be expressed in the form

$$\mathbf{x} = \lambda\mathbf{i} + \mu\mathbf{j},$$

knowledge of the effect of T upon **i** and **j** enables us to predict the effect of T upon **x**; for

$$T(\mathbf{x}) = T(\lambda\mathbf{i} + \mu\mathbf{j})$$
$$= \lambda T(\mathbf{i}) + \mu T(\mathbf{j}).$$

Now suppose we have two linear transformations S, T whose matrices are respectively **A** and **W** where

$$\mathbf{A} = \begin{pmatrix} a & b \\ c & d \end{pmatrix}, \quad \mathbf{W} = \begin{pmatrix} w & x \\ y & z \end{pmatrix}.$$

If we define a new transformation U, called the *sum* of S and T by the equation

$$U(\mathbf{x}) = S(\mathbf{x}) + T(\mathbf{x})$$

it may be shown that

  (i) U is a linear transformation;
  (ii) U has matrix
$$\begin{pmatrix} a+w & b+x \\ c+y & d+z \end{pmatrix}.$$

For we have

  (i) $U(\lambda\mathbf{x}+\mu\mathbf{y}) = S(\lambda\mathbf{x}+\mu\mathbf{y}) + T(\lambda\mathbf{x}+\mu\mathbf{y})$, by definition of U,

$$= \lambda S(\mathbf{x}) + \mu S(\mathbf{y}) + \lambda T(\mathbf{x}) + \mu T(\mathbf{y}), \quad \text{since } S, T \text{ are linear,}$$

$$= \lambda(S(\mathbf{x}) + T(\mathbf{x})) + \mu(S(\mathbf{y}) + T(\mathbf{y}))$$

$$= \lambda U(\mathbf{x}) + \mu U(\mathbf{y}), \quad \text{by definition of } U,$$

and U is a linear transformation.

Again, (ii) to find the matrix of U, we have simply to find $U(\mathbf{i})$ and $U(\mathbf{j})$.

$$U(\mathbf{i}) = S(\mathbf{i}) + T(\mathbf{i}), \quad \text{by definition of } U,$$

$$= (a\mathbf{i} + c\mathbf{j}) + (w\mathbf{i} + y\mathbf{j})$$

$$= (a+w)\mathbf{i} + (c+y)\mathbf{j}.$$

Similarly
$$U(\mathbf{j}) = (b+x)\mathbf{i} + (d+z)\mathbf{j}$$

and the result (ii) follows.

244

Ex. 9. If $\qquad A = \begin{pmatrix} 1 & 2 \\ 2 & 3 \end{pmatrix}, \quad W = \begin{pmatrix} 2 & 1 \\ 1 & -1 \end{pmatrix}$

and P is the point $(1, 1)$ sketch in a diagram the effects of S, T and U upon the point P.

*Ex. 10. The transformation L is defined by

$$L(\mathbf{x}) = cT(\mathbf{x}).$$

(L is sometimes written as cT.) Prove that L is a linear transformation and that its matrix is

$$\begin{pmatrix} cw & cx \\ cy & cz \end{pmatrix}.$$

*Ex. 11. The transformation M is defined by

$$M(\mathbf{x}) = S[T(\mathbf{x})],$$

that is, $\mathbf{x}$ is first transformed under T into $T(\mathbf{x})$, and $T(\mathbf{x})$ is then transformed under S into $M(\mathbf{x})$. (M is called the *product of S and T* and may be written as ST.) Prove that M is a linear transformation and that its matrix is

$$\begin{pmatrix} aw+by & ax+bz \\ cw+dy & cx+dz \end{pmatrix}.$$

All the transformations mentioned so far have transformed points in a plane into points in the same plane. It is not difficult to generalize the concept of transformations of points in space to points in space. For example, the equations

$$x' = x,$$
$$y' = y,$$
$$z' = -z$$

define a transformation whose matrix is

$$\begin{pmatrix} 1 & 0 & 0 \\ 0 & 1 & 0 \\ 0 & 0 & -1 \end{pmatrix}.$$

Ex. 12. Give a geometrical interpretation for the transformation T whose matrix is

$$\begin{pmatrix} 1 & 0 & 0 \\ 0 & 1 & 0 \\ 0 & 0 & -1 \end{pmatrix}.$$

Exercise 13(a)

1. The transformation T is defined by the equations

$$x' = 2x-y,$$
$$y' = x-3y.$$

245

What is the image of the point $P(-1, 3)$? What point Q gives rise to the point $Q'(3, 5)$?

2. A transformation is represented by the matrix

$$\begin{pmatrix} 3 & -1 \\ -2 & -3 \end{pmatrix}.$$

Find the image of the point $(-1, 2)$ and also the point whose image is $(14, 9)$. What points are invariant under this transformation? (A point is *invariant* under a transformation if it maps into itself.)

3. What points are invariant under the transformation whose matrix is

$$\begin{pmatrix} 4 & -6 \\ 1 & -1 \end{pmatrix}?$$

4. A transformation whose matrix is

$$\begin{pmatrix} 1 & k \\ 0 & 1 \end{pmatrix}$$

is called a *shear*. Consider its effect upon the square with vertices $(0, 0)$, $(1, 0)$, $(1, 1)$, $(0, 1)$ and suggest a reason for the name.

5. Prove that the shear transformation defined in Question 4 is linear.

6. Describe the following transformation in geometrical terms:

$$x' = y,$$
$$y' = 0.$$

Draw a sketch to illustrate the transformation; mark in a number of points and their images.
  Prove that the transformation is linear.

7. Answer the same questions as in Question 6 for the transformation

$$x' = 2y,$$
$$y' = 2x.$$

8. Sketch a diagram to illustrate the effect of the transformation which has matrix

$$\begin{pmatrix} a & b \\ c & d \end{pmatrix}$$

on the four points $P(0, 0)$, $Q(1, 0)$, $R(1, 1)$, $S(0, 1)$.
  Determine the area of the image quadrilateral $P'Q'R'S'$.
  What can you say about the particular transformation in which $ad - bc = 0$?

9. Prove that the translation transformation defined by

$$x' = x,$$
$$y' = y + 1$$

is not a linear transformation.

246

10. Find the matrix of the linear transformation which maps the points U, J whose position vectors are given by

$$\mathbf{u} = \begin{pmatrix} 1 \\ 1 \end{pmatrix}, \quad \mathbf{j} = \begin{pmatrix} 0 \\ 1 \end{pmatrix}$$

into the points U', J' whose position vectors are given by

$$\mathbf{u}' = \begin{pmatrix} p \\ q \end{pmatrix}, \quad \mathbf{j}' = \begin{pmatrix} r \\ s \end{pmatrix}.$$

11. Write down the matrix for the shear, S, given by

$$x' = x + ky,$$

$$y' = y;$$

and the matrix for the reflection R, given by

$$x' = x,$$

$$y' = -y.$$

Two new transformations T_1 and T_2 are defined as follows. To find $T_1(P)$, find $R(P) = Q'$, say, and then find $S(Q')$; to find $T_2(P)$, find $S(P) = Q''$, say, and then find $R(Q'')$. Prove that T_1 and T_2 represent different transformations.

4. THE ALGEBRA OF MATRICES

The results we proved in the last section for the sums, numerical multiples and products of linear transformations and their associated matrices suggest that definitions should be given for the sums, numerical multiples and products of matrices so that, for example, the sum of two matrices **A** and **W** is the matrix of the sum of the two transformations whose matrices are respectively **A** and **W**. In this section we shall give some definitions for combining and manipulating matrices which are indeed motivated by the corresponding rules for linear transformations (proved only in the plane, but holding more generally). In Section 5 we shall show how the definitions of this section tie up with our previous work on linear transformations.

We begin by defining *equality of matrices*. Notice that such a definition is required: it is intuitively fairly clear that

$$\begin{pmatrix} 1 & 2 \\ 5 & 7 \end{pmatrix} \quad \text{and} \quad \begin{pmatrix} -4 & 6 \\ 1 & 2 \end{pmatrix}$$

are different matrices, but are

$$\begin{pmatrix} 0 & 2 \\ 5 & 1 \end{pmatrix} \quad \text{and} \quad \begin{pmatrix} 0 & 2 & 0 \\ 5 & 1 & 0 \end{pmatrix}$$

different?

(i) *Equality of matrices.*

Since column vectors are 3×1 matrices (in three dimensions) we must ensure that our rule for the equality of matrices includes as a special case the rule for equality of vectors.

Two matrices **A** and **B** are *equal if and only if*

(*a*) *they have the same number of rows and the same number of columns*;

(*b*) *the i, jth element of* **A** *equals the i, jth element of* **B**, *for all possible values of i and j.*

Example 2. If
$$\begin{pmatrix} 2 & a & 3 \\ 1 & 0 & b \end{pmatrix} = \begin{pmatrix} c & -2 & 3 \\ d & e & 4 \end{pmatrix},$$

then $a = -2$, $b = 4$, $c = 2$, $d = 1$, $e = 0$. The two matrices

$$\begin{pmatrix} 0 & 2 \\ 5 & 1 \end{pmatrix}$$

and
$$\begin{pmatrix} 0 & 2 & 0 \\ 5 & 1 & 0 \end{pmatrix}$$

are not equal.

(ii) *Addition of matrices.*

Two matrices are said to be *conformable for addition* if they have the same number of rows and the same number of columns.

By analogy with the corresponding rule for column vectors, we make the following definition: *if two matrices are conformable for addition,* **A**+**B** *is the matrix whose i, jth element is the sum of the i, jth elements of* **A** *and* **B**. *If* **A** *and* **B** *are not conformable for addition,* **A**+**B** *is not defined.*

Example 3. If
$$\mathbf{A} = \begin{pmatrix} 1 & -3 & 2 \\ 4 & 0 & 3 \\ 1 & -1 & 2 \end{pmatrix}, \quad \mathbf{B} = \begin{pmatrix} 2 & 2 & -3 \\ 1 & -3 & 4 \\ 3 & -3 & 1 \end{pmatrix},$$

then
$$\mathbf{A}+\mathbf{B} = \begin{pmatrix} 1+2 & -3+2 & 2-3 \\ 4+1 & 0-3 & 3+4 \\ 1+3 & -1-3 & 2+1 \end{pmatrix} = \begin{pmatrix} 3 & -1 & -1 \\ 5 & -3 & 7 \\ 4 & -4 & 3 \end{pmatrix}.$$

If
$$\mathbf{C} = \begin{pmatrix} 1 & 3 \\ 1 & 1 \\ 2 & 4 \end{pmatrix},$$

then **A**+**C** is not defined.

(iii) *Multiplication of matrices by numbers.*

Again working by analogy with column vectors, *if* **A** *is any matrix and k is any number, k***A** *is a matrix, conformable for addition with* **A**, *whose i, jth elements is k times the i, jth element of* **A**.

248

Example 4. If

$$A = \begin{pmatrix} 1 & 2 \\ 3 & -1 \\ 1 & -1 \end{pmatrix}, \quad 3A = \begin{pmatrix} 3 & 6 \\ 9 & -3 \\ 3 & -3 \end{pmatrix}, \quad -2A = \begin{pmatrix} -2 & -4 \\ -6 & 2 \\ -2 & 2 \end{pmatrix}.$$

We may now define the *subtraction* of two matrices **A** and **B** which are conformable for addition by the equation $A - B = A + (-1) B$.

Example 5. With the matrices **A** *and* **B** *of Example 3*

$$A - B = \begin{pmatrix} -1 & -5 & 5 \\ 3 & 3 & -1 \\ -2 & 2 & 1 \end{pmatrix}.$$

(iv) *Zero matrices.*

A *zero matrix is a matrix all of whose elements are zero.* Provided no confusion is likely to arise, a zero matrix may be written **0** but note that there are many different zero matrices; for example,

$$\begin{pmatrix} 0 \\ 0 \end{pmatrix} \quad \begin{pmatrix} 0 & 0 \\ 0 & 0 \end{pmatrix} \quad \begin{pmatrix} 0 & 0 & 0 \\ 0 & 0 & 0 \end{pmatrix}$$

are all zero matrices, and are all different.

(v) *Multiplication of matrices.*

Two matrices **A** and **B** are said to be *conformable for the product* **AB** if the number of columns in **A** is the same as the number of rows in **B**. We now define *the product* **AB** *of two matrices* **A** *and* **B** *which are conformable for the product* **AB** *as follows: the i, jth element of* **AB** *is obtained from the ith row of* **A** *and the jth column of* **B** *by multiplying together the corresponding elements and adding. If* **A**, **B** *are not conformable for the product* **AB**, *then* **AB** *is not defined.*

Example 6. If

$$A = \begin{pmatrix} 1 & 3 & 2 \\ 5 & -1 & 3 \\ 1 & 1 & 2 \end{pmatrix} \quad \text{and} \quad B = \begin{pmatrix} -1 & 1 & -1 \\ 2 & 0 & 2 \\ 0 & 3 & 1 \end{pmatrix},$$

then

$$AB = \begin{pmatrix} (1)(-1)+(3)(2)+(2)(0) & (1)(1)+(3)(0)+(2)(3) \\ (5)(-1)+(-1)(2)+(3)(0) & (5)(1)+(-1)(0)+(3)(3) \\ (1)(-1)+(1)(2)+(2)(0) & (1)(1)+(1)(0)+(2)(3) \end{pmatrix}$$

$$\begin{pmatrix} (1)(-1)+(3)(2)+(2)(1) \\ (5)(-1)+(-1)(2)+(3)(1) \\ (1)(-1)+(1)(2)+(2)(1) \end{pmatrix}$$

$$= \begin{pmatrix} 5 & 7 & 7 \\ -7 & 14 & -4 \\ 1 & 7 & 3 \end{pmatrix}.$$

If

$$C = \begin{pmatrix} 1 & 2 \\ -1 & 0 \\ 2 & 3 \end{pmatrix} \quad \text{then} \quad AC = \begin{pmatrix} 2 & 8 \\ 12 & 19 \\ 4 & 8 \end{pmatrix}$$

but **CA** is not defined.

Ex. 13. If

$$A = \begin{pmatrix} 3 & 2 & -1 \\ 1 & 0 & 3 \\ 2 & 2 & -1 \end{pmatrix}, \quad B = \begin{pmatrix} 6 & 0 & 2 \\ 1 & 1 & -1 \\ 2 & 3 & 0 \end{pmatrix}$$

find

(i) **A+B**; (ii) **2A−3B**; (iii) **AB**; (iv) **BA**.

Ex. 14. If

$$A = \begin{pmatrix} 1 & -1 \\ 2 & 1 \\ 0 & 2 \end{pmatrix}, \quad B = \begin{pmatrix} 2 & 3 & 1 \\ 3 & -2 & 0 \end{pmatrix}$$

find

(i) **AB**; (ii) **BA**.

*Ex. 15. If

$$A = \begin{pmatrix} 1 & -1 \\ 2 & 1 \end{pmatrix}, \quad B = \begin{pmatrix} 0 & 2 \\ 2 & 1 \end{pmatrix}, \quad C = \begin{pmatrix} 1 & 2 \\ 0 & 3 \end{pmatrix},$$

verify that

(i) **A+B = B+A**; (ii) **(A+B)+C = A+(B+C)**;

(iii) **A(BC) = (AB)C**; (iv) **A(B+C) = AB+AC**.

Show also that **AB ≠ BA**.

In Ex. 15 above, certain of the basic laws of algebra have been shown to hold good for the particular matrices **A, B, C**. With the definitions of equality, addition and multiplication we have given, the following laws may be shown to hold good for all matrices **A, B, C**, provided all the sums and products are defined:

(i) Matrix addition is
    (*a*) Commutative: **A+B = B+A**;
    (*b*) Associative: **A+(B+C) = (A+B)+C**.
(ii) Matrix multiplication is
    (*a*) Associative: **A(BC) = (AB) C**;
    (*b*) Distributive over addition: $\begin{cases} \mathbf{A(B+C) = AB+AC,} \\ \mathbf{(A+B)C = AC+BC.} \end{cases}$

However, matrix multiplication is non-commutative; indeed, two matrices **A, B** may be conformable for the product **AB** and yet **BA** is not defined. This is not to say that matrix multiplication is never commutative.

Ex. 16. If

$$A = \begin{pmatrix} 1 & 2 \\ 4 & 3 \end{pmatrix} \quad \text{and} \quad B = \begin{pmatrix} -1 & 4 \\ 8 & 3 \end{pmatrix},$$

verify that **AB = BA**.

250

A *unit or identity matrix* is a square matrix in which the elements of the leading diagonal (top left to bottom right) are all unity and every other element is zero. Thus, the 2×2 identity matrix is

$$\begin{pmatrix} 1 & 0 \\ 0 & 1 \end{pmatrix}$$

while the 3×3 identity matrix is

$$\begin{pmatrix} 1 & 0 & 0 \\ 0 & 1 & 0 \\ 0 & 0 & 1 \end{pmatrix}.$$

Provided that no confusion is likely to arise and the correct size (2×2, 3×3, ...) is obvious from the context, an identity matrix is denoted by the letter **I**.

Ex. 17. Show that, if **A** is any 2×2 matrix, **B** is any 3×2 matrix and **I** is the 2×2 identity matrix, (i) **AI** = **IA** = **A**; (ii) **BI** = **B**.

Ex. 18. Show that, if **I** is the 3×3 identity matrix and **A** is any matrix with three columns, **AI** = **A**.

5. LINEAR TRANSFORMATIONS
AND THEIR MATRICES (CONTINUED)

The rules for matrix addition and multiplication given above enable us to obtain a deeper insight into the machinery of linear transformations. If P has coordinates (x, y) and its image, P', has coordinates (x', y') then the position vectors (in column vector form) of P and P' are respectively

$$\mathbf{P} = \begin{pmatrix} x \\ y \end{pmatrix} \quad \text{and} \quad \mathbf{P'} = \begin{pmatrix} x' \\ y' \end{pmatrix}.$$

If we have a transformation P to P' defined by the matrix

$$\mathbf{A} = \begin{pmatrix} a & b \\ c & d \end{pmatrix}$$

then x, y, x', y' are related by the equations

$$x' = ax + by,$$
$$y' = cx + dy$$

and these may be written, on using the definition of multiplication of matrices, in the form of the matrix equation

$$\begin{pmatrix} x' \\ y' \end{pmatrix} = \begin{pmatrix} a & b \\ c & d \end{pmatrix} \begin{pmatrix} x \\ y \end{pmatrix}$$

or, more briefly, $\mathbf{p'} = \mathbf{Ap}.$ (1)

Furthermore, **A** *always represents a linear transformation*, for
$$\mathbf{A}(\lambda\mathbf{x}+\mu\mathbf{y}) = \lambda\mathbf{A}\mathbf{x}+\mu\mathbf{A}\mathbf{y}.$$
A second linear transformation p' to p'' with matrix **B** has the form
$$\mathbf{p}'' = \mathbf{B}\mathbf{p}' \tag{2}$$
and so, combining (1) and (2),
$$\mathbf{p}'' = \mathbf{B}(\mathbf{A}\mathbf{p})$$
$$= (\mathbf{B}\mathbf{A})\,\mathbf{p}.$$

Thus, if the linear transformation whose matrix is **A** is followed by the linear transformation whose matrix is **B**, the combined effect is a linear transformation whose matrix is **BA**.

In three-dimensional space, precisely similar results hold. Indeed, if **p**, **p**' are the position vectors (in column vector form) of the point P and its image P', and if **A** is a 3×3 matrix, then the linear transformation defined by **A** takes the matrix form $\quad \mathbf{p}' = \mathbf{A}\mathbf{p},$

which is precisely equation (1), although **p**', **A**, **p** have different meanings.

Example 7. The linear transformation P to P' of points in three-dimensional space is defined by the matrix:
$$\mathbf{A} = \begin{pmatrix} 0 & 2 & 1 \\ 3 & 1 & 2 \\ 3 & -1 & 1 \end{pmatrix}.$$

Show that, under this transformation,
  (i) *any point P is mapped into a point lying in a certain plane;*
  (ii) *all points of the line*
$$\frac{x-1}{1} = \frac{y+1}{1} = \frac{z-2}{-2}$$

are mapped into the same point.
  (iii) *Find the set of points that are mapped into the origin.*

  (i) The transformation is given by the equations
$$x' = 2y+z,$$
$$y' = 3x+y+2z,$$
$$z' = 3x-y+z.$$

But $y'-z' = x'$ and so all points map into the plane $x-y+z = 0$.

  (ii) A general point P of the given line has coordinates $(\lambda+1, \lambda-1, -2\lambda+2)$. Thus, the position vector of the image of P is given by
$$\begin{pmatrix} 0 & 2 & 1 \\ 3 & 1 & 2 \\ 3 & -1 & 1 \end{pmatrix} \begin{pmatrix} \lambda+1 \\ \lambda-1 \\ -2\lambda+2 \end{pmatrix} = \begin{pmatrix} 0 \\ 6 \\ 6 \end{pmatrix},$$

and so all points of the given line map onto the point $(0, 6, 6)$.

252

(iii) If the image of the point $P(x, y, z)$ is the origin, then x, y, z satisfy the equations

$$(a) \qquad 2y + z = 0,$$
$$(b) \quad 3x + y + 2z = 0,$$
$$(c) \quad 3x - y + z = 0.$$

Planes (a) and (b) meet in the line $x = y = -\frac{1}{2}z$ which clearly lies also in plane (c). Thus, all points with coordinates of the form $(\lambda, \lambda, -2\lambda)$ map into the origin.

Exercise 13(b)

1. If
$$A = \begin{pmatrix} 3 & 2 & 4 \\ -1 & 3 & 2 \end{pmatrix} \quad \text{and} \quad B = \begin{pmatrix} -1 & 3 & 0 \\ 2 & -2 & 4 \end{pmatrix},$$
evaluate

(i) $A + B$;   (ii) $A - B$;   (iii) $2A - B$;   (iv) $2A + 3B$.

2. If
$$A = \begin{pmatrix} -1 & 2 & 1 \\ 3 & 0 & 3 \\ 1 & 2 & -1 \end{pmatrix} \quad \text{and} \quad B = \begin{pmatrix} 1 & 2 & 1 \\ 1 & 1 & 3 \\ 2 & -1 & 2 \end{pmatrix},$$
evaluate

(i) $A + B$;   (ii) $2A - 3B$;   (iii) $3A - B$;   (iv) $4A - 2B$.

3. If
$$A = \begin{pmatrix} -1 & 2 \\ 2 & 3 \end{pmatrix}, \quad B = \begin{pmatrix} 3 & 0 \\ 1 & 1 \end{pmatrix}, \quad C = \begin{pmatrix} 0 & 1 \\ 1 & 2 \end{pmatrix},$$
evaluate

(i) $A - 3B + 2C$;   (ii) $2A(B - C)$;   (iii) $A^2 - AB + AC$.

Verify that $(A + B)^2 = A^2 + AB + BA + B^2$; can this be put in the simpler form $A^2 + 2AB + B^2$?

4. A, B, C are all 3×3 matrices. Remove brackets in the following expressions:

(i) $A(B - 2C)$;   (ii) $(A + B)(A - C)$;   (iii) $(A - B - C)(A + B + C)$.

5. If
$$A = \begin{pmatrix} 1 & 1 \\ 2 & -3 \\ 1 & 2 \end{pmatrix}, \quad B = \begin{pmatrix} 2 & 1 & 2 \\ 3 & -1 & 0 \end{pmatrix},$$
find AB and BA.

6. If
$$A = \begin{pmatrix} 1 & 0 & 2 \\ 0 & -1 & -1 \\ 2 & 1 & 1 \end{pmatrix}, \quad B = \begin{pmatrix} 3 & 1 & -2 \\ 1 & -1 & -2 \\ 1 & 1 & 1 \end{pmatrix},$$
find

(i) AB;   (ii) BA;   (iii) A^2;

(iv) B^2;   (v) $(2A - B)^2$;   (vi) $(A + 2B)(A - B)$.

7. If
$$A = \begin{pmatrix} 2 & 1 & -1 \\ 1 & 1 & 2 \\ -1 & 2 & 1 \end{pmatrix}, \quad B = \begin{pmatrix} 0 & 2 & 1 \\ 1 & 3 & 0 \\ -2 & -1 & 2 \end{pmatrix},$$

find

(i) **AB**; (ii) **BA**; (iii) **A²**;

(iv) **B²**; (v) **A² − 4B²**; (vi) **(A − 2B) (A + 2B)**.

8. If

$$A = \begin{pmatrix} 1 & 3 & 4 \\ -2 & 1 & -2 \\ 1 & 2 & 3 \end{pmatrix}, \quad B = \begin{pmatrix} -1 & 0 & 1 \\ 2 & 1 & 0 \\ 0 & 2 & 3 \end{pmatrix}, \quad C = \begin{pmatrix} 1 & -1 \\ 2 & 1 \\ -2 & 1 \end{pmatrix},$$

evaluate

(i) **AC**; (ii) **BC**; (iii) **A + 2B**.

Verify that **(A + 2B) C = AC + 2BC**.

9. If

$$A = \begin{pmatrix} 1 & 2 \\ -3 & 0 \\ 2 & -1 \end{pmatrix}, \quad B = \begin{pmatrix} -1 & 2 & 0 \\ 1 & 0 & 1 \end{pmatrix},$$

find

(i) **AB**; (ii) **BA**; (iii) **ABA**; (iv) **BAB**.

10. A matrix **M** is said to be *transposed* into the matrix **M′** if the first row of **M** becomes the first column of **M′**, the second row of **M** becomes the second column of **M′**, and so on. Write down the transposes of the matrices:

$$M = \begin{pmatrix} x \\ y \\ z \end{pmatrix}, \quad T = \begin{pmatrix} 0 & b & 0 \\ 0 & 0 & c \\ a & 0 & 0 \end{pmatrix}.$$

Calculate the matrix products **M′M** and **TM**; show also that **(TM)′ = M′T′**.

If the elements of **M** are the Cartesian coordinates of a point P, what information is provided by the element of **M′M**?

If the matrix **T** describes a transformation of the point P of three-dimensional space, interpret geometrically the equation:

$$(TM)' \, (TM) = M'M,$$

and find all appropriate values of a, b and c. (SMP)

11. Show that under the linear transformation defined by the matrix

$$A = \begin{pmatrix} 3 & -1 & -1 \\ 2 & 2 & 1 \\ 8 & 0 & -1 \end{pmatrix}$$

any point P in space is mapped into a certain plane, and find the equation of this plane.

Show further that all points of the line

$$\frac{x-1}{1} = \frac{y-1}{-5} = \frac{z-3}{8}$$

are mapped into a certain point, and find the coordinates of this point.

12. Show that, under the linear transformation defined by the matrix

$$A = \begin{pmatrix} 2 & 1 & 1 \\ 3 & 2 & 1 \\ 1 & 1 & 0 \end{pmatrix},$$

any point P in space is mapped into a certain plane, and find the equation of this plane.

254

Show also that all points of the line

$$\frac{x-1}{1} = \frac{y-2}{-1} = \frac{z-1}{-1}$$

map into a certain point and find the coordinates of this point.

13. The linear transformation T of three-dimensional space into itself maps the point P into the point P' and the point Q into the point Q'. The points P and Q are distinct. Show that
  (i) if P' and Q' are distinct, then all points of the line PQ map into points of the line $P'Q'$.
  (ii) if P' and Q' coincide, then all points of the line PQ map into P'.

14. The linear transformation T of the plane into itself has matrix

$$\mathbf{A} = \begin{pmatrix} 1 & -2 \\ 1 & -1 \end{pmatrix}.$$

Show that T maps the interior of the triangle $O(0, 0)$, $P(2, 0)$, $Q(1, 1)$ into the interior of another triangle $O'P'Q'$ and find the coordinates of the vertices O', P', Q'.
  Prove also that the image of the centroid of the triangle OPQ is the centroid of the triangle $O'P'Q'$.

Miscellaneous Exercise 13

1. If

$$\mathbf{A} = \begin{pmatrix} a & b \\ c & d \end{pmatrix}, \quad \text{does} \quad \begin{pmatrix} x' \\ y' \end{pmatrix} = \mathbf{A} \begin{pmatrix} x \\ y \end{pmatrix}$$

map a set of parallel lines into another set of parallel lines when $ad \neq bc$?
  What happens to the transformation defined by $\mathbf{A}$ when $ad = bc$? Is it still one-one? (A transformation is said to be *one-one* if each image P' arises from a unique P.)

2. What are the position vectors of the images of the points whose position vectors are $\mathbf{i}$, $\mathbf{j}$, $\mathbf{k}$ under the linear transformation whose matrix, $\mathbf{A}$, is given by

$$\mathbf{A} = \begin{pmatrix} a_1 & a_2 & a_3 \\ b_1 & b_2 & b_3 \\ c_1 & c_2 & c_3 \end{pmatrix}?$$

Describe geometrically the linear transformation whose matrix is

$$\begin{pmatrix} 1 & 1 & 0 \\ 0 & 1 & 0 \\ 0 & 0 & 1 \end{pmatrix}.$$

3. Describe the effect of the linear transformations whose matrices are:

(i) $\begin{pmatrix} 1 & 1 \\ 1 & 0 \end{pmatrix}$;   (ii) $\begin{pmatrix} 2 & -1 \\ -4 & 2 \end{pmatrix}$;   (iii) $\begin{pmatrix} 0 & 0 \\ 0 & 0 \end{pmatrix}$.

For each transformation determine the set of vectors which are transformed into the zero vector.

4. **A** is the matrix of the transformation that rotates all points in the plane through an angle α; **B** is the matrix of the transformation that rotates all points in the plane through an angle β. Calculate **BA** and simplify the resulting matrix. What result does this illustrate?

5. Can you find a point P with position vector **x** which is mapped into itself by the tranformation whose matrix is **A**, where

$$\mathbf{A} = \begin{pmatrix} 8 & 13 \\ -2 & -2 \end{pmatrix}?$$

Can you determine any real values of λ which would enable you to find non-zero vectors **x** such that $\mathbf{Ax} = \lambda \mathbf{x}$? If you can, find both λ and the corresponding vectors.

6. Answer the same questions as in Question 5 for the linear transformations with matrices

(i) $\begin{pmatrix} 3 & 5 \\ 7 & 5 \end{pmatrix}$;

(ii) $\begin{pmatrix} 2 & -1 \\ -4 & 5 \end{pmatrix}$.

7. The transpose of the matrix **A**, denoted by **A′**, is defined as the matrix whose ith row is the same as the ith column of **A**. For example, if

$$\mathbf{A} = \begin{pmatrix} 1 & -3 & 2 \\ 1 & 4 & 5 \end{pmatrix}, \quad \mathbf{B} = \begin{pmatrix} 2 & 1 & 3 \\ 4 & 2 & 1 \\ 3 & -5 & -2 \end{pmatrix},$$

then

$$\mathbf{A'} = \begin{pmatrix} 1 & 1 \\ -3 & 4 \\ 2 & 5 \end{pmatrix} \quad \text{and} \quad \mathbf{B'} = \begin{pmatrix} 2 & 4 & 3 \\ 1 & 2 & -5 \\ 3 & 1 & -2 \end{pmatrix}.$$

If **C** and **D** are both 2×2 matrices, prove that $\mathbf{(CD)'} = \mathbf{D'C'}$.

8. A symmetric matrix **A** is a matrix such that $\mathbf{A'} = \mathbf{A}$. If **A** and **B** are two symmetric matrices, find a further condition that **A** and **B** must satisfy to ensure that **AB** is a symmetric matrix.

9. A square matrix is said to be *diagonal* if its only non-zero elements lie on the leading diagonal (that is, top left to bottom right). For example, the following two matrices are diagonal:

$$\begin{pmatrix} 2 & 0 \\ 0 & -3 \end{pmatrix}, \quad \begin{pmatrix} 2 & 0 & 0 \\ 0 & 3 & 0 \\ 0 & 0 & 1 \end{pmatrix}.$$

Prove that, if $\mathbf{D_1}$, $\mathbf{D_2}$ are two 3×3 diagonal matrices, then

(i) $\mathbf{D_1 D_2}$ is a diagonal matrix;   (ii) $\mathbf{D_1 D_2} = \mathbf{D_2 D_1}$;

(iii) $\mathbf{D_1'} = \mathbf{D_1}$.

If A is a 3×3 matrix and **D** any diagonal 3×3 matrix, what can you say about A if $\mathbf{AD} = \mathbf{DA}$?

10. A linear transformation is given by the matrix

$$\begin{pmatrix} 1 & 3 & 2 \\ 2 & 1 & 1 \\ 0 & 5 & 3 \end{pmatrix}.$$

256

Show that
   (i) all points are mapped into points on a certain plane;
   (ii) all points on the line
$$\frac{x-1}{1} = \frac{y-1}{3} = \frac{z-1}{-5}.$$
are mapped into the same point.

11. Let **A, B, C** be real 2×2 matrices and write

$$[A, B] = AB - BA, \text{ etc.}$$

Prove that

   (i) $[A, A] = 0$;

   (ii) $[[A, B], C] + [[B, C], A] + [[C, A], B] = 0$;

   (iii) $[A, B] = I \Rightarrow [A, B^m] = mB^{m-1}$ for all positive integers m.

At each step you should state clearly any properties of matrices which you use.
   The *trace Tr(A)*, of a matrix

$$A = \begin{pmatrix} a_{11} & a_{12} \\ a_{21} & a_{22} \end{pmatrix}$$

is defined by $Tr(A) = a_{11} + a_{22}.$
Prove that:

   (iv) $Tr(A + B) = Tr(A) + Tr(B)$;

   (v) $Tr(AB) = Tr(BA)$;

   (vi) $Tr(I) = 2$.

Deduce that there are no matrices satisfying $[A, B] = I$. Does this in any way invalidate the statement in (iii)?   (M.E.I.)

12. If **M** denotes the matrix $\begin{pmatrix} 1 & 0 \\ 1 & 2 \end{pmatrix}$

and **I** denotes the matrix $\begin{pmatrix} 1 & 0 \\ 0 & 1 \end{pmatrix}$

prove that $M^2 = 3M - 2I.$

Prove further that, if n is any positive integer,

$$M^n = (2^n - 1)M - 2(2^{n-1} - 1)I. \qquad \text{(M.E.I. adapted)}$$

13. Prove that a linear transformation T of three-dimensional space into itself maps the interior of a tetrahedron into the interior of the image tetrahedron. Prove further that the image of the centroid of the given tetrahedron is the centroid of the image tetrahedron.

14. *Matrices* 2

1. THE INVERSE OF A MATRIX

The reader has seen that a definition of multiplication of matrices may be formulated which has some of the properties of multiplication of real numbers. Notably, if the matrices are square and of the same order (say three, for the sake of argument), then the matrix **I**, where

$$\mathbf{I} = \begin{pmatrix} 1 & 0 & 0 \\ 0 & 1 & 0 \\ 0 & 0 & 1 \end{pmatrix},$$

has some of the properties of the number 1.

Ex. 1. The linear transformation T maps points of the x-axis according to the rule
$$T(x) = kx.$$
Interpret T in the case where $k = 1$.

Ex. 2. The linear transformation T maps points in a plane into points in the same plane according to the rule
$$T(\mathbf{X}) = \mathbf{A}x \quad \text{where} \quad \mathbf{A} \text{ is a } 2 \times 2 \text{ matrix.}$$
Interpret T in the case where
$$\mathbf{A} = \begin{pmatrix} 1 & 0 \\ 0 & 1 \end{pmatrix}.$$

Ex. 3. Interpret the matrix
$$\mathbf{I} = \begin{pmatrix} 1 & 0 & 0 \\ 0 & 1 & 0 \\ 0 & 0 & 1 \end{pmatrix}$$
as the matrix of a linear transformation.

The question thus naturally arises: 'Is there a matrix analogue to the reciprocal of a number?'; that is, 'given a square matrix **A**, does there exist a matrix **B** such that $\mathbf{BA} = \mathbf{I}$?'

We begin our investigation by actually constructing such a matrix **B** for a given 2×2 matrix **A**. Suppose

$$\mathbf{A} = \begin{pmatrix} 1 & 3 \\ 2 & 7 \end{pmatrix}.$$

We effect the construction in two stages: we first form a matrix $\mathbf{C}_1$ such that

258

the product $C_1 A$ has as its first column $\begin{pmatrix} 1 \\ 0 \end{pmatrix}$; we then form a matrix C_2 such that $C_2(C_1 A) = I$. By associativity, it follows that $C_2 C_1 = B$.

Since the element a_{11} of A is already 1, we have only to assume that $C_1 A$ makes the element of the second row and first column of the product zero. Choose

$$C_1 = \begin{pmatrix} 1 & 0 \\ -2 & 1 \end{pmatrix}; \quad \text{then} \quad C_1 A = \begin{pmatrix} 1 & 3 \\ 0 & 1 \end{pmatrix}.$$

Next choose

$$C_2 = \begin{pmatrix} 1 & -3 \\ 0 & 1 \end{pmatrix}; \quad \text{then} \quad C_2(C_1 A) = \begin{pmatrix} 1 & 0 \\ 0 & 1 \end{pmatrix}.$$

Thus if we take

$$B = C_2 C_1 = \begin{pmatrix} 7 & -3 \\ -2 & 1 \end{pmatrix} \quad \text{we have} \quad BA = I.$$

We write $B = A^{-1}$ and call A^{-1} the *inverse of* A.

(Notice that we have not yet justified the use of the definite article 'the': in fact, B *is* unique, although the intermediate matrices C_1 and C_2 are not. Notice also that we have shown that $BA = I$ but not that $AB = I$ although this latter equation does indeed hold, as we shall soon show.)

In this example, the choice of C_1 and C_2 was determined by trial and error. Whilst this is easy for 2×2 matrices, in more complicated cases we shall need a more general method. This is given by considering the so-called *elementary row operations* on a matrix.

We shall consider the 3×3 matrix

$$A = \begin{pmatrix} a_{11} & a_{12} & a_{13} \\ a_{21} & a_{22} & a_{23} \\ a_{31} & a_{32} & a_{33} \end{pmatrix}$$

although our results will easily be seen to generalize to the $n \times n$ case (and, in particular, to cover the 2×2 case).

(i) *The first elementary row operation*: *the interchange of two rows of* A.
Consider the matrix

$$E_1 = \begin{pmatrix} 1 & 0 & 0 \\ 0 & 0 & 1 \\ 0 & 1 & 0 \end{pmatrix},$$

$$E_1 A = \begin{pmatrix} a_{11} & a_{12} & a_{13} \\ a_{31} & a_{32} & a_{33} \\ a_{21} & a_{22} & a_{23} \end{pmatrix}$$

and the effect of pre-multiplication by E_1 has been to interchange row 2 and row 3 of A. A can be any 3×3 matrix; taking $A = I$, since $E_1 I = E_1$, E_1 is formed by interchanging row 2 and row 3 of I. If r_i, r_i' represent the ith rows of $\mathbf{A}$ and $\mathbf{E}_1\mathbf{A}$ respectively, the effect may be symbolically expressed by $r_1' = r_1, r_2' = r_3, r_3' = r_2$.

Similarly

$$\mathbf{E}_2 = \begin{pmatrix} 0 & 0 & 1 \\ 0 & 1 & 0 \\ 1 & 0 & 0 \end{pmatrix}$$

has the effect of interchanging the first and third rows of

$$\mathbf{A} \; (r_1' = r_3, r_2' = r_2, r_3' = r_1.)$$

Ex. 4. Show that $\mathbf{E}_1$ is the matrix of the linear transformation which reflects points in the plane $y = z$.

Ex. 5. Interpret $\mathbf{E}_2$ as the matrix of a linear transformation.

(ii) *The second elementary row operation: the multiplication of a row of* $\mathbf{A}$ *by a non-zero constant c.*

Consider

$$\mathbf{C}_1 = \begin{pmatrix} c & 0 & 0 \\ 0 & 1 & 0 \\ 0 & 0 & 1 \end{pmatrix},$$

$$\mathbf{C}_1\mathbf{A} = \begin{pmatrix} ca_{11} & ca_{12} & ca_{13} \\ a_{21} & a_{22} & a_{23} \\ a_{31} & a_{32} & a_{33} \end{pmatrix}$$

and the effect of pre-multiplication by $\mathbf{C}_1$ has been to multiply the first row of $\mathbf{A}$ by c ($r_1' = cr_1, r_2' = r_2, r_3' = r_3$). Notice again that $\mathbf{C}_1$ has been obtained by performing the required elementary row operation on $\mathbf{I}$. (The reader may wonder why the restriction $c \neq 0$ has been imposed; so far as the result is concerned, this is of course unnecessary, but multiplication of a row by zero must be specifically excluded when we use elementary row operations to determine inverses.)

Ex. 6. Interpret $\mathbf{C}_1$ as the matrix of a linear transformation.

(iii) *The third elementary row operation: addition to any one row a constant multiple c of another row.*

Consider

$$\mathbf{M}_1 = \begin{pmatrix} 1 & 0 & 0 \\ 0 & 1 & 0 \\ 0 & c & 1 \end{pmatrix},$$

$$\mathbf{M}_1\mathbf{A} = \begin{pmatrix} a_{11} & a_{12} & a_{13} \\ a_{21} & a_{22} & a_{23} \\ a_{31}+ca_{21} & a_{32}+ca_{22} & a_{33}+ca_{23} \end{pmatrix}$$

and we have a matrix whose first two rows are those of $\mathbf{A}$, but whose third row is obtained by adding to each element of the third row of $\mathbf{A}$, c times the corresponding element of the second row ($r_1' = r_1, r_2' = r_2, r_3' = r_3+cr_2$).

260

Ex. 7. Interpret $\mathbf{M}_1$ as the matrix of a linear transformation.

Matrices such as $\mathbf{E}$, $\mathbf{M}$ and $\mathbf{C}$, which effect elementary row operations are called *elementary matrices*. Let us now reconsider the reduction of

$$\mathbf{A} = \begin{pmatrix} 1 & 3 \\ 2 & 7 \end{pmatrix}$$

to a unit matrix in terms of pre-multiplications by elementary matrices. We wish to effect the transformations

$$\begin{pmatrix} 1 & 3 \\ 2 & 7 \end{pmatrix} \to \begin{pmatrix} 1 & 3 \\ 0 & 1 \end{pmatrix} \to \begin{pmatrix} 1 & 0 \\ 0 & 1 \end{pmatrix}.$$

The first transformation may be obtained by leaving the first row as it is and subtracting from the second row twice the first row

$$(r_1' = r_1, \; r_2' = r_2 - 2r_1)$$

that is, by multiplying by the elementary matrix

$$\mathbf{C}_1 = \begin{pmatrix} 1 & 0 \\ -2 & 1 \end{pmatrix}.$$

Operating thus on $\mathbf{A}$ we obtain

$$\begin{pmatrix} 1 & 3 \\ 0 & 1 \end{pmatrix}.$$

We now leave the second row as it is and subtract from the first row three times the second row $(r_1' = r_1 - 3r_2, \; r_2' = r_2)$; that is, we multiply by

$$\mathbf{C}_2 = \begin{pmatrix} 1 & -3 \\ 0 & 1 \end{pmatrix}$$

and the reduction is complete.

If we attempt a reduction of any square matrix $\mathbf{A}$ to unit form by a succession of row operations represented by the elementary matrices $\mathbf{X}_1 \ldots \mathbf{X}_n$, then

$$\mathbf{X}_n \mathbf{X}_{n-1} \ldots \mathbf{X}_2 \mathbf{X}_1 \mathbf{A} = \mathbf{I}$$

and $\quad \mathbf{X}_n \mathbf{X}_{n-1} \ldots \mathbf{X}_2 \mathbf{X}_1 \mathbf{I} = \mathbf{X}_n \mathbf{X}_{n-1} \ldots \mathbf{X}_2 \mathbf{X}_1 = \mathbf{A}^{-1}.$

Thus, in a practical reduction we perform the successive row operations on two series of matrices, one side starting with $\mathbf{A}$ and finishing with $\mathbf{I}$, the other side starting with $\mathbf{I}$ and finishing with $\mathbf{A}^{-1}$ (see Example 1).

Ex. 8. If A is the matrix of a linear transformation T, and if A^{-1} exists, interpret A^{-1} as the matrix of a linear transformation.

Example 1. If $\qquad \mathbf{A} = \begin{pmatrix} 3 & 4 \\ -1 & 2 \end{pmatrix},$

find $\mathbf{B}$ *such that* $\mathbf{BA} = \mathbf{I}.$

$$\begin{pmatrix} 3 & 4 \\ -1 & 2 \end{pmatrix} \qquad\qquad \begin{pmatrix} 1 & 0 \\ 0 & 1 \end{pmatrix}$$

$$\begin{pmatrix} -1 & 2 \\ 3 & 4 \end{pmatrix} \begin{matrix} r_1' = r_2 \\ r_2' = r_1 \end{matrix} \qquad \begin{pmatrix} 0 & 1 \\ 1 & 0 \end{pmatrix}$$

$$\begin{pmatrix} -1 & 2 \\ 0 & 10 \end{pmatrix} \begin{matrix} r_1' = r_1 \\ r_2' = r_2 + 3r_1 \end{matrix} \qquad \begin{pmatrix} 0 & 1 \\ 1 & 3 \end{pmatrix}$$

$$\begin{pmatrix} -5 & 10 \\ 0 & 10 \end{pmatrix} \begin{matrix} r_1' = 5r_1 \\ r_2' = r_2 \end{matrix} \qquad \begin{pmatrix} 0 & 5 \\ 1 & 3 \end{pmatrix}$$

$$\begin{pmatrix} -5 & 0 \\ 0 & 10 \end{pmatrix} \begin{matrix} r_1' = r_1 - r_2 \\ r_2' = r_2 \end{matrix} \qquad \begin{pmatrix} -1 & 2 \\ 1 & 3 \end{pmatrix}$$

$$\begin{pmatrix} 1 & 0 \\ 0 & 10 \end{pmatrix} \begin{matrix} r_1' = -r_1/5 \\ r_2' = r_2 \end{matrix} \qquad \begin{pmatrix} \frac{1}{5} & -\frac{2}{5} \\ 1 & 3 \end{pmatrix}$$

$$\begin{pmatrix} 1 & 0 \\ 0 & 1 \end{pmatrix} \begin{matrix} r_1' = r_1 \\ r_2' = r_2/10 \end{matrix} \qquad \begin{pmatrix} \frac{1}{5} & -\frac{2}{5} \\ \frac{1}{10} & \frac{3}{10} \end{pmatrix}$$

Thus
$$\mathbf{B} = \begin{pmatrix} \frac{1}{5} & -\frac{2}{5} \\ \frac{1}{10} & \frac{3}{10} \end{pmatrix}.$$

Notice that, in the third transformation, we multiplied the first row by 5 to avoid introducing fractions for a little longer—an artifice worth remembering. With practice, the reader will learn to contract some of the working, though it is best to write it out in full at first. It is always advisable to check one's working by computing **BA.**

Ex. 9. Find, using elementary row operations, matrices **B** such that **BA** = **I** in each of the following cases:

(i) $\mathbf{A} = \begin{pmatrix} 5 & 2 \\ 7 & 3 \end{pmatrix};$ (ii) $\mathbf{A} = \begin{pmatrix} 2 & 3 \\ -2 & -4 \end{pmatrix};$

(iii) $\mathbf{A} = \begin{pmatrix} 12 & -5 \\ 5 & -2 \end{pmatrix};$ (iv) $\mathbf{A} = \begin{pmatrix} 2 & 5 \\ 3 & 9 \end{pmatrix}.$

Example 2. *If*
$$\mathbf{A} = \begin{pmatrix} 1 & 2 & 5 \\ 2 & 3 & 4 \\ 1 & 1 & 2 \end{pmatrix},$$

find **B** *such that* **BA** = **I.**

$$\begin{pmatrix} 1 & 2 & 5 \\ 2 & 3 & 4 \\ 1 & 1 & 2 \end{pmatrix} \qquad\qquad \begin{pmatrix} 1 & 0 & 0 \\ 0 & 1 & 0 \\ 0 & 0 & 1 \end{pmatrix}$$

$$\begin{pmatrix} 1 & 2 & 5 \\ 0 & -1 & -6 \\ 1 & 1 & 2 \end{pmatrix} \quad r_2' = r_2 - 2r_1 \quad \begin{pmatrix} 1 & 0 & 0 \\ -2 & 1 & 0 \\ 0 & 0 & 1 \end{pmatrix}$$

$$\begin{pmatrix} 1 & 2 & 5 \\ 0 & -1 & -6 \\ 0 & -1 & -3 \end{pmatrix} \quad r_3' = r_3 - r_1 \quad \begin{pmatrix} 1 & 0 & 0 \\ -2 & 1 & 0 \\ -1 & 0 & 1 \end{pmatrix}$$

$$\begin{pmatrix} 1 & 2 & 5 \\ 0 & -1 & -6 \\ 0 & 0 & 3 \end{pmatrix} \quad r_3' = r_3 - r_2 \quad \begin{pmatrix} 1 & 0 & 0 \\ -2 & 1 & 0 \\ 1 & -1 & 1 \end{pmatrix}$$

$$\begin{pmatrix} 1 & 0 & -7 \\ 0 & -1 & -6 \\ 0 & 0 & 3 \end{pmatrix} \quad r_1' = r_1 + 2r_2 \quad \begin{pmatrix} -3 & 2 & 0 \\ -2 & 1 & 0 \\ 1 & -1 & 1 \end{pmatrix}$$

$$\begin{pmatrix} 1 & 0 & -7 \\ 0 & -1 & 0 \\ 0 & 0 & 3 \end{pmatrix} \quad r_2' = r_2 + 2r_3 \quad \begin{pmatrix} -3 & 2 & 0 \\ 0 & -1 & 2 \\ 1 & -1 & 1 \end{pmatrix}$$

$$\begin{pmatrix} 1 & 0 & 0 \\ 0 & -1 & 0 \\ 0 & 0 & 3 \end{pmatrix} \quad r_1' = r_1 + \tfrac{7}{3}r_3 \quad \begin{pmatrix} -\tfrac{2}{3} & -\tfrac{1}{3} & \tfrac{7}{3} \\ 0 & -1 & 2 \\ 1 & -1 & 1 \end{pmatrix}$$

$$\begin{pmatrix} 1 & 0 & 0 \\ 0 & 1 & 0 \\ 0 & 0 & 3 \end{pmatrix} \quad r_2' = -r_2 \quad \begin{pmatrix} -\tfrac{2}{3} & -\tfrac{1}{3} & \tfrac{7}{3} \\ 0 & 1 & -2 \\ 1 & -1 & 1 \end{pmatrix}$$

$$\begin{pmatrix} 1 & 0 & 0 \\ 0 & 1 & 0 \\ 0 & 0 & 1 \end{pmatrix} \quad r_3' = \tfrac{1}{3}r_3 \quad \begin{pmatrix} -\tfrac{2}{3} & -\tfrac{1}{3} & \tfrac{7}{3} \\ 0 & 1 & -2 \\ \tfrac{1}{3} & -\tfrac{1}{3} & \tfrac{1}{3} \end{pmatrix}$$

Thus
$$\mathbf{B} = \begin{pmatrix} -\tfrac{2}{3} & -\tfrac{1}{3} & \tfrac{7}{3} \\ 0 & 1 & -2 \\ \tfrac{1}{3} & -\tfrac{1}{3} & \tfrac{1}{3} \end{pmatrix}.$$

Ex. 10. Find, using elementary row operations, matrices $\mathbf{B}$ such that $\mathbf{BA} = \mathbf{I}$ in each of the following cases:

(i) $\mathbf{A} = \begin{pmatrix} 6 & 8 & 5 \\ 3 & 5 & 3 \\ 2 & 3 & 2 \end{pmatrix}$; (ii) $\mathbf{A} = \begin{pmatrix} 4 & 7 & 3 \\ 2 & 5 & 2 \\ 5 & 13 & 5 \end{pmatrix}$;

(iii) $A = \begin{pmatrix} 4 & 3 & 5 \\ 4 & 2 & 3 \\ 6 & 3 & 5 \end{pmatrix};$
(iv) $A = \begin{pmatrix} 4 & 1 & 1 \\ 3 & 2 & 3 \\ 4 & 3 & 4 \end{pmatrix}.$

Having determined the inverses of some specific matrices, we next consider whether all square matrices **A** have an inverse. The perceptive reader may have observed that the process outlined above breaks down if a complete row of zeros is obtained. In fact, if this occurs at any stage, **A** has no inverse. Matrices for which no inverse can be found are called *singular matrices*; matrices which have an inverse are called *non-singular matrices*. The proof of a necessary and sufficient condition for singularity is deferred to the next section.

Before leaving the consideration of elementary row operations it should be pointed out that entirely analogous elementary column operations exist and post-inverses (that is, matrices **C** such that **AC = I**) may be found by post-multiplication by elementary matrices.

Exercise 14(a)

1. Find matrices **B** such that **BA = I** in each of the following cases:

(i) $A = \begin{pmatrix} 2 & 1 \\ 3 & 2 \end{pmatrix};$
(ii) $A = \begin{pmatrix} 2 & 3 \\ 5 & 4 \end{pmatrix};$
(iii) $A = \begin{pmatrix} 0 & -1 \\ -2 & 3 \end{pmatrix};$

(iv) $A = \begin{pmatrix} 3 & 5 \\ 2 & 7 \end{pmatrix};$
(v) $A = \begin{pmatrix} h & h+1 \\ h-1 & h \end{pmatrix}.$

2. Find matrices **C** such that **AC = I** for each of the matrices **A** of Question 1.

3. Show that the matrix $\begin{pmatrix} 3 & 2 \\ 6 & 4 \end{pmatrix}$

is singular.

4. Find matrices **B** such that **BA = I** in each of the following cases:

(i) $\begin{pmatrix} 1 & 0 & 2 \\ 3 & 1 & 1 \\ 4 & 1 & 4 \end{pmatrix};$
(ii) $\begin{pmatrix} 4 & 8 & 3 \\ 3 & 5 & 1 \\ 1 & 4 & 3 \end{pmatrix};$
(iii) $\begin{pmatrix} 2 & 2 & -1 \\ 3 & 7 & 2 \\ 2 & 5 & 2 \end{pmatrix};$

(iv) $\begin{pmatrix} 3 & 4 & 1 \\ 2 & 3 & 1 \\ 3 & 7 & 2 \end{pmatrix};$
(v) $\begin{pmatrix} 3 & 4 & 5 \\ 4 & 3 & 11 \\ 1 & 0 & 3 \end{pmatrix};$
(vi) $\begin{pmatrix} 3 & 6 & 2 \\ 1 & 4 & 2 \\ 2 & 4 & 2 \end{pmatrix}.$

Verify in each case that **AB = I.**

5. Show that the matrix $\begin{pmatrix} 1 & 2 & 3 \\ 2 & 3 & 1 \\ 1 & 1 & -2 \end{pmatrix}$

is singular.

264

6. A matrix of the form
$$\begin{pmatrix} 1 & a & b \\ 0 & 1 & c \\ 0 & 0 & 1 \end{pmatrix}$$

with zeros in every entry below the leading diagonal and 1 as each element of that diagonal is called an *echelon matrix*.

Prove that every echelon matrix is non-singular and that, if **A** is echelon and **BA** = **I**, then **B** is also echelon.

7. If
$$\mathbf{A} = \begin{pmatrix} 6 & 9 & 8 \\ 3 & 5 & 4 \\ 2 & 4 & 3 \end{pmatrix},$$

find **B** such that **BA** = **I**.

If
$$\mathbf{v} = \begin{pmatrix} x \\ y \\ z \end{pmatrix}, \quad \mathbf{w} = \begin{pmatrix} 1 \\ 3 \\ 2 \end{pmatrix},$$

show that the system of equations
$$\begin{cases} 6x+9y+8z = 1, \\ 3x+5y+4z = 3, \\ 2x+4y+3z = 2 \end{cases}$$

may be written in the matrix form
$$\mathbf{Av} = \mathbf{w}.$$

Pre-multiply both sides of this equation by **B** and hence solve the equations.

8. Solve the equations
$$\begin{cases} 3x+2y+3z = 17, \\ 2x-3y+4z = -7, \\ 2x- y+3z = 1 \end{cases}$$

by the method of Question 7.

9. For what value of a is the matrix
$$\begin{pmatrix} 4 & -3 & -1 \\ 2 & 4 & a \\ 3 & -5 & -4 \end{pmatrix}$$

singular?

10. If **AX** = **B** where
$$\mathbf{A} = \begin{pmatrix} 3 & 4 & 4 \\ 1 & 3 & 2 \\ 2 & 3 & 3 \end{pmatrix}, \quad \mathbf{B} = \begin{pmatrix} 1 & 1 & 3 \\ 2 & 0 & 1 \\ 3 & 1 & -5 \end{pmatrix},$$

find **X**.

2. DETERMINANTS

Recall that a square matrix **A** is non-singular if a (pre- or post-) inverse may be found; otherwise it is singular. We now establish a simple criterion for singularity for 2×2 matrices.

Theorem 14.1. *If* **A** *is the matrix*

$$\begin{pmatrix} a_{11} & a_{12} \\ a_{21} & a_{22} \end{pmatrix},$$

then **A** *is non-singular* $\Leftrightarrow a_{11}a_{22} - a_{12}a_{21} \neq 0.$

Proof. (i) Suppose **A** is non-singular.

A is non-singular $\Rightarrow$ a matrix $\mathbf{B} = \begin{pmatrix} x & y \\ z & w \end{pmatrix}$

exists such that $\qquad\qquad \mathbf{BA} = \mathbf{I},$

$$\Rightarrow \begin{cases} a_{11}x + a_{21}y = 1 \\ a_{12}x + a_{22}y = 0 \end{cases} \text{ and } \begin{cases} a_{11}z + a_{21}w = 0, \\ a_{12}z + a_{22}w = 1, \end{cases}$$

$$\Rightarrow \begin{cases} x(a_{11}a_{22} - a_{12}a_{21}) = a_{22}, \\ y(a_{11}a_{22} - a_{12}a_{21}) = -a_{12}, \\ z(a_{11}a_{22} - a_{12}a_{21}) = -a_{21}, \\ w(a_{11}a_{22} - a_{12}a_{21}) = a_{11}. \end{cases}$$

But the matrix **A** is non-singular and thus $\mathbf{A} \neq 0$, from which it follows that at least one of the elements of **A** is non-zero and hence that

$$a_{11}a_{22} - a_{12}a_{21} \neq 0.$$

(ii) Suppose $a_{11}a_{22} - a_{12}a_{21} \neq 0.$
Consider

$$\begin{pmatrix} a_{22} & -a_{12} \\ -a_{21} & a_{11} \end{pmatrix} \begin{pmatrix} a_{11} & a_{12} \\ a_{21} & a_{22} \end{pmatrix} = \begin{pmatrix} a_{11}a_{22} - a_{21}a_{12} & 0 \\ 0 & a_{11}a_{22} - a_{21}a_{12} \end{pmatrix},$$

then

$$a_{11}a_{22} - a_{12}a_{21} \neq 0 \Rightarrow \frac{1}{a_{11}a_{22} - a_{12}a_{21}} \begin{pmatrix} a_{22} & -a_{12} \\ -a_{21} & a_{11} \end{pmatrix} \begin{pmatrix} a_{11} & a_{12} \\ a_{21} & a_{22} \end{pmatrix} = \mathbf{I}$$

$$\Rightarrow \mathbf{BA} = \mathbf{I} \quad \text{where} \quad \mathbf{B} = \frac{1}{a_{11}a_{22} - a_{12}a_{21}} \begin{pmatrix} a_{22} & -a_{12} \\ -a_{21} & a_{11} \end{pmatrix}$$

$$\Rightarrow \mathbf{A} \text{ is non-singular.}$$

The quantity $a_{11}a_{22} - a_{12}a_{21}$ is called the *determinant* of **A** and is written

$$\begin{vmatrix} a_{11} & a_{12} \\ a_{21} & a_{22} \end{vmatrix} \quad \text{or, more shortly,} \quad \det \mathbf{A} \quad (\text{or } |\mathbf{A}|).$$

266

Thus the result of Theorem 14.1 may be stated as:

'**A** is a non-singular 2×2 matrix $\Leftrightarrow$ det **A** $\neq$ 0'.

If the elements of **A** are real numbers then det **A** is a real number and we have a mapping **A** $\rightarrow$ det **A** from the set of all 2×2 matrices with real elements to the set of real numbers. Similarly, we have mappings **A** $\rightarrow$ det **A** from the set of all 2×2 matrices with rational/integral elements to the set of all rationals/integers.

The rule for determining the value of det **A** must be carefully memorized: products of the elements are formed diagonally (the leading diagonal first) and then subtracted. Thus

$$\begin{vmatrix} 1 & 2 \\ 3 & 4 \end{vmatrix} = -2; \qquad \begin{vmatrix} 2 & -1 \\ -3 & -2 \end{vmatrix} = -7; \qquad \begin{vmatrix} \cos\alpha & \sin\alpha \\ -\sin\alpha & \cos\alpha \end{vmatrix} = 1.$$

Ex. 11. Evaluate:

(i) $\begin{vmatrix} 3 & 1 \\ 0 & 1 \end{vmatrix}$;   (ii) $\begin{vmatrix} 1 & -2 \\ 2 & 1 \end{vmatrix}$;   (iii) $\begin{vmatrix} 1 & -2 \\ 3 & 1 \end{vmatrix}$.

The construction of the determinant of a 2×2 matrix has thus given us a test for singularity. We now define determinants of higher orders; although the definition will no doubt appear complicated, the motivation for their introduction should be clear—we shall use them to extend the result of Theorem 14.1.

If **A** is the 3×3 matrix $\begin{pmatrix} a_{11} & a_{12} & a_{13} \\ a_{21} & a_{22} & a_{23} \\ a_{31} & a_{32} & a_{33} \end{pmatrix}$,

then the *determinant of* **A**, written

$$\begin{vmatrix} a_{11} & a_{12} & a_{13} \\ a_{21} & a_{22} & a_{23} \\ a_{31} & a_{32} & a_{33} \end{vmatrix} \qquad \text{or, more briefly,} \quad \text{det } \mathbf{A} \quad \text{(or } |\mathbf{A}| \text{)}$$

is defined by

$$\text{det } \mathbf{A} = a_{11} \begin{vmatrix} a_{22} & a_{23} \\ a_{32} & a_{33} \end{vmatrix} - a_{12} \begin{vmatrix} a_{21} & a_{23} \\ a_{31} & a_{33} \end{vmatrix} + a_{13} \begin{vmatrix} a_{21} & a_{22} \\ a_{31} & a_{32} \end{vmatrix}$$

$$= a_{11}a_{22}a_{33} - a_{11}a_{23}a_{32} - a_{12}a_{21}a_{33} + a_{12}a_{23}a_{31} + a_{13}a_{21}a_{32} - a_{13}a_{22}a_{31}.$$

It is simply verified by direct calculation that det **A** may be expressed in the two alternative forms

$$\text{det } \mathbf{A} = -a_{21} \begin{vmatrix} a_{12} & a_{13} \\ a_{32} & a_{33} \end{vmatrix} + a_{22} \begin{vmatrix} a_{11} & a_{13} \\ a_{31} & a_{33} \end{vmatrix} - a_{23} \begin{vmatrix} a_{11} & a_{12} \\ a_{31} & a_{32} \end{vmatrix},$$

267

or

$$\det \mathbf{A} = a_{31} \begin{vmatrix} a_{12} & a_{13} \\ a_{22} & a_{23} \end{vmatrix} - a_{32} \begin{vmatrix} a_{11} & a_{13} \\ a_{21} & a_{23} \end{vmatrix} + a_{33} \begin{vmatrix} a_{11} & a_{12} \\ a_{21} & a_{22} \end{vmatrix}.$$

These three forms give the *expansion of the determinant by rows*. The determinant may also be expanded by columns; for example, expanding by the first column

$$\det \mathbf{A} = a_{11} \begin{vmatrix} a_{22} & a_{23} \\ a_{32} & a_{33} \end{vmatrix} - a_{21} \begin{vmatrix} a_{12} & a_{13} \\ a_{32} & a_{33} \end{vmatrix} + a_{31} \begin{vmatrix} a_{12} & a_{13} \\ a_{22} & a_{23} \end{vmatrix}.$$

The term

$$\begin{vmatrix} a_{22} & a_{23} \\ a_{32} & a_{33} \end{vmatrix}$$

is called the *minor* of a_{11}; similarly, the minor of a_{12} is

$$\begin{vmatrix} a_{21} & a_{23} \\ a_{31} & a_{33} \end{vmatrix}$$

(see expansion by first row) while the minor of a_{32} is

$$\begin{vmatrix} a_{11} & a_{13} \\ a_{21} & a_{23} \end{vmatrix}$$

(from the expansion by the third row). To find the minor of any term, write down the determinant and cross-out the row and column containing the term under consideration; the required minor is the 2×2 determinant that remains. See Figure 14.1, where the minor of a_{23} is being sought: it is

$$\begin{vmatrix} a_{11} & a_{12} \\ a_{31} & a_{32} \end{vmatrix} \quad \text{or} \quad (a_{11}a_{32} - a_{12}a_{31}).$$

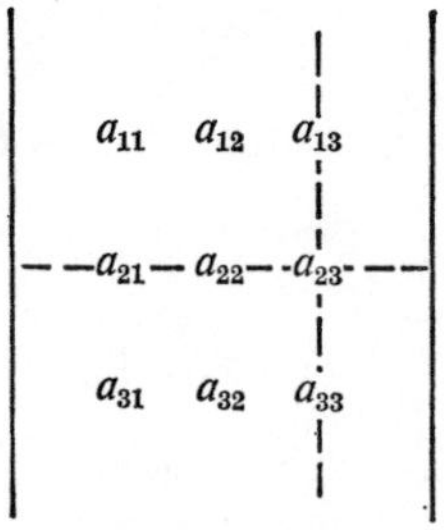

Fig. 14.1 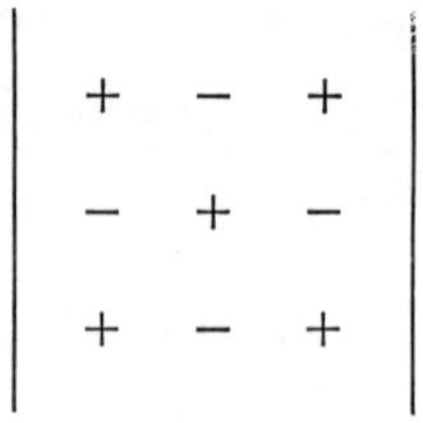   Fig. 14.2

To find the sign to be attached to each minor in the expansion of a determinant, draw the chess-board pattern, as shown in Figure 14.2, starting with + along the leading diagonal. Thus, if we were expanding by the second row, or by the third column, we should include the term

$$-a_{23} \begin{vmatrix} a_{11} & a_{12} \\ a_{31} & a_{32} \end{vmatrix}.$$

A minor, together with its correct sign as given in Figure 14.2, is called a *cofactor*, the cofactor of the term a_{ij} being written A_{ij}. Thus

$$A_{22} = \begin{vmatrix} a_{11} & a_{13} \\ a_{31} & a_{33} \end{vmatrix} = a_{11}a_{33} - a_{13}a_{31};$$

$$A_{32} = -\begin{vmatrix} a_{11} & a_{13} \\ a_{21} & a_{23} \end{vmatrix} = a_{13}a_{21} - a_{11}a_{23}.$$

In terms of cofactors, the expansion of the determinant may be written

$$\det \mathbf{A} = a_{11}A_{11} + a_{12}A_{12} + a_{13}A_{13} \quad \text{(first row)},$$

or $\qquad \det \mathbf{A} = a_{12}A_{12} + a_{22}A_{22} + a_{32}A_{32}$ (second column), etc.

Determinants of orders 4, 5, 6, ... may be defined similarly. Thus, for the 4×4 determinant

$$\begin{vmatrix} a_{11} & a_{12} & a_{13} & a_{14} \\ a_{21} & a_{22} & a_{23} & a_{24} \\ a_{31} & a_{32} & a_{33} & a_{34} \\ a_{41} & a_{42} & a_{43} & a_{44} \end{vmatrix}$$

each cofactor is a 3×3 determinant, obtained by rejecting the row and column in which the corresponding element stands and attaching the required sign, obtained from the chess-board pattern, to the remaining determinant. Thus

$$A_{22} = \begin{vmatrix} a_{11} & a_{13} & a_{14} \\ a_{31} & a_{33} & a_{34} \\ a_{41} & a_{43} & a_{44} \end{vmatrix} ; \quad A_{43} = -\begin{vmatrix} a_{11} & a_{12} & a_{14} \\ a_{21} & a_{22} & a_{24} \\ a_{31} & a_{32} & a_{34} \end{vmatrix}.$$

The expansion of this determinant by the third column is

$$a_{13}A_{13} + a_{23}A_{23} + a_{33}A_{33} + a_{43}A_{43}.$$

Ex. 12. Evaluate the determinants:

(i) $\begin{vmatrix} 1 & 0 & 5 \\ 2 & 1 & 6 \\ 1 & 1 & 3 \end{vmatrix}$;   (ii) $\begin{vmatrix} 1 & 2 & -1 \\ 2 & 3 & 0 \\ 1 & 1 & 4 \end{vmatrix}$;   (iii) $\begin{vmatrix} -1 & 1 & 2 \\ 1 & 1 & 3 \\ -2 & 4 & 9 \end{vmatrix}$;

(iv) $\begin{vmatrix} 1 & 1 & 0 & 0 \\ 2 & 1 & 3 & 4 \\ 1 & -1 & 3 & 2 \\ 1 & 2 & 1 & 3 \end{vmatrix}$;   (v) $\begin{vmatrix} a & h & g \\ h & b & f \\ g & f & c \end{vmatrix}$.

3. PROPERTIES OF DETERMINANTS

We shall now develop some simple properties of determinants, restricting ourselves to the 3×3 case for simplicity, although the results and proofs all extend to $n \times n$ determinants.

First observe that the interchange of rows and columns does not affect the value of a determinant: for we may expand in the first case by the first row and in the second case by the first column and, in either case, the corresponding cofactors remain the same. Thus, any property possessed by the rows of a determinant is possessed equally well by the columns.

For brevity, we shall denote the determinant

$$\begin{vmatrix} a_{11} & a_{12} & a_{13} \\ a_{21} & a_{22} & a_{23} \\ a_{31} & a_{32} & a_{33} \end{vmatrix} \text{ by } \Delta.$$

Property 1.

$$\begin{vmatrix} a_{11}+x & a_{12}+y & a_{13}+z \\ a_{21} & a_{22} & a_{23} \\ a_{31} & a_{32} & a_{33} \end{vmatrix} = \begin{vmatrix} a_{11} & a_{12} & a_{13} \\ a_{21} & a_{22} & a_{23} \\ a_{31} & a_{32} & a_{33} \end{vmatrix} + \begin{vmatrix} x & y & z \\ a_{21} & a_{22} & a_{23} \\ a_{31} & a_{32} & a_{33} \end{vmatrix}.$$

For

$$\text{L.H.S.} = (a_{11}+x) A_{11} + (a_{12}+y) A_{12} + (a_{13}+z) A_{13} = \text{R.H.S.}$$

Property 2. *If two rows (or columns) are identical,* det $\mathbf{A} = 0$.

For, if two rows are the same, expanding by the third row the corresponding cofactors are all zero.

Property 3. *If an elementary row operation is performed on* $\mathbf{A}$, *the determinant of the new matrix is equal to the product of* det $\mathbf{A}$ *and the determinant of the corresponding elementary matrix.*

Case (i): the interchange of two rows (columns).

If, for example, we interchange rows 2 and 3, on expansion by row 1 the cofactors all change sign but remain the same in magnitude; but

$$\begin{vmatrix} 1 & 0 & 0 \\ 0 & 0 & 1 \\ 0 & 1 & 0 \end{vmatrix} = -1.$$

The result may similarly be verified for any other interchange of two rows (columns).

Case (ii): the multiplication of a row (column) by a non-zero constant.

$$\begin{vmatrix} ca_{11} & ca_{12} & ca_{13} \\ a_{21} & a_{22} & a_{23} \\ a_{31} & a_{32} & a_{33} \end{vmatrix} = c \det \mathbf{A},$$

by expanding by the first row.

270

But the corresponding elementary matrix is

$$\begin{pmatrix} c & 0 & 0 \\ 0 & 1 & 0 \\ 0 & 0 & 1 \end{pmatrix} \quad \text{and} \quad \begin{vmatrix} c & 0 & 0 \\ 0 & 1 & 0 \\ 0 & 0 & 1 \end{vmatrix} = c.$$

Case (iii): the addition to any one row (column) a constant multiple of another row (column).

Suppose, for example, that we add to row 1 c times row 2

$$\begin{vmatrix} a_{11}+ca_{21} & a_{12}+ca_{22} & a_{13}+ca_{23} \\ a_{21} & a_{22} & a_{23} \\ a_{31} & a_{32} & a_{33} \end{vmatrix} = \det \mathbf{A} + c \begin{vmatrix} a_{21} & a_{22} & a_{23} \\ a_{21} & a_{22} & a_{23} \\ a_{31} & a_{32} & a_{33} \end{vmatrix}$$

by properties 1 and 3 (case (ii))

$$= \det \mathbf{A}, \quad \text{by property 2.}$$

But the corresponding elementary matrix is

$$\begin{pmatrix} 1 & c & 0 \\ 0 & 1 & 0 \\ 0 & 0 & 1 \end{pmatrix} \quad \text{and} \quad \begin{vmatrix} 1 & c & 0 \\ 0 & 1 & 0 \\ 0 & 0 & 1 \end{vmatrix} = 1,$$

on expanding by the first column.

Other possibilities are dealt with in a precisely similar manner.

Property 3 may clearly be extended to a sequence of elementary row (column) operations on $\mathbf{A}$.

Property 4. $\det (\mathbf{AB}) = \det \mathbf{A} \det \mathbf{B}$.

Write
$$\mathbf{B} = (b_{ij}),$$
then

det $\mathbf{AB}$

$$= \begin{vmatrix} a_{11}b_{11}+a_{12}b_{21}+a_{13}b_{31} & a_{11}b_{12}+a_{12}b_{22}+a_{13}b_{32} & a_{11}b_{13}+a_{12}b_{23}+a_{13}b_{33} \\ a_{21}b_{11}+a_{22}b_{21}+a_{23}b_{31} & a_{21}b_{12}+a_{22}b_{22}+a_{23}b_{32} & a_{21}b_{13}+a_{22}b_{23}+a_{23}b_{33} \\ a_{31}b_{11}+a_{32}b_{21}+a_{33}b_{31} & a_{31}b_{12}+a_{32}b_{22}+a_{33}b_{32} & a_{31}b_{13}+a_{32}b_{23}+a_{33}b_{33} \end{vmatrix}.$$

But this may be expressed, by an extension of property 1, as the sum of twenty-seven determinants, twenty-one of which are zero. (For example, one of the vanishing determinants would be

$$\begin{vmatrix} a_{11}b_{11} & a_{11}b_{12} & a_{13}b_{33} \\ a_{21}b_{11} & a_{21}b_{12} & a_{23}b_{33} \\ a_{31}b_{11} & a_{31}b_{12} & a_{33}b_{33} \end{vmatrix} = b_{11}b_{12}b_{33} \begin{vmatrix} a_{11} & a_{11} & a_{13} \\ a_{21} & a_{21} & a_{23} \\ a_{31} & a_{31} & a_{33} \end{vmatrix} = 0 \quad \text{by property 2.)}$$

We are left with six determinants which do not have two identical columns. However, using properties 1 and 3 we get

det $\mathbf{AB} = \det \mathbf{A} \, (b_{11}b_{22}b_{33}-b_{11}b_{23}b_{32}+b_{12}b_{23}b_{31}-b_{12}b_{21}b_{33}+b_{13}b_{21}b_{32}$

$$-b_{13}b_{22}b_{31}) = \det \mathbf{A} \det \mathbf{B}.$$

271

One simple but useful result that follows immediately from property 2 can now be derived. It will be recalled that $a_{11}A_{11}+a_{12}A_{12}+a_{13}A_{13} = \det \mathbf{A}$ and similarly for other rows and columns. Now suppose we multiply each element of some row (or column) by the cofactors of the corresponding elements of another row (or column); for example

$$a_{11}A_{21}+a_{12}A_{22}+a_{13}A_{23}.$$

Now

$$a_{11}A_{21}+a_{12}A_{22}+a_{13}A_{23} = \begin{vmatrix} a_{11} & a_{12} & a_{13} \\ a_{31} & a_{32} & a_{33} \\ a_{11} & a_{12} & a_{13} \end{vmatrix} = 0 \quad (r_1 = r_3).$$

A similar result holds for any other combination of rows (or columns). Such an expansion is called an *expansion by alien cofactors* and we have demonstrated that *expansion by alien cofactors gives the value zero*.

Example 3. Evaluate the determinant

$$\begin{vmatrix} 8 & 4 & 12 \\ 9 & 3 & 3 \\ 5 & 15 & 10 \end{vmatrix},$$

$$\begin{vmatrix} 8 & 4 & 12 \\ 9 & 3 & 3 \\ 5 & 15 & 10 \end{vmatrix} = 4.3.5 \begin{vmatrix} 2 & 1 & 3 \\ 3 & 1 & 1 \\ 1 & 3 & 2 \end{vmatrix} \quad \text{(removing factors)}$$

$$= 60 \begin{vmatrix} 2 & 1 & 3 \\ 1 & 0 & -2 \\ 1 & 3 & 2 \end{vmatrix} \quad r_2' = r_2 - r_1$$

$$= 60 \begin{vmatrix} 2 & 1 & 7 \\ 1 & 0 & 0 \\ 1 & 3 & 4 \end{vmatrix} \quad c_3' = c_3 + 2c_1$$

$$= -60 \begin{vmatrix} 1 & 7 \\ 3 & 4 \end{vmatrix} \quad \text{(expanding by second row)}$$

$$= (-60)(-17)$$

$$= 1020.$$

Example 4. Express the determinant

$$\begin{vmatrix} 1 & 1 & 1 \\ a^2 & b^2 & c^2 \\ bc & ca & ab \end{vmatrix}$$

as the product of factors.

272

If we set $b = c$, the given determinant is zero (two columns identical) and so $(b-c)$ must be a factor. By symmetry, $(c-a)$ and $(a-b)$ must also be factors. But the expansion of the determinant clearly gives an expression of degree 4, in a, b, c and so the remaining factor must be linear and symmetrical, i.e. $(a+b+c)$.

$$\therefore \quad \begin{vmatrix} 1 & 1 & 1 \\ a^2 & b^2 & c^2 \\ bc & ca & ab \end{vmatrix} = \lambda(b-c)\ (c-a)\ (a-b)\ (a+b+c).$$

By comparing the term in ab^3 on both sides, the value of λ is clearly 1.

Ex. 13. Evaluate the following determinants:

(i) $\begin{vmatrix} 3 & 7 & -4 \\ -1 & 1 & -3 \\ 1 & 3 & -1 \end{vmatrix}$;   (ii) $\begin{vmatrix} 2 & 1 & -1 \\ 4 & 2 & 1 \\ -5 & -1 & -2 \end{vmatrix}$;

(iii) $\begin{vmatrix} 11 & 3 & 5 \\ 2 & -3 & 2 \\ 16 & 15 & 4 \end{vmatrix}$;   (iv) $\begin{vmatrix} 8 & 13 & 3 \\ 1 & 14 & 8 \\ 19 & 55 & 22 \end{vmatrix}$.

With the properties of determinants that we have just proved we are almost in a position to extend our theorem on the necessary and sufficient condition for a matrix to be non-singular to matrices of order higher than two. However, before we do so, we shall introduce a further concept, the *adjugate* (or *adjoint*) of a matrix, since there is an intimate connection between the adjugate and inverse of a non-singular matrix.

Given any square matrix $\mathbf{A}$, where

$$\mathbf{A} = \begin{pmatrix} a_{11} & a_{12} & a_{13} \\ a_{21} & a_{22} & a_{23} \\ a_{31} & a_{32} & a_{33} \end{pmatrix},$$

the *adjugate* (or *adjoint*) of $\mathbf{A}$, written adj $\mathbf{A}$, is defined by

$$\text{adj } \mathbf{A} = \begin{pmatrix} A_{11} & A_{21} & A_{31} \\ A_{12} & A_{22} & A_{32} \\ A_{13} & A_{23} & A_{33} \end{pmatrix},$$

that is, the adjugate is obtained by substituting for each element its co-factor and transposing (see Miscellaneous Exercise 13, Question 7).

Theorem 14.2. *For any square matrix* $\mathbf{A}$

$$\mathbf{A} \text{ (adj } \mathbf{A}) = \text{(adj } \mathbf{A})\mathbf{A} = \text{(det } \mathbf{A}) \mathbf{I}.$$

Proof. (3×3 matrices)

$$A \, (\text{adj } A) = \begin{pmatrix} a_{11} & a_{12} & a_{13} \\ a_{21} & a_{22} & a_{23} \\ a_{31} & a_{32} & a_{33} \end{pmatrix} \begin{pmatrix} A_{11} & A_{21} & A_{31} \\ A_{12} & A_{22} & A_{32} \\ A_{13} & A_{23} & A_{33} \end{pmatrix} = \begin{pmatrix} \Delta & 0 & 0 \\ 0 & \Delta & 0 \\ 0 & 0 & \Delta \end{pmatrix},$$

since each term in the product is either an expansion of the determinant, or an expansion by alien cofactors;

$$= \Delta I, \quad \text{where} \quad \Delta = \det A.$$

A precisely similar result holds for (adj A) A.

Corollary. If $\det A \neq 0$, $\det (\text{adj } A) = (\det A)^2$ (3×3 matrix).

Proof. Take determinants of both sides of $A \, (\text{adj } A) = (\det A) \, I$ and divide both sides by $\det A$.

It can be shown that, in fact,

$$\det A = 0 \Rightarrow \det (\text{adj } A) = 0$$

and so the restriction that $\det A$ must be non-zero may be dropped.

If $\det A \neq 0$ we have now obtained an inverse for A, namely

$$\frac{\text{adj } A}{\det A}, \quad \text{since} \quad A . \frac{\text{adj } A}{\det A} = I.$$

We note further that multiplication of this inverse with A is commutative. To obtain a complete picture about inverses we need to clear-up two final points:

(i) Can a matrix A have an inverse even if $\det A = 0$?

(ii) If $\det A \neq 0$, can we find an inverse of A other than adj $A/\det A$?

Theorem 14.3. *If A is any* 3×3 *matrix, we have*:

the matrix A is non-singular $\Leftrightarrow \det A \neq 0$.

Proof (i). To prove the implication $\Rightarrow$ we show that $\det A = 0 \Rightarrow A$ is singular (see Chapter 9).

$$\det A = 0 \Rightarrow \text{for any matrix } B, \quad \det (AB) = \det A \det B = 0$$

$$\Rightarrow AB \neq I, \quad \text{since} \quad \det I = 1$$

$$\Rightarrow A \text{ is singular};$$

(ii) $\det A \neq 0 \Rightarrow \dfrac{\text{adj } A}{\det A}$ exists

$$\Rightarrow A \text{ is non-singular, by Theorem 14.2.}$$

Theorem 14.4.

$$A^{-1} = \frac{\text{adj } A}{\det A}$$

is the unique inverse of the non-singular matrix **A**.

Proof. Suppose **L** is a left inverse other than A^{-1}; that is, suppose that $LA = I, L \neq A^{-1}$. Then

$$L = LI = L(AA^{-1}) = (LA) A^{-1} = IA^{-1} = A^{-1},$$

which contradicts the assumption that $L \neq A^{-1}$. Similarly for right inverses.

Exercise 14(b)

1. Evaluate the following determinants:

(i) $\begin{vmatrix} 1 & 3 \\ 2 & 4 \end{vmatrix}$;

(ii) $\begin{vmatrix} 2 & -7 \\ -1 & 3 \end{vmatrix}$;

(iii) $\begin{vmatrix} 6 & 5 \\ 5 & 4 \end{vmatrix}$;

(iv) $\begin{vmatrix} -2 & 3 \\ -4 & -5 \end{vmatrix}$.

2. Evaluate the following determinants:

(i) $\begin{vmatrix} -4 & 7 & 4 \\ 3 & 1 & 2 \\ 5 & -9 & -4 \end{vmatrix}$;

(ii) $\begin{vmatrix} 1 & 2 & 3 \\ 12 & 13 & 14 \\ -7 & -3 & 1 \end{vmatrix}$;

(iii) $\begin{vmatrix} 3 & 4 & 8 \\ 2 & 7 & 1 \\ 5 & 17 & 3 \end{vmatrix}$;

(iv) $\begin{vmatrix} 4 & 3 & 1 \\ 3 & 4 & 2 \\ 10 & 8 & 3 \end{vmatrix}$;

(v) $\begin{vmatrix} 3 & 7 & 4 \\ 2 & 7 & 3 \\ 5 & 4 & 9 \end{vmatrix}$;

(vi) $\begin{vmatrix} -4 & -5 & 2 \\ 2 & -3 & 3 \\ 7 & 2 & 1 \end{vmatrix}$;

(vii) $\begin{vmatrix} 1 & 3 & 5 \\ 2 & 7 & 1 \\ 5 & 16 & 19 \end{vmatrix}$;

(viii) $\begin{vmatrix} 5 & 6 & 7 \\ 3 & -2 & 5 \\ 4 & 5 & 6 \end{vmatrix}$;

(ix) $\begin{vmatrix} 7 & 17 & 16 \\ 13 & 33 & 30 \\ 10 & 21 & 23 \end{vmatrix}$;

(x) $\begin{vmatrix} 112 & 129 & 104 \\ 67 & 78 & 62 \\ 99 & 114 & 92 \end{vmatrix}$.

3. Determine which of the following matrices are non-singular:

(i) $\begin{pmatrix} 9 & 6 & 10 \\ 1 & 3 & 5 \\ 3 & 2 & 1 \end{pmatrix}$;

(ii) $\begin{pmatrix} 10 & 7 & 24 \\ 23 & 14 & 29 \\ 4 & 1 & 6 \end{pmatrix}$;

(iii) $\begin{pmatrix} 16 & 6 & 31 \\ 17 & 9 & 29 \\ 11 & 5 & 20 \end{pmatrix}$;

(iv) $\begin{pmatrix} -1 & 8 & 6 \\ 3 & 1 & 2 \\ 11 & -7 & 0 \end{pmatrix}$.

4. Find the adjugate of each of the following matrices and, in each case, evaluate the product of the matrix with its adjugate. Write down the determinant of each matrix.

(i) $\begin{pmatrix} 1 & 2 & 1 \\ 3 & 7 & 5 \\ 5 & 13 & 9 \end{pmatrix};$ (ii) $\begin{pmatrix} 5 & 1 & -2 \\ -2 & 5 & 4 \\ 3 & 6 & 2 \end{pmatrix};$

(iii) $\begin{pmatrix} 1 & 3 & 1 \\ 3 & 10 & 5 \\ 1 & 4 & 5 \end{pmatrix};$ (iv) $\begin{pmatrix} 4 & 11 & 5 \\ 1 & 4 & 2 \\ 1 & 2 & 1 \end{pmatrix}.$

5. Find the inverses of the following matrices by the adjugate-determinant method:

(i) $\begin{pmatrix} 1 & -2 & 1 \\ 3 & -1 & 5 \\ -1 & 4 & 0 \end{pmatrix};$ (ii) $\begin{pmatrix} 2 & 5 & 1 \\ 1 & 0 & 3 \\ 3 & 1 & 2 \end{pmatrix};$

(iii) $\begin{pmatrix} 3 & 7 & 2 \\ 2 & 6 & 3 \\ 1 & 4 & 2 \end{pmatrix};$ (iv) $\begin{pmatrix} 2 & 4 & 1 \\ 1 & 4 & 2 \\ 1 & 2 & 1 \end{pmatrix}.$

6. Find the values of a which make the following matrices singular:

(i) $\begin{pmatrix} 1 & 3 & 7 \\ 4 & 2 & 5 \\ 5 & 5 & a \end{pmatrix};$ (ii) $\begin{pmatrix} 7 & 13 & 1 \\ -1 & a & 3 \\ 3 & 7 & 2 \end{pmatrix};$ (iii) $\begin{pmatrix} 1 & -3 & 5 \\ -2 & 6 & a \\ 4 & -11 & 16 \end{pmatrix}.$

7. Factorize the following determinants:

(i) $\begin{vmatrix} 1 & 1 & 1 \\ a & b & c \\ a^2 & b^2 & c^2 \end{vmatrix};$ (ii) $\begin{vmatrix} 1 & 1 & 1 \\ a & b & c \\ a^3 & b^3 & c^3 \end{vmatrix};$ (iii) $\begin{vmatrix} a & b & c \\ a^2 & b^2 & c^2 \\ bc & ca & ab \end{vmatrix}.$

8.
$$A = \begin{pmatrix} 1 & 2 & 7 \\ 0 & 1 & 2 \\ 1 & 2 & 8 \end{pmatrix}, \quad B = \begin{pmatrix} 2 & 0 & 0 \\ 1 & 1 & 0 \\ 0 & 2 & -1 \end{pmatrix}.$$

Solve for X the matrix equation
$$A^2 + AX = B.$$

9.
$$A = \begin{pmatrix} 3 & 4 & 4 \\ 2 & 1 & 5 \\ 1 & 8 & 8 \end{pmatrix}, \quad B = \begin{pmatrix} 0 & 2 & 1 \\ 1 & 1 & 0 \\ 3 & -2 & 1 \end{pmatrix},$$

$$C = \begin{pmatrix} 2 & 1 & 2 \\ 1 & -2 & 2 \\ -1 & 1 & 2 \end{pmatrix}, \quad D = \begin{pmatrix} 1 & 3 & 1 \\ 2 & 2 & 1 \\ 3 & 0 & 1 \end{pmatrix}.$$

Solve for **X** the matrix equation

$$\mathbf{AX} - \mathbf{B} = \mathbf{CX} + \mathbf{D}.$$

10.
$$\mathbf{A} = \begin{pmatrix} 2 & 1 & -4 \\ 1 & 1 & 3 \\ 0 & 2 & -1 \end{pmatrix}, \quad \mathbf{B} = \begin{pmatrix} -4 & 2 & 1 \\ 11 & -5 & -3 \\ -16 & 7 & 5 \end{pmatrix}.$$

Solve for **X** the matrix equation

$$\mathbf{B}^{-1}\mathbf{XB} = \mathbf{A}.$$

Miscellaneous Exercise 14

1. Prove that

$$\begin{pmatrix} 1 & 0 \\ -1 & 1 \end{pmatrix} \begin{pmatrix} -1 & 0 \\ 0 & 1 \end{pmatrix} \begin{pmatrix} 1 & -1 \\ 0 & 1 \end{pmatrix} \begin{pmatrix} 1 & 0 \\ 1 & 1 \end{pmatrix} \begin{pmatrix} a & b \\ c & d \end{pmatrix} = \begin{pmatrix} c & d \\ a & b \end{pmatrix}.$$

Deduce that the rows of a 2×2 matrix can be interchanged by operations which add multiples of one row of the matrix to the other, together with operations changing the sign of a row.

Find a 2×2 matrix **X** such that

$$\begin{pmatrix} a & b \\ c & d \end{pmatrix} \mathbf{X} = \begin{pmatrix} b & a \\ d & c \end{pmatrix}.$$

2. Do 2×2 matrices **A, B** with integer entries, exist such that

    (a) $\mathbf{AB} = 0, \quad \mathbf{BA} \neq 0$?

    (b) $\mathbf{AB} = \mathbf{BA} = 0, \quad \mathbf{A} \neq 0, \quad \mathbf{B} \neq 0, \quad \mathbf{A} \neq \mathbf{B}$?

    (c) $\mathbf{AB} = \mathbf{BA} \neq 0, \quad \mathbf{A}, \mathbf{B} \neq \mathbf{I}, \quad \mathbf{A} \neq \mathbf{B}$?

In each case, if your answer is 'yes', justify it by giving examples of suitable **A, B**. (M.E.I.)

3. If

$$\mathbf{a} = \begin{pmatrix} a \\ b \\ c \end{pmatrix}$$

so that the transpose **a**′ is given by

$$\mathbf{a}' = (a \quad b \quad c)$$

write down the 3×3 matrix **aa**′ and prove that the determinant of this matrix has value zero.

Obtain the analogous result when

$$\mathbf{a} = \begin{pmatrix} a & 0 \\ b & 1 \\ c & 2 \end{pmatrix}.$$
    (SMP)

4. If **A** is any 3×3 matrix and **P** is a non-singular 3×3 matrix, prove that

$$\det(\mathbf{A} - \lambda\mathbf{I}) = \det(\mathbf{B} - \lambda\mathbf{I}), \quad \text{where} \quad \mathbf{B} = \mathbf{P}^{-1}\mathbf{AP}.$$

5. S is a *skew-symmetric matrix* if $S+S' = 0$; A is an *orthogonal matrix* if $AA' = I$. If S is a given skew-symmetric matrix and A, B given orthogonal matrices, prove the following results:

(i) $\det A = \pm 1$;

(ii) AB is orthogonal;

(iii) $(I-S)(I+S)^{-1}$ is orthogonal.

6. If

$$A = \begin{pmatrix} a & b \\ 0 & 1 \end{pmatrix},$$

prove by induction that

$$A^n = \begin{pmatrix} a^n & \dfrac{a^n-1}{a-1}b \\ 0 & 1 \end{pmatrix} \quad (a \neq 0).$$

Prove also that the nth power of the matrix

$$B = \begin{pmatrix} 1 & b \\ 0 & 1 \end{pmatrix} \quad \text{is} \quad \begin{pmatrix} 1 & nb \\ 0 & 1 \end{pmatrix}.$$

Do these results hold if $n = -1$?

7. Prove that

$$\begin{vmatrix} b^2c^2+a^2d^2 & bc+ad & 1 \\ c^2a^2+b^2d^2 & ca+bd & 1 \\ a^2b^2+c^2d^2 & ab+cd & 1 \end{vmatrix} = (b-c)(c-a)(a-b)(a-d)(b-d)(c-d).$$

Also prove that

$$\begin{vmatrix} a_1 & x & x & x \\ x & a_2 & x & x \\ x & x & a_3 & x \\ x & x & x & a_4 \end{vmatrix} = (a_1-x)(a_2-x)(a_3-x)(a_4-x)\left(1+x\sum_{r=1}^{4}\frac{1}{a_r-x}\right).$$

(O & C)

8. If

$$M = \begin{pmatrix} a & h & g \\ h & b & f \\ g & f & c \end{pmatrix}$$

and $\det M \neq 0$, prove that, if λ is a root of the equation

$$\begin{vmatrix} A+\lambda & H & G \\ H & B+\lambda & F \\ G & F & C \end{vmatrix} = 0,$$

where A is the cofactor of a, etc., then $\det M/\lambda$ is a root of the equation

$$(x+a)(x+b) = h^2.$$

(O & C)

9. Factorize the determinant

$$\begin{vmatrix} 1+a^2+a^4 & 1+ab+a^2b^2 & 1+ac+a^2c^2 \\ 1+ab+a^2b^2 & 1+b^2+b^4 & 1+bc+b^2c^2 \\ 1+ac+a^2c^2 & 1+bc+b^2c^2 & 1+c^2+c^4 \end{vmatrix}.$$

(O & C)

10. Prove that

$$\begin{vmatrix} 1 & 1 & 1 \\ yz & zx & xy \\ (y+z-x)^4 & (z+x-y)^4 & (x+y-z)^4 \end{vmatrix} = -16xyz(y-z)(z-x)(x-y).$$

(O & C)

11. If

$$A = \begin{pmatrix} a & 0 & 0 & d \\ 0 & b & 0 & e \\ 0 & 0 & c & f \\ d & e & f & x \end{pmatrix},$$

where $a, b, \ldots, f$ are real and $a > b > c$, prove that the equation

$$\det (A - xI) = 0$$

has real roots.

(O & C adapted)

12. If A and B are square matrices such that $AB = 0$, prove that either $A = 0$ or $B = 0$ or $\det A = \det B = 0$.

13. Two matrices A and B are said to commute if $AB = BA$. Let

$$A = \begin{pmatrix} 2 & 1 \\ 1 & 0 \end{pmatrix};$$

prove that every matrix B that commutes with A can be expressed in the form $B = \lambda A + \mu I$, where λ and μ are scalars and I is the unit matrix. Obtain expressions of this form for A^2 and A^{-1}.

(M.T.)

14. Prove that, if a is a 3×3 matrix, with adj $a = A$ and det $a = \alpha$, that

$$aA = Aa = \alpha I.$$

Assuming that $\alpha \neq 0$, prove that:
  (i) $\det A = \alpha^2$;
  (ii) $X = A$ is the only solution of the matrix equation $aX = \alpha I$;
  (iii) adj $A = \alpha a$.
  Which, if any, of the above results, are still valid if the restriction on α is removed?

15. If A is a 3×3 matrix with $a_{11} \neq 0$, and if the cofactor of every element of A is zero (that is, if adj $A = 0$), prove that A has the form

$$\begin{pmatrix} a_{11} & a_{12} & a_{13} \\ ka_{11} & ka_{12} & ka_{13} \\ la_{11} & la_{12} & la_{13} \end{pmatrix}.$$

16. What is meant by the statement that multiplication of real numbers is associative and is distributive over addition? Prove that, if $a_{ij}, b_{ij}\ c_{ij}$ $(i, j = 1, 2, 3)$ are real numbers, then

$$\sum_{\beta=1}^{3} \left(\sum_{\alpha=1}^{3} a_{i\alpha} b_{\alpha\beta} \right) c_{\beta j} = \sum_{\alpha=1}^{3} a_{i\alpha} \left(\sum_{\beta=1}^{3} b_{\alpha\beta} c_{\beta j} \right).$$

Deduce that multiplication of 3×3 real matrices is associative and that, if A is a 3×3 real matrix, then the notation A^3, A^4, A^5, ... may be interpreted unambiguously.

If the 3×3 real matrices B and $A^2 + A + I$ are non-singular (I is the identity matrix) why would the notation A/B be ambiguous, but

$$\frac{A}{A^2 + A + I}$$

not so? (M.E.I.)

17. The non-singular matrix B has the property $BB' = B'B$, where B' is the transpose of B. Prove that $B'B^{-1} = B^{-1}B'$. Prove also that, if $C = B^{-1}B'$, then CC' is the identity matrix.

Find B', BB', B^{-1} and C when

$$B = \begin{pmatrix} 2 & 2 & 1 \\ -2 & 1 & 2 \\ 1 & -2 & 2 \end{pmatrix}.$$ (M.E.I.)

15. *Linear equations*

1. LINEAR EQUATIONS IN TWO UNKNOWNS; INTRODUCTION

Given perpendicular coordinate axes Ox, Oy in a plane, any linear equation connecting the two variables x and y is the equation of some straight line in the plane; that is, the linear equation defines the set of points (x, y) comprising the line. Two such sets of points will have as their intersection a single point, in general, whose coordinates may be obtained by solving the equations simultaneously, or, in other words, by requiring the defining properties of the sets of points comprising the two lines to hold simultaneously.

For example, the pair of straight lines

$$\begin{cases} 2x+5y = 1, \\ x-3y = 6 \end{cases}$$

intersect at the point $(3, -1)$, a result derived by solving the simultaneous equations in the usual way.

Consider now the pair of straight lines

$$\begin{cases} 2x+3y = 1, \\ 2x+3y = 2. \end{cases}$$

It is immediately obvious algebraically that these equations have no solutions. Geometrically, they represent parallel straight lines, with no finite point of intersection.

Again, consider the 'pair' of straight lines

$$\begin{cases} x+2y = 1, \\ 2x+4y = 2. \end{cases}$$

The second equation is a thinly disguised re-write of the first so any point of the single line represented has coordinates satisfying the equation. In fact, setting $y = \lambda$ and solving the first equation for x, we see that $(1-2\lambda, \lambda)$ is a solution, for all values of λ. Since we may assign values of the single parameter λ arbitrarily, our equations are said to have *one degree of freedom* (or to be a *one parameter system*). Geometrically, we have a pair of coincident straight lines.

The reader may feel this last case somewhat frivolous, and its extensive discussion pedantic. However, if the coefficients are unknown, this possibility must be remembered.

To summarize; given two equations in two unknowns, one of three possibilities occurs:

(i) The equations have a unique solution. (The two lines are distinct and intersect.)

(ii) The equations have no solution. (The two lines are distinct and parallel.)

(iii) The equations have one degree of freedom. (The two lines coincide.)

Example 1. *Solve the equations*

$$\begin{cases} x+ y = 2, \\ ax+2y = b. \end{cases}$$

Eliminating y, we have
$$(2-a) x = 4-b.$$

Case (i). If $a \neq 2$, we have the unique solution

$$x = \frac{4-b}{2-a}, \quad y = \frac{b-2a}{2-a}.$$

Case (ii). If $a = 2$, we have $0.x = 4-b$.

Sub-case (ii$a$). If $b \neq 4$, no solution for x exists.

Sub-case (ii$b$). If $b = 4$, x may take any value, y then being determined from the equation $x+y = 2$.

Thus, the complete solution of the equations takes the form

$$a \neq 2: x = \frac{4-b}{2-a}, \quad y = \frac{b-2a}{2-a};$$

$$a = 2, \quad b \neq 4: \text{ no solution;}$$

$$a = 2, \quad b = 4: \text{ one-parameter solutions } (\lambda, 2-\lambda).$$

The reader would be wise to consider the meaning of this solution geometrically.

The reader is probably so accustomed to solving pairs of simultaneous equations that it may not have occurred to him to ask what happens if he is given three (or more) equations in two unknowns. From geometrical considerations it should be fairly clear that, in general, no values of x and y satisfy all three equations simultaneously. However, consider the system
$$\begin{cases} x+2y = 5, \\ 3x- y = 1, \\ x-5y = -9. \end{cases}$$

Solving the first two equations we get $x = 1$, $y = 2$ and these values certainly do satisfy the third equation. Geometrically, these three equations represent three straight lines through the point $(1, 2)$ (see Figure 15.1).

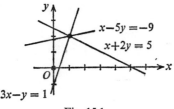

$$3x-y = 1$$

Fig. 15.1

It will be recalled that, if

$$a_1 x + b_1 y + c_1 = 0, \quad a_2 x + b_2 y + c_2 = 0$$

are two non-parallel straight lines, then any line through their point of intersection has the form

$$\mu(a_1 x + b_1 y + c_1) + \lambda(a_2 x + b_2 y + c_2) = 0.$$

Thus, in the particular case we are considering, any straight line through the point $(1, 2)$ has an equation of the form

$$\mu(x + 2y - 5) + \lambda(3x - y - 1) = 0.$$

Setting $\lambda/\mu = -\frac{1}{2}$ we obtain the third equation. This example illustrates the general result, that, if three equations in two unknowns have a solution, then any one equation is a linear combination of the other two (see Chapter 2.4).

2. LINEAR EQUATIONS IN TWO UNKNOWNS; CONTINUED

We consider pairs of equations of the form

$$\begin{cases} a_{11} x + a_{12} y = b_1, \\ a_{21} x + a_{22} y = b_2. \end{cases} \tag{1}$$

Writing

$$\mathbf{A} = \begin{pmatrix} a_{11} & a_{21} \\ a_{21} & a_{22} \end{pmatrix}, \quad \mathbf{x} = \begin{pmatrix} x \\ y \end{pmatrix}, \quad \mathbf{b} = \begin{pmatrix} b_1 \\ b_2 \end{pmatrix}$$

the equations (1) may be rewritten in the matrix form

$$\mathbf{Ax} = \mathbf{b}. \tag{2}$$

If we regard **A** as the matrix of a linear transformation T, equation (2) tells us that the image of the point P, with position vector $\begin{pmatrix} x \\ y \end{pmatrix}$, is the point B, with position vector $\begin{pmatrix} b_1 \\ b_2 \end{pmatrix}$. Thus, the problem of solving a pair of simultaneous equations may be reinterpreted as the problem of finding the point P whose image, under a given linear transformation, is a given point B.

If **A** is non-singular, that is, if det **A** $\neq$ 0, we have, for any point B,

$$\mathbf{Ax} = \mathbf{b}$$
$$\Leftrightarrow \mathbf{A^{-1}Ax} = \mathbf{A^{-1}b}$$
$$\Leftrightarrow \quad \mathbf{x} = \mathbf{A^{-1}b}$$

and we see that the unique point P, whose position vector is $\mathbf{A^{-1}b}$, has image B under the linear transformation T.

Ex. 1. Show that $\mathbf{A^{-1}}$ is the matrix of a linear transformation S.
[You must show that, for every point Q with position vector **y**, the image $S(\mathbf{y})$ exists and is unique and that $S(\lambda\mathbf{y}+\mu\mathbf{z}) = \lambda S(\mathbf{y})+\mu S(\mathbf{z})$.] The linear transformation S so defined is called the *inverse of the transformation* T; S and T satisfy the relations
$$S[T(\mathbf{x})] = \mathbf{x}; \quad T[S(\mathbf{y})] = \mathbf{y} \quad \text{for all } \mathbf{x}, \mathbf{y}.$$

As an example of the solution of equations whose matrix, **A**, is non-singular, consider
$$\begin{cases} 3x-2y = 4, \\ 2x+5y = 1. \end{cases}$$
Write
$$\mathbf{A} = \begin{pmatrix} 3 & -2 \\ 2 & 5 \end{pmatrix}, \quad \mathbf{b} = \begin{pmatrix} 4 \\ 1 \end{pmatrix},$$
then det **A** $= 19 \neq 0$ and
$$\mathbf{A^{-1}} = \tfrac{1}{19}\begin{pmatrix} 5 & 2 \\ -2 & 3 \end{pmatrix}$$
and we have
$$\begin{pmatrix} 3 & -2 \\ 2 & 5 \end{pmatrix}\begin{pmatrix} x \\ y \end{pmatrix} = \begin{pmatrix} 4 \\ 1 \end{pmatrix}$$
$$\Leftrightarrow \begin{pmatrix} x \\ y \end{pmatrix} = \frac{1}{19}\begin{pmatrix} 5 & 2 \\ -2 & 3 \end{pmatrix}\begin{pmatrix} 4 \\ 1 \end{pmatrix}$$
$$\Leftrightarrow \begin{pmatrix} x \\ y \end{pmatrix} = \frac{1}{19}\begin{pmatrix} 22 \\ -5 \end{pmatrix}.$$

The solution may be stated in the form $x = \tfrac{22}{19}$, $y = -\tfrac{5}{19}$ or, in terms of the linear transformation T whose matrix is **A**, the unique point $(\tfrac{22}{19}, -\tfrac{5}{19})$ maps into (4, 1).

284

Ex. 2. Solve the equations $\qquad 3x - 2y = 4,$
$$2x + 3y = 1$$
by using the inverse matrix method.

Suppose now that det $\mathbf{A} = 0$. Before discussing the existence of a point P whose image is B under the linear transformation T, consider the effect of T upon the unit square $OIMJ$. For a general transformation

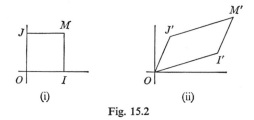

Fig. 15.2

(det $\mathbf{A} \neq 0$) $OI'M'J'$ is a parallelogram whose area is det $\mathbf{A}$ (see Chapter 13)—depicted in Figure 15.2, but, if det $\mathbf{A} = 0$, the parallelogram collapses and O, I', J', M' are collinear as shown in Figure 15.3.

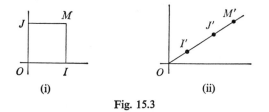

Fig. 15.3

Ex. 3. If det $\mathbf{A} = 0$, show that every point P of the plane maps into a point of the line OI'.

Since, in this latter case, T maps every point P into a point of the line OI', a point B not lying on the line cannot be the image of any point under T: the equations $\mathbf{A}x = \mathbf{b}$ are inconsistent.

However, if B does lie on OI', we may write the position vectors of J', I', B as $\mathbf{r}$, $m\mathbf{r}$, $c\mathbf{r}$ respectively; that is

$$\mathbf{Aj} = \mathbf{r}, \quad \mathbf{Ai} = m\mathbf{r}, \quad \mathbf{b} = c\mathbf{r}.$$

Then, $P(x, y)$ is a point which maps into B

$$\Leftrightarrow \qquad c\mathbf{r} = \mathbf{A}(x\mathbf{i} + y\mathbf{j})$$
$$\Leftrightarrow \qquad c\mathbf{r} = x(\mathbf{Ai}) + y(\mathbf{Aj})$$
$$\Leftrightarrow \qquad c\mathbf{r} = (mx + y)\,\mathbf{r}$$
$$\Leftrightarrow P \text{ lies in the straight line } y + mx = c,$$

and infinitely many points map into B, by the reversibility of the argument.

To summarize for the case det $\mathbf{A} = 0$:

(i) the equations $\mathbf{Ax} = \mathbf{b}$ have no solution (are *inconsistent*; equations with one or more solutions are said to be *consistent*).

⟺ there is no point which maps into B under T

⟺ B does not lie on the line OI';

(ii) the equations $\mathbf{Ax} = \mathbf{b}$ have infinitely many solutions

⟺ there are infinitely many points P which map into B under T

⟺ B does lies on the line OI'.

Ex. 4. Show that the equation $ax = b$ is uniquely soluble only if $a \neq 0$, in which case, the unique solution is $x = a^{-1}b$.

Discuss the case $a = 0$, showing that failure to obtain a unique solution can occur in two different ways.

Ex. 5. What can you say about the equation $\mathbf{Ax} = \mathbf{b}$ if $T(I) = T(J) = 0$? (T is the linear transformation with matrix $\mathbf{A}$.)

Exercise 15(a)

1. Solve, using the inverse matrix, the following pairs of simultaneous equations:

(i) $\begin{cases} 3x - y = 1, \\ 2x + 3y = 19; \end{cases}$ (ii) $\begin{cases} 3x + 2y = 1, \\ 2x + 7y = 29; \end{cases}$ (iii) $\begin{cases} 70x + 105y = 12, \\ 5x - 7y = 5. \end{cases}$

2. Solve for x the following equations, commenting upon any special cases that arise in the two cases:

(i) $ax + a^2 = b^2 - bx$; (ii) $ax + b = bx + c$.

3. Solve for x, y the following pairs of equations, commenting upon any special cases that arise for particular values of the coefficients a:

(i) $\begin{cases} 3x + ay = -2, \\ 3x + 2y = 3; \end{cases}$ (ii) $\begin{cases} x + 2y = 4, \\ 2x + ay = 2a; \end{cases}$ (iii) $\begin{cases} 3x + ay = 1, \\ ax + 12y = 2. \end{cases}$

4. Solve for x, y the following pairs of equations, commenting upon any special cases that arise for particular values of the coefficients a, b:

(i) $\begin{cases} ax + by = 2, \\ 12x - 4y = a + b; \end{cases}$ (ii) $\begin{cases} ax + 3y = 6; \\ x - by = 2; \end{cases}$ (iii) $\begin{cases} ax + by = 1, \\ bx + ay = -1. \end{cases}$

5. Discuss the solution of the following simultaneous equations for various values of a:

$$\begin{cases} x + y = 1, \\ 2x + ay = 5, \\ ax + y = -3. \end{cases}$$

6. Discuss the solution of the following simultaneous equations for various values of the coefficient a:

$$\begin{cases} ax + 3y = 4, \\ 3x - ay = 6, \\ x - 2y = a. \end{cases}$$

7. Discuss fully the solution of the following simultaneous equations for the unknowns x, y:

$$\begin{cases} ax+ by = c, \\ a^2x+b^2y = c^2. \end{cases}$$

8. Under what conditions do the *homogeneous equations*

$$\begin{cases} a_1x+b_1y = 0, \\ a_2x+b_2y = 0 \end{cases}$$

have a non-trivial solution (that is, a solution other than $x, y = 0$)? Solve the equations fully in the case where non-trivial solutions exist.

9. Solve for x, y the equations:

$$\begin{cases} x\cos\theta+y\cos\phi = \cos\alpha, \\ x\sin\theta+y\sin\phi = \sin\alpha. \end{cases}$$

10. Sketch the set, E, of points in the plane whose coordinates satisfy the inequality $x+y > 0$. The linear transformation, T, has matrix $\mathbf{A}$ where

$$\mathbf{A} = \begin{pmatrix} 1 & 2 \\ 5 & 0 \end{pmatrix}.$$

Sketch the image set $T(E)$.

11. T is a linear transformation whose matrix is $\mathbf{A}$, where

$$\mathbf{A} = \begin{pmatrix} 3 & -1 \\ 2 & -1 \end{pmatrix}.$$

If E is the set of points whose coordinates satisfy the inequality $y > 0$, sketch the image set $T(E)$.

3. SYSTEMS OF LINEAR EQUATIONS IN THREE UNKNOWNS; INTRODUCTION

Given perpendicular axes Ox, Oy, Oz in space, a linear equation connecting the three variables x, y, z is the equation of some plane. Two linear equations represent two planes which may be parallel (same unit normal vector) but otherwise intersect in a straight line. In general, three planes intersect in a unique point and thus, in general, three equations in three unknowns possess a unique solution; see Figure 15.4.

For example, the three planes

$$\begin{cases} x+ y+ z = 0, \\ x+2y+3z = -3, \\ x+ y- z = 4, \end{cases}$$

Fig. 15.4

have in common the single point $(1, 1, -2)$—a result readily derived by successively eliminating two of the variables.

However, just as in the case of two lines, complications may occur. Consider the equations

$$\begin{cases} x+ \ y+3z = 1, \\ x-2y+ \ z = 1, \\ 2x- \ y+4z = 2. \end{cases}$$

If we write

$$L_1 \equiv x+y+3z-1, \quad L_2 \equiv x-2y+z-1, \quad L_3 \equiv 2x-y+4z-2,$$

then it is readily seen that $L_3 = L_1+L_2$; thus, these three equations represent three planes through a common line (see page 62) and so possess infinitely many solutions (one degree of freedom); see Figure 15.5.

Again, the system

$$\begin{cases} 2x+y+3z = 6, \\ x+y+4z = 1, \\ x- \quad z = 1, \end{cases}$$

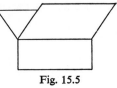

Fig. 15.5

has no solution, for by subtracting the first two equations we obtain $x-z = 5$, which is inconsistent with the third equation. Geometrically, $x-z = 5$, which is a plane through the line of intersection of the two planes

$$2x+y+3z = 6 \quad \text{and} \quad x+y+4z = 1,$$

is parallel to the third plane $x-z = 1$ and thus the line of intersection of the first two planes is parallel to the third plane. A similar result would hold whatever line of intersection was chosen and so the three planes form a triangular prism of uniform cross-section; see Figure 15.6.

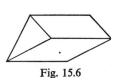
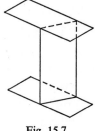

Fig. 15.6   Fig. 15.7

Another possibility is illustrated by the system

$$\begin{cases} x+ \ y+ \ z = 1, \\ 2x+2y+2z = 3, \\ x+ \ y+3z = 1, \end{cases}$$

which clearly has no solution, the first pair of equations being inconsistent. Geometrically, the first two planes are parallel to one another but not to the third plane; see Figure 15.7.

Again, we may have equations in the form:

$$\begin{cases} x+y+z = 1, \\ x+y+z = 2, \\ x+y+z = 3. \end{cases}$$

The equations are manifestly inconsistent and thus have no solution. Geometrically, they represent three parallel planes.

Finally, we may have two or three equations which reduce to the same equation, in which case we have one or two degrees of freedom—geometrically, two or three coincident planes. (Or, possibly, two coincident planes and the other plane parallel—giving no solution.)

To summarize: given three equations in three unknowns one of four possibilities may occur:

(i) The equations have a unique solution (no two of the planes are parallel and the planes do not have a common line of intersection).

(ii) The equations have no solution (either at least two of the planes are parallel or the three lines of intersection are parallel but not coincident or two of the planes coincide and the third is parallel).

(iii) The equations have a one-parameter solution (the planes have a common line of intersection).

(iv) The equations have a two-parameter solution (the planes all coincide).

The situation is more complicated than in two dimensions, as was to be expected but, if the reader keeps the various geometrical possibilities in his mind, he should avoid confusion.

Example 2. Solve completely the equations

$$\begin{cases} 3x+y+ z = a, & (1) \\ 2x+y- z = 4, & (2) \\ 5x+y+bz = 1. & (3) \end{cases}$$

$(1)-(2)$ gives $\qquad x \qquad +2z = a-4,$

$(1)-(3)$ gives $-2x+(1-b)z = a-1,$

$\therefore \qquad\qquad\qquad (5-b)z = 3(a-3).$

If $b \neq 5$, $\quad z = \dfrac{3(a-3)}{5-b}$

and substitution back gives

$$x = \frac{-a-2-ab+4b}{5-b}, \quad y = \frac{15+5a-12b+2ab}{5-b}$$

corresponding to the case of unique solution.

If $b = 5$, $a \neq 3$ there is no finite solution for z—we have a triangular prism of planes (clearly no two of the planes are parallel).

If $b = 5$, $a = 3$ the equations are consistent: putting $x = \lambda$ in (1) and (2) we have $2y = 7 - 5\lambda$, $2z = -1 - \lambda$ and the line of intersection of the first two planes is

$$\frac{x}{2} = \frac{y - \frac{7}{2}}{-5} = \frac{z + \frac{1}{2}}{-1} = \mu.$$

By substitution, the general point $(2\mu, \frac{7}{2} - 5\mu, -\frac{1}{2} - \mu)$ of this line lies on plane (3) for all μ. Since no pair of the planes coincide, we have three planes with a common line of intersection and the general solution may be taken as

$$x = 2\mu, \quad y = \tfrac{7}{2} - 5\mu, \quad z = -\tfrac{1}{2} - \mu$$

(or any comparable form).

If we are given four equations in three unknowns, we have, geometrically four planes and these will not, in general, have a common point. However, it is not impossible for four equations in three unknowns to be consistent; consider, for example, the four planes given by the equations

$$\begin{cases} x + y + z = 0, \\ 2x - 3y + z = -3, \\ x + 3y + z = 2, \\ 3x + 14y + 4z = 9, \end{cases}$$

all of which contain the point $(1, 1, -2)$. In practice, the best way of tackling such a system is to solve three of the equations and check whether or not the fourth equation is satisfied.

Ex. 6. Show that the system of equations

$$\begin{cases} x + y + z = 2, \\ 2x - 5y + z = -1, \\ x + 2y + 3z = -1, \\ 3x - 3y + 2z = 2 \end{cases}$$

is consistent.

4. SYSTEMS OF LINEAR EQUATIONS IN THREE UNKNOWNS; CONTINUED

As in the case of two unknowns, we may write the system

$$\begin{cases} a_{11}x + a_{12}y + a_{13}z = b_1, \\ a_{21}x + a_{22}y + a_{23}z = b_2, \\ a_{31}x + a_{32}y + a_{33}z = b_3, \end{cases} \tag{3}$$

in the matrix form $\qquad\qquad \mathbf{Ax = b.} \qquad\qquad\qquad (4)$

Regarding $\mathbf{A}$ as the matrix of a linear transformation T, equation (4) tells us that the image of the point P, whose position vector is

$$\begin{pmatrix} x \\ y \\ z \end{pmatrix},$$

is the point B, whose position vector is

$$\begin{pmatrix} b_1 \\ b_2 \\ b_3 \end{pmatrix}.$$

Again, the problem of solving a set of simultaneous equations may be interpreted as the problem of finding the point P whose image, under a given linear transformation, is a given point B.

If $\det \mathbf{A} \neq 0$ we have, as in section 2,

$$\mathbf{Ax} = \mathbf{b}$$
$$\Leftrightarrow \mathbf{A}^{-1}\mathbf{Ax} = \mathbf{A}^{-1}\mathbf{b}$$
$$\Leftrightarrow \quad \mathbf{x} = \mathbf{A}^{-1}\mathbf{b};$$

the unique point P, whose position vector is $\mathbf{A}^{-1}\mathbf{b}$, has image B under the linear transformation T.

Ex. 7. Show that $\mathbf{A}^{-1}$ is the matrix of a linear transformation S—the inverse of the transformation T.

As an example of the solution of equations whose matrix, $\mathbf{A}$, is non-singular consider

$$\begin{cases} x + y + z = 4, \\ x - y - z = -2, \\ x + 2y - z = 1, \end{cases}$$

$$\mathbf{A} = \begin{pmatrix} 1 & 1 & 1 \\ 1 & -1 & -1 \\ 1 & 2 & -1 \end{pmatrix}; \quad \mathbf{A}^{-1} = \begin{pmatrix} \frac{1}{2} & \frac{1}{2} & 0 \\ 0 & -\frac{1}{3} & \frac{1}{3} \\ \frac{1}{2} & -\frac{1}{6} & -\frac{1}{3} \end{pmatrix}$$ (by the usual inversion process)

and we have

$$\begin{pmatrix} x \\ y \\ z \end{pmatrix} = \begin{pmatrix} \frac{1}{2} & \frac{1}{2} & 0 \\ 0 & -\frac{1}{3} & \frac{1}{3} \\ \frac{1}{2} & -\frac{1}{6} & -\frac{1}{3} \end{pmatrix} \begin{pmatrix} 4 \\ -2 \\ 1 \end{pmatrix}$$

$$= \begin{pmatrix} 1 \\ 1 \\ 2 \end{pmatrix}.$$

The solution is $x = 1$, $y = 1$, $z = 2$ or, in terms of the linear transformation whose matrix is $\mathbf{A}$, the point $(1, 1, 2)$ maps into the point $(4, -2, 1)$.

291

The analysis of the case in which det $\mathbf{A} = 0$ follows the same pattern as the two-dimensional case and is pursued in the following series of exercises.

Ex. 8. Show that, under the linear transformation T whose matrix is given by

$$\mathbf{A} = \begin{pmatrix} a_1 & a_2 & a_3 \\ b_1 & b_2 & b_3 \\ c_1 & c_2 & c_3 \end{pmatrix}$$

the images of the points I, J, K, whose position vectors are $\mathbf{i}, \mathbf{j}, \mathbf{k}$, are I', J', K', whose position vectors are respectively the first, second and third columns of $\mathbf{A}$.

Ex. 9. Show that, under T, the unit cube, three of whose edges are OI, OJ, OK, transforms into a parallelepiped (a figure all of whose faces are parallelograms).

Ex. 10. Show that the volume of the parallelepiped obtained in Ex. 8. is det $\mathbf{A}$. (This result is necessary for the remaining exercises in this section, but its proof is rather hard and may be omitted at a first reading. The best proof depends upon the triple scalar product, which will be met in Book 2.)

Ex. 11. If det $\mathbf{A} = 0$, show that O, I', J', K' are coplanar. What does this tell us about the columns of $\mathbf{A}$?

Ex. 12. If the point D, with position vector $\mathbf{d}$, is the image of a point P under a linear transformation whose matrix is singular, what can be said about
  (i) the point D;   (ii) the vector $\mathbf{d}$?

Ex. 13. Show that, if det $\mathbf{A} = 0$, and if D lies in the plane $OI'J'K'$, then all the points of a certain line map into D.

Ex. 14. In the extreme case in which O, I', J', K' are collinear, what can be said about the columns of $\mathbf{A}$? If $\mathbf{Ax} = \mathbf{d}$ has a solution in this case, what can be said about (i) the point D; (ii) the vector $\mathbf{d}$?

In an actual example, det $\mathbf{A}$ should be calculated and the various cases in which det $\mathbf{A} = 0$ should be treated by reverting to the original equation. Matrix methods are admirably suited to studying the structure of systems of equations but rarely constitute an efficient procedure for their solution in individual cases.

Example 3. *Discuss the solution of the system of linear equations*

$$\begin{cases} x + ay + z = b, \\ ax + 3y + z = 1, \\ 5x + 8y + 3z = 1 \end{cases}$$

for various values of a and b.

$$\mathbf{A} = \begin{pmatrix} 1 & a & 1 \\ a & 3 & 1 \\ 5 & 8 & 3 \end{pmatrix} \quad \text{and so} \quad \det \mathbf{A} = -3a^2 + 13a - 14.$$

Thus det $\mathbf{A} = 0$ if $a = 2$ or $\frac{7}{3}$.

Case (i). $a \neq 2$, $a \neq \frac{7}{3}$.

The equations have a unique solution for all values of b.

Case (ii). $a = 2$.

The equations reduce to

$$\begin{cases} x+2y+\ z = b, & (1) \\ 2x+3y+\ z = 1, & (2) \\ 5x+8y+3z = 1. & (3) \end{cases}$$

Eliminating z between (2) and (3), and between (1) and (2),

$$\begin{cases} x+\ y \quad\ = 2, & (4) \\ x+\ y \quad\ = 1-b. & (5) \end{cases}$$

Thus, the equations are consistent if and only if $b = -1$, in which case we have a one-parameter solution $x = \lambda$, $y = 2-\lambda$, $z = \lambda - 5$ (on using equations (4) and (1)).

Case (iii). $a = \frac{7}{3}$.

The equations reduce to

$$\begin{cases} 3x+7y+3z = 3b, & (6) \\ 7x+9y+3z = 3, & (7) \\ 5x+8y+3z = 1. & (8) \end{cases}$$

(6)+(7)−2(8) gives $\qquad 0 = 3b+3-2.$

Thus, the equations are consistent if and only if $b = -\frac{1}{3}$, in which case we have a one-parameter solution $x = \lambda$, $y = 2(1-\lambda)$, $z = \frac{1}{3}(11\lambda - 15)$ (from equations (7) and (8)).

5. HOMOGENEOUS EQUATIONS

We now consider the system of linear equations

$$\begin{cases} a_{11}x+a_{12}y+a_{13}z = 0, \\ a_{21}x+a_{22}y+a_{23}z = 0, \\ a_{31}x+a_{32}y+a_{33}z = 0, \end{cases}$$

or $\qquad\qquad\qquad\qquad \mathbf{Ax = 0.}$

Such a system is said to be *homogeneous*. If $\mathbf{A}$ is regarded as the matrix of a linear transformation T we seek these points which are mapped into the origin under T. It is easy to see that the origin maps into the origin under any linear transformation; that is, that $\mathbf{x} = \mathbf{0}$ is always a solution for a set of homogeneous equations—we call this the *trivial solution*—but it is of more interest to look for *non-trivial solutions* $\mathbf{x} \neq \mathbf{0}$.

Ex. 15. Show that the linear transformation T whose matrix is

$$A = \begin{pmatrix} 3 & 7 & 1 \\ 1 & -1 & -3 \\ 1 & 3 & 1 \end{pmatrix}$$

maps all points of the line $\quad \dfrac{x}{2} = \dfrac{y}{-1} = \dfrac{z}{1}$

into the origin.

What does this tell us about the system of homogeneous equations

$$\begin{cases} 3x+7y+ \ z = 0, \\ x- \ y-3z = 0, \\ x+3y+ \ z = 0? \end{cases}$$

We conclude this chapter by proving a necessary and sufficient condition for the existence of non-trivial solutions of the homogeneous equations $\mathbf{Ax} = \mathbf{0}$.

Theorem 15.1

$$\mathbf{Ax} = \mathbf{0} \text{ has a non-trivial solution} \Leftrightarrow \det \mathbf{A} = 0.$$

Proof. (i) If $\det \mathbf{A} \neq 0$, $\mathbf{A}^{-1}$ exists and $\mathbf{x} = \mathbf{0}$ is the only solution.

Thus, if $\mathbf{Ax} = \mathbf{0}$ has a non-trivial solution, then $\det \mathbf{A} = 0$, and we have proved that a necessary condition for the existence of a non-trivial solution is $\det \mathbf{A} = 0$ (the implication $\Rightarrow$).

(ii) If $\det \mathbf{A} = 0$ and all the cofactors are zero then, by the result proved in Miscellaneous Exercise 14, Question 15, the rows of $\mathbf{A}$ are in proportion and the three equations reduce to a single equation, which has a two-parameter solution.

If $\det \mathbf{A} = 0$ and at least one cofactor, say A_{11}, is non-zero, then

$$\begin{aligned} a_{11}A_{11}+a_{12}A_{12}+a_{13}A_{13} &= 0 \quad (\det \mathbf{A} = 0), \\ a_{21}A_{11}+a_{22}A_{12}+a_{23}A_{13} &= 0, \\ a_{31}A_{11}+a_{32}A_{12}+a_{33}A_{13} &= 0, \end{aligned} \Bigg\} \text{ expansion by alien cofactors.}$$

We have thus constructed a solution

$$x = A_{11}, \quad y = A_{12}, \quad z = A_{13}$$

which is non-trivial, since $A_{11} \neq 0$.

The condition $\det \mathbf{A} = 0$ is sufficient to ensure the existence of a non-trivial solution (the implication $\Leftarrow$).

Exercise 15 (b)

1. Solve the equations $\quad \begin{cases} 3x+ \ y+ \ z = -2, \\ 2x+2y+3z = 8, \\ x+3y+2z = 6 \end{cases}$

(i) by successive elimination; (ii) by using the inverse matrix.

294

2. Calculate the inverse of the matrix

$$\begin{pmatrix} -3 & 11 & 7 \\ -1 & 4 & 3 \\ 2 & -7 & -5 \end{pmatrix}$$

and hence solve the equations

$$\begin{cases} -3x+11y+7z = a, \\ -x+4y+3z = b, \\ 2x-7y-5z = c \end{cases}$$

(i) when $a = 4$, $b = 1$, $c = -2$;   (ii) when $a = 1$, $b = 1$, $c = -1$;
(iii) when $a = 1$, $b = -6$, $c = 0$.

3. Solve the equations

$$\begin{cases} x-2y+z = 1, \\ 3x+2y-3z = 7, \\ 5x-2y-z = 9 \end{cases}$$

and interpret your result geometrically.

4. Show that the matrix

$$A = \begin{pmatrix} 3 & -1 & 2 \\ 2 & 3 & -1 \\ 1 & -15 & 10 \end{pmatrix}$$

is singular.
   Discuss the solution of the equations

(i) $\begin{cases} 3x-y+2z = 4, \\ 2x+3y-z = 1, \\ x-15y+10z = 8; \end{cases}$ (ii) $\begin{cases} 3x-y+2z = 4, \\ 2x+3y-z = 1, \\ x-15y+10z = 9, \end{cases}$

and interpret your results geometrically.

5. Show that the equations

$$\begin{cases} 3x-y+z = 3, \\ ax+y+z = 4, \\ 8x-y+3z = b \end{cases}$$

are consistent and have a unique solution, provided $a \neq 2$.
   Discuss the solution of the equations for the case $a = 2$.

6. Discuss the solution of the equations

$$\begin{cases} x+y+z = 1, \\ ax+ay+2z = 1, \\ 3x+3y+(a+1)z = b \end{cases}$$

for various values of a, b.
   Interpret your various results geometrically.

7.

$$A = \begin{pmatrix} 3 & -1 & 1 \\ 2 & 1 & -1 \\ 1 & -4 & -1 \end{pmatrix}, \quad B = \begin{pmatrix} 2 & -1 & -1 \\ 3 & -1 & 2 \\ 5 & -1 & -2 \end{pmatrix}.$$

A maps the point P into the point Q and B maps the point Q into the point R, whose coordinates are $(-5, 0, 0)$. Find the coordinates of P.

8. Discuss the solution of the equations

$$\begin{cases} 3x+2y+az = 2a, \\ ax+\ y+6z = 15, \\ \ x+2y+3z = 8 \end{cases}$$

for various values of a.

Interpret your results geometrically.

9. Find the value of a for which the homogeneous equations

$$\begin{cases} 6x+2y-\ z = 0, \\ 3x+ay-2z = 0, \\ 3x-2y+\ z = 0 \end{cases}$$

have a non-trivial solution, and find solutions for this case.

10. Prove that, if det $\mathbf{A} = 0$ and if $\mathbf{A}\mathbf{x}_1 = \mathbf{b}$ and $\mathbf{A}\mathbf{x}_2 = \mathbf{0}$, then $\mathbf{x}_1+\lambda\mathbf{x}_2$ is a solution for the equation $\mathbf{A}\mathbf{x} = \mathbf{b}$, for all values of λ.

Find a solution of the equations

$$\begin{cases} x+\ y+\ z = a, \\ 3x-5y-\ z = b, \\ 2x-8y-3z = c \end{cases}$$

when $a = b = c = 0$ and hence write down the general solution of the equations when $a = 1, b = 3, c = 2$.

11. A linear transformation T has matrix

$$\mathbf{A} = \begin{pmatrix} 3 & 1 & 2 \\ 1 & 4 & 1 \\ 2 & -3 & 1 \end{pmatrix}.$$

Show that T maps all points of the line

$$\frac{x}{7} = \frac{y}{1} = \frac{z}{-11}$$

into the origin, and find the line of points that maps into the point $(6, 6, 0)$. What is the relation between these two lines?

12.

$$\mathbf{A} = \begin{pmatrix} a_1 & b_1 & c_1 \\ a_2 & b_2 & c_2 \\ a_3 & b_3 & c_3 \end{pmatrix}.$$

A_1 is the cofactor of a_1, etc., and det $\mathbf{A} = \Delta$. If

$$a_1x+b_1y+c_1z = d_1,$$
$$a_2x+b_2y+c_2z = d_2,$$
$$a_3x+b_3y+c_3z = d_3,$$

prove that $\Delta x = d_1 A_1+d_2 A_2+d_3 A_3.$

If $\Delta = 0$, what does the value of the expression $d_1 A_1+d_2 A_2+d_3 A_3$ tell you about the solution of the given system of equations?

296

13. Prove that, if

$$A = \begin{pmatrix} a_1 & b_1 & c_1 \\ a_2 & b_2 & c_2 \\ a_3 & b_3 & c_3 \end{pmatrix}, \quad d = \begin{pmatrix} d_1 \\ d_2 \\ d_3 \end{pmatrix}, \quad x = \begin{pmatrix} x \\ y \\ z \end{pmatrix}$$

and if $\det A \neq 0$, then the unique solution of the equation

$$Ax = d$$

is given by

$$\frac{x}{\begin{vmatrix} d_1 & b_1 & c_1 \\ d_2 & b_2 & c_2 \\ d_3 & b_3 & c_3 \end{vmatrix}} = \frac{y}{\begin{vmatrix} a_1 & d_1 & c_1 \\ a_2 & d_2 & c_2 \\ a_3 & d_3 & c_3 \end{vmatrix}} = \frac{z}{\begin{vmatrix} a_1 & b_1 & d_1 \\ a_2 & b_2 & d_2 \\ a_3 & b_3 & d_3 \end{vmatrix}} = \frac{1}{\det A}.$$

14. The linear transformation, T, has matrix A where

$$A = \begin{pmatrix} 3 & 1 & 2 \\ -1 & 2 & -1 \\ 5 & -1 & 4 \end{pmatrix}.$$

E is the set of points in space whose coordinates satisfy the inequalities $x > 0$, $y > 0$, $z > 0$, $x+y+z < 1$. Determine the image set $T(E)$.

Miscellaneous Exercise 15

1. Find the inverse of the matrix

$$\begin{pmatrix} 1 & 0 & 3 \\ -1 & 2 & -1 \\ 2 & -4 & 1 \end{pmatrix}.$$

Given the equations

$$\begin{cases} 2x_1 - 4x_2 + x_3 = a, \\ x_1 \qquad\;\; + 3x_3 = b, \\ -x_1 + 2x_2 - x_3 = c, \end{cases}$$

find the solutions

(i) when $a = 1, b = 1, c = -1$;   (ii) when $a = -\frac{1}{2}, b = 2, c = 0$.

(M.E.I.)

2. Let A be a 3×3 real matrix and b a three-rowed column vector. It is proposed to solve the equation

$$Ax = b$$

and a particular solution $x = x_0$ is noted. Prove that any other solution may be written in the form

$$x = x_0 + u,$$

where u is a solution of the equation $Ax = 0$. Prove conversely that any vector $x_0 + u$ is a solution of the equation, where x_0 is a fixed particular solution of the equation and u is any vector such that $Au = 0$.

Interpret geometrically the equation and its solutions if A is singular (i) when x_0 exists, and (ii) when there is no such particular solution x_0.   (M.E.I.)

3. If

$$\mathbf{M} = \begin{pmatrix} 2 & 3 & 6 \\ 6 & 2 & -3 \\ 3 & -6 & 2 \end{pmatrix},$$

form the product $\mathbf{MM'}$ and show that $\mathbf{M'} = 49\mathbf{M}^{-1}$.

Without multiplying out, state the product $\mathbf{M'M}$, giving reasons for your answer. Hence, or otherwise, find the solution of the equations:

$$2x_1 + 3x_2 + 6x_3 = 1,$$
$$6x_1 + 2x_2 - 3x_3 = 1,$$
$$3x_1 - 6x_2 + 2x_3 = 2. \qquad \text{(M.E.I.)}$$

4. The simultaneous equations

$$x + 2y = 4,$$
$$2x - y = 0,$$
$$3x + y = 5$$

may be written in matrix form as

$$\begin{pmatrix} 1 & 2 \\ 2 & -1 \\ 3 & 1 \end{pmatrix} \begin{pmatrix} x \\ y \end{pmatrix} = \begin{pmatrix} 4 \\ 0 \\ 5 \end{pmatrix} \quad \text{or} \quad \mathbf{AX} = \mathbf{B}.$$

Carry out numerically the procedure of the following three steps:

(i) $\mathbf{A'AX} = \mathbf{A'B}$;

(ii) $(\mathbf{A'A})^{-1}\mathbf{A'AX} = (\mathbf{A'A})^{-1}\mathbf{A'B}$;

(iii) $\mathbf{IX} = \begin{pmatrix} x \\ y \end{pmatrix} = (\mathbf{A'A})^{-1}\mathbf{A'B}.$

Verify that the values of x, y so found do not satisfy all the original three equations. Suggest a reason for this.

Under what circumstances will the procedure given above, when applied to a set of three simultaneous equations in two variables, result in values which satisfy the equations? (SMP)

5. By systematic elimination, find values of A, B, C in terms of a, b, c, such that

$$\begin{cases} x + y + z = 1, \\ ax + by + cz = a+b+c, \\ a^2x + b^2y + c^2z = bc+ca+ab, \end{cases}$$

if and only if

$$\begin{cases} x+y+z = 1, \\ Ay + Bz = b+c \\ Cz = a^2+b^2. \end{cases}$$

Solve the equations, assuming a, b, c are all different.

Describe geometrically the configuration of planes, in three-dimensional Euclidean space, with equations:

$$x + y + z = 1,$$
$$x + 2y + 2z = 5,$$
$$x + 4y + 4z = 8. \qquad \text{(SMP)}$$

6. Solve the simultaneous equations

$$x+\ y+\ z = 3,$$
$$x+2y+3z = 6,$$
$$x+3y+kz = 4+k$$

(i) when $k \neq 5$;

(ii) when $k = 5$, giving the general solution. (SMP)

7. If **A** is the matrix $\begin{pmatrix} a & b \\ c & d \end{pmatrix}$ and **X** is the non-zero matrix $\begin{pmatrix} x \\ y \end{pmatrix}$, show that, if $\mathbf{AX} = \lambda\mathbf{X}$, where λ is a number, real or complex, then

$$\lambda^2 - (a+d)\lambda + (ad-bc) = 0.$$

Show that **A** itself satisfies this quadratic equation, in the sense that

$$\mathbf{A}^2 - (a+d)\mathbf{A} + (ad-bc)\mathbf{I} = \mathbf{0},$$

where **I** is the matrix $\begin{pmatrix} 1 & 0 \\ 0 & 1 \end{pmatrix}$ and **0** is the matrix $\begin{pmatrix} 0 & 0 \\ 0 & 0 \end{pmatrix}$. (Oxford)

8. By considering $\det(\mathbf{A} - \lambda\mathbf{I})$, extend the result of Question 7 to a 3×3 matrix **A**.

9. Factorize the determinant $\begin{vmatrix} 1 & 1 & 1 \\ a & b & c \\ a^2 & b^2 & c^2 \end{vmatrix}.$

Show that, if no two of a, b, c are equal, the equations

$$x+\ y+\ z = a,$$
$$ax+\ by+\ cz = ab,$$
$$a^2x+b^2y+c^2z = abc,$$

have unique solutions for x, y, z, and find them.

Discuss the special cases

(i) $a = b \neq c$; (ii) $b = c \neq a$; (iii) $a = b = c$. (M.T.)

10. Prove that the only value of λ allowing a real non-trivial solution of the simultaneous equations

$$x\ \ \ \ \ -z = \lambda x,$$
$$y+z = \lambda y,$$
$$4x+2y-z = \lambda z,$$

is $\lambda = 1$. (M.T.)

11. If A, B are 3×3 matrices and x a three-rowed column vector such that there exist numbers λ, μ such that

$$\mathbf{Ax} = \lambda\mathbf{x}, \quad \mathbf{Bx} = \mu\mathbf{x},$$

prove that there exists a number ν such that

$$\mathbf{ABx} = \nu\mathbf{x}.$$

Prove further that, if x_1, x_2, x_3 are three linearly independent column vectors with this property, then A and B are commutative for multiplication.

12. Write the two sets of three equations

$$a_{i1}x_1 + a_{i2}x_2 + a_{i3}x_3 = c, \quad b_{i1}y_1 + b_{i2}y_2 + b_{i3}y_3 = x_i \quad (i = 1, 2, 3)$$

in matrix form, and prove that they can be solved uniquely for $x_1, x_2, x_3, y_1, y_2, y_3$ if and only if det $\mathbf{AB} \neq 0$, where $\mathbf{A}$ and $\mathbf{B}$ are the 3×3 matrices of coefficients in the two sets of equations.

Show that the equations

$$x_1 + 2x_2 = 2, \quad x_1 + x_2 + x_3 = 1, \quad 3x_2 - x_3 = k,$$

$$3y_1 + y_2 + 4y_3 = x_1, \quad -y_1 + 2y_2 - 3y_3 = x_2, \quad y_1 + 5y_2 - 2y_3 = x_3$$

are inconsistent if $k \neq 7$, and find the most general solution for $x_1 \ldots y_3$ if $k = 7$.
(M.T.)

13. Prove that, if $k \neq 0$, the system of equations

$$2x + y \quad = a,$$
$$x + ky - z = b,$$
$$y + 2z = c$$

has a unique solution (x, y, z) for every choice of (a, b, c).

Show also that, when $k = 0$, the system is consistent if and only if (a, b, c) satisfy a certain linear relation, and find this relation.

Verify that the system is consistent when $k = 0$ and $(a, b, c) = (1, 1, -1)$ and find an expression for the general solution of the system in this case.
(M.T.)

14. Find, for all values of the parameter λ, the number of solutions of the equations

$$x + 2y + \lambda z = 0,$$
$$2x + 3y - 2z = \lambda,$$
$$\lambda x + y + z = 3.$$
(M.T.)

16. *Discrete probability distributions*

1. INTRODUCTION:
THE UNIFORM DISTRIBUTION

In Chapter 7 we discussed the concept of an outcome space for a random experiment. To each elementary event we ascribed a probability and the entire set of probabilities was described as a *probability distribution for the outcome space*. In this chapter we shall enumerate various possible probability distributions that find frequent use as mathematical models for random experiments. We shall generally define our outcome space in terms of an associated random variable X (see Chapter 10), and we shall thus be able to talk about the mean and variance of the distribution; however, it must be remembered that, for example, the mean is defined as $\mathscr{E}(X)$ and so, if a new random variable, Y, is chosen, the mean naturally changes, too. Unless there is any possibility of confusion, we shall refer to the mean and variance of X as μ and σ^2 respectively.

Suppose we have an outcome space consisting of n elementary events, with associated random variable, X, where

$$X = \{1, 2, 3, ..., n\}.$$

Perhaps the simplest assumption we can make about the n possible outcomes is that each one is as likely to occur as any other. Thus we take

$$\Pr(X = r) = 1/n. \tag{1}$$

Equation (1) defines the *uniform distribution for n possible outcomes.*

The uniform distribution is, in a way, fundamental, for we may often subdivide the elements of an outcome space in such a way that the new outcome space may reasonably be given a uniform distribution. This is not always possible, however; a simple counter-example might be the fall of a biased coin.

The mean, μ, of the random variable X with a uniform distribution is given by

$$\mu = \mathscr{E}(X)$$

$$= \sum_{r=1}^{n} r \cdot \frac{1}{n}$$

$$= \tfrac{1}{2}(n+1). \tag{2}$$

Again, the variance, σ^2, is given by

$$\sigma^2 = \mathscr{E}[(X-\mu)^2]$$
$$= \mathscr{E}[X^2]-\mu^2$$
$$= \sum_{r=1}^{n} r^2 \cdot \frac{1}{n} - \tfrac{1}{4}(n+1)^2$$
$$= \tfrac{1}{6}(n+1)(2n+1)-\tfrac{1}{4}(n+1)^2$$
$$= \tfrac{1}{12}(n^2-1). \tag{3}$$

The reader will find a large number of examples on the uniform distribution at the end of Chapter 7.

Ex. 1. A man spins a coin and throws a die. For a head he scores -1, for a tail $+1$, and this he adds to the score showing on the uppermost face of the die. The values of the random variable, X, where

$$X = \{0, 1, 2, ..., 7\}$$

represent his total score. Why do you think a uniform distribution would be an unsuitable mathematical model for this eight-point space? Suggest a way of subdividing the sample space so that a uniform distribution would be suitable.

2. THE BINOMIAL DISTRIBUTION

The simplest possible type of random experiment is one that has just two possible outcomes, which we may conveniently designate success and failure. An experiment of this type is called a *Bernoulli trial*. (J. Bernoulli, 1654–1705, one of a family of distinguished mathematicians, whose famous work on probability, the *Ars Conjectandi*, was published posthumously in 1713.). Some examples of Bernoulli trials are
   (i) a coin is tossed : does it show heads or tails?;
   (ii) a person is tested for disease: has he got the disease or not?;
   (iii) the height of a person is measured: is it less than six feet or not?;
   (iv) a marksman fires at a target: does he hit or miss the bull?
   If the probabilities of the two possible outcomes of a Bernoulli trial are p (success) and q (failure) (where $p+q = 1$) and n independent repetitions of the trial are made, we may define the random variable X as the number of successes obtained in the n trials and calculate $p(r) = \Pr(X = r)$, $r = 1, 2, 3, ..., n$.
   Method I. Suppose first we assign some specific order in which we should obtain the r successes: for sake of argument, suppose the first r trials result in success and the final $(n-r)$ trials in failure. Then, by independence,

the probability of obtaining this sequence is $p^r q^{n-r}$. But there are $\binom{n}{r}$ different sequences possible. Thus

$$p(r) = \Pr(X = r) = \binom{n}{r} p^r q^{n-r}. \tag{4}$$

Method II. The p.g.f. for a single Bernoulli trial is given by

$$\mathscr{E}(t^r) = p \cdot t^1 + q \cdot t^0$$
$$= pt + q.$$

Thus, the probability generating function for n independent Bernoulli trials is given by
$$G(t) = (pt + q)^n.$$

Thus $p(r) = $ coefficient of t^r in the expansion of $(pt + q)^n$

$$= \binom{n}{r} p^r q^{n-r}.$$

The probability distribution defined by equation (4) is called the *binomial distribution*. It is easily verified that (4) does indeed define a valid probability distribution. For $\Pr(X = r) > 0$ and also

$$\sum_{r=0}^{n} \binom{n}{r} p^r q^{n-r} = (p+q)^n, \quad \text{by the Binomial Theorem;}$$
$$= 1, \quad \text{since} \quad p + q = 1.$$

It finds a wide field of application as a probability model but the reader must always take care to remember the binomial distribution applies only if we have n *independent* repetitions of a Bernoulli trial. A binomial distribution is known completely if the two parameters n and p are given; the phrase 'the binomial distribution arising from n repetitions of a Bernoulli trial with probability of success p' is often abbreviated to $B(n, p)$.

Example 1. *Six unbiased dice are thrown. What is the probability of securing three or more sixes?*

The dice may be assumed to fall independently and so the random variable X (= number of sixes showing) has a binomial distribution with probability $\frac{1}{6}$ of success on each of the six Bernoulli trials.

Thus

$$\Pr(X \geqslant 3) = 1 - p(X < 3)$$
$$= 1 - \left\{ \left(\frac{5}{6}\right)^6 + \binom{6}{1}\left(\frac{5}{6}\right)^5\left(\frac{1}{6}\right) + \binom{6}{2}\left(\frac{5}{6}\right)^4\left(\frac{1}{6}\right)^2 \right\}$$
$$\approx 0 \cdot 06.$$

303

We next derive expressions for the mean, μ, and variance, σ^2, of the number of successes in a binomial distribution. We shall give two methods, the first one using the definition (4) directly, the second employing the probability generating function (and using Theorem 10.5).

Method I. By definition

$$\mu = \mathscr{E}(X) = \sum_{r=0}^{n} r \binom{n}{r} p^r q^{n-r}$$

$$= \sum_{r=1}^{n} n \binom{n-1}{r-1} p^r q^{n-r}, \quad \text{since} \quad \binom{n}{r} = \frac{n!}{r!(n-r)!} = \frac{n}{r}\binom{n-1}{r-1}$$

$$= np \sum_{r=1}^{n} \binom{n-1}{r-1} p^{r-1} q^{n-r}$$

$$= np(p+q)^{n-1}, \quad \text{by the Binomial Theorem,}$$

$$= np, \quad \text{since} \quad p+q = 1.$$

Again

$$\sigma^2 = \mathscr{E}[(X-\mu)^2] = \mathscr{E}[X^2] - \mu^2, \quad \text{by Theorem 10.1,}$$

$$= \sum_{r=0}^{n} r^2 \binom{n}{r} p^r q^{n-r} - n^2 p^2, \quad \text{using the first part,}$$

$$= \sum_{r=1}^{n} nr \binom{n-1}{r-1} p^r q^{n-r} - n^2 p^2$$

$$= \sum_{r=2}^{n} n(n-1) p^2 \binom{n-2}{r-2} p^{r-2} q^{n-r}$$

$$+ \sum_{r=1}^{n} np \binom{n-1}{r-1} p^{r-1} q^{n-r} - n^2 p^2,$$

$$\text{on writing} \quad r = (r-1)+1,$$

$$= n(n-1) p^2 + np - n^2 p^2, \quad \text{since} \quad p+q = 1,$$

$$= npq.$$

Thus we arrive at the important result: the mean and variance of the number of successes in a binomial distribution $B(n, p)$ are given by

$$\mu = np, \quad \sigma^2 = npq. \tag{5}$$

Method II. Since the p.g.f. for the binomial distribution is given by

$$G(t) = (pt+q)^n$$

we have

$$G'(t) = np(pt+q)^{n-1}, \quad G''(t) = n(n-1) p^2(pt+q)^{n-2} \quad (n \geqslant 2).$$

Putting $t = 1$, $\mu = np$, $\sigma^2 + \mu^2 - \mu = n(n-1) p^2$ and the results follow.

304

Example 2. A very large number of balls are in a bag, one-eighth being black and the rest white. Twelve balls are drawn at random. Find
    (i) *the probability of drawing three black balls and nine white balls;*
    (ii) *the probability of drawing at least 3 black balls;*
    (iii) *the expected number of black balls in the sample;*
    (iv) *the most likely number of black balls in the sample.*

Drawing a ball from the bag and noting its colour may be regarded as a Bernoulli trial (a black ball drawn being a success, $p = \frac{1}{8}$). Since a ball is not replaced before its successor is drawn, the twelve Bernoulli trials constituting our sample are not strictly independent; however, since the number of balls in the bag is very large, we may assume that Pr (*black ball drawn*) remains sensibly constant at $\frac{1}{8}$; that is, each trial is independent of what has previously occurred. Thus the random variable

$X =$ number of black balls contained in a sample of 12

has a binomial distribution $B(12, \frac{1}{8})$.

(i) $\Pr (X = 3) = \dbinom{12}{3} \left(\dfrac{1}{8}\right)^3 \left(\dfrac{7}{8}\right)^9$

$$\approx 0{\cdot}129;$$

(ii) $\Pr (X \geqslant 3) = 1 - \left\{ \left(\dfrac{7}{8}\right)^{12} + \dbinom{12}{1} \left(\dfrac{7}{8}\right)^{11} \left(\dfrac{1}{8}\right) + \dbinom{12}{2} \left(\dfrac{7}{8}\right)^{10} \left(\dfrac{1}{8}\right)^2 \right\}$

$$\approx 0{\cdot}182;$$

(iii) $\mathscr{E}(X) = np$

$$= 1{\cdot}5.$$

(iv) Write $p(r) = \Pr (X = r) = \dbinom{12}{r} p^r q^{12-r}.$

Then $\dfrac{p(r+1)}{p(r)} = \dfrac{\dbinom{12}{r+1} \left(\dfrac{1}{8}\right)^{r+1} \left(\dfrac{7}{8}\right)^{11-r}}{\dbinom{12}{r} \left(\dfrac{1}{8}\right)^{r} \left(\dfrac{7}{8}\right)^{12-r}}$

$$= \dfrac{12!}{(r+1)!\,(11-r)!} \dfrac{r!(12-r)!}{12!} \left(\dfrac{\frac{1}{8}}{\frac{7}{8}}\right)$$

$$= \dfrac{12-r}{7(r+1)}.$$

Thus $\dfrac{p(r+1)}{p(r)} < 1$ if $r \geqslant 1$

and so $p(1) = \dfrac{12-0}{7(0+1)} p(0) = \dfrac{12}{7} p(0)$

is the maximum of the $p(r)$; that is, the most likely number of black balls is 1.

[Notice that the ratio deduced in Example 2(iv) enables us to express $p(r)$ in terms of p_0. Thus:

$$p_1 = \tfrac{12}{7}p_0,$$

$$p_2 = \tfrac{11}{16}p_1 = \tfrac{33}{28}p_0,$$

$$p_3 = \tfrac{10}{24}p_2 = \tfrac{55}{112}p_0, \quad \text{etc.}$$

This is a particularly useful device for calculating binomial probabilities if a hand calculating machine is available.]

Ex. 2. Find the values of Pr $(X = r)$ in terms of Pr $(X = 0)$ for the binomial distribution $B(4, \tfrac{1}{6})$.

Ex. 3. If fifteen dice are thrown what is
   (i) the expected number of sixes showing;
   (ii) the most likely number of sixes showing?

Ex. 4. Calculate the mean and variance for the binomial distribution $B(9, \tfrac{1}{5})$.

Ex. 5. In a family of four children, what is the probability of there being two boys and two girls? What is the probability that the eldest two are boys and the youngest two girls? What are the odds against having all four children of the same sex?

Exercise 16(a)

1. A coin is tossed four times. Find the probability that heads appear
   (i) at the first two tosses, followed by two tails;
   (ii) just twice in the four throws;
   (iii) at least twice.

2. 10 % of the very large number of articles produced by a machine are faulty. What is the probability that a random sample of ten articles will
   (i) be free of faulty articles;
   (ii) contain more than two faulty articles?

3. From a packet containing a large number of seeds, 40 % of which are advertised to give red flowers and the others white, 10 plants are produced. What is the probability
   (i) that all the plants have red flowers;
   (ii) that all the plants have white flowers;
   (iii) that half the plants have red flowers and half white?

4. 10 % of the very large number of articles produced by a machine are faulty. If articles are taken at random and tested, how many articles will be tested, on average, before the first faulty article is found? What is the probability that the testing procedure will have to go on longer than this before the first faulty article is found?

5. (i) In a trial, eight coins are tossed together. In one hundred such trials how many times should one expect to obtain three heads and five tails?

(ii) If 8 % of articles in a large consignment are defective, what is the chance that a sample of thirty articles will contain fewer than three defectives?

(O & C)

6. A battery of four guns is firing on to an enemy emplacement. It is reckoned that each gun should score on the average one direct hit in every five shots, and that three direct hits are needed to destroy the emplacement. If each gun fires one shell, calculate the probability that the emplacement will be destroyed. With new gun crews it is reckoned that two of the guns should score one direct hit in every three shots and that the other two guns should score one direct hit in every four shots. If each gun now fires one shell, calculate the probability that the emplacement will be destroyed. (Cambridge)

7. Nine unbiased dice are thrown. Find $p(r)$, the probability that r sixes appear, and hence determine the value of $p(r+1)/p(r)$. Find
  (i) the expected number of sixes;
  (ii) the most likely number of sixes;
  (iii) the probability of obtaining more than one six.

8. (i) In a binomial distribution where the probabilities of the occurrence of an event are given by the terms of the expansion of $(p+q)^m$, the mean μ and the standard deviation σ of the distribution are given by the formulae

$$\mu = mp; \quad \sigma = \sqrt{(mpq)}.$$

Prove these formulae in the case where $m = 3$.
  (ii) Two men A and B play a game in which A should win eight games to every seven won by B. If they play three games, show that the probability that A will win at least two games is approximately 0.55. (Cambridge)

9. Playing a certain 'one-arm bandit', which is advertised to 'increase your money tenfold', costs 5p a turn; the player is returned 50p if more than eight balls out of a total of ten drop in a specified slot. The chance of any one ball dropping is p. Determine the chance of winning in a given turn, and for $p = 0.65$, calculate the mean profit made by the machine on five hundred turns. Evaluate the proportion of losing turns in which the player comes within one or two balls of winning ($p = 0.65$). (Cambridge)

10. Prove that, in the binomial distribution $B(2n, \frac{1}{2})$, the probability of scoring an even number of successes is $\frac{1}{2}$.

11. An experiment consists of tossing an unbiased coin twelve times and counting the number of heads obtained (X). If the mean and variance of X are μ and σ^2 respectively, find the value of

(i) Pr $(|X-\mu| > \sigma)$; (ii) Pr $(|X-\mu| > 2\sigma)$.

3. THE GEOMETRIC AND NEGATIVE
BINOMIAL DISTRIBUTIONS

We must now consider two further probability distributions associated with the independent repetitions of Bernoulli trials. However, instead of repeating the trial a fixed number of times and asking how many successes

307

have been obtained, we reverse the process by asking how long we must go on repeating the trial until a stipulated number of successes is obtained.

First, suppose we wish to calculate the probability that the first success occurs at the rth repetition of a Bernoulli trial, the probability of success in any one trial being p. (As in Section 2, we assume that each trial is independent of what has previously occurred.) We take as our random variable X, where

X = number of trials up to and including the trial which results in the first success.

There is no upper limit to the value X may take: we can theoretically continue obtaining failures for ever, although the probability of doing so steadily decreases.

Now Pr $(X = r)$ = Pr (*initially $(r-1)$ failures, followed by a success*), i.e.

$$\text{Pr } (X = r) = q^{r-1}p. \tag{6}$$

Equation (6) defines the *geometric distribution* for the random variable $X = \{1, 2, 3, ...\}$. It is easily seen that this is a valid probability distribution, for

$$\sum_{r=1}^{\infty} q^{r-1}p = \frac{p}{1-q}$$

$$= 1.$$

The mean, μ, and variance, σ^2, of the random variable X for a geometric distribution may be derived without undue difficulty: we give two possible methods.

Method I.
$$\mathscr{E}(X) = \sum_{r=1}^{\infty} rpq^{r-1},$$

$$q\mathscr{E}(X) = \sum_{r=1}^{\infty} rpq^r = \sum_{r=2}^{\infty} (r-1)\, pq^{r-1}.$$

Subtract:
$$p\mathscr{E}(X) = p + \sum_{r=2}^{\infty} pq^{r-1}$$

$$= p + \frac{pq}{1-q}$$

$$= 1, \quad \text{since} \quad p + q = 1,$$

$$\therefore \quad \mu = \mathscr{E}(X) = 1/p.$$

Again
$$\mathscr{E}(X^2) = \sum_{r=1}^{\infty} r^2 pq^{r-1},$$

$$q\mathscr{E}(X^2) = \sum_{r=1}^{\infty} r^2 pq^r = \sum_{r=2}^{\infty} (r-1)^2 pq^{r-1}.$$

Subtract:
$$p\mathscr{E}(X^2) = p + 2\sum_{r=2}^{\infty} rpq^{r-1} - \sum_{r=2}^{\infty} pq^{r-1}$$

$$= p + 2(\mu - p) - \frac{pq}{1-q}$$

$$= p + 2\{(1/p) - p\} - (1-p)$$

$$= (2/p) - 1,$$

$$\therefore \quad \sigma^2 = \mathscr{E}(X^2) - \mu^2$$

$$= \frac{2}{p^2} - \frac{1}{p} - \frac{1}{p^2}$$

$$= q/p^2.$$

Thus, for the geometric distribution,

$$\mu = \frac{1}{p}, \quad \sigma^2 = \frac{q}{p^2}. \tag{7}$$

Method II. The p.g.f. for the geometric distribution is given by

$$G(t) = \mathscr{E}(t^r)$$

$$= \sum_{r=1}^{\infty} pq^{r-1}t^r$$

$$= pt/(1-qt).$$

Thus
$$G'(t) = p/(1-qt)^2, \quad G''(t) = 2pq/(1-qt)^3$$

and results (7) follow on substituting $t = 1$ and using Theorem 10.5.

The geometric distribution is a suitable probability model in a number of practical examples; for example, in *inverse sampling*, articles are tested until a faulty article is found.

Example 3. 5% of the output of a certain machine is faulty. Articles are taken at random from the output and tested, the process stopping when the first faulty article is obtained. Find
(i) the expected duration of this sampling process;
(ii) the probability that the process will terminate before the expected value is reached.

We shall assume that the total output of the machine is large and so the individual Bernoulli trials of testing articles are independent, each with probability of success (that is, of finding a faulty article) equal to $\frac{1}{20}$. Adopting the geometric distribution as a suitable mathematical model, we have
  (i) mean length of sampling process $= 1/(\frac{1}{20}) = 20$;

(ii) $\Pr (X < 20) = 1 - \Pr (X \geqslant 20)$

$$= 1 - \sum_{r=20}^{\infty} (\tfrac{19}{20})^{r-1}(\tfrac{1}{20})$$

$$= 1 - [(\tfrac{19}{20})^{19} (\tfrac{1}{20})]/[1 - \tfrac{19}{20}]$$

$$\approx 0.623.$$

The concept underlying the geometric distribution may be generalized by asking how many Bernoulli trials will be required up to and including the kth success. Taking as our random variable $X = \{1, 2, 3, ...\}$ we observe that, if $X = r$, the rth outcome must be the kth success, probability p, and the previous $(k-1)$ successes are binomially distributed $B(r-1, p)$. Thus

$$\Pr (X = r) = p\left\{\binom{r-1}{k-1} p^{k-1}q^{(r-1)-(k-1)}\right\} \quad (p, r \geqslant k)$$

$$= \binom{r-1}{k-1} p^k q^{r-k} \quad (r \geqslant k). \tag{8}$$

Equation (8) defines the *negative binomial distribution*; to appreciate the reason for this name and also to facilitate the verification that this is indeed a valid probability distribution, we first observe that

$$X = X_1 + X_2 + ... + X_i + ... + X_k,$$

where X_i is the number of trials after the $(i-1)$th success up to and including the ith success. Thus, the p.g.f. for a negative binomial distribution is the kth power of the p.g.f. for a geometric distribution, i.e.

$$G(t) = p^k t^k (1-qt)^{-k}.$$

Writing
$$G(t) = a_k t^k + a_{k+1} t^{k+1} + a_{k+2} t^{k+2} + ...$$

we have for $r \geqslant k$,
$$\Pr (X = r) = a_{k+r},$$

$$\sum_{r=k}^{\infty} \Pr (X = r) = \sum_{s=0}^{\infty} a_{k+s}$$

$$= G(1)$$

$$= 1.$$

Furthermore,
$$G'(t) = kp^k t^{k-1}/(1-qt)^{k+1},$$

$$G''(t) = \frac{k(k-1+2qt) p^k t^{k-2}}{(1-qt)^{k+2}},$$

and it follows that
$$\mu = \frac{k}{p}, \quad \sigma^2 = \frac{kq}{p^2}. \tag{9}$$

310

Ex. 6. Devise an experiment for which you feel the negative binomial distribution would constitute a suitable mathematical model.

Ex. 7. Dice are thrown in succession until two sixes have appeared; find
  (i)   the probability that two dice in all are thrown;
  (ii) the probability that more than four dice are needed;
  (iii) the expected number of throws required.

4. THE POISSON DISTRIBUTION

Another distribution of common applicability associated with an infinite outcome space and random variable

$$X = \{0, 1, 2, 3, \ldots\}$$

is the *Poisson distribution*, defined by the equation

$$\Pr(X = r) = e^{-a} \cdot \frac{a^r}{r!} \quad (a > 0).$$

Since
$$\sum_{r=0}^{\infty} \Pr(X = r) = e^{-a} \sum_{r=0}^{\infty} \frac{a^r}{r!} \tag{10}$$

$$= e^{-a} e^{a}$$

$$= 1$$

and $\Pr(X = r) > 0$, for all r, equation (10) does constitute a valid probability distribution.

We shall show that the Poisson distribution arises as the limit of a binomial distribution in which $n \to \infty$ and $p \to 0$, in such a way that $np = a$ remains constant. Thus the Poisson distribution will form a suitable probability model, not only to situations where the binomial distribution applies directly and n is very large and p very small but also to situations where the binomial distribution is not directly applicable. For example, consider requests for trunk call connections made at a telephone exchange. Suppose that, for the period 7.00 a.m. to 8.00 a.m. they average out at three and suppose further that the request takes a negligible time to make. Dividing the hour up into a large number of short time intervals (say 720 of 5 seconds each), the probability of there being a call in any one of the intervals may be taken as $\frac{1}{240}$, on the assumption that the calls arrive independently throughout the hour, and the probability of two calls in the interval is negligible. Thus we have 720 independent repetitions of a Bernoulli trial ('Is there a call or not in a given 5 second interval?') with small probability of success $p = \frac{1}{240}$, and the Poisson distribution may be regarded as a good mathematical model to employ.

We must now verify our original assertion that a binomial distribution

$B(n, p)$ tends to a Poisson distribution as $n \to \infty$ and $p \to 0$ in such a way that $np = a, a > 0$. First, for $B(n, p)$

$$\Pr (X = r) = \binom{n}{r} p^r q^{n-r}$$

$$= \frac{n(n-1)\,(n-2)\, \ldots\, (n-r+1)}{r!} p^r (1-p)^n\, (1-p)^{-r}$$

$$= \frac{1\left(1-\frac{1}{n}\right)\left(1-\frac{2}{n}\right) \ldots \left(1-\frac{r-1}{n}\right)}{r!} a^r \left(1-\frac{a}{n}\right)^n (1-p)^{-r},$$

$$\text{since} \quad np = a.$$

Since r is a fixed number, the product of the r factors in the numerator of the first fraction tends to 1 as $n \to \infty$, and $(1 - p)^{-r}$ tends to 1 as $p \to 0$. Furthermore,

$$\left(1-\frac{a}{n}\right)^n \to e^{-a} \dagger$$

and we have

$$\Pr (X = r) \to \frac{e^{-a} a^r}{r!}$$

as required.

The Poisson distribution is completely described if we are given the value of a; thus, a Poisson distribution is a *one-parameter distribution* and a Poisson distribution with parameter a may be referred to as $P(a)$.

The mean, μ, and the variance, σ^2, of the Poisson distribution $P(a)$ may be found by the direct computation of $\mathscr{E}(X)$ and $\mathscr{E}(X^2)$. Thus

$$\mu = \mathscr{E}(X)$$

$$= \sum_{r=0}^{\infty} r \cdot \frac{e^{-a}\, a^r}{r!}$$

$$= \sum_{r=1}^{\infty} \frac{a^{r-1}}{(r-1)!} \cdot a e^{-a}$$

$$= a.$$

Similarly,

$$\sigma^2 = \mathscr{E}(X^2) - \mu^2$$

$$= a \quad \text{as above.}$$

For the Poisson distribution $P(a)$,

$$\mu = a, \quad \sigma^2 = a, \tag{11}$$

i.e. the mean and variance of the Poisson distribution $P(a)$ are both equal to a.

† For the proof of this and other results concerning the exponential function, see one of the books on calculus mentioned in the bibliography.

312

Ex. 8. Prove that, if the random variable $X = \{0, 1, 2, ...\}$ has equal mean and variance, this does not necessarily mean that X has a Poisson distribution.
   (*Hint*: consider a suitable uniform distribution.)

Example 4. *Traffic accidents are reported in a certain town at an average rate of four in a week. Estimate the probabilities:*
   (i)   *of a given week being accident free;*
   (ii) *of there being three or fewer accidents in a given week;*
   (iii) *of there being more than four accidents in a given week.*

To produce reasonable estimates of these probabilities we have first to set up a mathematical model of the situation. The assumption that accidents occur independently of one another is arguable but, without more detailed data, it would be difficult to make a more plausible assumption. With this hypothesis, a Poisson distribution for the number, X, of accidents per week would appear to be a reasonable model, for the reason outlined earlier. Thus we have

(i) $\mathrm{Pr}\,(X = 0) = e^{-4}$

$$\approx 0{\cdot}018;$$

(ii) $\mathrm{Pr}\,(X \leqslant 3) = e^{-4}\left(1 + 4 + \dfrac{4^2}{2!} + \dfrac{4^3}{3!}\right)$

$$\approx 0{\cdot}433;$$

(iii) $\mathrm{Pr}\,(X > 4) = 1 - e^{-4}\left(1 + 4 + \dfrac{4^2}{2!} + \dfrac{4^3}{3!} + \dfrac{4^4}{4!}\right)$

$$\approx 0{\cdot}371.$$

Exercise 16(b)

1. The random variable X can take values 0, 1, 2, 3, ... Given that X has a Poisson distribution, mean 2, calculate the probabilities

$$\mathrm{Pr}\,(X = 0), \quad \mathrm{Pr}\,(X = 1), \quad \mathrm{Pr}\,(X = 2), \quad \mathrm{Pr}\,(X = 3),$$

$$\mathrm{Pr}\,(X = 4), \quad \mathrm{Pr}\,(X = 5), \quad \mathrm{Pr}\,(X > 5).$$

2. Samples of forty articles at a time are taken periodically from the continuous production of a machine and the number of samples containing 0, 1, 2, ... defective articles are recorded in the following table:

No. defective per sample	0	1	2	3	4	5	6	Total
No. of samples	30	23	27	14	4	2	0	100

Find the mean number of defectives per sample.

Assuming that this is the mean of the population and that the Poisson distribution applies, find the chance of:

(*a*) a sample containing four or more defectives;

(*b*) two successive samples containing between them four or more defectives.

(O & C)

3. The following table shows the results of recording the telephone calls handled at a village telephone exchange between 1.00 p.m. and 2.00 p.m. on each of a hundred weekdays (e.g. on thirty-six days no such calls were made):

Calls	0	1	2	3	4 or more
Days	36	35	22	7	0

Assuming that calls arrive independently and at random, estimate

(i) the mean m of the corresponding Poisson probability distribution;

(ii) the probability that if the operator is absent for ten minutes no call will be missed;

(iii) the probability that if the operator is absent for ten minutes two or more calls will be missed. (Cambridge)

4. In an examination 60 % of the candidates pass but only 4 % obtain distinction. Use the binomial distribution to calculate the chance that a random group of ten candidates should contain at most two failures.

Use the Poisson distribution to calculate the chance that a random group of fifty candidates should contain more than one distinction. (Cambridge)

5. The road accidents in a certain area occur at an average rate of one per two days. Calculate the probability of 0, 1, 2, ..., 6 accidents per week in the district.

What is the most likely number of accidents per week?

How many days in a week are expected to be free of accidents? (M.E.I.)

(*Note.* This question is best attempted using a hand calculating machine, if one is available.)

6. Explain briefly what is meant by a Poisson distribution and show that for such a distribution the mean is equal to the variance.

In a bakery 3600 cherries are added to a mixture which is later divided up to make 1200 small cakes.

(i) Find the average number of cherries per cake.

(ii) Assuming that the number of cherries in each cake follows a Poisson distribution, estimate the number of cakes which will be without a cherry and the number with five or more cherries. (O & C)

7. 10 % of the output of screws from a machine are faulty. If screws are taken at random from the output until two faulty screws are found, what will be the average number of screws tested? What is the probability that precisely this number of screws will be needed?

8. 20 % of the butterflies in a district are of type A. If a random sample of size 10 is taken, find the probability

(i) that there will be just two butterflies of type A in the sample;

(ii) that the tenth butterfly caught will be the second one of type A.

314

9. Mass-produced articles are taken at random from a batch and tested until a faulty article is found. If the twenty-first article proves to be the first defective, is this at variance with the assumption that 10 % of all the articles are faulty?

10. If X is distributed according to a Poisson distribution with mean λ, write down the probability that $X = r$.

How is this probability modified if the values $X = 0$ are unobservable? Prove that the mean is now $\lambda/(1 - e^{-\lambda})$, and find the second moment† about $X = 0$.

(Oxford)

11. Evaluate $\Pr(X = r+1)/\Pr(X = r)$ for the Poisson distribution $P(a)$. If the numbers of misprints on pages of an uncorrected proof have a Poisson distribution with mean 2·7, what is the most likely number of misprints to be found on a given page?

12. The average proportion of bad eggs in an egg packing station is one in 2000. The eggs are packed in boxes containing six eggs each.

(i) Evaluate to two significant figures the probability that a box contains one bad egg.

(ii) A housewife complains if she obtains two or more boxes, with one bad egg each per hundred boxes. What is the probability that she complains.?

(M.E.I.)

13. During World War II, 537 flying bombs fell on south London. The distribution of the number of hits in 576 areas, each of 0·25 km², is given in the table. Compare the actual frequency with the theoretical frequency obtained by assuming that the aim was effectively random and followed a Poisson distribution with the same average number of hits.

No. of hits	0	1	2	3	4	5	6 or more
Frequency	229	211	93	35	7	1	0

(M.E.I. adapted)

5. SAMPLING INSPECTION SCHEMES

Suppose a machine produces a large number of articles and it is required to keep a check upon the number of articles produced which do not attain some prescribed standard; for convenience, we shall describe such articles as 'faulty'. The most obvious method is to check each article individually, but such a process suffers from several drawbacks; for example

(i) the process of testing might be very costly;

(ii) the process would almost certainly be time consuming;

(iii) by the very nature of the test, the article tested might be destroyed (consider, for example, the testing of photographic flash bulbs).

A more economic approach is to take a random sample from the total output, to test each article of the sample and to deduce, from a probabilistic argument, the quality of the whole output. The process of selecting a random sample is not as straightforward as it might appear; we shall,

† The *second moment* about $X = 0$ is $\mathscr{E}(X^2)$.

however, here assume that such a sample has been drawn, and concentrate upon the second part of the problem: inferring the quality of the population.

A simple approach would be to take a sample of size n, test each article and reject the batch as sub-standard if, say, more than m of the articles prove faulty. We begin by assuming that we have some percentage, $100p$ say, as an upper limit to the number of faulty articles which may be allowed before the manufacturing process is stopped and corrected for any fault.

Example 5. Samples of size 20 *are taken from a large batch of articles produced by a machine; if more than two faulty articles are discovered the batch is withdrawn, otherwise it is accepted. What is the probability that, if the machine is producing* 5 % *of faulty articles, the batch will be accepted? If the proportion of faulty articles rises to* 10 % *of the total output, what is the probability the batch will now be rejected?*

Since the batch is large, we may assume that the removal of twenty articles does not sensibly alter the proportion of defectives and so the binomial distribution $B(20, 0·05)$ may be taken as a suitable mathematical model for the experiment, where our random variable is the number, X, of defectives in a sample of size 20.

(i) If Pr (*article faulty*) $= \frac{1}{20}$, then
  Pr (*not more than* 2 *faulty articles in* 20)

$$= \left(\frac{19}{20}\right)^{20} + 20\left(\frac{19}{20}\right)^{19}\left(\frac{1}{20}\right) + \frac{20.19}{1.2}\left(\frac{19}{20}\right)^{18}\left(\frac{1}{20}\right)^2$$

$$\approx 0·925.$$

(ii) If Pr (*article faulty*) $= \frac{1}{10}$, then
  Pr (*more than* 2 *faulty articles in* 20)

$$= 1 - \left(\frac{9}{10}\right)^{20} - 20\left(\frac{9}{10}\right)^{19}\left(\frac{1}{10}\right) - \frac{20.19}{1.2}\left(\frac{9}{10}\right)^{18}\left(\frac{1}{10}\right)^2$$

$$\approx 0·649.$$

Thus, if only 5 % of the articles produced are faulty, the chance of accepting the batch is about $92\frac{1}{2}$%, whereas, if the number of faulty articles increases to 10 %, there is a 65 % chance of rejecting the batch.

Ex. 9. Comment upon the efficiency of the test given in Example 5. Suggest ways in which you feel it could be improved.

The testing procedure exhibited above is an example of a *single sampling inspection scheme*. Any sampling inspection scheme is open to two types of error:

(I) A batch with an acceptable number of faulty articles may be rejected.

(II) A batch with an unacceptable number of faulty articles may be accepted.

316

If $\alpha = \text{Pr}$ (error of Type I), $\beta = \text{Pr}$ (error of type II), then, in Example 1 above, $\alpha \approx 0.075$, $\beta \approx 0.351$, if we regard 5 % faulty as acceptable, but 10 % faulty as unacceptable.

It can be shown that, if the size of the sample is held fixed, but the standard of rejection is altered, either α increases and β decreases or vice versa. Thus, there is an unavoidable margin of error in any inspection scheme; the decision whether to minimize α or β depends upon such external arguments as whether it is economically more desirable to withdraw good batches or allow sub-standard batches on to the market. Of course, if the sample is increased, more accurate information about the population may be obtained and both α and β may be decreased.

Ex. 10. What objections are there to increasing the sample size in order to reduce α and β?

If the probability, p, that an individual article is faulty is now regarded as a variable, and the testing procedure is defined (that is, the sample size and number of faulty articles required for rejection are given), the probability P of accepting the batch is a function of p. The curve obtained by plotting P against p is called the *operating characteristic* for the testing plan. For example, with the test outlined in Example 5, the operating characteristic has the following shape:

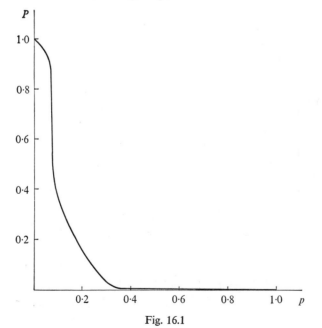

Fig. 16.1

From this graph, the probability of accepting (or rejecting) a sample given the proportion of defectives in the population may be read off. An increase in the sample size causes the operating characteristics to fall off more steeply, thereby improving the test.

Other schemes are possible, besides single sampling schemes. For example one can devise *double sampling schemes* as outlined in the next example.

Example 6. A sample of size 8 is taken from a large batch of articles produced by a machine. If the sample contains no faulty article the batch is accepted, if more than one, it is rejected; if, however, the sample contains a single faulty article, a second sample of eight articles is taken. The batch is now accepted if this second sample is free of faulty articles, otherwise it is rejected. Find

   (i) *the probability of accepting a batch containing 1 % of faulty articles;*
  (ii) *the probability of rejecting a batch containing 10 % of faulty articles;*
 (iii) *the average size of sample tested in case* (ii).

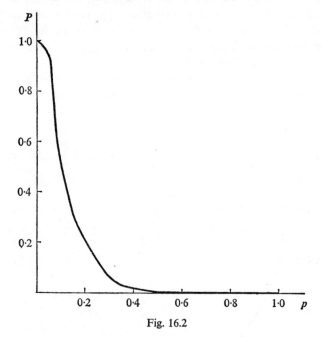

Fig. 16.2

Since the batch is large, the binomial distribution constitutes a suitable mathematical model. Thus, if p is the probability of a randomly chosen article being faulty, the probability, P, of accepting the batch is given by

318

$$P = (1-p)^8 + [8(1-p)^7 p] (1-p)^8$$
$$= (1-p)^8 + 8p(1-p)^{15};$$

(i) if $p = 1/100$, $P \approx 0.99$;

(ii) if $p = 10/100$, $1 - P \approx 0.55$;

(iii) a first sample of size 8 is always taken; the probability that a second will be required is $8(0.9)^7(0.1) \approx 0.382$ and so the expected sample size is

$$8 + 8 \times 0.382 \approx 11.$$

As in the case of single sample inspection schemes, the operating characteristics curve can be drawn in this case too; see Figure 16.2.

Ex. 11. What advantage does a double sampling scheme possess over a single sampling scheme? Are there any disadvantages?

6. HYPOTHESIS TESTING

Probability theory finds a further application in the testing of statistical hypotheses. Consider the following problem.

Example 7. A coin is tossed ten times and shows nine heads. Is this sufficient evidence to support the claim that the coin is biased?

In order to attack this problem, we adopt the approach made in testing scientific theories: we make a hypothesis and then consider whether or not observational evidence supports this hypothesis. In problems of statistical inference, our hypothesis is generally called the *null hypothesis* (because it often takes the form of an assumption about the absence of bias in the population): in this example, we shall take as our null hypothesis the statement 'the coin is unbiased; that is, Pr (*heads on any toss*) = $\frac{1}{2}$.

Having set up our null hypothesis we may ask the question 'Is the probability of obtaining a result as bad as or worse than, the observed result so small that we are reluctant to ascribe it to chance?' If it is, we agree to reject our null hypothesis in favour of some alternative hypothesis.

To complete the framework of our solution we must further decide what numerical value to prescribe to the indefinite phrase 'so small'; following common practice, we shall define $p = \frac{1}{20}$ as a small probability (the so-called '5 % significance level'); in other cases it might be more reasonable to take $p = \frac{1}{100}$ ('1 % significance level').

Returning to the given example, our null hypothesis, H_0, is given by

$$H_0: p = \frac{1}{2};$$

we may take as our alternative hypothesis

$$H_1: p \neq \frac{1}{2}.$$

319

Our question now takes the form 'What is the probability of obtaining a result as bad as, or worse than, nine heads with an unbiased coin?' Since we are comparing the hypothesis $H_0 : p = \frac{1}{2}$ with the alternative hypothesis $H_1 : p \neq \frac{1}{2}$, we are simply testing for absence of bias and thus we have no reason to distinguish between an apparently abnormal number of heads or tails; it follows that a result 'as bad as, or worse than, nine heads' is to be interpreted as the result 'nine or ten heads or tails'.

We adopt as our probability model for the situation the binomial distribution. Thus we have

$$\text{Pr } (9 \text{ or } 10 \text{ heads or tails}/H_0) = 2[(\tfrac{1}{2})^{10} + 10(\tfrac{1}{2})^9(\tfrac{1}{2})]$$
$$\approx \tfrac{1}{47}.$$

Since this is less than $\frac{1}{20}$, we infer that the result is significant at the 5 % level: we have reason to believe that the coin is biased.

Sometimes a test of a statistical hypothesis is constructed before the observational evidence is obtained. For instance, in our last example, we might have compared the null hypothesis:

$$H_0 : p = \tfrac{1}{2}$$

with the alternative hypothesis:

$$H_1 : p \neq \tfrac{1}{2}$$

and so decided what results we should require before accepting or rejecting H_0.

In Example 7, our null hypothesis took the form of a statement about the probability of an event; more generally, a *null hypothesis is a statement about the probability distribution of a population.* We conclude this chapter with a further example, in which our null hypothesis is a statement about the mean of a random variable.

Example 8. Batteries are sent out by manufacturers in batches of five hundred. On average, 2·4 batteries per batch are faulty. How many batteries would we need to find faulty in a particular batch before we could adduce evidence that more faulty batteries were appearing than could be ascribed to pure chance?

Since we are here concerned only with the question of finding more than the expected number of faulty batteries, we take as our null hypothesis

$$H_0 : \text{mean number of batteries per batch} = 2 \cdot 4,$$

and as our alternative hypothesis

$$H_1 : \text{mean number of batteries per batch} > 2 \cdot 4.$$

We adopt as a mathematical model of the situation the Poisson distribution (there is a large number of batteries in every batch and the prob-

320

ability of any particular battery being faulty is small), with random variable X, where $X = r$ when there are r faulty articles in a batch.

Thus we have $$\Pr(X = r|H_0) = e^{-2\cdot4} \times \frac{(2\cdot4)^r}{r!}$$

and we wish to find the least integer n such that

$$\Pr(X > n|H_0) < 0\cdot05.$$

Equivalently we have to find the least integer n such that

$$\Pr(X \leqslant n|H_0) \geqslant 0\cdot95.$$

By direct computation

$$\Pr(X \leqslant 4|H_0) = e^{-2\cdot4}\left(1 + 2\cdot4 + \frac{2\cdot4^2}{2!} + \frac{2\cdot4^3}{3!} + \frac{2\cdot4^4}{4!}\right)$$

$$\approx 0\cdot0907(1 + 2\cdot4 + 2\cdot88 + 2\cdot304 + 1\cdot382)$$

$$\approx 0\cdot90,$$

$$\Pr(X \leqslant 5|H_0) = \Pr(X \leqslant 4|H_0) + \Pr(X = 5|H_0)$$

$$\approx 0\cdot96.$$

Thus, $n = 5$: if we were to find 5 or more faulty batteries in a batch, we should have reason for rejecting our null hypothesis H_0 in favour of our alternative hypothesis H_1.

Exercise 16(c)

1. A machine is believed, on average, to produce 0·1% of faulty articles. Estimate, to 2 D.P., the probability of finding a batch of five hundred articles free of defectives
    (i) by using a binomial distribution;
    (ii) by using a suitable Poisson distribution.
    A batch of five hundred is tested and found to contain two faulty articles. Comment.

2. A large batch of manufactured articles is accepted if either of the following conditions is satisfied:
    (i) a random sample of 10 articles contains no defective article;
    (ii) a random sample of 10 articles contains one defective article and a second random sample of ten is then drawn which contains no defective articles. Otherwise the batch is rejected.
    If, in fact, 5% of the articles in a batch to be examined are defective, find the chance of the batch being accepted $[(0\cdot95)^{10} = 0\cdot5987]$.   (O & C)

3. From a batch of manufactured articles a sample of ten is taken and each article is examined. If two or more articles are found to be defective the batch is

rejected; otherwise it is accepted. Show that, if p is the proportion defective in a batch and P its chance of being accepted,

$$P = (1-p)^9 (1+9p).$$

Find an expression for P if it is now decided to modify the scheme so that when one defective is found in the sample a second sample of ten is taken and the batch rejected if this second sample contains any defectives.

In the second case, what will be the average number sampled per batch over a large number of batches when $p = 0.05$? (M.E.I.)

4. In a certain inspection scheme a sample of fifty items is selected at random from a very large batch and the number of defectives is recorded. If this number is more than three the batch is rejected; if it is less than three the batch is accepted. If the number of defectives is exactly three a further sample, this time of twenty-five items, is taken and the batch is rejected if there is more than one defective in the second sample but accepted otherwise.

If the proportion of defective items in the batch is 1% determine the values of the following probabilities:

(i) that the batch is accepted as a result of inspection of the first sample;

(ii) that a further sample has to be taken and the batch is accepted as a result of inspection of that sample;

(iii) that the batch is rejected.

Take $(0.99)^{48}$ as 0.6173. (M.E.I.)

5. State the formula for the probability that a variable following a Poisson distribution of mean m takes the value r. Prove that the variance of r is m.

Past experience has shown that the number of defective items produced in a shift by a certain machine is a Poisson variable of mean 4. A new employee in his first shift produced six defectives. Is this clear evidence that he is operating the machine inefficiently? (Cambridge)

6. The probability $P(r)$ that there will be r damaged tomatoes in a crate can be taken as

$$P(r) = \frac{e^{-m} m^r}{r!},$$

where m is the expectation of r. Over a large number of crates the value of m has been found to be 10. In the first crate from a new supplier the value of r was 4. Test whether this is significant evidence that the value of m for this supplier is less than 10; explain carefully the logic of your argument.

(Cambridge)

7. A die is thrown six times. If a score of six is made on three of these occasions, have you any reason for believing that the die is biased?

8. A cubical die with faces marked 1 to 6 is thrown n times. Show that on the hypothesis that the die is unbiased the chance that the face marked 4 will appear uppermost not more than once is p, where

$$p = \left(\frac{n+5}{5}\right)\left(\frac{5}{6}\right)^n.$$

If $n = 40$ and the face marked 4 comes uppermost exactly once, test whether the hypothesis that the die is unbiased is contradicted

(a) at the 1 % significance level;

(b) at the 0·1 % significance level.   (Cambridge)

9. A bag contains ten balls, each of which is either black or white, but otherwise the balls are indistinguishable one from another. Three balls are drawn without replacement, and all are found to be white. Test the hypothesis

H_0: there is an equal number of black and white balls in the bag.

The three balls are now replaced and three more are drawn; these are found to be two white and one black. Test the hypothesis H_0 again.

10. A sampling inspection scheme is operated by taking a random sample of size 10 from each large batch of a product. The batch is rejected if more than one defective is found and otherwise the batch is accepted. Plot the operating characteristic of the given plan.

Explain the applications of operating characteristics when choosing a suitable plan.   (M.E.I.)

[You are advised to use a hand calculating machine for the first part, if you have one available.]

11. A double sampling inspection scheme is devised as follows: a sample of size 15 is drawn from a batch of articles; if the sample contains none or one faulty article the batch is accepted, if more than three, it is rejected. If it contains two or three faulty articles a second sample is taken; the batch is now rejected if this second sample contains more than one faulty article. If the batch contains $100p$ % faulty articles, find

(i)   the probability that the batch will be accepted;

(ii) the value of p which gives the largest expected sample size;

(iii) the size of this largest expected sample.

12. An assembled instrument contains two critical components A and B. Sample tests show that we may expect one in ten of A and one in eighteen of B to be defective. Estimate and compare the costs of the following inspection plans, per hundred fully tested instruments:

(i)   to test every component before assembly at a cost of 2p for each A tested and 3p for each B tested; or

(ii) to test every instrument after assembly, if this test adds nothing to the cost but making good a defective instrument costs on average 24p.   (M.E.I.)

Miscellaneous Exercise 16

1. A pack of cards is cut and the suit of the exposed card noted; the pack is then well shuffled and the process repeated. Find

(i)   the probability that a spade will appear for the first time on the fourth cut;

(ii) the average number of cuts required before the first spade appears;

(iii) the average number of cuts required to expose cards of all four suits.

2. Show that the probability of r successes in n independent trials is the coefficient of t^r in the expansion of $(q+pt)^n$, where p is the chance of success in a single trial and $q = 1-p$. Prove that the mean number of successes is np.

Samples, each of eight articles, are taken at random from a large consignment in which 20 % of the articles are defective. Find the most likely number of defective articles in a single sample and the chance of obtaining precisely this number.

If a hundred samples of eight are to be examined, calculate the number of samples in which you expect to find three or more defective articles.   (O & C)

3. Two coins are identical in appearance, but one is unbiased while the other gives, on the average, heads three times as often as it does tails. One of the coins is taken at random and tossed four times. If two heads and two tails appear, what is the probability that it is the unbiased coin?

4. Explain briefly what is meant by a Poisson distribution of rare events and its relation to the binomial distribution. Prove that the mean of the distribution is equal to its variance.

A shopkeeper's sales of washing machines are four per month on the average. Assuming that the monthly sales fit a Poisson distribution, find to what number he should make up his stock at the beginning of each month so that his chance of running out of machines during the month will be less than 4 %.   (O & C)

5. A machine depending for its energy upon four complexes of solar cells, each complex functioning independently of the others, will work provided one of the four complexes is working. Each complex has probability p of failing. The machine is redesigned to have six complexes and will function if two of the six complexes are working. Is the new design an improvement on the old?

6. A and B play N games, each of which must result in a definite win to one or other player. A's chance of success in any one game is p. For his rth win, A receives from B £r, for his sth loss, he gives B £s. Find A's expected gain.

7. A coin is tossed repeatedly an even number, $2n$, times. Show that, whatever the bias (provided $\Pr(H) \neq 0$ or 1) the probability of obtaining the same number of heads as tails decreases as n increases.

8. In lawn tennis a set is won by the first player to win six games, except that if the score reaches 5–5 the set is won by the first to lead by two games. Two players have chances respectively p and q of winning in any game ($p+q = 1$); games may be treated as independent. Find the chance that a set lasts exactly $2n+2$ games ($n \geqslant 5$).   (Cambridge)

9. The number of eggs laid by an insect has Poisson distribution with mean μ. If the probability that an individual egg survives is p, show that the number of eggs surviving has Poisson distribution, and determine its mean value. (You may assume that the survival of an egg is independent of the fate of the other eggs laid.)

10. An experiment has probability p of success. In n independent trials, p_n is the probability of an even number of successes ($p_0 = 1$). Prove that

$$p_n - (1-2p)\,p_{n-1} = p.$$

If $f(t) = \sum_{n=0}^{\infty} p_n t^n$, prove that

$$f(t) = [1-(1-p)\,t]/\{(1-t)\,[1-(1-2p)\,t]\}.$$

Deduce that $p_n = \tfrac{1}{2}[1+(1-2p)^n].$

11. Two machines, A and B, produce large numbers of articles, with 10% of those from A and 20% of those from B defective. Machine B produces 50% more articles than machine A. A batch of ten taken from one of the machines contains two defective articles. What is the probability it came from A? (Give to 1 D.P.)

12. In a simplified probability model of the service in a barber's shop, it is supposed that all haircuts take exactly six minutes and that a fresh batch of customers arrives at six-minute intervals. The number of customers in a batch is described by a Poisson probability function, the mean number being three. Any customer who cannot be served instantly goes away and has his hair cut elsewhere. The shop is open for forty hours a week. Calculate the theoretical frequencies with which batches of 0, 1, 2, 3, 4, 5 and more than 5 customers will arrive.

The proprietor reckons that it costs him £25 a week to staff and maintain each chair in his shop, and he charges 25p for each haircut. Calculate his expected weekly profit if he has
(i) three; (ii) four; (iii) five chairs. (SMP)

13. A sample of n coins is drawn at random from a large collection in which a fraction p are pennies. What is the probability that just r of the n coins are pennies?

If the probability that a penny is a Queen Elizabeth one is q, what is the probability that there are exactly s Queen Elizabeth pennies among the r pennies of this sample?

Write down the probability that a sample of n coins will contain $s+k$ 10p pieces, only s of which are Queen Elizabeth ones, and calculate the sum of these probabilities for all possible values of k. (C.S.)

14. A bag contains a large number of red, white and blue dice in equal numbers. If n are drawn at random, show that the probability $P(n, r)$ of drawing exactly r red dice is equal to the term containing $(\frac{1}{3})^r (\frac{2}{3})^{n-r}$ in the expansion of $(\frac{1}{3} + \frac{2}{3})^n$.

If r dice are thrown, find the probability $Q(r, s)$ of throwing exactly s sixes.

If n dice are drawn from the bag and the red dice drawn are thrown, show that the probability of throwing exactly s sixes is

$$\sum_{t=0}^{n-s} P(n, s+t)\, Q(s+t, s)$$

and prove that this is equal to a term in a binomial expansion. Explain why a binomial distribution is obtained. (C.S.)

15. A random sample of size 10 is taken from a batch of a thousand components and one defective is found.
   (i) What is the largest possible percentage of defectives in the batch?
   (ii) p is the smallest proportion of defectives in the batch such that the probability of obtaining not more than one defective is not less than 95%. Find the value of p to two decimal places by trial of suitable values of p.
   (iii) Find the most likely percentage of defectives in the batch (i.e. such that the probability of obtaining one defective in the sample is a maximum).
(M.E.I.)

16. In sampling inspections of batches of manufactured articles a random sample of twenty is taken; if none or one defective occurs in the sample the batch is accepted, if three or more defectives occur the batch is rejected. If two defectives occur a second random sample of twenty is taken and if in the combined sample of forty less than four defectives occur the batch is accepted; otherwise it is rejected.

Assuming that the proportion p of defectives in a batch is sufficiently small for the Poisson distribution to apply, show that the chance P of the batch being accepted is given by

$$P = e^{-20p} (1+20p) (1+200p^2 e^{-20p}).$$

(i) Find the chance of a batch which is 2 % defective being rejected.

(ii) Find the chances of batches which are respectively 5 and 10 % defective being accepted.

(iii) Sketch the operating characteristic curve for the inspection scheme. Determine the average sample size per batch if $p = 0.05$.   (O & C)

17. The number of a certain type of organism in a given volume of water has Poisson distribution with mean 2. A test, applied to indicate absence of the organism has a 90 % chance of success if the organism is in fact absent, but also indicates absence in 10 % of those cases in which they are present. If the test is applied and indicates absence, what is the probability that the water is free of the organism?

18. The probability that a source emits r α-particles in a given time is proportional to $\mu^r/r!$, where μ is a constant. Obtain the constant of proportionality and calculate the mean of r.

The probability of the same source emitting s β-particles in the same time is proportional to $\nu^s/s!$. Assuming that the two types of particle are emitted independently, write down the probability that r α-particles and s β-particles are given off in this time and show that the probability that a total of n particles of the two types are emitted is

$$e^{-(\mu+\nu)} (\mu+\nu)^n/n!.$$ (Cambridge)

19. The probability that any randomly chosen rat from the colony used in a certain laboratory will show a certain undesirable characteristic is p; it is known that the value of p for the colony is either 0·4 or 0·6 and it is desired to set up a sampling scheme to decide which value is correct. The procedure is to take rats one at a time at random and test for the presence of the characteristic; after n rats have been tested, let r be the number with the characteristic.

Show how to determine limits L_n and U_n such that for known n

$$\Pr (r \leqslant L_n | p = 0.6) \approx \alpha \quad \text{and} \quad \Pr (r \geqslant U_n | p = 0.4) \approx \beta$$

where α and β are specified.

Use the table of partial binomial sums below to determine L_n and U_n for $n = 5, 7, 9, 11, 13, 15, 17$ where α and β are less than 0·1 and as close to it as possible. Mark these values on a plot of $n-r$ against r, and explain how such a diagram could be used in the decision procedure.

326

Partial binomial sums

r \ n	5	7	9	11	13	15	17
3	317	580	768	881	942	973	988
4	87	290	517	704	831	909	954
5	10	96	267	467	647	783	874
6		19	99	247	426	597	736
7		2	25	99	229	390	552
8			4	29	98	213	359
9			0	6	32	95	199
10				1	8	34	92
11				0	1	9	35

Table of $10^3 \times \sum_{s=r}^{n} \binom{n}{s} (0\cdot4)^s (0\cdot6)^{n-s}$.   (Cambridge)

20. At a certain seed testing station it is found that a proportion $0\cdot4$ of a certain type of seed is fertile. By accident the remaining stock of this seed (whose total amount is very large) is completely mixed with an equal quantity of a second type of seed which is believed to be completely infertile. If this latter assumption is true, what is the probability that a seed taken at random from the mixture will germinate?

Each of seven pots is planted with two seeds taken at random from the mixture. Six pots eventually produce one or more plants each. Is this result consistent, at the 5 % level of significance, with the infertility postulate for the second type of seed?   (Cambridge)

21. Derive the probability $p(r)$ of obtaining exactly r successes in n independent trials, the probability of a success being p at each trial. Determine the mean and variance of this distribution.

Find an expression for $[p(r)]/[p(r-1)]$ and hence or otherwise find the conditions that r_m must satisfy if $p(r_m)$ is such that no other value of $p(r)$ is greater than $p(r_m)$.

Show that the mode of a binomial distribution differs from the mean by less than unity.   (M.E.I.)

Revision exercise B

1. Find the equation of the line L_1 through the origin with gradient $\frac{1}{2}$, and also the equation of the line L_2 perpendicular to L_1 and passing through the point $(4, -\frac{1}{2})$.

2. In a large university, one-third of the men and one-quarter of the women read science. If four men are selected at random, what is the probability that not more than one reads science? If two men and two women are selected at random what is the probability that not more than one of the four reads science?

What is the probability that, in a mixed group, one man reads science and the other man and the two women read something else?

3. A square lamina $ABCD$ of side a is held with the corner A on a horizontal plane. The feet of the perpendiculars from B, C, D on to the plane are B', C', D' and the angles $B'AB$, $D'AD$ are α, β. The angle $B'AD'$ is θ. Prove that
  (i) $\cos \theta = -\tan \alpha \tan \beta$;
  (ii) the area of the triangle $B'AD'$ is $\frac{1}{2}a^2(\cos^2 \alpha \cos^2 \beta - \sin^2 \alpha \sin^2 \beta)^{\frac{1}{2}}$;
  (iii) the inclination of the lamina to the horizontal can be expressed in the
form
$$\arccos \, [\cos (\alpha + \beta) \cos (\alpha - \beta)]^{\frac{1}{2}}. \qquad \text{(O \& C)}$$

4. If $\alpha \neq \frac{1}{4}(4n+1)\pi$, find x if $\sin (x+\alpha) = \cos (x-\alpha)$.
  What can you say about x if $\alpha = \frac{1}{4}(4n+1)\pi$?

5. Find the sum to infinity, S, of the geometric series
$$1 + \frac{1}{\sqrt{10}} + \frac{1}{10} + \frac{1}{10\sqrt{10}} + \dots .$$

If S_N denotes the sum of the first N terms of this series, find the least value of N such that S and S_N are the same correct to 3 D.P.

6. A tennis match usually consists of either three or five sets, and ends when one side has won a majority of the sets. If the probability of a side winning a set is p, and if the result of each set is independent of any previous results, show that the probability of a match going its full legth is $2pq$ in the case of a three-set match and $6p^2q^2$ in the case of a five-set match ($q = 1-p$).
  Show that the first probability is always greater than the second, if $p \neq 0$ or 1.

7. The function $f: R \to R^+$ is defined by
$$f(x) = |x+1| + |2x-1| + |x-2|.$$
Sketch the graph of f and determine the least value of $f(x)$.

8. Call a matrix of the form $\begin{pmatrix} x & y \\ y & x \end{pmatrix}$

which is symmetrical about both diagonals 'super-symmetrical'. If **A**, **B**, ... are super-symmetrical 2×2 matrices and $m, n,$ ... are non-negative integers, prove that $\mathbf{A}^m \mathbf{B}^n$ ... is super-symmetrical.

Does this result hold for 3×3 matrices?

9. Factorize into linear factors the expression $2x^2 + 5xy - 3y^2 - 3x + 5y - 2$ and describe geometrically the set of points $\{(x, y): 2x^2 + 5xy - 3y^2 - 3x + 5y - 2 = 0\}$.

Describe geometrically the sets of points

(i) $\{(x, y): x^2 - 2y^2 = 0\};$ (ii) $\{(x, y): x^2 + 2y^2 = 0\}$.

10. i, j, k are unequal positive integers and x, y, z are real numbers. Prove that $x(j-k) + y(k-i) + z(i-j) = 0 \Leftrightarrow x, y, z$ are respectively the ith, jth, kth terms of an arithmetic sequence.

11. Prove by mathematical induction, or otherwise, that

$$n.1^3 + (n-1).2^3 + (n-2).3^3 + \ldots + 1.n^3 = \tfrac{1}{60}n(n+1)(n+2)(3n^2 + 6n + 1).$$

(Oxford)

12. Find the inverse of the matrix

$$\begin{pmatrix} 5 & 3 & 7 \\ 3 & 4 & 6 \\ -1 & 2 & 1 \end{pmatrix}.$$

Hence solve the simultaneous equations

$$\begin{cases} 5x + 3y + 7z = a, \\ 3x + 4y + 6z = b; \\ -x + 2y + z = c; \end{cases}$$

(i) when $a = -1, b = 2, c = -3;$ (ii) when $a = b = 1, c = 2$.

13. What are the first three terms in the expansion of $(1-2x)^{24}$ in ascending powers of x?

Find the value of 0.98^{24}, correct to 4 D.P.

14. Show that, whatever value is chosen for k, the equation

$$(3 + 5k)x + (2 - 7k)y + (5 - 4k) = 0$$

represents a straight line through a fixed point A.

Find the particular line of the system

(i) which passes through the origin;

(ii) which is parallel to the y axis.

15. The polynomial $P(x)$ leaves a remainder of $x + 1$ on division by $x^2 - 2$ and the polynomial $Q(x)$ leaves a remainder of $2x + 3$ on division by $x^2 - 2$. New polynomials $R(x) \equiv P(x) + Q(x)$ and $S(x) \equiv P(x) Q(x)$ are defined. Find the remainder

(i) when $R(x)$ is divided by $x^2 - 2;$

(ii) when $S(x)$ is divided by $x^2 - 2$.

16. If A is the point $(a \cos \alpha, b \sin \alpha)$ and B is the point $(a \cos \beta, b \sin \beta)$, show that the equation of the line AB is

$$\frac{x}{a} \cos \frac{\alpha+\beta}{2} + \frac{y}{b} \sin \frac{\alpha+\beta}{2} = \cos \frac{\alpha-\beta}{2}.$$

What is the connection between α and β if AB passes through the origin?

17. Prove that the number of spheres that can be drawn to pass through three given points and touch a given plane is 2 or 1 or 0, explaining how the three cases arise.

18. OA, OB, OC are three concurrent straight lines lying in one plane. P is a point outside the plane such that the angles POA, POB, POC are equal. Prove that PO is perpendicular to the plane.

19. Find the matrix of the linear transformation which reflects all points in the plane $x+y+z = 0$.

20. $ABCDA'B'C'D'$ is a parallelepiped, with opposite faces $ABCD$, $A'B'C'D'$ and edges AA', etc., $AB = BB' = B'C'$, and the mid-points of BB', $A'D'$, $A'B'$ are respectively F, G, H. Find the ratio in which the plane $AD'H$ divides the line FG.

21. Two boxes each contain one hundred cards, numbered 1 to 100. A card is taken from each box, the numbers on the two cards noted, and they are then returned to their respective boxes. If the process is repeated fifty times, find the probability that at no stage a pair of cards bearing the same number will be drawn. How many draws are needed for the probability to be $> \frac{1}{2}$?

22. Prove that $\lg 15$ is irrational. ($\lg 15$ means $\log_{10} 15$.) Is it true that $\lg x$ is irrational $\Leftrightarrow x$ is not a power of 10?

23. Evaluate the following determinants:

(i) $\begin{vmatrix} b-c & c-a & a-b \\ c-a & a-b & b-c \\ a-b & b-c & c-a \end{vmatrix}$;

(ii) $\begin{vmatrix} (x-p)^2 & (y-p)^2 & (z-p)^2 \\ (x-q)^2 & (y-q)^2 & (z-q)^2 \\ (x-r)^2 & (y-r)^2 & (z-r)^2 \end{vmatrix}$.

24. Define the projection of a vector in a given direction. $ABCD$ is a quadrilateral in which $\angle A = \angle C = 90°$. The feet of the perpendiculars from B, D to AC are X, Y respectively. Prove that $AX = CY$.

25. In a large crate of oranges, $100p\%$ are bad. A random sample of ten oranges produces two bad ones. On the assumption that this is the most likely number of bad oranges to find in the sample, what can you say about the possible values of p?

26. $ABCD$ is a square lying in the plane $2x-y-2z = 5$. If A has coordinates $(1, 1, -2)$ and C has coordinates $(5, 5, 0)$, find the coordinates of B and D.

27. The function, f, defined by

$$f(x) = \sin x + \cos x$$

has for its domain the set of real numbers $\{x \in R : 0 < x < \pi\}$. Find the range of f.

28. Factorize the expression $ax^2 + (ac + b - c)\,x + c(b - c)$ into two linear factors. Hence factorize the expressions

   (i) $a + b - c + bc + ca - c^2$;

   (ii) $a - b + c + bc - ca - c^2$;

   (iii) $a^3b^2 + a^2bc + ab^2 - abc + bc - c^2$.

29. Describe geometrically the transformation of three-dimensional space represented by premultiplying the position vector of the point (x, y, z) by the matrix

$$\begin{pmatrix} \frac{1}{2} & 0 & -\frac{1}{2} \\ 0 & 1 & 0 \\ -\frac{1}{2} & 0 & \frac{1}{2} \end{pmatrix}.$$

Which points are left unaltered by this transformation?   (O.S.)

30. When A and B play chess the chance of either winning a game is always $\frac{1}{4}$ and the chance of the game being drawn is always $\frac{1}{2}$. Find the chance of A winning at least three games out of five.

   If A and B play a match to be decided as soon as either has won two games, not necessarily consecutive games, find the chance of the match being finished in ten games or less.   (J.M.B)

31. Solve the equations

   (i) $2 \sin^2 x + \sin 2x = 0$;

   (ii) $\sin x = \cos(\frac{1}{3}\pi - x)$;

giving all solutions in the interval $0 \leqslant x \leqslant 2\pi$ in each case.

32. Solve the inequality $\qquad \dfrac{x^2 - 1}{x^2 - 4} \leqslant \dfrac{1}{5}$

and illustrate your solutions by means of a sketch of the curve

$$y = \frac{x^2 - 1}{x^2 - 4}.$$

33. The base AB of a triangle ABC is fixed and K is a fixed point on AB. The vertex C of the triangle moves so that the perpendicular distances of K from CA and CB are always equal in length. Prove that, in general, the locus of C is a circle through K.

   What is the exceptional case?   (Cambridge)

34. A pitcher is taken daily to a well and back. Its chance of being broken on an outward trip is p_1. If it survives the outward journey it has a further chance p_2 of being broken on the return. Show that on any day its change of being broken is P, where

$$P = p_1 + p_2 - p_1p_2.$$

   Show that the chance that the pitcher will survive for at least n days is Q^n, where $Q = (1 - p_1)(1 - p_2)$, and find the chance it will survive $(n - 1)$ days but be broken on the nth day.

   If two such pitchers are each taken independently to the well and back daily, prove that the chance that they survive for exactly the same number of days is $P/(1 + Q)$.   (C.S.)

35. Find the image by reflection of the point $(4, 3, 1)$ in the plane

$$3x + 2y + 3z + 1 = 0.$$

36. A and B are two towers, B being four miles due east of A. The true bearings of a flagpole C from A and B are $\alpha°$ east of north and $\alpha°$ west of north respectively; the true bearings of a second flagpole D from A and B are $(\alpha + \beta)°$ east of north and $(\alpha - \beta)°$ west of north respectively. Draw a sketch-plane to indicate the positions of A, B, C, D.

Assuming that A, B, C and D are on level ground, prove that D is $4 \sin^2 \beta \operatorname{cosec} 2\alpha$ miles south of C and $2 \sin 2\beta \operatorname{cosec} 2\alpha$ miles east of C. (O & C)

37. If $ax^4 + 3x^3 + bx^2 + cx + 2$ is exactly divisible by $(x + 2)(x^2 - 1)$, find the values of a, b, c.

38. Sketch the graph of the function defined by

$$f(x) = x + |x| \quad (x \in R).$$

In a separate diagram, shade in the set of points satisfying simultaneously the three inequalities

$$y \geqslant x + |x|, \quad y \geqslant |x| - x, \quad x - y + 1 \geqslant 0.$$

What is the maximum value of the expression

$$E = x + y + 1$$

if x and y are subject to the three given inequalities?

39. Prove that, if $\mathbf{A}$, $\mathbf{B}$ are two non-singular 3×3 matrices, then $\mathbf{AB}$ is a non-singular matrix and $(\mathbf{AB})^{-1} = \mathbf{B}^{-1}\mathbf{A}^{-1}$.

If

$$\mathbf{A} = \begin{pmatrix} 6 & 3 & 5 \\ 2 & 5 & 2 \\ -3 & 4 & -2 \end{pmatrix}, \quad \mathbf{E}_1 = \begin{pmatrix} 1 & 0 & 0 \\ 0 & 0 & 1 \\ 0 & 1 & 0 \end{pmatrix}, \quad \mathbf{E}_2 = \begin{pmatrix} 1 & 0 & 0 \\ 0 & 1 & 0 \\ 1 & 1 & 1 \end{pmatrix}$$

find $\mathbf{A}^{-1}$, $\mathbf{E}_1^{-1}$, $\mathbf{E}_2^{-1}$.

What are the inverses of the following matrices:

(i) $\begin{pmatrix} 6 & 3 & 5 \\ -3 & 4 & -2 \\ 2 & 5 & 2 \end{pmatrix}$;
(ii) $\begin{pmatrix} 6 & 3 & 5 \\ -3 & 4 & -2 \\ 5 & 12 & 5 \end{pmatrix}$?

40. Using the formula for $\tan(A + B)$ in terms of $\tan A$ and $\tan B$, show that, if A, B, C are the angles of a triangle, then

$$\tan A + \tan B + \tan C = \tan A \tan B \tan C.$$

Calculate, in degrees and minutes, the angles of a triangle ABC if

$$\tan A : \tan B : \tan C = 1 : 2 : -6. \qquad \text{(Cambridge)}$$

41. Find the equation of the plane containing the origin, the point $(1, 1, 1)$ and the point $(3, 1, -1)$. Find also the direction ratios of the line of intersection of this plane with the plane $x + y - z - 4 = 0$.

42. In a game of tennis one point is scored either by A or by his opponent B. The winner of the game is the player who first scores four points, unless each player has won three points, when 'deuce' is called and play proceeds until one player is two points ahead of the other and so wins. If A's chance of winning any point is $\frac{2}{3}$ and B's chance is $\frac{1}{3}$ calculate the chance of

(i) A winning the game without 'deuce' being called;

(ii) a similar win by B;

(iii) 'deuce' being called.

If 'deuce' is called, prove that A's subsequent chance of winning the game is $\frac{4}{5}$.

Deduce that A's chance of winning the game is nearly six times that of B.

(Cambridge)

43. Prove that
$$\sum_{r=0}^{n} \binom{n}{r} = 2^n.$$

If $\mathbf{A}$ is a square matrix such that $\mathbf{A}^2 = \mathbf{A}$, express $(\mathbf{A}+\mathbf{I})^n$ in the form

$$\alpha\mathbf{A}+\beta\mathbf{I}.$$

44. Use the method of mathematical induction to prove that

$$k! + \frac{(k+1)!}{1!} + \frac{(k+2)!}{2!} + \ldots + \frac{(k+n-1)!}{(n-1)!} = \frac{(k+n)!}{(k+1)\,(n-1)!}.$$

45. Show that the equations

$$\begin{cases} (k+2)\,x+2y+3z = 7, \\ x+(k+2)\,y+z = 0, \\ 5x+2y+(6-k)\,z = 13 \end{cases}$$

have a unique solution for all but three values of k.

Discuss the solution of the equations in the three exceptional cases.

46. Prove the formula $\cos 3A = 4\cos^3 A - 3\cos A$. (Formulae for $\cos 2A$ and $\sin 2A$ may be assumed.)

Substitute $x = \frac{1}{2}+\cos\theta$ in the equation $8x^3-12x^2+1 = 0$ and, with the aid of the above formula, solve the resulting equation in θ, giving values between $0°$ and $180°$.

Hence find the three roots of the cubic equation in x, correct to two decimal places.

(Cambridge)

47. $A_1 A_2 \ldots A_n$ is a regular polygon of side 1 unit. Two (distinct) vertices are selected at random. Taking as random variable X, the shorter distance measured along the perimeter between the two points, find $\mathscr{E}(X)$

(i) when n is odd; (ii) when n is even.

48. When n is a positive integer the coefficient of $a^{n-r}b^r$ in the binomial expansion of $(a+b)^n$ is denoted by $\binom{n}{r}$. Write down an expression for $\binom{n}{r}$ and prove that

$$\binom{n}{r} < n\binom{n-1}{r-1} \quad \text{for} \quad r = 2, 3, \ldots, n.$$

By comparing the binomial expansions, or otherwise, prove that, when $a > 0, b > 0$,
$$(a+b)^n - a^n < nb(a+b)^{n-1}.$$

(O & C)

49. Factorize the determinants

(i) $\begin{vmatrix} a^2 & (a+1)^2 & (a+2)^2 \\ b^2 & (b+1)^2 & (b+2)^2 \\ c^2 & (c+1)^2 & (c+2)^2 \end{vmatrix}$,
(ii) $\begin{vmatrix} x & a & b & c \\ a & x & c & b \\ b & c & x & a \\ c & b & a & x \end{vmatrix}$.
(O & C)

50. Find the image by reflection of the plane $x = 0$ in the plane $x+y+z = 4$.

51. Using the same axes draw the graphs of $y = \sin x°$ and $y = 1-\dfrac{x}{270}$ for values of x from 0 to 360. Estimate from your diagram the roots of the equation

$$\sin x° + \frac{x}{270} = 1.$$

The equation $\sin x° = mx + c$, where m and c are constants, has roots $x = 60$, $x = 330$. With the aid of your diagram estimate
  (i) the other root of the equation;
  (ii) the values of m and c. (Cambridge)

52. Prove that, when any polynomial $f(x)$ is divided by $(x-a)$, the remainder is $f(a)$.
  The remainder, when $f(x)$ is divided by $(x-a)(x-b)$ is written in the form $A(x-a)+B(x-b)$; prove that

$$A = \frac{f(b)}{b-a}, \quad B = \frac{f(a)}{a-b}.$$

When $\alpha x^3 + \beta x^2 + \gamma x + \delta$ is divided by x^2-1, the remainder is Kx where K is a constant; when it is divided by x^2-4, the remainder is K. Prove that

$$\alpha = -\beta = -\tfrac{1}{4}\gamma = \delta = -\tfrac{1}{3}K.$$
(O & C)

53. Let $A(\theta)$ and $B(\theta)$ denote the matrices

$$\begin{pmatrix} \cos\theta & \sin\theta \\ \sin\theta & -\cos\theta \end{pmatrix}, \quad \begin{pmatrix} \cos\theta & -\sin\theta \\ \sin\theta & \cos\theta \end{pmatrix}$$

respectively.
  (i) If

$$\begin{pmatrix} X' \\ Y' \end{pmatrix} = A(\theta) \begin{pmatrix} X \\ Y \end{pmatrix}$$

show that the point (X', Y') is the mirror image of (X, Y) in the line $y = x \tan\tfrac{1}{2}\theta$.
  (ii) Prove that
$$A(\theta_1)\,A(\theta_2) = B(\phi),$$

where ϕ is some angle (to be determined), and hence, or otherwise, explain the relation between the points (X', Y') and (X, Y) when

$$\begin{pmatrix} X' \\ Y' \end{pmatrix} = B(\theta) \begin{pmatrix} X \\ Y \end{pmatrix}.$$

  (iii) Prove that $\quad A(\theta_1)\,A(\theta_2)\,A(\theta_3) = A(\theta_3)\,A(\theta_2)\,A(\theta_1)$

and interpret this result geometrically. (C.S.)

334

54. One side of a hill has the form of an inclined plane, the line of greatest slope, AB, being due north. A man starts from A and walks to B, the distance being d_1 km. At B he walks for a distance d_2 km in a straight line, inclined at an acute angle θ to AB, reaching a point C. The vertical heights of B and C above the level of A are h_1 km and h_2 km respectively. Prove that

$$\cos\theta = \frac{d_1(h_2-h_1)}{h_1 d_2}.$$

The bearing of C from A is ϕ east or west of north. Prove that

$$\tan\phi = \frac{h_1 d_2 \sin\theta}{h_2\sqrt{(d_1^2-h_1^2)}}.$$ (O & C)

55. Show that, for all but two specific values of k, the equations

$$\begin{cases} x-ky+2z = 3, \\ 3x+ y-2z = 1, \\ kx-9y+2z = 7, \end{cases}$$

represent three planes with a single common point.
Interpret geometrically the two special cases.

56. In how many different ways may a red balls, b white balls and c black balls (indistinguishable apart from colour) be arranged in a straight line?
Find the coefficient of $x^4y^4z^4$ in the expansion of $(x+y+2z)^{12}$.

57. Solve the inequality

$$\left| \frac{5x+1}{x^2-x-6} \right| < 1$$

and illustrate your solution by drawing a sketch of the curve

$$y = \frac{5x+1}{x^2-x-6}.$$

58. Three spheres of radii 1, 2, 3 units, touch each other externally. Prove that a plane which touches each sphere makes an angle $\arcsin(\frac{1}{6}\sqrt{13})$ with the plane containing the centres of the spheres. (O & C)

59. Find all values of x, y and z which satisfy the equations

$$-y+z = u,$$
$$x\quad -z = v,$$
$$-x+y\quad = w,$$

where
$$v-2w = a,$$
$$-u\quad +3w = b,$$
$$2u-3v\quad = c.$$ (C.S.)

60. If I deal cards one by one from a well-shuffled pack, find the expectation of the number of cards I shall have to deal
(i) to secure a spade; (ii) to secure all the spades.

61. $ABCDA'B'C'D'$ is a rectangular box with faces $ABCD$, $A'B'C'D'$ and edges AA', etc. $AA'D'D$ is a square of side 1 unit, $AB = 2$ units and M is the midpoint of $C'D'$. By setting up a suitable coordinate system, or otherwise, find the acute angle between the planes BMA', $AB'D'$, correct to the nearest degree.

62. Prove that
$$\begin{vmatrix} (a-x)^2 & (a-y)^2 & (a-z)^2 & (a-w)^2 \\ (b-x)^2 & (b-y)^2 & (b-z)^2 & (b-w)^2 \\ (c-x)^2 & (c-y)^2 & (c-z)^2 & (c-w)^2 \\ (d-x)^2 & (d-y)^2 & (d-z)^2 & (d-w)^2 \end{vmatrix} = 0. \qquad \text{(C.S.)}$$

63. If θ denotes the angle between two intersecting lines with direction cosines l, m, n and l', m', n' respectively, show that
$$\cos\theta = ll' + mm' + nn'.$$
Prove that the lines $\qquad x = y+3 = z+1$
and $\qquad x = \frac{1}{2}(y+4) = \frac{1}{3}(z+3)$
intersect. If P is the point of intersection, find the equation of the line through P perpendicular to both given lines. (J.M.B.)

64. Two jars, one white and the other black, contain $a+b$ balls each; in the white jar there are a white and b black balls and in the black jar b white and a black. Single draws are made as follows: at the rth draw a ball is drawn from the white or black jar according as the $(r-1)$th ball drawn was white or black, the colour of the ball noted and then returned. If p_n is the probability that the nth draw is white, show that
$$(a+b)p_n = b+(a-b)p_{n-1}.$$
By means of the substitution $\qquad p_n = \frac{1}{2}+q_n,$
or otherwise, determine p_n, when the jar from which the first draw is made is (i) chosen at random, (ii) white. What is the probability in the two cases that both jars have been drawn after three draws? (O.S.)

65. The number n whose digits in the scale of 10 are a, b, c, d in that order is the same as the number whose digits in the scale of 9 are d, b, c, a in that order; in other words, we have
$$10^3a+10^2b+10c+d = 9^3d+9^2b+9c+a$$
and the digits a, b, c, d all lie between 0 and 8 inclusive. Prove that there is exactly one number n ($\neq 0$) with this property, and find n. (C.S.)

66. Prove that, if
$$A = \begin{pmatrix} \lambda & 1 & 0 \\ 0 & \lambda & 1 \\ 0 & 0 & \lambda \end{pmatrix},$$
then
$$A^n = \begin{pmatrix} \lambda^n & n\lambda^{n-1} & \frac{1}{2}n(n-1)\lambda^{n-2} \\ 0 & \lambda^n & n\lambda^{n-1} \\ 0 & 0 & \lambda^n \end{pmatrix}$$
where n is a positive integer.

If A^0 is defined to be I, is the result still true for *any* integer n?

67. The points P_1 and P_2 on the surface of the earth (assumed to be a sphere of radius r and centre O) are at the same (northern) latitude λ, and their respective longitudes are L_1 and L_2. Show that the length C of the route from P_1 to P_2 via a circle centre O (called a great circle) satisfies the equation

$$\cos\left(\frac{C}{r}\right) = \sin^2 \lambda + \cos^2 \lambda \cos(L_2 - L_1).$$

If the separation in longitude is $90°$ show that either

$$C = 2r \arcsin\left(\frac{\cos \lambda}{\sqrt{2}}\right) \quad \text{or} \quad C = 2\pi r - 2r \arcsin\left(\frac{\cos \lambda}{\sqrt{2}}\right).$$

(Cambridge)

68. If λ is a real number, show that the equations

$$\lambda x + y + z = 2,$$
$$x + \lambda y + z = -1,$$
$$x + y + \lambda z = -1,$$

have a unique solution (x, y, z) for all but two exceptional values of λ.

Show that, for one of the exceptional values of λ, the equations have no solution and that, for the other exceptional value of λ they have infinitely many solutions. (O.S.)

69. Determine θ so that the line

$$lx + my + n = \theta (l'x + m'y + n')$$

is perpendicular to the line $\lambda x + \mu y + \nu = 0$.

Prove that the perpendiculars from the vertices A_1, A_2, A_3 of the triangle formed by the lines

$$l_i x + m_i y + n_i = 0 \quad (i = 1, 2, 3)$$

on to the sides $B_2 B_3$, $B_3 B_1$, $B_1 B_2$ respectively, of the triangle formed by the lines

$$\lambda_i x + \mu_i y + \nu_i = 0 \quad (i = 1, 2, 3)$$

are concurrent if

$$(l_1\lambda_2 + m_1\mu_2)(l_2\lambda_3 + m_2\mu_3)(l_3\lambda_1 + m_3\mu_1)$$
$$= (l_1\lambda_3 + m_1\mu_3)(l_2\lambda_1 + m_2\mu_1)(l_3\lambda_2 + m_3\mu_2).$$

Deduce that, in this case, the perpendiculars from the vertices of $B_1 B_2 B_3$ on to the respective sides of $A_1 A_2 A_3$ are also concurrent. (C.S.)

70. A hill $0\cdot3$ km high is in the shape of a spherical cap, with a horizontal circular rim, the radius of the sphere being $0\cdot6$ km. A man walks up from a point of the rim to the peak at a steady speed of $1\cdot6$ km per hour but never ascending at a gradient of more than $\arcsin\left(\frac{2}{3}\right)$. Find the minimum time the walk can take him, and sketch roughly a possible minimum path (as seen from above); does it necessarily have no sharp corners? (C.S.)

71. In a population of identical elements, an element produces no or one progeny with equal probabilities $\frac{1}{2}$. If the population consists of 0, 1, 2, ...

337

elements with probabilities $p_0, p_1, p_2, \ldots$ show that the probability P_r of r progeny is given by the coefficient of t^r in $G(t)$, where

$$G(t) = \sum_{n=0}^{\infty} p_n \left(\frac{1+t}{2}\right)^n.$$

When

$$p_n = \frac{1}{2^{n+1}}$$

find the probability that the number of progeny is greater than or equal to N. By considering $G(t)$ and its derivatives, or otherwise, find $\bar{r}$, the expected value of r, the number of progeny, and the expected value of $(r-\bar{r})^2$.   (O.S.)

72. A, B and C are the three angles of a triangle. Show that

$$\begin{vmatrix} \sin A & \sin B & \sin C \\ \cos A & \cos B & \cos C \\ \sin^3 A & \sin^3 B & \sin^3 C \end{vmatrix} = 0. \qquad \text{(C.S.)}$$

73. If n is a positive integer and p a prime number, $\alpha_p(n)$ denotes the greatest integer k such that p^k divides n. If n is written in the form

$$n = \sum_{r=0}^{N} a_r p^r \quad (0 \leqslant a_r \leqslant p-1),$$

show that

$$\alpha_p(n!) = \frac{n - \sum_{r=0}^{N} a_r}{p-1}. \qquad \text{(C.S.)}$$

74. $ABCD$ is a parallelogram and E a point not necessarily in the plane $ABCD$. Show that $a^2 + c^2 + g^2 + h^2 = b^2 + d^2 + e^2$, these being the lengths shown in the figure, and find a relation involving only a, b, c, e, f. (You may use vector geometry.)   (C.S.)

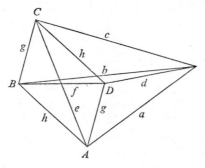

Bibliography

GENERAL

Allen, R. G. D. *Basic Mathematics* (Macmillan). A broad survey of mathematical ideas—useful as a reference book.

Backhouse, J. K. and Houldsworth, S. P. T. *Pure Mathematics* (Longmans, 2 volumes). Written some years ago, with traditional 'A' levels in mind—consequently rather old-fashioned, but workmanlike in its approach and contains a great number of examples for the student.

Kemeny, J. G., Murkill, H., Snell, J. L. and Thompson, G. L. *Finite Mathematical Structures* (Prentice-Hall). An introductory survey of some modern topics, containing a much more thorough account of the ideas sketched in Ch. 9.1 and also including chapters on linear algebra and probability.

S.M.P. *Advanced Mathematics*. (Cambridge, 4 volumes). Specifically written for the new S.M.P. 'A' level, these books are full of new ideas, presented in a lively and stimulating manner.

ALGEBRA

Beckenbach, E. F. and Bellman, R. *An Introduction to Inequalities* (Random House.) A readable introduction to the subject.

Birkhoff, G. D. and Maclane, S. *A Survey of Modern Algebra* (Macmillan, New York). Really a university text book, but beautifully written and containing much that can be read with profit by sixth-formers. Gives a much more thorough account of the ideas outlined somewhat sketchily in Ch. 1.

Cohn, P. M. *Linear Equations* (Routledge and Kegan Paul). A sound introduction at low cost.

Durell, C. V. and Robson, A. *Advanced Algebra* (Bell, 3 volumes). Written a long time ago, but these books wear well and still contain a great deal of valuable reading; they also contain an excellent selection of problems, many of which are stimulating and challenging.

Ferrar, W. L. *Higher Algebra for Schools* (Oxford). A good introductory course in traditional sixth-form algebra.

Maxwell, E. A. *Algebraic Structures and Matrices* (Cambridge). Carries the work beyond 'A' level standard; contains some good exercises.

Neill, H. and Moakes, A. J. *Vectors, Matrices and Linear Equations* (Oliver and Boyd). Covers the course of linear algebra required for the M.E.I. 'A' level examinations. Approaches the subject from a rather different standpoint to that adopted in this book.

Niven, I. *Numbers: Rational and Irrational* (Random House). A comprehensive account of the work of Ch. 1.

CALCULUS

Hardy, G. H. *Pure Mathematics* (Cambridge). A very famous book. Not easy reading, but repays careful study. A work for the specialist.

Matthews, G. *Calculus* (Murray). An excellent modern text.

Maxwell, E. H. *Calculus* (Cambridge, 4 volumes). A comprehensive text, useful as a work of reference.

Quadling, D. A. *Mathematical Analysis* (Oxford). An excellent introduction to university work: presupposes some acquaintance with the calculus.

Scott, D. B. and Timms, S. R. *Mathematical Analysis* (Cambridge). A university text, but contains much good reading for the serious sixth-form student.

Siddons, A. W., Snell, K. S. and Morgan, J. B. *A New Calculus* (Cambridge, 3 volumes). A standard text-book; volume 3 is a particularly good introduction to advanced work.

Toeplitz, O. *The Calculus, A Genetic Approach* (Chicago). A stimulating approach to calculus by tracing its historical development.

GEOMETRY AND TRIGONOMETRY

Barton, A. *Introduction to Coordinate Geometry* (London). A good account of two-dimensional coordinate geometry.

Cohn, P. M. *Solid Geometry* (Routledge and Kegan Paul). See Cohn: *Linear Equations*.

Forder, H. G. *Higher Course Geometry* (Cambridge). Full of excellent material—fascinating for the keen geometer.

Kazarinoff, N. *Geometric Inequalities* (Random House). Stimulating reading: contains a good selection of problems, with hints on solutions.

Macbeath, A. M. *Elementary Vector Algebra* (Oxford). Despite its title, this is really an introduction to vector geometry. Very clearly written.

Maxwell, E. A. *Coordinate Geometry with Vectors and Tensors* (Oxford). A good introduction to three-dimensional coordinate geometry—takes the subject well beyond 'A' level.

Nobbs, C. G. *Trigonometry* (Oxford). A good introduction to 'A' level work.

Tuckey, C. A. and Rollett, A. P *Trigonometry* (Murray). A sound introductory text, with many interesting digressions.

PROBABILITY

Feller, W. *An Introduction to Probability Theory and Its Applications*, Volume 1 (Wiley). An advanced text, but highly recommended for the serious post-'A' level student.

Mosteller, F. *Fifty Challenging Problems in Probability* (Addison-Wesley). Some good material here for the problem addict.

Mosteller, F., Rourke, R. E. K. and Thomas, G. B. *Probability and Statistics* (Addison-Wesley). A very elementary introduction to probability—wordy at times, but thorough.

Parzen, E. *Modern Probability Theory and its Applications* (Wiley). A very thorough introduction, carrying the subject well beyond 'A' level.

Whitworth, W. A. *Choice and Chance* (Hafner). Published seventy years ago, the bookwork is distinctly old-fashioned, but it ends with a delightful collection of problems, some distinctly tricky. Excellent bedside reading for the inveterate problem-solver; a key is published to prevent insomnia.

BOOKS FOR GENERAL READING, COLLECTIONS OF PROBLEMS, ETC.

Abramowitz, M. and Stegun, I. A. *Handbook of Mathematical Functions* (Dover). Over a thousand pages of mathematical tables (most to sixteen or eighteen significant figures), formulae and graphs, together with extensive notes. A marvellous reference book and not at all expensive for what it contains.

Ball, W. W. R. *Mathematical Recreations and Essays* (Macmillan). First published in 1892 but it still provides excellent reading material.

Bell, E. T. *Men of Mathematics* (Pelican, 2 volumes). A racy and amusing account of the lives of great mathematicians.

Boyer, C. B. *A History of the Calculus* (Dover). A readable account of the subject.

Burkill, J. C. and Cundy, H. M. *Mathematical Scholarship Problems* (Cambridge). A good collection of problems at university scholarship level.

Cadwell, J. H. *Topics in Recreational Mathematics* (Cambridge). Digressions on the underlying mathematics in fifteen different problems: it makes very good reading.

Courant, R. and Robbins, H. *What is Mathematics?* (Oxford). A famous book, which discusses a number of mathematical situations in some depth.

David, F. N. *Games, Gods and Gambling* (Griffin). An excellent book on the early history of probability.

Dorrie, H. *100 Great Problems of Elementary Mathematics* (Dover). Extended discussion of 100 problems of considerable historical interest, together with their solutions—excellent value.

Gardner, M. *Mathematical Puzzles and Diversions* (Pelican). Entertaining reading in hexaflexagons, polyominoes, the games of nim and hex, etc.

Lockwood, E. H. *A Book of Curves* (Cambridge). A delightful collection, with historical notes and comments on the geometrical properties. A good book for browsing.

Maxwell, E. A. *Fallacies in Mathematics* (Cambridge). Will be read with interest and enjoyment by any mathematician.

Moakes, A. J. *Core of Mathematics* (Macmillan). An elementary account of mathematical structure and methods of proof: easy to read but stimulating.

Newman, J. R. *World of Mathematics* (George Allen and Unwin). An extensive anthology of mathematical writings—good browsing material.

Polya, G. *How to Solve It* (Doubleday). An analysis of the art of problem solving

Polya, G. *Mathematics and Plausible Reasoning* (Princeton, 2 volumes). The title is self-explanatory. Compulsory reading for the serious student, while the more frivolous will be able to skip through with profit.

Salkind, C. T. *The Contest Problem Book* (Random House). A collection of multiple choice problems, not all of which are easy.

Sawyer, W. W. *Prelude to Mathematics* (Pelican). A book for the layman, but can be read by the specialist with profit. Strongly recommended to all sixth-formers.

Smith, D. E. *A Source Book in Mathematics* (Dover, 2 volumes). Contains excerpts from the writings of great mathematicians of the past—all within the understanding of the sixth-former.

Weston, J. D. and Godwin, H. J. *Some Exercises in Pure Mathematics* (Cambridge). A fine collection of problems, based on the Welsh 'A' level (alternative syllabus). Contains detailed solutions.

Answers

CHAPTER 1

2 **Ex. 2.** 100101001. **Ex. 3.** 100, remainder 111.

Exercise 1(a)

1. (i) 10; (ii) 1110; (iii) 10000; (iv) 101.

2. 100010011, 101012, 1*te*.

3. 8*e*242.   **4.** 3*e*, remainder 19.

5 **Ex. 7.** Yes, unless $a^2 = b^2 \neq 0$.

7 **Ex. 12.** (i) 7/9; (ii) 134/333; (iii) 283/45.

  Ex. 13. (i) 11·11; (ii) 0·101101; (iii) $100 \cdot \dot{1}00\dot{1}$;
(iv) $0 \cdot 1\dot{1}010001111010111000\dot{0}$.

  Ex. 15. (i) $0 \cdot \dot{3}$; (ii) $1 \cdot \dot{7}14285\dot{5}$.

Exercise 1(b)

9 **4.** (i) $0 \cdot \dot{3}$; (ii) $0 \cdot \dot{0}\dot{1}$.

  6. (i) True; (ii) True; (iii) False; (iv) True; (v) True (provided rational number is not zero); (vi) False.

11 **Ex. 17.** (i) $2\sqrt{2}$; (ii) $3\sqrt{2}$; (iii) $3\sqrt{6}$; (iv) $5\sqrt{10}$; (v) $42\sqrt{3}$.

  Ex. 18. (i) $11+4\sqrt{6}$; (ii) $3\sqrt{6}$; (iii) $2\sqrt{3}$; (iv) 8.

  Ex. 19. (i) $\frac{1}{3}\sqrt{3}$; (ii) $\frac{1}{2}(2+\sqrt{2})$; (iii) $\frac{1}{2}(2+\sqrt{2})$; (iv) $3+\sqrt{6}$; (v) $7-4\sqrt{3}$.

Exercise 1(c)

12 **1.** (i) $5\sqrt{2}$; (ii) $11\sqrt{3}$; (iii) $20\sqrt{6}$; (iv) $8\sqrt{3}$; (v) $22\sqrt{3}$.

  2. (i) $6-2\sqrt{5}$; (ii) $14-4\sqrt{6}$; (iii) $10+6\sqrt{3}$; (iv) $9\sqrt{3}-11\sqrt{2}$;
(v) $28-16\sqrt{3}$.

  3. (i) $2\sqrt{2}$; (ii) $3\sqrt{5}$; (iii) $5\sqrt{3}$; (iv) $\sqrt{13}$; (v) $(3\sqrt{3})/2$.

13 **4.** (i) $\sqrt{5}/5$; (ii) $\sqrt{21}/3$; (iii) $2(\sqrt{7}+2)/3$; (iv) $(13+4\sqrt{3})/11$;
(v) $\sqrt{6}+\sqrt{3}-\sqrt{2}-2$.

13 **5.** (i) $\sqrt{5}-1$; (ii) $\sqrt{6}-2$; (iii) $3\sqrt{2}+2\sqrt{3}$; (iv) $3\sqrt{3}-2\sqrt{5}$;
(v) $\sqrt{5}+\sqrt{2}$.

6. (i) 4; (ii) ± 2; (iii) -5.

7. (i) $\frac{1}{4}(2+\sqrt{2}-\sqrt{6})$; (ii) $\frac{1}{4}(\sqrt{10}+\sqrt{5}-\sqrt{2}-3)$.

9. (i) 0·44721 (5 d.p.); (ii) 0·27395 (5 d.p.).

10. 0·98560 (5 d.p.).   **11.** $\frac{1}{4}(3-\sqrt[3]{9}+\sqrt[3]{3})$.

12. (i) $\{\sqrt{(x+1)}+\sqrt{(x-1)}\}/2$; (ii) $(x+2)\sqrt{(x+1)}/(x+1)$;
(iii) $\{\sqrt{(2x-a)}-\sqrt{(2x+a)}\}\sqrt{(4x^2-a^2)}/(4x^2-a^2)$;
(iv) $\{x\sqrt{(x-1)}-(x-2)\sqrt{(x+1)}-2(x-1)\}/(x^2-2x)$.

14 **Ex. 20.** (i) $\{1, 2, 3, 4, 5\}$; (ii) $\{1, 4, 9\}$.

15 **Ex. 21.** (i) Odd integers; (ii) integers ≥ 2; (iii) multiples of 10;
(iv) the integer 6; (v) $\varnothing$.

16 **Ex. 26.** $\left\{x \in \mathfrak{U}: \dfrac{x}{6} \in \mathfrak{U}\right\}$.

Ex. 27. (i) $\mathfrak{U}$; (ii) $\varnothing$; (iii) $\mathfrak{U}$; (iv) A; (v) A; (vi) $\varnothing$; (vii) $\varnothing$;
(viii) $\mathfrak{U}$.

Ex. 28. (i) $\{a, e\}$; (ii) $\{a, b, d, e\}$; (iii) $\{c\}$.

Ex. 29. (i) $\{2\}$; (ii) $\{2\}$; (iii) $\{-\frac{1}{2}, 2\}$; (iv) $\{\sqrt{2}, 2\}$;
(v) $\{-\sqrt{2}, -\frac{1}{2}, \sqrt{2}, 2\}$.

18 **Ex. 31.** (i) $x < -2$; (ii) $x < 1$; (iii) $x < \frac{1}{2}$.

Exercise 1(d)

20 **2.** (i) R; (ii) $\{x \in R: 3 < x < 4\}$; (iii) $\{x \in R: x < 4\}$.

3. (i) $\{x \in Z: x < 0\}$; (ii) $\{x \in Z^+: x/6 \in Z^+\}$;
(iii) $\{x \in Z: x \leq -3 \text{ or } x \geq 3\}$.

4. (i) $\{x \in R: 2 \leq x < 3\}$; (ii) $\{x \in R: x > 3\}$;
(iii) $\{x \in R: -1 \leq x \leq 3\}$; (iv) $\{x \in R: -1 \leq x \leq 3\}$;
(v) $\{x \in R: x > 3\}$; (vi) $\{x \in R: x < -1 \text{ or } x \geq 3\}$;
(vii) $\{x \in R: 3 < x < 4\}$.

21 **5.** (i) $\{x \in R: 0 < x < 1\}$; (ii) $\varnothing$; (iii) $\{x \in R: 1 \leq x < 2\}$;
(iv) $\{x \in R: -2 \leq x \leq -1\}$.

6. (i) $\{x \in R: x < -5\}$; (ii) $\{x \in R: x > 2\}$; (iii) $\{x \in R: x < 7\}$;
(iv) $\{x \in R: x > 0\}$; (v) $\{x \in R: x < 0 \text{ or } x > 1\}$.

7. (i) $\{x \in R: x < -3 \text{ or } x > 1\}$; (ii) $\{x \in R: x < -\frac{1}{3} \text{ or } x > \frac{1}{2}\}$;
(iii) $\{x \in R: -\frac{3}{2} < x < 3\}$; (iv) $\varnothing$; (v) $\{x \in R: -1 < x < 5\}$.

21   **8.** $\{x \in R: -3 < x < -\frac{1}{2} \quad \text{or} \quad x > 2\}$.

    9. (i) 1;   (ii) 3;   (iii) $\frac{1}{2}$.   **10.** (i) Negative;   (ii) positive.

    11. $x < -4; \quad -2 < x < 1; \quad x > 3$.

    12. 10.   **13.** 12.   **14.** 1.   **15.** 600.

    16. 20 m.   **17.** $\frac{2}{3}$ m²; $AB = 1$ m, $AD = \frac{2}{3}$ m.

Miscellaneous Exercise 1

    1. 1111000; Seven: $\frac{1}{2}$p, 1p, 2p, 4p, 8p, 16p, 32p.

22   **2.** $a = 2, \quad b = 3$.   **6.** $a = 1, b = 4, c = 3$.

    8. $1 - 1/\sqrt{7}$.   **9.** (i) 10;   (ii) $\frac{2}{3}$.   **10.** Unaltered.

    11. (Expressions not unique) (i) $A \cap C$;   (ii) $A' \cap B'$;   (iii) $C' \cap B$; (iv) $B \cap (A' \cup C')$.

23   **12.** $k = -7, a = 8, b = \frac{1}{2}; k = 3, a = -2, b = -2$.

    13. (i) Expressions equal; (ii) strict inequality.

    14. 1/162, 4/27.

CHAPTER 2

28   **Ex. 5.** (i) 8 units N;   (ii) 3 units W;   (iii) $4\sqrt{2}$ units NW; (iv) $2\sqrt{17}$ units N 14° 2′ E;   (v) 10 units N 36° 52′ W.

    Ex. 6. $x = (2a+b)/7, y = (a-3b)/7$.

    Ex. 7. (i) $\sqrt{7}$ units N 19° 6′ E;   (ii) $\sqrt{3}$ units S 30° E; (iii) 1 unit S 60° E;   (iv) $\sqrt{7}$ units S 40° 54 W.

    Ex. 8. (i) $2\sqrt{2}$ units at 45° with downward vertical in plane through SN line; (ii) $3\sqrt{2}$ units at 45° with downward vertical in plane through EW line; (iii) $6\sqrt{3}$ units at 45° to N, E and upward vertical; (iv) $6\sqrt{3}$ units at 45° to N, W and downward vertical.

    Ex. 9. (i) $2\mathbf{a}+\mathbf{b}$;   (ii) $2\mathbf{a}-\mathbf{b}$;   (iii) $\mathbf{a}+\mathbf{b}$;   (iv) $\mathbf{a}-\mathbf{b}$.

30   **Ex. 12.** $\mathbf{x} = \mathbf{b}+\frac{1}{2}\mathbf{a}, \mathbf{y} = \mathbf{b}-\frac{1}{2}\mathbf{a}, \mathbf{a} = \mathbf{x}-\mathbf{y}, \mathbf{b} = \frac{1}{2}(\mathbf{x}+\mathbf{y})$.

30   **Ex. 13.** Yes, no.

Exercise 2(a)

    1. (i) $3\mathbf{a}+\mathbf{b}$;   (ii) $8\mathbf{a}+\mathbf{b}$;   (iii) $-5\mathbf{a}+5\mathbf{b}$,   (iv) $-2\mathbf{a}+6\mathbf{b}$.

    2. $\mathbf{a} = (\mathbf{u}+3\mathbf{v})/7, \mathbf{b} = (2\mathbf{u}-\mathbf{v})/7$.

30 **3.** (i) $3\mathbf{a}+2\mathbf{b}$; (ii) $-\mathbf{a}+2\mathbf{c}$; (iii) $2\mathbf{a}+5\mathbf{b}+5\mathbf{c}$; (iv) $6\mathbf{a}+2\mathbf{b}-3\mathbf{c}$.

      4. $\mathbf{a}=\frac{1}{3}(\mathbf{u}+\mathbf{v})$, $\mathbf{b}=(-\mathbf{u}-4\mathbf{v}+3\mathbf{w})/9$, $\mathbf{c}=(-7\mathbf{u}-\mathbf{v}+3\mathbf{w})/9$.

      5. (i) 2 units E; (ii) 3 units S; (iii) 5 units N 36° 52′ E;
      (iv) $\sqrt{2}$ units SE; (v) 5 units N 36° 52′ W.

31 **6.** (i) 13 units S 67° 23′ E; (ii) 13 units N 67° 23′ E;
      (iii) $\sqrt{29}$ units N 21° 48′ W.

      7. (i) 1·53 units N 22° 30′ E; (ii) 2·8 units S 59° 38′ E;
      (iii) 1·47 units S 16° 20′ E; (iv) 7·4 units N 67° 30′ W.

      8. $-20\mathbf{x}-10\sqrt{2}\mathbf{y}$.

      9. $\lambda=2\sec 70°$, $\mu=-2\tan 70°$; $\lambda'=\mu'\approx 1\cdot02$.

      10. 9 units: (i) 12° 45′; (ii) 125° 28′.

      11. OP: (i) $\mathbf{a}+\mathbf{b}$; (ii) $2\mathbf{a}+\mathbf{c}$; (iii) $2\mathbf{b}-\mathbf{c}$.
        OQ: (i) $2\mathbf{a}+3\mathbf{b}$; (ii) $5\mathbf{a}+3\mathbf{c}$; (iii) $5\mathbf{b}-2\mathbf{c}$.
        OR: (i) $3\mathbf{a}+4\mathbf{b}$; (ii) $7\mathbf{a}+4\mathbf{c}$; (iii) $7\mathbf{b}-3\mathbf{c}$.
        $PQ=\mathbf{a}+2\mathbf{b}$; $RQ=-2\mathbf{b}+\mathbf{c}$.

      12. $\frac{1}{3}\mathbf{u}+\frac{1}{4}\mathbf{v}$, $\frac{2}{3}\mathbf{u}+\frac{3}{4}\mathbf{v}$, $\mathbf{u}+\mathbf{v}$, $\mathbf{w}=-\frac{1}{3}\mathbf{u}-\frac{1}{2}\mathbf{v}$.

      13. $\mathbf{b}-\mathbf{a}$, $-\mathbf{a}$, $-\mathbf{b}$, $\mathbf{a}-\mathbf{b}$.

      14. $\mathbf{a}-2\mathbf{b}$, $2\mathbf{a}+2\mathbf{b}+2\mathbf{c}$, $\mathbf{a}+2\mathbf{b}+2\mathbf{c}$, $\mathbf{b}-2\mathbf{c}$, $-\mathbf{a}-\mathbf{b}-4\mathbf{c}$.

32 **15.** $-\mathbf{a}+2\mathbf{b}+4\mathbf{c}$, $\mathbf{a}+\mathbf{b}+4\mathbf{c}$, $\mathbf{a}+2\mathbf{b}+2\mathbf{c}$;
      $(-3\mathbf{ED}'+2\mathbf{EG}+2\mathbf{EF})/7$, $(\mathbf{ED}'-3\mathbf{EG}+4\mathbf{EF})/7$, $(\mathbf{ED}'+4\mathbf{EG}-3\mathbf{EF})/14$.

      16. (i) $\mathbf{j}+\mathbf{k}$; (ii) $\mathbf{i}+\mathbf{j}+2\mathbf{k}$; (iii) $\mathbf{i}-\mathbf{j}-2\mathbf{k}$; (iv) $2\mathbf{i}+\mathbf{j}+2\mathbf{k}$;
      (v) $\mathbf{i}+\mathbf{k}$; (vi) $\mathbf{i}+\mathbf{j}+\mathbf{k}$.

      17. (i) $a\mathbf{q}-a\mathbf{p}$; (ii) $a\mathbf{p}-a\mathbf{q}+a\mathbf{r}$.

      18. (i) $(4\mathbf{u}-2\mathbf{v})/3$; (ii) $(4\mathbf{v}-2\mathbf{u})/3$; (iii) $2(\mathbf{v}-\mathbf{u})$.

      19. (i) $\mathbf{u}-\frac{1}{2}\mathbf{v}-\frac{1}{2}\mathbf{w}$; (ii) $\frac{1}{2}(\mathbf{v}-w)$; (iii) $\frac{1}{2}(\mathbf{u}+\mathbf{w})$, (iv) $\frac{1}{2}(\mathbf{v}-\mathbf{u})$.

      21. $\mathbf{AC}'-2\mathbf{AD}'$, $2\mathbf{AC}-\mathbf{AC}'$.

      22. $\mathbf{b}\sqrt{2}-\mathbf{a}$, $\mathbf{b}-\mathbf{a}\sqrt{2}$, $-\mathbf{a}$, $-\mathbf{b}$, $\mathbf{a}-\mathbf{b}\sqrt{2}$, $\mathbf{a}\sqrt{2}-\mathbf{b}$.

35 Ex. **16.** $\alpha+\beta=1$.

Exercise 2(b)

40 **1.** $2\mathbf{b}-\mathbf{a}$, $\frac{1}{3}(2\mathbf{c}+\mathbf{a})$, $\frac{1}{3}(-\mathbf{a}+3\mathbf{b}+\mathbf{c})$.   **5.** $\lambda(\mathbf{b}+\mathbf{c})$, $\lambda(2\mathbf{c}+\mathbf{a})$.

      6. $\frac{2}{3}\mathbf{b}$, $\frac{1}{2}(\mathbf{a}+\mathbf{b})$, $2\mathbf{a}$, $OA=AX$.

41 **7.** $\frac{2}{3}\mathbf{a}+\frac{1}{3}\mathbf{c}$, $\frac{1}{3}\mathbf{a}+\frac{2}{3}\mathbf{b}$; $\mathbf{x}=\frac{1}{7}(2\mathbf{a}+4\mathbf{b}+\mathbf{c})$.

PAGE

41 **8.** $\frac{1}{3}$**a**′, $\frac{2}{3}$**b**+**d**+**a**′, **b**+$\frac{1}{3}$**d**+**a**′; the point of trisection of DD' nearer D'.

  9. **u**+**v**, $\frac{1}{2}$(**v**+**w**), $-\frac{1}{3}$(**v**+2**u**); point X on WO produced such that $OX = \frac{1}{3}WO$.

  10. 3:1.   **11.** 2**i**+3**j**, 6**i**+4**j**, 6**j**−**i**.

42 **15.** $\frac{4}{5}$, $\frac{2}{5}$.

Miscellaneous Exercise 2

  1. **b**+2 cos 72° **a**, **a**+2 cos 72° **b**.

  3. (i) Parallelogram; (ii) equal diagonals; (iii) rectangle.

43 **14.** 3:1:2.

  15. $(\alpha\delta_2 - \beta\delta_1)/(\gamma_1\delta_2 - \gamma_2\delta_1)$, $(\beta\gamma_1 - \alpha\gamma_2)/(\gamma_1\delta_2 - \gamma_2\delta_1)$; **c**, **d** not parallel.

CHAPTER 3

47 **Ex. 2.** $\begin{pmatrix} -\frac{5}{2} \\ \frac{3}{2} \\ \frac{3}{2} \end{pmatrix}$. **Ex. 3.** $\begin{pmatrix} 3 \\ 1 \\ -2 \end{pmatrix}$, $\begin{pmatrix} -4 \\ -3 \\ 1 \end{pmatrix}$, $\begin{pmatrix} -9 \\ -6 \\ 3 \end{pmatrix}$.

  Ex. 4. $-2, 6$.

48 **Ex. 6.** (2, 1).   **Ex. 7.** $(\frac{7}{3}, -\frac{7}{3})$, $(\frac{11}{3}, -\frac{11}{3})$.   **Ex. 8.** (1, 1, 2).

  Ex. 9. (0, 4)   **Ex. 10.** $(-2, 3, 9)$, $(0, -1, -5)$.   **Ex. 11.** $(\frac{8}{3}, \frac{10}{3})$.

  Ex. 12. $\frac{5}{2}$**i**+**j**+$\frac{1}{2}$**k**, $(\frac{5}{2}, 1, \frac{1}{2})$.

50 **Ex. 13.** $2\sqrt{5}$, $\sqrt{6}$, $\sqrt{(2a^2 + 3k^2)}$.   **Ex. 15.** (2, 4, 3).

  Ex. 16. (0, 0, 0), $\sqrt{2}$.

Exercise 3(a)

51 **1.** (i) $\begin{pmatrix} 0 \\ 2 \\ 2 \end{pmatrix}$; (ii) $\begin{pmatrix} 5 \\ 4 \\ -8 \end{pmatrix}$; (iii) $\begin{pmatrix} 4 \\ -3 \\ -1 \end{pmatrix}$; (iv) $\begin{pmatrix} 5 \\ 0 \\ -1 \end{pmatrix}$; (v) $\begin{pmatrix} 0 \\ -3 \\ 8 \end{pmatrix}$.

  2. (i) $\begin{pmatrix} -3 \\ -1 \\ -4 \end{pmatrix}$; (ii) $\begin{pmatrix} -3 \\ 13 \\ -14 \end{pmatrix}$; (iii) $\begin{pmatrix} -10 \\ 18 \\ -25 \end{pmatrix}$.

  3. (i) $\begin{pmatrix} -1 \\ -1 \\ -\frac{1}{2} \end{pmatrix}$; (ii) $\begin{pmatrix} \frac{2}{3} \\ 2 \\ \frac{1}{3} \end{pmatrix}$.

  4. (i) **x** $= \begin{pmatrix} \frac{2}{7} \\ \frac{20}{7} \\ -\frac{19}{7} \end{pmatrix}$, **y** $= \begin{pmatrix} -\frac{1}{7} \\ \frac{11}{7} \\ -\frac{8}{7} \end{pmatrix}$; (ii) **x** $= \begin{pmatrix} 0 \\ 4 \\ -5 \end{pmatrix}$, **y** $= \begin{pmatrix} 2 \\ 0 \\ 1 \end{pmatrix}$, **z** $= \begin{pmatrix} 2 \\ -4 \\ 6 \end{pmatrix}$.

PAGE

51 **5.** $\begin{pmatrix}1\\1\end{pmatrix}$, $\begin{pmatrix}1\\-1\end{pmatrix}$, $\begin{pmatrix}3\\-1\end{pmatrix}$, $\begin{pmatrix}3\\1\end{pmatrix}$.

6. $\begin{pmatrix}-\frac{1}{2}\\\frac{1}{2}\\\frac{1}{2}\end{pmatrix}$, $\begin{pmatrix}\frac{1}{2}\\\frac{1}{2}\\\frac{1}{2}\end{pmatrix}$, $\begin{pmatrix}2\\1\\1\end{pmatrix}$, $\begin{pmatrix}4\\-4\\0\end{pmatrix}$.

7. (i) $(3, 5)$; (ii) $(1, 3)$; (iii) $(\frac{1}{2}, -\frac{7}{2})$; (iv) $(\frac{5}{2}, -\frac{3}{2}, -\frac{5}{2})$; (v) $(a, 0, -b)$.

52 **8.** (i) $(2, 6), (3, 8)$; (ii) $(-1, \frac{10}{3}), (0, \frac{17}{3})$; (iii) $(a+b, b-a), (a, b)$; (iv) $(\frac{4}{3}, \frac{5}{3}, -\frac{7}{3}), (\frac{5}{3}, \frac{4}{3}, -\frac{11}{3})$; (v) $(a-\frac{1}{3}b, \frac{2}{3}a+\frac{1}{3}b, \frac{1}{3}a+b)$, $(a-\frac{2}{3}b, -\frac{2}{3}a+\frac{2}{3}b, \frac{2}{3}a+b)$.

9. (i) $\sqrt{8}$; (ii) $\sqrt{40}$; (iii) $\sqrt{10}$; (iv) $\sqrt{51}$; (v) $\sqrt{(8a^2+4b^2)}$.

10. $(5, 3), (1, -3)$.   **11.** $\frac{25}{2}$.

12. $(2, -1, 3), (\frac{3}{2}, \frac{1}{2}, \frac{1}{2})$.   **13.** 20.   **14.** $1:2$.

55 **Ex. 18.** (i) $2x-y-7 = 0$;   (ii) $2x+3y+5 = 0$.

Ex. 19. (i) $5x-y-13 = 0$; (ii) $x+y-1 = 0$; (iii) $3x-2y+7 = 0$; (iv) $y-2 = 0$.

Ex. 20. (i) 2; (ii) -1; (iii) $-\frac{3}{4}$.

57 **Ex. 23.** $3x-y-22 = 0$, $x+2y-5 = 0$, $(7, -1)$.

Ex. 24. $11x+5y+1 = 0$.   **Ex. 25.** $x+3y-1 = 0$.

Ex. 26. $3\sqrt{29}$.

Exercise 3(b)

1. (i) $2x-y-2 = 0$; (ii) $2x+y+3 = 0$; (iii) $x+2y-1 = 0$; (iv) $ax+by-(a^2+b^2) = 0$.

2. (i) $3x-y-5 = 0$; (ii) $7x-y+11 = 0$; (iii) $y+1 = 0$; (iv) $3bx+2ay-5ab = 0$.

3. (i) $\frac{2}{3}$; (ii) $-\frac{1}{2}$; (iii) 5; (iv) $(b+a)/(b-a)$.

4. (i) $2x-y-7 = 0$, $x+2y-1 = 0$; (ii) $5x+4y-11 = 0$, $4x-5y-17 = 0$;   (iii) $x-3 = 0$, $y+1 = 0. \ 2\sqrt{5}$.

5. (i) $(3, -2)$; (ii) $(-(a^3+b^3)/(a^2+b^2), -ab(a-b)/(a^2+b^2))$.

6. (i) $43x+3y = 0$; (ii) $7x-y-2 = 0$; (iii) $10x-6y-9 = 0$.

58 **7.** $(-3, 10)$.   **8.** $(5, -9), (3, -1), (1, 3)$.   **9.** $(2, -3)$.

10. $(-5, 4), (-5\pm2\sqrt{21}, 0), (0, 4\pm5\sqrt{3})$.

11. $x-\lambda y = 1-2\lambda$; a circle on $(-2, 1)$, $(1, 2)$ as diameter.

PAGE

58 **12.** $3:4$. **13.** $(3, -4)$. **14.** $(2, 1)$. **15.** Lies on AB.

16. (i) $2x+3y+6 = 0$; (ii) $2x+3y-6 = 0$; (iii) $2x-3y-6 = 0$;
(iv) $2x-3y-12 = 0$.

62 **Ex. 27.** (i) $z = 0$; (ii) $z = 2$.

63 **Ex. 31.** $3y-5z = 0$. **Ex. 32.** $(2\lambda+3, -\lambda-2, -3\lambda-5), (1, -1, -2)$.

Ex. 33. $\frac{1}{5}(x+3) = y-1 = -\frac{1}{2}(z-1)$.

Exercise 3 (c)

1. (i) $[1, 1, 1]$, $[1/\sqrt{3}, 1/\sqrt{3}, 1/\sqrt{3}]$. The direction ratios only are given in
the remaining seven parts; (ii) $[1, -2, 1]$; (iii) $[-2, 2, 1]$; (iv) $[1, 0, -1]$;
(v) $[-1, 1, 1]$; (vi) $[1, 2, 3]$, (vii) $[0, a, b+c]$; (viii) $[1, 0, -1]$.

2. (i) $x+y+z = 1$; (ii) $x+y-2z = 5$; (iii) $2x+y-z = 4$;
(iv) $3x-y-2z = 4$; (v) $5x+3y-2z = 2$; (vi) $5x-z = 2$.

3. (i) $\frac{1}{4}x = y = -\frac{1}{3}z$; (ii) $x-1 = y-2 = -\frac{1}{2}(z+1)$;
(iii) $\frac{1}{2}(x-1) = -\frac{1}{3}(y-1) = -\frac{1}{3}(z+1)$; (iv) $\frac{1}{2}(x+2) = -\frac{1}{3}(z-3), y = 1$;
(v) $x = 1, z = 2$; (vi) $\frac{1}{2}(x-a) = y-2a = z-3a$.

4. (i) $3x-3y+z = 0$; (ii) $5x-4y-1 = 0$; (iii) $3y-5z-3 = 0$.

5. (i) $7x+3y+5z = 0$; (ii) $4x-4y-5z+5 = 0$; (iii) $11x-y+5 = 0$.

64 **6.** $3y+2z-7 = 0$; $7x-4y-5z = 0$.

7. $2x+y+2z+7 = 0$.

8. $(3\lambda+8, \lambda+1, 1), (5, 0\ 1)$. **9.** $(1, 1, 0)$.

10. $x-2 = \frac{1}{2}(y-1) = -(z-1), (3, 3, 0)$.

11. $[1/\sqrt{5}, 0, -2/\sqrt{5}], (1, -4, 3)$.

13. $(-7, -7, 4), x-4y-z-17 = 0$.

14. $(1, 1, 3), 3x-4y-2z+7 = 0$.

65 **15.** $(1, -2, -1)$. **16.** $(-3, -4, 2)$. **17.** $(7, 5, 0)$.

Miscellaneous Exercise 3

2. $2:1, 5\frac{1}{3}$. **4.** $mx-y+(b-am) = 0$.

66 **8.** $x = -y = \frac{1}{2}z$.

10. (i) Planes form a prism;
(ii) planes all pass through the line $x - z + 1 = 0$, $y = 4$.

11. $2:1$; $2:1$. **12.** $18\lambda\mu+2\lambda-5\mu = 0$.

67 **14.** $\alpha(\beta+\gamma)/(a-\alpha)$. **15.** $x \pm z\sqrt{3}-2 = 0$.

CHAPTER 4

PAGE

68 **Ex. 1.** 3, 6, 6.　　**Ex. 2.** 8, -1, 5.

69 **Ex. 4.** 1, -1, 0.

Exercise 4(a)

1. 10, 2, $3\frac{7}{8}$, 82. **2.** 1, -9, 26, -24. 　　　　　**3.** 0.

4. 3, 4, -5. 　**5.** 7, 20, 22, 5. 　**6.** 4, 0, -6, 2. 　**7.** 3, -7, -6, 0;

3, 20, 33, 0; $-1\frac{2}{3}$, -1, 2. 　　　　**8.** 1, k, $-2k^2$, $-k^3$.

70 **11.** -9, 27, 3.

Exercise 4(b)

72 **1.** (i) 62; (ii) 8; (iii) -2; (iv) -241; (v) $1\frac{1}{4}$; (vi) $4\frac{1}{2}$.

2. $(x-2)(x-3)(x+1)$.

73 **3.** (i) $(2x+1)(x+4)(x-1)$; (ii) $(x+1)(3x-4)(4x+3)$;
(iii) $(x+5)(x-2)(2x+1)$; (iv) $(x+3)(x^2-2)$; (v) $(x-2)(x^2+x+1)$;
(vi) $(x+1)(x-3)(x-5)$; (vii) $(x-2)(x^2+4x+1)$;
(viii) $(2x-1)(2x+1)(2x+3)$.

4. As for Qu. 3 except (iv) $(x+3)(x-\sqrt{2})(x+\sqrt{2})$;
(vii) $(x-2)(x+2-\sqrt{3})(x+2+\sqrt{3})$.

5. 2. 　　　　**6.** -5.

7. $-6\frac{3}{4}$. 　　**8.** 4, -5. 　　**9.** 2, -2.

11. (i) $(x-1)(x-2)(x^2+6x+1)$;
(ii) $(x-1)(x-2)(x+3+2\sqrt{2})(x+3-2\sqrt{2})$.

12. 0, 4; $2(x+1)(x-1)(x-2)$.

Exercise 4(c)

75 **6.** x^3-x^2+3x+2. 　　　　**7.** $2x^3-5x^2+x+1$.

8. x^3-x-5.

Miscellaneous Exercise 4

76 **2.** $R=-2$, $S=-3$.

3. (i) $18x+6$; (ii) $1261x+2777$. **4.** $P(b)/(b-a)$, $P(a)/(a-b)$.

5. $(b+c)(c+a)(a+b)$. (i) $3(p+2q-3r)(-3p+q+2r)(2p-3q+r)$;
(ii) 2, 3, 13, 47, 73.

ANSWERS

77 **8.** (i) $-(b-c)(c-a)(a-b)$; (ii) $(b+c)(c+a)(a+b)$;
(iii) $(a+b+c)(b-c)(c-a)(a-b)$.

10. x^3+3x^2+5x+5.

CHAPTER 5

78 **Ex. 1.** *mn*.

80 **Ex. 3.** $2, 3, -12, -13$; $0, (3\pm\sqrt{29})/2$.

Ex. 4. $2, 3, -12, -13$; 0.

Exercise 5(a)

81 **1.** $-1, -1, 5, 23, -1$.   **2.** $1\frac{1}{2}, 2\frac{1}{3}, 3\frac{1}{4}$.

3. $\{y \in R : y \geqslant 0\}, \{y \in R : y \leqslant 0\}$.

82 **4.** $-1, 1$.   **6.** $2\frac{7}{9}, \{z \in R : 2 \leqslant z \leqslant 5\}$.

9. (i) $0, 0$; (ii) $\{y \in R : -\frac{1}{4} \leqslant y < 2\}$; (iii) $\{(3-\sqrt{5})/2, (3+\sqrt{5})/2\}$;
(iv) $\varnothing$.

10. $\{y \in R : -4\sqrt{2} \leqslant y \leqslant 4\sqrt{2}\}$.   **11.** $f^{-1}(y) = 1+y^{\frac{1}{3}}$.

12. $\frac{1}{2}$.   **14.** (i) No; (ii) no.   **15.** Reflection in $x = y$.

Exercise 5(b)

86 **1.** $x < 0$ or $x > \frac{1}{2}$.   **2.** $x < 0$ or $x > 1$.

3. $x < 0$ or $x > 1$.   **4.** $x < -2$ or $x > -1$.

5. $1 \leqslant x < 3$.   **6.** $x < \frac{2}{3}$ or $x > 1$.

7. $x \leqslant -1$ or $1 < x \leqslant 2$.   **8.** $x > 3$ or $x = 2$.

9. $-1 < x < \frac{1}{2}$.   **10.** $x < 1$ or $2 < x < 3$ or $x > 4$.

11. $-2 < x < -1$ or $1 < x < 1\frac{1}{2}$.

12. $-3 < x < -2$ or $-1 < x < 1$.

13. $x < -2$ or $0 < x < 1$ or $x > 2$.

14. $x < -5$ or $-3 < x < 0$ or $1 < x < 2$ or $x > 5$.

15. $x < -\frac{1}{2}(\sqrt{13}+1)$ or $x > \frac{1}{2}(\sqrt{13}-1)$.

16. $-\sqrt{3} < x < -\sqrt{2}$ or $\sqrt{2} < x < \sqrt{3}$.

17. $x < 1\frac{1}{2}$ or $x \geqslant 3$.   **18.** $x > 2\frac{2}{3}$.

19. $x < -\frac{1}{3}$ or $x > 1\frac{2}{3}$.   **20.** $x < -\sqrt{2}$ or $x > \sqrt{2}$.

21. $x \leqslant 0$ or $1\frac{1}{2} \leqslant x \leqslant 2$.   **22.** $x < -1\frac{1}{2}$ or $3\frac{6}{7} < x < 5$.

CHAPTER 6

PAGE

87 **Ex. 1.** $\dfrac{\pi}{6}, \dfrac{\pi}{3}, \dfrac{\pi}{4}, \dfrac{5\pi}{12}, \dfrac{3\pi}{4}, \dfrac{5\pi}{4}, \dfrac{11\pi}{6}$.

Ex. 2. 45°, 150°, 120°, 40°, 105°, 36°, 48°.

Exercise 6(a)

88 **1.** $\dfrac{\pi}{9}, \dfrac{\pi}{4}, \dfrac{7\pi}{12}, \dfrac{5\pi}{6}, \dfrac{7\pi}{6}, \dfrac{3\pi}{2}, \dfrac{7\pi}{4}, \dfrac{11\pi}{6}, \dfrac{5\pi}{2}, \dfrac{19\pi}{6}$.

2. 30°, 60°, 135°, 75°, 210°, 810°, 54°, 900°, 50°, 63°.

3. 0·445, 1·244, 2·552.　　　　　**4.** 27·5°, 37·2°, 124·9°.

6. 6080 feet—the 'nautical mile'.　　**7.** 18·5 cm.

8. (i) 10·5 cm; (ii) 43·3 cm²; (iii) 9·1 cm².

9. $2r \sin \theta$, $\pi r \theta / 90$.　　　　　**10.** 1·7 m, 8 m².

89 **11.** 9·6 cm, 26·5 cm².

12. (i) 216°; (ii) 47·1 cm²; (iii) 6·24 cm.

Exercise 6(b)

94 **1.** $-\frac{1}{2}$, -1, 2, $-\sqrt{3}/3$, $-\sqrt{2}/2$, 2, 0, $\sqrt{3}/3$, $-\sqrt{2}$, $-2\sqrt{3}/3$.

2. $\sqrt{2}/2$, -1, -2, $-\sqrt{2}/2$, $\sqrt{3}/3$, -2, $\sqrt{3}/2$, $-2\sqrt{3}/3$, $-\sqrt{3}/3$, $-\sqrt{3}/2$.

3. $-0\cdot5736$, $-0\cdot6157$, $-0\cdot8391$, $3\cdot0716$, $0\cdot3420$.

4. (i) $\dfrac{7\pi}{6}, \dfrac{11\pi}{6}$; (ii) $\dfrac{3\pi}{4}, \dfrac{7\pi}{4}$, (iii) $\dfrac{2\pi}{3}, \dfrac{4\pi}{3}$; (iv) $\dfrac{\pi}{6}, \dfrac{7\pi}{6}$;

(v) $\dfrac{\pi}{3}, \dfrac{2\pi}{3}, \dfrac{4\pi}{3}, \dfrac{5\pi}{3}$; (vi) $\dfrac{13\pi}{12}, \dfrac{17\pi}{12}$; (vii) $\dfrac{3\pi}{4}, \dfrac{7\pi}{4}$;

(viii) $\dfrac{\pi}{18}, \dfrac{5\pi}{18}, \dfrac{13\pi}{18}, \dfrac{17\pi}{18}, \dfrac{25\pi}{18}, \dfrac{29\pi}{18}$; (ix) $\dfrac{5\pi}{3}$; (x) $0, \frac{2}{3}\pi, \pi, \frac{5}{3}\pi, 2\pi$;

(xi) $\dfrac{\pi}{6}, \dfrac{7\pi}{6}$, (xii) $\dfrac{\pi}{6}, \dfrac{\pi}{3}, \dfrac{2\pi}{3}, \dfrac{5\pi}{6}$.

5. (i) $-\pi, -\dfrac{5\pi}{6}, -\dfrac{\pi}{6}, 0, \pi$; (ii) $-\dfrac{5\pi}{6}, -\dfrac{\pi}{6}$; (iii) $-\dfrac{\pi}{2}, \dfrac{\pi}{6}, \dfrac{5\pi}{6}$;

(iv) $-\pi, 0, \pi$; (v) $-\dfrac{5\pi}{8}, \dfrac{3\pi}{8}$; (vi) $-\dfrac{\pi}{2}, \dfrac{\pi}{2}$; (vii) $-\dfrac{7\pi}{12}, -\dfrac{\pi}{12}, \dfrac{5\pi}{12}, \dfrac{11\pi}{12}$

(viii) no solution; (ix) $-\dfrac{\pi}{2}$; (x) $-\dfrac{3\pi}{4}, -\dfrac{5\pi}{8}, -\dfrac{\pi}{8}, \dfrac{\pi}{4}, \dfrac{3\pi}{8}, \dfrac{7\pi}{8}$.

94 **6.** (i) 3, 1;   (ii) 4, 0;   (iii) 5, 1.

7. (i) $-2\sqrt{2}/3, -\sqrt{2}/4$;   (ii) $\sqrt{5}/5, -2\sqrt{5}/5$;
(iii) $-\frac{1}{3}, 2\sqrt{2}$;   (iv) $-\sqrt{15}/15, -4\sqrt{15}/15$;   (v) $-4\sqrt{15}/15, -\sqrt{15}/15$.

95 **11.** $-\frac{5}{12}, \frac{35}{12}$.   **12.** $3 \pm 6\sqrt{10}/10$.

13. (i) 45, 123·7, 225, 303·7;   (ii) 70·5, 289·5;   (iii) 45, 225, 153·4, 333·4;
(iv) 38·2, 141·8;   (v) 36·9, 143·1, 216·9, 323·1;   (vi) 30, 150;
(vii) no solution;   (viii) 0, 63·4, 180, 243·4, 360.

14. (i) $9x^2 + 4(y-3)^2 = 36$;   (ii) $x^2 + y^2 = 2$;   (iii) $2x^2 - 2xy + 5y^2 = 9$;
(iv) $x^2(16 - y^2) = 9y^2$;   (v) $y(2-y)(1+x)^2 = 1$.

15. (i) $(\sin \epsilon, 0)$;   (ii) $(\pm 1, 0)$;   (iii) π/ω seconds.   **16.** $\alpha = \frac{1}{4}\pi$.

96 **19.** 4, 1⅓.   (i) 0;   (ii) 2.

98 **Ex. 12.** arccot: $R \to \{y \in R : 0 < y < \pi\}$;
arcsec: $\{x \in R : |x| \geqslant 1\} \to \{y \in R : 0 \leqslant y \leqslant \pi, y \neq \frac{1}{2}\pi\}$.

Ex. 13. $\frac{1}{6}\pi, \frac{1}{4}\pi, -\frac{1}{4}\pi$.

Exercise 6(c)

99 **2.** 0, $\frac{2}{3}\pi, \pi, \frac{4}{3}\pi, 2\pi$.   **3.** 35·2.   **4.** 65°.

100 **5.** 35·3, 144·7.   **6.** 0·4, 3·32, 5·14.   **7.** 0·90, 2·25.

15. (i) $\sqrt{3}/2$;   (ii) $\sqrt{3}/2$;   (iii) $\sqrt{3}/3$;   (iv) $-\sqrt{2}/2$;   (v) $\frac{1}{2}$;   (vi) 3;
(vii) 4;   (viii) $-\sqrt{3}/3$.

16. (i) $x/\sqrt{(1-x^2)}$;   (ii) $x/\sqrt{(1+x^2)}$.   **17.** $\sqrt{2}/2$.

18. $x, |x| \geqslant 1$.   **19.** $x^2 + y^2 = 1$.

Miscellaneous Exercise 6

1. 0·967.

101 **2.** $2a^2(\frac{1}{3}\pi - \sqrt{3}/4)$.   **3.** 11, -1.   **4.** 0·73, 2·41, 3·99, 5·43.

5. 54·4 cm.   (i) 12·25 cm;   (ii) 75·5°;   (iii) 13·2 cm.

6. 0.   **7.** $\sin x \neq \pm \sin y$

8. $(\frac{17}{36}\pi, \frac{7}{36}\pi)$ or $(\frac{23}{36}\pi, \frac{1}{36}\pi)$.   **9.** $(x^2 - y^2)^2 = 16xy$.

102 **11.** $0·88\pi, 0·78\pi, 0·69\pi, 0·60\pi, 0·50\pi$.

12. $0·46\pi, 1·63\pi, 2·31\pi, 3·95\pi, 4\pi$.

13. $2n\pi \pm \alpha, n\pi + \alpha$.

14. (i) $\frac{1}{6}(3n+1)\pi$;   (ii) $\frac{2}{3}(3n \pm 1)\pi$ or $2k\pi$.   **16.** $0·39\pi$, 2·3 cm.

353

CHAPTER 7

103 **Ex. 1.** 120, 720, 5040.

104 **Ex. 2.** 12, 60, 720. **Ex. 3.** 120, 6.

105 **Ex. 4.** 10, 20. **Ex. 5.** 1. **Ex. 7.** 364, 165.

106 **Ex. 8.** 210. **Ex. 9.** 5^{10}.

Exercise 7(a)

1. 120. **2.** 870.

107 **3.** 665 280. **4.** 216. **5.** 120, 48, 30. **6.** 495, 135.

7. 5005, 420 420. **8.** 34 650. **9.** 120, 85.

10. (i) $48!/(9!39!)$; (ii) $48!\,16/(9!\,39!)$. **12.** $\frac{1}{6}n!$, 840.

13. 30, 12. **14.** 19 958 400. **15.** $\frac{1}{2}n(n-3)$. **16.** 90.

108 **17.** $n!/(p!\,q!\,r!)$, $n!/\{3(n-2p)!\,(p!)^2\}$. **18.** $\frac{1}{2}n(n-1)$.

109 **Ex. 10.** $\{HH, HT, TH, TT\}$, $\{0H, 1H, 2H\}$, {coins fall the same, coins fall differently}.

112 **Ex. 20.** $\frac{3}{8}$. **Ex. 21.** $\frac{1}{12}$. **Ex. 22.** $\frac{1}{50}$.

Ex. 23. (i) $13^2(39!)^2/(27!\,52!)$; (ii) $13\,(39!)^2/(27!\,51!)$.

Ex. 24. (i) $\frac{3}{4}$; (ii) $\frac{1}{5}$; (iii) $\frac{1}{4}$.

Exercise 7(b)

1. 64, 20, $\frac{5}{16}$.

113 **2.** $\{\frac{1}{64}, \frac{6}{64}, \frac{15}{64}, \frac{20}{64}, \frac{15}{64}, \frac{6}{64}, \frac{1}{64}\}$.

3. (i) $\frac{2}{5}$; (ii) $\frac{9}{20}$. **4.** $\frac{135}{323}$. **5.** $\frac{135}{323}$.

6. $\Pr(0) = \frac{1}{10}$, $\Pr(r) = (10-r)/50$, $r = 1$ to 9. **7.** $\frac{9}{25}$.

8. (i) $\frac{1}{17}$; (ii) $\frac{4}{17}$.

9. $\{2, 3, 4, ..., 20\}$, $\{\frac{1}{100}, \frac{2}{100}, \frac{3}{100}, ..., \frac{9}{100}, \frac{10}{100}, \frac{9}{100}, ..., \frac{1}{100}\}$; $\frac{37}{100}$.

10. $\frac{1}{12}$.

115 **Ex. 26.** $\frac{2}{13}$. **Ex. 27.** $\frac{4}{13}$. **Ex. 28.** (i) $\frac{1}{2}$; (ii) $\frac{1}{3}$; (iii) $\frac{1}{6}$; (iv) $\frac{1}{3}$.

Ex. 29. $\frac{49}{50}$.

119 **Ex. 31.** (i) $\frac{1}{8}$; (ii) $\frac{1}{28}$; (iii) $\frac{3}{14}$. **Ex. 34.** $\frac{119}{144}$.

Exercise 7(c)

119 **1.** $\frac{625}{1296}$, $\frac{671}{1296}$. **2.** 0·784. **3.** $\frac{120}{343}$.

4. (i) $\frac{6}{11}$; (ii) $\frac{1}{22}$; (iii) $\frac{9}{22}$. **6.** $\frac{2}{9}$, $\frac{16}{81}$. **7.** $\frac{14}{39}$.

120 **8.** (i) $\frac{28}{55}$; (ii) $\frac{13}{55}$. **9.** 5!, 20, $\frac{11}{120}$. **10.** $\frac{1}{221}$.

11. $\frac{47}{66}$. **12.** At least 12. **13.** $\frac{15}{52}$. **14.** 0·22.

16. $\frac{14}{45}$. **17.** 13 times.

121 **20.** 0·956. **21.** (i) $\frac{3}{11}$; $\frac{3}{44}$; (ii) $\frac{5}{36}$, $\frac{5}{18}$.

123 **Ex. 35.** $\frac{5}{8}$, $\frac{4}{5}$. **Ex. 36.** $\frac{5}{18}$, $\frac{1}{6}$.

124 **Ex. 37.** $\frac{95}{491}$. **Ex. 38.** $\frac{25}{29}$, $\frac{5}{58}$, $\frac{3}{58}$.

Exercise 7(d)

125 **1.** $\frac{64}{307}$. **2.** 0·1997. **3.** $\frac{4}{19}$. **4.** $\frac{1}{4}$, $\frac{4}{17}$, $\frac{48}{217}$. **5.** $\frac{1}{5}$.

126 **6.** $\frac{95}{10094}$; **7.** $\frac{8}{11}$. **8.** $\frac{40}{73}$, $\frac{24}{73}$, $\frac{9}{73}$.

9. $p/(p+q-pq)$.

Miscellaneous Exercise 7

1. (i) $\frac{18}{37}$; (ii) $\frac{1}{37}$; (iii) 0·065; (iv) 0·036.

2. $\dfrac{1}{n!}$, 0, $\dfrac{1}{2(n-2)!}$, $\dfrac{1}{3(n-3)!}$.

127 **3.** No difference in either case. **4.** Approx. $\frac{1}{3}$. **5.** $\frac{1}{5}$.

6. Replacement $\frac{1}{36}$; no replacement $\frac{1}{66}$.

7. Probability of securing no prize greater for B, but this is compensated by greater probability of two prizes.

9. (i) 1; (ii) $\frac{2}{9}$. **10.** $(2^r-1)/3^{r-1}$.

128 **11.** (i) $m/(m+n)$; (ii) $m(m-1)/\{(m+n)(m+n-1)\}$; (iii) $n/(m+n-1)$; (iv) $m/(m+n)$.

12. $\frac{78}{115}$, $\frac{5}{17}$.

13. $\frac{1}{5}$. (i) $\frac{64}{125}$, $\frac{48}{125}$, $\frac{12}{125}$, $\frac{1}{125}$; (ii) $\frac{1}{125}$, $\frac{12}{125}$, $\frac{48}{125}$, $\frac{64}{125}$; $\frac{12}{13}$.

14. (i) 0·09; (ii) 0·111; (iii) 0·336; (iv) small; (v) no.

16. $(p_1+\lambda)(p_2+\lambda)(p_3+\lambda) = \lambda^2$.

17. $\frac{5}{12}$, 0, $\frac{7}{12}$; exactly and oppositely synchronized; $\frac{1}{4}$, 0, $\frac{3}{4}$; $\frac{1}{4}$, $\frac{1}{2}$, $\frac{1}{4}$.

18. $\frac{55}{243}$.

128 **19.** λ, $(1-q)(1-q^4)$; $\frac{4}{5}\lambda$, $(1-q)q^4$; $\frac{3}{4}\lambda$, $(1-q)q$; $\frac{2}{3}\lambda$, $(1-q)q^2$;
$\frac{1}{2}\lambda$, $(1-q)q^3$; $\frac{2}{5}\lambda$, q^4.

20. $1-(n-1)!\,(n^2-n)!\,n^{n-1}/(n^2-1)!$.

CHAPTER 8

131 **Ex. 1.** (i) 0, 1, 4, 17; (ii) 2, 5, 16, 65.

Ex. 2. (i) 1, 2, 4, 8; (ii) 1, 2, 3, 4; (iii) 0, 4, 21, 100; (iv) 1, 2, 5, 17;
(v) 1·5, 1·4, 1·41, 1·414, (approx.).

Ex. 3. (i) 3, 6, 9, 12, 15, 18; (ii) -2, 1, 4, 7, 10, 13;
(iii) 1, 2, 4, 8, 16, 32; (iv) 0, 6, 24, 60, 120, 210; (v) 0, 2, 0, 2, 0, 2;
(vi) $\frac{1}{2}$, $\frac{1}{6}$, $\frac{1}{12}$, $\frac{1}{20}$, $\frac{1}{30}$, $\frac{1}{42}$; (vii) 1, $\frac{1}{2}$, 1, 4, 25, 216;
(viii) -1, 5, -1, 9, -1, 13.

132 **Ex. 5.** 1, 1, 1, 1, 25.

Ex. 6. (i) $1+4+9$; (ii) $0+2+6+12$; (iii) $1+6+21+60$;
(iv) $-1+2-3+4-5$; (v) $2+3+10+29$; (vi) $3+0-1+0+3+8$;
(vii) $0+\frac{1}{3}+\frac{1}{2}+\frac{3}{5}+\frac{2}{3}$.

133 **Ex. 7.** (i) 18; (ii) 14; (iii) 100; (iv) 6; (v) $1\frac{1}{12}$; (vi) -15;
(vii) 31; (viii) $\frac{3}{10}$;

Ex. 8. (i) $\sum\limits_{r=1}^{4} r$; (ii) $\sum\limits_{r=1}^{4}(-1)^{r+1}r$; (iii) $\sum\limits_{r=1}^{4}2r$; (iv) $\sum\limits_{r=1}^{5}2^{r-1}$;
(v) $\sum\limits_{r=1}^{6}r^{-1}$; (vi) $\sum\limits_{r=1}^{6}r(r+1)$; (vii) $\sum\limits_{r=1}^{8}(-1)^{r+1}$; (viii) $\sum\limits_{r=1}^{n}r$.

Ex. 11. *cn.*   **Ex. 12.** $3r-2$, $\frac{1}{2}(3r-1)$, $4-2r$.

Ex. 13. (i) 46; (ii) 35; (iii) 86; (iv) 40; (v) 100.

134 **Ex. 14.** (i) $\sum\limits_{r=1}^{n}(3r-2)(3r+1)(3r+4)$; (ii) $\sum\limits_{r=1}^{n}6r^2(4r+1)$; (iii) $\sum\limits_{r=1}^{n}(2r)^{3r-2}$;
(iv) $\sum\limits_{r=1}^{n}(2r-1)(4r-1)(3r-1)^{-1}$; (v) $\sum\limits_{r=1}^{n}(-1)^{r+1}r\{(2r-1)(3r-1)(7r-4)\}^{-1}$.

Exercise 8(a)

135 **1.** (i) 112; (ii) $2\frac{1}{12}$; (iii) 15.

2. (i) $\sum\limits_{r=1}^{n}3r(3r-2)$;

(ii) $\sum\limits_{r=1}^{n}(-1)^{r+1}r(r+1)(r+2)$; (iii) $\sum\limits_{r=1}^{n}(-1)^{r+1}(2r-1)^2$.

PAGE

135 **3.** (i) 1, 4, 13, 40; (ii) 1, 1, 1, 1; (iii) 2, 2^2, 2^4, 2^8; (iv) 1, 2, $1\frac{3}{4}$, $1\frac{41}{56}$.

 4. $s_n - 2s_{n-1} + s_{n-2} = d$.

 5. (i) $9r - 6$; (ii) $\frac{1}{4}(2r-1)$; (iii) $20 - 8r$.

 6. (i) 51; (ii) 70; (iii) 30.   **7.** (i) 2601; (ii) 17045; (iii) -1155.

 8. $6 - 5r$, -930.   **9.** $8r + 1$, $n(4n+5)$.   **10.** $\frac{1}{2}(5r+3)$, $\frac{1}{4}n(5n+11)$.

136 **11.** 40.   **12.** 36.   **14.** 2, 4, 6.   **17.** $11\frac{2}{3}$, $20\frac{1}{3}$.

 18. 63.

 Ex. 15. (i), (ii), (iv) and (vi).   **Ex. 16.** (i) 8; (ii) 7; (iii) 32.

Exercise 8(b)

138 **1.** (i) $\frac{1}{3}(4^{12}-1)$; (ii) $-\frac{1}{3}(2^{20}-1)$; (iii) $(2+\sqrt{2})(2^8-1)$;
  (iv) $\frac{1}{2}[3 - 3^{-49}]$.

 2. $1\frac{1}{4}$, 2.

 3. $1\frac{1}{8}$, $2\frac{1}{4}$, $4\frac{1}{2}$, ... or $-1\frac{1}{8}$, $2\frac{1}{4}$, $-4\frac{1}{2}$, ...   **4.** 18.

 5. 21.   **6.** 29.   **7.** 27.   **8.** 16.

 9. $1 \cdot 126 \times 10^8$ km.   **10.** $\frac{1}{3}$, 1, 3.

139 **11.** £316·1.   **12.** £313·07.   **13.** (i) $1\frac{1}{3}$; (ii) 6; (iii) $\frac{2}{3}$.

 14. $\frac{35}{111}$.   **15.** $23\frac{1}{2}$ years.   **16.** $\{\rho a(\rho^n - 1) - an(\rho - 1)\}(\rho - 1)^{-2}$.

 17. $u_r = \rho u_{r-1}$.   **18.** $a_1^2(1-r)(1-r^{2n})(1+r)^{-1}$.

140 **Ex. 21.** $\frac{1}{6}n(n+1)(n+2)(n+3)(n+4)(n+5)$.

141 **Ex. 22.** $\frac{1}{96} - \frac{1}{4}\{(n+1)(n+2)(n+3)(n+4)\}^{-1}$.

Exercise 8(c)

142 **1.** (i) 650; (ii) 6084; (iii) 2865; (iv) $\frac{1}{3}n(4n^2-1)$.

 2. $\frac{1}{12}n(n+1)(n+2)(3n+13)$, $\frac{1}{12}n(n+1)(n+2)(3n+17)$.

 3. $\frac{1}{12}n(n+1)(n+2)(3n+1)$.

 4. $\frac{1}{4}n(n^3 + 2n^2 + 3n + 10)$.   **5.** $\frac{1}{12}n^2(n^2-1)$.

143 **6.** $\frac{1}{6}n(n+1)(2n+7)$.   **7.** $\frac{1}{4} - \frac{1}{2}(2n+3)\{(n+2)(n+3)\}^{-1}$.

 8. $\frac{1}{36} - \frac{1}{6}(3n+1)\{(n+1)(n+2)(n+3)\}^{-1}$.

 9. $\frac{13}{288} - \frac{1}{12}(4n+13)\{(n+1)(n+2)(n+3)(n+4)\}^{-1}$.

 10. (i) $n(3n^2 + 3n - 2)$; (ii) $\frac{1}{12}n(n+1)(n+2)(3n+1)$.
 (iii) $\frac{3}{4}n(n+1)(3n+1)(3n-2)$; (iv) $\frac{1}{20}n(n+1)(n+2)(n+3)(4n+1)$.

ANSWERS

PAGE

143 **11.** $\frac{1}{4}$, $-\frac{1}{4}$; $\frac{1}{2}n(n+1)^2(n+2)$.

12. $\frac{1}{2}(2n+1)(2n+3)\{(n+1)(n+2)\}^{-1}-\frac{3}{4}$.

14. $\frac{1}{4}-\frac{1}{2}\{n(n+1)\}^{-1}$.   **15.** $\frac{1}{3}n(4n^2-1)$.

144 **Ex. 23.** 1, 6, 15, 20, 15, 6, 1;   1, 7, 21, 35, 35, 21, 7, 1;
1, 8, 28, 56, 70, 56, 28, 8, 1.

145 **Ex. 26.** (i) $81x^4-108x^3y+54x^2y^2-12xy^3+y^4$;
(ii) $64x^6+192x^5y+240x^4y^2+160x^3y^3+60x^2y^4+12xy^5+y^6$;
(iii) $128x^7-448x^6+672x^5-560x^4+280x^3-84x^2+14x-1$;
(iv) $243x^5+810x^4y+1080x^3y^2+720x^2y^3+240xy^4+32y^5$.

Exercise 8(d)

146 **1.** (i) $x^6-6x^5y+15x^4y^2-20x^3y^3+15x^2y^4-6xy^5+y^6$;
(ii) $32x^5+40x^4y+20x^3y^2+5x^2y^3+\frac{5}{8}xy^4+\frac{1}{32}y^5$;
(iii) $1+14x+84x^2+280x^3+560x^4+672x^5+448x^6+128x^7$;
(iv) $64(x^6+18x^5y+135x^4y^2+540x^3y^3+1215x^2y^4+1458xy^5+729y^6)$.

2. (i) 54;   (ii) 672;   (iii) 264;   (iv) 19440.

3. (i) $1+16x+112x^2$;   (ii) $1+\frac{15}{2}x+\frac{105}{4}x^2$;   (iii) $256(4-20x+45x^2)$;
(iv) $-y^7+21y^6x-189y^5x^2$.

4. $\binom{8}{r}2^r x^{2r-8}$, 1120.

147 **5.** $\frac{5}{27}$.   **6.** (i) 1·0615;   (ii) 0·98411;   (iii) 0·99501;   (iv) 235·01.

7. 322.   **8.** 120, 4200.

9. (i) $1+4x+10x^2$;   (ii) $1-6x+21x^2$;   (iii) $1+10x+35x^2$;
(iv) $16(4-12x-9x^2)$.

10. $\pm1\frac{1}{2}\%$.   **11.** 2^n.   (i) 81;   (ii) 1.

Miscellaneous Exercise 8

1. (i) $\frac{1}{2}(3^n-1)$;   (ii) $3^{\frac{1}{2}n(n-1)}$ **2.** $\frac{1}{10}$, 19·99998, 9.

148 **3.** $\frac{5}{8}$.   **4.** $\{nx^{n+1}-(n+1)x^n+1\}(x-1)^{-2}$,
$\{n^2x^{n+2}-(2n^2+2n-1)x^{n+1}+(n+1)^2x^n-x-1\}(x-1)^{-3}$.

5. $\binom{n+1}{p+1}$.   **6.** 4, 12, 36; 2.3^{n-1}.

149 **12.** $\{(1-b^n)-nb^n(1-b)\}(1-b)^{-2}$.

13. $(r-1)$ digits 1, followed by r digits 0 and finally the digit 1.

PAGE

149 **15.** 627500.

150 **17.** (i) $15n(n+83)/2$; (ii) $45(19n-40)$. 18720, $10dn+720n-55d$; 30.

18. $(n-1)^2$.

Revision Exercise A

151 **1.** $5, 3; x-1$. **2.** $(-5, -5)$. **4.** (i) 1110; (ii) 17·3.

5. 120, 24. **6.** 40·9°. **7.** $7x+7y-29 = 0$.

8. $0, 4$; $(x^2+2\sqrt{2}x+4)(x^2-2\sqrt{2}x+4)$.

9. $3\mathbf{RQ}-2\mathbf{BC}$, $3\mathbf{RQ}-\mathbf{BC}$.

10. (i) $-\sqrt{5}/3$; (ii) $-2\sqrt{5}/5$; (iii) $1\frac{1}{2}$.

152 **11.** 5, 15. **12.** 11, $(3x+1)(x+1)$.

13. 0·036, 0·12. **16.** 28, $\frac{1}{2}(n+1)(n+2)$.

18. 10 cm, 9·6 cm, 37·25°, 9·75 cm. **19.** $\frac{57}{1000}$, $\frac{15}{19}$.

21. $2x+3y+4z-9 = 0$; $3\sqrt{13}/13, -2\sqrt{13}/13, 0$.

153 **23.** $(bc'+b'c)^2(ca'-c'a)^2 = (ab'+a'b)^2[(bc'+b'c)^2+(ca'-c'a)^2]$.

24. $\frac{1}{4}(5-\sqrt{97}) < x < -1$ or $\frac{1}{4}(5+\sqrt{97}) < x < 4$.

25. $\frac{1}{6}n(n+1)(n+2)(3n+7)$.

26. $\{-2 \leqslant x \leqslant 2\}, \{-3 < x \leqslant 1\}, \{2 < x < 3\}, \{1 < x \leqslant 2\}$, $\{-3 < x \leqslant 2\}$.

27. 1·03. **28.** $\frac{3833}{5625}$. **29.** $-\mathbf{i}-\mathbf{j}-3\mathbf{k}$.

30. $2E_1 = E_2+E_3$.

154 **31.** $\frac{2}{3}$. **32.** $\mathbf{r} = \mu(\hat{\mathbf{a}}-\hat{\mathbf{b}})$, $ab(\hat{\mathbf{a}}+\hat{\mathbf{b}})/(a+b+c)$.

33. (i) $\frac{1}{2}(\sqrt{5}+1)$, (ii) 2; $4n+1$ is a perfect square. **34.** $\frac{1}{49}$.

CHAPTER 9

158 **Ex. 6.** ABC is right-angled at A. **Ex. 7.** Not 'only if'.

Ex. 8. Not 'if'. **Ex. 9.** Yes.

Exercise 9(a)

160 **4.** 13. **5.** 0 or 4. **6.** 13.

10. No solution if $a = -1$ unless $b = 0$.

15. No: e.g. right-angle at B and M coincident with B.

CHAPTER 10

171 **Ex. 2.** $1000 - X, -X$.

173 **Ex. 3.** $1\frac{4}{7}$.   **Ex. 4.** Lose.   **Ex. 5.** Yes, if $x = 1$.

Exercise 10(a)

174   **1.** (i) $2\frac{3}{5}$;   (ii) $-\frac{3}{10}$;   (iii) $3\frac{13}{20}$;   (iv) $5\frac{1}{2}$.   **2.** (i) $4\frac{1}{5}$;   (ii) $-1\frac{3}{5}$;   (iii) $6\frac{3}{10}$;   (iv) 10.

    3. 3p.   **4.** $\frac{161}{36}$.   **5.** £100.   **6.** 0, 3·3.

175   **8.** 9p.   **9.** 7p.   **12.** £1·32.   **13.** 2.

    14. (i) 8·75;   (ii) 5·25.

176   **15.** $27\frac{1}{2}$p.   **16.** $22\frac{1}{2}$p.   **17.**

X	3	8	13	15	16	17
16p	2	3	3	2	3	3

178   **Ex. 6.** 2, $1\frac{1}{2}$.   **Ex. 7.** $\frac{3}{4}$.   **Ex. 8.** (i) $\mu + c$;   (ii) σ^2.

181   **Ex. 9.** $\frac{1}{4}$, 0.   **Ex. 10.** $\mathscr{E}(X)^3 - 3\mu\sigma^2 - \mu^3$.

183   **Ex. 11.** $\frac{1}{8}(1+t)^3$, $1\frac{1}{2}$, $\frac{3}{4}$.

185   **Ex. 12.** 2p.

Exercise 10(b)

    1. (i) $-\mu, \sigma$;   (ii) $\mu + 1, \sigma$;   (iii) $3\mu - 1, 3\sigma$;   (iv) 0, 1.

    2. (i) 2·81, 4·41;   (ii) 3·7, 2·01;   (iii) 0·15, 3·53;   (iv) 150, 3000.

    3. (i) 12·31, 121·1;   (ii) 15·7, 102·8;   (iii) 3·55, 16·75;   (iv) $2·55 \times 10^4$, $2·83 \times 10^8$.

    4. $4\frac{1}{3}$, $2\frac{2}{9}$.   **5.** $\frac{1}{2}(n+1)$, $\frac{1}{12}(n^2 - 1)$.

186   **6.** $\frac{36}{91}, \frac{30}{91}, \frac{25}{91}$.   **7.** $\frac{6}{35}$.   **9.** $(t^5 + t^3 + t + 3)^n/6^n$, $\frac{3}{2}n$.

    10. $\frac{5}{18}$, 7, 2·415, 1·71.   **11.** $\frac{85}{13}, \frac{1680}{169}, \frac{15}{169}$.

    12. 6·5, 2·36.   (i) $\frac{4}{9}$;   (ii) 0.

Miscellaneous Exercise 10

    1. £7·33.   **2.** 4p favours player, $4\frac{1}{2}$p favours banker.

187   **3.** Just over £3.   **4.** $-1\frac{1}{18}$.   **5.** Yes, if X, Y independent.

    7. $2(n-r)/\{n(n-1)\}$.   **10.** θp^{-1}.   **11.** $\frac{1}{2}(\sigma^2 + \mu^2 - \mu)$.

188   **14.** $3^{-14}\left\{\binom{13}{4} + \binom{9}{1}\binom{13}{5} + \binom{8}{2}\binom{13}{6} + \binom{7}{3}\binom{13}{7}\right.$

$$\left. + \binom{6}{4}\binom{13}{8} + \binom{13}{9}\right\}.$$

    16. $\frac{1}{4}$, 71.

CHAPTER 11

192 **Ex. 1.** Yes, provided $\mathbf{a} \neq \mathbf{0}, \mathbf{b} \neq \mathbf{0}$.　**Ex. 2.** OA^2.

Ex. 3. (i) Pythagoras;　(ii) Extension of Pythagoras (Cosine Rule).

Exercise 11 (a)

193 **3.** Sphere, centre A, radius $|\mathbf{c}|$.

195 **Ex. 4.** -5.　　**Ex. 6.** $(3\mathbf{i}+\mathbf{j}+\mathbf{k})/\sqrt{11}$.

199 **Ex. 9.** 1, 1; lies on angle bisector.

Ex. 11. $3x+2y-10 = 0$, $(2, 2)$.　　**Ex. 12.** $(-a, -b)$, $|c|$.

Ex. 13. $8x+6y+13 = 0$, $8x+6y-7 = 0$.

Exercise 11 (b)

1. (i) $2, \frac{11}{5}$;　(ii) $2, \frac{17}{5}$;　(iii) $3, \frac{3}{5}$;　(iv) $b, (3a-2b)/5$.

200 **2.** (i) $2\sqrt{5}/5$;　(ii) $\sqrt{65}/65$;　(iii) $8\sqrt{17}/85$;　(iv) $|(a^2-b^2)/(a^2+b^2)|$.

3. (i) $\sqrt{17}/17$;　(ii) $12\sqrt{13}/13$;　(iii) $6\sqrt{10}/5$;　(iv) $(h+k)^2 (h^2+k^2)^{-\frac{1}{2}}$.

4. (i) $2\sqrt{5}/5$;　(ii) $9\sqrt{5}/10$;　(iii) $2\sqrt{26}/13$;　(iv) $(a+b)(a^2+b^2)^{-\frac{1}{2}}$.

5. (i) $3x-4y+16 = 0$,　$3x-4y-14 = 0$;
(ii) $8x+6y+35 = 0$, $8x+6y-25 = 0$;　(iii) $5x+12y+41 = 0$,
$5x+12y-37 = 0$;　(iv) $3x+2y+1\pm3\sqrt{13} = 0$.

7. (i) $2x-y = 0$;　(ii) $7x-7y-3 = 0$;　(iii) $128x+16y+69 = 0$.

8. $x-7y-18 = 0$.　　　　　**9.** (i) $(9, -9)$;　(ii) $52\frac{1}{2}$;　(iii) $+\frac{1}{2}$.

10. $(-p, -q)$.

201 **11.** $x+2y-11 = 0$, $x-y+1 = 0$, $\arccos(8\sqrt{145}/145)$, $(\frac{11}{3}, \frac{7}{3})$.

12. 37.

202 **Ex. 14.** (i) $\frac{1}{3}(\mathbf{i}-2\mathbf{j}+2\mathbf{k})$;　(ii) $(3\mathbf{i}-\mathbf{j}+\mathbf{k})/\sqrt{11}$;　(iii) $(3\mathbf{i}+2\mathbf{j}+\mathbf{k})/\sqrt{14}$.

Ex. 15. (i) $x-3y+z = -5$;　(ii) $x-y+z = 2$;　(iii) $2x+3y-5z = -16$.

Exercise 11 (c)

205 **1.** $110{\cdot}9°$.　　　　**2.** (i) $x-y+z = 0$;　(ii) $2x+y-3z = 13$;
(iii) $3x-z = 1$;　(iv) $6x-3y-2z = 2$;　　(v) $4x+y-3z = -1$;
(vi) $ax+by+cz = a^2+b^2+c^2$.

3. (i) $2\sqrt{70}/35$;　(ii) $\sqrt{28}/84$;　(iii) $2/29$;　(iv) $1/2$.

ANSWERS

206 **4.** (i) $3\sqrt{11}/11$; (ii) $\sqrt{15}/15$; (iii) $\sqrt{66}/11$; (iv) $17\sqrt{58}/174$;
(v) $ab(a^2+b^2)^{-1}$; (vi) $|ab-bc-ca|\,(a^2+b^2+c^2)^{-1}$.

5. (i) $\sqrt{7}/7$; (ii) $\sqrt{105}/15$; (iii) 1; (iv) 40/41; (v) $\sqrt{3}/2$.

(vi) $\sqrt{\{\sum(ql-pm)^2\}}/\sqrt{\{(l^2+m^2+n^3)(p^2+q^2+r^2)\}}$.

6. (i) $\frac{1}{3}(2\mathbf{i}-2\mathbf{j}+\mathbf{k}), 2x-2y+z=-1$;
(ii) $\frac{1}{7}(3\mathbf{i}-2\mathbf{j}+6\mathbf{k}), 3x-2y+6z=0$;

(iii) $\dfrac{\sqrt{2}}{6}(\mathbf{i}+\mathbf{j}-4\mathbf{k}), x+y-4z=1$;

(iv) $\dfrac{\sqrt{21}}{21}(4\mathbf{i}-\mathbf{j}-2\mathbf{k}), 4x-y-2z=6$;

(v) $\dfrac{\sqrt{26}}{26}(3\mathbf{i}-4\mathbf{j}+\mathbf{k}), 3x-4y+z=1$;

(vi) $(a^2\mathbf{i}-b^2\mathbf{j}+c^2\mathbf{k})/\sqrt{(a^4+b^4+c^4)}, a^2x-b^2y+c^2z=0$.

207 **7.** (i) $(2, 3, -1)$; (ii) $(4, 7, -5)$; (iii) $(1, 1, 1)$; (iv) $(0, -1, 3)$.

8. (i) $(9, 5, 3)$; (ii) $(7, -10, -3)$; (iii) $(-6, 16, 6)$; (iv) $(-9, 9, 12)$;
(v) $(15, -13, -2)$; (vi) $(-2ad(a^2+b^2+c^2)^{-1}, -2bd(a^2+b^2+c^2)^{-1}, -2cd(a^2+b^2+c^2)^{-1})$.

9. (i) $(1, 1, 3)$; (ii) $(2, 3, 4)$; (iii) $(6, 2, 4)$; (iv) $(6, 4, 1)$.

10. $(8, 2, 0)$. **11.** $(1, 4, 3), \frac{1}{3}(x-1)=y-4=z-3$.

12. $\frac{1}{3}(x-1)=-\frac{1}{3}(y-5)=\frac{1}{8}(z-2)$. **13.** $x=y-3=-(z+6)$.

208 **14.** $3: -1:2, \sqrt{14}$.

16. $\frac{1}{2}(\sqrt{3}-1), \frac{1}{2}(\sqrt{3}+1), \sqrt{3}(1-\sqrt{3})/6, \sqrt{3}(1+\sqrt{3})/6, \frac{2}{3}\sqrt{3}$.

17. $5\lambda=2\mu, \mathbf{a}=5\mathbf{i}+29\mathbf{j}+2\mathbf{k}, \mathbf{b}=-(\mathbf{i}+5\mathbf{j}+\mathbf{k})$.

209 **18.** $2x-y+2z=9$, arccos $\frac{4}{5}$. **19.** $(1, 5, 0)$, arccos $\sqrt{(\frac{5}{11})}$.

20. (i) $(4, -1, -3), (\frac{22}{9}, \frac{8}{9}, -\frac{17}{9})$; (ii) $\frac{4}{3}; (\frac{8}{3}, \frac{4}{3}, -\frac{7}{3})$.

Miscellaneous Exercise 11

1. $|p-x_1\cos\alpha-y_1\sin\alpha|$.

2. $3x+11y+19=0, \quad 11x-3y-17=0$.

210 **3.** $14x+8y-57=0$. **5.** $3\cdot75, 1$. **6.** $(-4, 3)$.

9. $1:2$.

211 **11.** $60°$. **15.** $x+2=\frac{1}{3}(y+5)=z-5$.

16. $\frac{1}{2}x=-\frac{1}{3}y=-z$. **17.** $\mathbf{s}+2|\mathbf{n}.\mathbf{s}-p|(\pm\mathbf{n})$.

362

212 **18.** $x^2 + y^2 = 1 \pm 2y \cot \theta$.

19. (i) $x - 5y + 4z = 0$; (ii) $x + y + z = 0$, $(6, -2, -4)$.

20. $-11, (1, -2, 3)$.

21. $B(-\frac{1}{2}, \sqrt{3}/2, 0)$, $C(-\frac{1}{2}, -\sqrt{3}/2, 0)$, $D(0, 0, \sqrt{2})$, $(0, 0, \sqrt{2}/4)$; $-4:0:\sqrt{2}$, $2:\pm 2\sqrt{3}:\sqrt{2}$, $0:0:1$.

22. 2.

213 **23.** $5x + 12y - 60 = 0$. **24.** $2\sqrt{6}$.

25. $x = [p(b^2 + c^2 - a^2) - 2a(bq + cr + d)] (a^2 + b^2 + c^2)^{-1}$, etc.; $(\frac{1}{12}, -\frac{5}{12}, \frac{2}{3})$, $(-\frac{7}{6}, -\frac{5}{6}, \frac{2}{3})$.

26. $15x - 9y - 3z = 0$, $1:2:-1$.

27. $\Sigma[(a^2 + b^2 + c^2) l - 2a(al + bm + cn) x] = 0$.

214 **28.** $y = z = 0$, $z = x = 0$, $x = y = 0$; $cy - bz = 0$. $120°$.

29. $\arcsin 8/\sqrt{82}$, $\arccos 4/\sqrt{82}$.

30. Intersection of planes with $\Sigma(m_2 n_3 - m_3 n_2) x = 0$.

32. $14 \cdot 2°$. **33.** Sphere, centre the centroid.

CHAPTER 12

215 **Ex. 1.** Yes, e.g. $A = B = 60°$.

216 **Ex. 2.** $\frac{1}{4}(\sqrt{6} - \sqrt{2})$, $\frac{1}{4}(\sqrt{6} + \sqrt{2})$. **Ex. 3.** $-\frac{1}{4}(\sqrt{6} + \sqrt{2})$, $\frac{1}{4}(\sqrt{6} + \sqrt{2})$.

Ex. 4. (i) $\frac{63}{65}, \frac{16}{65}$; (ii) $\frac{33}{65}, -\frac{56}{65}$; (iii) $-\frac{63}{65}, \frac{16}{65}$.

Ex. 5. $-2 \sin A \sin B$.

217 **Ex. 6.** (a) $\theta - \phi \neq (2k + 1) \frac{1}{2}\pi$; (b) $\theta \neq \frac{1}{2}n\pi \pm \frac{1}{4}\pi$.

219 **Ex. 7.** (i) $\pm\sqrt{10}$; (ii) $\pm\sqrt{5}$; (iii) $10, 0$; (iv) $1 \pm \sqrt{2}$; (v) $\frac{1}{2}(2 \pm \sqrt{2})$.

Ex. 8. (i) $0, 270, 360$; (ii) $53 \cdot 1$; (iii) $90, 323 \cdot 1$; (iv) $4 \cdot 9, 220 \cdot 5$.

Ex. 9. $1, 7$. **Ex. 10.** $\frac{3}{5}$.

220 **Ex. 11.** $-\frac{7}{9}, \frac{4}{9}\sqrt{2}$. **Ex. 12.** $1\frac{1}{2}, \frac{1}{3}$. **Ex. 13.** $\frac{1}{6}\pi, \frac{5}{6}\pi$.

Ex. 14. $\sqrt{2} - 1$. **Ex. 15.** $2x\sqrt{(1 - x^2)}, 2y^2 - 1$. **Ex. 17.** $\arcsin \frac{56}{65}$.

221 **Ex. 18.** $(1 + 2t - t^2)(1 + t^2)^{-1}$.

223 **Ex. 19.** (i) $2 \sin 2x \cos x$; (ii) $2 \cos 3x \cos x$; (iii) $-2 \sin 2x \sin x$; (iv) $\sqrt{2} \sin(\frac{1}{4}\pi + x)$; (v) $\sqrt{2} \sin x$.

224 **Ex. 20.** $0, \frac{1}{2}\pi, \frac{2}{3}\pi, \pi, \frac{4}{3}\pi, \frac{3}{2}\pi, 2\pi$. **Ex. 21.** $0, \frac{2}{3}\pi, \pi, \frac{4}{3}\pi, 2\pi$.

Exercise 12(a)

224 **1.** (i) $\frac{1}{4}(\sqrt{6}+\sqrt{2})$; (ii) $-\frac{1}{4}(\sqrt{6}-\sqrt{2})$; (iii) $-(2+\sqrt{3})$; (iv) $2-\sqrt{3}$.

2. (i) $\frac{1}{4}(\sqrt{5}-1)$; (ii) $\frac{1}{4}\sqrt{(10+2\sqrt{5})}$; (iii) $\frac{1}{4}(\sqrt{5}+1)$;
(iv) $-\frac{1}{4}(\sqrt{5}+1)\sqrt{(10+2\sqrt{5})}$.

225 **5.** (i) $28\cdot6°, 208\cdot6°$; (ii) $120°, 300°$; (iii) $37\cdot5°, 217\cdot5°$; (iv) $18\cdot3°, 198\cdot3°$.

6. (i) $225°$; (ii) $90°, 330°$; (iii) $29\cdot5°, 256\cdot7°$; (iv) $22\cdot6°, 90°$.

7. (i) $0°, 116\cdot6°, 180°, 296\cdot6°, 360°$; (ii) $180°$; (iii) $45°, 120°, 135°$, $225°, 240°, 315°$; (iv) $0°, 45°, 90°, 225°, 360°$.

8. $|\sin\alpha| \leqslant \frac{2}{3}$; $9\cdot3°, 50\cdot7°, 189\cdot3,° 230\cdot7°$.

10. $4\cos^3\theta - 3\cos\theta$, $8\cos^4\theta - 8\cos^2\theta + 1$.

226 **13.** (i) $\pm(a^2-b^2)(2ab)^{-1}$; (ii) $a = 8\frac{1}{2}$, $b = 6\frac{1}{2}$; $\tan\theta = \frac{5}{12}$.

16. $R = \sqrt{5}$, $\alpha = 26\cdot6°$. (i) $140\cdot5°, 346\cdot3°$;
(ii) $0°, 63\cdot4°, 180°, 243\cdot4°, 360°$.

17. $-97\cdot6°, 0°, 90°, 171\cdot3°$.

227 **18.** $(\frac{23}{12}\pi, \frac{7}{12}\pi)$, $(\frac{7}{12}\pi, \frac{23}{12}\pi)$.

Exercise 12(b)

232 **1.** 76 m.   **3.** (i) 84; (ii) $\frac{56}{65}$; (iii) $8\frac{1}{8}$.

233 **4.** $101\cdot2°, 44\cdot8°$. **5.** $14\cdot8°$.   **6.** $9\cdot3$ m.   **7.** $36°$ **8.** $127\cdot8°$.

9. (i) $h(h^2+2a^2)^{-\frac{1}{2}}$; (ii) $h(h^2+a^2)^{-\frac{1}{2}}$;
(iii) $2ah(h^2+a^2)^{-1}$; (iv) $\sqrt{(h^2+2a^2)}/\sqrt{(2h^2+2a^2)}$.

10. (i) $35\cdot3°$; (ii) $64°$.   **11.** (i) 77 m; (ii) S $46°$ W.   **12.** 121 m.

234 **13.** 529 cm^2.   **14.** (i) $64\cdot9°$; (ii) $69\cdot4°$; (iii) $31\cdot6°$.

16. $1\cdot12r$.   **17.** $1\cdot96, 56\cdot8°$.

235 **19.** $\arccos\{(c^4-a^4-b^4+2a^2b^2)^{\frac{1}{2}}(2b^2c^2+2c^2a^2+2a^2b^2-a^4-b^4-c^4)^{-\frac{1}{2}}\}$.

Miscellaneous Exercise 12

2. (i) $\frac{1}{8}$; (ii) $\frac{3}{4}, -\frac{1}{4}$.   **4.** $2n\pi < x < (2n+1)\pi$, $n \in Z$.

236 **8.** $(\frac{1}{4}\pi, \frac{1}{12}\pi)$, $(\frac{1}{12}\pi, \frac{1}{4}\pi)$, $(\frac{11}{12}\pi, \frac{3}{4}\pi)$, $(\frac{3}{4}\pi, \frac{11}{12}\pi)$.   **13.** $0, \frac{1}{2}\pi, \pi$.

14. $\frac{1}{2}(1\pm\sqrt{2})$. ' **15.** $\tan\frac{1}{2}\alpha = a/b$.

237 **17.** $c > 4$.

(i) $\theta = 2n\pi \pm \arccos\frac{4}{5}$, $\phi = 2m\pi + \arcsin\frac{1}{5}$;
(ii) $\theta = 2n\pi \pm \arccos\frac{4}{5}$, $\phi = (2m+1)\pi - \arcsin\frac{1}{5}$;
(iii) $\theta = 2n\pi \pm \arccos\frac{1}{5}$, $\phi = 2m\pi + \arcsin\frac{4}{5}$;
(iv) $\theta = 2n\pi \pm \arccos\frac{1}{5}$, $\phi = (2m+1)\pi - \arcsin\frac{4}{5}$.

CHAPTER 13

245 **Ex. 9.** $S(P) = (3, 5)$, $T(P) = (3, 0)$, $U(P) = (6, 5)$.

Ex. 12. Reflection in Oxy plane.

Exercise 13(a)

1. $(-5, -10)$, $(\frac{4}{5}, -\frac{7}{5})$.

246 **2.** $(-5, -4)$, $(3, -5)$; $(0, 0)$.   **3.** The line $x - 2y = 0$.

6. Reflect in $x = y$ and then project on to x axis.

7. Reflect in $x = y$ and stretch by factor 2.

8. $|ad - bc|$; all points map into line $cx - ay = 0$.

247 **10.** $\begin{pmatrix} p-r & r \\ q-s & s \end{pmatrix}$.   **11.** $\begin{pmatrix} 1 & k \\ 0 & 1 \end{pmatrix}$, $\begin{pmatrix} 1 & 0 \\ 0 & -1 \end{pmatrix}$.

250 **Ex. 13.** (i) $\begin{pmatrix} 9 & 2 & 1 \\ 2 & 1 & 2 \\ 4 & 5 & -1 \end{pmatrix}$;   (ii) $\begin{pmatrix} -12 & 4 & -8 \\ -1 & -3 & 9 \\ -2 & -5 & -2 \end{pmatrix}$;   (iii) $\begin{pmatrix} 18 & -1 & 4 \\ 12 & 9 & 2 \\ 12 & -1 & 2 \end{pmatrix}$;

(iv) $\begin{pmatrix} 22 & 16 & -8 \\ 2 & 0 & 3 \\ 9 & 4 & 7 \end{pmatrix}$.   **Ex. 14.** (i) $\begin{pmatrix} -1 & 5 & 1 \\ 7 & 4 & 2 \\ 6 & -4 & 0 \end{pmatrix}$;   (ii) $\begin{pmatrix} 8 & 3 \\ -1 & -5 \end{pmatrix}$.

Exercise 13(b)

253 **1.** (i) $\begin{pmatrix} 2 & 5 & 4 \\ 1 & 1 & 6 \end{pmatrix}$;   (ii) $\begin{pmatrix} 4 & -1 & 4 \\ -3 & 5 & -2 \end{pmatrix}$;

(iii) $\begin{pmatrix} 7 & 1 & 8 \\ -4 & 8 & 0 \end{pmatrix}$;   (iv) $\begin{pmatrix} 3 & 13 & 8 \\ 4 & 0 & 16 \end{pmatrix}$.

2. (i) $\begin{pmatrix} 0 & 4 & 2 \\ 4 & 1 & 6 \\ 3 & 1 & 1 \end{pmatrix}$;   (ii) $\begin{pmatrix} -5 & -2 & -1 \\ 3 & -3 & -3 \\ -4 & 7 & -8 \end{pmatrix}$;   (iii) $\begin{pmatrix} -4 & 4 & 2 \\ 8 & -1 & 6 \\ 1 & 7 & -5 \end{pmatrix}$;

(iv) $\begin{pmatrix} -6 & 4 & 2 \\ 10 & -2 & 6 \\ 0 & 10 & -8 \end{pmatrix}$.

3. (i) $\begin{pmatrix} -10 & 4 \\ 1 & 4 \end{pmatrix}$;   (ii) $\begin{pmatrix} -6 & -2 \\ 12 & -10 \end{pmatrix}$;   (iii) $\begin{pmatrix} 8 & 5 \\ -2 & 18 \end{pmatrix}$.

4. (i) $AB - 2AC$;   (ii) $A^2 - AC + BA - BC$;

(iii) $A^2 + AB - BA + AC - CA - (B + C)^2$.

253 **5.** $\begin{pmatrix} 5 & 0 & 2 \\ -5 & 5 & 4 \\ 8 & -1 & 2 \end{pmatrix}, \begin{pmatrix} 6 & 3 \\ 1 & 6 \end{pmatrix}.$

6. (i) $\begin{pmatrix} 5 & 3 & 0 \\ -2 & 0 & 1 \\ 8 & 2 & -5 \end{pmatrix}$; (ii) $\begin{pmatrix} -1 & -3 & 3 \\ -3 & -1 & 1 \\ 3 & 0 & 2 \end{pmatrix}$; (iii) $\begin{pmatrix} 5 & 2 & 4 \\ -2 & 0 & 0 \\ 4 & 0 & 4 \end{pmatrix}$;

(iv) $\begin{pmatrix} 8 & 0 & -10 \\ 0 & 0 & -2 \\ 5 & 1 & -3 \end{pmatrix}$; (v) $\begin{pmatrix} 20 & 8 & 0 \\ 2 & 2 & -6 \\ -1 & -3 & 19 \end{pmatrix}$; (vi) $\begin{pmatrix} -18 & -7 & 30 \\ -6 & -2 & 5 \\ -8 & -4 & 19 \end{pmatrix}$.

7. (i) $\begin{pmatrix} 3 & 8 & 0 \\ -3 & 3 & 5 \\ 0 & 3 & 1 \end{pmatrix}$; (ii) $\begin{pmatrix} 1 & 4 & 5 \\ 5 & 4 & 5 \\ -7 & 1 & 2 \end{pmatrix}$; (iii) $\begin{pmatrix} 6 & 1 & -1 \\ 1 & 6 & 3 \\ -1 & 3 & 6 \end{pmatrix}$;

(iv) $\begin{pmatrix} 0 & 5 & 2 \\ 3 & 11 & 1 \\ -5 & -9 & 2 \end{pmatrix}$; (v) $\begin{pmatrix} 6 & -19 & -9 \\ -11 & -38 & -1 \\ 19 & 39 & -2 \end{pmatrix}$; (vi) $\begin{pmatrix} 10 & -11 & -19 \\ -27 & -40 & -1 \\ 33 & 43 & -4 \end{pmatrix}$

254 **8.** (i) $\begin{pmatrix} -1 & 6 \\ 4 & 1 \\ -1 & 4 \end{pmatrix}$; (ii) $\begin{pmatrix} -3 & 2 \\ 4 & -1 \\ -2 & 5 \end{pmatrix}$; (iii) $\begin{pmatrix} -1 & 3 & 6 \\ 2 & 3 & -2 \\ 1 & 6 & 9 \end{pmatrix}$.

9. (i) $\begin{pmatrix} 1 & 2 & 2 \\ 3 & -6 & 0 \\ -3 & 4 & -1 \end{pmatrix}$; (ii) $\begin{pmatrix} -7 & -2 \\ 3 & 1 \end{pmatrix}$;

(iii) $\begin{pmatrix} -1 & 0 \\ 21 & 6 \\ -17 & -5 \end{pmatrix}$; (iv) $\begin{pmatrix} 5 & -14 & -2 \\ -2 & 6 & 1 \end{pmatrix}$.

10. $(x \ y \ z)$, $\begin{pmatrix} 0 & 0 & a \\ b & 0 & 0 \\ 0 & c & 0 \end{pmatrix}$; T preserves lengths; each ± 1.

11. $2x + y - z = 0$, $(-1, 7, 5)$.

12. $x - y + z = 0$, $(5, 8, 3)$.

255 **14.** $(0, 0)$, $(2, 2)$, $(-1, 0)$.

Miscellaneous Exercise 13

2. Shear; x, z coordinates fixed.

3. (i) $(0, 0)$ only; (ii) line $2x - y = 0$; (iii) all points in the plane.

256 **5.** $(0, 0)$ only; no.

6. (i) $(0, 0)$ only; $\lambda = 10$: line $7x - 5y = 0$, $\lambda = -2$: line $x + y = 0$;
(ii) all points of line $x - y = 0$; $\lambda = 6$: line $4x + y = 0$.

PAGE

256 **8.** $AB = BA$.

9. A diagonal, provided non-zero elements of **D** distinct.

257 **11.** No.

CHAPTER 14

262 **Ex. 9.** (i) $\begin{pmatrix} 3 & -2 \\ -7 & 5 \end{pmatrix}$; (ii) $\begin{pmatrix} 2 & \frac{3}{2} \\ -1 & -1 \end{pmatrix}$;

(iii) $\begin{pmatrix} -2 & 5 \\ -5 & 12 \end{pmatrix}$; (iv) $\begin{pmatrix} 3 & -\frac{5}{3} \\ -1 & \frac{2}{3} \end{pmatrix}$.

263 **Ex. 10.** (i) $\begin{pmatrix} 1 & -1 & -1 \\ 0 & 2 & -3 \\ -1 & -2 & 6 \end{pmatrix}$; (ii) $\begin{pmatrix} 1 & -4 & 1 \\ 0 & -5 & 2 \\ -1 & 17 & -6 \end{pmatrix}$;

(iii) $\begin{pmatrix} -\frac{1}{2} & 0 & \frac{1}{2} \\ 1 & 5 & -4 \\ 0 & -3 & 2 \end{pmatrix}$; (iv) $\begin{pmatrix} \frac{1}{3} & \frac{1}{3} & -\frac{1}{3} \\ 0 & -4 & 3 \\ -\frac{1}{3} & \frac{8}{3} & -\frac{5}{3} \end{pmatrix}$.

Exercise 14(a)

264 **1.** (i) $\begin{pmatrix} 2 & -1 \\ -3 & 2 \end{pmatrix}$; (ii) $\begin{pmatrix} -\frac{4}{7} & \frac{3}{7} \\ \frac{5}{7} & -\frac{2}{7} \end{pmatrix}$; (iii) $\begin{pmatrix} -\frac{3}{2} & -\frac{1}{2} \\ -1 & 0 \end{pmatrix}$;

(iv) $\begin{pmatrix} \frac{7}{11} & -\frac{5}{11} \\ -\frac{2}{11} & \frac{3}{11} \end{pmatrix}$; (v) $\begin{pmatrix} h & -h-1 \\ -h+1 & h \end{pmatrix}$.

2. As in Qu. 1. **4.** (i) $\begin{pmatrix} 3 & 2 & -2 \\ -8 & -4 & 5 \\ -1 & -1 & 1 \end{pmatrix}$; (ii) $\begin{pmatrix} 11 & -12 & -7 \\ -8 & 9 & 5 \\ 7 & -8 & -4 \end{pmatrix}$;

(iii) $\begin{pmatrix} \frac{4}{3} & -3 & \frac{11}{3} \\ -\frac{2}{3} & 2 & -\frac{7}{3} \\ \frac{1}{3} & -2 & \frac{8}{3} \end{pmatrix}$; (iv) $\begin{pmatrix} \frac{1}{2} & \frac{1}{2} & -\frac{1}{2} \\ \frac{1}{2} & -\frac{3}{2} & \frac{1}{2} \\ -\frac{5}{2} & \frac{9}{2} & -\frac{1}{2} \end{pmatrix}$; (v) $\begin{pmatrix} \frac{9}{8} & -\frac{3}{2} & \frac{29}{8} \\ -\frac{1}{8} & \frac{1}{2} & -\frac{13}{8} \\ -\frac{3}{8} & \frac{1}{2} & -\frac{7}{8} \end{pmatrix}$;

(vi) $\begin{pmatrix} 0 & -1 & 1 \\ \frac{1}{2} & \frac{1}{2} & -1 \\ -1 & 0 & \frac{3}{2} \end{pmatrix}$.

265 **7.** $\begin{pmatrix} -1 & 5 & -4 \\ -1 & 2 & 0 \\ 2 & -6 & 3 \end{pmatrix}$, $\mathbf{v} = \begin{pmatrix} 6 \\ 5 \\ -10 \end{pmatrix}$. **8.** $\begin{pmatrix} -5 \\ 7 \\ 6 \end{pmatrix}$.

9. 6. **10.** $\begin{pmatrix} -9 & -1 & 29 \\ -3 & -1 & 14 \\ 10 & 2 & -35 \end{pmatrix}$.

367

267 **Ex. 11.** (i) 3; (ii) 5; (iii) 7.

Ex. 12. (i) 2; (ii) -3; (iii) 0;
(iv) -3; (v) $abc + 2fgh - af^2 - bg^2 - ch^2$.

273 **Ex. 13.** (i) 12; (ii) -9; (iii) 0, (iv) 1.

Exercise 14(b)

275 **1.** (i) -2; (ii) -1; (iii) -1; (iv) 22.

2. (i) -30; (ii) 0; (iii) 0; (iv) 1; (v) 24; (vi) -9; (vii) 3;
(viii) -12; (ix) 8; (x) 6.

3. (iii) Singular.

276 **4.** (i) $\begin{pmatrix} -2 & -5 & 3 \\ -2 & 4 & -2 \\ 4 & -3 & 1 \end{pmatrix}$, $-2\mathbf{I}$, -2; (ii) $\begin{pmatrix} -14 & -14 & 14 \\ 16 & 16 & -16 \\ -27 & -27 & 27 \end{pmatrix}$, $\mathbf{O}$, 0;

(iii) $\begin{pmatrix} 30 & -11 & 5 \\ -10 & 4 & -2 \\ 2 & -1 & 1 \end{pmatrix}$, $2\mathbf{I}$, 2; (iv) $\begin{pmatrix} 0 & -1 & 2 \\ 1 & -1 & -3 \\ -2 & 3 & 5 \end{pmatrix}$, $\mathbf{I}$, 1.

5. (i) $\begin{pmatrix} -20 & 4 & -9 \\ -5 & 1 & -2 \\ 11 & -2 & 5 \end{pmatrix}$; (ii) $\frac{1}{30}\begin{pmatrix} -3 & -9 & 15 \\ 7 & 1 & -5 \\ 1 & 13 & -5 \end{pmatrix}$;

(iii) $-\frac{1}{3}\begin{pmatrix} 0 & -6 & 9 \\ -1 & 4 & -5 \\ 2 & -5 & 4 \end{pmatrix}$; (iv) $\begin{pmatrix} 0 & -1 & 2 \\ \frac{1}{2} & \frac{1}{2} & -\frac{3}{2} \\ -1 & 0 & 2 \end{pmatrix}$.

6. (i) 12; (ii) 1; (iii) -10. **7.** (i) $(b-c)(c-a)(a-b)$;
(ii) $(b-c)(c-a)(a-b)(a+b+c)$; (iii) $(b-c)(c-a)(a-b)(bc+ca+ab)$.

8. $\begin{pmatrix} 5 & -10 & -4 \\ 5 & -4 & 0 \\ -3 & 0 & -9 \end{pmatrix}$. **9.** $\begin{pmatrix} -3 & 33 & 4 \\ 0 & -8 & 0 \\ 2 & -2 & -1 \end{pmatrix}$.

277 **10.** $\begin{pmatrix} 39 & 66 & 36 \\ -100 & -173 & -95 \\ 147 & 249 & 136 \end{pmatrix}$.

Miscellaneous Exercise 14

1. $\begin{pmatrix} 0 & 1 \\ 1 & 0 \end{pmatrix}$. **2.** (a) Yes; (b) yes; (c) yes.

3. $\begin{pmatrix} a^2 & ab & ac \\ ba & b^2 & bc \\ ca & cb & c^2 \end{pmatrix}$; $\begin{pmatrix} a^2 & ab & ac \\ ba & b^2+1 & bc+2 \\ ca & cb+2 & c^2+4 \end{pmatrix}$.

278 **6.** Yes. **9.** $(b-c)^2(c-a)^2(a-b)^2$.

279   **13.** $A^2 = 2A+I$, $A^{-1} = -A+2I$.

280   **17.** $\begin{pmatrix} 2 & -2 & 1 \\ 2 & 1 & -2 \\ 1 & 2 & 2 \end{pmatrix}$, $9I, \frac{1}{9}\begin{pmatrix} 2 & -2 & 1 \\ 2 & 1 & -2 \\ 1 & 2 & 2 \end{pmatrix}$,

$\frac{1}{9}\begin{pmatrix} 1 & -4 & 8 \\ 4 & -7 & -4 \\ 8 & 4 & 1 \end{pmatrix}$.

CHAPTER 15

285   **Ex. 2.** $(\frac{38}{39}, -\frac{7}{13})$.

286   **Ex. 5.** True for any **x** provided **b** = **0**.

Exercise 15(a)

1. (i) $(2, 5)$;   (ii) $(-3, 5)$;   (iii) $(\frac{3}{5}, -\frac{2}{7})$.

2. (i) If $a \neq -b$, $x = b-a$;   if $a = -b$, true all x.
(ii) If $a \neq b$, $x = (c-b)(a-b)^{-1}$;   if $a = b \neq c$, no solution;
if $a = b = c$, true all x.

3. (i) $x = (4+3a)(3a-6)^{-1}$, $y = 5(2-a)^{-1}$, provided $a \neq 2$.
If $a = 2$, equations inconsistent.
(ii) If $a \neq 4$, $x = 0$, $y = 2$; if $a = 4$, $x = 2(2-\lambda)$, $y = \lambda$, all λ.
(iii) If $a \neq \pm 6$, $x = 2(6+a)^{-1}$, $y = (6+a)^{-1}$.
If $a = 6$, $x = \lambda$, $y = \frac{1}{6}(1-3\lambda)$;   if $a = -6$, equations inconsistent.

4. (i) If $a \neq -3b$, $x = (b^2+ab+8)(4a+12b)^{-1}$, $y = (24-ab-a^2)(4a+12b)^{-1}$.
If $a = -3b$, $b^2 \neq 4$, equations inconsistent; if $b = 2$, $x = \lambda$, $y = 3\lambda+1$;
if $b = -2$, $x = \lambda$, $y = 3\lambda-1$.
(ii) If $ab \neq -3$, $x = 6(1+b)(ab+3)^{-1}$, $y = 2(3-a)(ab+3)^{-1}$.
If $a = 3$, $b = -1$, $x = \lambda$, $y = 2-\lambda$; if $ab = -3$, $a \neq 3$ equations inconsistent.
(iii) If $a^2 \neq b^2$, $x = (a-b)^{-1}$, $y = (b-a)^{-1}$. If $a = b$, equations inconsistent;
if $a+b = 0$, $x = \lambda$, $y = (a\lambda-1)a^{-1}$.

5. Inconsistent unless $a = 3$ or -1;
if $a = 3$, $x = -2$, $y = 3$; if $a = -1$, $x = 2$, $y = -1$.

6. Inconsistent unless $a = 1$, 2 or -3. If $a = 1$, $x = \frac{11}{5}$, $y = \frac{3}{5}$;
if $a = 2$, $x = 2$, $y = 0$; if $a = -3$, $x = \frac{1}{3}$, $y = \frac{5}{3}$.

287   **7.** (i) $a \neq 0$, $b \neq 0$, $a \neq b$, $x = c(b-c)a^{-1}(b-a)^{-1}$, $y = c(c-a)b^{-1}(b-a)^{-1}$;
(ii) $a = 0$, $b \neq 0$, $c \neq 0$, equations inconsistent unless
$b = c$, when $x = \lambda$, $y = 1$;   (iii) $a = 0$, $b \neq 0$, $c = 0$, consistent,
$x = \lambda$, $y = 0$;   (iv) $a \neq 0$, $b = 0$, $c \neq 0$, equations inconsistent unless

287　$a = c$, when solution is $x = 1$, $y = \lambda$; (v) $a \neq 0$, $b = 0$, $c = 0$, consistent, $x = 0$, $y = \lambda$; (vi) $a = b \neq 0$, $c \neq 0$, inconsistent unless $a = b = c$, when solution is $x = \lambda$, $y = 1-\lambda$; (vii) $a = b = 0$, $c \neq 0$, inconsistent; (viii) $a = b = c = 0$, consistent, $x = \lambda$, $y = \mu$.

8. $a_1 b_2 - a_2 b_1 = 0$, $x = \lambda a_1^{-1}$, $y = -\lambda b_1^{-1}$.

9. If $\theta \neq k\pi + \phi$ (k integral), $x = \sin(\phi - \alpha) \operatorname{cosec}(\phi - \theta)$, $y = \sin(\theta - \alpha) \operatorname{cosec}(\theta - \phi)$; if $\theta = k\pi + \phi$, equations inconsistent unless θ and ϕ both differ from α by an integral multiple of π. If $\theta = \alpha + 2m\pi$, $\phi = \alpha + 2n\pi$, $x = \lambda$, $y = 1-\lambda$; if $\theta = \alpha + 2m\pi$, $\phi = \alpha + (2n+1)\pi$, $x = \lambda$, $y = \lambda - 1$; if $\theta = \alpha + (2m+1)\pi$, $\phi = \alpha + 2n\pi$, $x = \lambda$, $y = \lambda + 1$; if $\theta = \alpha + (2m+1)\pi$, $\phi = \alpha + 2(n+1)\pi$, $x = \lambda$, $y = -1-\lambda$.

292　**Ex. 12.** (i) Lies in plane $OI'J'K'$; (ii) can be expressed in terms of any two of $\mathbf{i}'$, $\mathbf{j}'$, $\mathbf{k}'$.

　　Ex. 14. Columns of A proportional; (i) lies on OI'; (ii) $\lambda \mathbf{i}'$.

Exercise 15(b)

294　**1.** $(-2, 0, 4)$.

295　**2.** $\begin{pmatrix} 1 & 6 & 5 \\ 1 & 1 & 2 \\ -1 & 1 & -1 \end{pmatrix}$. (i) $(0, 1, -1)$; (ii) $(2, 0, 1)$; (iii) $(-35, -5, -7)$.

3. Any point of line $\frac{1}{2}(x-1) = \frac{1}{3}(y+1) = \frac{1}{4}(z+2)$.

4. (i) Line λ, $\frac{1}{5}(6-7\lambda)$, $\frac{1}{5}(13-11\lambda)$; (ii) inconsistent: planes form prism in direction $5\mathbf{i} - 7\mathbf{j} - 11\mathbf{k}$.

5. $b = 10$, line; $b \neq 10$, inconsistent.

6. $a = 2$, inconsistent; $a \neq 2$, consistent only if $b = a+2$, giving line.

7. $(2, 1, -3)$.

296　**8.** $a = 5$, inconsistent; $a = -\frac{3}{2}$, line; unique point otherwise.

9. 4, $(0, \lambda, 2\lambda)$.　　**10.** $(\lambda, \lambda, -2\lambda)$, $(1+\lambda, \lambda, -2\lambda)$.

11. $\frac{1}{7}(x+6) = y = -\frac{1}{11}(z-12)$, parallel.

297　**14.** Tetrahedron $7x - 6y - 5z > 0$, $x - 2y - z < 0$, $9x - 8y - 7z < 0$, $3x - 4y - 3z > -2$.

Miscellaneous Exercise 15

1. $\begin{pmatrix} 1 & 6 & 3 \\ \frac{1}{2} & \frac{5}{2} & 1 \\ 0 & -2 & -1 \end{pmatrix}$, $(-2, -1, 1)$, $(\frac{1}{2}, \frac{1}{2}, \frac{1}{2})$.

2. (i) Line or plane; (ii) inconsistent.

298   **3.** $(\frac{2}{7}, -\frac{1}{7}, \frac{1}{7})$.

      5. $A = b-a$, $B = c-a$, $C = (b-c)(c-a)$;
$x = (b^2+c^2)(a-b)^{-1}(c-a)^{-1}$, $y = (c^2+a^2)(a-b)^{-1}(b-c)^{-1}$,
$z = (a^2+b^2)(b-c)^{-1}(c-a)^{-1}$.

299   **6.** $(1, 1, 1)$, $(\lambda, 3-2\lambda, \lambda)$.

      9. $(b-c)(c-a)(a-b)$, $x = ab(b-c)(c-a)^{-1}(a-b)^{-1}$; $y = a^2(a-b)^{-1}$,
$z = ab(c-a)^{-1}$; $a = b \neq c$, inconsistent unless $a = 0$; $a \neq b = c$, line;
$a = b = c$, plane.

300   **12.** $-4, 3, 2, -11(1+\lambda)/7, 5(1+\lambda)/7, \lambda$.

      13. $a-2b-c = 0$, $(\lambda, 1-2\lambda, \lambda-1)$.

      14. $\lambda \neq \frac{1}{3}$, -1, unique; $\lambda = \frac{1}{3}$, inconsistent; $\lambda = -1$, line.

CHAPTER 16

306   **Ex. 2.** $\frac{4}{5}p_0, \frac{6}{25}p_0, \frac{4}{125}p_0, \frac{1}{625}p_0$.   **Ex. 3.** (i) 2·5;   (ii) 2.

     Ex. 4. 1·8, 1·44.   **Ex. 5.** $\frac{3}{8}, \frac{1}{16}$, 7 to 1.

Exercise 16(a)

  1. $\frac{1}{16}, \frac{3}{8}, \frac{11}{16}$,   **2.** 0·348, 0·071.   **3.** 0·000105, 0·00605, 0·201.

  4. 9, 0·387.   **5.** (i) $\frac{700}{32}$; (ii) 0·566.

307   **6.** $\frac{17}{625}, \frac{11}{144}$.   **7.** $(9-r)(5r+5)^{-1}$. (i) 1·5; (ii) 1; (iii) 0·46

  9. $p^9(10-9p)$, £3·52, 46·8%.   **11.** (i) 0·388;   (ii) 0·0386.

311   **Ex. 7.** (i) $\frac{1}{36}$; (ii) $\frac{125}{144}$; (iii) 12.

Exercise 16(b)

313   **1.** 0·135, 0·271, 0·271, 0·180, 0·090, 0·036, 0·017.

    2. 1·45; (a) 0·06; (b) 0·33.

314   **3.** (i) 1; (ii) 0·846; (iii) 0·013.   **4.** 0·167, 0·594.

    5. 0·030, 0·106, 0·185, 0·216, 0·188, 0·132, 0·077; 3, 4·25.

    6. 3; 60, 222.   **7.** 20, 0·029.   **8.** 0·302, 0·060.

315   **9.** No: $\Pr(X \geqslant 21) \approx 0.121$.   **10.** $(\lambda^2+\lambda)/(1-e^{-\lambda})$.

    11. $a(r+1)^{-1}$, 2.   **12.** 0·0030, 0·0379.

    13. 226·8, 211·4, 98·6, 30·6, 7·1, 1·5.

Exercise 16(c)

321   **1.** (i) 0·63;   (ii) 0·61. Pr (2 or more) $\approx$ 0·09.   **2.** 0·79.

        3. $(1-p)^{10} \{1+10p(1-p)^9\}$, 13·15.

322   **4.** 0·9860, 0·0119, 0·002.   **5.** No.

        6. Pr $(r \leqslant 4|m = 10) = 0.029$; yes.   **7.** Pr (3 or more sixes) = 0·062.

        8. Yes; no $(p \approx 1/163)$.

323   **9.** Not significant in either case.

        11. (i) $(1-p)^{14} (1+14p) \{1+105p^2(1-p)^{13}+455p^3 (1-p)^{12}\}$;
        (ii) 0·164;   (iii) 17·5.

        12. £2·25, £1·50.

Miscellaneous Exercise 16

        1. (i) $\frac{27}{256}$;   (ii) 4;   (iii) $8\frac{1}{3}$.   **2.** 1, 0·335; 20.

324   **3.** $\frac{16}{25}$.   **4.** 8.   **5.** Yes, if $p < \frac{1}{5}$; no otherwise.

        6. $\frac{1}{2}N(N+1) (2p-1)$.   **8.** $\frac{63}{8} (2pq)^n (p^2+q^2)$.

        9. μp.

325   **11.** 0·3.

        12. 20, 60, 90, 90, 67, 40, 33. (i) £157·50;
        (ii) £167·50;   (iii) £160·75.

        13. $\binom{n}{r} p^r(1-p)^{n-r}$,

$$\binom{r}{s} q^s(1-q)^{r-s}, \binom{s+k}{s} \binom{n}{s+k} p^{s+k}q^s(1-p)^{n-s-k}(1-q)^k,$$

$$\binom{n}{s} (pq)^s (1-pq)^{n-s}.$$

        14. $Q(r, s) = \binom{r}{s} (\frac{1}{6})^s (\frac{5}{6})^{r-s}$.

        15. (i) 99·1%;   (ii) 0·03;   (iii) 0·1.

326   **16.** 0·011, 0·870, 0·516; 23·7.   **17.** 0·585.

        18. $e^{-\mu}, \mu, e^{-(\mu+\nu)}\mu^r\nu^s\{r!s!\}^{-1}$.

327   **20.** 0·2;   no.   **21.** $p(n-r+1) (r-rp)^{-1}, r_m = [p(n+1)]$.

Revision Exercise B

328   **1.** $x-2y = 0, 4x+2y-15 = 0.$ **2.** $\frac{16}{27}, \frac{2}{3}, \frac{1}{4}.$ **4.** $\frac{1}{4}(4k+1)\pi.$

     5. $\frac{1}{9}(10+\sqrt{10}), 7.$ **7.** 3.   **8.** No.

329   **9.** $(2x-y+1)(x+3y-2)$, two lines; (i) two lines; (ii) origin.

     12. $\frac{1}{3}\begin{pmatrix} -8 & 11 & -10 \\ -9 & 12 & -9 \\ 10 & -13 & 11 \end{pmatrix}.$ (i) $(20, 20, -23)$;   (ii) $(-\frac{17}{3}, -5, \frac{19}{3}).$

     13. $1-48x+1104x^2, 0\cdot6158.$ **14.** (i) $37x-27y = 0;$
     (ii) $31x+27 = 0.$

     15. (i) $3x+4$;   (ii) $5x+7.$

330   **16.** $\alpha \sim \beta = (2k+1)\pi.$ **19.** $\frac{1}{3}\begin{pmatrix} 1 & -2 & -2 \\ -2 & 1 & -2 \\ -2 & -2 & 1 \end{pmatrix}.$

     20. $3:1.$ **21.** About $\frac{3}{5}, 69.$

     23. (i) 0;   (ii) $2(q-r)(r-p)(p-q)(y-z)(z-x)(x-y).$

     25. $\frac{2}{11} < p < \frac{3}{11}.$ **26.** $(2, 5, -3), (4, 1, 1).$

     27. $\{y \in R: -1 < y \leqslant \sqrt{2}\}.$

331   **28.** $(x+c)(ax+b-c).$ (i) $(1+c)(a+b-c)$;   (ii) $(c-1)(b-c-a);$
     (iii) $(ab+c)(a^2bc+b-c).$

     29. Plane $x+z = 0.$

     30. $\frac{53}{512}, \frac{1981}{2048}.$ **31.** (i) $0, \frac{3}{4}\pi, \pi, \frac{7}{4}\pi, 2\pi$;   (ii) $\frac{5}{12}\pi, \frac{17}{12}\pi.$

     32. $-2 < x \leqslant -\frac{1}{2}$ or $\frac{1}{2} \leqslant x < 2.$ **34.** $Q^{n-1}P.$

332   **35.** $(-2, -1, -5).$ **37.** $2, -4, -3.$ **38.** 4.

     39. $\begin{pmatrix} -18 & 26 & -19 \\ -2 & 3 & -2 \\ 23 & -33 & 24 \end{pmatrix}, \begin{pmatrix} 1 & 0 & 0 \\ 0 & 0 & 1 \\ 0 & 1 & 0 \end{pmatrix}, \begin{pmatrix} 1 & 0 & 0 \\ 0 & 1 & 0 \\ -1 & -1 & 1 \end{pmatrix}.$

     (i) $\begin{pmatrix} -18 & -19 & 26 \\ -2 & -2 & 3 \\ 23 & 24 & -33 \end{pmatrix}$;   (ii) $\begin{pmatrix} -18 & 26 & -19 \\ -2 & 3 & -2 \\ 43 & -62 & 45 \end{pmatrix}.$

     40. $26° 34', 45°, 108° 26'.$ **41.** $x-2y+z = 0, 1:2:3.$

333   **42.** (i) $\frac{496}{729}$;   (ii) $\frac{73}{729}$;   (iii) $\frac{160}{729}.$ **43.** $\alpha = 2^n-1, \beta = 1.$

     45. $k = 1$, line; $k = -2$ or $k = 3$, inconsistent.

     46. $20°, 100°, 140°; 1\cdot44, 0\cdot33, -0\cdot27.$

     47. (i) $\frac{1}{4}(n+1)$;   (ii) $\frac{1}{4}n^2(n-1)^{-1}.$

334   **49.** (i) $-4(b-c)(c-a)(a-b)$;

(ii) $(x+a+b+c)(x+a-b-c)(x-a+b-c)(x-a-b+c)$.

50. $x-2y-2z+8 = 0$.

51. $53°, 155°, 344°$.   (i) $158°$;   (ii) $m = -0·005, c = 1·7$.

53. $\phi = \theta_1 - \theta_2$.

335   **55.** $k = 5$, line; $k = -7$, prism.   **56.** 554400.

57. $x < -5, -1 < x < 1, x > 7$.

59. $u+v+w = 0$ and $3a+2b+c = 0$ for consistency;
line $(\lambda, \lambda+\tfrac{1}{6}(b-a), \lambda-\tfrac{1}{3}(2a+b))$.

60. $3\tfrac{11}{14}, 49\tfrac{3}{14}$.

336   **61.** $47°$.   **63.** $x-1 = -\tfrac{1}{2}(y+2) = z$.

64. (i) $\tfrac{1}{2}$;   (ii) $\tfrac{1}{2}+\tfrac{1}{2}(a-b)^n (a+b)^{-n}$; $b(b+2a)(a+b)^{-2}$ in both cases.

65. 5567.   **66.** Yes, provided $\lambda \neq 0$.

337   **68.** $\lambda = -2$, line; $\lambda = 1$, inconsistent.

69. $(\lambda l'+\mu m')(\lambda l+\mu m)^{-1}$.   **70.** 23 min.

338   **71.** $3^{-N}, \tfrac{1}{2}, \tfrac{3}{4}$.   **74.** $2a^2+2c^2+f^2 = 2b^2+2d^2+e^2$.

Index